A STRANGER IN BLOOD

# A STRANGER IN BLOOD

*The Case Files on*

*Dr John Bodkin Adams*

Pamela V. Halliday Cullen

Elliott & Thompson

London

# CONTENTS

———

For my sons, Roderick and Alasdair, and for my parents,
who would have taken pleasure in this book.

# ACKNOWLEDGEMENTS

—

This book would not have been written had it not been for my GP, Dr Hugh Thomas. He is a partner in the College Road, 'Red House' practice in Eastbourne – the same practice which Dr Adams joined in 1922. In conversation during one visit, Dr Thomas mentioned that he had always wanted to know the truth about Dr Adams. His remark sparked my curiosity and I began what turned out to be two years of research into the case. Sussex Police were the first to agree that I could see their closed archives and Elizabeth Hughes and her staff at East Sussex Record Office were most helpful to me.

The Metropolitan Police were very generous in opening their closed archives on the case, which were due to remain closed till 2033. A special thanks is due to Margaret Bird, archivist at Scotland Yard, who devoted much time to helping me and who has taken such a personal interest in the case and the book. The National Archive staff provided much help with the handling and guarding of these archives and I am particularly indebted to David Priest for his advice and assistance.

In Eastbourne, Haine's Undertakers afforded me free access to their fascinating records, Eastbourne College provided information about Gwilym Lloyd-George and Councillor David Stevens, a former Mayor of Eastbourne, provided much background information about the town. Richard James gave me many intriguing insights into his father and Dr Adams. In Co. Antrim, Northern Ireland, Jim Rankin and Randalstown History Society were welcoming and helpful, as were the staff of the Irish Room in Coleraine. Dr Christopher Woods, University College, Dublin contributed information on Irish history and families and my thanks also go to his daughter, Nellie Woods, who, bubbling with enthusiasm, provided timely assistance with research in Dublin.

Joe and Nicky Henson, the sons of Leslie Henson, also deserve my particular thanks. They provided the vivid description of their father and his involvement in triggering the police investigation into the death of Bobbie Hullett, that serves as the perfect introduction to the whole story. Artemis Cooper generously gave me essential contacts and the late 11th Duke of Devonshire kindly responded to enquiries about his father and Dr Adams. The Attorney General, Lord Goldsmith, and his office supplied very detailed information about the role of the Attorney General and its dual aspect.

I am particularly grateful to Dr Jane Mercer, pathologist at Eastbourne District General Hospital, who freely provided her professional opinion on the 'Nurses' Notes' in the Morrell case for inclusion in this book.

Martin Gwynne and his wife, Frederica, were extraordinarily generous with their time and hospitality. Martin lent his energetic support and provided free access to his family archives. Another member of the Gwynne family, Rupert Grey, has also been extremely helpful to me with information about his great-uncle, Lt Col Roland Gwynne, with whom Dr Adams had such a significant relationship.

My Editor, David Elliott, has shown much patience and understanding and has been full of sage advice. His professionalism and support have been unfailing since the day he learned I was researching a book about Dr Adams. 'Do you have a publisher?' he asked. 'No.' I replied. 'You do now,' he rejoined and has remained true to his word ever since.

Members of my own family and close circle have also been extremely supportive. Most of all, the book could not have been written without the help of my partner in crime, Lyall Davidson: he has lived with the Dr Adams story from the beginning, participating in the research, reading through each draft, helping with revisions and contributing analysis and ideas. Above of all, he has helped breathe life into the main characters.

# PREFACE

———

When the idea for this book was first suggested to me by my own GP, Dr Hugh Thomas, I was struck by his interest in having an historian examine the case in an effort to get at the truth. At the time I did not know what archives – if any – would be made available to me. In the event, there was a veritable mountain of material as the closed archives of Sussex Police, and then Scotland Yard – closed until 2033 – were opened, and those of the Director of Public Prosecutions. It is the first time that any writer has been able to study these documents. One can only speculate as to why the archives of the firms of solicitors for the defence, Coles & James (now incorporated into Cornfield Law) and Hempsons, have not been made available to me. The title of the book made its appearance early in my research: it was on a 1935 probate form: the executor was asked if they were kin of the deceased or 'A Stranger in Blood'. Dr Adams had, of course, replied that he was 'A Stranger in Blood'.

It is evident that the controversy surrounding the case – and the notoriety achieved by Dr Adams – still lives on in Eastbourne; one can still discern traces of the old battle lines between those who thought him innocent and those who thought him guilty. Not too difficult in a town where people still refer to Kent Lodge in Trinity Trees as 'Bodkin Adams' place', where the nearby chemist's shop (now an interior design boutique) where he bought his supplies of drugs still bears the original name of the owners picked out in mosaic tiles on the doorstep, or where the undertakers who were responsible for organising the burials and cremations of most of his patients are still in business and have preserved records going back over a century.

I approached the archives as an historian of crime, police and punishment, not knowing what I would find, but in an attempt to discover the truth; it was of particular interest to me to examine the police procedures, and the trial itself, and to recreate what exactly had happened during the whole case and in the life of Dr Adams, so far as it could be known. I had no notion that the matter would turn out to have such amazing political and personal links with the elite of the land, or that there might be aspects of the case which seemed in some respects more sinister than the serial murders which might be discovered. The life of John Bodkin Adams spans the major part of the 20th Century and his story is interwoven with many of its significant events.

*One owes respect to the living*
*but to the dead we owe only the truth.*

Voltaire

**Première Lettre sur Oedipe**

# PUBLISHER'S NOTE

———

Because of the vast amount of original source material – much of it previously sealed – made available during the research for this book, both the author and her publishers felt that the length of the text should not be compromised.

The case of Dr Bodkin Adams was remarkable in many ways. One of the first murder trials to attract the burgeoning interest of an increasingly vociferous media, there are few people now approaching the autumn of their days who will not remember the myriad photographs of the portly doctor nor the huge publicity which surrounded the trial and its aftermath. Given that, to them, the circumstances of the story are so well known, *A Stranger in Blood* does not employ a conventional narrative structure. Those younger readers who may wish to avail themselves first of the actual sequence of events may care to follow the route outlined below.

By avoiding those sections which record the extensive quotations from Police reports undertaken as the case against Dr Adams was compiled, some readers may find it more beneficial to return to that body of evidence, after they have first read the descriptive narrative detailed in the order below:

Part One – All
Part Two – Chapters 17–20, 22–29
Part Three – All
Part Four – All

*You will not come again, your song is done,*
*The white waves leap upon the Antrim shore,*
*The fields are bright beneath the westering sun,*
*But you will come no more.*

Moira O'Neill

**Songs of the Glens of Antrim**

# PART I

---

# Prologue

———

# Dublin

## 23 July 1956

———

It is approaching midnight on a Monday evening. A young garda is marching down the warm, silent corridor of a hotel in Dublin. The pile of the carpet beneath his feet is so thick that his boots make practically no sound. These are unfamiliar surroundings, but he finds the suite easily and halts outside. He knocks on the door. After a short delay, it opens. The garda is a head taller than the stocky, middle-aged man who stands before him, dressed informally in sweater and slacks. He has the features and expression of a disgruntled frog and is smoking a cigarette through a short black holder. They consider each other in silence.

It is the resident, the well-known actor, not his visitor, who speaks first. A simple salutation. Nothing more. His tone is measured, even friendly. The accent is upper-class; the voice deep, warm and gravelly. It is as familiar to the garda as Churchill's. He catches just a whiff of Johnnie Walker.

> 'Mr Leslie Henson,' says the Garda 'I have reason to believe… that you have just made… an anonymous telephone call… to the headquarters of the constabulary in Eastbourne, England…'

Leslie Henson had not given his name to Eastbourne Police, but his voice was far too distinctive not to be recognised. He was an extremely popular musical comedy star who had become a household name between the wars; he had appeared in two films, both made in 1943: *Adventure for Two* and *The Demi-Paradise*. During the war, he helped form ENSA and travelled the world entertaining the troops. Even today, his sons, Nicky and Joe, are still buttonholed by elderly gentlemen recalling their father's glamourous musical shows in far-flung corners of the theatre of war. The son of a wealthy man, he was educated at Emmanuel public school, where his physical appearance earned him the nickname 'Froggie'. Later, as a young man, he had had to undergo a career threatening operation to his vocal chords, which left him with the throaty delivery that became his fortune and incidentally betrayed him to the Eastbourne Police. It did not take them long to discover that he was appearing in *Small Hotel* at the Olympia Theatre in Dublin.

He may not have left his name, but Leslie Henson's message was clear enough. It concerned Gertrude Joyce (known as 'Bobbie') Hullett, who had died earlier that day, and her husband, Alfred John Hullett, known as Jack, who had died only three months previously. The circumstances of both deaths were suspicious and needed to be investigated.

Leslie Henson had known Jack Hullett for a long time and they were close friends. Jack was a member of Lloyds and was extremely wealthy. He had a great love of the theatre and was the treasurer of an actors' charity – the Royal Actors' Benevolent Society, which owned Denville Hall, a retirement home for actors, which was in Northwood in Middlesex. Leslie Henson was chairman of the charity. For years, they had been meeting regularly to go over the charity's accounts. The Hensons were frequent visitors to Eastbourne and probably stayed regularly with the Hulletts in their large house on the sea front, in full view of the promontory, Beachy Head, the most chic address in town. St Bede's Preparatory School was next door and Jack Hullett recommended it to Leslie Henson when he was looking for a prep school for his son, Nicky (Nicky Henson followed his father into show business and is a very successful comedy actor).

The friendship between Jack Hullett and the Hensons began just after the war. At that time, Jack Hullett was married to Mabel Theodora Hullett. Mabel died in 1951. The Hulletts' doctor was Dr Adams. The Hulletts would have known Bobbie Tomlinson, the wife of the headmaster at St Bede's. Her husband, Vaughan, died in August, 1954. Bobbie was a buxom, vivacious woman, with something of the Mediterranean about her. At fifty, she was twenty years younger than Jack Hullett. Nevertheless, a romance flourished between them. According to Dr Adams' statements to the newspapers, it was a relationship he had actively encouraged. He claimed to have suggested that Jack should take Bobbie on a winter cruise early in 1955. It was on their return from that cruise that the couple were married, in the Spring of 1955.

By all accounts, they were extremely happy together; their home was one of the centres of society life in Eastbourne. The theatre having always been one of Jack Hullett's passions, they frequently entertained actors, actresses, directors and producers. They were generous hosts and their 'showbiz' parties were popular, drawing in the wealthy and well-connected residents and visitors to Eastbourne. They supported various local charities and were frequently seen at society events at the Grand Hotel.

The Hensons continued to visit. Dr Adams was also a frequent guest at the Hulletts' parties, so they met him regularly. But something about him always made them feel uneasy.

Jack Hullett's sudden death from a cerebral thrombosis at the age of 71 in March, 1956, came as a great shock. The Hensons' concern transferred immediately to Bobbie. Not surprisingly, although she had been left a very wealthy woman, she was deeply depressed. She seemed to have become heavily dependent on Dr Adams and was constantly in a drugged, confused state from the medication he prescribed. Their concern was not assuaged by the news that Bobbie had been persuaded to go on holiday to Ireland with a party of people from Eastbourne, a party which included Dr Adams. But in deference to Bobbie and her daughter, Patricia, they did not interfere. It was a decision they perhaps came to regret.

Bobbie Hullett died on 27 July, 1956, practically four months to the day after Jack Hullett's funeral, having never really emerged from mourning. The cause of death, reported by Dr Adams on the death certificate, was Barbitone poisoning. Her death was suspected to be suicide.

When his wife telephoned him in Dublin with the news, Leslie Henson was devastated. The couple found it hard to comprehend that, in the space of a few months, they had lost first Jack, now Bobbie. They had always harboured grave suspicions of the Hulletts' podgy doctor with his large pink hands, his dark Saville Row suits and thick-rimmed spectacles. Perhaps they had also heard the dark rumours which circulated about him in Eastbourne. Partly fuelled by his own indiscretions in revealing how frequently he received legacies from his dear departed patients, the rumours speculated whether their deaths were entirely due to natural causes. Perhaps Leslie had also heard not only the dark mutterings about Dr Adams' liberal use of dangerous drugs to gain control over his elderly patients but also the whispers of drug peddling and euthanasia killings. Maybe he remembered how the normally vivacious Bobbie had looked, heavily sedated, on the Hensons' last visit.

Whatever the case, he found the circumstances just too suspicious to ignore. After all, the doctor had motive, means and, God knew, plenty of opportunity. But what could he do? He was committed to a season in Dublin; travelling to England and seeing to the matter personally was out of the question. But in his grief, he had a strong impulse to communicate, to do something. He had to talk to somebody. Doubtless the Hensons' frequent social visits meant that they had the home telephone numbers of the Great and the Good in Eastbourne but it would have been difficult to broach a subject like this even at the best of times, let alone out of the blue, late at night. Anyway, given the characteristic British diffidence, could he actually have relied on them to take any action? Still, he did owe it to his old friend to do something…

He felt driven to sharing his suspicions with someone in authority. He considered calling the police. Probably not the Chief of Police, since he was known to be a close friend of Dr Adams. Perhaps just the police station. There was no need to give them his name… a friend of the family… a word to the wise… rum business… thought they should look into it… that sort of thing. Perhaps his wife, who was in England at the time, could get the number for him; no need to trouble the switchboard in Dublin to speak to Directory Enquiries and start too many hares. He picked up the telephone.

Though rumours had simmered locally in Eastbourne for over twenty years, it was Leslie Henson's anonymous call on 23rd July to Eastbourne Police that triggered a chain of events, which would culminate in the arrest and trial of Dr John Bodkin Adams on a charge of murdering one of his patients.

The police investigation was to attract huge media interest. Eastbourne police quickly recognized that they were out of their depth. Perhaps the Chief of Police also knew the rumours which linked one of his senior police officers to Dr Adams. In any event, he called Scotland Yard, Britain's premier police authority, who nominated the charismatic Herbert Hannam to take charge of the case.

Chapter One

—◆—

# Genesis

—◆—

John Bodkin Adams was born on the 21st January in 1899: he was a Victorian, by a whisker. He was born in a bedroom over his father's shop in the High Street of Randalstown, a small market town with less than 3,000 inhabitants in County Antrim, in what is today, Northern Ireland. The main work in the town was linen-bleaching, which employed 1,000 at its height. His father was Samuel Adams, a tall, handsome man with dark hair and a moustache, a man brimming over with the confidence of the Victorian age, a watchmaker[1], and the son of a watchmaker, a man who had a passionate interest in new inventions and a man with a lay preacher's profound knowledge of the bliss of heaven and the bonfires of eternal damnation. In the tradition of Irish sons, Samuel Adams had married late.

He was already thirty-nine when he married Ellen Bodkin on 17th December, 1896 at the Methodist Church at Magherafelt, near Randalstown. She was the twelfth child in a family of fourteen and was a small, plain woman; being already thirty, she might not have been considered marriage material. Had her family not owned scutch[2] mills and had money, she might have been condemned to spinsterly dependence. Samuel Adams had taken over his father's business as a watchmaker and jeweller and the house and shop, and in such a poor community, he probably also operated as the town's pawnbroker. It generated sufficient profit for them to buy a plot of land further up the main street in Randalstown and build cottages on it, which were rented out to local mill workers. Dr Adams always described his father as a jeweller and a Justice of the Peace – an ancient but minor civic appointment – and also as a property developer. Intriguingly, he rarely talked about his mother.

It was into this comfortable middle class environment that the Adams' first son was born. In a society riven even today by sectarian divisions, the Bodkins and the Adams were Plymouth Brethren. This small protestant movement began in Dublin in the late 1820s, when the Rev. J.N. Darby, a curate in Wicklow, left the Anglican communion and joined others in Dublin who called themselves 'Brethren'; it was later when he went to Plymouth in England and had great success in persuading many others to join him that they began to be called 'Plymouth Brethren'.

[1] Directories of Randalstown  /  [2] flax-dressing for linen-making

Its teachings, which have continuously evolved since its foundation, were extremely austere: as Calvin and Knox had protested against the extravagances and dogma of Rome, so the Plymouth Brethren rejected what they considered the trappings of Christianity – elaborate buildings, decoration, music, ceremony and priests or ministers. Each day began and ended with prayer; each meal was preceded by grace. Sunday observance was absolute, as were evening prayer meetings during the week. Meetings were held in the homes of members, five times on a Sunday; all members attended wearing dark clothing and 'Sunday best'. There would be a sermon based on the Scriptures and preached by a male member of the congregation. There was no written body of orthodox teaching or any central organisation – each congregation was guided by the teachings of lay preachers. The most important books of the Bible for them were the Epistles of Paul and *Revelation* from the New Testament and those of *Genesis*, *Exodus*, and *Ecclesiastes* from the Old Testament. The Bible was – and is – regarded as literally true: from the story of Adam and Eve to the Second Coming. All their actions were based upon their interpretation of the Scriptures in the confidence that the Divine Will was revealed to them in direct answer to their prayers.

Women obeyed men in all things. As Edmund Gosse observed:

'My Mother always deferred to my Father, and in his absence spoke of him to me, as if he were all-wise. I confused him in some sense with God.'[3]

Gosse also recorded that illnesses and accidents were interpreted as the Lord's hand 'extended in chastisement' and that there would be much prayer so that 'it might be explained to the sufferer, or to his relations, in what he or they had sinned.'

The movement observed the cycle of the Christian Year but without the celebrations common to the Catholic, Protestant or Orthodox traditions. Consumption of alcohol or tobacco was also abjured and anything regarded as frivolous, which often included books of fiction and games. Children, 'dedicated' as infants, were usually forbidden to mix with others who were not of their persuasion. Their central notion was simple enough: those who accepted the teachings of the Brethren were 'saved'; once they were baptised, they became 'Saints' and would be raised to eternal bliss – which was to be infinitely preferred to this earthly life – and being then saved by grace, nothing in their subsequent behaviour on earth could change their eternal destiny of sainthood. The movement took firm root in Ireland about the time of the potato famine. Ellen Adams had a brilliant brother, Dr John Bodkin, who had graduated at twenty-two with honours and distinction in Medicine from Queen's University; in the tradition of the Plymouth Brethren, he had been called as a medical missionary to China. The Chinese had so appreciated his efforts to rescue their souls and improve their public health system that they had made him a Mandarin. So Samuel and Ellen Adams named their infant son after this religiocrat: Samuel did so out of respect, but Ellen harboured quite a different ambition – the 'Bodkin' label would prove to be an albatross round the neck of her first born.

[3] Gosse, *Father and Son*

He would also learn early on that the wrath of God is exercised through all too human hands. His earliest memory was of being chastised as a three year old by his father. The dispassionate observer might have deemed his offence trivial – he had refused an apple, which had been offered to him by a friend. In his parents' eyes, however, he had refused to accept a 'gift of God' and retribution followed as night does day. Dr Adams would later defend his father's action, saying it helped to keep him on the straight and narrow. From today's perspective, Samuel Adams' behaviour teetered on the edge of abuse. Dr Adams' *post hoc* justification rings very hollow, particularly since it was a statement made to a reporter for the edification of newspaper readers. He recalled crossing his father only once more, but vouchsafed no details of the second incident. It is likely, however, that his father was merely the executioner. John Adams' real Svengali was his mother. Like many tyrants, she was small but had a will of iron.

Not that life in the Adams' household was devoid of pastimes or amusement. Samuel Adams was a sportsman and his prizes were for the pot. He was an excellent game and wild fowl shot and an expert fisherman. These skills he passed on to his elder son and John's younger brother, William Samuel, born in 1903. More endearingly, he also had the Victorians' passion for machines: neighbours recalled seeing him aloft, on a penny-farthing bicycle. There followed a rapid succession of new-fangled cycles, then a motorbike and finally, a motor car – a shiny new Wolseley. He became a car enthusiast and, in 1906, had an article published in the *Motor News* of Dublin. Mrs Adams cycled; Dr Adams also claimed that she had played golf and went sailing with her husband on Lough Neagh, Co. Tyrone. Dr Adams inherited his father's interest in shooting, cars, radios and cameras, and he played a little golf. But shooting was his passion. Having started at a tender age and having the benefit of a stocky figure, he became a first-class shot, in spite of his poor eyesight. In later life, he also loved owning expensive motor cars and photographic equipment but his skill and knowledge of such grown-up toys never matched his father's.

John Adams was somewhat unlucky in other aspects of his genetic inheritance. He managed a remarkable metamorphosis: his appearance favoured his father when he was young and his mother as he grew older. . His father was tall and rangy; photographs of John Adams at university show that he was not particularly tall, but was quite slim. However, his mother's heavier build asserted itself in later life. He broadened out, especially after his mother died .

When John was four, Samuel and Ellen Adams had made sufficient money to sell up their business interests in Randalstown and retire. They moved to Ballinderry Bridge on the shores of Lough Neagh, buying 'Fairview', the biggest house in the hamlet. Samuel Adams then devoted his life to preaching. John Adams attended his first year in the Methodist primary school in Ballinderry in 1903 – the same year his brother was born. On Sundays the family would travel miles to the nearest Plymouth Brethren meeting place, where Samuel Adams would preach. A certain Paddy McCosher, who once lived near 'Fairview' is quoted as saying: 'He [John Adams] never seemed to play with the others. He was a wee bit mean'[4]; evidence of a childhood made lonely by his parents' prohibition against playing with children from

---

[4] Hallworth

families other than Plymouth Brethren. But his relationship with his younger brother evidently became very close.

Many of the Bodkins were and had been, doctors. in the tradition of the Brethren. The family believed in education and academic prowess was expected of them. In 1911, when John was twelve, the family made their second move: they settled in Coleraine so that he could attend the Coleraine Academical Institution. In addition to his preaching commitments, Samuel Adams took up the appointment as Justice of the Peace. On Sundays, the family would travel miles in the Wolseley – William Samuel in the front next to his father, John Bodkin with his mother in the back – to the nearest Plymouth Brethren meeting place where Samuel Adams would preach.

In 1914, shortly before the outbreak of the First World War, came the first great blow to this little family: at the age of 57, Samuel Adams had a stroke. The obituary in the 'Coleraine Chronicle' described what had occurred:

'Sudden Death of Mr Samuel Adams J.P.

Feelings of surprise and sorrow were occasioned in Coleraine by the death, which took place on Wednesday night [30th September, 1914] of Mr Samuel Adams J.P., Ebenezer House, Mountsandel. Deceased had been for a motor run to Portstewart on the same evening and returned about 5 o'clock. Later he complained of a pain in his head. Grave symptoms developed and Dr J.T. Creery was speedily summoned, but Mr Adams died shortly before midnight. Deceased who was 57 years of age, was regularly in attendance at the petty sessions court and was much esteemed by his magisterial colleagues. He formerly resided at Fairview House, Ballinderry Bridge, Moneymore and came to Coleraine four years ago. He leaves a wife and family to mourn his loss.'

Within a matter of a few hours, John's father had died in a coma; the funeral followed rapidly, just thirty-eight hours later, and his body was buried in a grave in the centre of Coleraine cemetery, high above the town.

His death gave Ellen Adams full responsibility for her sons' upbringing. Before her marriage she had been an active worker in the temperance organisation. Her first action after her widowhood was to make them both sign the pledge, rejecting gambling and intoxicating drink.

'In God's name and with His help, I do promise to abstain absolutely from every form of intoxicating drink; also from gambling in every form. Knowing this to be the wishes of my late father, and mother's.

Signed J.B. Adams. W.S. Adams'

In an article in the *Daily Express*, Dr Adams would later claim that '…to the time of my mother's death there was never a bottle of spirits in my house…' and that he remained faithful to the pledge. The first part of the claim was undoubtedly true, but the second was not.

In 1916, shortly after the Battle of the Somme, the trio moved to Belfast where, at the age of seventeen, John Bodkin Adams matriculated at Queen's University to begin his medical studies. He joined the Officer Training Corps, apparently with the ambition of obtaining a commission as a surgeon probationer in the Royal Navy. This ambition was thwarted by a serious illness, which he would later suggest was a 'virulent septic infection', mentioning that, at the time, he was thought to have tuberculosis. It was this long period of sickness, he said, which forced him to resign from the O.T.C. The illness also affected his studies. One of his lecturers at the faculty remembered him as a 'plodder' and a 'lone wolf' rather than a brilliant student, and he was advised to abandon his medical career. He made a better than anticipated recovery and was ultimately able to qualify by the scheduled date in 1921. But the break in his studies meant he had to cram two years into one and this denied him the possibility of an honours degree. The writing was already on the wall for his ambition to emulate the glorious career of the great John Bodkin.

It was his brother William who had inherited the Bodkin genius. He was a sensitive, attractive boy. He sailed effortlessly through life, in his brother's wake. He also intended to follow the family tradition by studying medicine at Queen's. At 15 years old, in 1918, he was already matriculated. He was also a gifted painter and was attending Art College in Belfast prior to going up to Queen's. There was an oil painting of William, probably a self-portrait, which would later hang in Dr Adams' waiting room in Eastbourne. He was to cherish the painting in lieu of the artist, for William died suddenly in the influenza pandemic at the end of the First World War, only three months after the portrait was completed.

—

If God had a recruiting sergeant for missionaries, it was Professor Rendle Short. He was a professor in the Faculty of Medicine at Bristol University, a deeply religious man, a philosopher, a great speaker and a member of the Plymouth Brethren. Still harbouring his childhood dream, John Adams attended a missionary study-class conference held at Larne on the Antrim coast during his last student holiday before graduation. The convenor was Professor Short.

After he qualified with an ordinary degree, the young Dr Adams travelled to Portrush with the intention of relaxing for two months and, no doubt, contemplating his future. But that Bodkin pedigree was too impeccable for Rendle Short to ignore. Hardly had Dr Adams settled in, than he received a telegram from Professor Short, offering him an appointment as an assistant houseman at the Bristol Royal Infirmary. Scarcely two weeks later, he was on duty in Casualty – what would today be called 'A & E' – Accident and Emergency. The accident department was not a popular option for career-minded doctors, since it did not lead naturally to a specialisation.

The assistant houseman was the lowest echelon of doctor in a hospital. Survive this intellectual and physical challenge as someone so inferior that you are barely acknowledged even by the nurses, so the wisdom ran, and you show yourself fit to be marked for future greatness. The assistant houseman was a denizen of the hospital, on call round the clock, with perhaps only one day off a week. Promotion depended on opportunity and impressing the professors and consultants. Only the truly dedicated followed this career path and the ambitious would also study for further degrees – particularly in a teaching hospital like Bristol – under the tutelage of senior doctors, who were usually also senior academics, probably also with lucrative private practices.

Dr Adams was studying to qualify for a diploma in public health, which took him six months.

> 'When I was working for my DPH the pathologist gave me the key to the fire escape door of the laboratory, so that I could go there out of hours and get the experience needed on the plating and culturing of bacteria. Pneumococci were important then because the organism killed lots of people. I know that they had the smallpox virus in the lab, without any of the fuss which came later. When my colleagues went out of an evening I worked at the books and obtained my DPH.'[5]

He had to work hard and had very little time for sleep. The one break he had was Sunday: he would go to a Brethren meeting in the morning, then take a five-mile walk into the country, returning to Bristol for the Plymouth Brethren services in the evening, where Professor Rendle Short often preached, and then home to bed. No problem for a young man brought up by his parents' tough regime.

It was at such a meeting on a Sunday that Professor Rendle Short handed him an advertisement which his wife had cut out of a Christian weekly. According to Dr Adams, Rendle Short told him: 'I don't want you to take this job but I have to show you the cutting'. This sentence attributed to Rendle Short perhaps to demonstrate a religious imperative; it seems likely that Rendle Short had decided that the best course for John Adams was to become a general practitioner. Taking the hint and perhaps fearing the consequences of refusing a gift from God Dr Adams decided to answer the advertisement:

> 'WANTED Christian young Doctor-assistant, with view to Partnership in a large South Coast practice – c.821, 12, Paternoster Bldgs. E.C.4.'

Dr Adams had two versions of what happened next: one told to the Police before the Trial, the other to Percy Hoskins, the crime reporter from the *Daily Express*, after the trial. He told Superintendent Hannam that a reply came to say the position was filled, but two weeks later, a telegram arrived on a Friday asking him to call next day for an interview. The Hoskins version makes no mention of the post being at first filled. Both versions agree that he arrived in Eastbourne the evening of the day following the receipt of the telegram: it was windy and pouring with rain and there was no one to meet him at the station. He was interviewed the following day, which was a Sunday, and he got the job.

[5] Surtees, quoting Dr Adams

Chapter Two

---

# Eastbourne in the 1920s

---

A young man  dressed in tweeds stepped from the London train and looked cautiously around, like someone in unaccustomed surroundings or perhaps a stag at bay. He was above medium height, but his build gave more the impression of girth. He wore spectacles with lenses like the bottom of a wine bottle; they had the effect of distorting and magnifying his eyes.

The small railway station in Eastbourne was pretty as well as practical, as if the architect had wanted to celebrate a memorable holiday in Austria. But the young man was more concerned about the heavy rain. He was something of an expert on bad weather, having been brought up on the Atlantic Antrim coast. He was sharply disappointed, having expected a much softer welcome from this resort town on the English Channel which was so renowned for its benign weather, that it had become a haven for the wealthy and the retired and in particular for those who were both. Doubts entered his mind; he wondered if he was making a mistake in coming here.

Eastbourne today has retained many of the features of the busy but sedate little town that first met his eye: the neat, tree-lined streets fanning outwards from the station; the comfortable, well-presented houses with tall windows on the first two floors capped by a row of smaller windows above; the efficiency and quiet discretion of a town used to caring for visitors and elderly residents. That evening, there might even have been a uniformed chauffeur holding an umbrella and ushering first class passengers off the train into a stately Rolls Royce. If so, the young man, who loved motorcars with almost the same passion he reserved for shooting, would certainly have noticed. Perhaps it was such a scene that persuaded him to stay. His first night in Eastbourne was probably spent in whichever of the small temperance hotels was open out of season and had been recommended by his future colleagues.

The young man's name was John Bodkin Adams. He was a recently qualified doctor who had grown up with the ambition of becoming a great missionary. His reason for travelling from Bristol to Eastbourne that day was to attend an interview. The interview would change the course of his life; he was destined to spend the rest of his long professional career in Eastbourne. In the course of that career, he would become the wealthiest GP in Britain and the accused in a sensational murder trial.

The British aristocracy is often endowed with commercial flair, particularly when confronted by falling rents or rising taxation. The Dukes of Devonshire fashioned Eastbourne from a cluster of small villages, which might otherwise have slept the nineteenth century out in tranquillity. By adding a fine esplanade, some equally fine hotels, some splendid houses and their own aristocratic cache, they created a haven which attracted in generations of retiring generals, ambassadors and industrialists. They in turn, applied their own considerable fortunes to building more houses, their charity to the creation of hospitals.

Eastbourne was not simply another commercial development; tacitly, it became a movement to preserve certain values and a way of life threatened by a changing world. It transformed itself into a coastal spa without the tackiness which often attends such places. Successive generations of the Dukes of Devonshire preserved the gentility of the place by controlling development, particularly along the sea front. People with wealth and influence had settled in large mansions to the west of the town; they and the hotels found their staff in the meaner streets on the east side. A pier had been built in 1865 at the point where the two communities met. Even today, locals characterise Eastbourne streets and neighbourhoods as being either east or west of the pier.

By the time Dr Adams arrived, the population had grown to 25,000, of whom perhaps 85% were involved directly or indirectly in looking after the remaining 15%. The town had also become a modestly popular tourist and holiday destination. Since it had been constructed over sixty years before, the railway had been bringing in visitors — mainly from London and the home counties.

The town praised God and celebrated the King's birthday and Empire Day. There was a social order underpinned by the Devonshire family, bolstered by Royal visits and upheld by common consent. The town expected to return Conservative members of Parliament now and forever. Eastbourne had been designated a county borough which gave the local council great powers and prestige, symbolised by heavy robes, gold chains of office, solemn portraits in the council offices and its own police force. The members of the council were exclusively Conservative and included local landowners and farmers, ex military officers, former diplomats and wealthy local businessmen. The local Member of Parliament was certainly a significant figure, but his — Eastbourne has never been represented in Parliament by a woman — local influence and power were not as significant as to those of the Mayor.

However well organised, life in Eastbourne was not untouched by crime. In 1920, the murder of seventeen-year-old Irene Munro made headline news. She had been on holiday in Eastbourne, staying at 393 Seaside — east of the pier — and her savagely battered body was found, partially buried, on the Crumbles, a stretch of shingle between Eastbourne and Pevensey Bay belonging to the Duke of Devonshire's estates. [The Crumbles has since been transformed into two large marinas full of luxury yachts, with extensive housing and restaurants.] Two local men in their twenties, Jack Field and William Gray, were convicted of her murder and hanged in February 1921, after an appeal.

In 1924, the Crumbles was the venue for another, rather more grisly murder. Emily Kaye, a thirty-seven-year old London typist, had been taken to a coastguard's cottage on the Crumbles by Patrick Mahon, a married man. His wife had found a ticket in her husband's pocket and hired a private detective who found a bag in the cloakroom at Waterloo Station, containing bloodstained clothing and a carving knife. Chief Inspector Savage of Scotland Yard took over, arrested Mahon, and then found the dismembered body of Miss Kaye in the cottage, part of it boiled in pans in the kitchen; the head was never found. Not only had Mahon – a handsome philanderer – obtained money from Emily Kaye, but she was pregnant. Sir Bernard Spilsbury, the Home Office pathologist, shattered the defence case by showing that Mahon's explanation of her death was a fabrication. Patrick Mahon was convicted and executed at Wandsworth prison, admitting his guilt in the end. While the cottage on the Crumbles still stood, visitors would peer over the wall to see where the slaughter had taken place.

Eastbourne's first seaside visitors – when it was separate hamlets – arrived in 1780, when King George III and Queen Charlotte, with their youngest children, Princesses Elizabeth and Sophia and Prince Edward, stayed at the Seahouses on the seafront. This wholesome, family visit set the tone of the place, in the same way that the visit of their eldest son, the pleasure-loving Prince Regent, set that of Eastbourne's neighbour, Brighton. This royal visit was followed by those of Princess Amelia in 1789 and 1790. The tradition of aristocratic visitors continued with the arrival of many refugees from the French Revolution; in one day alone during the Terror, three hundred emigrés landed on the beach.[1]

William Wilberforce enjoyed a seaside holiday in Eastbourne in 1808, following the success of his anti-slavery campaign, and Jane Austen used Eastbourne as the location for her unfinished novel *Sanditon*. Following the Napoleonic Wars, there was little development until the 1830s; in 1831 Charles Dickens came to visit and Jenny Lind, the 'Swedish Nightingale' stayed at Cliff Cottage, which was in the town centre, on two occasions. Alfred, Lord Tennyson stayed at Mount Pleasant in 1843 and at the Seahouses in 1845.

During this period, the journey from London was interminable. The coming of the railway in 1849 lent huge impetus to the town's development as a resort but it was the enclosure of the land by the Cavendish and Davies Gilbert families which enabled its expansion.[2]

On 30th June, 1883, the Prince and Princess of Wales (later Edward VII and Queen Alexandra) opened Western Parade and the Princess Alice Hospital. Princess Alice of Hesse, mother of the last Tsarina, after whom the hospital is named, had a great interest in the care of the sick, visiting the aged and infirm, and spent the last year of her life in Eastbourne, where she died in 1878 of diphtheria at the age of 35. Both Edward VII and George V came to Eastbourne to visit as friends of the Dukes of Devonshire.

Lewis Carroll (Charles Lutwidge Dodgson), the author of Alice in Wonderland, was an enthusiastic visitor, who stayed at 7, Lushington Road and at 2, Bedfordwell Road, for twenty-two summers between 1876 and 1897; *Sylvie and Bruno* was written in Eastbourne. Mrs Dyer,

---

[1] Surtees, *Eastbourne: A History*

[2] Rich landowners normally promoted Inclosure Bills in Parliament for agricultural purposes, depriving yeomen farmers, smallholders and villagers of their common law rights and forcing them off their land; this was a very late enclosure for development purposes, and the ancient strip farming system was still extant in the area up to 1840.

his landlady in Lushington Road was 'a good motherly creature' and his accommodation consisted of 'a nice little front sitting room and adjoining bedroom', but he brought with him some rather cumbersome luggage as it included his own tin bath. [3] Thomas Huxley, the biologist, and Friedrich Engels were late 19th Century resident and visitor respectively; it is a fine irony that the co-author of *The Communist Manifesto* later had his ashes scattered from Beachy Head.

In 1905, Claude Debussy stayed at the Grand Hotel (completed in 1877) with his pregnant mistress, Emma Bardac, fleeing from the scandal of deserting his wife. He found the Grand 'a peaceful and charming spot, where he could relax like an animal'. [4] He was apparently 'very shy and was hardly ever seen in the public rooms.' [5] He completed his composition *La Mer*, partly inspired by the English Channel. Another piece, *Reflets dans l'eau*, the first of his *Images pour Piano*, is said to have been inspired 'by his watching the interplay of sun and cloud on an ornamental pool in Devonshire Park'. [6]

The Grand Hotel's visitors in the early 20th Century included: Lord Lytton 1902, Lord and Lady Curzon 1904, Lord Kelvin 1905, Lord Abercorn 1906, Campbell Bannerman, Prime Minister, 1907, Lord Willingdon 1910 (later Viceroy of India), Count Togo (Prime Minister of Japan) 1911, the Prince and Princess of Hesse 1913, King Constantine of Greece and Queen Sophie 1913, Sir Ernest Shackleton 1914, the Prince of Wales (later Edward VIII), Sir George Robey, and Max Aitken (later Lord Beaverbrook).

Other musicians and composers followed Debussy to the Grand Hotel: Eugene Ysaye, the great Belgian violinist, conductor and composer; the Czech violinist and composer, Jan Kubelik – the second Paganini; Jan Paderewski, pianist, composer and statesman of Poland; Fritz Kreisler, the Austrian violinist; Paolo Tosti, Italian composer of many famous songs; Enrico Caruso and Dame Nellie Melba. The prima ballerina *assoluta* Anna Pavlova came to stay at the Grand, the pianist Dame Myra Hess, the conductors, Sir Henry Wood and Sir Thomas Beecham, Sir Edward Elgar, and two Russians: the bass Chaliapin and the pianist Vladimir de Pachmann.

Rupert Brooke, First World War poet and the enduring image of the lost generation of that conflict, made several visits to Eastbourne and stayed at the Beachy Head Hotel in 1911. A later socialist afficionado of Eastbourne was George Bernard Shaw, who apparently learned to ride a bicycle in the town. [7]

Dr Adams started his career in 1922 making calls to patients by bicycle, but soon migrated to a motor cycle. Being ever watchful and knowledgeable about such things, he might have noticed a Brough Superior, the Rolls Royce of motorbikes, outside Number 18 Southfields Road. The owner of the Brough Superior was Lawrence of Arabia. He was a regular visitor to the home of Charles Doughty, the distinguished Arabist and author of *Arabia Deserta*, and corresponded with him regularly. [8]

The aristocratic, the rich and famous and the merely rich continued to visit Eastbourne during the 1920s and even during the depressed 1930s, staying in particular at the Grand Hotel. Queen Marie of Yugoslavia and her son – later King Peter, Amy Johnson and her husband Jim

---

[3] Surtees, *Eastbourne: A History* / [4] Pugh / [5] Ibid / [6] Ibid / [7] Surtees, *Eastbourne: A History* / [8] Enser, *Eastbourne Medical Gazette Centenary Edition*

Mollison, Paul Robeson, the Duke and Duchess of York (later King George VI and Queen Elizabeth), the Emperor and Empress of Japan and the King and Queen of the Hellenes. Small wonder that Dr Adams would aspire to the post of doctor to the Grand and the other large hotels. Small wonder that, in 1929, he borrowed money from a wealthy patient, bought a house in Trinity Trees, a prestigious address opposite the private Esperance Hospital, and established his own practice.

Chapter Three

---

# The War Years in Eastbourne

## 1939–1945

---

At the beginning of the Second World War, the prevalent view was that Eastbourne would be a safe haven – after all, wisdom had it, why would Hitler want to bomb a quiet little civilian town of no strategic importance? In 1939, Eastbourne's M.P., Charles Taylor, even made a somewhat complacent speech expressing views which he was later to regret, stating that he ' – did not think that Eastbourne need worry about being bombed in time of war'. As a consequence, in September, 1939, around 17,000 children and hospital patients duly arrived as evacuees from London. It would not be long before they were being hurriedly evacuated out again. By the time war broke out, Dr Adams was a well-established society doctor. Although many of his patients had left Eastbourne, his workload increased exponentially; first, there were the evacuees to care for; then his partner, Dr Harris, was called up for service in India; then his other partner, Dr Snowball,[1] had to do extra surgical work at the hospital.

In the event, the war reached Eastbourne on 21st March, 1940, with the bombing of a merchant ship, the S.S. *Barnhill*, off Beachy Head. Shortly after, came the end of the 'phoney war' on April 8th-9th, when Germany invaded Denmark and Norway. The 21st (Eastbourne) Battalion of the Sussex Home Guard was formed on the 14th May, 1940 just before the German army reached the French coast in June. On Sunday, July 7th, without warning, a Dornier Do. 17 aeroplane dropped ten bombs on Whitley Road in the centre of Eastbourne; two people died in this raid, which was the start of the intensive bombing of Eastbourne. The town – in common with many others along Britain's southern and eastern seaboards – was a so-called ' target of opportunity'. In the overall context of the war in Europe, the attacks on Eastbourne may not have been remarkable for their ferocity or the damage they caused. After all, the damage and death toll suffered Eastbourne was hardly on a scale with Coventry or Dresden. But the shock for those living in Eastbourne, who had enjoyed the security and tranquillity of the place, was nonetheless devastating.

---

[1] The convention is to designate surgeons as 'Mr', but for purposes of clarity, 'Dr' is used.

George Humphrey, in his book, describes what happened: [2]

> 'Why was Eastbourne deliberately bombed? Primarily because it was a key feature in the German invasion plans, but this held good for only a few days in September 1940. After that, with one or two exceptions the bombing took place because the Luftwaffe crews who made the trip across the Channel were mostly trainees who found Beachy Head easy to locate. Once found, Eastbourne was conveniently to hand; once Eastbourne was found the protruding pier made a useful point of reference. It was as simple as that according to ex-Luftwaffe sources. Raiders aborting raids on London played little part in the attacks, generally simply unloading their bombs hereabouts at night because they were making Beachy Head their point of reference for departure from British airspace. Our real ordeal came in daylight and it was deliberate, not the 'wides, over-throws and leg-byes' from London raids. People died, were injured, bereaved – generally without adequate warning.'

It was after a running fight down the coast on 16th August, when a Messerschmitt Me110 was shot down over the Meads area and twenty-five bombs were dropped in the town that the *Eastbourne Gazette and Herald* sponsored a Spitfire Fund to buy one of the aircraft in the town's name: the cost was £5,000 and £6,000 was raised in ten days. The bombing continued, and just after the London Blitz began on Saturday, 7th September, 1940, a Home Office proclamation recommended that those with no official duties should voluntarily evacuate from Eastbourne. Even while crowds of people were waiting on the station platforms, bombs were dropped without warning on the town centre, including a junior school. The bombing over three days in September 1940 illustrates its intensity: Friday, September 13th: 18 HE, 1 oil bomb, 4 others. The town centre was hit, the technical institute and the library. [The beginning of the preliminary bombardment for the proposed invasion.] Saturday, September 14th: 2 bombers dropped 8 bombs in the town centre, 3 aircraft dropped 16 bombs also in the centre; 8 more bombs, then 30 H.E. bombs and 24 incendiaries all in residential areas. 'Anti-aircraft fire was virtually non-existent, just a few 40mm Bofors guns – the only viable weapons were on London's perimeter.' [3] Sunday, September 15th, Battle of Britain day: 3 enemy planes dropped 17 HE bombs, one oil bomb and a large number of 2kg Thermite incendiaries on the town.

Eastbourne felt that it was totally undefended: it really was reliant upon the Captain Mainwarings and Corporal Jones of its Home Guard: 'The town felt it was on its own – but all the stronger for that.' [4]

The Germans decided to postpone their invasion until the Spring of 1941, but as for Eastbourne: 'Our private squabble with the Luftwaffe came to life with a long series of air raids having no connection with the defunct invasion and serving no observable military purpose.' [5] These were quite deliberate and indiscriminate attacks: on Monday September 23rd, 28 bombs were strewn by a number of aircraft, which approached the town singly, from the direction of

---

[2] Humphrey, *Eastbourne at War – Portrait of a Front Line Town* / [3] Ibid / [4] Ibid / [5] Ibid

the railway station, and dropped the bombs over residential areas from east of the pier to the Duke of Devonshire's home, Compton Place. With the evacuation, the town's population fell drastically from its normal 60,000; many of Dr Adams' private patients – including Mrs Morrell, who would figure so significantly in his later life – removed themselves.

Saturday, September 28th, 1940, was yet another day of deliberate attack upon the town when 8 bombs were dropped, but it was one which was notable for the most arduous rescue attempt. People were trapped in the cellars in Cavendish Place and the rescue took 36 hours: Dr Snowball crawled under the wreckage near an unexploded bomb and, contending with a burst water main, had to amputate the legs of a seventeen -year-old girl guide, Peggy Harland. She died and was awarded the Girl Guides' VC posthumously; Dr Snowball received a commendation.

Responsibility for organising wartime medical services in Eastbourne, deciding which GPs were available for the armed forces and which should stay in the town fell to a certain Dr Mathew. Those patients whose doctors had gone into the forces could select another GP until their own returned and the selected GP would receive half the fee. Dr Mathew chose twelve doctors for this pool system. He deliberately excluded Dr Adams. It is quite clear from the statements which he would make years later to the police, why Dr Mathew made this decision. He was concerned for the well-being of the patients and did not want to be responsible for the consequences of sending patients to Dr Adams. Dr Adams was of course furious: '…I was the thirteenth, the only one not to receive any pay from the kitty.'[6]

In 1942, Dr Adams sent his elderly mother to stay in the countryside for safety at a cottage in Lower Dicker nearby in Sussex. She died there in March 1943 and he accompanied her body back to Ireland for burial in the family plot in Coleraine.

He had a large and very strong air-raid shelter built in the garden of Kent Lodge and also reinforced the basement. 'Snowball and I slept there in safety through the worst of the raids.'[7] With his reduced workload, he found more time to study for his Diploma in Anaesthetics, which he gained in 1941. At least this meant that he was able to be of more assistance to the war effort in Eastbourne: 'Until Dr Linacre came, I was the only one who could intubate; needed for the facial injuries in the early part of the war.'[8/9]

The bombing continued unabated throughout the rest of 1940. On Sunday, November 10th, 20 bombs were dropped, in two raids, on the seafront and the residential area just east of the pier, and on the 12th the streets were machine-gunned by low-flying aircraft, and bombs were rained on to a council housing estate. 1941 brought more raids, with 300 incendiaries and 4 bombs on March 13th alone. Then, after June 7th, there was a lull and the Luftwaffe left Eastbourne alone for nearly eleven months. Then on 4th May, 1942:

> '13.55 hours. 9 Messerschmitt ME 109s, each carrying 250kg of high explosive bomb, found their way across the Channel, lifted up over Beachy Head and, turning, swept down across the town with cannon and machine guns blazing.'[10]

[6] Surtees, *The Strange Case of Dr. Bodkin Adams* / [7] Ibid / [8] Ibid / [9] Dr. Mathew, however, was an anaesthetist. / [10] Humphrey, *Eastbourne at War – Portrait of a Front Line Town*

It was in June of the same year that the town won from the Home Office, an agreement for a local warning system, as opposed to the normal siren alert for air raids. Instead of the usual portamento between the two notes, they were separated, the result being 'a cuckoo warning' – which became a local term.[11]

On 11th August 1942, came Eastbourne's worst night-raid. It prompted 'many questions and recriminations about the ill-fated Dieppe Raid eight days later.' Twenty-four bombers attacked central residential areas, which included Eastbourne College, one bomb falling on a boarding house of the school. Fifty-seven high explosive bombs and over 2,000 Thermite incendiary bombs were dropped. The incendiaries were fitted with burster charges to scatter flaming fragments. The casualty list was surprisingly low, with only eleven dead. This was:

> '…a deliberate night raid; it was intense; target illuminating flares were used for the first time over the town to ensure accurate identification of target areas; Canadian troops were in dispersed billets throughout each of the areas hit.'[12]

One week after this, the 2nd Canadian Division and British commandoes, together with other units, embarked on the Dieppe Raid. Towards the end of the year, on Friday December 18th, during the daytime, a low-flying bomber dropped four bombs, chained together, onto the shopping centre. The Canadian 1st Infantry Division helped to rescue those buried in the wreckage; eighteen were killed. The last major air raid on the town was on Sunday, June 6th, 1943, by fourteen aircraft, and the last time manned aircraft dropped bombs was on 31st March, 1944.

Six days after D-Day, at 4 a.m. on the night of June 12th/13th, 1944, observers at Beachy Head were able to see the first V1 flying bomb – a Doodle-Bug. 'A few nights later there were a few more – a trickle which rapidly became a stream and later a flood which lasted ten weeks.'[13] Although they were meant for London, London's defence systems were inadequate, and anti-aircraft batteries were moved to the coast to destroy the V1s in flight. When the guns opened fire and hit a V1: 'suddenly there would appear a massive dark cloud with a vivid red centre and the ram-jet engine would come cartwheeling out as the V1 died.'[14]

During the war, the town of Eastbourne had been hit by 671 high explosive bombs, 90 unexploded bombs, 28 oil bombs and over 4,000 incendiary and phosphate incendiary bombs, and 15 V1 flying bombs, apart from the machine gun and cannon fire attacks. This was apart from those which had exploded in the sea. There had been a surprisingly low number of casualties: 172 civilian deaths and 28 servicemen, but there was much damage to housing: 475 destroyed, 1,000 severely damaged and 10,000 slightly damaged.

Scaffolding had been put up on the beach to prevent vehicles landing during the war, and when this was removed, together with the anti-tank and anti-landing mines, the children returned with their buckets and spades, at least to part of the beach. Eastbourne was returning to a semblance of normality.

[11] Ibid / [12] Ibid / [13] Ibid / [14] Ibid

In the immediate post-war period, there was a dramatic surge in public sentiment in Britain away from the Conservative party and a Labour Government was eventually installed in Westminster. This swing was not reflected in the local politics of Eastbourne, where the Conservatives remained resolutely in power and the town continued to return a Conservative MP to Parliament.

Chapter Four

# Eastbourne in the 1950s

By the early 1950s, Eastbourne had become once more home to the wealthy and influential. The bombing – Eastbourne was the most bombed town on the south coast – and deprivations of the War were now distant memories and the scars had been mainly removed from the town centre. The council was launching school building programmes to cope with the baby boom which followed the War. Small crocodiles of children in the school uniforms of the various private preparatory schools wound their comforting way through the town. There were some 40 churches in Eastbourne and Sunday attendances were heavy. The *jeunesse doré* of Eastbourne, had re-established the pleasant routines of tennis club dances, car rallies in ancient Fords and healthy walks along the Downs. Older generations, who had taken the business of leading their nation so seriously, now took to their pleasures with equal intensity and enjoyed the influence they had over the social whirl. Their favourite watering holes were the Grand Hotel and the Cumberland Hotel, which had re-emerged fully restored following their wartime service and were now the venues for famous dinners and celebrations. The town was still in the hands of a Conservative council. Even the Eastbourne herring gulls were thought by some people to be better behaved than their counterparts in other coastal towns.

There was cricket at the Saffrons and tennis in Devonshire Park. The regimental bands played on the seafront under a bandstand with a turquoise dome (emulating the Royal Pavilion in Brighton). They entertained the promenade crowds with familiar tunes from musicals or Gilbert and Sullivan or performed military marches to stiffen backs and set pulses racing. Every Sunday evening, the music from the 'Palm Court' of the Grand Hotel, perhaps with Max Jaffa and his string quartet or such singers as Anne Ziegler and Webster Booth, were broadcast to the nation over the wireless. In 1953, when the Light Programme Director of the BBC had moved the 'Grand Hotel Music Hour' from 7.30 to 9 p.m. because it was affecting church attendance, it was reported in the London *Evening Standard* that:

> 'Whenever the BBC have tried to drop this light music marathon they have been abused by every kind of listener from choleric colonels to irate ironmongers. Grand Hotel is the programme the BBC DARE NOT take off.' [1]

[1] Pugh, *Grand Hotel*

Post-war Eastbourne re-established itself with visitors and holiday makers, but it has never sought to match the brashness of other seaside resorts which had a more popular appeal, where visitors might buy saucy seaside postcards, eat candyfloss or wear kiss-me-quick hats. The railway still brought many holidaymakers and day-trippers; middle-class fathers would drive their families down to Eastbourne in hired black Ford Prefects and bring a picnic lunch to spread out on the cliffs near the Beachy Head end of the seafront.

Perhaps the children might have preferred Brighton where there was the attraction of the new 'Mobo' horses – painted metal horses which 'walked' when you pressed down on the pedals – on a rink by the Aquarium on the seafront, and the little railway which went all the way to Black Rock. But there was still the pier in Eastbourne and the prospect of a high tea in Fuller's tearooms: Welsh rarebit, poached egg, or soft herring roes on toast, scones with strawberry jam and cream, and cakes.

Eastbourne's caché was indeed that it did not attract hoi-polloi; it had retained the sedate elegance which the Victorian planners of the Dukes of Devonshire had intended, their restrictive covenants banning shops along the seafront. It did not have the fusty atmosphere of Folkestone, the seediness of Hastings, or the slightly exciting, verging-on-the-edge-of-something-illegal air of Brighton. The gentility of the town was fiercely protected; bad behaviour was simply not tolerated in public and would win a rebuke from neighbours, passers-by and complete strangers. The authoritarian instinct and the confidence of the 19th Century middle class still epitomised Eastbourne, perhaps even more so in to the face of the radical social change taking place in the rest of the country.

On their visits, the middle classes were rarely drawn east of the pier. West of the pier, the wealthy lived in their enormous houses of red brick and stucco. Today, most of these houses have been divided into flats, but in the '50s, wealthy retirees still maintained staffs of cook-housekeepers and maids, whose quarters were in the top floors.

The best properties were in the Meads area where, in 1956, the residents included Sir Percy Sillitoe – retired director of M.I.5, Sir John Ellerman, shipping millionaire, Brigadier W.W. Linny, O.B.E., Viscount Claremont, Sir Henry Dalton, and Mr Clarkson Rose, the impresario. The retired remnants of the Raj were here, the widows of Colonial Governors and of those who had built the great businesses of the Empire.. Nearly one person in four in the town was over sixty-five. The town encouraged the retired: 'Why not live here?', said the town's official guide. 'Charming, elegant Eastbourne. The Place to Come and Live.' The Town's motto was *Meliora Sequimus* – We Strive for Better Things.'

There were still some permanent residents in the larger hotels. The Grand Hotel had fourteen in 1960, but the number gradually dwindled till they were no longer a paying proposition. Some permanent residents were notorious for terrifying the staff and for their amazing eccentricities. Among the most notorious were a brother and sister, Mrs Benson and Mr Myers, who occupied a suite. They refused to eat in the dining room and the staff had to buy a chicken every day from Sainsbury's. 'This had to be taken to their room for inspection. It then had to be cooked with a cup of water but no salt and placed in a casserole topped off with a covering of pastry so that no waiter could touch it.' All the staff dreaded going to their suite and, over the years, they had used up all the staff by dismissing each, saying 'That man's useless.' Mr and Mrs Brodie James required the porters to wear gloves to put logs on their fire. The permanent residents were given a portion of the dining room with an elderly waiter to look after them, who would order their meals without consulting them. They, on the other hand, had no regard for the hotel and its other guests at all. The sarcasm of a particular Major Blair, for instance, was said to be able to 'fell the chef at a hundred paces', and the rather deaf Mrs Pearson would proclaim to all and sundry in a loud voice: 'I think this fish is a bit orf.', causing other diners immediately to cancel their orders.[2]

The Grand continued to have its share of famous guests: Viscount Montgomery of Alamein, Field Marshall Slim, Gwilym Lloyd-George, Viscount Tenby, who came down to Eastbourne regularly as Chairman of the Council of Eastbourne College; Harold Macmillan also came to stay because of his Eastbourne connection as brother-in-law of the Duke of Devonshire. Other politicians stayed, including Clement Attlee, Ernest Bevin, Edward Heath and Harold Wilson; royalty: Princess Margaret, the Duke of Edinburgh and Princess Alexandra, and many from the world of show business, films and sport.

Buying a house in Eastbourne was an expensive proposition: in 1956, quite a small house on the outskirts of the town cost in the range of £3000 to £3500. In the Meads, new houses cost between £6,000 and £10,000. The rates level was the lowest in Britain at 12 shillings in the pound, which was an indication of the wealth of the population and the influence of the Conservative council. New building, particularly of estates of bungalows, began around 1955 as it did in many parts of the country; the idea of retiring to the seaside became a dream for the many, particularly as the population became more mobile with the acquisition of cars. The exclusive houses on the new Ratton Manor estate, once owned by William Mawhood, a patient of Dr Adams, were priced between £3000 and £10,000. Eastbourne had become a boom town.

If anything, the new development accentuated the social divide, since it took place mainly to the west of the town. East of the pier might as well have been the other side of the moon, with its narrow terraced houses, built to house servants or to accommodate people who provided services to those living west of the pier. Some modest boarding houses appeared with notices proclaiming 'hot and cold in every room', distinguishing themselves from those other establishments which survived on in their Victorian gloom of aspidistras and green plush tablecloths with the landladies knocking on the bedroom doors in the mornings with a ewer of hot water for use in the china basin decorated with roses. The huge mahogany wardrobes and the edifying religious oil paintings on the walls added to the atmosphere of dark depression which pervaded the rooms. My own childhood memory is of the feather beds which smelled of camphor and threatened to swallow me completely so I felt I would never escape and would drown in their dusty folds. These were the days before even some of the largest hotels had en suite bathrooms, so a chamber-pot would lurk somewhere under the bed, or in a bedside cupboard. The alternative was a perilous walk down a dimly lit corridor and over cold and fraying linoleum to an icy shared lavatory, lit by a 40 watt bulb.

[2] Ibid

On beaches in other towns – such as Brighton or Hastings - you could discover the fabled British holidaymakers, still caricatured in traditional humorous postcards: men with knotted handkerchiefs on their heads and rolled-up trousers and large ladies in polka-dot swimsuits, dozing in the hired deckchairs. In Eastbourne, the holidaymakers on the beach seemed somehow more restrained, as if united in a conspiracy of moderation.

By contrast, the pier was always ablaze with lights and a centre of activity and excitement. The slot machines winked and flashed and made thrilling, stacatto clicking noises; the players almost invariably lost, but the machines still did great business. The sound of end-of-the-pier concerts with musicians, singers, magicians and comedians drifted ashore across the water. For children with buckets and spades, seeking the traditional beach on which to build sandcastles, Eastbourne was a disappointment - it was a struggle to find a sufficiently sandy patch amongst the stones. Eventually, this pursuit would give way to collecting shells and the pebbles, which, polished up, might turn out to be gemstones, and the cloudy pieces of glass which had become rounded and fogged by the action of the waves and the salt in the water.

The social climate might have been changing in the rest of the country, but Eastbourne was oblivious to such trends. Teddy Boys – rebellious young men with extravagant hairstyles, long jackets, tight trousers, thick crepe soled shoes and a penchant for knife-fights – existed only in such far off places as London or Glasgow. The era of rock 'n roll and skiffle – yet more young men in outrageous clothing playing mainly popular American music and dancing with outrageously immodest young women – simply passed Eastbourne by, at least west of the pier.

The cinema was as popular in Eastbourne as everywhere else. This was still the age of patriotism, innocence and moral tales in which the guilty were always punished and the good were rescued in the final reel. Films had simple plots and polarised characterisation. In September 1956, while the police were investigating Dr Adams, audiences in Eastbourne were being entertained by Jack Hawkins, starring as Superintendent Halliday of Scotland Yard in *The Long Arm*; in December of that year, cinema audiences could see *Where no Vultures Fly* with Anthony Steel, go *Underwater* with Jane Russell; or, for the denizens of the back row, watch the siren of British '50s' glamour, Diana Dors, in *Miss Tulip Stays the Night*. Alec Guinness – who was a regular guest at the Grand – appeared in *Kind Hearts and Coronets*, a light-hearted comedy about murder, and Gregory Peck appeared in *The Man in the Grey Flannel Suit*, a drama about a war hero whose liberation of an Italian woman threatens his marriage but who saves the day by confessing all, doing the right thing and putting his family life before his business career.

The town's many theatres were played by some great names: those of the music hall, Sandy Powell, Norman Evans; of variety: Rawicz and Landauer the piano duettists, with twelve John Tiller Girls, and of drama: Anna Neagle, Peggy Ashcroft, Alec Guinness. Eastbourne visitors could attend 'Henry Hall's Guest Night' at the Winter Garden – 'This *is* Henry Hall speaking', heard every Saturday night on the Light Programme of the BBC – or perhaps the Grand Hotel Dance at 17/6d. a ticket, with Henry Loveday and the Grand Hotel Dance Orchestra.

There were fascinating department stores – such as Plummers and Bobbys - with distinct identities. Automation and security meant that the shop assistant put the bill and the customer's money into a screw-topped container, attached this to an overhead wire and pulled a handle to send the container whizzing along to the cashier sitting high in a small cabin. The cashier would then send the change and receipt whizzing back to the counter assistant. Alternatively, a shop might have a vacuum system where the container was sucked down a pipe to wend its way to the cashier. Alstons Corset Shop was supplying the trendier lady shoppers with Berlei girdles and corselettes 'from 47/6 to 75/-' or the Little X silhouette roll-on. Still available for the more conservative customers were those flesh-pink corsets boned within an inch of their lives, even long-sleeved woolly spencers, and, of course, the directoire knickers which would ensure complete coverage of suspenders and stocking-tops. For the more sporting , 'Harry Hall' riding clothes were available at Hope & Co., and there was innovation at the hairdressers' with a 'Bubble Cut Perm with the Callinan system'. East of the pier, the girls had a home 'Which twin has the Toni?' perm.

Maids, cooks, housekeepers and gardeners advertised their availability in the local newspaper, The *Eastbourne Herald* and there was the odd specialist: 'Careful Lady driver takes invalids out 1/- a mile'. Then there were the legions of private nurses. In July 1956, the newspaper recorded the service and good fortune of one of their number:

> 'A warm tribute has been paid by Miss P. Elizabeth Turner, his nurse: Mr Frank Bolam of 12, Lascelles Terrace, who died on April 8th, leaving her some £12,000, the residue of his estate. For three years off and on, she had nursed Mr Bolam. "He was a charming, delightful, aristocratic gentleman", she said.'

The *Eastbourne Herald* informed its readers that the NHS statistics for 1955 showed that there were now 54,339 patients registered with local doctors and – unsurprisingly, perhaps – that the average cost of prescriptions in Eastbourne was higher than the average for England. Nevertheless, each week the newspaper reported that someone had either jumped off Beachy Head and died of multiple injuries or had drowned himself or herself in the sea off Holywell.

A review recommended the purchase of crime writer Nicholas Blake's book *A Tangled Web* which was based on the true story of the murder of Inspector Walls in South Cliff Avenue (in the Meads) in October 1912. A burglar named John Williams had been convicted of shooting the policeman. After the murder, Williams and his girl Flo, had gone to the Picture Palace to see *Dante's Inferno*. He was hanged the following year.

—•—

In 1956, while the nation was pre-occupied with the Suez crisis, Leslie Henson made his call to the Police in Eastbourne. Suddenly, the talk in Eastbourne was of huge legacies, a serial killer, hundreds of victims, an inquest and an investigation by Scotland Yard. The business of the town's hotels and restaurants was boosted in late season by an influx of British and foreign journalists, all looking for angles on Eastbourne's latest celebrity, Dr John Bodkin Adams, who was rumoured to be a murderer.

Chapter Five

# Hannam of the Yard
# and the Police Inquiry

## 17 August 1956

Detective Superintendent Herbert Hannam was chosen for this enquiry for very particular reasons: he was an exceptionally intelligent and innovative detective and he was personable enough to be acceptable to Eastbourne society, yet not someone to be overawed by anybody or deterred by status.

Herbert Hannam was described by the *Daily Mail* journalist, Rodney Hallworth, as 'a man whom you either liked or disliked', 'sartorially elegant', with expensive tastes in clothing and cigars: he was nicknamed by his colleagues at the Yard as 'The Count'. He first became known to the general public as the detective who solved the Teddington Towpath Murders in 1953, and thereafter was known as 'Hannam of the Yard'. If he had written a biography he might have rivalled 'Fabian of the Yard' and been the subject of a television series as Robert Fabian was, but his line continued after him when both his son and grandson became policemen. Hallworth also described him as an intellectual with 'a reputation for thoroughness, patience and, if necessary, cunning'. He was also one of Scotland Yard's best lecturers.

It is instructive to see how the meticulous Hannam, then Chief Inspector, dealt with the Teddington Towpath Murders, for which he received his promotion to Superintendent during the course of the investigation. On the day before the Coronation of Queen Elizabeth II, the body of sixteen-year-old Barbara Songhurst was discovered floating in the River Thames. She had been stabbed in the back four times and beaten about the head; she had also been raped. Both a knife and an axe had been used by her killer. Her friend, Christine Reed, with whom she had been cycling on the towpath, was missing. While the Coronation was proceeding on June 2nd, 1953, Hannam started an exhaustive inquiry throughout Surrey, including camps of the British Army and American forces. Hundreds of statements were taken.

Meanwhile, police were searching through the mud of the foreshore, and found Christine's cycle that same day. Barbara's cycle has never been found, nor the knife with which she was stabbed. Police launches dragged the river and police dog patrols searched the fields and woodland on the Surrey bank; mine-detectors were used in the hunt for the weapons. At the Yard, Hannam and his assistants studied the medical evidence, issued a public appeal and later in that day arranged for auditory tests to be carried out near the lock-keeper's lodge at Teddington: the noise of the water through the lock sluices drowned out all sound. Plans were made to drain the Thames between Teddington and Richmond, and a new system devised for taking prints from the cycle.

By the 5th June, the case had attained newspaper headlines. Hannam inaugurated a new procedure for questioning every householder in the area. Each detective had a printed questionnaire to be filled in by the detective himself, with seventeen questions. This part of the inquiry was expected to take a fortnight. Hannam had to be patient and not to overlook anything. He was, by now, certain that the killer was a man living a semi-nomadic lifestyle; that he was young and physically fit. On the following day, a Saturday, Christine's body was found two miles from the murder scene. She also had been savagely stabbed with a knife and raped.

All psychiatric hospitals in the country were checked; detectives visited dance-halls and cinemas; statements were now numbered in thousands. Hannam was now directing the largest force of detectives ever used on a murder hunt in Britain. He concentrated on the door-to-door inquiries because he was certain that he was looking for a local man, and that man must have been covered with blood.

Hannam went through reports of other attacks by unknown assailants in the Surrey area and found one which had occurred on May 24th, a week before the murders, when a fifteen-year-old girl had been attacked on Oxshott Heath and had given a description of the man. In March 1952, there had been a serious attack in the same place when a woman with a child was hit with an iron bar and raped. An emergency operation saved her life. A similar attack then occurred on 12th June in Windsor Great Park. Two workmen, who had seen the appeals published by the police, were crossing Oxshott Heath when they saw a young man loitering who matched the police description of the girl's attacker. They told the local police and a patrol car picked him up. While he was in the police car, somehow he managed to secrete an axe under the driver's seat. A police driver found this on the following day, thought nothing of it and took it home where he used it at least once to chop wood. On this occasion the police were unable to detain him and Alfred Whiteway, a married man with a family, was released, but after the incident on 12th June and the fresh information it brought, he was arrested on June 28th and remanded in custody.

Before Whiteway appeared in court again, Hannam questioned him about the towpath murders. It appeared that, since he was a schoolboy, he had had a passion for knives, and practised throwing them. He also threw axes and kukris. The axe from the police car was eventually handed to Hannam on July 15th. He visited Whiteway in Brixton Prison and showed him the axe. This shocked Whiteway and he made a statement which he later tried to retract. Defence Counsel, Mr Peter Rawlinson, accused Hannam of faking the statement. The Judge admitted the statement as evidence. The Jury found Whiteway guilty after an hour and a half's deliberation and he was sentenced to death. His appeal was heard by Lord Chief Justice, Lord Goddard and the appeal was dismissed. Hannam was totally vindicated – as he was entitled to be – and the case has been described as one of Scotland Yard's most notable triumphs in a century. Whiteway was hanged at Wandsworth on November 22nd, 1953. The axe is in the Black Museum at Scotland Yard, but the knife is still in the mud of the River Thames.

Lord Devlin, in his unprecedented book (an account of a trial by the judge of that trial) about the Adams' proceedings, described Hannam as liking to 'take charge' in the witness-box, and coming near to a 'duel' with the defence counsel, Mr Lawrence. What impresses from the archive material is that Hannam was an upright man who, in the mode of Luther, knew where he stood with regard to the truth, and that he would not, if it were in his power, deviate from this. He really was what we all like to think of as the archetypal detective in search of the truth and, having found it, trusting that the law would take its course and justice be done. He could not have foreseen the obstacles which would arise in the Bodkin Adams' case.

Enquiries concerning Dr Adams were first taken over by Scotland Yard at the request of the Chief Constable of Eastbourne, on the 17th August, 1956. At that time there had already been worldwide press headlines about 'preliminary matters already discovered in Eastbourne' and since then press publicity had escalated 'on a fantastic scale'.

The police team which Detective Superintendent Hannam had was a small one, consisting of himself and Detective Sergeant Charles Hewett from the Yard and the head of the Eastbourne Borough C.I.D., Detective Inspector Brynley Pugh, and they had a very short time in which to conduct the police enquiry. It was a very unusual enquiry in that there is normally a particular crime which is committed and the police set out to discover who committed the crime. This case was infinitely more difficult because Hannam had a named person who was suspected of a type of crime, for which the motive was also suggested: that Dr Adams had murdered patients in order to benefit from their wills. Hannam should also have been given much longer to conduct such a complicated investigation, but he was put under pressure to bring the matter to a conclusion very rapidly because the Government did not want it to drag on.

It is difficult to see that Hannam had any alternative to the way in which he set about the search for evidence: a search was made at Somerset House for all the death certificates which had been signed by Dr Adams over a period of a little more than ten years – from the beginning of 1946 to the death of Mrs Hullett in July 1956. He decided it was of little use to go back further than this, although the rumours most certainly dated from more than twenty years previously, because most witnesses were likely to be dead as well as the possible victims. The death certificates which were found for this period amounted to 316, but there were some which were not found. On comparing the nurses' statements with the death certificate list, there were three missing. A search was then made for the wills relating to those death certificates and 132 were found in which Dr Adams' name appeared; an odd one or two of these were of an earlier date than 1946, e.g. his mother's will, and Mrs Whitton's.

This painstaking work having been completed, relatives, neighbours, nurses had to be found, visited, and statements written out. Letters came in from the public, and telephone calls as publicity mounted: all had to be followed up.

On 23rd August, 1956, Hannam held a press conference in Eastbourne, at the request of the press; he was making a personal statement which he did not want quoted as he had no authority to give an official statement. The reason was that 'quite a number of you gentlemen are greatly embarassing me' with undesirable publicity and he just wanted to tell them where the enquiry was going He was 'making enquiries on behalf of the Chief Constable into certain matters which arise out of the death of a lady named Hullett.' Apparently it had been suggested that he had 40 officers making searches at Somerset House 'on his behalf' which was nonsense. He did not know 'where this enquiry is going to lead or if it is going to lead anywhere at all' and so was not in a position to give any information.

A Press Member asked if Detective Superintendent Hannam's enquiries were concerned with one death only as the Coroner had requested that he investigate the deaths of several women. Hannam replied that he was looking into 'impropriety in the deaths of any other cases' but at the moment was 'extremely doubtful'. Another Press Member asked about the '400 women who died in this town in the last ten years' and Hannam responded that he was 'as amazed as others' at reading this in the press.

Hannam wrote on the same day to Chief Superintendent Findlay at the Yard in his very beautiful handwriting – a flowing cursive script of which he was doubtless very proud. The letters are preserved together with the stamped addressed envelopes showing the date stamps.

'The enquiry is going very well and we have made good progress today.

Percy Hoskins [the *Daily Express* reporter] visited here today and spent quite a time with the Chief Constable. I discussed with Mr Walker [the Chief Constable] the terrible publicity and I feel that I now have the situation under control. I hope within a day or so I can close down the Press interest very considerably. [!] There are some sixty press fellows here and scores of photographers. We have a back way out of the H.Q. and have shaken them off all day.

I held a press conference at 5 p.m. in an endeavour to kill the whole affair and had a shorthand note taken of the whole proceedings. I enclose the note herewith for the information of the Commander. [George Hatherill]

Internal co-operation here is absolutely 1st class and I think the C.C. has seen the red light and we shall have no more trouble. I insisted that he was present at the talk with the Press. All the press lads feel he has mislead them.

I have no further worries, all is well.
Respectfully,
[Signed]. H. Hannam.'

There was rather a strange diversion in the enquiry, described in a letter written on 30th August, 1956, by Detective Sergeant Hewett to Chief Superintendent Findlay and endorsed by Detective Inspector Pugh. It was suggested in more than one of the statements taken from witnesses, particularly nurses, that Dr Adams had used hypnotic techniques upon his patients:

'During the course of the enquiry at present proceeding in Eastbourne regarding the suspicious deaths in which the name of Dr Bodkin Adams has been mentioned, information was received that he had been visiting a Mr Maynell BLOOMFIELD a Hypnotist, residing at Ocklynge Priory, Peartree Lane, Little Common, Cooden, Bexhill-on-Sea, and obtaining instruction in hypnotism.

You directed that during the course of the enquiry Mr Bloomfield should be seen and this matter enquired into.

On the 29th August, 1956, at 11.30 a.m. during your absence in London, Detective Inspector Pugh of Eastbourne suggested that this enquiry should be dealt with and I went with him and together we interviewed Mr Bloomfield. As a result of our conversation with him, we regard him as a fraud.

He was born in 1881 and, for the past 30 years, had been practicing [sic] what he calls Auto-suggestion and Hypnosis. At one time Mr Bloomfield was a patient of Dr Adams' as a result of a spinal injury sustained in a railway accident in London. At no time has he ever given instruction to Dr Adams in the technique of hypnosis. In view of the fact that information he was in a position to supply had no bearing upon the investigation you are conducting, the interview was terminated.

Mr Bloomfield said that he had dealt with eight or nine of Dr Adams' patients at his request.

I have read in the daily press to-day, particularly in the *Daily Mirror* and the *Daily Mail*, that Mr Bloomfield practiced hypnotism on myself and the whole story as published has no truth in it whatsoever. Whilst in Mr Bloomfield's presence I used my handkerchief several times and he asked if I had a cold. I told him I had an attack of catarrh and no further comment was made about it. There was at no time any suggestion that Mr Bloomfield even requested me to submit to his treatment.
C. Hewett
Detective Sergeant.


I was present with Detective Sergeant Hewett at the time of this interview and agree that the suggestion in the press is utterly false and that the contents of his above report are accurate. DI Pugh.'


'Detective Inspector
To Chief Superintendent Findlay:
This Mr Bloomfield was seen on my directions, although I wasn't aware that he was being interviewed while I was in London. The information he supplied to the officers about treating 8 or 9 of Dr Adams' patients is, I believe, untrue. I have discovered that after the officers had visited him he got in touch with the press himself and asked them to call on him. The *Evening Standard* representative called as I believe did also the representative of the *Daily Mail*. He made this alarming statement to them as a form of advertisement and I accept the officers' information that no such thing took place.

Just before 11 a.m. to-day Mr James the Solicitor of Dr Adams here in Eastbourne telephoned me and told me that he had read in the press about Bloomfield, that Dr Adams had only sent two patients to him, both of whom desired to stop their habit of smoking. One of these patients Bloomfield gave some treatment to and the second he referred to a Psychiatrist at Worthing. Mr Bloomfield frequently calls on Dr Adams in Eastbourne touting for patients and he has even called on Mr James personally asking him for recommendations in the same way. I understand from local police records he is well known and is frowned upon by the British Medical Association. It is unfortunate that this publicity took place but we have no control over it and I would further add that some 18 members of the press are enjoying themselves in Eastbourne and are visiting the Registrars of Deaths in the neighbourhood and are obtaining numerous copies of death certificates and interviewing relatives of the persons named upon them. They have, therefore, in their possession many names which are not, and never will be, of interest to us, and although I have to-day made a request to one or two members of the press that this should cease, again I have no control over it.
H. Hannam
Detective Superintendent.'

There is a note accompanying a letter to Chief Superintendent Findlay dated '30.VIII.56', both from Hannam. Not only was Hannam supposed to conduct a very complicated enquiry but also to control the press and placate those in authority as well. The note reads:

'Sir,
Herewith as requested and I hope it allays A.C.C.'s [Asst. Chief Constable] fears of any lack of caution on our part.
It is extremely difficult here with all this Press interest and I will do my utmost to keep it to a minimum and safeguard our interests.'

The letter to Chief Superintendent Findlay reads as follows:

'This afternoon several of the Press fellows have worried me about their own references to exhumations following the known conference of yesterday.
I saw four of them and said:
"The question of any exhumation has not arisen, it may never arise and no thought can be given to such a possibility until the enquiries are more advanced and their results studied."
I also told the fellows that I should not see them again on any issue in connection with this investigation. To make no comment at all would only cause them to hang around here with cameras and the like. I understand staff of cemeteries have already been approached and offered cash for information. I sincerely trust this will end the matter and thought it right to inform you at once as this whole case is so electric.

Everything else in Eastbourne is going fine.
Respectfully,
H. Hannam, Supt.'

Hannam wrote a brief note on 31st August, addressed to 'Commander C' [C Division at Scotland Yard]:

'These are the reports I called for yesterday. They should be kept by Chief Supt. C. with the short hand notes of the press conference etc.'

There follows in this bundle of the archives a note of Hannam's, dated 4.9.56, of some figures:

'Searches made on wills: 148. Searches to be made as at 4.9.56: 52. Wills in which suspect is mentioned – approx. 16. A.C.C. & C.C. informed by me 5.25 p.m. 4.9.56.'

An extract from the *Daily Herald* of 13th September, entitled 'Yard man gets advice on exhumations' informs readers that Dr Francis Camps, the Home Office pathologist had driven to Eastbourne on the previous day to confer with Hannam to discuss the possibility of exhuming the bodies of Mrs Julia Bradnum and Miss Clara Neil Miller. The articles mentions that 'Soil samples taken from Ocklynge cemetery, where Mrs Bradnum is buried, have been analysed by Dr Camps' and 'Her body was embalmed...'

Hannam has underlined these statements and annotated them as 'quite untrue' and the last paragraph which mentions that Hannam has nearly reached the stage where his investigations into 21 deaths of wealthy women will require 'exhumations to complete the picture' he has annotated as 'Pure nonsense'.

An extract from *World's Press News* of September 14, 1956, pasted up by Hannam, throws curious light on what was happening in Eastbourne; it is headed 'No sneer':

'It was a change to read an *Express* piece from Eastbourne which didn't have a sneer running through it at every other paper's versions. If only one-tenth of the confidential memos being churned out and duplicated in Eastbourne are true, the *Express* looks like having it on its front page a lot more. Unfortunately, as the inquiries drag on relationships between Fleet Street and the local police deteriorate. It doesn't help either when a reporter carelessly leaves a copy of one of the most damaging of the confidential memos at the police station.'

There follows a personal memorandum of Hannam's, in his own handwriting:-

'For years – putting patients under hypnotics (dangerous drugs)
Wills and powers of attorney.

24 Open files – each relating to separate persons all A's patients.

_'_

{400 Certificates – almost all cerebral haemorrhage
{1st January 1946 – to date.

_'_

{Treatment likely to induce cerebral haemorrhage.
MB Ireland }
MD Bristol }
B.S. Bristol }

_'_

{Supt. Seekings                                    }
{D/I Pugh                                          }          Holiday together
{L/Col Gwynne – {Standing Joint Ctee.             }
        {Chairman of J.J. (Magistrates)

_'_

Francis Camps, – GMC -

_____

under drugs – mentally unable to do any business.

Never seen Editor.

C.C. (Chief Constable of Eastbourne) Phoned Editor of *Mail*.'

Hannam was clearly worried about the policemen in Eastbourne: Chief Constable Walker, Superintendent Seekings, DI Pugh, and the Chairman of the Magistrates, Lieutenant-Colonel Gwynne. Both Gwynne and Walker, the Chief Constable, were friends of Dr Adams, and, at weekends, Adams would shoot game on Gwynne's estate. If he thought of this as a major complication, he did not know what was to lie ahead.

If Hannam was worried, in due course Colonel Gwynne would become worried as well about his 'friendship' with Dr Adams. The relationship was on the minds of others as well: a Mr Sawyer of Convent House, Wartling, sent Hannam a letter on 28th January 1957:

'I may be striking my neck out rather far but since Dr Adams' cheque and prescriptions have been missing, [from the Hullett inquest] something tells me that his bosom pal Gwynne may be concerned. Now Gwynne since his recent car accident has been taken to the Princess Alice Hospital and has demanded that [Superintendent] Seekings shall do this, that and the other for him and in addition, take care of his wallet, etc. It all seems to tie up together somehow. I only hope that his mishap was caused by the after effects of his celebration luncheon at Lewes and that he won't be able to wrongly blame some one else, as he successfully did twice before…'

On 21st September, Hannam reported to Commander George Hatherill at the Yard that he had 'four concrete cases, very watertight, against Dr John Bodkin Adams', though these, he believed, were not very serious offences. However, the sequence of them would make the technique adopted more serious. There was still 'an enormous amount of work to be done'. Two of the cases, those of Devey and Crisford, were forgeries of NHS prescriptions for private patients, and one, the case of Mr James Priestley Downs, a false statement on a cremation form – all eventually dealt with at Lewes Crown Court after the Old Bailey trial – the last was that of Mrs Edith Morrell in relation again to the statement on the cremation form. Commander Hatherill had apparently suggested to Hannam that immediate efforts should be confined to completing some minor cases so that Adams could be charged as quickly as possible on these matters.

Hannam wrote from the Chief Constable's Office in Eastbourne on 26th September, an informal note to 'Wilf' in his office at Scotland Yard to let him know he would travel up on the Friday for a meeting with the A.C.C. and Commander Hatherill that afternoon, and return the following week to Eastbourne to 'tie up a couple of additional offences I have discovered'. He signs himself 'Bert H.'

# PART II

# Author's Note

*In tracing Dr Adams' years from the time he arrived in Eastbourne in 1922 to the time of the police investigation and trial in 1956 and 1957, I have relied primarily on the Police archives, particularly the several hundred witness statements collected during 1956, including statements made by Dr Adams himself. I have taken key information from the statements and the police notes and reports. Only a small number of witnesses – such as Mrs Mawhood, Lt. Col. Gwynne, Sister Stuart-Hemsley, and some other nurses, had known Dr Adams from the early days to the time of the trial itself. Consequently, other witnesses made statements which covered much shorter periods of time, ranging from a few days to a few months, and usually dealing with the treatment Dr Adams had given their relatives, or patients in their care.*

*Inevitably, the picture the statements paint of Dr Adams' earlier years in Eastbourne is more patchy than for the later years. The Police themselves concentrated huge effort into finding the several hundred death certificates signed by Dr Adams during the period 1946-1956 and the wills relating to them. Detective Superintendent Hannam ruled out investigating any earlier period – except for the odd case – because most of the potential witnesses would have already died and the possibility of collecting any useful evidence was remote.*

*These statements were given under oath and would have been given by witnesses well aware of the seriousness of the outcome for Dr Adams, and the penalties for perjury or for deliberately misleading the Police, so they are not in the same category as 'gossip' or 'opinions', but were evidence to lay before the Director of Public Prosecutions.*

*Like all investigations into suspected serial killings, the case against Dr Adams was prepared from a large number of witness statements which dealt with different alleged victims and different times. In order to give more of a flavour of the investigation itself I have chosen to keep each statement integral rather than fragment them. The statements are organised roughly into four decades: the period up to 1930, when Dr Adams set up his own practice; the subsequent period up to the time of the Second World War; the War years; the post-War years, and the 1950s. Some of the statements fit rather untidily into this linear framework, but for clarity the time span of each case is shown.*

*From the trolley-loads of boxes and bundles of dusty typewritten and handwritten archive material – most of which was not used in the Old Bailey trial itself – there emerged a fascinating story… and some astonishing conclusions.*

Chapter Six

—•—

# The Early Years

## 1922 – 1949

—•—

### Mary Stuart Hemsley

Sister Mary Gwendoline Stuart-Hemsley related her strange experiences of Dr Adams to the police. When she first came to Eastbourne to work she asked the matrons she encountered to recommend a good GP. Having heard Dr Adams' name, she asked Miss Mackintosh, the Matron of Upperton Maternity Home what she thought of Dr Adams, and she said, 'You don't want that pig.' 'I asked her what she didn't like about him and she told me of an occasion some time in the early days (early 1920s) he was in Eastbourne, when she had remonstrated with him for damaging some flowers in the front of the nursing home by throwing his bicycle among them and he said, 'If you live in this town long enough you will see me riding in my Rolls.' This was because she had said to him: 'You won't have a bike if you do that again.'

'I did not meet Dr Adams until the summer of 1939 when local children were being evacuated overseas. I was at the clinic to see the children who were being examined by four doctors. Eventually there was just one boy left and the time was seven minutes to one. I sent the boy in to the doctor, who, whilst using the stethoscope, was ticking me off for insisting that he examine the boy when he wanted to go for his lunch. I gathered the opinion that he was a very indifferent doctor as I knew that he could not listen to the chest wall properly at the same time as he was talking to me.

After the child had gone out, I said 'Are you from Canada?' as I thought he might have been one of the doctors who had come from Canada to assist in the scheme. Then he said: 'No, I am Irish' and I said, 'What's your name?' and he said 'Dr John Bodkin Adams.'

### Mrs Elsie Muddell

Detective Sergeant Sellars called on Mrs Elsie Muddell, the wife of the Bank Manager at Lloyds Bank; she had intimated that she had some interesting information to impart to the police. Mrs Muddell had known Dr Adams for thirty-five years – ever since he had arrived in

Eastbourne. One of his partners, Dr Rainey, was her doctor and he had introduced Dr Adams to her: 'I did not like Dr Adams from the start.'

Thirty-one years previously, in 1925, her daughter had been born and she was being attended by Dr Rainey. The day before her daughter was born, Dr Adams came to see her, as Dr Rainey was attending a conference. 'I well remember Dr Adams gave me a mixture to ease my pains but I was definitely worse after I took his mixture and after one dose I refused to take any more. Dr Adams was furious when he knew and prescribed the hot water treatment for me – sitting on a pail of hot water.'

Mrs Muddell and Dr Adams were both involved with the YMCA so they came into contact with each other quite often. She was forthright: 'I always put people against Dr Adams whenever I could.'

Hannam remarks in his report that her great dislike of Dr Adams because of his treatment of her, might well colour 'other matters' and that they should bear this in mind.

Mrs Muddell related that Dr Adams was attending Miss Wills (of the tobacco family), who lived in Willingdon Road. He had had a discussion with her about her will and she told him she would leave him £1,000. Dr Adams suggested she should let him have this whilst she was alive and Miss Wills agreed and wrote out a cheque for the £1,000. Then he said that he had not rendered an account for his medical treatment of her for some time and suggested she write the cheque for £1,250, which she duly did. Hannam records in his Report: 'Four other persons told this story but declined to make statements. Miss Wills died in 1941.'

Another incident concerned the widow of a Metropolitan Gas Official who lived in Pashley Road. This had occurred around 1941. Dr Adams sold the lady's car for her. He told her it was worth £100 but he sold it for £300 and kept the £200 for himself. Mrs Muddell added: 'Mr Spears of East Dean Road Garages can tell you something about this because Dr Adams hired one of his lock-up garages for a month to store the car, but he sold it before he used the garage and wanted Mr Spears to reduce the rent of the garage.'

Now Mrs Muddell got to her *pièce de résistance*: the three mistresses: Miss Betty Cradock of Little Hall, East Dean, who had been left a lot of money by her uncle, Percy Cradock; Miss Norah O'Hara, the discarded fiancee, whose engagement with Dr Adams had been broken off by him in 1935 after all the preparations had been made and the house and furniture bought; and Miss Ella Leach of 30 Vicarage Drive 'another of his lady loves. She was put into 30 Vicarage Drive by Dr Adams. The house belongs to him but he has now given her over in favour of the woman at East Dean, although he still remembers her birthday and gives her presents at Christmas. She suffers from heart trouble and is supposed to be a sick woman.'

### Elsie Orange Randall

A woman with the unusual name of Miss Elsie Orange Randall, who was Principal of the School of Domestic Economy in Eastbourne, made a sworn statement to the police about a lady, Mrs Donnet, then 92 years of age in 1956, whom the police considered was so aged that she might be upset by their questioning. The incident occurred in 1934: a tennis ball had struck her in the eye and Dr Adams examined it and told her that she would be unable to sign cheques and manage her affairs. He said he would take out Power of Attorney. She was upset and sent for Miss Randall and went with her to her bank manager at Barclays Bank. He gave her forms and she appointed the bank manager and Miss Randall to have Power of Attorney. The following morning Dr Adams called with a Power of Attorney form and when he was told that it had already been done, he became extremely annoyed. The Power of Attorney, Miss Randall said, was still in existence.

### Dr Adams and Motors Cars

Over the years, Dr Adams bought and sold many cars, using his hobby to make money. Mr Rippon, a solicitor, confirmed that Dr Adams had sold a Lanchester car to Mr Mawhood in 1945 for £332:6s.6d. Walter Elfick, his chauffeur from 1949 to 1953 confirmed that the Doctor bought and sold cars 'all the time.' The Doctor was 'a man who never conversed very much and he never once discussed any of his patients with me. He visited his patients on Sundays the same as any other day of the week. He visited patients before I started at 8 a.m.' The car he had received from the Morrell estate was black and Dr Adams had sold it after a few months. There was also a 'grey Rolls Royce with the number JK 1600'.

Hannam comments in his Report that Elfick described his employer as 'uncommunicative'. When Elfick first worked for Dr Adams in 1949, the Doctor owned a Hillman Minx, an Armstrong-Siddeley and a 1.5 litre Riley. He had later sold the Minx and bought a Humber Hawk and then sold the Armstrong-Siddeley and acquired a Rolls Royce.

Walter had 'only known him to be friendly with three women. First Miss O'Hara of Carlisle Road and I understood that he was engaged to her and intended marrying her and living in Prideaux Road. The second was Miss Chatty of the Cumberland Hotel. 'Dr Adams used to send him to collect her car and 'take it to my garage to wash.' Dr Adams always asked him if he received anything from Miss Chatty – this was usually ten shillings and this was deducted from his wages. 'He never would give me a rise. He was a very temperamental man and a fanatic as far as cars were concerned. His third lady friend was a single middle-aged lady from East Dean. [Miss Betty Cradock] I have forgotten her name – this lady used to go shooting with him. At the shoot of Eastbourne Gun Club at Berwick. On Saturday afternoons he used to go shooting at the home of Lieutenant Colonel Gwynne.' Often, whilst he was driving him, the Doctor would open a whole box of chocolates and never offer one to him.

### Peter Hurrington

The police had taken a statement from Peter Hurrington of Sackville Works, Old Shoreham Road, in Hove, a garage service manager. Hannam stated in his Report that this statement 'sheds a little light on the mind of Adams when he received such gifts'. In the early summer of 1952, Dr Adams approached Mr Hurrington and subsequently brought in a Rolls Royce, registration number FXU 1 and gave instructions that the rear wings of the car were to be altered in shape: it was to be completely resprayed in a different colour; the exterior mirrors were to be altered and the registration number to be changed to JH1600. The Doctor had told him that the car had belonged to one of his patients, that he had acquired it and was anxious to have the appearance changed as much as reasonably possible so that residents would not recognise it. The work was carried out for £290.

### David Jenkins

David Jenkins was Dr Adams chauffeur from 1928 to 1939. He was loaned to various families apart from his normal duties: to Mrs Whitton of Kenilworth Court Hotel (who died in 1935). He often took her and Dr Adams' mother for drives and Mrs Whitton to Northampton on business trips and to see friends. She paid his expenses and Dr Adams his wages. The Doctor also offered him the job of looking after Mrs Whitton's car and servicing it in addition to his normal duties and Mrs Whitton paid him extra.

The friendliness of Dr Adams with his patients had been a standing joke: he had driven them on shopping trips using the Doctor's car and the Doctor would drive his other car. Mrs Young of 14 Upperton Road had given the Doctor a pair of twelve bore sporting guns for a birthday present in gratitude for this service. Yes, the Doctor had been a guest at many shooting parties in estates in England and Scotland. One family, the Rawlings, owned racehorses and Jenkins had taken Mr Rawlings to race meetings.

### Mrs Dorothy Abbot-Anderson

The police took a statement from Mrs Dorothy Abbot-Anderson who was friendly with the senior assistant at Brufords, the jewellers in Cornfield Road. Dr Adams regularly bought diamonds there and put them in the bank. He also had a contract with Brufords to pierce ladies' ears for five shillings a time. Hannam comments: 'Local doctors regard this as revolting.'

### Dr Adams and Alcohol

It has been said in previous books on Dr Adams that he did not drink and, certainly, he had signed the pledge as a boy. There is plenty of evidence that he was fond of a sherry and used to call at 'sherry time' on the Mawhoods and other patients. Sister Henagulph mentions in her statement that she was at a champagne party which Mrs Brierley gave in her room at the Grand Hotel. After he had left the party, Mrs Brierley told Sister Henagulph that Dr Adams had consumed a bottle of champagne. When the police searched Kent Lodge when the Doctor was arrested they found a considerable wine cellar: 'wines and spirits were stored in quantity'.

### Mrs Beryl Galloway

When the police were taking a statement from Mrs Beryl Galloway of Grove Road, where she and her husband owned a millinery shop, on the matter of a forged National Health Service prescription, she told them of an odd incident concerning Dr Adams. When Mrs Morrell died, they had a bill outstanding for her millinery; it was a little more than £2. 'Dr Adams happened to call at my home to see me and I heard my husband tell him that it was strange that he was making out a bill for a lady who had just died. Dr Adams said he was the executor of her will and added "Whatever the bill is, make it out for double, she has plenty of money". We did not do this and the matter was not raised again.'

## Mrs Lucille Murray

One of the various letters received by the police due to press publicity was from Mrs Lucille Murray. Dr Adams had attended her father for the last three years of his life when he was ill in the Cumberland Hotel. He eventually had a stroke and for two weeks afterwards Dr Adams had insisted on keeping the old gentleman alive by forcibly feeding him through a tube.

Mrs Murray told Dr Adams that it was going to be awkward if her father's illness was prolonged as she had no resources to meet nursing home fees. The Doctor said: 'Don't worry, as soon as we can get the old chap conscious enough to make his mark we can get hold of the money all right.' Hannam says: 'This is the only complaint we have received about Adams keeping a patient alive longer than appeared necessary.'

## The Mawhoods

A letter to Eastbourne Police Headquarters from an ex-senior police official prompted Detective-Superintendent Hannam to visit Mrs Edith May Mawhood, now seventy-seven years old, living in Rottingdean near Brighton, and disabled. She had been left £57,000 by her husband when he died in June 1949.

They lived for many years in Ratton, an estate of 320 acres. She first met Dr Adams in 1923 when she broke her leg. He was then a young GP and had arrived in Eastbourne only the previous year. He tried to get friendly with her husband, but in fact became a nuisance to them. He visited for many years and his habit was to come at mealtimes so that they had to feed him, or arrive even earlier at sherry time in the morning. Frequently he would bring his mother and sometimes his cousin, Miss Henry, as well. When he did this he would leave them on the terrace and the servants would have to serve them tea and refreshments.

When Dr Adams bought Kent Lodge, it was Mr William Mawhood who loaned him the money – £2,000; this was subsequently repaid. Often in the early days, Dr Adams told Mrs Mawhood he was hard up and she sometimes gave him a £1 or a 10 shilling note to tide him over. After her leg was improving, she decided to go for a holiday to a house she owned in Lynton, Devonshire. She normally made the journey in her own car with her chauffeur driving. The Doctor said that he thought he should go with her: he drove half the journey and the chauffeur drove the remainder. When they arrived Dr Adams said that he would like to stay at the house. Mrs Mawhood found that he had brought no luggage with him and she loaned him some of her husband's 'sleeping things'.

Mrs Mawhood regarded Dr Adams 'as a real scrounger'. On one occasion when her husband had bought a mackintosh, he admired it, went and obtained one at the same shop and had the bill added to Mr Mawhood's account and never paid for it. He used exactly the same technique when he bought a new pair of boots. Mrs Mawhood's brother was in the steel trade in Sheffield and Dr Adams asked if he could purchase a case of medical instruments. Mr Mawhood obtained them from his brother-in-law – a very expensive set in a case with compartments – and 'to this day Adams has never paid a penny for them'.

The Mawhoods were now living at Hanmer Lea in the town, and Dr Adams attended Mr Mawhood, who had always been a healthy man, for a few weeks before he died, sometimes twice daily and always at sherry or mealtimes. The patient was lying in bed, very feeble, a few days before he died, and the bedroom door was ajar. Mrs Mawhood heard Adams ask her husband if he would leave to him the whole of his money and said that he would then see that Mrs Mawhood was well-looked after and regularly provided for. When Mrs Mawhood heard this, she went into the bedroom, and, even though she limped, chased the Doctor around the bed, threatening him with her stick. He ran down the stairs and she threw her stick at him and smashed a valuable flower pot as a result. Dr Adams fled into his car and went. She returned to her husband in the bedroom and he said that Dr Adams had written something on a piece of paper and had asked him to sign it, but he was too weak to do so. Mrs Mawhood immediately contacted her solicitor, Mr Hart of Hart, Reade & Rippon of Eastbourne, and instructed him to arrange with the bank manager to stop all her husband's cheques and to accept nothing 'under his alleged signed authority'.

A day or two previously, Mrs Mawhood had asked for a bill from Dr Adams to settle the medical expenses up to date. He suggested that she make a cheque out for £100 or £200, preferably the latter. She made this out to the partnership name and he told her to make it out to him. She informed him that this was cheating and tore the cheque up, saying he wouldn't get one at all.

Mr Mawhood died on 8th March 1949, aged 89, and Dr Adams certified the cause of death as 'Carcinoma recti'. Dr Adams returned to the house to see her and made quite a fuss because he was not a beneficiary of the will. He also attended the funeral and, while he was there, shouted at one of the mourners that he had been cut out of the will. Mr Hart, the solicitor, had, some time previously, declined to deal with the will if Dr Adams was mentioned.

Some time after the funeral, Dr Adams came back to Ratton, when Mrs Mawhood was in bed ill. He was not invited or sent for as she had decided not to have him again. He walked into the bedroom and she told him that she would have nothing to do with him. On the dressing table was a 22 carat gold pencil which had belonged to her husband. Dr Adams said to her that he wanted something of her husband's, picked it up and walked away with it. She had not seen him since.

As Hannam pointed out in his report, this taking an article from the house of the deceased was far from an isolated incident, but he could not in 1956 have realised just how significant this habit was. Adams had got nothing from the will, but he was unable to resist going back and taking a souvenir when he knew he could not be stopped from doing so. The real question is: why was this a death which was significant enough to him to demand a souvenir?

## Henrietta Hatton

Mr Hurst, a solicitor, of Stapley & Hurst in Gildredge Road, provided the police with a complete set of papers to prove that 'Dr Adams justified his reputation'. Mr Hurst regarded Dr Adams' activities as 'unprofessional' and, in many cases, fraudulent. He said that 'not a few' solicitors in the town declined to deal with any will in which Dr Adams was mentioned. Amongst these papers – demonstrating that Dr Adams had been acting in a similar way for at least 23 years prior to the police investigation – was the case of Henrietta Hatton.

Miss Hatton was a spinster, aged 87 years of age in 1933. She lived at Down View in Grange Road, and was senile. Dr Adams arranged for her removal to Southfields Nursing Home, Eastbourne. Her assets included: an annuity of £350 pounds per annum, £102.11s.8d cash at the Westminster Bank, £400 in War Bonds, and the house Down View.

Miss Hatton's two maids said that Dr Adams had ordered them out of the room when he was visiting, and had whispered conversations with Miss Hatton over financial matters. The maids found him giving them small amounts of money for household expenses, and the matter was brought to the attention of her relations. It was discovered that Dr Adams had obtained Power of Attorney, was drawing cheques on her bank account and completely supervising her financial affairs. He was also spending above her income. Mr Hurst visited her, at the request of her relatives, and he found her totally incapable of managing her affairs.

Mr Hurst informed Miss Hatton's relatives and then went to see Dr Adams, who 'insisted to the point of being extremely abusive', that the patient was capable and, in fact, controlling her own finances. Mr Hurst prepared an 'Affidavit of Kindred and Fortune' for the High Court. Doctors were consulted in respect of this Affidavit and confirmed Miss Hatton's incapability. Nevertheless, Dr Adams furnished an affidavit stating that she was mentally alert and clear in her mind. A Process was served on Dr Adams, and he immediately withdrew and accepted the appointment made by the Receiver.

Miss Hatton died on 13th February, 1935. Her later will did not include Dr Adams, although an earlier one did.

Detective Superintendent Hannam thought this was a valuable case for demonstrating Dr Adams' technique. He wondered why, apart from the financial gain accruing, would Dr Adams 'so encumber himself with and strive to hold on to the control of finances of some of his patients'. It is very clear, however, that what was most important to Dr Adams was having power and control over a patient; the more total it was, the more satisfying to him. This was a stage in the process of complete control. This case also demonstrates his loss of temper immediately he is crossed.

## Mrs Matilda Whitton

Elsie Gander was 57 years old in 1956 – the same age as Dr Adams, and a bath attendant on RMS *Queen Mary*, when she made her statement to police. In 1935, she was a chambermaid at the Kenilworth Court Hotel in Wilmington Square. Mrs Matilda Whitton was a permanent resident at the hotel and Elsie looked after her for about two years. Dr Adams would call every morning to see her in her room. Elsie would frequently enter and find Dr Adams either holding her hand, or, with his hand on her knee. Mrs Whitton seemed to have no energy and was tired and lifeless, spending many days, sometimes weeks at a time, in bed.

When Dr Adams was away on holiday, Elsie noticed that her condition improved and she would be up most of the time and seemed much better. This was so noticeable it was discussed by all the staff. On the day of Mrs Whitton's death, she had walked to the bathroom and she did not appear to be any worse than she had been during the past two or three years. She had joked with Elsie about putting her slippers on. She came back from the bathroom and Elsie helped put her to bed again. She then left the room. Another member of staff, Mrs Flint, came to Elsie at about 8 p.m. and shocked her by telling her that Mrs Whitton was dead. Mrs Flint said that Dr Adams had given her a one pound note and told her to keep the death quiet. Elsie did not know whether Dr Adams had been with Mrs Whitton when she died but Mrs Flint also said that, some time prior to the death, Dr Adams had left a bottle of pills for Mrs Whitton. After Mrs Whitton's death, Mrs Flint noticed that about half of them were gone and that Dr Adams then put the bottle into his pocket. 'We discussed this matter at some length as we were very suspicious and had been for some time.'

When Dr Adams was away, another doctor used to visit Mrs Whitton and Elsie remembered that on one occasion after a visit, he said to her, on coming out of Mrs Whitton's room, 'Why doesn't the old fool get up?' She also recalled that a masseuse used to visit Mrs Whitton and that, on one occasion, Mrs Whitton told her that the masseuse was Dr Adams' cousin. Elsie described the masseuse as 'a small woman aged about 30 or 35 years'. The exact age of Florence Henry, his cousin, would have been 35 years at this time.

From 1924 to 1934 Beryl Buck from Bexhill used to visit her family in Eastbourne, where they went to school, and always stayed at the Kenilworth Court Hotel. She got to know Mrs Whitton and became very friendly with her, often sitting with her in her room. Mrs Whitton had two enlarged photographs of Dr Adams in her room. She was obviously very attached to him and, at one time, she told Mrs Buck that she thought Dr Adams would marry her. He had told her to have her car 'an old-fashioned high two-seater, sent down from Northampton'. Some time later, she had seen it outside the hotel and Mrs Whitton told her that she had bought a new car for herself and had given the old car to Dr Adams as a present. Mrs Whitton also confided that Dr Adams was arranging her affairs and was helping her with her investments. Miss Atkins, the Manageress of the Hotel had told Mrs Buck that, on one occasion, Mrs Whitton had asked her to witness a document and Miss Atkins had suggested that the Doctor would be a better person to do this. She was told, 'Oh, no, he could not witness this document.'

One day, Mrs Whitton was most anxious for Mrs Buck to come and see her. She did not look at all well and told Mrs Buck that she was very ill. Dr Adams had just visited, she said, and had given her an injection and she thought that this had upset her. He was coming back that same evening to give her a further injection and she asked Mrs Buck to leave a message with the management saying that she did not wish to see the Doctor when he called that evening. Having some acquaintance with Dr Adams, Mrs Buck was curious to see what his reaction would be and positioned herself to see him when he arrived. 'I saw him come in and, having received the information, he appeared very annoyed, threw his bag on to a chair with such force that it rebounded; he grabbed his coat, went out and really slammed the door.'

Mrs Lucy Maud Atkins had been manageress of the Kenilworth Hotel for eighteen years, up to 1934. She had known Mrs Whitton very well indeed: her home was in Northampton and she was a regular visitor to the hotel. Indeed, when Mrs Atkins retired, Dr Adams arranged for his car and driver to bring Mrs Whitton on a trip to Bushey to see her. Dr Adams' chauffeur, David Jenkins, recalled that he often took Mrs Whitton and Mrs Adams out for drives. He also took her on business trips to Northampton and to see friends. She paid his expenses and Dr Adams his wages, as usual. The Doctor had offered him the job of looking after Mrs Whitton's car and servicing it in addition to his normal duties, and Mrs Whitton paid him extra for this.

Mrs Whitton had always referred to the Doctor as 'my John', and was always calling upon his mother. Mrs Atkins knew about the will, but had not witnessed it because she was one of the beneficiaries. But Mrs Atkins did have one great concern about Mrs Whitton: 'The thing that worried me was that she was always ill after arriving at Eastbourne.'

On one occasion when Mrs Whitton was very ill, Dr Adams indicated that she might not last through the night. The Manageress, Mrs Atkins, asked him to call her relatives and Dr Adams replied that she had no relatives at all. Detective-Superintendent Hannam notes that this was a lie, as the will, of which he was the executor, 'shows what a liar he was', and that the Doctor invariably prevented relatives and close friends from visiting a patient who was ill and over whose finances he was beginning to exert or gain control.

Mrs Whitton died on 11th May, 1935: Dr Adams signed the death certificate and arranged the burial. She left estate of £11,465, consisting of money, stocks and shares, some in Northampton companies, such as Northampton Brewery and British Shoe Company, and others in great national companies – reminding us of past stability and loyalty of shareholders to the companies they invested in. She remembered various charities in her will, endowing a bed at Northampton General Hospital for £1,000 in her name; leaving the Vicar and Churchwardens of All Saints Church, Northampton £1,000; and the Bethany Homes in Northampton £100. This was still a time when, as in centuries past, people left their charitable legacies to local charities in their home town or village. A few relatives received legacies of £500, £100 and smaller amounts. Sarah Henry, Dr Adams' cousin received £500. Dr Adams was the sole executor and received a legacy of £2,000, and was also the sole residual legatee, receiving £7,385:10s.5d in all. Mr James, his solicitor, was one of the witnesses of the will, which was made on 5th January, 1933. The will was opposed by Mrs Whitton's relatives, but upheld: The Hon. Sir George Langton Knight, one of the Justices of the High Court, having on 22nd July, 1935, by his final decree in an action entitled 'Adams against Horton and Another' pronounced 'for the force of validity of the said Will'.

## Thomas Horsley Angus

Mr George Whitfield Plummer of Hyde Gardens in the town centre, had been a chartered accountant for forty-two years and was the senior partner in an accountancy firm – which still exists as Plummer, Parsons at the same address. He felt very strongly that he should make a statement to the police about Dr Adams' activities in the early 1930s.

Mr Thomas Horsley Angus, a widower, had been a client of Mr Plummer's firm. Some time during the month of November, 1933, his housekeeper, a Miss Douch, telephoned him to say that Mr Angus would like to see him. Mr Plummer went to his house in Derwent Road, where he found his client under the influence of drugs. He understood that he was dying of cancer, and managed to tell his accountant that he desired that his body should be cremated. Mr Plummer wrote a request to his Executors to that effect, which, with difficulty, he was able to sign. On leaving him, Mr Plummer saw the housekeeper and commented on Mr Angus' condition. Miss Douch said that Dr Adams had been that morning and had written some business letters for him and had told her that Mr Angus seemed worried about his will and that he, Dr Adams, was going to telephone to Mr Angus' solicitors in London to get them to come down.

This information surprised and annoyed Mr Plummer considerably: he was in Mr Angus' confidence and 'knowing his clear business ability, I could not imagine that a will which he had quite recently made would need any serious alteration such as to cause him any anxiety'. Under this Will, he had appointed Mr Plummer and the Westminster Bank as his Executors and Trustees and, subject to an annuity for his housekeeper of about £100 per annum, he had left his estate equally divided between his nephews.

On returning to the town centre, Mr Plummer saw Dr Adams' car in Cornfield Road and, ascertaining from his chauffeur that he was in the Midland Bank, he waited on the steps of the bank until the Doctor came out. Mr Plummer told him that he had seen Mr Angus that morning that that he had heard of his intentions to get the solicitor down – to which, of course, he strongly objected. Dr Adams replied that he thought the old man seemed worried about his will, to which Mr Plummer rejoined: 'I am his advisor and, being in his confidence, I am satisfied that the will is in order and that nothing, so far as I know, in regard thereto could cause him any anxiety, and further, in any case in my opinion, he is not now in a condition to make either a will or a codicil.'

Dr Adams then responded by telling Mr Plummer that he would not rescind buying a row of cottages in Lower Willingdon, which were owned by Mr Angus. Mr Plummer told the Doctor that 'his function was to care for the patient's health and mine to look after his affairs', and walked away from him.

Chapter Seven

# Mrs Pike and her Vigilant Relatives

## Late 1930s – 1945

Despite the letter from the BMA to all the GPs in the town, Dr Mathew of 'The White House' practice, had grave concerns and invited Detective Superintendent Hannam and his colleagues 'to chat' as he was anxious to provide information on Dr Adams' technique in dealing with patients. He made a sworn statement to the police. Towards the end of the War a firm of London solicitors had contacted him and asked him to see a Mrs Pike who lived in a small hotel in Eastbourne. Relatives had instructed that he should take over this patient from Dr Adams. He had agreed on condition that he first meet with Dr Adams and consult with him.

The solicitors forward to him a bundle of prescriptions written by Dr Adams and dispensed for Mrs Pike; all contained hypnotic drugs. Dr Mathew visited the hotel and met with Dr Adams. The patient had two private nurses looking after her. When he examined the patient, Dr Mathew could find no disease present, but concluded that she was 'very deeply under the influence of drugs.' Her pupils were pinpoint and she was completely incoherent in speech and confused, having no idea of her name and giving her age as 200 years. During the examination Dr Adams was present and he suddenly approached the patient and gave her a hypodermic injection. Dr Mathew – amazed – asked him why he had done this and what the injection was. Dr Adams replied 'morphia' and in explaining why he had done it said: 'because she might be violent.' Dr Mathew retorted that the patient was already 'flat out' and this was ridiculous. He later questioned the nurses who said that they had been told by Dr Adams that all the patient's relatives were forbidden to see her.

Within a few days Dr Mathew moved the patient out of the hotel and put her under his personal care. He withdrew all drugs and at the end of eight weeks Mrs Pike was able to do her own shopping and regained her full faculties. Dr Mathew had discovered that 'Dr B. Reid, consulting psychiatrist at Hellingly Mental Hospital had seen the patient but had told Adams that he could not assess her mental state until the drugs were very much diminished.' Dr Mathew's view was that 'It was a case devoid of any reason other than ulterior in its method of medical treatment.'

Two other statements from friends of Mrs Pike and her daughter Nan: Miss Ethel Cockshott and her sister Adeline, both confirmed Dr Mathew's view that Mrs Pike was 'very much under the influence of drugs' and recovered when they were withdrawn.

Well after the main police investigation, and during the committal proceedings in Eastbourne, the police took further statements in this case. Detective Inspector Pugh visited one of the nurses who had cared for Mrs Pike, Edna Baldock, now aged 56, who lived in the village of Friston near Eastbourne. She had started private nursing in Eastbourne in 1929, joining Miss Appleton's Jevington Gardens Nursing Association. Early in 1939 she was asked to nurse Mrs Pike at the Lathom House Hotel, Howard Square in Eastbourne. Mrs Pike and her daughter Nan were in a double bedroom at the front of the hotel. For the first month, Nurse Baldock was on night duty:

'I remember the first night I was on duty because Doctor Adams arrived between 9 p.m. and 10 p.m. I did not know what was wrong with the patient. Doctor Adams stayed for about 15 minutes and to the best of my recollection I remained in the bedroom whilst he was with the patient. On that night the room was dimly lit and I saw Doctor Adams taken a syringe from his bag. He filled it, or I should say he drew some liquid from a bottle, a small bottle and then injected the contents into Mrs Pike's arm. The patient was quiet until between three and four in the morning when she became restless and irritable and tried to get out of bed. This lasted for about an hour and then she fell off to sleep. I remained on duty until 9 a.m. when I was relieved by Nurse Doyle, who died about 3 years ago. I now remember that on my first night of duty I asked Doctor Adams, after he had given the injection to Mrs Pike, what it had contained. I wanted this information so that I could put it in my night report. He told me it was something to keep the patient quiet and make her sleep. The Doctor was rather abrupt when he told me this. During the month I was on night duty I think Doctor Adams visited Mrs Pike about five times after I had come on duty. On each of these occasions he took a syringe from his bag, drew some liquid from a small bottle and then injected into the patient's arm. I asked the Doctor again on one of these occasions what the injection was and again he told me it was something to keep the patient quiet. I do know that on the remaining nights I was on duty at Lathom House, Nurse Doyle informed me that Doctor Adams had been and given the injection to Mrs Pike. After the month of night duty I changed duties with Nurse Doyle and for the next two weeks I looked after Mrs Pike from 9 a.m. to 9 p.m. During the whole of the time, that is about six weeks, Mrs Pike never appeared sensible. I couldn't hold a conversation with her because her mind always appeared a blank. To me Mrs Pike always appeared to be in a stupor. There were short periods, usually in the afternoon, when she would brighten up a little and converse with me. Her conversation was always childish. I cannot say that Mrs Pike was suffering from any kind of complaint or disease whilst I nursed her. At the end of six weeks Mrs Pike was taken away by ambulance to a Mental Home. I do recollect that Nurse Doyle told me that during the last two weeks she was on night duty, Mrs Pike became rather noisy and Miss Parker, the owner of Lathom House Hotel, had objected.'

Nurse Baldock considered that was the only reason Mrs Pike had been removed to the Mental Home, not that she had a mental problem. She had seen no medicine or tablets in the patient's bedroom during the whole of the time she had nursed her. She had absolutely no recollection of Dr Adams leaving or writing out any prescription for Mrs Pike.

'On the few occasions I was able to hold any kind of conversation with Mrs Pike, I felt that she had something on her mind and that she was trying to tell me what it was. Her speech was always slurred and she was unable to convey to me what was on her mind. I have been asked if on any occasion I found Mrs Pike in a drunken stupor. I can say definitely that there was [sic] no wines, spirits or beer in the bedroom, and had the patient taken any such refreshment whilst I was off duty I would have most probably found out when I came on duty by the smell of her breath. Had Mrs Pike taken anything alcoholic during my absence I feel sure that Nurse Doyle would have told me or put it in her report which I read on each occasion I reported for duty. I would like to include in this statement that when Doctor Adams visited Mrs Pike on the few occasions I was on night duty, he would give the injection almost immediately and then sit at the bedside and look at the patient. I would say the Doctor stared more than looked at Mrs Pike. There was very little conversation as the patient was unable to converse.'

Whilst she had nursed Mrs Pike, Nurse Baldock had been paid by her daughter, Nan, by weekly cheque. She did not know if Mrs Pike was wealthy, but there had never been a question over the fees and she had been paid regularly. Nurse Baldock seems to have had a very good memory and she was able to recall Miss Parker the owner of the hotel, the name of the hotel, and the housekeeper and where she lived, and was still living, in Eastbourne. DI Pugh asked about Nan, Mrs Pike's daughter: Nurse Baldock was unable to say 'if she was a mental case' but remembered that 'on one occasion I stopped Nan from seeing her mother' as she was 'an excitable type' and 'she immediately went up to her bedroom on the top floor (to where she had removed when nurses were called in for her mother) and started screaming'. In 1940, Nurse Baldock had given up nursing and become a companion-housekeeper for a Mrs Bridge at 'Friston Field'.

On the 29th February, DI Pugh went to see Miss Gladys Parker, the former part-owner of the Lathom House Hotel, who was now a Director of the Imperial Hotel, and an Alderman of Eastbourne. She remembered Mrs Agnes Pike and her daughter, Nan; they had stayed at Lathom House Hotel on two occasions, in the middle thirties for about four months, and then, she thought, in 1938 or 1939. During that stay, the daughter had been ill and the Doctor 'made a routine visit once each week, but there were occasions when he was called to the Hotel if the patient became a little worse'.

'I do remember the daughter Nan paying a visit to London where she stayed for several days. Immediately Mrs Pike was alone she went out, purchased a quantity of liquor which I feel sure was brandy, and took it to her bedroom. She then commenced an orgy of drinking which lasted for a few days and culminated in her falling in her room and receiving an injury to her head. She was found unconscious and Doctor Adams was called as he had been attending Miss Pike. Mrs Pike was, of course, confined to her bed and Doctor Adams obtained two nurses, one for day duty and the other for night duty.'

The patient had been unconscious for about two days and then had periods where she was 'uncontrollable and noisy'. As the other guests were upset by this, Miss Parker had asked Dr Adams about moving her to a nursing home. He had informed her that he was arranging for Dr Shera to do a lumbar puncture 'so as to relieve the pressure on the brain'. Miss Parker did not recall seeing Dr Shera visit Mrs Pike.

'During the two months Mrs Pike was in her room and under the care of Doctor Adams, she had patches of recovery and was able to sit up and hold a conversation. I would like to add that her speech was slow, slurred and rather disjointed…

Doctor Adams gave the patient an injection between 9 p.m. and midnight and before 9-0'clock each morning. I was present on some of these occasions, which was usually at night. I saw Doctor Adams take a syringe from his bag, fill it with a liquid which also came from his bag and inject it into the patient's arm. There were several occasions when Mrs Pike was uncontrollably noisy in the daytime and the nurse on duty was unable to control, or I should say quieten the patient as she had no sedative. It was therefore necessary to get in touch with Doctor Adams, who would attend and give her an injection which was always taken from his bag. I was always under the impression that the injection given by Doctor Adams at night-time was a strong one as we were never disturbed at night. I always made a practice of visiting Mrs Pike last thing at night and again first thing in the morning, and I never received a bad report from the night nurse. It did appear that the injection given at night kept the patient quiet. It is possible that the injections given to Mrs Pike by Doctor Adams night and morning were to assist the patient in her recovery, but the continued drugged stupor that Mrs Pike remained in, alarmed me. I was so concerned that I communicated with a Miss Robertson who was a friend of the patient, and she travelled down from London and stayed at my hotel for a few days. She was shocked at the appearance and condition of Mrs Pike and promised to contact a friend. I think the outcome of this was that Doctor Adams was approached about a second opinion. He immediately dropped the case and another, a Doctor P. Mathew, took over the case. Shortly afterwards Mrs Pike was moved to a flat in College Road, Eastbourne, (presumably after a short stay in a Mental Home) and I visited her several times and found she had improved in health and was able to converse quite normally. After about 6 months Mrs Pike moved to London. The last I heard of Mrs Pike was that she had died and her daughter Nan was in a Mental Hospital, I think at Virginia Water.'

DI Jones saw Dr Shera on 2nd February, 1957. Dr Shera checked his records and found that on 30th August, 1939, he had called to see Mrs Pike at the Lathom House Hotel, at Dr Adams request, and took a blood test to estimate her kidney efficiency. 'On the same day I received from Doctor Adams a specimen of the spinal fluid for analysis, but I have no record of having done the lumbar puncture myself.' He could not recall the clinical condition of the patient when he had seen her.

# Chapter Eight

—

# Control and Fraud

## 1928 – 1948

—

### Mrs Ada Harris

Miss Ellen Edith Vooght and Miss Annie Bowden Vooght, aged 85 and 87 years, told the police about the case of their sister, Mrs Ada Harris, who, in 1948, made a claim against Dr Adams. The whole story had started nearly thirty years before Detective Superintendent Hannam's investigation began, but it was Dr Philip Mathew who suggested that these ladies might have valuable information for him. Hannam comments that he has only included this case 'for the purpose of removing the cloak from Dr Adams and revealing the man and his dealings with these elderly ladies'.

Mrs Harris first met Dr Adams through his mother, Mrs Ellen Adams, in 1928 at Marine Hall, Seaside, in Eastbourne. They both attended meetings of the Plymouth Brethren and Mrs Harris used to visit Mrs Adams at Kent Lodge. She also knew Miss Florence Henry – in her 1948 Statement she relates that Florence was 'a child of one of Mrs Adams' sisters, who had run away from home in her youth and has since been looked after by Mrs Adams'. Some years after she first met them, Ada went, on several occasions, to stay at Kent Lodge for some three weeks at a time, twice a year. Each time she found there was no medical receptionist for the private practice and acted as temporary receptionist. She did not pay for her board and was not paid anything for her assistance.

Dr Adams had attended Ada professionally since 1931. She was sent one or two accounts when he first became her doctor and she paid these, but the money was returned to her by Mrs Adams, who said that she was not to be charged because she had helped out as receptionist. Early in 1930 or in the late 1920s Dr Adams had to have an operation for appendicitis in London; he sent his mother and cousin, Miss Henry, for a holiday and asked Mrs Harris to live in at Kent Lodge and look after it and the servants whilst they were all away. At the time she first met the Dr and Mrs Adams she had been living with her sisters but she found this difficult and in 1933 she had a house built: Torbay, Marshfoot Lane in Hailsham, a village very near to Eastbourne, and she went to live there alone.

When the air raids started at Eastbourne during the Second World War, Mrs Adams and Florence Henry evacuated to Yew Tree Cottage, The Dicker, a few miles outside of Eastbourne, the Doctor staying at Kent Lodge. Mrs Harris used to visit Mrs Adams from time to time, but she died in 1943, and she went to stay with Miss Henry for a month or so at her request. Miss Henry, apparently, 'did not want to be called up' so she went in to Eastbourne daily and drove a YMCA canteen van, returning to the cottage each night. When Mrs Harris left Miss Henry's sister-in-law came with her child to stay, but, after a while, they quarrelled and then left. Mrs Harris returned to stay for a short period.

It was in February 1945 that she decided that she needed help in her Hailsham house and she took on a married couple, who came to live in to run the house and cook. By August, however, she was taken ill with 'nervous trouble' and she went to stay with her sisters in their flat in Spencer Road, Eastbourne. Dr Adams visited four or five days a week for six or seven weeks and prescribed drugs in powder form in sachets. When she felt better, Mrs Harris went to stay with Miss Henry at 30, Victoria Drive and remained there for several weeks before returning to her house again. By now, the housekeeping couple had become very possessive of the house and she found the situation impossible. She told the couple she would be selling the house and went back to Miss Henry, staying with her until May 1946. Dr Adams took over the selling of the house and put it on the market. Her sisters approached him and asked him to prevent her selling as they thought she should keep a home. Nevertheless, it was sold for £2,000.

Coles & James, the Doctor's solicitors, handled the sale. Mrs Harris could not recall signing anything or seeing the solicitors. The sale was completed in May 1946. She got the cheque for the sale amount: £1,901:7s.11d., and when Dr Adams called the morning after, she endorsed the cheque as he requested and handed it back to him in Miss Henry's presence. She did not know why she did this, but perhaps: 'When I gave the doctor the cheque it was by way of investment. I thought I intended, and was intending to have a half share in the house.' She must have meant the house at Victoria Drive. Prior to the house sale, Dr Adams had sold, on behalf of Mrs Harris, some stair and landing carpet and seven opal electric lamp shades to another of his patients. These were valued at £12, but, at no time did he account for that sum to Mrs Harris.

Perhaps it was because Mrs Harris was reluctant to take any action against a fellow 'Saint', a member of the Brethren, but she did not pursue a claim until September 1948 when she wrote to Dr Adams and asked him for a document telling her what had happened to the cheque for such a large sum of money. He replied that he had not got any documents to help her but would deal with it at some later date. She wrote again two months later, asking for the money. In response, Dr Adams said it was due to his efforts that she had got so good a price for the house and that he had retained the money against her account whilst she was living with his cousin Miss Henry.

It was at this point that Mrs Harris, now 81 years of age, went to her solicitor, Mr Berry of Hillman, Burt & Warren. She was loath to say anything to Dr Adams' prejudice. Mr Berry wrote to Dr Adams on several occasions, and in one reply Dr Adams said that she had given the money to him as a gift. On 30th November, 1948 he called on her solicitors, again stating to them that the money was a gift. He admitted selling the items from her home and said he would pay for those, but adding that if Mrs Harris wanted some money from the sale of her house he would have to charge for her accommodation with Miss Henry.

The solicitors were disgusted at this and threatened proceedings. Dr Adams' solicitors, Coles & James at first supported his 'gift' story, but then gave way and sent a cheque for the full amount plus the £12 for the other items sold. Mr Berry told the police that he had taken Counsel's Opinion on the matter and this was that it was a clear case of fraud, but advised no further action after the money was repaid.

Mrs Harris understood that the house at Victoria Drive belonged to Miss Henry or Dr Adams – but she did not like it and could not settle down there. Dr Adams owned a property, 42, Carew Road, which was requisitioned by the authorities late in 1945, redecorated and repaired. She and Miss Henry had been looking for a smaller house but could not find one, and they finally moved into the Doctor's house early in May 1946. Mrs Harris had two rooms in Carew Road, which she completely furnished and also provided some other furniture for the rest of the house. She had asked the Doctor what she could pay to Miss Henry and he had said 'Thirty shillings a week.'

Mrs Harris had made a will in June of 1945, in which she appointed Miss Henry as Trustee and, after legacies, left the residue to her. She had not worried about the cheque until the Doctor became ill when he was on holiday in Ireland in 1946: she remembered that she had no written acknowledgement. He had gone away with Miss Henry; Miss Henry was repeatedly going away and Ada could not manage on her own. In September 1946 she was surprised to find various people coming to view the house and, when questioned, Miss Henry said that she was trying to sell the property. She then found out that Miss Henry had previously been approaching friends of Mrs Harris hoping to arrange other accommodation for her without her knowledge. She had not been asked by Miss Henry or the Doctor to get out.

The Misses Vooght added to this information when they were questioned in 1956: the house in Hailsham had been sold for £2,000. They had not known about the 'loan' to Dr Adams until about October 1943 when a friend told them that she 'had to tell them about it'. 'Our sister told us that when she received the cheque, she endorsed it and handed it to Dr Adams. She used to be very careful about money and we are quite certain that, unless she had been drugged, she would not have parted with the cheque.' Whilst she was living with Miss Henry at Victoria Drive: '…at one time, we believe, before the house was sold, we remonstrated with Adams about giving our sister drugs. We also knew later, because our sister told us, that she had made a will and left her effects to Miss Henry and Dr Adams.' The Doctor was, in fact, the main legatee of this will.

Miss Ellen Vooght was a trained nurse. She had on more than the one occasion warned Dr Adams that her sister was 'not normal' yet he had actually then proceeded to give her twelve more drug cachets in the street! She was definitely of the opinion that her sister was under the influence of drugs and she went to Adams' house to wait for him. She confronted him: 'Do you realise you gave her the cachets after I had said she wasn't normal and fit to have them?' Miss Vooght told him about Mrs Harris getting out of bed at night and just taking another cachet and that she was not taking responsibility until she had control of the cachets, otherwise her sister must go into a nursing home. She added that she would also report him to the General Medical Council. He replied with some exaggeration: 'Do you wish to dictate to me who have been a doctor for thirty years?' She replied: 'I have been a nurse for fifty years.', and then left. She went home and told Ada what she had done and that if she did not have control of the cachets then she would have to go into a nursing home. The next day Mrs Harris asked for the Doctor, saw him at 9 a.m. on the Sunday at his house, returned with the cachets and handed them to her sister. She stayed with them just six or seven weeks and then went to live at Victoria Drive with Miss Henry.

Whenever she subsequently came to visit her sisters it was obvious from her condition that she was taking heavy amounts of sleeping tablets. The Misses Vooght wanted to say that their sister had never been normal from childhood: it wasn't that she was backward, but – well – just peculiar and very difficult to get on with.

## Sister Stuart-Hemsley

Sister Stuart-Hemsley came into contact with Dr Adams near the end of the War when a Miss Beryl Durban, with whom she was then friendly, asked her to go with her to see a friend whose husband was ill. She told her that the friend was not satisfied with his condition. 'Then I found out that the doctor was Bodkin Adams. I went with Miss Durban to a house in Osborne Road and told the woman that it was irregular from the professional point of view for me to be asked to see a patient who was under a doctor's care. Then she said "Well, you need not worry because the doctor has said he is not to have any visitors." We devised a scheme whereby I went into the garden and then, as if by accident, I went through the French doors into the patient's room. I made an excuse and got into a discussion with the patient and had a good look at him. I thought he looked extremely ill and emaciated; he was supposed to be 'gastric'. When I got back to the wife I suggested that she should obtain a second opinion but she said that the doctor had refused one and that he had said that the patient should be kept in a darkened room with little nourishment, but medicine. After that she mentioned that they had bought or taken a house in Rustington, but that the doctor had said that to move her husband would kill him and I said that I thought he should be moved. I left after that and shortly afterwards there was a difference of opinion between Miss Durban and myself over a private matter and I did not hear the result of the case.'

During the War Dr Adams bought a motor cycle and 'he worried my husband for a week to paint the number plates. I happened to be in the yard one morning when he came into the garage: he asked if the number plates were done and I said, "No, my husband is much too busy. Go and get one of the seven cars you've got planted away." He went very red, said "All right, all right", and the next morning he brought a packet containing about 4lbs of tea into the garage and asked my husband to give it to me with his compliments as he had made me very cross the day before. I returned the tea to his housekeeper.

'We did not come up against each other again until Mrs Norton-Dowding [see Ch 14], who had all through the war worked continuously in the maternity unit at All Saints' Hospital, complained she could not understand why her health seemed to be failing. She had several periods of illness and one or two visits to the Esperance Nursing Home. I told her that while she paid fat bills to the doctor she would stay ill. On one occasion I was visiting her at the Esperance when Dr Adams came in and threw a bed jacket on the bed. I said to her "What, is he making you presents now?" And she said, "No, he has the keys to my house and he is most helpful in looking after my affairs and getting my linen." After that, on another occasion when she was at home, she was unwell and said that she did not seem to be getting any better, I told her she would not while she had that doctor and she said "Oh, you misjudge him. He is really a very good doctor and if he does not know how to treat you he kneels down by the bed and prays for guidance." Not so very long after that she died.'

Sister Stuart-Hemsley heard no more about him and had nothing to do with him until the year she was interviewed by police, 1956. In June, her husband had an operation in the Princess Alice Hospital. The surgeon was Mr Henry Wilson and Dr Adams was the anaesthetist. 'My husband was very deeply anaesthetised and had many hours of retching afterwards. Some weeks after that my husband was in bed with thrombosis when I met Dr Adams in Beneys' in South Street. He said "How is your good man?" And I said"He isn't good. What did you do to him? You gave him enough to sink an ox, didn't you?" He spun around and said, "What?" Then he said, "He was a very nervous man and took a lot of getting under." Then he just told me to give my husband his compliments and out he went.

'I, as a nurse, have always wondered why he, with the good practice he has, has always been an anaesthetist at the local hospital.'


### Mrs Irene Herbert

Mrs Frances Player, now aged 68, first became acquainted with Mrs Irene Herbert in 1922, when she was engaged as an occasional cook for Mrs Herbert and her husband, Gerald. They were living in Shottermill, near Haslemere, Surrey at the time, but in 1936 Mrs Herbert obtained a divorce – an unusual occurrence for a middle-class lady in the 1930s – and moved to another house in Surrey, Inwoods at Knapp Hill. Mrs Player then went to live with her as her housekeeper, and they moved again to Byeways, Maybury Hill, at Woking. Frances remained with Mrs Herbert until about 1944, sometime near the end of the War. Unfortunately, Mrs Herbert had taken to drinking excessively. Fairly often, Mrs Herbert had taken holidays in Eastbourne and her doctor there was Dr Adams, whom she also counted as a friend, so Mrs Player, unable to cope with Mrs Herbert's perpetual drunkenness, telephoned him and he arranged for her to be taken to an Eastbourne Nursing Home. Mrs Player returned to her home and just visited Byeways from time to time to tidy up and clean the house, and sometimes to meet with Mrs Herbert when she visited the house. Mrs Player thought she was much better and that the treatment was doing her good.

Mrs Player had known Dr Adams since Mrs Herbert bought Byeways in the late 1930s, and in fact, Mrs Herbert had continued to visit Eastbourne frequently in order to see him. She stayed for periods at flats and hotels there. On most of these occasions Mrs Player went with her, and this is when she had met Dr Adams. Frances formed the opinion that Dr Adams was purely a friend and medical advisor, nothing more intimate. There was an air-raid whilst they were staying at the Beaulieu Hotel and Mrs Herbert said she had been so frightened that she had decided to make her will. She told Mrs Player that Dr Adams was Trustee of her will, but no, she did not mention where Dr Adams was during the air-raid – whether he had been with her or not. She said she would leave everything to the Merchant Navy. She had suggested to her solicitors, Summers and Henderson of Leadenhall Street, London, that when she was taken to the mental hospital, she would much prefer to have Adams as Trustee than her ex-husband, whom they suggested. Poor woman, she went to the mental hospital at Haywards Heath in Sussex, and soon after to Otto House, Sydenham Hill in South London, where she died, aged 50 on 5th August, 1944. Otto House was a home for inebriates and the death certificate, signed by a Dr WM Percy, gave the causes of death as 'myocardial degeneration, chronic alcoholism – alcoholic psychosis'. The 'treatment' had done no good at all, and it is surprising that a woman who was reasonably well off should have been sent from a private nursing home to the county mental asylum, especially if she was suffering from a heart condition. Did she still have access to alcohol while she was in the nursing home to help her on her way? Evidence from another case history suggests that this was a possibility.

Mrs Player received notification of her death from Dr Adams, and also that she had been left £100. Later Dr Adams went to Byeways at Woking to sort out the contents. Mrs Player asked him for a nest of three walnut tables which Mrs Herbert had promised to her, but Adams said no, as such a gift was not mentioned in the will. The will had been made on 15th April, 1943 and witnessed by Mr James, Dr Adams' solicitor. Mrs Herbert left £11,062; Dr Adams was sole executor and there were three bequests, including £100 to Mrs Player, and £1,000 to Dr Adams 'as a slight token for all his kindness to me which I can never repay'. The whole of the residue was left to King George's Fund for Sailors. The police received an anonymous letter during the investigation, informing them that a firm of furniture removers, Downs of Eastbourne, had collected some of the furniture from the house at Woking and taken it to Eastbourne. Messrs. Downs confirmed that on 3rd October, 1944, on the instructions of Edgar Horn, auctioneers, they had collected certain items and delivered them to Kent Lodge. No-one could remember exactly what items these were, and James, the solicitor, declined to help the police. Hannam was convinced that this was fraudulent conversion, otherwise why would the items not have been delivered to Edgar Horn's auction rooms in Eastbourne so that the proceeds would go to the charity?

# Chapter Nine

## Suspicious Wartime Cases

### Mrs Emily Louise Mortimer

The family of Mrs Emily Louise Mortimer had still not got over it all ten years after her death – the will, that is. They were a military family on both sides and it was all certainly not in the order they would have wished. Mary Phyllis Spranger, eighty-one, was the widow of Colonel F. J. Spranger of Castle Keep, Reigate Surrey; Colonel Henry Beaufoy Mortimer was her paternal uncle and she had certainly understood that he meant to leave his money to his nephew, Frederick Mortimer, who was then in Canada. Sometime in 1922, her uncle, then about seventy-five years of age, married Emily Mockler, whose father was a General in the British Army. After her uncle died, her aunt lived at a hotel in Eastbourne. When she had visited her aunt there, she had said that her uncle had wanted her to leave Mary some money in her will. She had not asked how much it was, but she had received nothing from the will.

Mrs Catherine Green of Virginia Water, was Mary's sister, and daughter of the late George Ferris Whidbourn Mortimer, a solicitor; she had another sister, Mrs Scott, and a brother, Arthur. She had received nothing from the estate and felt most strongly that the residue should have reverted to the family. Aunt's funeral was the first time she had met Adams. Geraldine Mockler, a second cousin of Emily, had known her well since 1912 and felt that she was a woman 'easily taken in by men': several had tried to take advantage of her and obtain money. Geraldine had, in fact, received £1,200 from her cousin's will.

Somewhat curiously, Dora Kincaid Jameson, whose husband was a first cousin of Mrs Mortimer and had known her since 1907, had been introduced to Dr Adams before the Mortimers' marriage and, indeed, he had visited the Jamesons' house, Doran Court, Redhill. At this time he did not know Mrs Mortimer. Emily Mortimer was living at the Hydro Hotel in Eastbourne and Mrs Jameson visited her frequently. She had been told that all the money left by Mr Mortimer was to come back to the Mortimer family, and that she herself would receive a legacy. Two or three weeks before Mrs Mortimer's death, Dora had had tea with her at the Hydro and she was then in perfect health and spirits. Dora was still not aware that her cousin knew Dr Adams. On the morning of 24th December, 1946, she received a telephone call from the Hydro to say that Mrs Mortimer had been moved to a nursing home and the same evening received a call from a nurse to say that Mrs Mortimer had died. On the 27th December, Dora went to Eastbourne to attend the funeral at Ocklynge Cemetery. Three other mourners, including Dr Adams were there. As soon as she saw him, she asked him why he was at the funeral and he told her that he had been Mrs Mortimer's medical advisor for the last five years. He attended the service and left immediately afterwards.

There was an auction of her effects by Barclays Bank: the furniture was at the Army and Navy Stores to be sold. Mrs Jameson received £500 from the will and the residue went to Dr Adams. The Mortimer family got nothing.

Mrs Jameson, while still in Eastbourne, then saw Dr Adams at the Burlington Hotel, when he came in to dinner with an elderly widow, who, she understood, had an apartment at the hotel. 'She was a nice-looking lady about seventy years of age. I did not speak to him.'

Mrs Mortimer had been taken from the hotel to Tredegar Nursing Home on 22nd December, on Dr Adams' instructions. Mrs Jessie Neale was the Proprietress, and said that she was very ill on admission with a heart condition. Dr Adams had attended the patient and came in on each of the two mornings she was in the nursing home. Mrs Neale was present at death and Dr Adams attended later, examining the body. The only treatment was nursing care, as far as she knew. She did know that Mrs Mortimer's solicitors were Coles & James.

Haines the undertakers confirmed that they had arranged the funeral on Dr Adams' instructions and the cemetery clerk, Ronald Scotcher, that he had an agreement with Dr Adams for cleaning the memorial annually.

The family business of the Mortimers was Carron Iron and Steel at Falkirk, Stirlingshire in Scotland. Mrs Mortimer held £2,250 worth of shares. The Assistant Secretary of the Company, Ian Scott Smith, received the will from Coles & James: Mrs Mortimer had bequeathed three twenty-firsts parts of her estate to Dr Adams. A Codicil revoked legacies to Mrs Spranger and Mrs Green and Mrs Mortimer also bequeathed to Dr Adams her two shares in the Carron Company. The family must have been outraged! Dividends were paid to shareholders twice yearly on Whitsunday and Martinmas and since Dr Adams had become a shareholder, he had been paid £1,950 in dividends, the last dividend of £100 having been made on 11th November, 1956 whilst the investigation was going on. Mr Scott Smith had read in the newspapers that Dr Adams had been arrested on a charge of murder and he called in at the Central Police Station in Edinburgh on 21st December 1956: 'I thought it right that the Police should have this information.'


### Mrs Ethel Helen Hunt

In Mrs Ethel Hunt, the mother of Sir John Hunt of Everest fame, Dr Adams had really misjudged his target. Mrs Hunt lived in Selwyn Drive in Eastbourne, and some time in 1944 she had called in Dr Adams to treat her for some temporary disorder. Two days later, he called again, told her that he knew she was a widow and hoped 'her affairs were in good hands'. He wanted to know whether her finances and securities were being properly looked after, and asked her if he could help her in that direction. She was quite taken aback and made it very clear to the Doctor that her financial position was far from an attractive one. She paid his bill for the visit and decided to call for another doctor next time she was unwell.

A day or so later, when Mrs Hunt was in her drawing-room playing bridge with three lady friends, the door bell rang. Her maid informed her that Dr Adams had called and insisted on seeing her. Mrs Hunt instructed her parlourmaid to tell him she was engaged and could not see him. The maid returned again and said that the Doctor was most insistent. Mrs Hunt left her friends and went to see him. He told her that his purpose in seeing her was to tell her that she was a most unsatisfactory patient, that she had not carried out his orders and that he thought she was slightly mentally deranged. Mrs Hunt was more than amazed at his words, and she told Dr Adams that she might be senile, but she had retained one grain of common-sense and that was that, as his bill was paid, she could show him the door and ask him to go. Mrs Hunt stated that: 'He became furious, bounded out of the house and slammed the gate and the door of his car.'

Mrs Hunt repeated the story to a *Daily Telegraph* reporter, standing 'at the door of her home in Arundel Road with her golden spaniel', at the beginning of September 1956, after Hannam had seen her, and gave some additional details. She was seventy-two at the time and had lived in Eastbourne for more than fifty years. At the bridge party had been her friend Lynett, Lady Tollemache, widow of the third Baron Tollemache. She had telephoned the Chief Constable, Mr Walker, 'a friend of my son, Sir John' – they had apparently served in Greece together during the War – and told him what had happened. She thought it her duty to do so, and he had sent Superintendent Hannam round to see her. Lady Tollemache told the reporter 'I attended the bridge party. There was an incident, and I offered my assistance to Mrs Hunt, but she said she and her maid could manage the situation'.

Detective Superintendent Hannam noted that he had come across other cases where this behaviour of Dr Adams was typical, but this was the only one which had been written down in a sworn statement. He also commented that he thought it 'clear that in many cases Dr Adams satisfied himself as to whether the patient is monied or not and, if not, declines to show further interest'. The Doctor was, however, also looking for rich patients who were compliant and could be controlled and dominated. What is most interesting is that, even although he already knew that Mrs Hunt did not fall into this category and that there was no point in pursuing her, he could not resist returning to see her. The only object he could have in doing so was to give vent to his anger: the uncontrollable anger he felt when he was crossed.

### Mr Leslie & Mrs Ada Cockhead – The Duel

In December 1939, Nurse Sarah McDermott was given an appointment by Miss Appleton's Nursing Co-operative of Jevington Gardens. She was instructed to go to the Queen's Hotel by the pier on Eastbourne seafront, and there she was employed by Mr Leslie Cockhead to nurse his wife. She was said to be receiving 'treatment for cerebral' – presumably 'cerebral accident'. Dr Adams was attending her and another two nurses were already being employed: Nurse Good on day duty and Nurse McKenna on nights.

Nurse McDermott recalled that Mrs Cockhead was 'in a coma on and off during the whole period that I was nursing her'. Sometimes she would be in a coma for a matter of a few days and on these occasions she would be fed artificially. She would be given a heart stimulant from time to time and sleeping draughts. The day nurse gave injections under Dr Adams' instructions. Due to the patient's mental condition it was difficult for Nurse McDermott to say whether the she was under the influence of drugs.

Nurse McDermott went on to day duty when Nurse Good left in 1940 and about six months later they all had to leave the Queen's Hotel and moved to Silverdale Lodge Hotel in Silverdale Road, and then moved again to Keymer Nursing Home in East Grinstead.

During all this, Mrs Cockhead's condition remained unchanged; due to wartime conditions, it was not possible for Dr Adams to visit a patient so far away. She died in 1941.

Mr Cockhead moved to a flat in Carlisle Grange, Carlisle Road. Mrs Harriett Brown obtained the post of housekeeper to him through her sister Miss Gardner (later Mrs Clegg). She cooked, dressed him and prepared him for bed at night. He was about eighty-five years of age and disabled, having a stiff leg; he used a wheelchair. The daily help was Gredwin Chappel.

Dr Adams visited Mr Cockhead about four times a week, and later, almost every day. On many occasions Mrs Brown saw Dr Adams give his patient injections and also tablets; she knew that her employer had heart problems.

Mrs Brown stated that Miss Gardner, Mr Cockhead's nurse, was a 'great friend'. Mr Cockhead would not hear a word against her and she devoted a considerable amount of her own time to him. He was a very alert, intelligent and 'venturesome' man, in full possession of his faculties until a few hours before his death

Mr Cockhead thought a great deal of Dr Adams, though 'I would say that Miss Gardner always came first with Mr Cockhead and then his niece, Mrs Myott, then Dr Adams'. Miss Gardner had a key to the flat. Oh, yes, there was a lot of trouble from the family. Miss Gardner had a lot of shares left to her and all the contents of the flat except for one hundred and fifty snuff boxes sold at Christies and certain books which went to Sothebys. Miss Gardner and Mrs Myott shared the residue of the estate. She could only say that Dr Adams gave Mr Cockhead every attention whilst he attended him and didn't hesitate to come when called out at night.

Gertrude Clegg, née Gardner, was sixty-five years of age in 1956. She was a State Registered Nurse, midwife and physiotherapist. She came to Eastbourne in 1937 and practised in Silverdale Road. The majority of her patients were sent to her by Dr Adams, to whom she had been introduced by Lieutenant-Colonel Gwynne of Wootton Manor. 'I do know the late Marchioness of Abergavenny wrote to the Colonel on my behalf.' Dr Adams sent, in all, between two and three hundred patients to her.

In May 1940, Dr Adams sent Mr Cockhead to Nurse Gardner for massage and ultra-short-wave therapy for his hip. This was while he was still at Silverdale Lodge Hotel. 'We became very good friends and I felt he relied on me.' Mr Cockhead was taken to a nursing home with a strangulated hernia. Nurse Gardner went to his room and took possession of his valuables, locked them in a case and kept the keys. She refused to give the keys both to his chauffeur, Mr Halls and to Dr Adams. 'He was very annoyed with me.' Next day she went to see Mr Cockhead at the nursing home and was informed by the Matron that the patient was allowed no visitors. She asked why and was told that this was on the instructions of Dr Adams. Matron was very frigid with her and she attributed this attitude to her refusal to hand over the keys to Mr Cockhead's case to Dr Adams. When she eventually was able to visit the patient, Mr Cockhead expressed his indignation that she had been prevented from seeing him, and the Doctor apologised.

Shortly after this incident Miss Gardner received a telephone call from Mr Duff, Mr Cockhead's brother-in-law and co-director with him of Pearce Duff Ltd – of blancmange and custard fame – inviting her out to lunch at the Sussex Hotel. This meeting, she believed, was to discuss with her the incident at the nursing home. She already knew Mr Duff as Mr Cockhead had taken her to visit him at his home in Hove.

Mr and Mrs Duff arrived at the Sussex Hotel for the arranged luncheon, and were surprised to find Dr Adams there. Shortly before they arrived Dr Adams had spoken to Miss Gardner and said that he had come to see Mr Duff and 'put things right'. She told him that, 'the one that had caused the trouble, meaning myself, must put it right... As Dr Adams was an uninvited guest to this luncheon party, Mr Duff was unable to discuss this incident and hear my side of the story.' During lunch, Mr Duff said to her in front of Dr Adams: 'We will have to arrange another luncheon.' This was obviously a hint to the doctor that he would not be wanted at the next luncheon. A few days later she saw Mr Duff and he told her that Dr Adams had 'phoned him and apologised for what he called "a misunderstanding at the nursing home."'

Dr Adams had told Mr Cockhead that he should try to find a ground floor flat and Mr Cockhead asked Miss Gardner to try to find one. She had heard that the ground floor flat in Carlisle Grange would be vacant. Mr Duff viewed it and thought it suitable. He also told her that Dr Adams had obtained the keys of two other houses and wanted him to look over them. On inspection Mr Duff decided on the flat at Carlisle Grange. Mr Cockhead then instructed Nurse Gardner to furnish the flat for his occupation and allowed her to spend up to £1,000. This was during 1943.

Mr Cockhead told Nurse Gardner that he had made a will and that his niece, Mrs Myott and she, would share equally in the residue, and added that he was leaving this residue to the two people that mattered most in his life. He also mentioned some others named in his will, among them Dr Adams, business associates, and Mr Halls, the chauffeur. She had actually suggested that the £250 he had left to Dr Adams should be increased to £500. He later showed to her that part of the will in which her name was mentioned. The will had been witnessed by Mr Glenister, a local solicitor, and his daughter. She added, somewhat defensively, 'I was more or less his companion and spent as much time as I could with him.' Mr Leslie Cockhead died on 15th December, 1947, aged eighty-six years. He was mentally alert and even played bridge in the evening within a few days of his death. As far as Dr Adams was concerned, he 'did his utmost to help Mr Cockhead to maintain a good degree of health. I could not possibly complain in any way of the medical attention he received from Dr Adams.' The body was cremated at Golders Green Crematorium.

Roland Halls, fifty-eight years old in 1956 and by then a clerk at the Dental Estimates Board, was, from 1924 to 1947, personal attendant to Mr Cockhead. His duties had consisted of driving him in his car, acting as valet and assisting him with clerical work. His employer had originally resided in London but had moved, with his wife, in 1932, to the Queen's Hotel, which had been closed down during the Second World War. Shortly after they moved to Silverdale Lodge Hotel he met Miss Gardner; he was given to understand that 'this woman was also giving treatment to Mrs Clegg who also lived there with her husband'. Miss Gardner, of course, later married Mr Clegg when he was a widower and Mr Cockhead had died. Roland Halls related an episode which had occurred soon after Mrs Cockhead's death in 1941. 'One afternoon I returned to Silverdale Lodge and on going into Mr Cockhead's apartment I found Miss Gardner there. She and Mr Cockhead were embracing each other and as I walked in Miss Gardner stepped away.' At this time she was forty-nine and he was seventy-eight.

This friendship between Roland's employer and Miss Gardner ripened very quickly and she became a regular visitor to Silverdale Lodge. She gave Mr Cockhead treatment for an arthritic hip and he became 'very attached to her.' Dr Adams was visiting his patient about two or three times a week, but sometimes less. It was in October 1941 that Mr Cockhead was taken to Southfields Nursing Home and operated on for hernia. Roland recalled that Miss Gardner had taken it upon herself to collect various articles in the apartment and retained the keys in her possession. He was 'naturally responsible for Mr Cockhead's personal belongings' and had asked Miss Gardner for the keys to the apartment at Silverdale lodge. She refused to give them to him and he had mentioned this to Dr Adams and together they got Mr Cockhead to write a note to Miss Gardner telling her to give the keys to Roland Halls. When he delivered this note to her, she handed the keys to him.

From his observation, 'it was quite clear to me that Dr Adams and Miss Gardner were jockeying for position with Mr Cockhead'. He knew that Dr Adams had given instructions to the nursing staff at Southfields Nursing Home not to let Miss Gardner see Mr Cockhead. This ban, however, only lasted for about two days and then Miss Gardner was allowed to see the patient. When Mr Cockhead was beginning to walk about, Miss Gardner was seen on several occasions to embrace and kiss him on the verandah of the nursing home.

On moving to the flat in Carlisle Grange, Mr Hall's wife was appointed as housekeeper. Dr Adams continued to visit as usual and, despite the previous friction between him and Miss Gardener, they were now on friendly terms. In April 1942, after they had only been at Carlisle Grange for three months, his wife and Miss Gardner 'failed to see eye to eye'. There was a disagreement over Miss Gardner interfering with the catering and Mr and Mrs Hall returned to their own home. As time went by, Miss Gardner took control and Mr Hall was relegated to taking his employer out in his wheelchair and doing a little shopping. Miss Gardner continued to run the flat and spent a great deal of her leisure time with Mr Cockhead. Dr Adams continued with his visits and everything appeared to be running smoothly. Mr Cockhead's general condition deteriorated; his one thought was Miss Gardner whom he had nicknamed 'Gee Gee', 'and she appeared to like it'.

Mr Hall had frequently seen Mr Cockhead's will lying about the lounge where anyone could see it, and he often changed it. About four or five years before he died he had told Roland that Dr Adams had had enough out of him in medical fees and that it was his intention to leave the Doctor only £200. He himself had received £500 and his wife £200, and the only gift was £50 from Miss Gardener to help with his daughter's school fees. Nurse Gardner inherited over £20,000.

During the investigation, the police received the following letter from Mrs Myott, Leslie Cockhead's niece:

'Dimsdale House, Wolstanton,
Newcastle, Staffs. 24.8.56

I have read with great interest in the press, that you are making enquiries into the death of several widows in the Eastbourne area. I also noticed a photograph of Dr Adams. He attended my uncle Mr L.G. Cockhead. Miss Gardner had telephoned to Mr and Mrs Duff in Hove that uncle was sinking and I went to Eastbourne immediately. Uncle died during the night and I waited for Dr Adams. Mr Duff asked me to read the Will over the telephone and I did. The Doctor arrived at 8 a.m. and, after examining the body, he came into the sitting room and wiped away a tear, which struck me as rather odd and then said 'I would like that…' 'Coffee?', I said. 'Oh, I mean the gold pen as a little reminder of a dear patient.' 'I am sorry it is not mine to give.' He replied 'Well, remember that I would like it.' I already knew that it had been left to my younger son in the Will but I did not tell him so.

I am telling you all this as I thought Dr Adams was a very greedy man. My uncle left him £500, he told me 'Adams expects something, why I do not know.' Miss Gardner, who had ingratiated herself with uncle was left co-beneficiary with me in the estate. I never forgave her for leaving him when he became unconscious. I felt that Dr Adams had become somewhat jealous that she had in a measure displaced him in the ménage, seeing that it was he who had introduced her there. I realised he [uncle] had parasites about him, especially after my aunt died.'

Leslie Cockhead died, aged eighty-six, on 15th December, 1947. Dr Adams certified cause of death as (a) Uraemia (b) chronic nephritis – a common cause-of-death certification for him. There were many prescriptions for pethedine – a pain-killer on the dangerous drugs list but not as strong as morphine, and also, during the month of his death, stilboestrol – an oestrogen substitute sometimes used in cases of prostate cancer as it is a female hormone which may reduce tumours of the prostate gland. Nephritis is inflammation of the kidneys and uraemia a symptom; kidney failure could be caused by cancer of the prostate. But why start a treatment a few days before death – if the patient was a dying man? If the patient's condition was prostate cancer the symptoms would have been apparent much earlier. There is other evidence of Dr Adams' use of a treatment just before death that could have no effect and was, perhaps, to rationalise to himself that he had been giving proper treatment to the patient to preserve life. The attempt to take a souvenir in this case failed, but that signature is, nevertheless, there.

Chapter Ten

# The Post-War Years

## 1945 – 1950

### Mrs Mary Jane Mouat

Mrs Olgar Mouat Smith was the widow of a former colonial judge – eighty years of age in 1956 – and Dr Adams had been her doctor for several years in the 1940s. 'I gave him up', she said, 'because I did not like his manner towards his patients and, in particular, his horrid manner towards his poorer panel patients and the expectant mothers'. Her husband had died in 1950 and she became an NHS patient. She also had a comment to make on Nurse Gardiner (now Mrs Clegg), the nurse who was left the very large legacy by Mr Leslie Cockhead – 'Miss Gardiner would never have a wrong word said against Dr Adams, and she was very much in his confidence'.

It was about her aunt, Mrs Mouat, she was concerned to see the police: 'Dr Adams tried to get my aunt, many times, to sell him the car: a Morris Minor. He said he wanted it for a Miss Chatty, who was connected with the YMCA, but my aunt wouldn't sell it to him, although he pestered her many times.' Her aunt also possessed many fine pieces of furniture which Dr Adams tried to buy from her, but she refused to part with them.

In 1948, Mrs Mouat had been badly burned when her nightdress caught alight from an electric fire. Dr Adams called and bandaged the legs. Two days before she died, Dr Adams was with her in her bedroom. Nurse Richards went in and out of the room several times and came to Mrs Mouat's niece, telling her that the Doctor was trying to get her aunt to sign her name on a blank piece of paper. She had seen him with the piece of paper on an attaché case on the bed and a pen in his hand attempting to get her to sign it and actually asking her to do so. The nurse had thought it strange as the patient was so feeble and unable to do anything.

When the Doctor had left the house, Mrs Mouat Smith went to her aunt, who said, 'Doctor wanted me to sign my name, but I couldn't'. She was far too ill, and she died two days later in the middle of the night – this was just one week after the accident and she had been in good health with no symptoms of any illness. Dr Adams was not present but he came later on in the morning and told the niece that the patient had died from a thrombosis. He said to her: 'It's lucky she died of thrombosis because otherwise there would have to be an inquest on the burning accident.' Mrs Mouat Smith thought this a most odd remark. When he was leaving the house he said to her: 'Don't forget about the car.' She thought this a callous demand, at such a time. Some weeks after her aunt's death, she saw Dr Adams and he again broached the matter of her aunt's car. She told him he could buy it if he wanted: he offered her £215 for it, which she accepted.

Nurse Marion Richards, physiotherapist and State Registered Nurse, had nursed Mrs Mouat, who was about ninety-two years of age, and had been giving her massage before the accident occurred. The patient would say of Dr Adams: 'He is very wonderful'. Nurse Richards joked with her about this. After the accident when Mrs Mouat sustained severe burns to the lower part of the body and upper limbs, she did the dressing and Mrs Mouat never complained about the burns, which were very bad. It was when she had just done the dressings one day and left the room when the Doctor came and waited. She eventually opened the bedroom door: 'I saw the doctor sitting by the bed, he had an attaché case on his knees, resting against the side of the bed. I saw a blank sheet of notepaper lying on the case. As I entered the room, the doctor looked up and waved to me to go out again, which I did. He did not say anything and neither did Mrs Mouat.' She waited until the Doctor left the room, but when she went back, Mrs Mouat said nothing about what the Doctor had said. When she returned that afternoon, Mrs Smith told her that her aunt had been delirious all day and saying she was sorry she could not sign the paper for the Doctor that morning.

Detective Superintendent Hannam concluded that this was a clear attempt to obtain a Power of Attorney, and also a case for the Coroner. Mrs Mouat left £22,391 and the comment in Hannam's Report to the Chief Superintendent was: 'He didn't manage it.'


### Mrs Julia Maud Thomas

Mrs Julia Maud Thomas of Cumballa in St. John's Road, was a wealthy widow, and Dr Adams had been her doctor since 1932. Miss Elizabeth Bryant was her 'Cook-general'. From about 1949, Dr Adams visited her in the evenings, but sometimes came for afternoon tea. She called him 'Bobbums'. Dr Adams was fond of chocolates and Mrs Thomas would always give him some. He would also help himself to those beside her bed. The Doctor often discussed her private affairs and gave financial advice. When her cat was run over in November 1952, she became very depressed and showed signs of mental disorder. The Doctor visited her every day and prescribed sleeping tablets during the last twelve months of her life.

On the Tuesday night, three days before she died, Mrs Thomas was sitting in a chair in the study and Dr Adams was with her. Miss Bryant overheard the Doctor say to Rose Figgett, the houseparlourmaid: 'I want her to have a good night's rest; she must take this medicine and will feel better for it in the morning.' He got Rose to fetch a glass of water, and the Doctor gave her tablets, and, with the houseparlourmaid, helped her upstairs to bed. She fell unconscious almost immediately and did not wake again until 2 p.m. on Wednesday when she had a drink and more of the tablets. She went into a coma. On Friday morning Dr Adams came and gave her an injection. He called again at 9 o'clock that night, saying to Mrs Bryant: 'I don't think she will last much longer. It will all be over soon.' She died at 3 a.m. in the morning. Dr Adams came at 9 a.m. It was on the day before she died, Dr Adams was in the house and Miss Bryant, standing in the hall with another lady when he said, 'Mrs Thomas has promised me her typewriter, I'll take it now.' Miss Bryant went into the drawing room, fetched the typewriter, gave it to Dr Adams and he took it away with him.

## Major Philip Christie

Major Philip Christie was still a relatively young man when he died in April, 1948. He was an underwriter and member of Lloyds and lived at the fashionable block of apartments, Keppelstone in Staveley Road, near the Beachy Head end of the seafront. Dr Adams certified the cause of death as 'Cerebral thrombosis'. Major Christie left the large sum of £57,088 but Dr Adams was not a beneficiary of the will. Thomas Etherington, the Head Porter of Keppelstone, reported that the Doctor came to him one day and asked him to go to Major Christie's flat. There was another gentleman also there, whom he did not know. Dr Adams produced a document with 'Power of Attorney' written at the top. The document was partly concealed by blotting paper, but the Head Porter could see that it gave Dr Adams Power of Attorney over Major Christie's affairs. He was told to sign his name against a cross as a witness. A few days later Major Christie died, leaving a widow, Mrs Daphne Christie.

## Mrs Margaret Pilling

Elaine Wilson stated that her mother, Margaret Pilling, lived at the Grand Hotel from 1948 to 1951. Early in 1951 she understood that her mother had been taken ill with influenza. As with many rich permanent guests at the Grand Hotel, Mrs Pilling was a patient of Dr Adams. He had called and arranged for two private nurses to attend her.

Nurse Brierly had first met the Pilling family in the 1920s in Cheshire and she had nursed the children of the younger daughters. In 1951 when Mrs Pilling was eighty-one years of age, the daughters had asked Nurse Brierly to go down to Eastbourne and nurse their mother. When she arrived she saw no symptoms of 'flu. Dr Adams told her nothing except that Mrs Pilling had some slight obstruction of the bowel, but the patient did not complain of any pain. She thought that too many sedatives were being given and did not know what the drugs were. Dr Adams manner was always 'casual'. He would tell her to carry on with the treatment, or just come in and sit on the bed and enquire from the patient how she was. 'His casualness struck me.'

On Monday 18th February, 1951, Miss Phayle, the Assistant Housekeeper of the Grand Hotel called Nurse Brierly to see another patient in the hotel, who was very ill – strangely a Mrs Brierley. Having seen the patient, Nurse Brierly telephoned Dr Adams and gave him her report. 'He said he could not come and see her until the next morning and would I give Mrs Brierley a dose of Mrs Pilling's night medicine.'

Nurse Brierly then spoke to her daughters about Mrs Pilling's desire to move from

Eastbourne. It was agreed that Nurse Brierly should speak to Dr Adams about this, but his response was that she was not fit to be moved and would not be for some time. She then told Dr Adams that the relatives had requested a second medical opinion as to Mrs Pilling's general health. Dr Adams told her that a specialist was coming from London to see another of his patients, Lord Burghley, and that he would make arrangements for the specialist to see Mrs Pilling on the same day. Time went on and no specialist ever came to see her.

Mrs Pilling improved and her daughter, Mrs Wilson, and the family, bought her a house at Ascot. Dr Adams remained in attendance. Nurse Brierly went away for three days rest and when she came back she found Mrs Pilling very ill and in a similar state to when she first saw her. When Nurse Brierly reported to the daughters they decided to move their mother. She was moved two days later and enjoyed the journey to Ascot. The medicine was stopped just before the journey: on arrival at Ascot she vomited a lot for a night and a day, saw another doctor and recovered completely. As Nurse Brierly related: 'Under Dr Adams' direction she was in a continuous coma and a demented state – I have never been able to account for.'

Chapter Eleven

—◆—

# Mrs Edith Morrell

## 13 November 1950

—◆—

The night before Mrs Morrell died, the Doctor looked at her 1939 Rolls Royce Silver Ghost, and said, 'That's a beautiful car.'

James Dean, seventy-three years old and a retired police officer, was the relief night watchman at Marden Ash, Mrs Morrell's house. Dr Adams frequently visited late in the evening and James Dean would open the garage gates for him. The other night watchman was also a retired police officer, Mr Simmons – Mr Dean had got the job for him. He was anxious to point out that Dr Adams had not only received one thousand pounds and the Rolls Royce, but had also had a lot of china which Mrs Morrell had brought from a previous home, Corner Cottage in Carlisle Road: she had not even unpacked it when the Doctor carted it away! Price later remembered that Mrs Morrell had bought a complete dinner service of one hundred and twenty or more pieces in a sale and for some time it was stored over the garage. Later he moved it to the lounge in the house and put it in the court cupboard. About a month before Mrs Morrell died, he went into the lounge and saw Dr Adams wrapping up a few of the plates of this set in paper. Later he looked in the court cupboard and nothing of the set was left.

Walter Elphick, Dr Adams' chauffeur mentioned in his second statement that, during the last twelve months of Mrs Morrell's life, the Doctor frequently brought away from Marden Ash brown paper parcels. They were of varying sizes and he did not know what they contained.

The chauffeur at the time of Mrs Morrell's death and for three and a half years previously, was Thomas Price, fifty-three years of age. During the last nine months of her life Price saw her every day and thought she was getting better. He knew that she had a stroke and was partially paralysed and he knew of Dr Adams frequent visits to the house. It was his habit to assist the Doctor in supporting Mrs Morrell when they walked her around her room for exercise. Price would push her around in the garden in a wheelchair and on one or two occasions got her into the car and took her for a drive. A special handrail was fitted on the staircase and he and Dr Adams helped her up the stairs on many occasions.

Price looked after his employer's Wolseley 18 and the Rolls Royce Silver Ghost: Dr Adams often commented to Price on how nicely the Rolls Royce was kept, 'A very lovely thing'. Hannam comments in the police report: 'From our knowledge of Adams' technique and his keenness on good motor cars it is not mere bias to say that this covetous comment appears quite usual.'

Mrs Morrell told Price that she was going to give Dr Adams, a chest of silver which was a treasure piece in the Morrell house. It was a large dark oak chest, standing on four legs with a wooden carved eagle as a handle. It contained two dozen of everything in silver and Mrs Morrell had previously told Price it was worth £800, but Mrs Morrell had thought the world of Dr Adams. He knew that the chest had been taken to Kent Lodge after Mrs Morrell's death, and he himself had delivered the Rolls Royce. He was a little incensed because Dr Adams did not even give him 6d. for doing so. Later, when Dr Adams opened it for Hannam to examine it at Kent Lodge, 'inside were eight narrow drawers, each containing silver, some still in tissue paper, and the bottom drawer held several service trays.'

The gardener, John Carter was a dedicated man and quite devoted. Mrs Morrell frequently spoke to him in the garden about the cultivation of flowers: 'her one ambition was to win the Samuel Argo Cup for Dahlias in the Eastbourne Summer Flower Show and on two occasions '49 and '50, I won it for her and she was as pleased as ever anyone could be. At that time she had between eight hundred and one thousand dahlias in her collection and they were entered for probate when she died. The whole collection was left to me when she died.' There is a dahlia named after her: 'Edith Morrell'.

John Carter was well aware of the Doctor's regular visits and, during her last illness he was there at least once a day; sometimes he went in Mrs Morrell's car for drives with her. About twelve months before she died, whilst she was staying with her son in Cheshire, she had a fall and hurt her head and Dr Adams travelled all the way to Cheshire with an ambulance and brought her back to Eastbourne.

The police later managed to trace the cook who was employed by Mrs Morrell: Miss Bessie Woodward, who was by then employed in Oxford. She was able to give details of the routine in Mrs Morrell's household, apparently 'at great length'. She would receive the drugs delivered by Browne's the Chemist, and she gave it as her strong opinion, and expressed her disapproval of Mrs Morrell's 'drugged condition' at various times. She mentioned that the dangerous drugs were kept in an unlocked drawer in the dining room. The police planned to see Miss Woodward once more because they were informed that it was she who had purchased the spirits kept in the house, and she had known that Mrs Morrell had the whisky with her lunch.

An interview with Rosaline Spray, a retired trained nurse who was for a while in 1949 a companion to Mrs Morrell and living at Marden Ash, was interesting if not providing concrete evidence. Mrs Morrell had given Dr Adams a pair of silver candlesticks for a Christmas present. On two occasions she went with Mrs Morrell for a drive in the Rolls Royce and Dr Adams accompanied them.

One morning, shortly after the second drive, the Doctor was visiting Marden Ash and, as he entered the bedroom, he was rubbing his hands together and said to Mrs Morrell: 'Good morning, me dear, there is one thing I envy you of, it's your beautiful Rolls. It's like sitting in an armchair.' Miss Spray felt 'utter contempt' for his behaviour. He then sat on the bed and conversed with Mrs Morrell.

A letter arrived on Detective Superintendent Hannam's desk, dated August 26th, 1956, from Lilian Myers '(Widow)' of The Old Barn, Swanage, Dorset:

> 'After seeing constant appeals in the newspaper, for any information relevant to the deaths of several ladies in Eastbourne during recent years, I thought perhaps it was my duty to send you what I knew about the late Mrs Morrell of Marden Ash, prior to her death. She had been a friend of my mother (who died some years ago) and myself for many years. I had visited her quite frequently when she lived in Beaconsfield and later at Eastbourne when I lived in Wallington in Surrey – after mother's death. To me she always seemed [of] a placid happy disposition and was so kind and always pleased when I went to see her. The last Christmas she was alive – I think she wrote to tell me that she would be spending it with her son and family, Mr Claude Morrell of West Kirby, and would I go and see her in Eastbourne when she returned in the New Year? I heard once or twice again after that, seemingly, she had been ill, but still wanted me to go. Eventually I wrote saying I'd call in for a short time on March 21st 1950 and if she wasn't feeling well I would only stay for a short time. To my surprise I was told on arrival that she was not well enough to see me. I told the nurse that I was an old friend and that she had said in her letter how much she wanted to see me. But the nurse said that she was very ill, and very difficult, and that she had just been given either an injection or a drug (I forget which) to calm her. She also said that Mrs Morrell turned against people and might not wish to see me at all, but if I liked to go for a walk and call again in two hours – she would see how things were. I did this – but was still told it would be most inadvisable for me to see her and I had to go back to Wallington very disappointed. I never saw her again, but received a notification of her death.
>
> That is all I can tell you and it can be of little use, I am sure, except that I had made a note of the date and was so puzzled at not being allowed even a few moments with her as I really did feel however ill she was she would have wished it.
>
> I hope that everything will soon be satisfactorily cleared up for you.'

This information was of no use as evidence but it does, of course, tally with the statements of other witnesses who were prevented from seeing their friends or relatives on the instructions of Dr Adams: anyone who might affect his position of dominance, notice the drugged state of the patient; interfere in any way with his arrangements.

'In view of the publicity which has recently been given to your investigations, I thought it right to pass on, in confidence, a little information...' Doreen Henagulph, a state-registered nurse, had volunteered to be interviewed because she had nursed four cases for Dr Adams. The first of these was that of Mrs Morrell, in about November, 1948, when she was in the Olinda Nursing Home for a short while. Sister Henagulph thought, at that time, that she was 'just a mild stroke case'. While she had paralysis of one leg, she was able to get up for exercise. At that time, Dr Adams had said he would get a bed from his own house, with a wooden rail round it so that she could exercise around the bed; 'that is the kind of thing he would do to ingratiate himself with patients'. Although there seemed to be nothing wrong that she could not recover from, Mrs Morrell told Sister Henagulph that she didn't want to live; 'she also said she would offer money if I would give her an overdose. Life certainly had no meaning for her.' When Sister Henagulph left at the end of the month – because Mrs Morrell had suggested that she could run errands in her off-duty time, which was unprofessional – Mrs Morrell was improving and the nurse considered that she might recover the use of her leg. Dr Adams visited every day and gave some intra-muscular injections, which she thought were vitamins.

Sister Henagulph was of the opinion that the Doctor tried to endear himself to patients and that he had a 'hypnotic influence over them. He sits very close to them and gazes into their eyes'.

Miss Florence Pearson had nursed Mrs Morrell in the early stages of her illness, at nights for one month, but also relieved the day nurses during their days off and holiday periods for one year. This was the last case she nursed for Dr Adams. She found Mrs Morrell a difficult patient, in fact impossible at times, but this was due to the fact that she was 'physically and mentally sick'. She was unable to remember the treatment in detail, and probably did not know, but she did know that the patient had medicines and injections. Sister Pearson had given her some injections but Dr Adams also gave injections, 'I saw him give many injections'. He had visited many times, during the day and night. 'Mrs Morrell liked Dr Adams very much but there were occasions when she was cross with the doctor.'

Mrs Morrell was the only patient Sister Beatrice May Barton had nursed for Dr Adams and this was for three months from April to June 1949 as a relief day nurse. She had found Mrs Morrell to be 'extremely charming' and got on well with her. She had really no information about the treatment given to her, but had understood that injections were administered by Dr Adams.

Even more briefly, Sister Margaret Methren had nursed Mrs Morrell for two days on 1st and 2nd September, 1950. She recalled that when Dr Adams visited the patient, 'he requested me to leave the bedroom. I considered this rather a breach of ethics and rather unusual.'

When Sister Caroline Sylvia Randall first nursed Mrs Morrell she was at the Cumberland Hotel, then at the Esperance Nursing Home and at Olinda Nursing Home. She was a very difficult patient and had 'brainstorms': she would get in a temper very quickly. Dr Adams came to see her every evening. He gave injections of morphia which were gradually increased. He also gave her phenobarbitone during the daytime and tablets for sleep. Sometimes he gave her heroin. Sister Randall asked Dr Adams 'if he could stop the heroin as she became ill and clammy during the night. Adams did not agree with me and he thought the condition was not resultant from the drug. Adams did not like unsolicited advice from nurses. Subsequently he ceased the heroin and the disturbed condition went.'

Annie Helen Mason-Ellis was the same age as Dr Adams and had nursed only two cases for him, one of these being Mrs Morrell. She would, of course, end up as a witness for the prosecution, but at the beginning of her statement she appears to soften the impression: '…this doctor was always very kind and attentive to his patients and he had a most attractive bedside manner. His very technique and approach of conduct appealed very much to his aged women patients.'

For the majority of the time, Mrs Morrell had been mentally alert, recovering from a stroke under treatment and able to walk with assistance. Dr Adams gave her medicine and injections and she had sedatives for sleeping. Although he was very attentive, Sister Mason-Ellis felt that he could have done more in the way of treatment and she was surprised that she was not having more exercise and massage to stimulate the nerves. She did, in fact, suggest this to Dr Adams and he allowed her to give the patient massage and showed her what he would like done. He did this by demonstration, but ultimately arranged for a trained masseuse to be called in, and the patient had massage and radiant heat treatment. Sister Mason-Ellis felt pleased that the patient was improving: Mrs Morrell was very keen to get well and most co-operative.

During the time Mrs Morrell was ill, the Doctor had gone up to Scotland for some shooting and she did not like him being away so long, even although Dr Harris visited as locum. During this Scottish holiday, Dr Adams paid one visit to the patient and Sister Mason-Ellis was told that he had flown back for the purpose. She remembered that Mrs Morrell was 'very thoughtful about her Will' and told the Sister that she had made a number of changes to it and codicils, and that she was going to leave Dr Adams some money and the silver chest and an old court cupboard: 'I have often seen them both stop and admire the silver chest and discuss it.' After Dr Adams left after a visit, Mrs Morrell would often tell her how very kind he was.

On one occasion, though, 'Mrs Morrell was very cross with Dr Adams and told me that she would wipe him out of her will.' This, however, was only a passing phase.

Towards the close of her life, Mrs Morrell's condition 'got more pronounced and she had brainstorms. Dr Adams gave injections and at no time did I know what he was administrating.' This is an important point Sister Mason-Ellis makes because she could not have entered in her nurse's notebook what this injection was as she had no idea. She continued: 'Mrs Morrell died suddenly and I did not expect her to die at that time. I think she was comatose for a day or two.' What had really surprised her was the lack of any real treatment.

Whilst Dr Adams was in Scotland, Sister Mason-Ellis had more professional freedom and had continued more vigorously with the massage and exercise and the patient had responded well. In the normal way 'Dr Adams always takes complete charge and did not take the nurse into his confidence, and I found I had to be very firm at the patient's bedside if I wanted to discuss the patient with the doctor.' However, 'Dr Adams preferred the nurse out of the room when he was with the patient.'

Dr Adams had paid Nurse Randall and Sister Mason-Ellis their fees each week 'which from my experience was very unusual'. In April, 1951, some time after Mrs Morrell's death, Sister Mason-Ellis had received a letter from her son, Mr Claude Morrell of Thor's Hill in Cheshire: 'It was a very nice and appreciative letter of my nursing of his mother and he enclosed a cheque for £50. He added a postscript that he had got my name from Dr Adams.'

Sister Helen Rose Stronach was another of the nurse witnesses: she was only with Mrs Morrell for about three weeks, leaving just before the patient died on 1st November, 1950, when she had been called home for family reasons. Mrs Morrell had been given pheno-barbitone, half a grain and codeine when she was in pain, and in the evening one sixth of a grain of morphia. Sister Stronach gave some of these injections and so did Sister Randall. But, in addition to these injections: 'The patient also had injections at night-time by Dr Adams. I have no idea what these injections were but they were always given by the Doctor.' The nurses would only record their own injections in the nurses' notebooks, not those given by the doctor as they had no idea of what these consisted. Dr Adams often called as late as 11 p.m. and sometimes later. Mrs Morrell always insisted that she and Dr Adams be left alone in the bedroom. Sister Stronach had found Mrs Morrell to be a very temperamental person 'she could at times be very horrid to her nurses', but she was very attached to Dr Adams, who was 'very good, kind and patient' with her. On a number of occasions Dr Adams had stood and admired a chest which contained a large quantity of Georgian silver.

Hubert Sogno of Lawson Lewis & Co., Solicitors of 11, Hyde Gardens, Eastbourne, was Mrs Morrell's solicitor. He was a witness for the prosecution in connection with the wills which his client had made. Most of his information was from notes which he made on each occasion, but 'one particular feature of my discussions with Mrs Morrell remains very vividly in my mind'. This was Mrs Morrell constantly mentioning to him that she was convinced that she would not still be alive were it not for Dr Adams' great skill. She felt that she owed him a great debt of gratitude.

Mr Sogno was first consulted by Mrs Morrell in February 1947 when she gave him instructions to prepare a new will for her: he was handed a copy of her existing will which was dated 17th August, 1946 and had been prepared by Messrs. Coles & James. Paragraph 5(j) of this will read as follows: 'To Dr John Bodkin Adams…the sum of One thousand pounds.' In accordance with Mrs Morrell's instructions he prepared a new will which she signed on 27th February, 1947 and this will did not contain any mention of Dr Adams. On 25th October, 1947 she had another will prepared which did not contain any mention of Dr Adams; a further one on 8th October, 1948 and a codicil of 19th March 1949, neither of which contained any mention of Dr Adams.

On 28th April, 1949, Mr Sogno had made the following notes:

> 'Attending Dr Adams on the telephone, when he said you were extremely anxious about the contents of your will and desired to see Mr Sogno urgently.
>
> Attending at Marden Ash, receiving instructions to amend your will in such a way that the bulk of your estate passes to Dr Adams. We urged you not to do this as strongly as we could but you were perfectly clear in your mind and the reason you wished to make the alterations was that your son had told you that he did not want you to leave him anything as he had already had too much – we pointed out that your son probably meant that he did not want it all to himself and could probably dispose of the money amongst your other relatives but you were adamant and requesting us to send your new will tonight. Writing to you with this.'

Although it was clear from his notes that a will was prepared and forwarded to Mrs Morrell, Mr Sogno could find no copy of it and it was never signed.

On 30th April, 1949, Mrs Morrell had written:

> 'Dear Mr Sogno, Many thanks… About the will, I won't do anything until my son
> returns as I agree with you the first will was best.'

He believed that Mrs Morrell had asked for the prepared will to be destroyed. The notes he
made when he saw Mr Morrell and received instructions for a new will included: 'residue Dr
Adams'. He recollected that he was very much perturbed by the contents of the will and told
Mrs Morrell so. He tried to get in touch with her son but he was in America, so he wrote a letter to be delivered to him on his return asking him to come and see his mother. Mr Claude
Morrell was a director of Martin's Bank and of the White Star Shipping Company and he visited the USA regularly, twice a month.

At about this time, without consulting anyone, Mrs Morrell had drawn up three very large
cheques in favour of three of her friends, though not including Dr Adams. She telephoned Mr
Sogno early one morning and asked him to stop them. After this incident, Mr Sogno had
charge of her chequebook on her instructions; she sent all the bills to him for payment and she
signed the cheques which were drawn up.

Mr Morrell came to see Mr Sogno on 2nd June, 1949 and approved what had been done for
his mother. Mr Sogno went to see her on the following day and she gave instructions for a new
will. This contained the following gift in paragraph 4(g):

> 'To Dr John Bodkin Adams the oak chest containing silver in my drawing room at
> Marden Ash, together with all the silver articles usually kept in it.'

On 8th March, 1950, the following entries appeared in Mr Sogno's notes:

> 'Attended Dr Adams who called without appointment and requested to see Mr Sogno
> urgently. An appointment was made for 12.50 p.m.
>
> Attending Dr Adams when he said that you [Mrs Morrell] had promised him many
> months ago that you would give him your Rolls Royce Car in your Will and you now
> remember that you had forgotten to add this and now wished to give the car to him and
> also the contents of a certain case in the locked box at the bank, the contents of the case
> Dr Adams did not know. Dr Adams stated that though you were very ill your mind was
> perfectly clear and he had no doubt that you were in a fit state to make a Codicil or new
> Will. After some discussion it appeared that the case at the Bank contained some arti-
> cles or article of jewellery and it was supposed that the two gifts together were of con-
> siderable value. We reminded Dr Adams of the gifts which you had made by cheque
> some months ago and had afterwards regretted and we suggested that as these proposed
> gifts were of considerable value the matter should wait until Mr Morrell visited
> Eastbourne at the end of the week. Dr Adams replied that you were very uneasy and
> wished to get the matter off your mind. We suggested that if this were the case he might

ease your mind by pretending to receive the case and hand it to the nurse in the other room to be preserved for you, but Dr Adams stated that you seriously wished him to enjoy the gift. He then suggested that we should prepare a codicil, that it should be executed and later destroyed if it did not meet with the approval of Mr Morrell but we pointed out that such a course was entirely impossible and it was arranged that we should call upon you this afternoon.'

Mr Sogno told the police that in all his experience as a solicitor, he had 'never come across such a blatant attempt as was made by Adams to ensure some advantage to himself' in the event of Mrs Morrell's death.

'Attending at Marden Ash at 3 p.m. discussing the matter with you reminding you of the gifts of cheques and suggested that you might well regret giving to Dr Adams the case at the bank (which you informed us is a blue case one inch wide and twelve inches long containing a diamond necklace of great value). You made it clear that what you have in mind is to give Dr Adams the case containing the necklace now as a personal gift and to alter your Will by giving him your Rolls Royce car after your death. We pointed out that Dr Adams would be embarrassed by gifts of such value as the necklace and eventually you agreed to wait until the week end and to discuss this with your son. If you passed away meanwhile we promised to tell your son what your wishes were.

On the 11th March, 1950: Attending your son at length when we informed him of all that had occurred and he approved what we had done and expressed the view that Dr Adams had given such great service that it was quite reasonable that you should give him your Rolls Royce Motor Car in your Will and even the diamond necklace but he was of the opinion that you ought not to start giving things away in your life time. Your son suggested that you should give him the list of articles which you wished to be given away after your death and this would avoid the necessity to make a Codicil but he confirmed that you were certainly able to make a Codicil and would let us know during the morning what you wished to do.

Subsequently attending Mr Morrell on the telephone when he said you had given him various instructions about the disposal of certain items and did not wish to make a codicil. He thought it most likely you would want to make a codicil next week giving a few articles to your Gardener and so on and confirming the two gifts to Dr Adams and providing the codicil did not go beyond this and attempt to dispose of the residue he saw no objection.'

Mr Sogno had another message on 17th July, 1950, asking him to go to Marden Ash. He telephoned Mr Claude Morrell, who said that:

'He had heard you were likely to alter your will by appointing another executor and what would happen if he (this executor) predeceased you. Indicated his opinion that you were in a fit state but to contact him if alterations for major proposals giving away the whole of your estate.'

Mr Sogno visited Marden Ash.

'You were wheeled into the lounge and discussed your will in a rational and, indeed, lively manner for about half an hour. Having told us about the new executor and one or two minor amendments to the legacies, you said that you wished to indicate what should happen to the residue if your son predeceased you; you informed us that you had no relatives for whom you cared; your brother had two children, a girl who had married very well and was not in need of money and never came near you, and a son who was a ne'er do well whom your son had attempted to help but who would not work; you did not wish them or any other relatives of you or your husband to benefit instead you wished charities to benefit and having mentioned three or four you favoured you asked us to suggest others for your consideration; we suggested perhaps twenty well-known charities, some of which you disliked and others you seemed to favour, and it was arranged that we should include these in the draft of your will for you to think over.'

On the same day a draft codicil was sent to Mrs Morrell.
   The next morning a letter arrived, dated Tuesday:

'Dear Mr Sogno,
I hope I made myself clear yesterday, but I feel very ill these days. If my son survives me I would like the chest of silver in the lounge to go to Dr Adams and if he died before me I would like all my special bequests given and then the house and all it contains and all residue afterwards to go to Dr Bodkin Adams and may I not leave £1,000 to yourself for your kindness? I know you don't want it but it would be a small acknowledgement for all you have done for me, unless you would rather have a picture. I am sure time for myself is shorter than I think now: My son was laid up in London on Saturday, although he had two doctors neither of them knew what was the matter, then Dr Adams went up on Sunday and diagnosed the trouble at once and before he left they had tea in the lounge and he goes home today. It takes a good deal to repay such extreme kindness – and none of my relations want anything. My daughter paid over £100,000 in death duties but I have not so much money.'

Mr Sogno, a man of honour, felt that he had not known Mrs Morrell 'sufficiently long or undertaken any special work for her which justified me in accepting a legacy and I declined it.'
   The relevant paragraph of the Codicil of 19th July, 1950 read as follows:-

'7. If my said son... predecease me then
   (a) I bequeath to John Bodkin Adams free of all duties

(1) My freehold dwelling house known as Marden Ash with all the grounds thereof
(2) All my personal chattels.'

Next day, Mr Sogno received a letter from Mrs Morrell dated Wednesday, July 19th:

'Dear Mr Sogno,

I enclose Mr Dowsett's name on a separate sheet. With regard to Dr Adams I want him to have my jewellery that is in Martins Bank in a box (Mr Murray has the key) and also the chest of silver goods that is in the lounge. If my son has predeceased me I would like Dr Adams to have the house and all the contents except the pictures bequeathed to the Walker Art Gallery, [Liverpool] and other bequests of goods and sums of money to different people mentioned in my Will. I know he has plenty of money and does not need it, but he has been the best friend I ever had, and I want to show my appreciation and then if you would kindly have all this written out…'

On 1st August Mr Sogno had made another note:

'Attending you at Marden Ash – when you informed us that you had decided that you were proposing to give Dr Adams far too much in the event of your son's death.'

Another new will was proposed. The new will dated 5th August, 1950 contained the following clause:

'4g. To Dr John Bodkin Adams the Oak chest containing silver in my drawing room at Marden Ash together with all the silver articles usually kept in it…

8. If my son should predecease me…
(b) I bequeath to the said Dr John Bodkin Adams in addition to the bequest in his favour contained in paragraph 4, my Rolls Royce car and the Elizabethan court cupboard in the lounge at Marden Ash.'

The new will was completed on 24th August, 1950.
Things changed, however, for on September 11th, Mr Sogno's notes read:

'Attending you on the telephone when you instructed us that you wished to cut out all benefits to Dr Adams.'

On the 12th September there was an urgent request for Mr Sogno to call on Mrs Morrell. Mr Sogno spoke to Mr Morrell on the telephone:

'You had told him your intention to cut out Dr Adams from your will and we explained that we proposed to try and persuade you not to do this.'

Mr Sogno then called upon Mrs Morrell:

'Attending you at Marden Ash when you instructed us that you wished to cut Dr Adams out of your will entirely. On enquiring into the position we found that what had happened was that, without previous warning, Dr Adams had called one day and said that he was leaving on his holiday and that Dr Harris would be attending you for the next fortnight. He had breezed in and out though you were very ill and you thought he should have given you some warning and in view of your serious illness at that time, deferred his departure for a day or two. You had asked him to do this and he had said that he must get away. We pointed out that Doctors probably needed a holiday more than most people and that the reason why he had not given you warning was that he thought you might worry about it. We were quite certain that if you cut Dr Adams out of your will you would very quickly regret it and did our best to persuade you to leave your will as it stands. We were unable to persuade you however, and you instructed us to make a Codicil accordingly.'

On 13th September the Codicil was completed.

A letter dated 21st October arrived from Mr Morrell:

'I was fortunate this morning to find her very clear in her mind and we talked for some time of various things. She said with much emphasis how wonderful Dr Adams had been, not only in the past week or two, but all through her illness. I thereupon reminded her that, only a few weeks ago she executed a Codicil cutting him out of her Will. For a moment or two she did not remember doing so, but afterwards clearly remembered and expressed a wish this codicil be cancelled.

At her request I therefore went to Martins Bank, extracted this codicil from her box there and, again making sure it was her wish, destroyed it on her behalf and in her presence. Her will of 24th August therefore stands with no codicil.

As you are probably aware, Mother has been far from well many days lately, and her health is visibly failing. It will not surprise me if there is now difficulty about signature of cheques. But occasionally she is suddenly better and very clear in her mind.'

Mr Sogno pointed out to Mr Morrell that the destruction of a codicil does not nullify it and there must be a new will or codicil in order to achieve that object. Mr Morrell asked for a new codicil to be drawn up to reflect his mother's wishes. The co-executors were not made aware of the codicil.

Following Mrs Morrell's death, Mr Sogno notified the District Probate Registrar of the position regarding the codicil, the torn pieces of which had been handed to Mr Sogno. The

Registrar asked Mr Sogno if the residuary legatee [Mr Claude Morrell] would challenge the gift of the oak chest. On being informed that Mr Morrell was well content that the gift should stand, the Probate Registrar said that it was not necessary to present the codicil to him at all and its existence would be ignored.

Mrs Morrell died, aged eighty-one years on 13th November, 1950 at her home, Marden Ash in Beachy Head Road. Her death certificate, signed by Dr Adams, showed the cause as 'cerebral thrombosis'. The forms filled in by Dr Adams under the Cremation Act 1902 provided his version of the circumstances of the death, which he would have also put on the Medical Certificate of Death. He had to answer various questions:

'Died 13.11.50 at 2 a.m.' He had been her 'medical attendant for about five years; the last illness continued for two years and four months'; he 'last saw the deceased alive at 10 p.m. on 12th November, about four hours previous to her death'.; he saw the body 'eight and a half hours after death' and made 'a general examination.' The cause of death was cerebral thrombosis and the mode of death: 'coma, about two hours'. Observations: 'based on own observations and Nurse Randall.' She had been nursed: 'Firstly in Esperance Nursing Home Later Olinda Nursing Home, 12 Grassington Road. After that in her own home until death. Had three nurses on duty in 24 hours, often changed. Nurse Randall, Nurse Mason, Nurse Bartlett.' 'Nurse Randall was present at death.'

Mrs Morrell was a senior shareholder in the White Star Shipping Company and had associations with Martins Bank Ltd. She left estate of £78,000. Her body was cremated and, at her request, her ashes were scattered in the English Channel. Dr Adams received the Rolls Royce and the antique oak chest containing Georgian silver. Although Mrs Morrell had wished him to have these, crucially, as explained in the foregoing paragraph, it was Mr Claude Morrell who permitted these gifts to pass to Dr Adams.

The movements of the oak chest after Mrs Morrell's death, were followed with statements from William Unsted, the Managing Director of John Pring & Co. House Furnishers of Cornfield Road. They had received instructions from Lawson & Lewis, the solicitors, to collect a carved oak canteen of cutlery and a bed from Marden Ash and to deliver these articles to Dr Adams, and they did this on 6th February 1951. The bed was presumably one loaned to Mrs Morrell.

The foreman of Pring Removals, Richard Steers, stated that he went to Marden Ash, where the cook was still in occupation. 'I collected an oak carved canteen of cutlery from the dining room. It was very heavy and took two of us to lift it and carry it out. My assistant was Mr Cowdry who works for Messrs Pring. I also collected a bed at the same time.'

Mr Sogno later gave the police the valuation for probate purposes of the oak chest and silver as '£276:5s.0d., the Jacobean court cupboard £80; and the Rolls Royce £1,500.' The valuation for the antiques was very low, but as the police report says, 'We have no doubt that the valuer in this case has a large practice with solicitors in probate matters and this may affect his valuation.'

When Detective Superintendent Hannam and his team first looked at the case of Mrs Morrell, they 'were doubtful as to whether her death was bone fide.' This doubt was not to go away.

Mr L.C. Nickolls, Head of the Metropolitan Police Laboratory at New Scotland Yard, wrote to Detective Superintendent Hannam when he had examined the chemists' lists of medicines and drugs prescribed by Dr Adams for Mrs Morrell. His comments were 'that there is no doubt that in the last week of life she was dispensed sufficient morphine sulphate and heroin to be lethal to anyone but a confirmed drug addict. The general level of drug prescription is extremely high and if, she did, in fact, consume all this material I feel that she must have been under the influence of drugs for the whole of the ten months.' He thought that a competent physician would be able to state that 'no qualified doctor could possibly prescribe drugs in the amount shown without some peculiar intent.' He also pointed out that there is always a problem in proving murder in such cases as 'there is a very good defence that it was not the drugs but old age that killed them.'

Professor Dr Francis Camps MD, one of the most famous of forensic pathologists, was supplied with the chemists' lists of prescriptions dispensed for Mrs Morrell, and on 1st October, 1956, he wrote to the Assistant Commissioner, setting out his views:

> 'The patient is alleged to have died of cerebral thrombosis. If the drugs prescribed were in fact administered, they contribute an enormous quantity of hypnotic and narcotic (heroin and morphine) drugs to one person. It is difficult to see for what condition they could have been administered other than inoperable cancer or some very painful disease. Such quantities spread over a period of a year would quite soon have caused the patient to be addicted to them. No attempt seems to have been made to withdraw but rather to continue in increasing quantities. Had withdrawal been attempted it would have produced several symptoms. One would have expected the person receiving these drugs to be certainly under their effects. The termination of such treatment with increasing doses would be expected to be either a respiratory complaint or coma. The cause of death given on the certificate would resemble clinical narcotic poisoning (it would be of interest to know the manner and length of time of death).'

The police re-interviewed the nurses who attended Mrs Morrell, particularly regarding the drug administration. This time, following Dr Adams' arrest, they were more communicative 'and have been reasonably frank'. Sister Anne Mason-Ellis confirmed that the patient was often semi-conscious, and that this condition was not physical but was induced by drugs and sedatives. Sister Helen Stronach said that, on Dr Adams' instructions, a bottle of codeine was left beside Mrs Morrell's bed so that she could take a tablet if she was in pain. However, the nurses were all agreed that the patient was not in pain. Not only did Sister Stronach give injections of morphine, but Dr Adams did so when he visited, and these injections were prepared from his own bag, so that the quantities then given were additional to those shown on the chemist's list of dispensings.

The police managed to trace the day nurse who was in charge towards the end of Mrs Morrell's life: Sister Brenda Hughes who now lived in Devon, but was single at the time and known as Sister Bartlett [the name used at the trial]. She spoke of 'excessive drug injection' by

Dr Adams, 'who used material from his own bag'. She was in charge of the day duty, and added that, to the Doctor's knowledge, Mrs Morrell often had half a tumblerful of whisky at lunchtime, which must have considerably increased the effect of the barbiturate intoxication. She confirmed Sister Randall's account [below] about the very large injections prepared by Dr Adams on the final night, and said that he also got that material from his bag. She thought that the quantity was, in her opinion, about 5 c.c. Sister Hughes also said that, after Mrs Morrell's death, Dr Adams took away an infra-red ray lamp which Mrs Morrell had bought for about £60. There was 'an excellent infra-red lamp on a standard' found in the Doctor's surgery during the police search.

Sister Randall was the nurse present on night duty at Mrs Morrell's death and she made an additional statement. Towards the close of the patient's life, drug and sedative administration was excessive, and Mrs Morrell never complained of pain. When Dr Adams visited at night, Sister Randall reported to him that she had given a morphine or heroin injection in accordance with his directions. If the patient had not settled down, the Doctor would give another injection himself, and he did this with drugs taken from his own bag. Sometimes she had to call him in the night and he would do the same again. Sister Randall was told by Dr Adams not to allow Mrs Morrell to regain consciousness during the last three days of her life.

On one occasion about three months before Mrs Morrell died, Sister Randall found her very comatose and could not rouse her. In the bed she saw a bottle minus its cap, and concluded that Mrs Morrell had helped herself to tablets, possibly the codeine.

Very late on the night of Mrs Morrell's death, Dr Adams had called at the house and the patient was having 'jerky spasms'. He prepared an unusually large quantity of drug in a hypodermic syringe and instructed Sister Randall to inject it. She did so. He then prepared a second syringe, also with a very large quantity of drug, and told her to inject that also if the patient did not quieten down. The patient did not quieten down, and, at about 1 a.m. she telephoned the Doctor and got no reply. She then carried out his instructions and gave the second injection, and the patient died in about half an hour. She thought the injection was too soon after the previous large dose, but she did what she was told to do. Detective Superintendent Hannam records that at this interview 'Sister Randall was very worried, for she knows full well that Adams killed Mrs Morrell.'

Chapter Twelve

─────

# The Tenth Duke of Devonshire

## 26 November 1950

─────

*Whoso removeth stones shall be hurt thereby;*
*and he that cleaveth wood shall be*
*endangered thereby.*

The Tenth Duke of Devonshire was often in residence at his home at Compton Place, Eastbourne, an attractive small Georgian summer mansion in the heart of Eastbourne. He divided his time almost equally between Eastbourne and his Derbyshire home at Churchdale Hall near Chatsworth, except for his visits to Bolton Abbey, Yorkshire for grouse shooting, or to Ireland for the salmon fishing. He had these country pursuits in common with Dr Adams, who was his GP when he was in Eastbourne.

Edward William Spencer Cavendish was chairman of the Chatsworth Estates Company, which included the Compton Estate at Eastbourne. The Duke had considerable business interests in the borough, and, like his forbears and his son, the Eleventh Duke took a keen interest in the development and prosperity of Eastbourne and its inhabitants and was generous to the town. It was the 7th and 8th Dukes of Devonshire who had been responsible for the creation of this 'Empress of Watering Places' with its beautiful planning.

As Marquess of Hartington, he was elected Conservative M.P. for West Derbyshire in 1923. He became Dominions Under-Secretary in 1936, was Under-Secretary for India and Burma from 1940 until 1942, and then Colonial Under-Secretary from 1943 until 1945. During the First World War the Duke was a lieutenant-colonel in the Derbyshire Yeomanry and served in Egypt, the Dardanelles and France. The elder son of the Duke and Duchess was killed in France in 1944, and the heir was their second son, the late Eleventh Duke, who sadly died during the preparation of this book.

The Duke was elected Grand Master of the English Freemasons in September 1947; he was installed by the King in March 1948 at the Albert Hall. He was re-elected Grand Master on

12th November, 1950, fourteen days before his death, and after his re-election he visited Malta as Grand Master.

The Duke, 55 years old, had not been ill: recently he had 'provided work for two unemployed men' in laying-out new flower gardens at Compton Place and had been working alongside them. A few days before the 26th November, the Duchess had opened the YMCA-YWCA Fair in Eastbourne. No doubt, Dr Adams was there as he was a member of the YMCA Committee.

On Sunday, 26th November, 1950, accompanied by the Duchess, the Duke attended the morning service at All Saints' Church, and, as usual, read the first Lesson. He read from the Authorised Version of the Bible. There was some significance in the reading: the 11th and 12th Chapters of Ecclesiastes. The 11th Chapter begins with well-remembered words:

'Cast thy bread upon the waters: for thou shalt find it after many days.'

Then the the 12th Chapter begins:

'Remember now thy Creator in the days of thy youth…'

From the end of Verse Five onwards, it continues:

'because man goeth to his long home,
and the mourners go about the streets:
Or ever the silver cord be loosed,
or the golden bond be broken,
or the pitcher be broken at the fountain,
or the wheel broken at the cistern.
Then shall the dust return to earth as it was;
and the spirit shall return unto God who gave it.'

Chapter 12 ends with these verses:

'Let us hear the conclusion of the whole matter:
Fear God and keep his commandments: for this
is the whole *duty* of man.
For God shall bring every work into judgment,
with every secret thing, whether *it be* good,
or whether *it be* evil.'

The Vicar, the Rev. Hewitt, said afterwards that 'several people had remarked that they thought the Duke read the Lesson with great feeling'. He appeared to be in excellent health, and he had told some people as he left the church how well he felt. It struck everyone that the words he had read from the lectern were prophetic.

The Duke and Duchess returned to Compton Place and, during the afternoon he went into the garden to saw up some logs for the fire,[1] 'a task he always enjoyed'. On returning to the house some time later, he collapsed and was found unconscious by the butler. Dr Adams was called. He was with the Duke when he died. It was just thirteen days after the death of Mrs Morrell.

His son, the new Duke, was in Australia when his father died and left Sydney on the Monday following his father's death, so he was unaware of the exact circumstances of his father's death and Dr Adams' involvement but it was 'very sudden'. He wrote the following letter to me, dated 15th September, 2003:

'How very nice to hear from you. However, I fear I can be of little help concerning Dr Bodkin Adam's involvement in my father's death, which was very sudden. I was in Australia at the time. Dr Adams was my father's doctor when he was in Eastbourne, but it should perhaps be noted that this doctor was not appointed to look after the health of my two younger sisters, who were then in their teens.'

The death was registered by Lady Elizabeth Cavendish at Eastbourne on Monday, 27th November. Dr Adams certified the cases of death as '1(a) Coronary Thrombosis (b) cardio vascular degeneration'. Dr Adams should have notified the Coroner and there should have been a post-mortem examination as this was a sudden death and the Duke was not being treated for any illness prior to his death. But there is a loophole in the law which permits the patient's General Practitioner to sign a death certificate, even in the event of sudden death and even if the GP has not been treating the patient during the previous fourteen days for the condition which was the cause of death. The record of the Duke's death appears in the list of death certificates, which the Police prepared of all the certificates signed by Dr Adams over the period 1946-56. They were cross-matching death certificates with patients' wills in which Dr Adams was named as a beneficiary, in an effort to identify suspicious deaths. As they found no will in the Duke's case, they did not examine this death at all. On the list it is actually marked 'no will found'. The reason for the gaffe seems childishly simple. The death was listed under the surname 'Cavendish', but the will was lodged in Somerset House under 'Devonshire', and apparently, no one made the connection. This would seem quite surprising to anyone local, as the name 'Cavendish' is everywhere in Eastbourne and on the statues of the 7th and 8th Dukes on the seafront and the link between the two is a basic part of local knowledge.

The circumstances of the Duke's death were never considered suspicious and were never the subject of an official investigation. The decision to curtail the enquiry into the death of one Edward William Cavendish, meant, coincidentally, that Hannam's investigation apparently stopped short of registering a bizarre connection: the sister of the Tenth Duke of Devonshire, Lady Dorothy, was also the wife of Harold Macmillan, who became Prime Minister during the investigation. It was a member of the Macmillan government – the Attorney-General – who

---

[1] Some reports say that he was removing an oak tree.

would eventually prosecute the case against Dr Adams. It is inconceivable that Hannam would not have known of this connection. Although there is no reference to it in the files, it must have been part of the background to this case from the outset.

At the very beginning of Hannam's First Report to the Chief Superintendent, one of the rumours he reports as circulating for over twenty years in Eastbourne was that of Dr Adams 'precipitating death and patients dying without proper medical treatment'. It would certainly not have been his usual practice to send a private patient to a hospital for any emergency treatment, and he did not in this case. What he would have done would have been to give the Duke an injection, as this was his invariable practice. And he would have told no-one what he had injected.

If the Duke was not fully informed of Dr Adams' religious views, he should have been. He was probably not aware of them as Dr Adams frequently attended the Church of England as well as the Plymouth Brethren meetings at Marine Hall. As all Brethren are 'priests', this is a recommended practice, aiming to convert those already attending Christian churches. It is likely that the Doctor attended All Saints' Church that Sunday morning and heard the Duke read the lesson; such occasions were significant events in the life of Eastbourne society and well-attended by the wealthy and well-connected, amongst whom Dr Adams sought acceptance. The Plymouth Brethren regard Freemasonry as inimical to the truth and to Christianity: they say that it is not possible to be a Freemason and a Christian. The 'Great Architect of the Universe' – worshipped by both Christians and those of other religions in Freemasonry – is described by the Brethren as 'Lucifer' and 'Baal', and a reversal of good and evil, exchanging darkness for light and light for darkness. The Brethren use the words of St. Paul in 2 *Corinthians* 11 v. 3-4 to warn against Freemasonry as an evil doctrine:

> 'But I fear, lest by any means, as the serpent beguiled Eve through his subtlety, so your minds should be corrupted from the simplicity that is in Christ.
>
> For if he that cometh preacheth another Jesus, whom we have not preached, or *if* ye receive another spirit which we have not received, or another gospel which ye have not accepted, ye might bear with *him*.'

The Grandmaster of England would certainly have been seen by some of the Plymouth Brethren as Satan incarnate and a corrupting and subversive influence.

All Brethren are well-acquainted with the Bible; they do not fail to read it daily. Given that all men who are Brethren are considered priests, their interpretation of the Bible is both individual and literal. For instance, they accept the stories of Adam and Eve and the Creation in *Genesis* as the literal truth and reject Darwinism. Interpreting the books of the Bible in a totally literal way, as opposed to a scholarly way, leads to the most startling misunderstandings of text, and none more so than the interpretation of the deeply spiritual and sometimes obscure Book of *Ecclesiastes*. Scholars still cannot really answer the question as to why this book was accepted into the canon of Biblical texts. The authorship was once attributed to Solomon, but the 'Wisdom of Solomon' and the 'Odes of Solomon' were rejected. It is now agreed that the author of *Ecclesiastes* was a sage named Qohelet, who lived around 225 to 250 B.C. Fragments of the text in Hebrew were discovered at Qumran and date from the middle of the second century B.C. There is a striking similarity between the text and the wonderful Sumerian *Epic of Gilgamesh* from ancient Mesopotamia.

'Life is profitless; totally absurd. This oppressive message lies at the heart of the Bible's strangest book.'[2] Qohelet is saying that old age and death will come soon enough, so life should be enjoyed while it is still possible. His message is essentially a pessimistic one: that God leaves humanity to its fate, which is chance and death, without any moral order. Nevertheless, the last two verses of *Ecclesiastes* suggest that Qohelet did equate the judgment of God with death.

Verse 5 of Chapter 12, quoted above, is a straightforward statement of man's departure to his eternal home and is followed by the beautiful and mystical verses 6 and 7. The 'silver cord' and 'the golden bowl' refer to a golden lamp hung by a cord on the wall and this being shattered as the cord breaks: the extinguished lamp represents death. The severing of the silver cord is exactly the same idea and is the thread of life in Greek mythology – the connection between the soul and the physical body. In verse 7 Qohelet says that the breath of God which gave life now withdraws it. The concluding part of *Ecclesiastes* runs from verse 7 of Chapter 11 to verse 7 of Chapter 12: 'Literal and symbolic language combine to depict the silencing of the inhabitants of a stately house'[3] with death affecting all within it.

Anyone who knew the Bible as well as Dr Adams would have realised that the preceding Chapter of *Ecclesiastes* had a verse which, taken literally and taken together with the verses of Chapter 12, seemed startlingly prophetic in the context of the Duke's reading that morning – it is actually a collection of proverbs on wisdom and folly. Chapter 10 verse 9 is an aphorism about the dangers of domestic chores and reads: 'Whoso removeth stones shall be hurt thereby; *and* he that cleaveth wood shall be endangered thereby.'

[2] Crenshaw / [3] Ibid

# Chapter Thirteen

# Mrs Julia Bradnum

## 1942 – 1952

## Pawns on the Chessboard

The Rev. Harry Ingham, Minister of the Congregational Church in Upperton Road, had a high regard for his Church members, Mr and Mrs Bradnum and considered them 'very devout Christian people'. He was pleased when the widowed Mrs Bradnum asked him to be co-executor of her will and knew she would bequeath the church some small sum. The bank manager, Percy Muddell, was also happy to be co-executor with the Minister.

For many years Mrs Julia Bradnum and her husband, Mr Chapman Bradnum, had run a boarding house in Eastbourne and, when they retired, bought a house at 24 Coopers Hill, Willingdon – on the outskirts of Eastbourne. After Mr Bradnum's death on 11th May 1940, his widow, Julia, had asked the husband of her friend Constance Beart to draft a will and he did so. She left some of her possessions to her niece, Mrs Onion, and to her adopted daughter Lily Love, but did not want to leave anything to her relations in London. Mr Beart refused any legacy but she left something to her friend. Mrs Bradnum then took the will to the bank.

Miss Emily Worthington and Miss Gwenelda Hine went to live with Mrs Bradnum at her home in Coopers Hill, in August 1942. They rented rooms from her. Mrs Bradnum was in very good health, could walk two to three miles, attended church and was very active. Dr Adams then visited once each month – not that she required the attention of a doctor – but just 'to keep an eye' on her since her husband's death. He continued these monthly visits up to 1952.

She confided to Miss Worthington that she had made a will which would benefit the church, Mrs Onion her niece and Lily Love, and that she didn't want her brothers or any other relations to have anything because they would drink it or squander it away. About twelve months before her death she became rather forgetful. She said she was going to make a new will, but didn't really want to. She didn't say in so many words that anybody forced her to make this will but Bertie Love, Lily's husband, came up to the house three times in one week. Mrs Bradnum said he made her ill and wanted her to change the executors from Dr Ingham and Mr Muddell to Dr Adams and she didn't want to do this. Shortly afterwards, Dr Adams, during one of his regular visits, pulled up a chair near Mrs Bradnum – she was a little deaf – and Miss Worthington heard him say 'Now you tell me just what you want', referring to the will. When he had gone, Mrs Bradnum told her that Dr Adams was going to do everything in connection with the will and that she would receive something.

During the six months prior to her death Mrs Bradnum's health was good. She continued to be active, did her housework and went for walks. She never complained about herself. On 10th May, 1952, the day before she died, she was quite active and they were all going on a church outing the following day. She was quite chatty and in her usual good spirits: she was really looking forward to going on the outing. They all went to bed as usual about 9 o'clock and the following morning Miss Worthington arose just after 7 o'clock, made a cup of tea and knocked on Mrs Bradnum's door. Receiving no reply, she thought she was asleep, and went to her hairdresser's appointment. She returned just after 10 a.m., noticed that the curtains of Mrs Bradnum's room were still drawn and went upstairs and knocked on the door. There was no reply, so she knocked again, then heard the door being unlocked. On opening it, she saw Mrs Bradnum getting back into bed and noticed that she looked ill. She said nothing, so Miss Worthington asked if she should ring the doctor and she just replied 'yes'. Miss Hine rang up Dr Adams immediately and he was at the house within twenty minutes. Emily Worthington was in the bedroom when he examined Julia Bradnum; she saw him pick up her left arm and inject something by hypodermic syringe. All he said was 'I am afraid she's gone.' After the injection it was only a matter of minutes before she died. 'Dr Adams made no other comment to me and left the room.' He wasn't in the house for more than a few minutes altogether.

The space of time between Mrs Bradnum's death and Dr Adams' previous visit? Miss Worthington couldn't recall. But when he had left the bedroom, Dr Adams did say he would inform Mr Love of what had happened and he said he would make all the arrangements. In September 1952 she and Miss Hine purchased 24 Coopers Hill and Coles & James, the solicitors acted for them.

Miss Hine had also known Mrs Bradnum since 1942 – such a hale and hearty woman with a very strong will and very active – a great churchgoer. She remembered her coming and asking her to witness her will. Miss Hine went downstairs and into the dining room and saw Dr Adams there with his secretary, Miss Henry, who was a relative of his – now dead. Dr Adams said to her 'Will you sign here please?' She signed her name and was then asked by the Doctor to leave the room. It was Miss Hine who had rung up Dr Adams' surgery and had been informed that the Doctor was not in, but they said they knew where he was and would get in touch with him at once. After telephoning she went to find a nurse she knew who would attend Mrs Bradnum. Having done this, she returned to the house only to find that Dr Adams had been and left and that Mrs Bradnum had died. It was such a shock!

Six months before Mrs Bradnum died, Miss Hine had made an offer of £1,800 for the house, giving Mrs Bradnum her own bedroom and sitting room and offering to look after her for the rest of her life. Julia had thought this a good offer and sought the advice of Mr Love, and, well, the matter fell through. When the house was put up for auction she and Miss

Worthington bid £2,475 to acquire it. Mr Love was an active bidder but she felt he had no real wish to buy the house.

Miss Hine had, of course, thought that Dr Adams' visits were unnecessary, but he was the family doctor and it was possible that his intentions were to keep an eye on Mrs Bradnum. It was her belief that Mr Bertie Love had got in league with Dr Adams to make Mrs Bradnum change her mind about their offer: she was rather weak-minded at the time.

Mabel Onion was a widow and a niece of Mr Bradnum and also a member of the Upperton Congregational Church. For many years she had been the mainstay of their boarding house, a 'maid of all work'. She was on good terms with Lily Love. The second will had been a surprise to all the Bradnum relatives. Her aunt had been worried about the outing as the two ladies wanted to accompany her and she thought she was really only allowed to bring one friend along. The worry of this caused her to have the bilious attack. Miss Worthington had described Aunt's illness as 'a bilious attack.' Fancy that such a thing could cause her death!

Mrs Onion was aware that Dr Adams was giving her aunt some medicine and she had often taken the prescriptions down to Forbes the chemist. It was a mixture in a bottle. She did think it odd that when Dr Adams came to see Auntie, he used to make very much more fuss of her than one would expect a professional man to do. 'I have seen Dr Adams on one knee, holding Mrs Bradnum's hand!'

Mr Bertie Love was a chauffeur, now 68 years old, and he and his wife, Lily, lived in Bakewell Road, Eastbourne. He and his wife had been on excellent terms with Mrs Bradnum for many years. In November 1951, Mrs Bradnum asked to see him in connection with her will and she came to visit him at home. Her house was over two miles away and he made arrangements for her to be collected by car. However, she had misunderstood and made her own way there by bus – still quite fit at the age of 85. When she arrived, Mrs Bradnum explained that she wanted to make an alteration to her will and asked Bertie's advice as to a good solicitor, saying she had no desire to go to Coles & James as they were too expensive in settling her husband's estate. Mr Love recommended a solicitor named Fairclough of Gildredge Road and, at Mrs Bradnum's request, he wrote down, in her presence, what he called a codicil to her existing will. The substance of that codicil was that his wife, Lily Love, was to benefit substantially under it.

The police were inclined to the view that Mr and Mrs Love had, for some time, had their eyes on 24 Coopers Hill, and noted that the 'codicil' firstly appointed Mr Love and his wife to take full charge of that house and its property until such time as legal formalities were settled, and included a direction 'that any persons staying in the house will kindly vacate it immediately'. Hardly a clause which any solicitor would have drafted.

Mrs Bradnum signed that document, dated 25th November, 1951. Mr Love took it to the solicitor, Mr Fairclough and explained Mrs Bradnum's wishes to him. He agreed to accept instructions for the codicil or a new will but said that Mrs Bradnum must attend upon him, or he upon her, personally, to receive her direct instructions. An appointment was made for 2.15 p.m. on the Tuesday following. On this day Mr Love went to Coopers Hill to collect Mrs Bradnum by car and, on arrival, she said to him 'I'm not feeling very well today. Dr Adams called and, after I told him I intended altering my will, he said 'Don't worry, I will do it all for you.' Bertie pointed out that he had made arrangements for her to see the solicitor Mr Fairclough and she replied 'I'm sorry, but Dr Adams has promised to do it all for me.' The appointment was cancelled and Mr Love eventually had to pay a fee to Mr Fairclough. An obviously annoyed Mr Fairclough, confirmed all this to the police.

The first Mr Love heard of Mrs Bradnum's death was on the day it occurred. 'I arrived home for lunch on 11th May, 1952, when Dr Adams met me on my own doorstep and said "Mrs Bradnum passed away this morning". He then continued, saying "I am the sole executor and have made arrangements with Haines the undertakers and all concerned". I was flabbergasted and made no comment.' Dr Adams attended the funeral and later Mr Love received a copy of Mrs Bradnum's will from Coles & James, Solicitors. Mr Love then wrote a letter to Dr Adams enclosing a copy of the 'codicil' dictated by Mrs Bradnum to him and Mr James later communicated with him and told him that it was of no use whatsoever as it had not been witnessed.

Miss Worthington called at Mr and Mrs Love's house a few days after the funeral and told them what had happened: that when Dr Adams answered Miss Hine's call and arrived at the house, Miss Worthington was in the bedroom and saw the Doctor give Mrs Bradnum an injection, and, after doing so, remarked 'It will all be over in three minutes'. According to Miss Worthington, Mrs Bradnum was dead within three minutes.

When Lily Overal Love, [43 years old at the time of Mrs Bradnum's death], was four years' old, her parents were killed in a railway crash and she was taken care of by Mrs Bradnum. She wasn't legally adopted but took her name and lived with her until her marriage in 1940. She always referred to her as 'auntie'. Dr Adams continued to visit Mrs Bradnum every month. She and auntie had discussed his visits and both thought it a waste of time and expense. Lily thought auntie was afraid, or didn't like to tell him not to call, but she thought he appeared to have her 'round his little finger'. She had seen Dr Adams, during these visits, sitting by the fire for a long time and 'holding auntie's hand'. She had told him all her troubles.

After Lily's marriage, Mrs Bradnum became lonely and expressed a wish to come and live near Lily in the town centre. She mentioned this on many occasions to Dr Adams, but he always advised her against it and told her to 'stay in her own little home.' She was in good health but Dr Adams continued his visits and certainly used to send in bills on a quarterly or half-yearly basis. Auntie kept mentioning that it was a great and unnecessary expense. When Dr Adams occasionally gave a prescription to Mrs Bradnum, it was often her habit to throw it on the fire, as she said she was quite well and needed no medical treatment.

Just after Christmas 1951, Auntie had told Lily that she had spoken to Dr Adams about making a new will. In fact, Dr Adams had brought the matter up, asking whether her will was correctly made out. He suggested that he should accompany her to the bank to look at it and they went to Barclays Bank together. After looking at the will, Dr Adams pointed out that, although it was signed, there were no addresses and he suggested that she should make a new will, saying that he would help her do this. Auntie thought he was so kind to help her in this manner and agreed to his suggestions. It was on a Sunday early in 1952 when they devised the new will, and Auntie said she mentioned to Dr Adams that she wanted to leave the house and contents to Lily, but the Doctor advised her to have the house sold and then share the money amongst those that she loved. Auntie thought this was a good idea and agreed. She told Lily that she felt she had to leave Dr Adams something because he had been so very kind to her and promised to do everything in connection with the will. Mrs Love knew that Dr Adams had consulted Coles & James in connection with the drawing up of the new will.

Shortly after the interview about the will with Dr Adams, Lily met Auntie in the town and she said: 'I am very worried and very upset'. Lily asked her why: 'I want to get those two women out of the house and I want to make a new will', she replied. It was just after this that she came and dictated the 'codicil' to Bertie.

On the Saturday afternoon, prior to the Tuesday when Auntie died, she visited Lily in hospital, and seemed in very good health. When Miss Worthington visited them, she had mentioned that Auntie had been in the garden talking to the neighbours on the evening before she died.

Mr Frank Potter of Leytonstone, London, was Mrs Bradnum's brother. In August 1951, following a letter he received from Bert Love, in which he was told of his sister's desire to alter her will, he went to Eastbourne to meet Mr Love and, together, they went to Mr Fairclough's office. Bert had told him that his sister was losing her memory and was in a bad way, but Frank found her quite normal, though she did tell him that she wanted to alter her will and leave a little to Miss Worthington, who had been such a good companion to her for so long. They then went to see Dr Adams at his house and he suggested that they meet at the bank on the Monday morning. Dr Adams got the will out at his sister's request, and read it. Frank did not see it. After reading it, the Doctor said 'It is all right and yet it is not all right.' Frank did not ask him what he meant but merely repeated this to his sister, and asked Dr Adams to arrange whatever his sister wanted. Dr Adams agreed, sealed up the will and gave it back to the bank clerk. Mr Potter asked him to write and let him know that everything was duly arranged, took his sister home, and she seemed satisfied. He knew that she liked Dr Adams and thought there was nobody like him, which was the reason that Frank had just left everything to the Doctor.

About a week later, Frank Potter received a letter from Dr Adams telling him that a new will had been properly drawn up and that the will was 'about the same as the previous one'. He had visited his sister several times after that August visit. In May 1952 when she died, Dr Adams had sent him a telegram giving him the news. He had attended the funeral with his brother Birt, and another nephew. Later that day, Adams had told him that he was the sole executor, that Miss Worthington would get £50, and that everything else was to be divided between Frank, his brother and sister, Lily Love, cousin Emily Theedom, and Dr Adams. Yes, Frank was very surprised that Dr Adams was the executor and sharing the estate with them. Since then he had received a letter from Coles & James, saying that all six had each received the sum of £661:1s.

On 27th May 1952, Haines received instructions from Dr Adams to arrange the interment of Julia Bradnum in Ocklynge Cemetery in the grave where her husband Chapman's body rested, and his mother, Maria Amelia's remains were buried in 1911.

Horace Bradnum, a radio engineer of Lushington Lane, Eastbourne, had been alerted by the newspapers, that enquiries were underway. Julia Bradnum was his aunt by marriage, though he hadn't seen her since his uncle died in 1940. He had always understood that both sides of the family would benefit under their wills, but no one on the Bradnum side had received a thing. The family were particularly outraged that poor Mrs Mabel Onion, who worked her fingers to the bone as a general maid at the boarding house, had been left nothing. His brother, Bertram, was Aunt Julia's favourite nephew, and, when he was on leave from East Africa, Aunt Julia had said he was have the gold hunter watch left to him by his uncle. Horace had just learned that the said watch had actually gone to a Bert Love, a person whom he did not know.

The comment by Dr Adams in the letter to Frank Potter that the new will 'was just about the same' as the previous one, was completely untrue. The new will appointed Dr Adams as sole executor. It contained directions concerning the memorial to her husband and herself and the inclusion of her name upon it. Miss Worthington was left £50 and Upperton Congregational Church £100. The whole of the residue following the sale of the house was to be divided between Mrs Lily Love, Mrs Bradnum's two brothers, named Potter in London, her sister, a Mrs Whitbread, her cousin, a Miss Theedom, and Dr John Bodkin Adams. Probate was granted for £4,662:10s.4d and Dr Adams benefited to the extent of £661:1s. as a residual legatee.

The police thought it significant that, although most witnesses said that Mrs Bradnum had always maintained that her own relatives, the Potters, would not benefit from her estate because of her abhorrence of intoxicating liquor, they should be residual legatees to the exclusion of Mrs Onion, who devoted a large proportion of her life to the service of Mrs Bradnum, and with whom she was on very good terms. Hannam commented: 'Why Dr Adams wanted any active part in the preparation of this will is difficult to understand. Apart from being his persistent technique in the many cases which have come to our notice in this investigation.'

On 19th December, 1956, Ralph Hall, the Cemetery Superintendent, received an exhumation warrant from HM Coroner, ordering the exhumation of the remains of Julia Bradnum, together with that for Clara Neil Miller. The grave was reopened at 7 a.m on 21st December in the presence of Detective Superintendent Hannam, Detective Inspector Pugh, Detective Sergeant Hewett, Dr Camps and the Coroner, Dr Somerville. The two grave diggers were Harold Lewes and Percy Croucher. The remaining six inches of soil was removed from the coffin and the plate read 'Julia Bradnum aged 85 years, died 27th May, 1952'.[1] Messrs. Haines brought a new coffin with the remains later that morning after the post mortem examination had been completed, and these were reverently reinterred.

Dr Adams had certified the cause of death as (a) Cerebral haemorrhage and (b) Cardio-vascular degeneration. Dr Camps performed the post-mortem examination. Very little of the organs of the body remained but 'the brain was in sufficiently good condition to exclude a cerebral haemorrhage'. Obviously he could not exclude other causes and it was not possible to perform tests for drugs. All the evidence pointed to Mrs Bradnum having been in good health and active right up till the day of her death. He noted that there was no record anywhere of what substance Dr Adams had injected into Mrs Bradnum just minutes before her death, and,

---

[1] The date on the plate differs from the date of death.

that for that injection to have killed her, it would have had to have been a deliberate terminal injection.

Not only did the post mortem not bear out the suggestion that cerebral haemorrhage was the cause of death of Mrs Bradnum, but neither did the facts collected by the police. She was seen to walk back to her bed after unlocking her bedroom door, and get into bed and within twenty minutes – following the arrival of the Doctor – she was dead. No one ever found out what the injection was which Dr Adams gave.

# Chapter Fourteen

# The Early Fifties

## Annabella Kilgour

Mrs Annabella Kilgour was in her ninetieth year in the final days of 1950. She was somewhat senile, Sister Margaret Todd Methren thought when she first saw her. She nursed the old lady from 21st to 29th December that year. She was able to get up and walk around her bedroom and the Doctor visited at least once a day, perhaps twice. The housekeeper had to put up a bed in the patient's bedroom to keep an eye on her; she became extremely tired from lack of sleep, doing this, and Sister Methren asked Dr Adams if he would give the patient a sedative.

On 23rd December, Sister Methren went off duty about 9 p.m., and was later told by the housekeeper that Dr Adams had visited the patient after she had left and had given her a hypodermic injection. The nurse did not know what the injection was and she had given no injections herself. When she had gone off duty that night, Mrs Kilgour's condition had been unchanged from when she had started nursing her.

Sister Methren went on duty at 9 a.m. the following morning, which was Christmas Eve, and the housekeeper informed her that Mrs Kilgour had been in a deep sleep since the injection had been given to her by Dr Adams the previous night. Upon examining the patient, Sister Methren was alarmed to realise that the sleep was unnatural: her pulse was good, her colour pale, she was quite warm but she could not be roused. Dr Adams arrived soon afterwards. Sister Methren had it in her mind that the injection which had been given was morphine, but she could not recall why she had thought that this was the case.

Dr Adams gave no treatment and Mrs Kilgour remained in this deeply comatosed condition all day. Later that same evening, about six or seven o'clock, the patient seemed to have some cerebral spasms and her body became rigid. This condition subsided very quickly but Mrs Kilgour remained completely unconscious until her death on the 28th December, 1950. Dr Adams attended the patient twice each day during this time, but no treatment was given, except for Sister Methren keeping Mrs Kilgour's mouth moist. 'I must say I was concerned about the death of Mrs Kilgour and the manner in which she had died.' What she said to the police, although she refused to put it in her statement was that she was 'quite certain that Dr Adams either gave an incorrect injection or of far too concentrated a type and sent the patient into a coma from which she could not recover.'

Mrs Kilgour had lived at Staveley Cross, in Staveley Road, Eastbourne and Miss Dorothy Badham, her friend, had known her for the best part of thirty years, and lived with her 'on and off' from 1931 until her death. Dr Adams was Mrs Kilgour's medical advisor in all the years Miss Badham knew her, but she never really needed a doctor until, in July 1950, she had a stroke and Miss Badham sent for Dr Adams. He came and gave her two 'pellets' to give Mrs Kilgour and she recovered in a few days. It was some time in the November that she had a second stroke, which affected her speech, and from which she never recovered properly: she couldn't manage to write. Miss Badham was paid as a companion to Mrs Kilgour for the first four years she lived with her at Staveley Cross, then war and illness intervened and Dorothy did not return to the house until 1947, when she received presents from time to time, then eventually a salary of £2 weekly. During her last illness, Dr Adams attended daily. There was, to her knowledge, nothing between Dr Adams and Mrs Kilgour: the relationship was that of patient and doctor. She had the greatest confidence in the Doctor and liked him, but he was not a personal friend. 'She was very careful about discussing her finances with anyone – she was a true Scotswoman.'

Margaret Bell was Annabella McDonald Kilgour's niece. Her aunt was one of a family of twelve, eight sisters and four brothers, from Glasgow. Aunt Annabella had first met Dr Adams in 1928 when she had trouble with an eye and had it removed. Apart from having colitis during the War, her aunt had been very well until the first stroke in July 1950. Her aunt's will was made in October 1949 and Margaret was executrix. Mrs Kilgour had left the Doctor £200 and a clock. She had not known him outside his professional capacity, although his mother came to tea on one occasion. Auntie might have mentioned to Dr Adams that he was to benefit under her will, but she could not imagine her doing so.

Thomas Stretton, Mrs Kilgour's gardener was not at all interested in what was going on in the house, only in the garden. As far as he was concerned she was a very good employer: he got his wages with extra at Christmas and a present, and it had been a real shock to him when she left him £20 in her will.

The chauffeur, James Honeysett, threw a rather different light on the relationship between Mrs Kilgour and Dr Adams. It had been a year or two after Mr Kilgour had died that his employer had asked him to take a parcel to Dr Adams at Kent Lodge. He had guessed from the feel of it that it contained pictures of some kind. The parcel was about two feet square: it was definitely two pictures rather than one. He had handed the parcel in to Dr Adams' maid.

Miss Kathleen Hunt had been cook to Mrs Kilgour from 1941 up until her death. 'She was a dear old lady and I liked her very much'. She was amazed to have been left £1,000 in her will, although such legacies to staff were thought of by employers as in lieu of pension, if they had served many years. Mrs Kilgour had told her cook that she suffered from colitis, and Miss Hunt would make her a cup of arrowroot once a day, and, occasionally, an arrowroot pudding. She knew that Dr Adams came once or twice a week at this time, although Mrs Kilgour was perfectly fit and able to get about. It was when she had the first stroke that 'something came over her' and she was not able to remember anything and lost the power of speech. Dr Adams told Miss Hunt that 'small blood vessels over the brain' were affecting her speech. Dr Adams was then a more frequent visitor, but Miss Badham was usually present.

About a week before she died, Miss Badham had found Mrs Kilgour looking out of her bedroom window in the middle of the night, and, next morning when Dr Adams came, she had told him about the incident. It was then that Mrs Kilgour was given the injection and went into a coma. She never woke up again and about four days later, died. Dr Adams came in once a day. Miss Badham, of course, was never keen on Dr Adams; 'I don't think she liked him very much.'

Sister Marguerite Roberts had just nursed Mrs Kilgour for two nights at the request of Dr Adams; the patient had been unconscious the whole time. The other nurse had told her that, a short while before, Dr Adams had given the patient an injection. Sister Methren had told Sister Roberts what the injection was and the strength of it. She could not remember the details of it but she did recall that the doseage was very strong because she made an exclamation when it was mentioned to her. Sister Methren had also told her that she thought the injection was too strong because it put the patient straight out and she didn't think Mrs Kilgour would come round again. The Doctor had called on one of the nights about 10 p.m., took the patient's pulse and asked how she was. Sister Roberts told him that she hadn't moved. Dr Adams made no comment and left the bedroom. 'To my mind it was a most unusual case: unusual because she never once stirred during the two nights I nursed her.'

Messrs. Haines, the undertakers, received their instructions from Mr James to arrange the funeral. A service was held at St. John's Church and her body laid to rest with that of her husband, John, in Ocklynge Cemetery.

Detective Superintendent Hannam reported: 'There is little further we can do. The suspicion will always remain that Adams disposed of Mrs Kilgour by his method of treatment, more quickly than might have been natural, even if, in fact, she was a dying woman.' He also commented that exhumation had 'crossed their minds in this case', but thought that there could be little success after six years, and that caution should be exercised.

### Annie Adelaide Norton Dowding

Annie Adelaide Norton Dowding was born on 8th September, 1874 and died in Eastbourne in November 1952. She was the widow of Charles Norton Dowding, who died in 1936 and their remains were buried in a brick vault at Willingdon Cemetery. Mrs Norton Dowding had been living at Valetta in Park Avenue on the outskirts of Eastbourne for over twenty years. She died at the Esperance Nursing Home. The only notification relatives had of her death was a telegram sent by her brother, Norman Miller. He, himself had received notice of the funeral from Mrs Norton Dowding's housekeeper 'on the instructions of the doctor, a man named Adams'. He and his sister, Mrs Maude Burton both went to Eastbourne and visited the Esperance Nursing Home. They were informed that the coffin had been closed on the Doctor's orders and were not allowed to view the body. They were shown the death certificate with the cause of death as 'Carcinoma of the lower bowel'. Death seemed to have occurred in a very short period, although, apparently, there were no previous symptoms or illness of which they had any knowledge.

After some pressure to receive details of the will, Mrs Burton had received a copy from Mr

Albert Scott of Messrs. Scott & Son, solicitors, of Staple Inn, London, and from this Mrs Burton and her brother learned that Dr Adams had received a legacy of £500. Mrs Norton Dowding had a private income from a trust fund of £59,000 and some private capital of her own of about £10,000. The will had been drawn up in August 1952, by Mr Scott who was the sole executor. Mr Miller noticed at the funeral that the age on the plate of the coffin, reading '65' instead of '78' and pointed this out to the solicitor, who apologised for his mistake.

Maude Burton had not seen her sister for nearly two years before her death. She had never made any complaint about her health and Mrs Burton had no idea she was ill. The first she had heard was the call from her brother; then she went to the funeral. Not only had Dr Adams received £500 but the solicitor had been left £300 and some articles of jewellery! Mrs Burton made many enquiries about her sister's death but learned absolutely nothing. They could get no information about her illness at her home; they finally went to see the Reverend Mother at the Esperance, but got no satisfaction there either. After this, they went to see the undertaker and Mr Miller asked if he could see his deceased sister's body, but was refused and told by the undertakers that Adams had said that under no circumstances was the coffin to be opened. He tried to see the Doctor but was unable to do so. Dr Adams had been recommended to their sister by a friend, Mrs Brierley, who had since died. She had thought highly of Dr Adams as a medical advisor. When she and her brother called at the house, they could get no information about their sister's illness, or the whereabouts of Miss Boston, the housekeeper.

Miss Florence Sankey said that she had been employed for four and a half years by Mrs Norton Dowding as a driver and companion. Her employer had frequently grumbled about not being able to afford the things she wanted and she had, indeed, been surprised to find that she had been left £125 in the will. She thought there was nothing seriously wrong with Mrs Norton Dowding. Dr Adams had visited frequently, not always in a professional capacity, but to discuss her problems, financial and otherwise. She always saw him alone, and she always seemed to be having medicine of some kind. Miss Sankey often took her prescriptions to Checkley's Pharmacy in Hampden Park, but what complaint warranted the prescriptions, she could not imagine. It was about two weeks before Mrs Norton Dowding died that she took to her bed, but on the Wednesday before she was taken to the nursing home – which was on the Friday – she was up and walking round the bedroom that Florence had just repapered for her. Florence thought that she should also mention that Mrs Norton Dowding was very friendly with a Nurse Clark who lived with her, on and off, the whole time she had been employed at the house.

In 1950, two years before her death, Mrs Norton Dowding had engaged Gertrude Boston as her housekeeper and companion, living-in on a full time basis. Dr Adams had visited at least once a week and always at about quarter to eight in the mornings. Mrs Norton Dowding was always in bed when he called: 'She never did get up before her breakfast and seldom was she downstairs before nine in the morning.' She saw the Doctor alone. Miss Boston asked why he called because her employer was not ill, and the reply was: 'He only comes to check up on me. He promised Mr Dowding that he would keep an eye on me.' She simply adored the Doctor. Miss Boston herself had taken an intense dislike to him from the very first time she met him at the house. It was instinctive: 'I don't know why I disliked him – I think it was because I considered him dishonest – seeing a woman when she was not ill. It was not from the immoral aspect but I just despised him because he struck me as a dishonest man.' She seldom spoke to him and more or less ignored him when he came to the house. Mrs Norton Dowding would tell her when the Doctor would be calling and Miss Boston just left the front door on the latch and he would walk in unannounced, going straight to her bedroom. As far as she was concerned, she really didn't know whether they had discussions about private or financial affairs. These were not matters which her employer had discussed with her, although 'she was a friendly soul' and often invited Miss Boston to go for rides in the car with her; 'She always treated me more as a friend than as an employee.'

Miss Boston had seen a change in Mrs Norton Dowding's health about six months before she died. She became lethargic and lost interest in life and the things around her. She complained about abdominal pains, and although she never articulated any such fears, Miss Boston felt that she suspected a malignant growth. As her condition worsened – about the time Dr Adams went on holiday – Dr Snowball visited in his stead and advised that she should have an X-ray. She was most annoyed at this suggestion and said that she was sure Dr Adams would not allow it. When he returned from his holiday, Mrs Norton Dowding told him what Dr Snowball had said and Dr Adams told her that an X-ray was not necessary.

Not long after this episode, Mrs Norton Dowding's condition got so bad that Dr Adams started giving her injections. Miss Boston did not know what they were, and the Doctor brought them with him although she was also receiving other prescriptions. She was not totally confined to bed until several days before she was removed to the Esperance Nursing Home. Dr Adams was visiting her twice a day and had been doing so for several weeks. The day before she was taken to the nursing home, Miss Boston was in the bedroom when Dr Adams came in. He gave her an injection in the arm. He sat with her for some time after giving her the injection: he rearranged her pillows himself, sat her up in bed and remained talking with her until she fell asleep. Miss Boston heard her say: 'When I get better we will take a cruise round the world together.' The Doctor's last words to her were: 'I'll meet you at the airport.' Miss Boston regarded this as 'the usual small talk'. Before he left the house, the Doctor asked her whether or not she would like nurses to be called in or if she preferred the patient to be taken to a nursing home. Gertrude said that she would prefer to see her taken to a nursing home where she would be properly looked after, and the Doctor said that if she was removed to the Esperance, his partner, Dr Snowball, would want to operate. However, he made the arrangements and she was moved the next day. She had never awakened from the time the Doctor gave the last injection on the Thursday morning until she was taken away on the Friday: she never regained consciousness before she died. Miss Boston noted that 'at no time did Dr Adams appear to be perturbed about the condition of Mrs Norton Dowding'. As Dr Adams had surmised, Dr Snowball did decide to operate on her, but the operation was unsuccessful as, by this time, she was inoperable.

On that same Thursday morning before Mrs Norton Dowding was taken to the Esperance, Dr Adams told Miss Boston that on no account must she write to any of Mrs Norton Dowding's relatives, and he clarified this by saying that he himself had received instructions from her to that effect. Miss Boston received a legacy of £110.

Two other members of the staff added footnotes. Elizabeth Hobbs was the daily help during the last year of Mrs Norton Dowding's life. She did not think her employer was a sick woman, although towards the end of her life she complained about stomach pains. She knew that Dr Adams visited early in the mornings and always saw Mrs Norton Dowding alone. Miss Boston had often said to her that she had tried to get Mrs Norton Dowding to change her doctor, but with no success. Elizabeth thought that Miss Boston did not like Dr Adams because she considered that he was not giving Mrs Norton Dowding the proper treatment. Edward Mead, the gardener, was the longest-serving member of staff: for thirty years he had spent two days a week tending the garden. He had been left a legacy of £500 in the will, and the garden tools. He did recall that, when Mr Norton Dowding died, Dr Adams had been given his fishing rods.

Mrs Eva Barham was the next-door neighbour in Park Avenue and Mrs Norton Dowding was already a widow and living alone when she first knew her. About two and a half years after Mrs Barham first knew her, she became ill and bed-ridden. Mrs Barham was told how good Dr Adams was, especially at sorting out financial problems. Mrs Norton Dowding's condition worsened and Mrs Barham visited daily and cooked meals for her. 'She never could pinpoint what her ailment was and she seemed to be simply slipping away'. One evening Mrs Barham was so worried that she telephoned Dr Adams and told him she did not feel she could be responsible for her. His attitude gave her the impression that she was worrying unnecessarily and that there was no need to worry as 'she was not as ill as I thought'. Dr Adams visited Mrs Norton Dowding that night and she slowly got better and eventually went away for a holiday. On her return, after two or three weeks, Mrs Barham advised her against living alone and she engaged a housekeeper, Miss Boston.

There was another bout of illness, and Mrs Norton Dowding was still unable to tell Mrs Barham what was wrong: 'She just used to lie there and she was desperately ill'. A nurse who was a friend of hers went to live with her. After a long time she recovered and went to recuperate in a hotel on the seafront where the Doctor used to visit her. She collapsed there and was taken to a nursing home, but recovered again, went home and was perfectly well, although the Doctor used to visit every day. When Mrs Barham and her family left Eastbourne for Oxford in September 1952, Mrs Norton Dowding 'came to see us all and was quite well'. Then a few weeks later they had a letter to say she was dead. They had discussed financial affairs upon occasion and Mrs Norton Dowding talked of her will and said she was not going to leave anything to her family as they were 'grasping'. She always gave the impression that, because of her trust in and devotion to Dr Adams, that he would receive some benefit from her will.

Mrs Norton Dowding had, all through the War, worked continuously in the maternity unit at All Saints' Hospital, and that is where she and Sister Marion Stuart-Hemsley had first met. They had always kept in touch with each other and during 1952 Mrs Norton Dowding had complained to Sister Stuart-Hemsley that she could not understand why her health seemed to be failing. She had several periods of illness and one or two visits to the Esperance Nursing Home.

Sister Stuart Hemsley told her 'that while she paid the fat bills to the Doctor she would stay ill.' On one occasion she was visiting Mrs Norton Dowding at the Esperance when Dr Adams came in and threw a bed jacket on the bed. 'I said to her, "What, is he making you presents now?" And she said "No, he has the keys to my house and he is most helpful in looking after my affairs and getting my linen."' After that, on one occasion when she was back home, she was unwell and told Sister Stuart-Hemsley that she did not seem to be getting any better. The Sister replied 'that she would not while she had that doctor', and she said, 'Oh, you misjudge him. He is really a very good doctor and if he does not know how to treat you, he kneels down by the bed and prays for guidance.' It was not long after this episode that she died.

### Miss Florence Emily Cavill

Miss Florence Cavill lived at Motcombe Road in Eastbourne's Old Town. Mrs Ada Pearson was one of her oldest friends, having known her for around forty years. Miss Cavill had two brothers who lived in South Africa and died in the 1930s, and a sister, Lilian, who had been a nurse in the First World War. They had lived together until Lilian's death in the early '40s. After this, her cousin, Edith, went to live with her; Edith had only recently died. Dr Adams had attended Miss Cavill all through the years, but she never had an illness which confined her to bed. He was, in fact, a very personal friend of hers. Indeed, Florence had told her that she was on very intimate terms with him. She confided all her personal matters to him and Ada formed the opinion that there was 'more to the friendship than mere doctor and patient'. She told Ada that in Dr Adams she had, for the first time, someone on whom she could depend and trust. About her financial state, Ada knew nothing, although 'she always gave the impression that she was not well off'.

On the 7th May, 1954, Ada went on holiday to Chesham in Buckinghamshire. Two days before she left home, she saw Florence, who then appeared to be 'as fit as she possibly could be'. Even in her eighty-seventh year she was a great walker and had walked all the way from the Old Town to Cornfield Road in Eastbourne town centre – about a mile – to say goodbye. Her last words to Ada were: 'When you come back we will spend a week together at a nice hotel in Hastings.' She was in the best of spirits.

The day after Ada arrived in Chesham, the police called to tell her that Florence had been found dead at her home. It was a great shock. At the end of two weeks, she returned to Eastbourne to find she had notification from Coles & James, the solicitors, that she was a beneficiary under the will for £300, and certain articles of furniture and linen. Other friends and Dr Adams had benefited, but Ada didn't know of any living relatives.

Miss Cavill's god-daughter, Doris Readhead, lived in Luton, Bedfordshire, and it had been three years since she and her husband had visited her godmother. Before 1925, Miss Cavill had made regular visits to Luton to see Doris and her mother and she would always say to them 'I will see you alright'. She was never ill, although Doris had received a letter from a cousin, Eddie Cavill, some years ago, saying that Miss Cavill had had a slight stroke whilst on holiday in Cornwall. Doris and her godmother exchanged letters four or five times a year, and she had received the usual letter six weeks before she died. The letter had mentioned her doctor being in frequent touch with her and her regular attendance at church. The police had called upon Doris' mother to inform her of Miss Cavill's death, and they had found an unfinished letter which Miss Cavill had been writing to her.

David Alcorn first met Miss Cavill in 1942: she and her sister were great friends of his wife's family and his wife was Edith's god-daughter. They had both always called the sisters, Auntie Edith and Auntie Flo, and visited them six times a year. The Aunties had been very well off through family legacies, and brother John, in particular, had been a very wealthy man. David recalled a particular incident: the Aunties had a very dear friend, Mrs Elinore Rowe-Thomas of Ditchling. There was an occasion when Auntie Edith became very ill and Mrs Rowe-Thomas visited her. As a result of their conversation, Auntie Edith was advised to change her doctor – which she did. The apparent reason for the change was, firstly, that she was not receiving the correct treatment, and, secondly, that there was 'a personal suggestion' made by Dr Adams. What this was, David never did find out. Eventually, Auntie Edith had died in a nursing home and her remains cremated at Brighton.

David and his wife continued to visit Auntie Flo, though she was rather deaf and it was difficult to have a conversation with her. He and his wife thought that Auntie Flo was rather wealthier than Auntie Edith – whose estate was £5,708:13s.7d. During one of their visits she sought David's advice regarding a will, although whether this was one she had made or was about to make he was unsure. Anyway, she told him that the Doctor had, or was suggesting that she make a will which she did not want to make, which would appoint him as executor and a beneficiary of the will. David advised her to consult a solicitor, but she made no reply. When Auntie Flo died, Mrs Rowe-Thomas had told him that Dr Adams was on holiday in Ireland, but had flown back by 'plane to take charge as executor of the estate. David considered that Dr Adams had been most unco-operative and failed to notify them correctly of the date and time of the funeral. Auntie Flo, of course, 'thought the world of Dr Adams. His influence over her was such that it definitely changed her personality.' David's wife had received £607:10s.10d. from Auntie Edith's will but nothing from Auntie Flo's will.

Elinore Beatrice Rowe-Thomas had known Edith and Flo since childhood as she lived in Eastbourne for over fifty years, in Vicarage Drive and Motcombe Road. In 1948 when Edith had a stroke, she had arranged for her to go into Mrs Pike's Nursing Home in The Avenue. From that time Flo had lived alone, but went to stay with her friend Ada in Cornfield Road quite often. Mrs Rowe-Thomas visited Flo quite regularly and, during one visit, they had discussed wills and Elinore had suggested that she make one. On a later visit, Flo told her that Dr Adams had brought a solicitor to the house for this purpose, and some time after that she told her friend that she wished she had left everything to Dr Adams. Would Elinore be satisfied with two or three hundred pounds? About a year before Flo died, she and her sister-in-law had become very worried and she had spoken to Dr Adams on the telephone, suggesting that Miss Cavill should be moved into a nursing home or have someone in the house to look after her. He had replied that 'that would not do at all'. Mrs Rowe-Thomas said there was no question about the expense being too much and he said, 'Oh,' in a rather surprised voice. She asked him to let her know if Flo became ill and gave the Doctor her telephone number.

The first Elinore heard of Flo's death was from Mrs Hold, her next-door neighbour, expressing surprise that she was not at the funeral. She had received £30 in the will.

Haines, the undertakers, confirmed that they had received instructions from Coles & James to arrange the funeral, and, that after a service on 14th May, 1954 at St. Mary's Church, Miss Cavill's body was interred in the same grave where her mother, Elizabeth Julia Ann Cavill, had been interred in 1930. No relatives had been contacted. An additional inscription had been added to the memorial on the instructions of Dr Adams.

Miss Cavill was found dead in the lavatory of her home at 3.30 p.m. on 9th May, 1954. She was fully clothed and had been dead for some twenty-four hours. Her body was discovered by police when her neighbours reported that the milk had not been taken in from her doorstep. A post-mortem examination was held and the pathologist found the cause of death to be 'cerebral haemorrhage due to rupture of an atheroschlerotic blood vessel': she had died of a stroke, and she also had some kidney disease.

The will had been made on 28th July, 1953 and it had been witnessed by Mr James, the solicitor. Dr Adams was the sole executor and a legatee.

Mrs Pearson, Miss Cavill's lifelong friend, told an even sadder story to the *Daily Sketch* reporter: Miss Cavill had fallen in love with Dr Adams and believed it was a romance: every time he was going to call, 'she would hurry round, making sure everything was just how he wanted it'.

# A Twist in the Will

## Mrs Harriet Maud Hughes

Mrs Alice Delves was one of the younger of the private nurses, aged 44 when she was interviewed on two occasions. She had nursed Mrs Hughes of Kepplestone a fashionable block of apartments at King Edward's Parade, in 1951. Mrs Hughes was a widow, not too elderly, who had a thrombosis in the leg and perhaps some heart condition, and was very depressed because her husband had died recently – in May of 1951. 'She had plenty of money' Nurse Delves commented. She had nursed her at nights as had a Nurse Carey during the day. She believed Nurse Carey had emigrated to Canada. She had only been with Mrs Hughes for about five days before she died and she only used to see Dr Adams about once each night, normally between 10 p.m. and 11 p.m. and he visited regularly during the daytime. Dr Adams signed the death certificate and the cause of death was shown as (a) cerebral thrombosis and (b) cardio-vascular degeneration.

Dr Adams would leave a couple of white tablets to be given to the patient if she could not sleep. No injections were given at this stage. About two or three days before Mrs Hughes died, Sister Carey had told Sister Delves that Dr Adams had 'been in and out of the house several times during the day' and that a lot of documents had been signed by Mrs Hughes. She also said that the Doctor held the patient's hand and coaxed her to eat. He had brought presents of eggs and loaned her a portable wireless set. At this stage injections were given during the day by Dr Adams, and the patient's condition worsened. Nurse Delves could certainly confirm that Mrs Hughes was comatose for a good forty-eight hours before she died, aged only sixty-six. She was not there when the patient passed away but she assisted at the Last Offices.

After Mrs Hughes died, Dr Adams told the nurses to go to Lloyds Bank to get their money, and from the way he spoke the nurses assumed he must be an executor as he seemed to have so much control over the deceased patient's affairs, and they knew he made the arrangements with Haines the undertakers for her funeral.

Mrs Irene Swain, who lived in Meads Village in Eastbourne, became acquainted with Mr and Mrs Hughes through Mr Tom Etherington, the Head Porter at Kepplestone Flats, and she provided domestic help for three mornings each week and did some cooking. Mr and Mrs Hughes had moved into the flat in June 1950; they were then both in good health and went out for drives in their motor car. Mrs Hughes' sister, Mrs Beard came to visit, and her close friends, Mr and Mrs Thurston.

Towards the end of 1950, Mr Hughes was taken ill and Mrs Swain suggested that Dr Harris be called to attend him. After a short illness, Mr Hughes died in the first few months of 1951. The sudden death was a great shock to Mrs Hughes and, when she first became ill, Dr Snowball attended on the first occasion, but then Dr Adams came. Dr Adams continued to visit as her GP and came regularly at about 10 or 11 o'clock in the morning. Mr and Mrs Thurston were then at the flat and had been there for a few weeks.

About two or three days before Mrs Hughes died, the day nurse [Carey] told Mrs Swain that Mrs Hughes wished to see her. 'I went into the bedroom and found Mrs Hughes in a kind of stupor'. She was talking of things that had happened in her life many years before. Whilst Mrs Swain was in the bedroom, Mrs Hughes told her that she had asked Dr Adams to kiss her and, 'pointing to her forehead she told me he had kissed her there'. From what Mrs Swain knew of Mrs Hughes, she regarded her as a reserved lady and 'not given to romancing'. The patient's voice died down to a whisper and Mrs Swain could not make out what she was saying. Then she suddenly pulled herself together and remarked 'I'm talking silly, aren't I!'

Sometime before Mrs Hughes died she had told Mrs Swain that she intended making Dr Adams her executor and she mentioned having taken him to her bank and introducing him to her bank manager. She remarked that the Bank Manager had been very surprised. Whilst she was very ill she had also told Mrs Swain that the Doctor had taken her to his house, which she had admired very much, and she thought a feminine hand had been responsible for the arranging of the furniture and decorations. She also said that, when she was better, Dr Adams had told her he was going to take her to London and entertain her to a dinner – a thing he often did for his patients.

A few days before Mrs Hughes died, Mrs Thurston sent for Mrs Beard, who remained in the flat until after the funeral. 'I must say that I was really surprised that Mrs Hughes died, although Mrs Thurston told me she would not get better.'

Mr Ernest Privett, the Bank Manager of the main Eastbourne Branch of Lloyds Bank, had retired the year prior to the investigation. Aged sixty-one, he lived at Ocklynge Farm House in Victoria Drive. The affairs of Mrs Hughes and her involvement with Dr Adams had caused him great concern.

Mr and Mrs Hughes had moved from Worthing to Eastbourne, and on 7th July 1950 had transferred their account to his branch of the Bank. After Mr Hughes' death, Mrs Hughes opened an account in her own name.

On the 24th November, 1951, Dr Adams called at the Bank, requesting Mr Privett to allow him to withdraw the will of Mrs Hughes, which was dated 18th June, 1951 and a Codicil, dated 6th July, 1951. He had no authority from Mrs Hughes and Mr Privett was reluctant to agree. However, he gave a temporary receipt and promised to obtain Mrs Hughes' discharge for Mr Privett, and so the documents were released to him . On the 27th November, a letter from Dr Adams enclosed a receipt for the will and codicil as agreed.

Mr Privett was worried and telephoned to Mayo & Perkins, the solicitors who prepared Mrs Hughes' will and spoke to Mr Perkins, informing him of Dr Adams' request. The will and codicil were returned to the Bank by hand on 30th November, when a second codicil dated 23rd November, was also handed in. In the meantime, Mrs Hughes had died on 29th November.

Mr Privett also recalled that, during the month of November, 1951, Lloyds Bank had required the signature of Mrs Hughes on a new lease of Flat 7, Kepplestone, Staveley Road, which Messrs. Mayo and Perkins had been asked to prepare. On 22nd November, Mr Privett wrote to the solicitors asking them to delay preparation of the new lease as he had ascertained from Dr Adams that Mrs Hughes would be 'quite incapable of undertaking any business transaction for some time to come in view of the state of her health'.

Dr Adams had rung up Mr Mayo, the solicitor, two or three evenings prior to the 30th November, 1951, saying that Mrs Hughes was very ill and worried about her will, and wished to know that it was in safe custody. He asked Mr Mayo to tell him where the will was – at Mrs Hughes' request – so that he could tell her. He was informed that it was in Lloyds Bank. Dr Adams did not mention anything about Mrs Hughes' wishing to make any alterations to the will, merely saying that she was anxious to know that she had made one and where it was. After Mrs Hughes' death, Lloyds Bank asked Mayo & Perkins to obtain probate of the will and they were surprised to see the second codicil.

Miss Beatrice Charity Beard, Mrs Hughes' sister, was eighty-four years old and lived in Chatham, a naval town in the county of Kent. Miss Beard had been to see her sister when she was ill, five or six weeks before she died. She had certainly not thought she was seriously ill and expected her to get better.

When Miss Beard heard that her sister was very ill, she went immediately to Eastbourne and arrived on 24th November. Mr and Mrs Thurston, who were great friends of her sister, and had been for over twenty years, were already there. Her sister was able to recognise her and, with difficulty, did say a few words: she mentioned the new codicil to her will and told Miss Beard that Dr Adams had advised her about it. He had said something to her about Mr Thurston 'only being a schoolmaster'. Mr Thurston had, at one time, been a schoolmaster in Chatham, but had retired.

Miss Beard was present when her sister died. Later, when her will was read, she was surprised that the second codicil had not been prepared by her own solicitor, Mr Perkins. Mr and Mrs Thurston told her that they were both very surprised that they had been left such big gifts in the will. They were, of course, very kind to her sister when she was ill. She and some other relatives had received some money from the will, but she couldn't remember how much it was. Miss Beard, herself, had remained on very friendly terms with the Thurstons, and had, in fact, stayed with them for a week at their new home in Folkestone and returned home only the previous night.

Mrs Elsie May Thurston and her husband had known Mrs Hughes and Mr Percy Hughes since 1923, and they had spent many holidays together and stayed at each other's homes. She thought that Mr Hughes' death had been a great shock to his wife and that she had never got over it – she had no real will to live. Mr and Mrs Thurston had actually lived with her at Keppelstone since the death of Mr Hughes – with the exception of one week. As far as the will was concerned, Mrs Hughes had mentioned that she wanted to leave some money to the Chatham Hill Mothers' Meeting and wanted to make some extra provision for her nephew's children.

Despite her depression at her husband's death, Mrs Hughes had been in good health: a few giddy turns perhaps, but otherwise getting out and about. It was only in September that she had a swollen leg and thought she ought to have a doctor call. As she had had Dr Snowball for her husband, Mrs Thurston telephoned his home but he was not there and Dr Adams came. Mrs Hughes had not seen Dr Adams before and, on this occasion, he came about three times. She was not quite sure but thought that it was at the beginning of November that he began calling twice a day, and, as Mrs Hughes' condition deteriorated, he increased his visits.

Mrs Thurston knew that Mrs Hughes had been 'a little anxious' after visiting her Bank Manager, when he discussed with her whether or not she could afford to live at Keppelstone. On one of Dr Adams' visits while Mrs Thurston was present, Mrs Hughes had to sign a cheque. The Doctor asked her if she had any worries on her mind, and she told him she hadn't. Mrs Thurston intervened and said that she had, mentioning the incident with the Bank Manager. Dr Adams' response was that he could not bring her back to health if she had worries of that kind.

In mid-November, about a fortnight before she died, Mrs Hughes told Mrs Thurston that she wanted to get her will from the bank so that she could make a small alteration. She wrote a note in rather shaky handwriting asking the Bank Manager for the will, and Mrs Thurston took this down to the bank and 'gave it to Mr Privett'. He did not give her the will. He had later 'sent the will up to Mrs Hughes'. Mr Privett did not recall this visit by Mrs Thurston. When the receipt was signed for the will, Dr Adams and Mrs Thurston were in the bedroom. Mrs Thurston 'saw him guide Mrs Hughes' hand in making her signature on the receipt'. He then asked Mrs Thurston to witness it and she signed. Afterwards, Mrs Hughes told her that Dr Adams had her will.

Mrs Thurston was adamant: Dr Adams had never had a discussion with her about Mrs Hughes' will and Mrs Hughes had never told her what her alterations were. She was convinced that these were in connection with the Chatham Hill Womens' Meeting and her nephew. Well… Dr Adams had said to her that Mrs Hughes had altered her will and that it was to the benefit of herself and her husband. This was said when he brought a solicitor with him. This solicitor and Dr Adams went into Mrs Hughes together and she had not been present. This was just a few days before Mrs Hughes died. Elsie had then telephoned to the Bank Manager to tell him that Mrs Hughes had died. Mr Privett had asked her where the will was and she told him she didn't know, but 'If you have not got it, Dr Adams must have it.' The following day he telephoned her to tell her that Dr Adams had brought the will in to him.

On the day of the funeral, a solicitor came to the flat and read out the will. It was only afterwards that she learned that her husband and herself were legatees for £1,000 each. She could only say that it was a great surprise to both of them, Dr Adams had never discussed this with them and 'no portion of the money was ever passed to Dr Adams'. Harry Thurston had been present during the interview for the whole afternoon and heard his wife's statement about the circumstances surrounding the death of Mrs Hughes. He had nothing to add and concurred completely with the contents of her statement. Detective-Superintendent Hannam regarded this case as a very interesting one and, from the financial point of view, 'the most suspicious of the whole lot'. He was looking for just 'that extra piece of evidence necessary to prove complicity on his part with others, or a conspiracy to defraud'.

Mrs Hughes left estate valued at £20,502. The Will prepared by Mayo and Perkins named the executors as Lloyds Bank Ltd, and it contained a legacy of £100 to the Chatham Hill Mothers' Meeting and named nine relatives as residuary legatees. The First Codicil of 6th July, 1951 stated that Mrs Hughes desired cremation and otherwise confirmed her will. Again, it was prepared by Mr Perkins of Mayo & Perkins. The Second Codicil of 23rd November, 1951, was prepared six days before Mrs Hughes' death, witnessed by Mr James of Coles & James, 'the solicitor whose name we are now becoming accustomed to' and by Dr Adams. In this, £1,000 was left to Mr Harry Thurston and £1,000 to his wife, Elsie. Lloyds Bank Executor Department, together with Mayo & Perkins, had approached the police on the matter of the last codicil as they were convinced that 'there was something undesirable in this case'. They also conveyed that they have been suspicious about Dr Adams in these financial transactions for many years and when this matter arose they were most anxious about it.

Mr Privett, the Bank Manager, had consulted Dr Adams about the new lease on the flat on 22nd November, 1951 and it was then that the Doctor had told him that Mrs Hughes was quite incapable of undertaking any business transaction for some time to come. Yet on 24th November Dr Adams called upon Mr Privett to request the Will to take to Mrs Hughes. On 27th November, Mr Privett received a letter from Dr Adams in his own handwriting, marked 'Private and Confidential' saying that he is glad to report that:

> 'Our mutual friend has rallied considerably over the week end but unfortunately is still unable to write very well although she is quite clear mentally and able to talk quite well. She wishes to retain the documents for a time and they are quite safe. I drew up a receipt to cover you and had her friend who is staying with her to witness her signature so that everything would be in order. I hope her improvement will be maintained and meanwhile I will endeavour to get her to sign a cheque to cover the expenses of nurses etc., with very many thanks for your kindness and consideration.'

With that letter was enclosed a receipt which he had prepared in his own handwriting, and signed by Mrs Hughes and Mrs Elsie Thurston.

On the 28th November, Mr Privett wrote to Mrs Hughes acknowledging the receipt for her Will and Codicil and, because of his concern about the matter, offered to call upon her and have a chat about her financial affairs.

Mr Mayo of Mayo & Perkins, the solicitors, had stated that 'two or three evenings before 30th November' he had received a telephone call from Dr Adams stating that Mrs Hughes was very ill and worried about her will – about the same time as he informed Mr Privett that she had improved considerably. He said nothing to either Mr Mayo or Mr Privett about a new codicil. It was, of course, only recently that the solicitors had dealt with Mrs Hughes' will and first codicil, so it was clearly odd that Mayo & Perkins should not have been consulted in the matter by Mrs Hughes, and Dr Adams had acted in a most suspicious manner.

Mrs Thurston had made several untrue statements to the police: that Mrs Hughes wrote a note which she had taken to the bank to get the will, but did not get it – which Mr Privett could not confirm; that Mr Privett had sent the will up to the flat – this was definitely not the case and she added that she believed the receipt the bank manager wanted for the will was a printed form and that she saw Dr Adams guide Mrs Hughes' hand in signing it. Hannam thought it a little strange that the receipt actually signed by Dr Adams on 24th November was a printed form, whereas the receipt signed by Mrs Hughes on 27th November was a written one in Dr Adams' handwriting, and 'either Mrs Thurston is mistaken or she is lying, for there is no alternative'.

Detective-Superintendent Hannam and Detective Inspector Pugh did manage eventually to extract an admission from Mrs Thurston that Dr Adams had told her and her husband that they were beneficiaries under the will: 'at first she emphatically denied it and we put it to her in no uncertain terms as to whether or not there had been an arrangement between Dr Adams and herself and her husband and asked whether Dr Adams had received any money from either of them after they had received their £2,000 from Mrs Hughes' will.' Hannam and Pugh believed that there was a conspiracy between Adams and the Thurstons to share out the money and pursued enquiries with the Co-operative Permanent Building Society where Mrs Thurston had deposited a cheque for £1,000 on 23rd April, 1952 and the Abbey National Building Society where Mr Thurston deposited £1,000 on the same date.

Later, the police continued with their search of the Thurstons' bank accounts: on 5th August, 1953, £500 was withdrawn by cheque from Mr Thurston's Abbey National account and made payable to his account at Westminster Bank, Chatham. On 6th September, 1955, £50 was withdrawn by cheque payable to Westminster Bank Ltd at Folkestone. They then changed their address to Dudley Court, Trinity Crescent, Folkestone. On 16th January, 1956, £100 was paid into the account and on 5th June 1956, £50 was withdrawn by cheque to Westminster Bank, Folkestone. As for Mrs Elsie Thurston, there had been only one withdrawal from the account to date when she moved £50 to the Westminster Bank in Folkestone.

The police did not pursue the matter any further: '…it can probably be left where it is.' because they were working from the motive for murder being personal gain by Dr Adams. They had, however, collected evidence, elsewhere, which pointed to the fact that the Doctor believed in redistributing wealth to the more deserving and, even more, he wanted to control and dominate people's lives – and deaths.

## Miss Sara Emily Watson

Head Constable B.A. Durkan took statements from a relative and a former employee of Dr Adams in late October, 1956 in Northern Ireland.

The relative was Miss Sara Emily Watson, sixty-six years old in 1956, and living where she had been born and bred, in Rock, Dungannon, Co. Tyrone. Her mother and his mother were sisters, so they were first cousins. She had known him since he was born in Randalstown, when his father was a jeweller; at Coleraine when his father died, and then when he was a student at Queens and his mother had secured a house at Malone Avenue, Belfast. Her cousin, Sarah Florence Henry had also lived with them. When Dr Adams secured the tenancy of 12, Upperton Road, Eastbourne, then his mother and cousin, Miss Henry, had moved there from Belfast. In 1930 he had purchased Kent Lodge for the sum of £3,000, and, 'after spending quite a sum of money in renovating and repairing it, he occupied it with his mother and Miss Henry'. Miss Watson mentioned that 'His mother was, even at that time, a person of independent means, and was considered a wealthy person.'

Miss Watson visited the Adams family regularly when they lived in Belfast, and, also in Eastbourne and spent holidays with them in Harrogate and Keswick on numerous occasions. She had always gone as their guest and Dr Adams had paid her fare and hotel bills on these occasions. She had corresponded with both Mrs Adams and Miss Henry on a regular basis until their respective deaths. In the summer of 1951, she went to spend two weeks' holiday in Eastbourne visiting Dr Adams and Miss Henry but on this occasion stayed at the Sandhurst Hotel paying for herself because 'Dr Adams was having some trouble with housekeepers and he did not want visitors staying at Kent Lodge.' This was just after Florence Henry had had an operation and was being treated three days a week at Brighton Clinic. Nobody told Miss Watson the nature of Florence's illness.

In January 1952 she received a telegram from Dr Adams asking her to go to Eastbourne as Florence was very ill. The trouble with his housekeepers was still continuing so Dr Adams paid for a hotel for her; she stayed for about a month, then returned to Rock. But on 19th March she had a telegram from Florence Henry asking her to go to Eastbourne again. This time she stayed at Kent Lodge because Florence was terminally ill, and died in June. Her body was cremated and the ashes were brought to the family burial ground in Coleraine Cemetery. Miss Watson stayed on for about three weeks in Eastbourne as she was 'badly shaken' by Florence's death. Dr Adams treated her with sedatives and tonics. Each time she had been in Eastbourne, he had given her the necessary medicine when she mentioned various ailments to him. So far as she was concerned each one always had the desired effect.

# Chapter Fifteen

---

# Mrs Ware and Mr Downs

## 1950 – 1955

---

Mr James Priestley Downs, a retired bank manager, his wife Jane Elizabeth I'Anson Downs and her sister Amy Constance Clavering I'Anson Ware, lived together in a detached mock-Tudor house in a private close in Eastbourne's Old Town.

Mrs Downs died on 26th October, 1949 at the Esperance Nursing Home, run by Anglican nuns. The death was certified by Dr Adams as 'carcinoma of the breast'. According to the Mother Superior she had been admitted for a secondary on the lung. She had been operated on the previous February for breast cancer. Dr Adams was not a legatee of her will but Mrs Downs had directed that all necessary steps should be taken to make sure she was dead, particularly requesting Dr Adams to examine her for this purpose. Mrs Downs left almost the whole of her estate to her husband.

Not long after Mrs Downs' death, her sister, Amy, was admitted to Edgehill Nursing Home, 6 Mill Road, Eastbourne, and died on 23rd February 1950. Dr Adams signed this certificate, giving the cause of death as '(a) cerebral thrombosis and (b) cardio-vascular disease.'

Mrs Ware left an estate of £8,993, leaving Dr Adams £1,000. A copy of the will showed that, at one time, he was to receive only £100, and the £100 had been crossed out and £1,000 substituted. The residue was left to Mr Downs. The will was witnessed by Mr Willoughby, an Eastbourne solicitor and Sister Stuart Rollings, the Matron of the nursing home, and dated 16th February, 1950, as also was a codicil attached to it – seven days before her death.

Mrs Agnew Margaret Sumpter and her husband, Glaven, lived in Chelsea Cloisters just off Sloane Avenue in Kensington. They were very concerned about Glaven's remaining aunt, Amy, and had been accustomed to corresponding regularly with her and visiting. They knew that she did not get on very well with her brother-in-law although she stayed on in the house with him after her sister's death. She had previously lived in the North of England, but had been most unhappy there, and it was Dr Adams who had brought her down to live with her sister.

On the 1st November, 1949, Mrs Sumpter received a letter from Mrs Ware, written in pencil, to say that Mrs Downs had died. She responded by going down to Eastbourne, where she saw both Mrs Ware and Mr Downs. On this occasion Mrs Ware told her to take certain jewellery, silver and glass, but she declined to do so.

On the 9th November, Mrs Sumpter received a further letter from Mrs Ware saying that she was very lonely and Mrs Sumpter sent a reply, saying that she would visit her on the following Saturday. On the 11th November a telegram was delivered to Mrs Sumpter: 'Not well, doctor says no visitors. Writing. Amy.' This was almost immediately followed by a letter from Mr Downs, stating that Mrs Ware was confined to her bed suffering from nervous prostration and that the doctor had ordered complete immunity from social activities and that, therefore, Mrs Sumpter's intended visit on Saturday could not take place.

Mrs Sumpter decided she must go down to Eastbourne and find out what was wrong. On the 1st December she took the train from Victoria and, on her arrival, discovered that Mrs Ware was out and had gone to the doctor's. Whilst she was in the house, Mrs Ware returned and Mrs Sumpter was shocked to find that she looked vacant and scarcely seemed to know her niece. Mrs Ware seemed to be 'in a trance'. Towards the end of the month, Margaret wrote to Mrs Ware inviting her to visit her in London, and she then received a letter card from Mr Downs, which was unsigned: 'We are advised that Amy is not to be troubled with correspondence or visitors.'

On 5th January, Glaven Sumpter wrote a very gently-worded letter to Dr Adams, pointing out that he and his wife had received unsigned letters stating that no visitors or correspondence were allowed, and appealing to the Doctor to give them some information about their aunt. The response was in Dr Adams' own handwriting, on his headed notepaper, dated 11th January, 1950, saying he was pleased to know of a near relative; that it was quite true that, as a result of the loss of her sister, she was very ill, and he had forbidden her to be troubled by business matters, especially those of a distressing character. He added that they would be glad to know that she was making satisfactory progress and, if occasion should arise, he would communicate with them again.

Five days later, they heard from Dr Adams again, saying that Mrs Ware was in a nursing home and that he proposed keeping her there for a complete rest, and suggested that a visit some time might help the patient.

A telegram from Dr Adams arrived a week later, dated 23rd February, 1950. It said: 'Mrs Ware passed away this morning. Adams.' Margaret was extremely distressed and telephoned Dr Adams the same day, telling him she would come to the funeral. He told her that Mrs Ware had died in the nursing home and that she did not want anyone at her funeral. He said she was not to worry and that both she and her husband were mentioned in Mrs Ware's will. Mrs Sumpter thought that it was very strange that Dr Adams should be aware of this on the very day Mrs Ware died. Later, this conversation was to be evidence of the fact that Dr Adams had made a false statement on the cremation form for Mrs Ware. Trusting his word that Mrs Ware wanted no-one to attend her funeral, she sat down and wrote a letter to Dr Adams, enclosing money for flowers to be purchased, on hers and her husband's behalf, for the funeral. Again, he replied, in his own handwriting, in a letter dated 25th February, saying how much he appreciated Mrs Sumpter's letter and adds that the funeral was held that day at Brighton

Crematorium, attended by Mr Downs and himself, but that, as there were no flowers – strictly at the request of Mrs Ware – he had not purchased any and therefore returned the money. It was an extraordinarily short interval between death and cremation, particularly for the 1950s.

Mrs Morag Stuart Rollings had been proprietress of the Edgehill Nursing Home from September 1949 to June 1954, and was retired by the time of the police enquiry. She recalled Mrs Ware being admitted as a patient, and that she had only lived one week after that. She seemed to remember that Mrs Ware was in generally poor condition and that she had been paralysed down one side. Mrs Ware had told Mrs Rollings that Dr Adams had always been kind to her and her sister, and told the tale of his bringing her down here from the North of England. She told the matron that she wanted to leave money to the Cats and Dogs Home and £1,000 to Dr Adams. Mr Priestley Downs was present when she made these remarks and he agreed with her that Dr Adams had been kind and should have some money.

Dr Adams was, of course, in complete charge of a patient when he arranged for admission to a nursing home. Matrons and proprietresses of nursing homes were on close terms with all the doctors in the town who had private patients. Mrs Rollings was not at the top of Dr Adams' list as he only ever sent her two patients; it is likely that, in the depth of winter, it was quite difficult to find a bed in one of Eastbourne's nursing homes.

Dr Adams visited the patient twice a day. Mrs Ware was rather noisy and Nurse Rollings asked the Doctor to give her some sedatives to quieten her down at night. She thought that this was Medinal 7 grams. Sister also remembered a solicitor named Willoughby coming to the nursing home and dealing with Mrs Ware's will. She had no knowledge of its contents but, whilst in the bedroom, on that occasion, she heard Mrs Ware tell Mr Willoughby and Mr Downs that she wanted Dr Adams to have £1,000 and the residue was to go to Mr Downs. Mrs Ware signed the will, and a few days later she had a severe heart attack and died soon after.

Mrs Muriel Leah Sleap was a particular friend of Mrs Ware and lived only a few yards away in Vicarage Road. In 1949, a few months before Mrs Ware's death, she was at the house in Park Close with Mrs Ware. Amy was always talking about Dr Adams and said that she had told him that she would look after him in her will. The Doctor had apparently told her that he was interested in the YMCA and other organisations in Eastbourne, and, whatever money was left to him in her will, he intended sharing it amongst these organisations. Mrs Ware told Muriel that she was going to leave him £1,000 for this purpose. Detective Superintendent Hannam comments in his report that if Mrs Sleap was right in saying this then '…it is a damnable technique and may be further reason why the false statement was on the cremation form.' Mrs Sleap also recalled that Amy had told her that, during one of the Doctor's visits to her, he patted her hand and said to her 'You're my pet, aren't you?' Mrs Ware seemed quite thrilled about this.

Mrs Sleap, however, was strongly of the opinion that 'on the day Mrs Ware signed her will, she was not fit to do so.' On the very day when Amy signed her will, Dr Adams gave instructions to Mr Downs that Muriel was not to be allowed to visit her friend again. After the cremation of Mrs Ware's body, Dr Adams sent an account to Mr Downs for his attendance on her, for a sum in the region of £60. Mr Downs was furious about this as his sister-in-law had only been ill for about eight days before she died. On this particular occasion, Mr Downs told Mrs Sleap that he 'would not leave the Doctor a penny.' Mrs Sleap was banned by Dr Adams from visiting Mr Downs at the Esperance Nursing Home, and this was communicated to her by a Mr Bell.

Nurse Phyllis Owen visited Mrs Ware at home and nursed her on the instructions of Dr Adams. Mrs Ware had confided in her that Dr Adams was looking after her affairs and sorting out articles of her property and making an inventory so that they could be included in the will. Mrs Ware said she had been uncertain in her own mind about how much money she ought to leave to Dr Adams, but he had resolved the matter by suggesting an appropriate amount to her. Sister Owen confirmed that Mrs Ware was not comatose while she was nursing her, but that she was most certainly under the influence of sedatives.

Lucy Lavendar was companion and daily help to Mr and Mrs Downs. Dr Adams had attended Mrs Downs and visited her each morning. After Mrs Downs died, the Doctor visited Mrs Ware sometimes twice, sometimes three times a week. He also continued to look after Mr Downs, who was very active. In October 1954 he was able to get about and went to his bank, the Midland in Eastbourne and obtained his will. When Mrs Lavender saw him that day at teatime he was very upset and was waving his will about. He asked her: 'What was I like in July? Was I well?' Mrs Lavender told him he was quite well then and he then showed her the will and said: 'I've made thousands of wills in my time [as a bank manager] but I've never seen one like this. The people who are getting well-paid for their work are getting everything but those who really matter are getting nothing. I am going to alter this.' Mr Downs told her on several occasions during the following weeks that he had seen Mr Willoughby, his solicitor, about preparing a new will. The Doctor had been visiting Mr Downs daily since the death of Mrs Ware, but during this time Dr Adams was visiting very early every morning and he had a habit of sitting on the bed and talking to Mr Downs: they were discussing 'business matters'.

When Mr Downs had the fall, injuring his ankle which was put in plaster, and he became rather difficult which was the reason for his being taken to the Esperance Nursing Home, Mrs Lavender was asked by 'a friend' if she could find Mr Downs' will – the one which he had taken from the Midland Bank. Mrs Lavender knew that the will had been hidden by Mr Downs in the back of the seat of an easy chair in his bedroom and, looking there, she found the envelope. On the outside were the words 'Draft Will', so she opened it and read just a little.

Mr Downs was very friendly with an estate agent from South Shields, a Mr Bell, who came to Eastbourne to see him quite often. Mr Bell had tried to get Mr Downs to make a will. When he came, Mr Bell would kiss Mrs Lavender on the cheek and tell her she was 'being looked after'. Mr Downs told Mrs Lavender that he was leaving her £2,000 and one sixth of the residue of his estate. Mr Downs made this alteration in her presence, according to Mrs Lavender. She then telephoned Mr Bell and told him she 'had found the draft will' and sent it to him by registered post. Some time later Mr Bell came to Eastbourne and searched for the July will, but did not find it. Lucy Lavender later recalled to the police that Mr Downs had told her he had burnt this will, but she did not tell Mr Bell of this as Mr Downs had asked her not to do so.

When Mr Downs was admitted to the Esperance Nursing Home and she and Mr Bell were visiting him, Mr Downs mentioned where the draft will was in the house. Mr Bell said 'Not that one'; Mr Downs did not say another word but just looked at her. Mrs Lavender then decided to speak to Dr Adams and met him at the Esperance the next morning. She told him that the July will could not be found but that they had found a draft will. Dr Adams asked if Mr Downs had left him anything, and she replied that she did not know, and asked if she should speak to the patient about it. She then deposited the draft will with the solicitor. As a result of Dr Adams' enquiry she asked Mr Downs if he had left anything to Dr Adams in his will and he said he had. She pursued the matter 'How much?' And, as he did not reply: '£500?' Mr Downs said 'No, £1,000.' On 7th April 1955, Mrs Lavender said that she was there when the will was read in Mr Downs' presence at the nursing home and signed. Mr Heath, the solicitor, and Dr Adams were there when Mr Heath read the will in a loud voice as Mr Downs was somewhat deaf. Mr Downs then said that Dr Adams was not only his doctor, but a very good friend. Yes, she had always considered that Dr Adams' treatment of Mr and Mrs Downs was always very good: he was very attentive and came day or night when called.

A Nursing Sister of the Holy Family of Bordeaux, Nora MacCarthy, had nursed Mr Downs at the Esperance Hospital, where she was known as Sister Raphael. In April 1954 Mr Downs was operated on to remove his prostate gland. He was troublesome and often climbed out of bed at night so was given injections, of which the foundation was morphia. She believed that the patient stayed at the nursing home for about twenty-six weeks, when his condition had improved enough for him to be discharged towards the end of December 1954.

The second time he had been admitted on 16th February, 1955 with a fractured ankle, and the only treatment was nursing care and sedative medicine. Sister Raphael remembered that Dr Adams had given the patient a sedative containing morphia. The instructions were that the patient was to be given two doses in the daytime and a double dose at night-time. She believed that the patient was also given soneryl tablets to quieten him. On several occasions he tried to get out of bed and, early one morning, she found him lying on the floor with a head injury. The medicine and the soneryl tablets were then increased.

Sister Raphael said that Mrs Lavender used to visit Mr Downs and that she had told her that she had placed an unsigned will on the top of the patient's pyjamas in a cupboard in the room. The Sister rather gathered that the will was there if Mr Downs wanted to sign it. She did just glance at the will and saw that Dr Shera's name was on it and also that of a Canon Jackson, but she could not remember the others. She did recall Mrs Lavender speaking to Mr Downs one morning in May and trying to persuade him to sign the will. However, one day, just before Mr Downs died, Dr Adams, Dr Barkworth, Mrs Lavender, Mr Heath the solicitor, and a young lady, came to the Esperance. They all went into the patient's bedroom and Mrs Lavender told her the will had been settled and all the business in connection with it had been cleared up.

Sister Raphael told the police that the patient's condition was, on this day, brighter than usual, although he was still a little confused. She had been told by Sister Miller, the private night nurse, that, a day or two before this happened, Dr Adams had given her a tablet with instructions to give it to Mr Downs so that he would be more alert when he signed his will. She also recalled that in April 1955 Mr Bell and Dr Adams had an argument and parted bad friends. Mr Downs' will had been on top of the cupboard in his room and the day before everyone came for him to sign it, he had been given an atropine injection by Dr Adams.

Sister Gladys Miller nursed Mr Downs for six months and remained with him until his death. She stated that he was definitely senile and in a confused state of mind and that his only treatment was sedatives at night. The patient never recognised her and used to call her 'Lily', which she believed was the name he called his wife.

Dr Adams would visit between 7 a.m. and 8 a.m. each morning and told her that he was very great friends with the patient. She knew that: 'During the last War, Mr Priestley Downs lived at Dr Adams' house in Trinity Trees.' Trinity Trees was at the epicentre of the bombing but it was a sensible place to be with the basement of the house reinforced as an air-raid shelter. Co-incidentally, it added to Dr Adams' prestige to remain there in war-time Eastbourne. Mrs Lavender also visited the patient and Sister Miller understood that she was Mr Downs' house-keeper. Three or four weeks before Mr Downs died, Dr Adams had confided in her that a will had been found in Mr Downs' house but it had not been signed; Mrs Lavender had found it and, on reading its contents had panicked and sought his advice in order to get it signed. He also told her that Mrs Lavender had looked after Mr Downs ever since his wife had died and she was certainly entitled to some money in the will. She had naturally inferred that Dr Adams was worried that Mrs Lavender would be left without a job and without any means.

One morning, about 7.30, Sister Miller was in the patient's bedroom when Dr Adams visited as usual. The Doctor spoke to Mr Downs: 'Now look here Jimmy, you promised me on the day Lily was buried and on the return journey in the car, that you would look after me and I see that you haven't even mentioned me in your will.' Sister Miller said that Mr Downs was, as she had mentioned, extremely confused in his mind and she heard him say to the Doctor: 'Well, I don't know. I can't remember what happened. I must have had a blackout.' Dr Adams retorted: 'You haven't signed your will, your nieces will get the lot and you don't want them to have it do you? They have never done anything for you.' No will was produced at this time, but Nurse Miller also heard the Doctor say to the patient: 'Jimmy, I have looked after you all these years and I have never charged you a fee.'

A day or so then went by, Sister Miller recollected, and then Dr Adams came into the patient's room and told her that a solicitor was coming to the Nursing Home that morning and asked her to give Mr Downs a tablet. It was white in colour and he asked her to give it before she went off duty. Dr Adams said he wanted Mr Downs to be more alert and the tablet was to prepare him for the signing of his will. She went off duty at 9 a.m. and just before this she gave the tablet to the patient and noticed that, shortly afterwards, he became brighter and more responsive, seeming to understand what was said to him. Oh, and on several occasions whilst she was nursing Mr Downs, she saw Dr Adams assisting the patient to sign cheques for the nursing home fees, the cheques having been prepared by the Doctor.

Mr James Clement Heath, the solicitor, had spoken to Dr Adams on the telephone on the morning of 7th April and had been told by him that Mr Downs was much more alert, and, because of that, he had arranged an appointment at the patient's room at the Nursing Home for 11 a.m. that day. According to Nurse Miller this improved condition had been engineered by the Doctor. When Mr Heath arrived, bringing with him the draft will in which there was no mention of Dr Adams, he found the Doctor with Mr Downs, who directed that he be included in the will as a legatee for £1,000. Mr Heath returned to his office and made an engrossment on the will and returned to the Esperance Nursing Home at 1 p.m. on the same day. Mr Heath was aware that the patient was under the care of Dr Adams and was very unwell, and he had taken the precaution of insisting that another doctor was present as well as Adams, and Mrs Lavendar. He had read over the will to Mr Downs twice and had satisfied himself that Mr Downs understood and agreed to its contents. The will was witnessed by himself and Dr Barkworth. Mr Heath was shown the cremation form in the handwriting of Dr Adams, where he had answered the question 'Have you, so far as you are aware, any pecuniary interest in the death of the deceased?' 'Of this I do not know.' Mr Heath agreed that this was quite obviously an untrue statement.

In the archives of the Director of Public Prosecutions there are copies of a few of the entries in Mr Heath's diary relating to April 1955 and Mr Priestley Down's will. The first relates to Mr Bell calling on Mr Heath and informing him that he could find no trace of a will; Mr Bell and Mrs Lavendar then went to see Mr Downs and thought he was 'more able to take notice of things being said' and had gathered that he had burnt the will and asked if Mr Heath would prepare another one. The second entry notes that Mr Heath went to see Mr Downs at the Esperance, when Mrs Lavendar was present, seeking to obtain his approval for the draft will, but his client was 'not sufficiently responsive'. Dr Adams called in and arranged with Mr Heath that 'Mrs Lavendar should take us in the afternoon' if Mr Downs' condition improved. Mr Heath returned in the afternoon, but Dr Adams was unable to be there. Mr Downs 'appeared to understand what we were saying' and endeavoured to sign his will but did not, in fact, do so. Mr Snowball, the surgeon and Dr Adams' partner, 'looked in and in his opinion you were not sufficiently capable of understanding what you were doing'. The third entry was the one for 7th April: Dr Adams telephoned Mr Heath to tell him that Mr Downs was 'much more alert this morning and asked us to meet him at Esperance at 11'. Mr Heath attended at the Esperance and Dr Adams and Mrs Lavendar were there. He ascertained 'that the will met your wishes except that you wished to include Dr Adams as a legatee for £1,000'. Arrangements were made to re-engross the will ready for signing at the Esperance at 1 p.m. Mr Heath returned with the will, meeting with Mrs Lavendar, Dr Adams and Dr Barkworth and explained the will to Mr Downs twice 'and on each occasion you replied "that's what I want".' Mr Downs executed the will by making his mark and Mr Heath and Dr Barkworth witnessed this. Dr Adams then asked Mr Heath to send Dr Barkworth his fee of 3 guineas for attending. Subsequently, Mrs Lavendar handed in the draft will she had received from Mr Bell to Mr Heath.

Dr Barkworth, the junior partner of Dr Adams stated that he had satisfied himself that Mr Downs understood what was happening and saw him sign the will with a cross. The reason for this was not due to his mental state but his physical weakness.

James Priestley Downs died, aged 88, at the Esperance Nursing Home on 30th May, 1955, a few weeks after the signing of the new will. He left estate of £27,032 net. The death certificate, which was signed by Dr Adams, shows the primary cause of death as cerebral thrombosis and the secondary cause as cardio-vascular degeneration. He entered the nursing home with a broken ankle. On the cremation form – which requires answers to some medical questions,

Dr Adams stated that the 'last illness' – presumably the fractured ankle – had a duration of four months. He had last seen the patient at 6 p.m. on 29th May, 1955, about twelve hours before death. He had seen the body one hour after death and made a 'general examination' to decide the cause of death. The mode of death had been coma of about thirty-six hours. Dr Adams stated that he had reported the case to the Coroner and had 'Permission to Proceed'. The Coroner had obligingly given his permission to go ahead with the cremation without requiring a post-mortem examination! The 'Confirmatory Medical Certificate' had been signed by another doctor, and the 'Authority to Cremate' had been signed by yet another doctor as Medical Referee to Brighton Crematorium. Three doctors had the opportunity to question the Death Certificate and Cremation Form, and Hannam's advice from Dr Thrower, Consultant Neurologist at the National Hospital in London, was that there was no question that there should have been a post-mortem examination in this case. If this had been a burial, the death was recent enough for an exhumation to have produced good forensic evidence.

The Chief Constable received a letter from Mr Priestley Downs' niece, Dorothy Young, dated 21st May, 1957:

'I have just been reading Dr John Bodkin Adams' case in the newspapers.

I am one of the two (and only) nieces of the late James Priestley Downs, the patient mentioned in the case yesterday the 20th.

I note that Dr Adams was heard to have said to my uncle, 'I have looked after you all these years, and I have never charged you a fee.'

This is quite untrue. My Uncle often spoke about his Doctor's bills and what a lot he had got out of him, and only on Friday (the 17th) I received the full Administration accounts of his will from the Executors and in the Schedule of Debts is the entry:-

For professional attendance of Dr J.B. Adams, of Kent Lodge, Trinity Trees £216.1s.6d.

So you see he is not speaking the truth. I would like to see you on the matter and show you these accounts.'

Chapter Sixteen

—•—

# The Neil Millers

## 1952 – 1954

—•—

## The Long Pursuit

**Isabel's Story**

There was just enough light from the bedside lamp for the doctor to read the Bible. An icy February wind blew through the wide-open sash window. The bed clothes were draped over the brass rail at the foot of the bed. The frail old lady in the bed was obscenely exposed with her nightdress pulled up to her neck. But she knew nothing; she never would know anything about it, mercifully. The door of the bedroom opened and closed again gently. The doctor was still engrossed in his Bible.

Isabel Neil Miller was the proprietress of a Nursing Home near Guildford when she first met the sisters, Hilda and Clara Neil Miller in 1930. She was nursing their sister-in-law, the first Mrs Neil Miller. Their brother, Thomas, a retired iron and steel merchant, thirty years Isabel's senior and now widowed, married her on 18th July 1935 at Bramley, Surrey. The sisters went off to Austria in 1931 and lived there for four years. They returned in May 1935 in time for the wedding.

Isabel said that they were delighted at her marrying their brother, and confided in her that they were not wealthy but whatever they had would be passed to her at their deaths. In August her sisters-in-law sent her the whole of the furniture from their father's library, some table silver and a dessert service and three fairly valuable pictures. By the October of that year they had moved to a flat in St. John's Court, St. John's Road in Eastbourne and Isabel and Thomas visited them. Hilda asked for advice on certain investments and enquired about annuities. 'I then realised how little their income was and my husband gave them a present of £50 each. On the way home I spoke to my husband about his sisters' affairs and suggested that he gave them each a sum of money to increase their income. He eventually made a gift of £1,000 each to his two sisters which was taken out of his capital, which was, of course, money which would come to me at his death.

There was an understanding between us all that the gift of £2,000 should come back to me at their deaths. They were going to buy some annuities and then leave £500 each to me.'

Isabel took a practical interest in her sisters-in-law. In 1936 she visited Hilda and Clara in Eastbourne when Clara was recovering from an attack of bronchitis and confined to her bed. There was some domestic trouble and they were not happy at the flat. They were considering going into a small hotel and whilst Isabel was there the doctor arrived. A discussion ensued regarding alternative accommodation and the doctor suggested that he knew of a very nice little place called Barton which was in the same road. He had a call to make there and he would enquire if there was accommodation for Hilda and Clara. They all went and viewed the rooms at Barton and thought them very suitable. Isabel met Mr and Mrs Sharpe, but was not particularly impressed, especially with Mrs Sharpe.

At Christmas 1937, Isabel and Thomas decided to stay at the Grand Hotel in order to see the sisters. Hilda appeared much bothered about Mrs Sharpe and said she was trying to borrow money from Clara and had already obtained £300 from her. The following Spring, Isabel was surprised to receive a letter from a friend of Hilda and Clara, Mrs Johnson, saying that Hilda was unwell and that she and her husband should go and see her. Isabel went alone and took them by surprise. 'There was a flaming row between Hilda and Mrs Sharpe, which resulted in my leaving sooner than I intended. Mrs Sharpe was apparently furious that I had not given her some notification of the visit.'

The sisters were generally known as 'Miss Hilda' and 'Miss Clara' and considered very refined and rather eccentric and old-fashioned. They were *very* Victorian: the younger of the two, Miss Clara, was born in 1867. In Isabel's opinion Miss Hilda was the stronger of the two sisters in character, and she managed all the money affairs. As far as their health was concerned Clara had never been known to suffer from a weak heart and in her younger days and, up to about 1930, she climbed, went horseriding, cycling, and was a keen dancer. As for Miss Hilda's suffering from severe headaches, these were apparently caused by severe disagreements with Miss Clara and Mrs Sharpe over money matters.

Some time in 1938 Isabel found out that Mrs Sharpe was trying to persuade Miss Clara and Miss Hilda to take out a mortgage on Barton. The sum mentioned was £5,000 and if this money was forthcoming they could stay at Barton for the rest of their lives, merely paying a nominal sum for their food. Isabel 'strongly advised' against this and the loan was not made. But it caused a terrible row between the two sisters: Miss Hilda had never taken to Mrs Sharpe, but, somewhat inexplicably, a strong bond seemed to have been forged between Miss Clara and Mrs Sharpe. After this, whenever Isabel mentioned Mrs Sharpe's name in conversation, Miss Clara would immediately change the subject as she would not hear a word against her.

In 1940, with the majority of Eastbourne's population, Miss Hilda and Miss Clara evacuated. Isabel found them accommodation in Guildford. After about seven months, Miss Clara went to Eastbourne to see Dr Adams about her headaches. She remained and, after about three weeks, then persuaded Miss Hilda to join her. They remained at Barton until 1945 when they had a 'frightful row' with Mrs Sharpe and departed in some haste.

This time they went to Hassocks in Sussex and then on to Bournemouth, where Isabel and

Thomas lived, and where they stayed for twelve months. They then moved to Helensburgh, a genteel little town on the River Clyde north of Glasgow, to join Dolly Wallis, their oldest friend who was also Clara's goddaughter. They stayed there till 1948 and after a short sojourn in Switzerland, returned again to Bournemouth on the South Coast.

Here they had a flat at Dundrel, Balcombe Road from March 1949 to March 1950. Then they had a very unexpected and strange visitor. A Miss Green arrived in June 1949, saying she had been recommended to them by Dr Adams in Eastbourne and moved in. She then proceeded to have a severe disagreement with the owners of the flat who promptly asked Miss Green, Miss Hilda and Miss Clara to leave.

During this period in Bournemouth, Miss Hilda was most unwell. She told Isabel that she was being given too many pills which made her feel dizzy. 'I spoke to Clara about these pills and she told me that they were quite harmless and had been given to her by her doctor in Eastbourne.' Hilda had been the more capable sister, but now she was under Miss Clara's complete domination and no-one was allowed to see Hilda without Miss Clara being present. The Doctor came to Bournemouth to see Miss Hilda and Miss Clara at their flat and Miss Green was sent out whilst he was there. Isabel promptly called in a local doctor, who thought the sisters should be separated and he gave instructions that the tablets Miss Hilda was taking should be stopped.

These instructions were carried out and Hilda appeared much better. Shortly before they moved out of the Bournemouth flat, Miss Clara went to London to see Dolly, her goddaughter and Miss Hilda went to see Isabel and Thomas at their flat. Hilda was in great distress and begged them to do everything possible to prevent her returning to Eastbourne. 'She told me there were people there she was frightened of and that she did not wish to go there.' Miss Clara had taken all her money and jewellery away from her and she was not even allowed to wear her watch.

Isabel thought that it was in 1950 that Miss Clara and Miss Hilda did return to Eastbourne, again taking up residence with Mrs Sharpe at Barton – though it might have been early in '51. A telegram arrived from Miss Clara 'In great trouble, can you come?' Unusually there was a telephone number on it and Isabel rang and arranged to meet her at Brighton Station the next day. She arrived in great distress. 'She seemed frightened and worried and several times during the day she appeared to be on the point of telling me something but each time stopped herself and said, "No, I must not tell you. I must not give you all my worries." I implored her to confide in me but was unsuccessful.'

In 1951 Clara and Hilda went to Chagford in Devonshire and Isabel visited them in May. She was pleased as they both seemed very comfortable and Miss Hilda appeared to be much better than for some time. But, during a short time alone with her, Miss Hilda implored Isabel not to let her return to Eastbourne, giving no reason and saying that Clara still took all her money and retained her jewellery. Clara said she definitely intended staying at Chagford for the summer and Isabel decided, with her husband's approval, to book accommodation in Chagford for herself and keep an eye on them. She wrote to Clara saying that she had booked rooms and three days later received a letter saying they would leave in ten days and return to Eastbourne. The whole situation was out of Isabel's control and she had a good idea who was in control.

It was a friend, Mrs Dorothy Wright, who found rooms in Eastbourne for them this time, yet a couple of months later there was a letter from Clara saying that they were returning to Mrs Sharpe at Barton. It was now autumn '51, and, although she wrote fortnightly to Clara and Hilda, Isabel got no replies. She was concerned as her husband's health was now failing and she wanted the sisters to see their brother before he died: he was now ninety years of age. Eventually, a letter arrived from Clara in which she made no mention of Thomas' health and Isabel realised that they were not receiving her letters. She was very worried as her husband had had two serious heart attacks. She resorted to subterfuge, asking her sister to send a registered letter from Reading to Miss Clara at Barton and received a reply by return of post, saying how distressed she was and that they would visit them in Bournemouth immediately after Christmas. They arrived on 17th January '52 and remained until Thomas died on 23rd January.

They were questioned about the letters Isabel had sent to them, but they had not received any of these. There was a discussion before Thomas died to remind them about returning the legacy to Isabel. It was understood that the loan of £2,000 would not revert to her until after the deaths of Clara and Hilda. Hilda said that, in her will, she had left three paintings and an emerald cross to Isabel. After the funeral they returned to Barton.

Shortly afterwards, Isabel's bank, the National Provincial, wrote several letters to her sisters-in-law and failed to get any reply until they enclosed a letter in a registered bank envelope. There was now proof that someone was intercepting the letters addressed to them and Isabel wrote to the Postmaster at Eastbourne complaining. The Postmaster launched an official investigation. Following this, a letter arrived from Miss Clara telling Isabel to send letters care of Mrs Dorothy Wright.

Late in April '52, Isabel went to Eastbourne and arranged to meet Miss Clara in Fullers Restaurant in the high street: 'She would not allow me to go to Barton to see Miss Hilda.' Fullers – the tea-rooms that so many remember with nostalgia: that unique fondant-iced walnut cake which no-one has managed to imitate. It was to be a final meeting: she never saw Clara or Hilda again.

Isabel wrote to them regularly once a month. At Christmas 1952 she sent both of them a present, not acknowledged immediately, but received a letter at the end of January '53, thanking her for the parcel in the name of them both and then saying how much they had enjoyed the clotted cream. The letter ended: 'Love from us both'.

Letters continued to arrive periodically, perhaps five or six up to November 1953. Although she did not know it at the time, this was about eleven months after Hilda had died. There was no announcement in a national newspaper – as was usual in this family – and Isabel sent the normal Christmas greeting addressed to Clara and Hilda, c/o Mrs Wright. This was acknowledged in January 1954 and was the last letter she received from Miss Clara.

While Isabel was being treated in a nursing home, on 22nd February, her sister saw the announcement of Miss Clara's death in the *Daily Telegraph*. She immediately wrote to Miss Hilda at Barton expressing sorrow and offering assistance. About two or three days later, she received a letter from Dr Adams saying that Hilda had died the previous January. She wrote to Dr Adams asking for information regarding the deaths of Clara and Hilda, where they were buried and the name and address of the lawyers who had acted for them. The address of the lawyers was all she received from Dr Adams.

## Dorothy's Opinion

Alice Dorothy Wright [always known as 'Dorothy'] was the widow of a medical practitioner; her daughter was also a doctor. Yes, she knew the sisters, Hilda and Clara Neil Miller, for about six years and sometimes went on holiday with them. Once upon a time Hilda was the stronger character of the two and very good at financial matters. The other sister was not.

She used to see quite a lot of them, living in the same road, and visited them quite frequently. They didn't have many friends. 'I think I was the closest.' As for Mrs Isabel Neil Miller: 'I saw her on only one occasion. It was not her habit to visit the sisters and I am under the impression that Mrs Sharpe would not have her at Barton.' She had heard that a number of letters had not reached Hilda and Clara and it was arranged that their letters should be addressed care of herself. Miss Clara usually called on Dorothy each day to see if there was any post for them. They had both mentioned to her that their brother had given each of them £1,000 for investment, but there was never any suggestion that these amounts were to be returned to Mrs Isabel Neil Miller upon their deaths. Frankly, they had told Dorothy that Mrs Neil Miller was a rather extravagant woman.

No, Dorothy had never heard from the sisters that Mrs Sharpe had borrowed any money from them or anything about supporting a mortgage on Barton. Mrs Sharpe had a reputation for being very kind to persons who were ill at her house and, at times, she nursed both the Misses Neil Miller. It was true, though, that they were not very fond of Mrs Sharpe and it was most unlikely that Miss Clara would think of giving Mrs Sharpe any money as a present.

Of course, Dorothy had known Dr Adams for many years and thought him the best doctor in town. He attended the Misses Neil Miller: 'I think he did them a lot of good'. Miss Clara never indicated to her that she was going to leave any money to him. She left Dorothy an unexpected legacy of £200. She had visited Barton at the time when Miss Hilda was very ill, just before her death. Miss Clara did not realise at the time that Hilda was dying. She also visited Miss Clara during her last illness, and thought she was in bed for about fourteen days. She had talked to her and seen Dr Adams with her on several occasions.

## Dolly's Story

Now sixty years of age, Dolly Wallis had first met Miss Clara when she was five years old – in 1901: her mother had taken in paying guests at the Old Mill at Eynesford, Kent. Miss Clara had lived there from time to time when she went for medical treatment in London. She had become great friends with Dolly's mother and was Dolly's godmother. The friendship continued over the years, after her mother's death and after her marriage. Miss Clara was a very refined person, somewhat delicate, but her general state of health was good.

It was early in 1953 that Dolly visited Barton and was then first introduced to Dr Adams.

Her immediate impression was not favourable: 'He did not strike me as the type of practition-er the Miss Millers would have chosen. They had heard of his wonderful skill through Mrs Dorothy Wright….I think she quite innocently had great faith in Dr Adams. When Hilda died I went to see if I could be of assistance. Clara then said to me "Dr Adams has done everything for us. He is a wonderful man". I understand he had arranged the funeral, the burial site, and everything in connection with Miss Hilda's death.'

Some months after Miss Hilda's death and not long before Miss Clara's death, Dolly received an alarming telephone message from Mrs Sharpe. Mrs Sharpe said: 'Strange things are going on here. He is locked in Miss Clara's room for twenty minutes at a time and she appears to be under the influence of drugs.' Dolly said she had better come at once and see her and Mrs Sharpe told her she should do so.

Dolly arrived at Barton, but Miss Clara appeared to be her normal self. When she told her of Mrs Sharpe's message, Clara was indignant and furious with Mrs Sharpe. She said: 'Don't listen to 'phone calls.' Dolly realised that Clara was completely under the Doctor's spell and prepared to listen to every suggestion he made. She told Clara that Mrs Sharpe had said the Doctor was often locked in the room with her. Clara did not deny this but riposted that it was no business of anyone else. She coyly mentioned that Dr Adams assisted her in many person-al matters, such as pinning on brooches, adjusting her dress, and she also said his fat hands were comforting to her. Dolly was suspicious that something very peculiar was amiss between Dr Adams and Miss Clara. There was nothing to be done, thought Dolly, Clara was completely under the Doctor's influence and she could not help her. Consequently her visits became painful and rather embarrassing.

A few years before her death, Clara had confided in Dolly that she was to be the chief ben-eficiary under her will and that one day she should be quite comfortably off. 'Therefore I was very surprised when Dr Adams benefited by £6,000 and I only by £1,000.' She went to her London solicitors but was not able to show them a copy of the first will, which she was sure had been destroyed. She then received a letter from Coles & James, Dr Adams' solicitors, informing her that, until the will was proven, she could not enter Clara's room, which was sealed against any intrusion. Mrs Sharpe promptly charged Dolly the sum of £40 as she could not relet the room. She tried to recover this from Dr Adams' solicitors but without success. When she was eventually able to visit the room, she felt it had been interfered with.

Dr Adams was always rather aloof with Dolly, but after she had spoken to Clara 'about this apparent resentment', his manner altered. He became courteous but false. 'He only once dis-cussed the ailments of my friends Clara and Hilda but I did not understand his medical terms. I attended the funerals and spoke to Dr Adams on both occasions. He arranged that the sole car at each of the funerals should not follow immediately behind the hearse.'

## Mrs Sharpe's Stories

'I first met Dr Adams when I ran a hotel, Norman Court, numbers 18 and 20 Seaside Road. He used to visit two guests of mine and they thought a great deal of him. He wasn't my doctor then.

In September 1931 I left there and came to Barton as the proprietress of this guest house.' It was about 1935 when Miss Hilda and Miss Clara came there as paying guests. They had separate bedrooms and had a private sitting room. She regarded them as very thrifty and secretive ladies and certainly she knew absolutely nothing of their private affairs. They paid Mrs Sharpe regularly one quarter in advance, which was as much as she was interested as regards money.

They definitely did not have a doctor when they arrived in 1935 and they did not trust the medical profession. They remained with Mrs Sharpe until about 1946 when they left and went to reside in Scotland. No, during the whole of that time they did not have a doctor and never visited one. They disliked doctors intensely.

During 1949, about June, Miss Hilda and Miss Clara returned to Eastbourne and wrote to Mrs Sharpe with a view to returning to Barton. She was unable to accommodate them as she had already taken bookings for the holiday. They stayed at Avonmore in St. John's Road, until she was able give them a twin-bedded room in the September. They had to use the public lounge and dining room with the other guests. Knowing the aversion to doctors of both the Misses Neil Miller, she would only accept them back to Barton on the condition that they had a doctor in case either of them became ill. They both accepted and appointed Dr Adams as their doctor – as private patients, naturally; they would never have dreamed of becoming patients under the new National Health scheme.

Until August of 1952, both ladies enjoyed good health. One day in that month, whilst both sisters were seated in deckchairs on the lawn, Miss Hilda was taken ill. Mrs Sharpe, finding her unconscious, telephoned for Dr Adams. By the time he arrived, she and Miss Clara had got her into bed. The Doctor examined Miss Hilda, asked for some water, and after crushing a small white tablet in the glass, they got Miss Hilda, who was then conscious, to drink it. Mrs Sharpe was instructed to give a further tablet to the patient at midnight, and another at three o'clock in the morning.

When Dr Adams arrived next morning at 7 a.m., he examined Miss Hilda, and said 'She's better. She'll be up and about in a few days.' Miss Clara followed him out of the bedroom, saying, 'You must not come again until I send for you.' 'Very well,' he said, 'I will be pleased to call any time you want me.' Miss Hilda improved and in due course came downstairs for her meals, but stayed indoors as the weather was cold for the time of year.

They all spent Christmas together at Barton, but on Christmas Day evening, Miss Clara called Mrs Sharpe to her sister, who was then in bed and in the same state as she had seen her on the lawn the previous August. She was unconscious. 'I suggested to Miss Clara that we should call Dr Adams, but she refused, saying her sister would get over it very quickly. I went downstairs and telephoned him and, in a very short time, he arrived at the house.' Miss Hilda had rallied by the time the Doctor had arrived. He examined her and left two small white tablets with the same instructions as before. He returned at 7.30 a.m. the next morning, looked at Miss Hilda and said she would soon be well.

Miss Hilda had one more similar attack about a month later and she died in February 1953, at the age of 86, after another of these turns and an illness of about three or four weeks. Miss Clara agreed to Dr Adams attending her sister about twice a week, with an understanding that if he was required urgently, he would be called. Shortly before Miss Hilda died, Mrs Sharpe asked Dr Adams if she would get well; he said: 'I'm afraid it's the end.' She had just given Miss Hilda brandy and glucose, as the Doctor instructed.

Miss Clara continued to occupy the same room at Barton, 'I do know that Miss Clara suffered from a weak heart and from time to time had heart attacks. During these bad turns she took brandy and water which revived her. Sometimes she was prostrate for a day or two after and confined to her room. Dr Adams never attended Miss Clara on these occasions; she did not want him too and I got so used to seeing her in this condition that I was not unduly worried.' Early in 1954, Mrs Sharpe heard Miss Clara ringing her bell and, going to the bedroom found her very ill and asking for the doctor. Mrs Sharpe called him and he arrived within fifteen minutes at about 3.15 a.m. and gave her an injection in her thigh. 'Dr Adams remained in the bedroom and said to me: "It's no good me going home and coming back because I want to see her again in two hours' time". He remained with the patient and I stayed in the room the whole time. Miss Clara slept.'

At the end of two hours, Dr Adams looked at the patient and found she was awake. She said she felt a little better and he went off home. 'Oh, yes, I nursed her – she refused Dr Adams' invitation to enter the Esperance Nursing Home because she hated nursing homes and the expense.' The Doctor visited every day and prescribed the same small white tablets. Mrs Sharpe took the prescriptions to Moss Chemists, Grand Hotel Building and administered the tablets.

Miss Clara was quite bright, sitting up in bed, reading and knitting, but didn't want to get up as she complained she was very tired. During this illness, according to Mrs Sharpe, 'instead of being downright rude to Dr Adams as she was in the beginning, she became very fond of him and looked forward to his visits between 7 and 8 o'clock in the morning.' Shortly after this recovery, Miss Clara had a very bad attack at 3 a.m. on a Sunday morning. Mrs Sharpe called Dr Adams' house and Dr Snowball answered and said Dr Adams was away and he would come at once. He examined her, gave her an injection in the buttock and watched her for fifteen minutes until she fell asleep. Dr Adams was back in Eastbourne that same night and called at 9.30 p.m. Miss Clara remained in this condition for about a week. Dr Adams increased his daily visits to 7 a.m., 2 p.m. and 8 p.m., but instructed that no tablets or medicine should be given to the patient.

On the night of 22nd February when Miss Clara died, Mrs Sharpe went into the bedroom and discovered that she had taken a turn for the worst and called the Doctor. He arrived shortly afterwards and Mrs Sharpe asked him not to leave because she felt Miss Clara was dying. He glanced at Miss Clara and said he had to hurry off to another patient at the Grand Hotel to give an injection. He returned about a quarter of an hour afterwards and Mrs Sharpe recalled waiting in the bedroom with him until Miss Clara died about 11.30 p.m. She was 87 years old.

'Of course, I knew nothing of Miss Clara's business affairs, Inspector. She never confided in me and I don't know if she made a will. All I do know is that Mr James of Trinity Trees is her solicitor. Nothing except a clock was left me by Miss Clara. It was a marble clock and she left my husband a grandfather clock. Oh, a long time before she died. I would like to say that during Dr Adams' attendance upon Miss Hilda and Miss Clara, he was kindness itself. Towards the end Miss Clara idolized him.'

## The Additional Story

Superintendent Hannam decided to call upon Mrs Sharpe with the Inspector. Neither he, nor Detective Inspector Pugh were convinced that her previous statement was true or complete. 'I have been asked if I can help regarding a sum of £200 which I am told appears on the Probate Records of Miss Clara as having been received by me on 11th February 1954.'

In all, the two sisters, Miss Clara and Miss Hilda, stayed at Barton for over eleven years. At one time each of them had a bedroom and private sitting room each and these rooms they furnished themselves. After they returned from Scotland Mrs Sharpe had emptied one room for them, which they furnished themselves, but had their meals in the dining room with the other guests – which was the position when both the Misses Neil Miller died. Some of their furniture was stored at Dickeson & French of Eastbourne.

Mrs Sharpe had expected that Miss Clara's friend Dolly, who used to visit once a fortnight and whose fare Miss Clara paid, would come and live here and look after her. Miss Clara had been broken-hearted when she wouldn't do this. Mrs Sharpe had had to do all the nursing, under Dr Adams' supervision, because Miss Clara refused to go into a nursing home even when he urged her to do so. Several times Miss Clara had said to her that she would give her a present because she didn't know what she would have done without her. She never said what the present would be.

Just over a week before Miss Clara died, Dr Adams had come down to Mrs Sharpe's sitting room in the basement of the house and asked if she could spare a minute. She thought Miss Clara was worse, but he said: 'My dear, I have got a nice surprise for you, Miss Clara wants you to have £200 and it can't be put into her will for you for that is all arranged.' She went up to thank Miss Clara for the lovely gift to be told that it was only a small thing considering what she had done for her. The next day or the day after, Dr Adams came down again to see her and handed her a cheque for £200 from Miss Clara, which she had paid into Lloyds Bank. And while she was at it she might say that, when they went to Scotland, many years ago, they had each given her £50 in cash.

The letters? Neither of the Misses Neil Miller had ever mentioned that any letters to them had gone astray. Well, she did vaguely remember that some letters addressed to guests at Barton did go amiss, but this was reported to the Post Office and a detective came.

Dr Adams was, indeed, her own doctor and sometimes visited another guest, a Mrs Prince, who was a friend of his.

## The Vicar

The Rev. John Gwynn Downward was Vicar of All Saints Church. Miss Clara Neil Miller had been a member of his congregation for some twelve months before her death. He remembered her as 'an eccentric both in dress and behaviour', but very active and interested in the church. When she did not attend for some time, he had visited Barton to make enquiries, but was not able to see her. He had spoken to Mrs Sharpe and she had made a comment to him that Miss Neil Miller had plenty of money or words to that effect. 'I cannot remember what gave rise to this remark but it certainly registered with me.'

The next thing he remembered was officiating at her funeral at Langney Cemetery on 25th February 1954. He had noted that there were no mourners present save Mrs Sharpe and Dr Adams and had received a gift of one guinea from Dr Adams. 'With my lengthy experience of conducting funerals I did feel that the circumstances were unusual, but gave no further thought to this until reading in the newspaper that enquiries were being made about the deaths of elderly people in Eastbourne, and that the Mayor, Mr Caffyn, had asked that anyone with any relevant information might give it. I therefore thought it my duty to bring this to the notice of the Chief Constable of Eastbourne.'

## The Deaths and Wills

Sister Phyllis Owen, a private nurse, visited Miss Hilda on a few occasions during her illness and performed the last offices. Whilst she was doing so, Dr Adams and Mrs Sharpe were present and she saw the Doctor pick up one or two articles in the room, examine them and put them into his pocket. Sister Owen was horrified. Detective Inspector Pugh saw Mrs Sharpe again to question her about this. She was in bed resting after what she said was a heart attack, but she was fully dressed. She denied the suggestion against 'her friend Dr Adams', but said that in Miss Clara's case, the Doctor did take away an electric bowl fire which he had loaned her because she felt the cold so much. Hannam remarks 'Mrs Sharpe is a hard woman and a little petty stealing would not affect her conscience.'

Dr Adams signed the death certificate for Miss Hilda, who died on 15th January 1953, giving the cause as cerebral thrombosis. He certified Miss Clara's cause of death as '(a) coronary thrombosis and (b) myocardial degeneration.'

Dr Thrower of the National Hospital for Neurology in London examined chemists' records and causes of death at the request of Hannam. He was particularly concerned about two cases, one of these being that of Clara Neil Miller. She either did or did not have something wrong with her heart. If she did, why bring in another disease unless there was good evidence of it? He noted the change of chemist and that there was no sign of any injections ordered, yet towards the end of her life she was given injections three times a day. Dr Thrower was emphatic that, in his view, the exhumation of Miss Clara Neil Miller's body would be a wise step.

The sisters made their wills on 11th June 1952 before Mr Norman Hurst of Stapley & Hurst, Solicitors. In each case the National Provincial Bank was appointed executor and trustee and the wills decreed that these solicitors should be employed and consulted in any matter connected with the wills. Both wills were identically worded and each sister devised and bequeathed all their real and personal estate to each other, and, in the event of the other's former death, that all should be left to Dolly, Mrs Wallis.

The last will of Miss Clara was prepared and signed on 30th October, 1953, less than four months before her death. In that will, Dr Adams was the sole executor. Mrs Dolly Wallis was left £1,000 and all her personal effects; her two children were also left small amounts. Touchingly, she did not forget her charitable duties and the horses she once loved riding, leaving £25 each to the 'War Horse Memorial Fund of Lloyds Bank', the 'Blue Cross Horse Protection Fund' and the RSPCA Dr Adams favourite charity, the YMCA (Eastbourne Branch) were bequeathed £100. Dr Adams received £500 and was also the residuary legatee absolutely. He actually benefited to the extent of £1,275:12s.2d. This was not all, however: within a few days of her death he had got a further £700 out of her by cheque. Hannam commented: 'One wonders what his explanation of this can be.' And also noted that: '...we observe once again that the solicitor James plays the ...part of engrossing and witnessing and Messrs. Stapley and Hurst, Miss Neil Miller's normal solicitors were quite unaware of any change as were her bankers, the National Provincial, who had been appointed executors under the former wills.'

As for Mrs Sharpe, the detectives were 'by no means satisfied that Mrs Sharpe was being wholly truthful with us'; they knew from the earlier investigation over the missing letters that Mrs Sharpe herself was responsible. Additionally: 'She had not the slightest intention of telling us about this £200, and it had to be dragged out of her.'

In Superintendent Hannam's Second Report to the Chief Superintendent it is recorded that Mrs Annie Sharpe died on 15th November, 1956. This was obviously at home as Dr Adams had signed her death certificate, stating the cause of death to be 'carcinomatosis of the peritoneal cavity'. The police had traced a prescription, dated 10th November 1956, for hyperduric morphine and 36 pethidine tablets. A statement from the chemist, Mr Harold Seath, showed that on the 10th November, Dr Adams called personally at his chemist's shop and left that prescription, which was dispensed and the drugs concerned had been delivered to Mrs Sharpe's address on the same day.

It appeared that Dr Adams had diagnosed cancer on 10th November and his patient died from it five days later. Hannam regarded this death as remarkably convenient and extremely suspicious as Mrs Sharpe was an important witness. Her body had been cremated, so there was no investigation into her death.

The question of Miss Clara being under the influence of drugs and the spell of Dr Adams became very interesting to Hannam when the chemists' records were examined. In a letter to Detective Superintendent Hannam, Mr Nickolls of the Metropolitan Police Laboratory, New Scotland Yard advised that the prescribing for Miss Clara Neil Miller was extremely heavy, and, in places, almost incomprehensible. Fresh supplies of hypnotics were being administered before previous supplies had been exhausted. 'One gets the impression that the general idea is to saturate the patient with barbiturates and then leave them in possession of a fatal supply and hope for the best.' It was his opinion that no qualified doctor could possibly prescribe drugs in the amount shown without some peculiar intent.

The memorial read:

Hilda Neil Miller

Very Dearly Loved and Missed
Who passed to rest 15th January, 1953
And
Clara Neil Miller
22nd February, 1954
The Lord is My Shepherd

The inscription for Miss Clara had been added on the instructions of her sole executor, Dr Adams.

The exhumation warrant, signed by HM Coroner, Dr Sommerville, was served upon the Cemetery Superintendent of Langney Cemetery, Ralph Hall, holder of the Military Cross, who had held the office for twenty-seven years. The grave was reopened by the foreman gravedigger, Walter Staplehurst and his assistants, Nathan Christmas and Edward Aukett, under his supervision and in the presence of Detective Superintendent Hannam, Dr Camps, Detective Inspector Pugh, Detective Sergeant Hewett and the Coroner. At 9.10 a.m. on 21st December, 1956, the last six inches of earth were removed, revealing the coffin inscription plate of brass 'Clara Neil Miller, 87 years died on 22nd February 1954'. Mr Charles Rason Haine, the funeral director, identified the coffin and confirmed that instructions for the burial and embalming had been received from Dr Adams. The ground was very water-logged; samples of earth were taken for chemical analysis.

The hearse and police cars processed to the Police Mortuary where John Ramsey, the embalmer identified the body and Dr Camps conducted the post-mortem examination.

Dr Camps found the body well-preserved in spite of the water. Photographs show that this was so. His conclusion was that it was evident that Clara Neil Miller had died from bronchopneumonia, which could have been due to drugs. He advised further microscopic and chemical examination, from which it would be possible to disprove the cause of death as shown on the certificate or prove the presence of drugs in the body. The chemists' registers of prescriptions showed no indication of any treatment for bronchopneumonia. The last prescription, dispensed twenty-four days previous to her death, was for sodium barbitone tablets.

The Metropolitan Police Laboratory at Scotland Yard received from Dr Camps various samples taken from the coffin and the body for analysis. There is a note of a telephone conversation between Mr Nickolls and the Director of Public Prosecutions' Office that very little morphine had been found: 'unable to identify amount owing to presence of embalming fluid' – Dr Adams, the Executor, must have ordered the embalming. Mr Nickolls had also found '0.3 milligrams per cent gross of barbitone acid in liver which indicates that amount was circulating. Body in water for two years. Therefore may have been more.' So both results were negative.

The funeral directors reverently reburied her body in a new coffin.

When Detective Superintendent Hannam arrested Dr Adams for the murder of Mrs Morrell on 19th December, 1956, he said to Dr Adams 'I am informed that a few days before Miss Clara Neil Miller died, you were in her room for forty minutes in the month of February and you had the bed clothes all off that lady and over the foot rail of the bed, her night gown up around her chest and the window in the room open top and bottom. That case we are now considering' The Doctor replied 'The person who told you that doesn't know why I did it.'

The Misses Neil Miller were known in Eastbourne as 'the inseparable sisters from Scotland', who were born within ten months of each other, and died within thirteen months of each other; 'a meek and gentle couple, careful with their money. Most fine days you would see them walking round the guest house garden, hand in hand.'

# Two Suspicious Deaths

## The Hullets

### Mr Jack Hullett

Mr Jack Hullett was the only patient of Dr Adams whom Sister Jane Stuart had nursed; this was from 15th December 1955 to 14th March 1956 when he died. The first week had been in the Esperance Hospital, but he was so anxious to go home that they allowed him to do so. She had continued to nurse him at home and lived at the house, Holywell Mount. Mr Hullett had a malignant tumour and he was operated on by Dr Snowball and made a recovery. Whilst Mr Hullett was ill Dr Adams visited him twice a day in the morning and in the evening. Dr Snowball visited until the wound was completely healed. Dr Adams gave Mr Hullett injections both in the Esperance and when he returned home until the pain diminished. Sister Stuart knew that the hospital injections were morphia, one quarter of a grain, but did not know the content of the injections given by the Doctor at home: she merely assumed these were a lesser amount of morphia. When the injections stopped, sleeping tablets were given to the patient.

Towards the end of February, 1956, Mr Hullett had pains in the chest and attacks of breathlessness and his general condition worsened gradually. Dr Adams called in 'a specialist from Brighton', who examined Mr Hullett and proclaimed his heart to be perfectly healthy. At the beginning of March the attacks of breathlessness became more frequent, most usually in the morning. The treatment for this breathlessness was 'Ethedrine' which was given with the sleeping tablets.

The night nurse, Sister Blackwood administered the Ethedrine and the sleeping tablets, but on the 26th February she left as the patient was having good nights and it was thought she would not be needed. The attacks of breathlessness continued up until Mr Hullett died though they wore off quickly and he would go out of doors and for long car rides every day with his chauffeur driving, or sometimes Mrs Hullett, and Sister Stuart accompanying them.

After dinner each night, it was one of Sister Stuart's duties to help Mr Hullett upstairs to his bedroom; sometimes he would go up the stairs with only one pause half way and on other occasions he would climb the stairs in stages, two or three steps at a time and then pause for a rest. It seems to have occurred to no-one that with such a large house a bedroom could have been arranged downstairs or a lift installed.

Sister Stuart recalled that, on the evening before Mr Hullett died, he had pains in his chest and breathlessness shortly after dinner and she had telephoned to Dr Adams. The Doctor arrived and examined Mr Hullett, who, in the meantime, had been resting on a settee. At 9 p.m. Mr Hullett said he wished to go to bed and Dr Adams assisted him up the stairs. Sister Stuart went on in front to prepare the bed and, upon looking back, 'I saw Mr Hullett and the doctor climbing the stairs without a pause. On reaching his room Mr Hullett seemed quite pleased and said 'I've done it in one tonight.' Shortly after he complained of pains in the chest.

On the evening of the 13th March, 1956, Mr Hullett complained of severe pains in his chest and had a very bad headache. Dr Adams was called and a night nurse, Sister Miller, came on duty for that night. Sister Stuart went off duty at 9 p.m. that evening and at about 7 a.m. the following morning Sister Miller came into her room and told her that Mr Hullett had died. Sister Stuart telephoned Dr Adams and he came soon after.

Sister Isobel Blackwood had first nursed a patient for Dr Adams in January 1949, but was not asked to nurse another case for him until that of Mr Hullett on 19th November, 1955, so neither nurse was one of the usual nurses whom Dr Adams would call upon. Sister Blackwood was the night nurse, and she had nursed Mr Hullett from the date of his operation for carcinoma of the colon, firstly at the Esperance Nursing Home and then at home. He was having 'a large amount of drugs both in tablet and injection form' and at the beginning she was to give an injection of omnopon in ampoule form early in the evening. This was found to have little effect and the treatment was changed: Dr Adams came in the evening and gave the injection himself and she had instructions to repeat the injection during the night if necessary; this was an injection of hypodermic morphia, three quarters of a grain. Dr Adams' treatment of Mr Hullett while he was at the Esperance seemed perfectly normal to her.

On 2nd January, Sister Blackwood returned to nurse Mr Hullett at his home and, by this time, he was convalescing and allowed up for periods during the day. He had sleeping tablets at night and pain pills when necessary: A.P.C. [aspirin], sacconal, medinal and nebutol, but he was not making a good recovery and his breathlessness was worrying him. There appeared to be no apparent reason for his breathlessness: Dr Adams told her that his heart was good and his lungs also. Sister Blackwood had to call in Dr Adams twice during the night because Mr Hullett was complaining of pains in his leg and Dr Adams gave him an injection of hypodermic morphia. She added that 'in addition he gave him two or three injections about 9 p.m. for the pain in his leg.'

'I always found him to be a man who was frightened by pain and was certainly always seeking the doctor's advice' was the opinion of Henry Burridge, the retired chauffeur. Mr and Mrs Hullett thought a great deal of Dr Adams: they both had great faith in him. He had never known them to have a disagreement with the Doctor.

The day before he died, Mr Hullett had been in the Pilot Inn, Meads, near to his home – he would drop in from time to time, perhaps with his wife, his nurse or with friends. Arthur Betts, the landlord was also a friend and sometimes invited to Holywell Mount. Arthur had a long conversation with Mr Hullett and 'he told me how much better he was feeling. He told me that he had seen a heart specialist and had been given a very good report.' He was very cheerful and Arthur thought he looked a lot better and more like his own self. He just had one glass of lager and then left the bar about quarter past one. 'That was the last I saw of him and I heard next day he had passed away. I was very much surprised.'

Mr Charles Haine, the funeral director went, with one of his staff, to collect Mr Hullett's body. He saw Mr Hubbard Ford, one of the executors, at Holywell Mount, and received his directions for cremation, firstly at Willingdon church for a service and then to the Downs Crematorium in Brighton. The ashes were then brought back to Willingdon Church for a service prior to interment. The medical forms for cremations were delivered to Dr Adams and Dr Brown of St. Mary's Hospital called to view the body for the second examination and completed his part of the forms.

## Mrs 'Bobbie' Hullett

The Hulletts' chauffeur mechanic was Henry Burridge, a man of 68 with an amazing forty-six years of driving experience in 1956. He had been employed with them since 1934, but had retired on a pension in February, 1956. On the day after his retirement, he visited Holywell Mount – he thought it was the Wednesday before Mrs Hullett was taken ill. He found her 'quite excited and jerky'; she was 'certainly not her normal self'. Just before he left her she shook hands with him and said 'Goodbye'. As he was leaving the room she called him back and, shaking his hand, said: 'Goodbye Burridge, don't forget to bring your wife up to see the gardens whenever you want to.' This was the last time he saw her alive. 'I was rather concerned after Mrs Hullett wished me goodbye. I realized something was radically wrong with her. She had never shaken hands with me before when I visited her, and it struck me at the time that I might not see her alive again…'

## Dr Adams' Version

Dr Adams sat down with Detective Inspector Pugh at Kent Lodge on 26th July, 1956, three days after Mrs Bobbie Hullett's death, to relate the events leading up to her death and that of her husband Jack. Dr Adams first met Mrs Hullett the day after the death of her first husband, Mr Vaughan Tomlinson, which was about six or seven years before the enquiry. He had attended her ever since that date. When he died she was heartbroken and didn't want to live. She had said to the Doctor 'What can I do to die?' According to Dr Adams, she was in poor physical condition and she had lost weight: 'She had worried for some time before her husband's death and her nerves were in a dreadful state, she couldn't sleep and was absolutely like a person demented.' Mrs Tomlinson was living with an old Nanny and her young daughter, Patricia, at a house named Wishanger and Dr Adams visited her every day. 'Because she was so bad I got her to the Reverend Copsey, the Vicar of Willingdon. He was a locum in Switzerland that year and I got her to go out to Switzerland to him for a change.' The Doctor believed this had helped her: '…she came back a lot happier and I again treated her and got her better.'

Mrs Tomlinson already knew Jack Hullett as her husband had been headmaster of St. Bede's School, which was next door to his home, Holywell Mount. He had lost his wife about four months before. Dr Adams related what happened next: '…so to help him and to help her, Mrs Hawkins and I managed to get him to take Mrs Hullett to the Saturday night dances at the Grand Hotel and they got very friendly. Then Hullett said, "I am going on a cruise and I don't know whom to ask". I used to visit Mr Hullett every Sunday morning. I said, "Why don't you ask Bobby Tomlinson. She is a cheerful person, you know her more or less, why don't you invite her to go on this cruise. There is no reason why you shouldn't go together. If you like each other, well, that's that." He said, "I think you are right, I'll ask her tomorrow." He asked her and they went for the cruise. It lasted about four to six weeks. The day after they came back from the cruise they came into my consulting room and said, "You are the first person to know, we are engaged". I said, "Fine, nobody could be happier than I am; you couldn't marry anybody better, good luck." They informed me they would have a quiet wedding so they got married from her mother's flat in Putney. I wasn't at the wedding, I just couldn't make it. I sent them a telegram and wished them all the best.'

They came back and everything continued as usual. Dr Adams called each Sunday morning on Mr Hullett as he had always done. He also saw Mrs Hullett because she had developed what he considered to be a nervous skin rash all over her body, but chiefly on the side of her neck. This worried her a lot and the Doctor sent her to Dr McKenna in London, who was apparently 'the greatest authority on skin'. He gave her an X-ray 'and we got the thing cleared up in the end but it was a tedious business.' The rash 'worried her to pieces' because of her inability to wear evening dresses whilst she had it.

Jack Hullett had taken Dr Adams aside on various occasions to thank him profusely. He had said: 'I have never been so happy in my life. Life is one long dream of happiness. We are happy in every way.' But he also said: 'She is going to break me with her minks and her jewels.' The Doctor had replied 'What's the good of money in the bank? You now have something to see for your money,' and Mr Hullett had replied, 'That's true, you are right.'

On Jack Hullett's 70th birthday, he gave a big dinner party for about one hundred people at the Savoy Hotel in London. 'I was invited and attended. Everybody was happy and their lives were ideally happy.'

Dr Adams continued to visit them every Sunday morning: 'He was a nervous man and I treated him for various functional nervous illnesses.' The Hulletts then went to Australia, New Zealand and America. One Sunday evening, after their return, Mr Hullett sent for Dr Adams urgently: 'I rushed up and he said, "I have a terrible pain in my stomach". I said, "have you had it before?" He said, "Yes, I had an attack on the boat, but the ship's doctor paid no attention to it and thought it was colic." I examined him and to my horror I found he had a sub-acute obstruction of the lower bowel and I thought it might be cancer. I then had X-ray investigations which proved my diagnosis. I took him into the Esperance. I had Sir Arthur Porritt to operate on him, I told Sir Arthur, "I have a patient with a ring carcinoma of the lower colon. I want you to come down and operate. He is one of my important patients and I want the best done for him". I didn't ask Snowball to do it because I knew it was going to be fatal and I thought if I had a local surgeon to operate, his relations might say, "Why didn't you get a London man?" So I had Porritt.' Sir Arthur Porritt came with his assistant and they operated on Jack Hullett at the Esperance Nursing Home. The operation did not go smoothly. 'In about ten days suddenly one afternoon, the whole abdomen burst. Snowball and I were called at once, got him into the theatre at the Esperance and operated immediately and repaired the burst.' For some days they had despaired of his life, but they got him through and out of danger.

Mr Hullett was anxious to get home for Christmas and so three nurses were engaged. 'He then became very nervy and apprehensive and a bad sleeper. All his life he had been a bad sleeper and he had to have sleeping draughts regularly. He had every kind of sleeping draught, Sodium Barbiturate, a mixture of Bromide, Cloral and Morphia and several of Eli-Lilley's Ltd, who make three or four different kinds. They were given by mouth but sometimes I even had to give him an injection and I always gave him this myself. The tablets were given to him by the nurses. I managed with him until March and then to my horror he began to get abdominal distention.'

Mrs Hullett was terrified that she would lose her husband when Mr Hullett went into hospital for the operation. She said to Dr Adams: 'Is it serious?' He replied, 'That obstruction is serious, that is why I am getting this surgeon. What is after I cannot at the moment tell, because it is one of those conditions which you cannot prophesy.' Dr Adams saw her every evening at the Esperance to give her a report on the patient's condition. She was 'in an absolutely desperate state'. Dr Adams gave her 'some single Barbiturate tablets from night to night out of my stocks, only one at a time – 5 grains'. She went home every night and the Doctor comforted her and said he hoped Jack was going to be all right. 'She was in a great state of agitation – half hysterics.' When her husband came home by ambulance at Christmas 'She was still in a state of agitation and worrying, she was unable to help nurse him at all. He agitated to get rid of the night nurse. He said, "I want Bobby back in my room." I said, "Well, we will try it." So the night nurse went and Mrs Hullett slept in the other bed in the room. This went on for about two weeks approximately and then she was getting into such a state again it was reacting on him and he was getting terrible pains in his chest at night and getting bad nights that I couldn't control, so I said, "This has got to finish, I must have the night nurse back again".'

A week before Jack's death, Dr Adams called 'Campbell Price over from Brighton to do a cardiograph and he did a routine examination of his heart and wasn't satisfied as to his heart condition.' This is at variance with Sister Stuart's understanding, when she said that the specialist found that his heart was all right.

The night nurse returned the same night that the Doctor had decided she should do so, and he called in last thing that night to check on Mr Hullett's condition. 'He had had a bad headache and I wasn't happy about him'. Dr Adams was rung the next morning by the nurse about half past seven to say that the patient had suddenly died. He immediately thought to himself: 'Thank goodness we have had the night nurse on, because if Mrs Hullett had been in the room when this happened I don't know what would have happened.' He went to Holywell Mount and, according to him, he told her of her husband's death: '…she jumped up and screamed and said "Has Jack died?" I just looked at her and nodded and said, "Yes, he is dead".'

She fell back on the bed and collapsed. Then she became quite impossible. I put her to bed and made her stay there and said that everything, the funeral arrangements, etc. will be dealt with by those responsible. The cause of death was cerebral haemorrhage, accompanied by coronary thrombosis.'

After Mr Hullett's death, Dr Adams called on Mrs Hullett at approximately 10 o'clock each morning, never later than eleven, and personally gave her the dose of sleeping tablets for each night. On 1st May, 1956, he was going on holiday and 'prescribed and left the prescription at Brownes for 36 tablets of Sodium Barbiturate of 7½ grains each to do her two each night while I was away until the 18th May.' After he returned from his holiday he called on 19th May to Holywell Mount and 'prescribed a further 24 tablets of 7½ grains Sodium Barbiturate which did her till the end of the month. I gave her those 36 while I was away, but the others afterwards I kept myself. Each morning I went to Holywell Mount and gave to Mrs Hullett myself, 2 sodium barbiturate tablets of 7½ grains. My instructions were that Mrs Hullett was to take these two tablets every night about 10 o'clock.' She said to Dr Adams at the end of May: 'these tablets are losing their effect, give me something stronger.' The Doctor said that he responded by giving her cachets of 7½ grains instead of tablets: 'In fact what I was giving to Mrs Hullett was the same treatment only in cachet form.' He visited every morning to give her two cachets to be taken before going to bed at night.

On the 12th June, Dr Adams decided to reduce the strength of the cachets to 6 grains and prescribed twelve, giving her two each day as before. She was still distressed and said to him 'I don't want to live'. The Doctor replied 'You must live, Jack would not want you not to live, you have got to live and I am going to help you medically and Bob Handscomb will attend to your business. I have helped you through your original bereavement, I have helped you through your troubles and I will help you always to get well, but pull yourself together.' Her response was, 'I won't and I don't want to.'

Mrs Hullett told Dr Adams that, several times after her husband's death, she took the car and went up to Beachy Head, but something stopped her and she couldn't go over. He said: 'That was Jack's influence, he would not let you do it.' She then said that, on other occasions, she thought that a car crash would be a solution but it might not be fatal, so she turned that down; then perhaps, as she was a reasonably good swimmer, she might swim out to sea and it would look more like an accident. That would be better as 'it would not come in as suicide and be a blot on her daughter, Patricia and that was the only one [person] she thought of.'

Dr Adams also prescribed Sodium Pheno barbitone grains, one eighth because Mrs Hullett said she felt ill at meal times and could not eat any food; he sent fifty to her and told her to take one or two at meal times to avoid nausea and sickness. On 25th June, the Doctor got the Sodium Barbiturate cachets down to 5 grains, but on 30th June Mrs Hullett said they were losing their effect again and he went back to 6 grains, but returned to 5 grains on 7th July, 12th July and 19th July – at this point he produced to the police, twelve cachets of Sodium Barbiturate contained in a bottle.

On Sunday 15th July, 1956, Mrs Hullett was very agitated and told Dr Adams she had had no sleep, so he gave her a half grain of Amytol to steady her and went to see the Handscombs, telling them that she was in a bad way and asked them to go up to Holywell Mount as 'I don't know what to do with her.' She had the same type of 'nerve storm' on Thursday morning the 19th July as she had on the previous Sunday morning, telling the Doctor that she 'would not go on and that she was just going to swim out to sea and probably the next I would see would be her rotting body coming in about four days after' That was the last time he spoke to her.

When the Doctor called at Holywell Mount on Friday, 20th July, he only went to the door of the bedroom. The maid told him that Mrs Hullett was sleeping peacefully and 'I could hear her normal respirations' If they had been abnormal 'I would have gone in at once and taken action'. However, he knew that she often slept late; he had even heard that she had once slept on until lunchtime. The room was in darkness with the curtains drawn and he could not see her lying in bed. 'I didn't expect her to be found in a sleep that was induced by drugs. I didn't expect anything abnormal.' The maid did not appear to be worried. Before he left the house, he told the maid to inform him if she was worried about her mistress.

That same afternoon Dr Adams was in Lewes, the county town of Sussex, attending a YMCA Committee Meeting. There was a telephone call from his receptionist at about 3.30 p.m. to tell him that the maid from Holywell Mount had rung up to say that she was very worried because Mrs Hullett was still asleep. 'Well, I at once thought, "There must be something wrong". I said, "Phone Dr Harris and tell him to go at once and I will go as soon as I can return."'

When Dr Adams arrived at Holywell Mount, it was about 5 p.m. and Dr Harris was already there and had examined Mrs Hullett. Dr Adams also made an examination: 'The heart when I examined her was regular and normal as I would expect of a person in normal health and the respirations also.' She also had a squint, 'I should not have expected to see a squint on Friday if her subsequent death was due to drugs.' But on the Friday afternoon at 5 o'clock 'I didn't suspect poisoning in any form when I examined Mrs Hullett.' He examined the room but saw no bottles on the side table, 'I did not go further, had there been any there I would have seen them.' Dr Adams told police that he had no record of the quantity of barbiturates he had prescribed for Mr Hullett and did not know if any of that supply was left over after his death.

At 9 p.m. that Friday evening Dr Adams returned to Holywell Mount. Mrs Higgins, the night nurse, had come on duty and Mrs Hullett's temperature was 102°F. He had omitted to take her temperature on his earlier visit. He decided to stay the night at Holywell Mount 'because I had had a tooth out and was feeling ill myself and I figured that if I was called out during the night I should be unable to go there.' He also stayed on for the nights of Saturday 21st and Sunday, 22nd, 'because I felt if Mrs Hullett became conscious she would have somebody there whom she could recognize and I said to Mr and Mrs Handscomb that they should be there for the same reason during the day.'

There was concern about the coma: 'On the Friday afternoon, Harris and I said, "We will have Dr Shera in the morning".' Early on Saturday Dr Adams got the nurse to collect all the urine in the bladder and he delivered the specimen to Dr Shera when he arrived and they decided that half would go to the hospital for analysis, 'in case by some distant means there was anything abnormal in the sample.' Dr Shera himself took cerebral spinal fluid by lumbar puncture and a blood specimen from a vein.

Just before 2 p.m. on Saturday, Dr Shera arrived at Kent Lodge to give Dr Adams a preliminary report, 'which I thought was inconclusive regarding the diagnosis of the urine.' The following words in his statement are important, because they indicate that some time *before 2* p.m. on Saturday, it had occurred to him that there was a possibility of barbiturate poisoning: 'So I said, in case there was any question of barbiturate poisoning, I will go and get some Megimide.' I decided to give a 10 cc dose of Megimide to Mrs Hullett intravenously, as I knew it would do no harm and it was the latest form of antidote for a barbiturate. I went to the Princess Alice Hospital, found the House Surgeon, who opened the dispensary and produced a bottle. I then went to Holywell Mount and carried this treatment out sometime during Saturday afternoon, I do not know the time. As the other tests were inconclusive I was concerned about barbiturate poisoning.'

Before Dr Shera arrived, at 12.30 p.m. on Saturday, Dr Harris arrived at Holywell Mount and he and Dr Adams examined Mrs Hullett: her temperature was between 102F and 103F and her chest showed definite signs of pneumonia; she was given a penicillin injection by Dr Harris. Dr Harris returned again at 10 p.m. and they examined the patient again and gave her crystamycin, a combination of penicillin and cloromycetin. Dr Harris gave the injection.

Dr Adams was sleeping in the house when the night nurse called him at 3 a.m. on Sunday morning as she was worried about Mrs Hullett's breathing: 'her respirations were laboured and unsatisfactory and I gave her then a coramine injection into her right upper arm.' There is some contradiction next, because at 7.30 a.m. the nurse reported that Mrs Hullett was better after the injection and she was again catheterised and Dr Adams handed the sample to Dr Harris for delivery to Dr Shera. Dr Adams then states: 'She was weaker, her temperature was very high and her lung condition was very poor and her breathing was bad.'

Dr Adams explained why he did not have Mrs Hullett admitted to a nursing home or hospital: 'she had always expressly said, "Never remove me to Esperance or hospital whatever may be my condition". Had I decided to remove her to Esperance, Dr Harris and I would still have carried out the same treatment there. Dr Harris and I thought it inadvisable to move her.' Neither did he call in a neurologist, a day nurse, or put the patient on a drip to rehydrate her.

Sunday morning 9 o'clock and Dr Adams decided to ring Dr Somerville, HM Coroner, as he 'was getting worried about the whole condition of Mrs Hullett and I wanted to know what I should do if the patient died and I felt I could not give a death certificate, as I had never had such a condition to deal with before. He said, "If you can't issue a certificate you should inform me in the usual way." I said, "Thank you, that's all I want." I asked Dr Sommerville's advice as to a post mortem examination on Mrs Hullett, in case I could not give a death certificate and I asked him could I instruct, at the expense of the relatives, Dr Shera, to make a post mortem examination as he had done a clinical investigation. I thought that this was in order as I understood it was hospital practice, and I had never had such a case before. Dr Sommerville replied, 'If you cannot issue a certificate, notify me in the ordinary way.' I said, "Thank you, that's all I want."'

9.30 and Dr Harris arrived to meet Dr Adams and see the patient. Dr Harris gave her an injection of crystamycin. She was thought to be somewhat better: the heart and the breathing.

'We felt the crystamycin was doing her good.' Dr Adams went to see her again at 3 o'clock on Sunday afternoon and reported to her friends, the Hawkins and the others at Holywell Mount that 'I am pleased that I can report some improvement.' The night nurse came on duty at 9 p.m. and at 9.30 he and Dr Harris met in the patient's bedroom. Mrs Hullett's temperature had gone up to 105F and her colour, heart and respirations were worse. Dr Harris gave her another injection of crystamycin. Dr Adams retired to bed but was called at 3.40 a.m. on Monday morning by the night nurse: 'I found respirations weaker, heart irregular, colour bad and a bubbling sound in the lung.' He gave an injection of coramine plus 100th grain of atropine to dry the mucus in the lung. At 6 a.m. the patient was worse and he decided to give oxygen; he also noticed a whiteness on the left side of the mouth, but the night nurse said she had applied some zinc and castor oil cream to the sore place on the lip – about a month previously she had had a peptic ulcer on both sides of the mouth and he had swabbed it each morning with surgical spirit. – by 7 o'clock 'respirations very weak, collapsed, cold'. Dr Adams went to ask her daughter, Patricia, 'whether she wanted to see her mother again as she was about to pass away, and she said "No, I would rather remember her as she was."' He returned to the bedroom. 'At 7.23 a.m. respirations ceased.' Dr Adams, Mrs Higgins the night nurse and Miss Reid were with Mrs Hullett when she died.

After he had related most of what had happened to Inspector Pugh, the Doctor recalled another episode: he had called to see Mrs Hullett and found he did not have the usual two cachets of sodium barbiturate to dole out to her. He said: 'I am sorry, I haven't got your cachets for the night, but I will send them up to you later.' She had replied, 'You need not mind, I have got some of Jack's which I can take tonight.' He did not ask her how many she had got, but did say: 'Don't take those, I will send you some up.' And later that day he sent his chauffeur, White, with the two cachets. He omitted, however, to collect the tablets left over after her husband's death, even though he had just been forcibly reminded that these were not only available to her, but that she was quite prepared to take them herself. He had also, when he went on holiday to Ireland on 19th May given Mrs Hullett thirty-six tablets of sodium barbiturate but he did not ask her, on his return, if she had any left over, but 'took it for granted she had followed my instructions of taking two each night.'

Additionally, and somewhat inexplicably, a fortnight before Mrs Hullett's death, he had given her 'sometimes' two calcium or A.P.C. [aspirin] tablets to take before her bath, but these were 'dummies and of no potency'.

Dr Adams thought that Mrs Hullett had 'looked upon me as one of her best friends, and she sought my advice on any topic and her relatives said I was the only one who had any influence over her.' He had no knowledge whatsoever as to whom would benefit under her will, which she had told him she was going to make with her London lawyers, 'but as to what was in her instructions, I know nothing.' She had asked him if he would be one of the executors, but 'I said I would rather not, as I wanted to have nothing to do with her finances.' She therefore asked Bob Handscomb whom he would like to be his co-executor. Inspector Pugh asked him if he knew Leslie Henson, the actor – a friend of the Hulletts – and the Doctor replied that he had met him at Holywell Mount during the past couple of years.

Despite the fact that he had decided to hold to his diagnosis of cerebral haemorrhage, Dr Adams 'would not be surprised if Mrs Hullett had taken her own life in view of what she had previously told me about how she portended to do it. She said quite definitely, "Life is Hell every day, I have been hoping that I will suffer from a serious illness or get a coronary thrombosis. I cannot go on and I will not go on without Jack."'

A copy of a *Daily Light* – a devotional book of the Plymouth Brethren – had been found beside Mrs Hullett's bedside by the police. Dr Adams volunteered that he 'gave Mrs Hullett a *Daily Light*, in the hope that she would derive comfort from it and when there were apt quotations, I often discussed them with her during my visit. I did underline a certain text which I thought would give her hope and stability.'

Did he know of anybody who wished Mrs Hullett harm, asked Inspector Pugh. 'I know of no-one who would do Mrs Hullett harm. She was a lovable type of person, a good mother, and popular with her friends.'

### Mr John Sherwood Dodd

Mr John Sherwood Dodd, an Eastbourne solicitor, first met Mrs Hullett in March, 1956, when he was instructed by her and Mr Hugh Hubbard Ford as Executors to her husband's will, to wind up his estate. He saw her several times and 'she struck me as being overwrought and in a nervous state. The loss of her husband appeared to be paramount in her mind and she consequently gave me the impression of being unable or unwilling to grasp details or to concentrate on what was being discussed at a particular moment.' Mr Hullett's estate was, even now, not finally settled. She telephoned Mr Dodd, worried that bills were unpaid, when her husband would always settle a bill within twenty-four hours of its arrival: 'I told her they would be paid as funds were released from the estate… she appeared satisfied with the position but I did not feel she really took it in…'

Mr Handscomb asked Mr Dodd to be an executor of her will and on 9th July, she attended his office, made a joke or two about 'having to be sworn'. Mr Dodd noticed that 'she appeared to be much more calm and attentive to detail… To my mind the change was noticeable.' He then organised the Trusts she wanted and her will and she came to the office to sign documents and produced her will, signed and witnessed and asked him to check it. Mr Dodd was 'favourably impressed with the change in her outlook and she was cheerful and more natural.'

Yet on the 15th July, Mr Handscomb told Mr Dodd that he was worried about Mrs Hullett's condition: she thought there was nothing else to do regarding the estate, and to retain her interest he should 'phone and tell her it was not finished. Mr Dodd telephoned her on 16th July and she seemed perfectly cheerful.

On Saturday 21st Mr Handscomb called at Mr Dodd's office to tell him that she had gone to bed and not woken up, and was in a coma. Mr Dodd (unlike Dr Adams) immediately 'asked him whether it was due to an overdose and his reply was that nobody knew but there was a suggestion of cerebral haemorrhage.' On the 23rd, there was a message for Mr Dodd to say that Mrs Hullett had died and the coroner had been notified.

### Nurse Higgins' Evidence

Nurse Agnes Higgins had a 'phone call from Miss Gartley on the afternoon of Friday 20th July, asking her to go to a case at Holywell Mount: a woman in a coma. Nurse Higgins arrived at the same time as Dr Adams and Dr Harris was already there. Dr Harris gave the patient a penicillin injection. Nurse Higgins looked around and asked Dr Adams if 'she was addicted to sleeping tablets and he said he had given her sleeping draughts but he gave them to her and there was no chance of her getting any more. By that I understood that he gave them out as required. He did not tell me what sort of drugs she was having.' The patient had shallow breathing, and the nurse thought her complexion was dark; she was cyanosed (a bluish tinge – where the blood is not properly oxygenated).

If Nurse Higgins was accurate, then she had immediately suggested to Dr Adams that this might be a case of overdose; this was on the first evening. By his own admission, he knew that Mrs Hullett had retained her late husband's supply of barbiturate tablets. As usual he did not tell the nurse what drugs he had supplied to the patient, yet the nurse was older than himself and vastly experienced. If Dr Harris gave a penicillin injection at this stage, this was presumably because he feared the development of pneumonia.

Dr Adams told Nurse Higgins to watch Mrs Hullett closely, not to move her too much 'because of her heart condition'. Coramine (a heart stimulant) had been given earlier in the day. He said that she should call him if there was any sign of change and not try to rouse her too much or move her; just to keep her warm. 'The doctors went away together and I looked around to see if there were any medicine bottles and there were none. There was a glass powder bowl on the chest of drawers and I saw one white tablet there.' She was still thinking that this was a case of drug overdose.

She also examined the patient and noticed a bruised place on the right hip, 'it was a queer looking place, it might have been caused by an injection or it might have been caused by a blow. I told Dr Adams about this and drew his attention to it and he did not seem to think much of it.' Both he and Miss Reid told her that 'she had had a fall in the garden but they did not tell me when this happened.' Nurse Higgins also got some details of Mrs Hullett's previous history from Miss Reid.

Nurse Higgins called Dr Adams at 3.15 a.m. in the early hours of Saturday morning as Mrs Hullett's breathing was very shallow and her pulse was too rapid; he gave her another injection of coramine. It was 7 a.m. when he came again, after he had had a cup of tea. They then took the sample of urine for analysis. She went off duty at 9 a.m. When she returned at 9 p.m. Saturday, Miss Reid and 'another woman' were in the bedroom with Mrs Hullett, who was lying in exactly the same position and in the same condition. Dr Adams and Dr Harris came in about 9.30 p.m. and Dr Harris gave another penicillin injection. Dr Adams was sitting in a chair. 'I asked about Mrs Hullett's condition and Dr Adams said, "It is something cerebral, it must be because of the temperature." She had a high temperature. He said, "Carry on the same tonight."' Nurse Higgins asked if she could move the patient; she got permission and gave her a blanket bath.

Again, towards 3 o'clock on Sunday morning, Nurse Higgins called Dr Adams, who gave another injection of coramine and returned to bed. At 6.30 a.m. Mrs Hullett was much worse and the nurse called Dr Adams and another injection of coramine was given. 'We both thought she would die that day.' When she returned to duty at 9 p.m. the following evening she thought there was a marked improvement in the patient's condition. The doctors arrived together half an hour later and Dr Harris gave another injection of penicillin. Dr Adams said he would stay at the house another night and left the room. He had brought a cylinder of oxygen into the bedroom that night.

Monday morning at 2.30 and Nurse Higgins had to call Dr Adams: Mrs Hullett's temperature was over 105°F. He came at once and gave her an injection of coramine and atropine, but there was no reaction, none at all from that time on. By 6.30 a.m. Nurse Higgins thought there was very little time left and called Dr Adams again. 'He came at once, looked at her and agreed with me. "We will give her oxygen as a last resort." He turned on the oxygen for me and we gave it to her in the mouth but it did not have any effect...' Dr Adams sat in a chair and Nurse Higgins suggested he return to his bedroom. 'He did so reluctantly as he was taking a very great interest in this patient...' Miss Reid came in and sat with Nurse Higgins; at 7.10 a.m. the nurse sent for Dr Adams. He came at once and they were waiting. 'We stopped the oxygen going for the end was in sight. The patient died about 7.25.'

Dr Adams instructed Nurse Higgins not to remove anything in the room, to leave everything just as it was: it would probably be a case for the coroner.

## Dr Francis Camps' Opinion

The autopsy was carried out and the findings of the analysis, together with statements and the Post Mortem Report and various tissues were passed by police to Dr Francis Camps, Professor of Forensic Medicine at The London Hospital and most famous of Home Office Pathologists.

He summarised the medical aspects of the case:-

1) G.J. Hullett was a woman of 50 years of age when she died. She was originally married to Vaughan Tomlinson who died of heart disease at the age of 45. Subsequently she married Hullett who was a rich widower considerably older than herself. This marriage was a great success and she appears to have been very happy until November '55 when he was found to have carcinoma of the colon. This condition was operated upon by Sir A. Porritt and later a complication developed which was relieved. Hullett returned home at Christmas but was never completely fit. In April he died suddenly during the night of what is believed to have been, in the opinion Dr Adams, 'cerebral haemorrhage accompanied by coronary thrombosis.' No autopsy was carried out nor was the coroner notified.

(2) Subsequent to Hullett's death Mrs Hullett was in a very poor state mentally, desperately upset and distressed. She was under the care of Dr Adams who had attended her husband and had also looked after her from time to time since her first husband's death. From his own statement she had apparently threatened suicide by throwing her-

self off Beachy Head and drowning herself but there is no evidence of any actual attempt. Dr Adams' statement about this is confirmed by another witness. Dr Adams had prescribed for her barbitone soluble (Medinal) to be taken at night and reference to Superintendent Seeking's examination of the Register of Messrs. H.R. Browne (Chemists) Ltd leaves little doubt that she had been having a steady and fairly large supply since May. It would appear that she was given 2-5 grain tablets and two aspirins in the morning by Dr Adams and took the aspirins before her bath in the evening and the other tablets (theoretically) after going to bed. No check is available as to whether she did, in fact, take them but there would be no difficulty for her to hide them away. It is a matter for comment that, in fact, no attempts have been made to recover any hypnotics used by her late husband after his death. In fact there were other barbiturates in the house. At one period in June the dose was increased to $7\frac{1}{2}$ grains and in the middle of June soluble pheno-barbitone was prescribed for her 'appetite'. From Adams' statement this was ordered in the form of 2 x $\frac{1}{8}$th grains twice a day. It seems safe to assume that she was taking barbiturates from May until her death. It seems also correct that she showed symptoms such as giddiness and drowsiness at times suggesting that she was under the influence of the drug during the daytime. Although later it is suggested that she would sleep to lunchtime in fact the evidence is that she always remained in bed late. This is not the same as sleeping and several witnesses contradict the statement that she did, in fact, 'sleep'.

(3) The evidence relating to Mrs Hullett's final illness may be stated as follows: they date from July 15th until July 23rd and are based upon Dr Adams' letter and statement with comments as to the reliability from other persons' statements. As has already been mentioned in paragraph 2. Mrs Hullett was very upset and depressed by her husband's death. From this time until her death she was under the care of Dr Adams who prescribed for her barbiturates (see separate list of prescriptions Appendix I)

(i) July 15th (Sunday) said by Dr Adams to be in a state of cerebral irritation – spasmodic twitching of face and limbs – mental excitement. He gave her Amytal grains $\frac{1}{2}$ which quietened her. Examination of the C.N.S. (central nervous system) showed no organic localising condition. She later fell down but was better later on (Note, – her maid (Yogna) describes her as very unsteady on occasions) but nobody else confirms the 'nerve storm' and Handscomb definitely does not mention it nor does Patricia.

(ii) July 16th (Monday) visited by Dr Adams (morning)

(iii) July 17th (Tuesday) visited by Dr Adams (morning)

(iv) July 18th (Wednesday) visited by Dr Adams (morning)

(v) July 19th (Thursday) visited by Dr Adams (morning) Said to have had a nerve storm during morning which passed off – she is said to have gone out but felt ill. At 10 p.m. said she had a bad headache and went to bed. (Mayo says on this morning she was asleep at 9 a.m. but at 9.50 a.m. she had washed and was getting into bed to have her breakfast. Said by Patricia to have had a headache at 10 p.m. and gone to bed early.

(vi) July 20th (Friday) 10 a.m. Dr Adams called at 10 a.m., found Mrs Hullett asleep and did not disturb her. Told maid to ring him if she was worried. 3.30 p.m. Message received by Dr Harris from Dr Adams' secretary – went at once to house. Found Mrs Hullett in comatose state and could not rouse her – lying on left side, slight squint, pupils contracted. Pulse 90 – respirations 24 – colour good. No physical signs. (Had history of Mrs Hullett complaining of severe headache previous night and slight attack of giddiness.) Diagnosed cerebro-vascular accident (haemorrhage) thrombosis or tumour. Could see no bottles etc. although he considered possibility of overdose – gave an injection of coramine (right deltoid) gave instructions to see to her breathing (regular) and that her chin did not drop. Said he would notify Dr Adams. 5 p.m. Dr Adams arrived and Dr Harris joined him. Agreed with probable diagnosis and arranged for night nurse.

At 9 a.m. 22nd July Dr Adams rang HM Coroner. She died at 7.23 a.m. on Monday, 23rd July, 1956.

(4) Summary of Dr Shera's findings. (Appendix 4)

(5) Post Mortem examination by Dr Philps (Appendix 5) I examined the organs with Dr Philps and my Opinion together with the material I removed is included in Appendix 6. There is no doubt that Mrs Hullett died of bronchopneumonia subsequent upon respiratory failure.

(6) Report upon histological examination of tissues (Appendix 7)

(7) Report upon analysis of material collected at autopsy (Appendix 8)

Opinion from the evidence in the Statements submitted to me and other examinations, the following is my Opinion:-

(1) Mrs Hullett died of the effects of Barbitone poisoning from an overdose probably ingested on the evening of July 19th. The actual cause of death was Broncho-pneumonia due to respiratorial depression due to Barbitone poisoning. Bronchopneumonia is a recognised fatal result of such poisoning. She had been prescribed Barbitone over a period in the form of -

(a) Barbitone sodium (Medinal-Veronal sodium) dispensed 1.5.56 -19.7.56 = 80 days, 1512 grains of Barbitone

(b) Phenobarbitone – 6 ¼ grains.

Although she may not have received all this, it represents a large quantity if ingested over the period and does not include any other barbiturate remaining in the house after her husband's death.

(2) From the clinical picture described (i.e. small pupils and coma without localising signs – and later the findings of Dr Shera, the picture is one of barbiturate poisoning.

(3) From the statement of Dr Adams and others there is a strong probability that Mrs Hullett might attempt suicide or make a gesture of attempting suicide.

(4) If this history is correct it might be a matter for clinical comment as to why precau-

tions were not taken to prevent any such occurrence. It is true that Dr Adams says that Mrs Hullett would not see a doctor but with such a risk, other precautions can be taken such as warning the persons around her or even insisting on psychiatric opinion.

(5) It may be a matter for comment that in view of this knowledge of Dr Adams, Barbiturate poisoning was not suspected at once. Or even after the presence of the drug was demonstrated in the urine. If the diagnosis was obscure it might have been wise to have had a further opinion. The administration of Megimide as one dose cannot be regarded as more than a gesture.

(6) The treatment given was symptomatic – (the antibiotics were given after the respiratory infection was obvious). Such treatment is quite proper for bronchopneumonia. In view of the coma and inability to take nourishment, it might be a matter for comment as to why no intravenous fluids or nourishment were given. In spite of the statements to the contrary, the report of Nurse Higgins shows evidence of cyanosis. Again it might be commented as to why no oxygen was given until the end was certain.

(7) The clinical history is one which could suggest Barbiturate intoxication. Barbitone being almost completely removed by excretion can accumulate. The attack of twitching described could be a withdrawal phenomenon.

Signed: F. E. Camps. Forensic Pathologist

## Detective Superintendent Hannam's View

Detective Superintendent Hannam considered the cases of three of the Hullett family as Dr Adams had been a legatee in the wills of Mabel, Jack and 'Bobbie' Hullett. The first wife of Jack, Mabel Theodora, had died, aged 67 years, on 20th May, 1951, leaving estate of £17,550; Dr Adams received £100. In the will of Mr Alfred John (Jack) Hullett, who died aged 71 on 14th March, 1956, leaving estate of £94,644, he received £500. Mrs Gertrude Joyce 'Bobbie' Hullett left estate of £142,000 and in her will Dr Adams received a Rolls Royce and 'we suggest that, on her death bed, he extracted from her a cheque for £1,000'.

Mabel Hullett was attended by Dr Adams at the Hullett family home, Holywell Mount, Dukes Drive, 'a magnificent house at the foot of Beachy Head'. The death certificate, signed by Dr Adams, shows the causes of death as '(a) myocardial failure, (b) high blood pressure and (c) cardio-vascular degeneration.'

Alfred 'Jack' Hullett had died, according to Dr Adams' certification, from cerebral haemorrhage. In November 1955 he had a carcinoma of the colon, was operated upon by Sir Arthur Porritt, but a complication developed and the abdomen burst and Dr Adams and Dr Snowball operated and remedied the problem. Mr Hullett returned home at Christmas but was never completely well again. Four state-registered nurses were in attendance: Miss Stuart, Miss Miller, Miss Blackwood and Miss Goodchild. Sister Stuart nursed him from 15th December until he died. He received injections of morphia from Dr Adams whilst his abdomen was painful, and he slowly improved. He was given sleeping tablets. A specialist was called in due to his having pain in his chest and breathlessness, and he said that Mr Hullett's heart was in good condition. Dr Camps had said that excessive administration of barbiturates may cause respiratory complications.

Mr Hullett had difficulty in going upstairs to the bedroom on his own and was usually helped by one of the nurses. On every second or third step he would pause and regain his breath. On the night prior to his death Dr Adams assisted him up the stairs himself, having arrived at the house to treat him for a slight heart attack. Sister Stuart saw the Doctor take him up the whole flight without pause, as a result, five to ten minutes later Mr Hullett had another heart attack. Sister Miller was on duty on the night of Mr Hullett's death and remembered Sister Stuart informing her about the distress occasioned to Mr Hullett by being hurried up the whole flight of stairs without a break. Sister Miller emphasised that she often had to assist Mr Hullett upstairs and that a rest on every second or third step was essential.

On that same evening Dr Adams returned to Holywell Mount at 10.30 p.m. and gave Mr Hullett an injection. Sister Miller saw that the hypodermic needle and syringe was filled from a bottle which she recognised as highly-concentrated morphia and she thought this rather dangerous. Having had the injection, Mr Hullett went into a deep sleep and his breathing was stertorous. She noticed him open his eyes at 6 a.m. in the morning; he dozed off again and at 6.45 a.m. heard his breathing cease, found he was gasping and within a matter of seconds he died. She informed Dr Adams who arrived at the house and walked into the patient's bedroom and, without looking at the body said, 'cerebral haemorrhage, in any case he was malignant, he complained of a headache last night.' Sister Miller told police that, although Mr Hullett was a sick man she thought his death was unusual and she was not happy about it. She performed the last offices upon Mr Hullett's body and, shortly before 10 o'clock the same morning, was passing Holywell Mount when she saw a coffin being removed from the house. Dr Camps' opinion was that 'this is an extremely doubtful death'.

Mr Charles Haine, the funeral director had received instructions by 7.30 a.m. to remove the body to his private chapel, and he went to Holywell Mount at 9.15 a.m. and met Mr Hubbard Ford, one of the executors. On 19th March took it for cremation to the Downs Crematorium in Brighton. The name of Dr John Bodkin Adams appeared on the wreath list compiled in his office.

Hannam notes that this was another case of a knowingly false statement in answer to Question 4 on the Cremation Form, the question which asks whether the doctor has any pecuniary interest in the will of the deceased. Dr Adams wrote 'No'. 'When I spoke about this instance to Dr Adams, he said, "Now, now, he was a lifelong friend. He was a very ostentatious man about his wealth. He liked to talk about it. There is no mystery about him. He told me long before his death that he had left me money in his will. I even thought that it would be more than it was."'

By the time Hannam submitted his report to Scotland Yard, there had been an investigation into the death of Mrs Bobbie Hullett by the officers of Eastbourne County Borough Police on behalf of the Coroner, an inquest had been held and a verdict of suicide had resulted. With his report, Hannam attached the transcript of the evidence given at the inquest and all the other documentation connected with the case.

Under Mrs Hullett's will, Dr Adams received her Rolls Royce limousine. One 'extremely damning' piece of evidence brought out at the inquest was that on the evening of 17th July, Dr Adams visited Mrs Hullett when she was apparently quite normal and healthy and obtained from her a cheque for £1,000 drawn in his favour. 'The action he took with this cheque was rather astounding and unfortunately he was not and never has been asked to explain the action he took following its receipt.'

Mr John Oliver, the manager of the Westminster Bank in Terminus Road, was called before the coroner and gave evidence that the cheque concerned was presented to him by post through the Midland Bank, Terminus Road, on 19th July. He was astounded to find that it had been specially and urgently cleared; his astonishment being that, in the banking world, Mrs Hullett, who had considerable financial interests, was known as a lady of substantial credit and a special clearance of any of her cheques was unthinkable. Dr Adams merely said, in connection with this cheque, that when Mr Jack Hullett was dying, he expressed a wish that the Doctor should have a new MG saloon car and Mrs Hullett gave him the cheque in accordance with her husband's wish. 'This could still not account for having the cheque specially cleared.'

Early in the morning of 19th July, the very same day that the specially cleared cheque arrived at her bank, Mrs Hullett was thought to be sleeping longer than usual and Dr Adams visited the house, slightly opened the door of her room and told the maid that, as she was breathing normally, he would let her sleep. Later in the day when she failed to awaken, the staff panicked and telephoned Dr Adams' house. Unfortunately, he was not at home and his partner, Dr Harris attended, Dr Adams arriving later. 'Adams knew full well if the evidence is to be believed that Mrs Hullett had threatened suicide on more than one occasion, he knew he was dispensing barbiturates and yet, according to him, he did not suspect barbiturate poisoning.'

Dr Shera, a consulting pathologist, was called in at Dr Harris' suggestion and he did, in fact, suspect barbiturate poisoning and told both doctors so, when he first saw the patient on 21st July. 'Dr Adams would not accept the suggestion and was quite certain that the condition was one of cerebral haemorrhage.'

Detective Superintendent Hannam draws this conclusion in his First Report:

'There appears to be no doubt whatever from a complete knowledge of this case and of the proceedings at the inquest at which I was present that Adams knew full well it was a case of barbiturate poisoning and gave no treatment whatsoever to counteract it. He gave no intravenous feeding and in point of fact allowed the patient to die without any treatment. The negligence, however, as the learned coroner directed the jury, was not of a sufficient degree to concern them, and there is no sufficient evidence to justify us in taking further action in that direction and indeed I have not made this case the subject of any personal investigation.'

Mrs Hullett was found to have 115 grains, or more than 22 tablets of barbitone circulating in her blood at the time of her death.

This was to be the case which would be prepared as the second murder charge but would lie forever in abeyance, a sword of Damocles over the Doctor's head as he was returned to practice in Eastbourne.

## The Letter to the Coroner

Dr Adams wrote his official letter to the Coroner about Mrs Hullett's death, on 23rd July, 1956, on a typewriter with a blue ribbon:

'Dear Sir,

The following are the particulars of a case I have been attending:-

    Name: Mrs Hullett, Holywell Mount, Meads, Eastbourne.

    Age: Fifty years.

History: Married about five years to an adoring and rich husband who died suddenly about four months ago after a major abdominal operation. Since then has been ill generally and lost the will to live.

I have attended her regularly and <u>strictly</u> doled out to her Sodium Barbiturate so that she could get a good nights sleep. Average dose gr. x [10] per night. She could not possibly have secreted any of this. She repeatedly refused to consult a Psychologist or other physician.

On Sunday morning, 15th July – I called as usual about 10 a.m. and found her in a state of cerebral irritation, spasmodic twitching of face and limbs, and mentally excited. I gave her Amytal gr. half which quieted her. I examined her C.N.S. carefully, reflexes, etc., but could not localize any organic disease. Her maid reported to me next day that she had fallen down during the Sunday morning but was better later on. I visited her Monday, Tuesday and Wednesday mornings, when she seemed better and had good nights sleep. Thursday morning she had another nerve storm which soon passed.

Her daughter, friend, and maid, stated later that she went out and about, but complained of feeling ill – unable to state in what manner she was ill. About 10 p.m. she said she had a bad head and felt ill, so went to bed.

Friday morning I called at 10 o'clock and her maid told me she was sleeping peacefully, so I listened at the bedroom door. The room was dark, and as her breathing sounded quite normal, I said 'I will not disturb her, but let me know if you are worried, or anything abnormal happens.'

When at Lewes Committee, about 3.30 p.m. I was rung up to say she was still asleep, so I said, 'Send Dr Harris at once' and he went immediately. I arrived about 5 o'clock and met Dr Harris and we found Mrs Hullett in a coma. All reflexes gone – small pupils, and a divergent squint. Respiration regular and heart normal. Colour good.

I arranged for a night nurse to come on duty. Examined room carefully for any empty bottles, or cartons, and found none and nothing to suggest poisoning.

The following investigations were carried out by Pathologist – Dr Shera. C.S.F. [cerebral spinal fluid] complete examination. And Blood Examination, including blood chemistry, also complete urine examination including Barbiturate estimation, which is not yet to hand.

All these investigations were inconclusive of a definite diagnosis. In view of the remote possibility of Barbiturate poisoning 10 c.c. of megimide were given intravenously. Full supporting treatment including Oxygen and anti-biotics were given.

In spite of above, after temporary improvement her temperature rose steadily to 105.5 F and her condition worsened and she died at 7.23 a.m. on 23.7.56.

In my opinion and Dr Harris's death was due to a cerebral lesion, probably involving the Pons with secondary complications in the lungs.

Because of the Pathologist's findings being inconclusive, and cremation requested, we are reporting the facts fully to you, as we do not feel in a position to issue a death certificate.

Yours sincerely,

J. B. Adams. R. V. Harris MD.'

Chapter Eighteen

# The Hullett Inquest

## 21 August 1956

The 26th July, 1956, when the police began their enquiries after the death of Mrs Hullett, was the day on which Nasser broke the Anglo-Egyptian Treaty and nationalised the Suez Canal. From that day the two affairs of Suez and Adams ran alongside one another.

The Suez Canal, which had been built between 1859 and 1869, was still under the ownership of Western shareholders. Under the Anglo-Egyptian Treaty of 1954, British troops had been withdrawn from the area, leaving it possible for Nasser to take the action he did. The British and French plotted with Israel to invade Egypt and retake the Canal: the Israelis would invade Egypt and the British and French demand a ceasefire, and when the Israelis proceeded with their invasion, they would follow in order to 'keep the peace'. The Attorney-General, Sir Reginald Manningham-Buller advised Eden against invasion, but Eden did not consult him and accepted the Lord Chancellor, Lord Kilmuir's advice. The first invasion was on 29th October, 1956 and the second on the 5th November. The Prime Minister, Anthony Eden, claimed that Nasser was a dictator comparable to Hitler, who threatened the civilised world, and expected that the country would back him. It did not, and three of his ministers resigned. After Hugh Gaitskell's, the Leader of the Opposition, call for Eden's resignation in the House of Commons, there were widespread public demonstrations backing him throughout the country.

There was great damage done to Britain's relationship with America, who were more concerned about their oil interests in Arab countries, and regarded this as an imperialist adventure. The Soviet Union had seen their opportunity to invade Hungary, sparking fears of another world war, and the cost to the economy was huge. The U.S. refused to help unless British forces were withdrawn from Egypt. On 30th November the Cabinet decided to comply, and on 20th December the Prime Minister lied to the House of Commons when he denied that the Government had known that the Israeli invasion would take place. Disgraced, and his health broken, Eden was forced to resign on 9th January 1957 and was replaced by Harold Macmillan. The whole affair had showed that Britain was now subservient to America, and dented the confidence of the nation in itself. Worse still, for the ruling elite, Eden's blatant dishonesty and his willingness to connive at such deception, was yet another nail in the coffin of the deference of the British people towards the clique who governed them. The middle classes had certainly expected government ministers to be as honest and upright as they themselves were.

The Hullett Inquest was held on 21st August, 1956 at Eastbourne Town Hall at 2.15 p.m. The first witness the Coroner called was Patricia, Mrs Hullett's daughter – so that she could leave the court if she wished and not hear all the painful evidence which was to follow. The Coroner, having been fully briefed, prepared the questions for her to make it easier. She knew her mother had been unhappy and had sleeping tablets; she suffered the odd attack of giddiness. She herself went to work from Monday to Friday and only saw her mother in the evenings, and so it was on the Thursday night, the 19th July that she last saw her. 'You went to business as usual on Friday the 20th and she was asleep in bed when you got back?' 'Dr Adams came. He was not sure what was the matter… Mother had been very depressed. She said she did not have anything to live for.' They got on very well. The Coroner remarked: 'She was well off and had you to look after, so she did have something to live for didn't she?' The reply seemed despondent: 'She did not feel she did.' Patricia had asked Dr Adams 'What's the matter with Mum?' and he had replied that he 'thought it was this pressure on the brain.'

She went to bed on the Sunday night, and about 6.30 on Monday morning heard someone walking about; she opened her door and saw Dr Adams, 'who told you that your mother would probably live only another hour. Did that surprise you?' 'No.'

Patricia did not go and see her mother. The Coroner asked: 'After she died that Monday morning did you ever think that she might have taken her own life?' 'It did cross my mind, yes.' Mr Handscomb had given her a letter from her mother, and she had read it, then they both put it in the safe.

The second witness was Dr Ronald Vincent Harris, Dr Adams' partner. That Friday afternoon at 3.30 p.m. was the first time he had ever seen Mrs Hullett, when he was called out in Dr Adams' absence. He found her in a comatose state, lying on her left side. He made a general examination to make certain there were no signs of injury. 'The only positive findings were this external strabismus (squint), the slightly contracted pupils, also the absence of reflexes.' Having been told by 'a lady there' that Mrs Hullett had had a severe headache the night before and complained of giddiness, and after checking pulse and respirations he diagnosed her as probably suffering from 'some cerebral vascular accident.'

The Coroner asked Dr Harris if he had considered barbiturate poisoning; Dr Harris had thought of this among other causes for coma, looked around the room for an empty container and questioned the lady there. He gave an injection of coramine and said he would contact Dr Adams. He returned to meet Dr Adams at the house just after 5 p.m. He attested that Dr Adams had told him nothing of Mrs Hullett's history or the fact that he had been prescribing barbiturates for her, merely agreeing that the clinical picture 'more than suggested some cerebral vascular lesion'.

The Doctors had discussed the question of moving Mrs Hullett to a hospital or nursing home and Dr Harris had recommended it, but Dr Adams said it would be unwise as she had an intense dislike of such places. Dr Harris had suggested that Dr Shera be called in to help with the diagnosis; he had arrived at 12.30 on the Saturday, found raised pressure of the cerebrospinal fluid and taken specimens. Signs of bronchopneumonic congestion had been found and Dr Harris gave the patient an injection of penicillin and one of crystomycin [compound of penicillin and streptomycin]. It was on Saturday night 'the possibility of barbiturate poisoning entered our minds. Although we had not discovered anything to suggest this.' Dr Harris had continued with the course of crystomycin but there was 'still no evidence on Sunday evening that she was suffering from barbituric poisoning?' 'No, no evidence.'

Dr Harris had been satisfied that the cause of death was bronchopneumonia and the primary cause cerebral vascular accident. It had been Dr Adams who suggested that the Coroner should be informed. The Coroner enquired whether the letter he had received, signed by both doctors, was Dr Harris' usual custom. Dr Harris replied that he had never had 'quite such a case as this'.

Dr Shera, the pathologist, had come to Holywell Mount on the 20th July about midday to take cerebrospinal fluid samples: he did a lumbar puncture, took blood and was handed a sample of urine by Dr Adams. Dr Adams had told him that the patient was 'very highly-strung, a nervy type of patient'. Dr Adams had suggested to him that the coroner should be informed. Dr Shera's own findings excluded uraemia and diabetic coma, but his department had not received any information until the 22nd that there was barbiturate present. He had not discussed the case with Dr Adams apart from the first interview: 'I had my ideas at the time.'

Dr Shera had in fact said to Dr Adams and Dr Harris: 'I can't help thinking this looks like a case of narcotic poisoning and don't you think we should have the stomach contents?' 'They were both strongly opposed to it and both strongly in favour of cerebral haemorrhage and I merely left the suggestion with them and I heard no more.'

> 'That was on Saturday when you went there that noon time?'
> 'Yes.'
> 'Of course, then afterwards you went off and made your examinations and didn't see the patient again. You got the second specimen…'
> 'That is correct, sir.'
> 'In your experience as a pathologist at hospitals here, would you like to express an opinion about the antidote treatment?'
> 'I have no experience of this latest treatment since I left hospital, but I understand that they have had some quite remarkable results.'
> 'Megimide?'
> 'There have been some remarkable cures.'
> 'What about replacement of fluid? That was essential?'
> 'Yes.'

The Foreman of the Jury asked:

> 'Dr Shera, why was the first sample of urine not tested for barbiturates?'

'Well, I don't know. I strongly suspected it in the colour of the second specimen, that arrested my attention. I wasn't actually asked to do it, but the colour of the second specimen was so remarkable that I did it off my own bat as it were. The second specimen was submitted without my asking for it. I was surprised to see it.'

Exhibit No. 15 was the request form for pathological examination signed by 'John B. Adams MD' but would appear to have been filled in by Dr Shera. Date is: July 21.7.56, headed 'Mrs Hullett', P.P. (private patient); Under: Dr Adams. Specimen: 'Urine'; Investigation suggested: 'Excess of Barbiturates', and 'Coma case' as the clinical notes. In the space for laboratory use, it shows that the presence of barbiturates is proved, and the date stamp is 23 Jul. 1956.

The Coroner questioned Dr Shera about the squint which the patient had, but which Dr Adams regarded as a symptom of cerebral accident:

'The occulus squint is characteristic in certain forms of cerebral catastrophe…'
'Were there any particular symptoms you noticed that pointed in the direction of barbiturate poisoning rather than cerebral catastrophe?'
'The absence of paralysis and the coma.'
'Would any coma be common to a case of cerebral damage?'
'In apoplectic coma the breathing is deep and stertorous, [noisy, like snoring] in this case it was shallow.'

Apoplectic coma – this was how Dr Adams' father had died – would he not have remembered hearing such breathing? Would it not be deeply imprinted on his memory? And so many patients whose deaths he had certified as occurring in this way – cerebral haemorrhage.

The fourth witness was Nurse Agnes Claire Eileen Higgins. She had gained the impression that the patient's husband had just died and she was lying in a coma. Dr Adams had arrived at the same time as herself. The Coroner stated: 'Dr Adams told you the history. Did you look around and ask Dr Adams if she were addicted to sleeping tablets?' 'Yes, Dr Adams said he gave them to her.'

Nurse Higgins said that the patient was lying on her side and in a deep sleep. Significantly, she was 'very dark coloured. There were bruises on the right thigh'. The Nurse had asked Miss Reed about these and 'she told me that the patient had fallen or something. I thought it looked like an injection; I was relieved to find it was not.' This, again, was an observation of some significance. Dr Adams just told her to watch the patient very closely and that he was sleeping at the house. There was no treatment; she could not take fluid.

Just before 3 a.m. Nurse Higgins noticed Mrs Hullett's breathing become more shallow and she called Dr Adams. He gave an injection of coramine and the Nurse had catheterised her during the night. When she returned on duty the following day, Saturday, the patient was much the same. Dr Adams told her he was rather worried about it all and said it was something cerebral. Mrs Hullett's temperature was 102°F and Dr Harris gave an injection. Nurse Higgins gave her a blanket bath and turned her. On Sunday morning about 3 a.m. the Nurse called Dr

Adams and he gave another injection of coramine. Again, at about 6 o'clock or shortly after-wards, Nurse Higgins thought the patient was much worse and called Dr Adams. The Coroner asked: 'you both came to the conclusion that she would die that day on the 22nd?' 'Yes' 'Was she cyanosed at all?' 'Her colour, yes. It is difficult to know because she was a very dark coloured woman.'

Having read Dr Adams' statement, the Coroner asked: 'On the Sunday afternoon, the 22nd she appeared much better?' Nurse Higgins replied, 'I thought she was very much the same.' 'You got the impression that the rest of the people thought that she was better?' 'I got that impression.' Dr Harris had given an injection that afternoon, while Dr Adams was sitting by the window.

Dr Adams brought a cylinder of oxygen on Sunday night.

'There didn't appear to be any need for it, so I did not use it until the morning. It was used in the early morning of Monday.'
'How?'
'Dr Adams put on the tube into her mouth.'
'Was there any mask over the face?'
'No, he put a tube into her mouth.'
'Not in the nose?'
'No.'
'That was given as a gesture more or less at the end?'
'Yes, I suppose it would be.'
'You called Dr Adams at 6.30 on Monday morning and he said "we will give her oxygen as a last resort".'
'Yes, but despite that she died.'
'She died at 7.25 on the 23rd July?'
'Yes.'

Witness No. 5 was Detective Inspector Pugh. He had identified the body and informed Dr Adams that there would be a post mortem examination by Dr Camps. 'What was his reply?' asked the Coroner. 'His reply was that he would not be there or words to that effect.' Inspector Pugh had been present when Mr Handscomb identified the body and at the post mortem examination by Dr Camps. He had, on the morning of 25th July, gone with Superintendent Seekings to Holywell Mount and examined the bedroom. The articles they found there (List B) were taken by police to Mr Moss at the Metropolitan Police Science Forensic Laboratory at New Scotland Yard.

Michael Moss of the Metropolitan Police Laboratory gave evidence on his chemical analysis of samples from the body: 'This concentration of barbitone in the liver indicates that at the time of her death the deceased had circulating in her body 115 grains of sodium barbiturate. This quantity of barbitone is in excess of the minimum recorded fatal dose.' He presented as exhibits the drugs which had been found in Mrs Hullett's possession. These included bottles of: fifty-nine tablets of Physeptone, seven 5 grain tablets of sodium barbitone, twelve one-eighth grain tablets of sodium phenobarbitone, a blue box of sixty-two tablets of phenobarbitone, an empty hypodermic syringe, clean hypodermic needles, one tablet of an anti-depressant Ritalin, and some odd tablets of Amytal, Physeptone and pheno-barbitone. It was not made clear why the syringe and needles were there.

Dr Camps' report was presented to the Court. The Coroner asked him if anyone could take twenty tablets accidentally: 'I think it highly improbable.' replied Dr Camps. He pointed out that contracted pupils occurred 'really in about three cases: lesion of pons (an area of the brain), morphine poisoning and barbiturate poisoning. There were no localizing signs as there would be for cerebral vascular accident.'

How should such a case as this be dealt with: '…it is a matter of maintaining an unobstructed airway. You must, if you have coma for any length of time. The absence of any form of nourishment will establish some introchemical upset, for they have to live on their own bodies and some form of intravenous treatment should be given.' As to the use of megimide, it 'can be given with glucose or any other form of intravenous fluid. The dose has to be more than the 10cc given. The normal method of giving it is to give intravenous saline or repeated injections through the tube.'

The Coroner asked Dr Camps how soon after taking a dose of twenty tablets would he expect coma to ensue. 'About an hour.' Would Dr Camps not have thought of barbiturate poisoning immediately in this case? He would have thought of it 'but then I may be unduly suspicious.' However, a suicide attempt should have been expected, especially with a person in a coma. With the proper treatment she might have been saved but 'it is possible that this woman would have died whatever the treatment.' The Foreman asked whether the continual taking of barbitone would cause depression. Dr Camps said that as she was taking barbitone at night, theoretically she would have been depressed during the day. Mr Bruce Cumming for the defence, asked Dr Camps whether the doctor, taking the trouble to go round daily and give the patient their daily amount of tablets, was the best way of doing things. Dr Camps said that his personal opinion was that 'It is better to get somebody else to give them and see that the patient takes them.'

The next witness was Mary Mayo, the House Parlourmaid at Holywell Mount, who had been employed there since 1950. There were periods when Mrs Hullett was up, then down: she managed to pull herself together when she had visitors. On Thursday, 19th July, she was gardening in the afternoon and then she and Mary arranged flowers indoors. About ten o'clock that evening Mrs Hullett came into the pantry, had some orange juice, gave Mary the newspapers and said she had an awful headache. She had looked her usual self and talked about breakfast the next day. Then she went up to bed.

The next morning, Friday, 20th July, Mary had gone into her room at about 8 a.m. and Mrs Hullett was asleep with the curtains drawn. She put her orange juice beside her and left the room; at 9 a.m. she took her breakfast up, put the tray on the stand and quietly left the room, going downstairs to have breakfast herself. At twenty to ten, Mary had gone up again, opened the door and seeing Mrs Hullett still asleep, thought she would let her sleep any headache off. But at quarter past twelve, Mary had gone again into the room, and started talking: 'Oh, you haven't had your breakfast'. She pulled the curtains aside and there was no answer. She went downstairs and told Cook, 'Hold back lunch'. She told Miss Reed[1] that she couldn't wake her mistress: Miss Reed said 'I will come up and have a look.'

The Coroner asked if the doctor had attended. 'Oh, yes, in the morning, at about a quarter to ten.' 'They went up to the bedroom together?' 'No, he didn't go right to the bed, he said, "Oh, we will let her sleep".' 'Did he tell you to ring him if you were worried?' 'No sir.' 'At 3 o'clock you said you had better ring for the doctor as she was still asleep and they sent for Dr Harris?' 'Yes, Dr Adams came back when he had finished, about a quarter to five. He went upstairs. I showed him to the door. Miss Reed was in the room. Later Mr and Mrs Handscomb arrived and Mary told them what had happened. She had rung Mrs Handscomb.' 'They sat in the room?' 'More or less, Sir…' 'Did anybody do anything for her?' 'Not that I know of.' 'So what happened on the Saturday was that they were all sitting in the room all day?' 'They had their meals downstairs and then we girls took it in turns while they had their lunch…'

Mary had never heard Mrs Hullett suggest taking her life; sometimes she said that life was not worth living. 'Was she ever in a drugged state during the day?' 'I don't think so Sir.' 'Was she ever confused?' 'Sometimes, yes.'

The Cook-Housekeeper, Kathleen Durrant followed Mary as a witness. She had seen Mrs Hullett on the morning of the 19th and thought she seemed better than usual. She had heard Mrs Hullett say on the odd occasion 'if I am here by then', but she was looking forward to the weekend because Miss Reed was coming to stay. Thursday was her afternoon off. On Friday morning she had breakfasted with Mary and Teresa and at 11.30 Mary had told her that Mrs Hullett was still asleep. She had gone to see Miss Reed about 12 o'clock and said to her 'Isn't it rather strange?' Miss Reed hadn't thought there was anything unusual. It was, though. It was in the evening when she was asked to prepare dinner for another two, Mr and Mrs Handscomb, that she was told Mrs Hullett still hadn't woken up. The Coroner asked Mrs Durrant if she had been surprised when Mary had told her on Monday morning that Mrs Hullett had died. 'Yes, I thought it was serious but I didn't expect her to die…'

The tenth witness was the Italian housemaid, Teresa Yogna; she had been at Holywell Mount for three years. 'You used to do the bedroom.' 'Yes Sir.' Teresa said that on Mrs Hullett's bedside table was an ash tray, pocket mirror, telephone directory and *The Daily Light*. This was a book of prayers marked with paper. Teresa had not seen any tablets on the table that day, but she usually did: sometimes three or four, one day eighteen.

The Coroner asked:

'On Thursday you saw and spoke to her. Did she appear to be all right?'
'No, she was looking strange. She looked drugged. In the morning she usually couldn't stand properly when she came down.'
'It would not be unusual for her to come down swaying about?'

---

[1] The spelling of this name varies in the police archives and the inquest transcript. I have used both spellings as they are recorded.

'No, nearly every morning.'

'Did she speak to you on Thursday?'

'Yes.'

'Did she give you the impression she wasn't well?'

'No.'

'When you went out about and you got up as usual on the Friday and during the course of the morning, several times, the parlourmaid said Mrs Hullett was still asleep?'

'Yes, Sir.'

'You went into the bedroom somewhere about lunch time with Miss Mayo and Miss Mayo went to Mrs Hullett, shook her shoulders and tried to arouse her?'

'Yes.'

'She looked very ill?'

'Yes.'

'Did you think something had happened to her? That she had taken something?'

'Yes.'

'With the others you watched her during the luncheon intervals and she appeared to get worse?'

'Yes, Sir.'

'You knew she was taking drugs every night?'

'Yes, Sir.'

'Did she say anything to you?'

'No, but I was talking with the other maids.'

'Would you say her general condition seemed to be getting worse over the last three months?'

'Yes, Sir.'

'Did she ever suggest to you that she would take her own life?'

'No, but she gave me the impression that she wished to die.'

'When you went to clear up the room after Mrs Hullett died the nurse told you to leave everything in the waste paper basket?'

'Yes.'

'You knew the doctor came every day to deliver tablets?'

'Yes, I think he was making injections.'

'Who told you that?'

'The Parlourmaid.'

'She [Mrs Hullett] used to walk unsteadily down the stairs?'

'Yes.'

'She was often late coming down.'

'Yes.'

'What time?'

'Mid-day, quarter to twelve, twelve o'clock.'

'Did she ever say anything to you about why she came down late?'

'She said, 'It is not my fault, it is the doctor's fault.'

Mr Bruce Cumming came in for the kill. Today his questions would be regarded as racist, but, even then, were hardly suitable for an inquest intended to discover the truth about a death:

'You are an Italian lady, are you?'

'Yes, Sir.'

'Have you found the circumstances of this death rather exciting? Have you been rather excited about it?'

'Yes, I found it exciting.'

'When did you first notice her stagger nearly every morning.'

'About three or four months. Since Mr Hullett died.'

'Then she got better didn't she?'

'No, she used to stagger nearly every morning.'

This was how vital evidence concerning the doctor and Mrs Hullett's condition was dismissed out of hand: this was not a young girl, but a woman of thirty-nine years.

It is worthwhile considering the statements which had been made to police by Teresa Yogna just after Mrs Hullett's death: there are two of these: the copy of the first is without a date, and the copy of the additonal statement is dated 26th July, the Thursday following Mrs Hullett's death, taken by Inspector Pugh. These statements are the most natural and least contrived of all the statements taken and this is an indication of their importance.

Teresa said that Mrs Hullett had read the *The Daily Light* every night and had it marked with a piece of paper since Mr Hullett had died. This was given to her by Dr Adams, a publication of the Plymouth Brethren. Mrs Hullett had been 'very charming' and Teresa got on well with her, but 'She never confided in me' – an indication of Teresa's transparent honesty. On Thursday, she had noticed nothing strange about Mrs Hullett; she looked a little depressed. 'I heard her in the hall and thought she was going out and said: "I have put fresh water in the vases ready for you when you do the flowers." She didn't answer straight away, but a little while after she said; "Thank you Teresa". She was far away, but she was often like that.'

On the Friday morning Teresa had kept enquiring if Mrs Hullett was up because she wanted to tidy and clean her bedroom. Up to 12 o'clock, she was not surprised at Mrs Hullett being in bed, as this was not unusual. Then, just before 1 o'clock, the Parlourmaid [Mary] had said 'things were a little strange'. Teresa had followed Mary and Miss Reed up to Mrs Hullett's bedroom. Now she gave a clearer picture of the situation in her statement than anyone else: 'I went into the bedroom with them and the Parlourmaid went over to Mrs Hullett and shook her by the shoulder and tried to rouse her and said: "Come on Mrs Hullett it's 12 o'clock," or words to that effect, but we failed to wake her, she didn't move at all, she looked like a sack. When I saw her I had a bad thought, I was horrified, I thought it was something very tragic. She didn't appear to be peacefully asleep. Her breathing was not difficult but she looked bad. Her skin was falling down towards her chin.'

Teresa had gone out on Friday afternoon and returned just after 5 o'clock, learning from Mary that Mrs Hullett was still asleep and that the doctor had been called. 'We were all preoccupied. Miss Patricia is not expressive usually and it did not appear to me that she was much worried. I wondered what Mrs Hullett had done, what had happened, because she was walking about the day before.' On the Saturday and Sunday Teresa had stayed alone with Mrs Hullett in her room for about half an hour to an hour. She 'looked at her closely and watched her. She kept on changing. Her face became smoother and she looked a little better. Her breathing was changing a lot and on Saturday her breathing seemed difficult on occasions while I sat with her, and on Sunday too.'

Her narrative concluded: 'I knew she was taking some tablets because she could not sleep and I had noticed that when she was coming downstairs in the morning sometimes she was a little unsteady on her feet and sometimes leant against the wall. She told the Parlourmaid that she could see her "small and far away." She was upset and sometimes when she was coming down she was very weak and after she had lost her husband she didn't like to live.

'I am very near to thinking, because she was taking tablets in the morning, that she might have done something to herself. When she died I thought that she had probably done it herself.'

The police realised that Teresa was an observant and careful witness, which is why they took the additional statement from her. Inspector Pugh asked her about a conversation with Mrs Henson [Leslie Henson, wife of the actor, Leslie Henson], which they had at Easter 1956. Teresa had spoken to Mrs Henson about Mrs Hullett. She was worried 'because she was looking so bad and coming down in the morning and not standing on her feet. I told Mrs Henson I didn't like Mrs Hullett taking drugs to sleep and the cook had the same idea.' Teresa had wanted her 'not to carry on with the treatment of the doctor' and to go away on holiday from Eastbourne. 'I thought that Dr Adams' treatment was doing her harm because she was not looking better.' Mrs Hullett had told them both that six months after her first husband had died, she had a red rash come out on her neck. She had got the Doctor to treat this and the spots disappeared but following this she had gum problems, went to the dentist who pulled a tooth, and had bleeding in her mouth for which the Doctor put some liquid inside her mouth.

When Teresa sat with Mrs Hullett on the first day she was in a coma – the Friday – she noticed that 'her mouth was almost closed. On the second day her mouth was a little more open and on the third day it was wider open and I could see more inside her mouth, it was like that of a dead person.' On the Sunday, 'as her head lay on a paper handkerchief, I noticed a dark place on the left inside her mouth and down from the corner of her mouth there was a streak of dark fluid like a yellow catarrh fluid running down her chin. I pointed this out to Mrs Hankin who had come into sit a while with Mrs Hullett and she wiped it away with a paper handkerchief.' All the contents of the wastepaper basket had been preserved as the nurse said they should not be touched.

Teresa added: 'If I was asked, do I think that the cause of Mrs Hullett's death was by some deliberate act of somebody or by herself, I should say by herself, because she said to everybody that she would like to be dead. She told it to everybody in the house and to friends.'

Inspector Pugh obviously then asked Teresa about Dr Adams and injections both for Mr Hullett and for Mrs Hullett because she cleaned the bedrooms. Teresa replied: 'When the doctor came to inject Mr Hullett I was upstairs after, cleaning, and I used to find a little bottle of the injection and the cotton. When Dr Adams started to come to see Mrs Hullett, nearly every day, one day I said to the Parlourmaid: 'What does he come for?' and she said 'He comes to do injections to Mrs Hullett.' I said I didn't find anything upstairs, I didn't find ampules, cotton wool or anything and this kept me wondering.' Pugh also must have asked again about Mrs Hullett's condition in the mornings as Teresa's statement finishes in this way: 'When Mrs Hullett was going downstairs one morning, she was walking unsteadily and she said: "I'm sorry I'm late, it isn't my fault, it is the doctor's fault," because I was waiting to do the bedroom. I said to her: "How do you feel?" and she said: "Oh, I don't know," in a very tired way. Then I said to her: "Do you think these tablets do you any good to your heart?" She said: "Of course I don't," and I took that to mean that she meant they didn't do her heart any good and that she realised it.'

The eleventh witness was Miss Reed. Kathleen was an old school friend of Mrs Hullett. She had previously seen her in early June and had arranged to come on the 19th July. She had arrived on Thursday evening at 6.30 p.m. and Mrs Hullett had greeted her in a normal way. They had dinner and chatted of old times, mutual friends, that kind of thing. Miss Reed knew that her friend was in a very depressed condition. They heard some thunder, and Mrs Hullett said she had a headache – she often had a headache when it was stormy. They both went upstairs.

The Coroner asked:

'Did she ever suggest taking her own life?'
'Not in so many words, but she did talk in a depressed way about wishing to die.'

Miss Reed understood that Mrs Hullett had implicit faith in the medical attention she was getting and 'she had been very unwell after her first husband died and in much the same condition and I knew she had the best advice at that time.'

'Did she ever suggest that one day she would go over Beachy Head?'
'I have heard her make that remark.'
'Did you ever suggest to her as an old friend, that it might be a good idea to start breaking the habit?' [of taking tablets]
'I had said some such thing to her and she said she thought the doctor reduced the quantity sometimes, but she had a horror of not sleeping.'

Miss Reed had not spoken to her again after the Thursday night. There was not treatment other than moistening her lips; she was not to be disturbed in any way.

'Knowing her as well as you did, as an old friend. Knowing that she had taken these tablets would you say that it would fit into the picture that she had taken an overdose?'
'Yes, I think it would.'
'Was she completely steady on her feet?'
'No, not always.'

No, there was no suggestion that another opinion should be called in. It was known that she had great trust in her medical adviser.

Mr Robert Percy Handscomb took the stand. He was one of the executors and he had known Mr Hullett for many years, and then the second Mrs Hullett. He agreed with the Coroner that 'her mental health was definitely bad.' The Coroner was pressing on the point of getting another medical opinion. Mr Handscomb had not seen the need: she had implicit faith in Dr Adams: 'Honestly, I didn't think it was necessary. I was quite satisfied.' She was apt to say things like 'Well, I may not be here, I may fall under a bus.' And he would say, 'Bobbie, you mustn't talk like that.'

As to her state of mind when he last saw her on Monday, 16th July, Mr Handscomb 'had his suspicions'. Yes, he had rather feared she might 'do something'. Even the Coroner felt obliged to ask if he did not suspect suicide when he was informed that Mrs Hullett was in a coma: 'I was rather relieved that it might be cerebral haemorrhage.' But nothing specific to the possible exchange of information with Dr Adams was enquired about. The Coroner returned to asking again if he was satisfied with the treatment or whether he did not suggest getting another opinion. 'No.'

The Coroner now asked about the estate and any bequests which the deceased had made. Half of the estate went directly to Patricia and the other half was held in trust. A Cresta car had been left to her sister; the Rolls Royce to Dr Adams. Mr Handscomb was asked if Dr Adams knew anything about the Will. 'No.'

'Mr Handscomb, on Monday morning, the 23rd, you went to the deed box and found some letters. On Tuesday the 24th I took evidence of identification from you. I said that we were worried about the death of the deceased. I asked you if you could help us then in any way. I think you said you had no idea what she had died from and were quite certain that she had never taken her own life?'

'I don't remember that statement… I don't think I would have made such a definite statement as that. I am afraid I cannot tell you exactly what I said and I don't wish to contradict you.'

'Why didn't you disclose the letter to the police?'

'Really, I didn't consider it had any bearing on the case at all.'

'You know of course that it is not for us ordinary lay people to consider whether these papers have any bearing in such a case as death, cause unknown, that has to be reported to the Coroner, and you know it is the duty of any citizen to disclose to the Coroner any details.'

'I didn't really think at the time that there was anything in these letters unusual for a person to write.'

The letters were produced and the most important of these was the one dated 11th April, 1956 and addressed to Mrs Hullett's daughter, Patricia, giving various instructions but beginning: 'My darling Patricia, If I should die and you read this please be happy for me. I love you very dearly but I don't want to go on living without Jack. You will be unhappy at first but it will pass…'

'There was one letter in which it stated: "I want you to settle the matter of the M.G. car", which was crossed out 17.7.56; the deceased became unconscious on the 20.7.56 and you didn't think this relevant?'

This letter was dated April 19th, addressed to Mr Handscomb, 'Dear Bob, If I should die please be happy… Please do one more thing for me and make sure Dr Adams' M.G. is paid for from Jack. I know it was his wish… Have done this 17.7.56.'

'I am afraid I only read that letter once and put it away.'
'What made you decide to report the matter to the police? '
'I thought, in view of the publicity, that I had better consult my co-executor who is a solicitor… On Friday morning I saw him at about quarter to nine.'
'Of course, he being a legal man, immediately advised you of the significance of these letters and to report them to the police?'

Mr Handscomb was then questioned by Counsel, Mr Peck, confirming that Mr Dodds, his co-executor knew nothing about the letters till that Friday morning, and that he was trying to avoid 'unpleasantness' for the family. At the time, Mr Handscomb did not know the cause of death, though had been told that there was a possibility of it being cerebral haemorrhage.

Mr Bruce Cumming, for Dr Adams, elicited a useful commendation from Mr Handscomb:

'It is right isn't it to say that he played a very great part in contributing to the five years she had of happiness which she had with her second husband?'
'He was instrumental in the introduction and he definitely was the cause of those four years of happiness. They were very happy indeed. After the death of the second husband he attended upon the widow continuously, almost daily. I would say that he even went beyond a doctor's duties, that he took a personal interest in her as though he were not a doctor. He did every mortal thing he possibly could for her.'

Witness No. 13 was Dr John Bodkin Adams. It is worth hearing everything he had to say, because his voice would never be heard in any trial on this case, or at the Old Bailey. The Coroner began the questioning:-

'Your name is John Bodkin Adams?'
'Yes.'
'Are you a Doctor of Medicine, MD, London?'
'MD Belfast.'
'Practising at Kent Lodge, Eastbourne?'

'Yes, Sir.'

'You knew the late Mr Hullett of course and Mrs Hullett when she was Mrs Tomlinson?'

'Yes, Sir.'

'You attended Mr Hullett when he died and have been attending Mrs Hullett ever since?'

'Yes, Sir.'

'On the 1st May, you went away for a holiday?'

'Yes, Sir.'

'You prescribed at Brownes the Chemist thirty-six tablets sodium barbiturate 7½ grains each and that was to take her over the time you were away – two at night?'

'Yes.'

'You also prescribed some A.P.C. [aspirin] tablets?'

'Yes.'

'She had two tablets of 7½ grains of sodium barbiturate beginning the 1st May, and then you came back on the 18th or 19th, you saw her, and by that time you would say that she had consumed the quantity of tablets if she had taken two each night.'

'I presumed so.'

'You then ordered twenty-four tablets of sodium barbiturate in cachets?'

'Yes, Sir.'

'You considered it was a good idea to give her a change?'

'Yes. Also with the cachets I could reduce the dose without her knowing.'

'On the 1st June you had another prescription of twenty-four – 7½ grain cachets, apart from the first thirty-six. You got those when you wanted them and doled them out two a day, each morning?'

'Yes.'

'You prescribed and dealt out to her two tablets of 7½ or 5 or 6 grains according to what you considered advisable?'

'She said it was essential for her to have her sleep, she could carry on in the day if she slept at night. So I reduced those in the cachet as far as possible and kept it down as far as possible.'

'Sometime during the 1st May to the 9th July she complained of feeling sick with her meals and you prescribed pheno-barbitone tablets one eighth grain?'

'Yes, Sir.'

'To be taken two a day?'

'Yes, Sir, when she felt sick. She carried them with her. In prescribing these quantities of barbiturates one is apt to produce large hoards and one can't guard against hoarding if you prescribe enough for a fortnight, that was why I endeavoured to guard against that.'

'Since the time of her husband's death she has been very depressed. Has she suggested suicide to you.'

'Yes.'

'Would you say that her suggestions were those of an exhibitionist or a person who would practice it?'

'After the death of her first husband she had threatened to commit suicide at that time, and after working with her for three months I managed to get her well enough to leave that all behind. This time she had likewise discussed the question or said that she couldn't go on without Jack and eventually she said, "I can't and will not go on without Jack." I reasoned with her and pointed out that it was her duty to her daughter and to Jack's memory and that she ought to live her life as he would like her to live it and interest herself in good works and take an active interest in the community. Sometimes she said "Yes" and sometimes she said "I won't and I can't go on without him." She said she had gone up to Beachy Head but something had held her back, she couldn't go over. I told her it was Jack's influence holding her back.'

'Did you consider any definite psychiatric treatment?'

'Yes, I said I wanted her to see a Psychiatrist. She refused, she said: "I want to get an illness, I don't want to get better. I'm not going to."'

'Did you take it up with her friends, that you could not carry on without a Psychiatrist's opinion?'

'No I didn't. I was dealing with her.'

'You didn't consult any specialist?'

'No, I had given her Ritalin [tranquiliser] tablets. In the mornings I gave her several courses of that. One was left in the bottle – a specimen – apparently. On the morning of the 19th July, I was earlier than usual, it was before 10. I opened the bedroom door and listened carefully to her respirations.'

'Was that customary?'

'I just wanted to satisfy myself that there was no untoward happening.'

'Did you say to the maid: "I'll not disturb her, but let me know if you are worried, or if anything abnormal happens?" Did you anticipate anything abnormal happening?'

'No, but I said: "I won't disturb her, let me know if there is anything wrong."'

This contradicted the evidence of Mary Mayo but the Coroner said nothing.

'When you got the call in Lewes and you couldn't attend, you sent your partner. You listened to your partner's diagnosis; your partner not having seen her, or known anything of her history, he came to the conclusion that there was some cerebral condition. Didn't barbiturate poisoning enter your mind at all?'

'No, she never mentioned that form of suicide to me. I thought I had the tablets tightly cleared up and she couldn't do.'

'Did you clear away the tablets her husband had? You have heard the list of tablets haven't you?'

'Yes, I didn't know.'

'Surely it is reasonable for a GP to have at first thought: "I wonder if she has taken something too much?"'

'Frankly and honestly, it didn't occur to me.'

In a statement in the Scotland Yard archives Kathleen Reed swears on oath that on that Friday afternoon Dr Adams said to her: 'I don't know where she got them from and I am not touching anything.'

The Coroner continued:

'You got a night nurse, and she appears to be a very excellent night nurse from her report. During the day the patient seems to have been left alone to completely untrained people.'

'Miss Reed was a maternity nurse and had nursing knowledge.'

'You as a doctor with a very well-known patient in your charge would know it was unwise to leave the patient in the hands of unqualified people.'

'I gave them the number of the Hostel [sic]. I left it to them.'

'During the course of the day, you didn't consider any replacement of fluid loss intravenously?'

During the course of what day does the Coroner mean? Nurse Higgins' Nursing Records show that by 5 a.m. on Saturday morning, Mrs Hullett was 'sweating a good deal.' The same condition is noted at 11p.m. Saturday 21st, at 5 a.m. on Sunday 22nd and at 1 a.m. on Monday 23rd. But Dr Adams replied:

'She wasn't perspiring. She had lost no fluids and I thought to leave her quietly. If it was a cerebral condition it was best to leave her quietly and watch her carefully.'

'Why did you get your partner to give all those injections?'

'He had the stuff there and I said: "It's all right, you have got it, you can give it to her."'

'This question of Megimide. I understand you went to the hospital and got some megimide and they opened a new box for you. Did you read the instructions.'

'No, I didn't.'

'You knew all about it?'

'I understood from those who used it that a 10cc was the dose and if it didn't do any good not to repeat.'

'Here you have a patient who is unconscious, who you suddenly think might have barbiturate poisoning, you give 10cc Megimide. Did you add any Daptazole with it?'

'No.'

'If you read the instructions you will see 'Inject 1cc every 3-5 minutes until the recovery. Total dose average is 100 to 200 cc.' Do you consider that, under the circumstances you did all that you possibly could?'

'The House Surgeon who used it, and had told me about it said that 10cc was the dose, and if it didn't work it would be no use.'

'How long have you been a qualified doctor?'

'33 years.'

'You asked the advice of the House Surgeon?'

'If I hadn't asked the House Surgeon I wouldn't have been aware of it.'

In a statement in the Scotland Yard archive, Dr Cook, the House Physician at the Princess Alice Hospital stated under oath:

'I told Dr John Bodkin Adams how to give an intravenous infusion for megimide in doses of 1 cc every five minutes. I asked Dr Adams if he had a case of barbiturate poisoning and he said he had.' Dr Cook gave Dr Adams 100ml of Megimide.

But Dr Cook was not called to give evidence at the Inquest.

Neither did the Coroner raise the important point that Dr Adams was qualified as an anaesthetist and that he would commonly have used barbiturates for anaesthesia. Additionally, the main use for Megimide was as an antidote in cases of barbiturate overdose in anaesthesia. Is it believable that a doctor who spent eight hours a week at the Princess Alice Hospital as an anaesthetist would not know about this development?

The Coroner continued on his planned course of questioning:

'Did you on Sunday afternoon say to the relatives there was a decided improvement?'
'Yes.'
'Did you believe that?'
'I did.'
'When you ordered oxygen given by the mouth, you will admit it is a mere gesture? You didn't give any oxygen until the last moment?'
'There didn't seem to be any necessity for it.'
'The antibiotic that you and Dr Harris carried out seemed to be all that was required for a bronchopneumonia. When did you first come to the conclusion that there was the possibility of barbiturate poisoning?'
'I didn't really come to that conclusion, but when Dr Shera came to me on the Saturday afternoon and said that the coma wasn't due to diabetes or kidneys, and then I had the preliminary report for cerebral spinal fluid, which was not conclusive, then I wondered. We had a coma which was not diabetes nor kidneys, then I thought, it may be the odd chance that it was that. I thought I will go for some Megimide, which I had heard was the best antidote for it. I knew it would do no harm and I thought it was doing the right thing, to give it.'
'Did you consider calling in another opinion?'
'I didn't really. By that time the lung condition was so active it seemed to account for it.'
'Did you expect her to die?'
'On Sunday at 3, she seemed to be a bit better and it [temperature] had dropped to normal. She didn't seem embarrassed [sic]. Her colour was better, her temperature had dropped and I thought well, this is fine.'
'She decided that she should settle for the M.G. car, that your late patient, Mr Hullett had promised to give you and this cheque was paid to you, when?'
'On Tuesday evening the 17th June.'

The Foreman of the Jury questioned Dr Adams:

'When did the patient tell you that she didn't want to go to hospital?'

'Within a fortnight after her husband's death.'

'Why within a fortnight?'

'She was ill at that time and she said to me, "If ever I am ill, don't send me to Esperance or the hospital."'

'Was that because of her experience of her husband?'

'Yes, of both husbands.'

'How long did you stay at the house?'

'When she was very ill I was there about half an hour on the Friday afternoon because I had to go to the dentist to have my tooth out and then I went back again and at 9 o'clock and then I went home and brought my things about 10 and stopped until 7.30 in the morning, when I left in the ordinary way and came back again during the day on two or three occasions and each night.'

'In this case, having such exceptional knowledge of your patient didn't you consider suicide at that time?'

'Not at all, it came out of the blue and to me it was quite a surprise.'

'You considered her illness to be a perfectly normal one?'

'Yes, intensely septic infection as her temperature soared up so and her blood count. Acute septic infection, that took one's mind off other things.'

'Is it a fact that both you and the nurse were there in the house during the night and thought Miss Reed had nursing knowledge?'

'I understood she had, at the time, and had asked them to get day and night cover from the Hostel.'

'You have taken exceptional precautions by night, and no precautions by day?'

'By night, everyone was in bed asleep. So that one had to have a professional person on. The first night I was very late myself, having had a septic tooth extracted at quarter to six. I had to go home to my bed and lie down for two and a half hours before I could do anything.

When I got back I said to the nurse: "If this patient shows signs of coming round I wouldn't be able to get up and come round tonight from my house." And that was why I said the first night I would stop. I had anticipated that I would probably get a night call and I thought if I was there on the spot I could get up, but if I wasn't there I would not be well enough to come round.'

'You did take a particular interest in this patient. Would you agree that you could have obtained the best possible advice within the country within a few hours, either on Friday night or Saturday morning?'

'Yes.'

'You didn't consider then the condition was serious, that you needed another opinion?'

'No the blood count was ample – a satisfactory condition.'

'If you wished to consult at the hospital would you expect to get the report rather sooner than Monday, if it is put in on Saturday?'

'Yes.'

'Did you ring up to find out what had happened to the report as it was a matter of urgency?'

'No I didn't. It didn't occur to me.'

'Then, whilst you had your suspicions that something was a little untoward in the case, you went to the hospital to consult on the Saturday but there was no report. What treatment did you give the patient between Friday night and the time of death?'

'Friday – I gave her an injection for irregular respiration. Saturday we gave her crysto-mycin, Sunday 3 a.m. coramine, Monday about 6 o'clock, atropine, that was the first time she showed any fluid in the tubes and that was to dry that up. The nurse did the necessary attention as to bed bath.'

'Did you see the nurse before she left on Saturday morning?'

'Yes I did.'

'Did she have any information for you about the state of the patient?'

'She said she was better after the injection.'...

Mr Bruce Cumming questioned his client:

'At one time you did consider the possibility of some narcotic poisoning and at that stage you did take action by the administration of Megimide. You knew that Megimide was the latest antidote for narcotics and you did go up to the hospital in order to obtain a supply?'

'Yes.'

'Did you, for good or ill, seek from the House Surgeon at the hospital information as to the way in which Megimide was administered at the hospital?'

'Yes, I asked him what was the usual dose and he told me – 10 cc.'

'So it is the result of that enquiry that you took the course you did?'

'Yes.'

'The learned coroner has referred you to the printed instructions which are issued by the makers of the product. In fact, again for good or ill, did they ever come into your hands?'

'No.'

'Did you think, when prescribing Megimide that you were acting in accordance with sensible reasonable practice?'

'Yes, I only wanted to do the best.'

'At the time, what was your conclusion as to the diagnosis?'

'I agreed with Dr Harris that there was some cerebral trouble there and as the lung trouble became more acute we focused more on the lung condition.'

'You identified that part cerebral condition as being a probable lesion present and concluded it was in the region of the pons, because of the condition of the pupils and the temperature. The pons is the middle brain?'

'Yes.'

'What influence did the pathological reports which you got from Dr Shera have on your mind?'

'Increase in the white cells confirmed in my mind the lung condition…'

'In your experience in practice have you at any time come across cerebral catastrophe occurring suddenly in people of about 50?'

'One unfortunately recently has had that experience in the younger age group.'

'Is there in fact anything by way of therapy treatment that one can do which is likely to be helpful in a case of a patient who is lying in a deep coma due to mid brain lesion?'

'See that they have clear airway, change the position gently at intervals, turn from one side to another. Be certain of having a clear airway and free respiration.'

HM Coroner did his utmost to avoid any sort of criticism of the Doctor, asking if he felt under any sort of duty to call in a consultant physician:

'I felt that there were ample signs and symptoms in the lung to account for it and I didn't think anything else could be done and the condition I felt was sufficient to account for the symptoms.'

HM Coroner encouraged him:

'For years you have been trying to do your best for this lady?'

'Since I met her first after the death of her first husband I have been her attendant when required.'

The Coroner turned to the matter of the pathological reports and the fact that Dr Shera had sent part of the specimen for tests for barbiturates. Leading the witness he asked if Dr Adams have expected them to contact him if they had any suspicion regarding narcotic poisoning. He was not, of course, criticising the hospital…

'Any doctor looking after a patient in a serious illness would take steps to get the result.'

'Did you before the death – did it ever occur to you that there was any pathological evidence which may have helped you had it become available in your diagnosis?'

'I don't think so.'

Mr Bruce Cumming rose to his feet to deal with a matter of vast importance to the inquest:

'In the letter which eventually came to light dated April 19th which had the last three lines scrawled out about Dr Adams' M.G. "Make sure Dr Adams' M.G. is paid for from Jack. I know it was his wish." That has in fact been no secret in the circle of people

around this lady that the husband had been very anxious for you to have the M.G. car.
Mr Handscomb knew all about that didn't he?'
'That is right.'
'The question was how that should be dealt with, by the estate or by the widow herself?'
'Yes. There is no secret about that.'

The next witness was called, John Oliver, Manager of the main branch of the Westminster Bank in Eastbourne. The Coroner asked if a cheque was drawn on the Westminster Bank, Meads branch, for £1,000 in favour of Dr Adams and presented by post through his bank, Midland Bank on the 19th July. Mr Oliver agreed.

'Is that normal clearance?'
'No sir, that would be an unusual clearance, in other words we call it special clearance.'
'That would be within the knowledge of the presenting banker?'
'Normally, it would mean that there was some necessity for expediting payment of the cheque. We received it by post on the 19th. It would have been presumably paid into the Midland Bank on the 18th and they would have dispatched it to us by post that day. Normally had one used the usual course, it would not have been paid in till the 19th, we would have got it back on the 20th and the fate of the cheque would not be known to the other banker until the following day. This was sent direct and we were asked to 'phone the fate.'

Dr Adams was not asked one question about his asking for special clearance for this cheque and the timing. The obvious inference was that he was expecting her to die.

Mr Oliver was not asked if he was surprised at this special clearance – as indeed he had been according to his statement.

Detective Superintendent Hannam was called:

'The Chief Constable has invoked the help of Scotland Yard and I understand that you are in charge. Do you wish me to adjourn this inquest?'
'I have no application to make to you.'

This seems truly amazing. Who had instructed that this travesty of an inquest should continue?

The Coroner turned to instructing the Jury in their duty: that they should clear their minds of all they had heard and read about Mrs Hullett's death. Then that they should accept the evidence of the tests and of Dr Camps which showed that the death was due to barbiturate poisoning of more than twenty tablets. The question was how did she come to take these tablets. The verdict could be one of three possible: accidental taking of an overdose, suicide, and, if suicide was the verdict, then the state of melancholy at the time she took the tablets.

The Jury were also to consider whether there was any negligence in this case. There are degrees of negligence ranging from 'criminal negligence' – negligence so gross that it falls just short of murder. The Court was not concerned with the lesser degree of negligence but the Coroner emphasised that for a verdict of 'criminal negligence' 'one wants negligence of so gross a nature that the person guilty of it does something or attempts to do something with a reckless disregard for human life and public safety.' Doctors have a special duty for the care of their patients, who have a right to expect a certain amount of skill – 'Not a great deal of skill, luckily for most of them.'

The Coroner drew the Jury's attention to the letters which Mrs Hullett left; it was up to them to decide if these were ordinary letters or suicide letters. 'You will remember that Mr Handscomb thought they weren't suicide letters and hence his very misguided action in concealing them.'

The Coroner then proceeded to give a succinct account of the events from the evening of 19th July, telling the Jury that Dr Harris quite reasonably 'comes to the conclusion that there must be some cerebral catastrophe' as Dr Adams told him nothing of the patient's history, and 'You may consider it extraordinary that the doctor, knowing the past history of the patient, did not at once suspect barbiturate poisoning. If he had suspected barbiturate poisoning, possibly the circumstances might have been otherwise.' Dr Adams had rightly asked Dr Shera to take specimens and carry out investigations; these had not been helpful because the finding of barbiturate in the urine was not known until after the patient's death. Normal treatment for cerebral stroke was carried out; the amount of Megimide was 'a mere gesture' and the oxygen of no importance. 'There you have treatment that you may consider was not the form of treatment that a reasonable person should expect from a reasonable doctor, but on the other hand, if the doctor was convinced in his own mind that there was no question of barbituric poisoning, then the treatment was quite normal for a cerebral catastrophe.'

Returning to the point about 'criminal negligence', the Coroner instructed the Jury that 'in considering criminal negligence one must know and believe and have proof that the death of the deceased is the direct cause of the doctor's negligence.' In this case they would 'no doubt come to the conclusion that this is not the case. If there has been an extraordinary element of careless treatment in so far as the doctor knew the history of the patient and then did not disclose it, that is not criminal negligence.'

The reason he had to instruct them very clearly on this point was because 'certain cheques have come out and other matters, the question might cross your minds as to motive. If there was a motive in any particular case, motive does not convert negligence of a lesser degree into negligence of a more serious degree.' This was the law.

It was a matter for the Jury to decide if the deceased died from her own act, whether this was accident or suicide. If their verdict was that of 'suicide', was the balance of her mind disturbed or did she just have no desire to live, and, in deciding this they were to consider whether the cheque she wrote on 17th July was in anticipation of suicide and whether or not the letters were suicide letters. The other course open to the Jury was to return an 'Open' verdict: 'If you do not think that she took the tablets herself, return an Open verdict. But there is no evidence that anybody else gave them.'

The Jury retired to consider their verdict. When they returned the Coroner asked the

Foreman if they had reached their verdict: 'We have, Sir.' 'Unanimously?' 'Yes, Sir, Our verdict is that she committed suicide.'

So the Coroner proclaimed; 'The verdict of the Court is that Gertrude Joyce Hullett died on the 23rd July after swallowing numbers of sodium barbiturate tablets of her own free will, and so the finding be 'SUICIDE'.

One of the Exhibits, the cheque for £1,000 made out to Dr Adams by Mrs Hullett disappeared from the Courtroom, never to be seen again. Scotland Yard carried out an investigation into its disappearance but did not discover what had happened to it.

It is quite clear that this Inquest should have been adjourned because this case was then prepared as a charge of murder against Dr Adams – the case that was to hang over him for the rest of his life when the Attorney General decided to enter a *nolle prosequi* on the charge that he murdered Mrs Hullett: the Queen withdrew her consent to bringing the prosecution – technically he was never tried for a murder he was charged with.

## The Disappearance of Evidence

The £1,000 cheque signed by Mrs Hullett and made out to Dr Adams, produced by Mr Dodd, the Bank Manager and various prescriptions were never seen again after the Inquest. Superintendent Alexander Seekings, Deputy Constable of Eastbourne made a statement, taken by Detective Superintendent Hannam on 18th January, 1957. Following the death of Mrs Hullett, he had taken charge of enquiries into the circumstances of her death, assisted by Detective Inspector Pugh.

In the initial stages of the enquiry he visited Browne's the chemists at Memorial Square on two occasions to check on the drugs prescribed for Mrs Hullett, examining the register and against it the prescriptions written by Dr Adams, particularly those for barbiturates. This was on the 25th July and he returned the next day, going back to prescriptions issued in 1954. He took possession of what he thought were all of the prescriptions, returned with them to the police station, put them in an envelope without counting them and handed them to Pugh to put in the file of the case. He had seen none of these again until the week previous to his statement in January, when there were two of them and the envelope in the office used by Hannam.

As for the cheque for £1,000, Seekings had 'no knowledge of this cheque being in Police possession.' The last time he had seen it was at the Inquest when it was 'passed across the table to Counsel representing Dr Adams. I do not know what happened to it and I have not seen it since.'

This statement was taken in the presence of the Chief Constable of Eastbourne.

Why anyone would have thought it useful to remove and destroy the £1,000 cheque is a mystery because there was plenty of evidence to show that it had existed and been expedited by Dr Adams. It does seem that it was an attempt to sabotage evidence as it is not the only occasion that this occurred.

When the police gathered evidence for the charge of the murder of Mrs Hullett against Dr Adams, the exhibits included: No. 10 – the ledger entry for Dr Adams' No. 2 Deposit Account with the Midland Bank, showing the paying in of the cheque for £1,000 from Mrs Hullett on 18th July, 1956, the day before she consumed the overdose of barbiturates; No. 12 is the Deposit Slip of Midland Bank in Dr Adams' handwriting with his signature also showing the paying in of the £1,000 cheque on 18th July; No. 13 is the Midland Bank office voucher showing that the cheque was sent direct to Westminster Bank, Meads, G.J. Hullett's Account on 18th July and underlined the words 'please phone fate', proving the special clearance of the cheque; No. 14 is the Midland Bank slip showing that the cheque was specially cleared by 19th July. No. 11 was the missing cheque itself.

## The Enquiry continues for the Murder Charge

Detective Superintendent Hannam continued with his enquiries: a further statement was taken from Dr Ronald Harris, Dr Adams' partner. Dr Harris was obviously very alarmed as Dr Adams was, at this stage, awaiting trial for the murder of Mrs Morrell. Dr Harris had not considered, when he was questioned by police on the first occasion and indeed at the Inquest into the death of Mrs Hullett, that any criminal offence might have been considered, and he had naturally been prepared to support his senior partner and 'if anything in what I have said appeared evasive or to contain possible inaccuracies, that is the only explanation.' He now wished to be frank: '…if Dr Adams did not intentionally mislead me in connection with Mrs Gertrude Hullett, he most certainly kept back material facts which I should have known about and which would have assisted me, and Adams and I together, in a proper diagnosis and treatment…' At no time did he have the slightest idea that barbiturates were being delivered to Mrs Hullett's house and that they were under her control. He had asked Adams if there was any possibility of her condition being due to an overdose of drugs and 'he told me that was not possible, as he was giving her a sleeping cachet each day.' He had not been told of Mrs Hullett's suicidal tendencies by Adams or anyone else in the house. 'Had I known that Mrs Hullett had suggested suicide or that she had access to excessive quantities of barbiturates, I should certainly have insisted that she was removed to hospital.'

The reason Dr Harris had continued to visit Mrs Hullett was because Dr Adams had asked him to cover him. Throughout the course of her illness 'Dr Adams was absolutely dogmatic that she was suffering from a cerebral haemorrhage and I did not feel that I was in a position to disagree with the diagnosis, with his superior knowledge as an anaesthetist of barbiturates and I felt that the treatment was entirely his responsibility.' Dr Harris was asked why he gave the antibiotic injections that were given to Mrs Hullett. He replied, 'I did so because I was doubtful as to whether they would have been given at all if I had not done so.'

Dr Harris said that he had signed the letter which Dr Adams wrote to the Coroner, but all the information about Mrs Hullett's previous history had been supplied by Adams and he had had no knowledge of Mrs Hullett as a person or as a patient.

Chapter Nineteen

# Hannam's Encounter with Dr Adams

## 1 October 1956

*At 9 p.m. on Monday, 1st October, 1956, whilst walking through Bolton Road in Eastbourne, I saw Dr J.B. Adams drive his motor car into his garage entrance in Lismore Road at the back of his private house. As I passed the garage he was just closing the gates. It was a casual, unplanned meeting. I said to him, 'Good evening, doctor, did you have a good holiday in Scotland?' Dr Adams said to me, 'Hello, yes, it was very good; only one afternoon when we were unable to get about.'*

*The Doctor then went on at great length to describe his holiday, mentioning various places such as Angus and Pitlocherie [sic] in Scotland, and said that he was one of a party of ten who went shooting, and that together they had a very good bag. It was a type of holiday he enjoyed immensely as a complete relaxation. He then went on to tell me about his life and I found him extremely loquacious. He said his father died when he was 14 years of age and that his brother died very suddenly, saying, 'like that', and he snapped his fingers. He said he studied medicine and worked too hard and had a breakdown. It was thought he had TB. When he was better he returned and did two years study in one, and then qualified. He told me he got a good job in Bristol under Dr Rendell [sic] Short. Whilst he was there he saw a position offered in Eastbourne and he wrote for it and had a reply back saying it was filled. Later on he said, he received a letter asking him to attend for an interview and sent photographs and testimonials. He said that one Sunday he was on duty at Bristol and he met Dr Rendell Short who asked him about the Eastbourne appointment and advised him to take it, and that was how he came to Eastbourne in the first place.*

*Dr Adams told me he had a Christian upbringing and his parents and himself were members of the Brethren movement. He told me he felt certain it was God's guidance and leading which brought him to Eastbourne. He mentioned the rumours circulating in Eastbourne and said, 'Those who know me know it is all untrue and those who believe it, well, there is nothing I can do. I think it is all God's plan to teach me a new lesson.'*

*Dr Adams went on to speak of his mother, and told me he found her a cottage at Lower Dicker and then she died and he described how he managed to get her back to Ireland via Stranraer because she did not want cremation and she wanted to be interred with her husband. He told me that he had interred her* with his father. Then he told me his cousin, who was a very sweet Christian soul, died after six months of terrible agony with cancer and said to me, 'I thank God for the sweet memory of such a dear woman. It is an inspiration to me even now.'

This type of conversation continued for some minutes and then the Doctor said to me, 'You are finding all these rumours untrue, aren't you?' I said to him, 'I am sorry to say that it is not my experience, Doctor.' He said to me, 'It is strange. I live for my work. I gave a vow to God that I would look after my National poor patients. I am not taking on any more, but I have kept my vow. Day and night I will turn out for them and I never asked anybody else to do it for me. I think this makes people jealous of me. I get up at 6.30 each morning, listen to the 7 o'clock news, then visit a patient or go to the Esperance. I have two patients there now, then I go to the hospital and get back here at 9 for private patients. Gwynne comes in then if he wants to. I go out until 12, then see private patients till 1, then I am out till about 10 p.m. This afternoon I went to Brighton for the general meeting of the YMCA with which I have always been connected. I am a bit earlier coming in tonight because I am a little tired after the journey. Then I do my desk till 12 o'clock. I also do more surgeries than my partners. If only the others worked as hard as I do. What have you been told about me?'

I said to him, 'I wonder how all you are telling me reconciles with forging Dr Emslie's name on the vaccine prescription for Mr Devey and the ones for Mrs Crisford and Mrs Galloway.' Dr Adams said to me, 'That was very wrong, the vaccine one. I have had God's forgiveness for it. All of them were only to help poor National Patients. I love helping these National patients for I gave a vow to God I would. The Health people can afford it and the vaccine would have cost a lot. You have not found anything else?' I said to him, 'Doctor, I have been anxious about some of the gifts you have received under wills from your patients.' He said to me, 'A lot of those were instead of fees, I don't want money. What use is it? I paid £1100 super tax last year.' I said to him, 'Some of the staff of Mrs Morrell told me that when you assisted her to walk in exercise you frequently took her to a valuable chest of old silver and admired it. She left that to you in her Will.' Dr Adams said 'Mrs Morrell was a very dear patient. She insisted a long time before she died that I should have that in her memory and I did not want it. I am a bachelor. I have never used it. I knew she was going to leave it to me and her Rolls Royce car. She told me she had put it in her Will. Oh, yes, and another cabinet.' I said to him, 'Mr Hullett left you £500.' And the Doctor said, 'Now, now, he was a life-long friend. He was a very ostentatious man about his wealth. He liked to talk about it. There is no mystery about him. He told me long before he died that he had left me money in his will. I even thought it would be more than it was.'

I said to him, 'I am thinking of Mr Priestley Downs, Doctor. If what I am told is true, you got him to include you in his Will when he was very ill and even suggested the amount to him.' The Doctor said, 'Superintendent, that is where rumour can get to. He told me several times that he wanted to look after me and leave me something. He forgot to sign his Will until he was ill and he told me then and other people that he must leave me something. I did not want it.' I said to him, 'I saw in the Will of a relation of Mr Priestley Downs, a Mrs Ware, that a £100 legacy to you had been increased to £1,000.' He said, 'She increased it twice. People are grateful for my kindness. I told her I did not want it but she said I had been so kind she must leave me something. It was no secret she was leaving me something. Every one of these dear patients I have done my very best for. I have only one thing in life, and God knows I have vowed to Him I would, that is to relieve pain and try to let these dear people live as long as possible.' I said to him, 'Doctor, I have examined the cremation certificate forms you filled in in your own handwriting for Downs, Ware, Jack Hullett and Mrs Morrell and you have said on them that you were not, or that you were not aware, that you were a beneficiary under their wills. That is quite a serious offence.' Dr Adams said, 'Oh, that wasn't done wickedly, God knows it wasn't. We always want cremations to go off smoothly for the dear relatives. If I said I knew I was getting money under the Will they might get suspicious and I like cremations and burials to go smoothly. There was nothing suspicious really. It was not deceitful.' I said to him, 'I hope I shall finish these enquiries soon and we will probably have another talk.' He said to me, 'Don't hurry, please be thorough, it is in my interests. Goodnight and thank you very much for your kindness.' I left Dr Adams at 9.35 p.m. and immediately recorded the notes of that conversation.

Chapter Twenty

# Suez Crisis

## July – November 1956

*There are events in the history of nations which gather about themselves
such a weight of significance that they are conveyed in a single word.
The Fifties added to their number the word Suez.*

Hopkins

## Suez Crisis July–August 1956

It is now almost fifty years since the Suez Crisis, but even those who were young at the time remember that it aroused passions and divided the nation more than the Iraq War – and not along party political lines. I recall a fellow fourteen-year-old pupil at school putting a poster of the photogenic Prime Minister, Anthony Eden, on the classroom wall to demonstrate her support.

Three years earlier, at Primary School, there had been the last celebration of Empire Day which I remember at school, when we sang 'I vow to Thee, my Country', raised the flag and considered the vast number of pink patches on the world atlas which marked the countries of the British Empire. It was always a celebration of civilisation rather than an exhibition of jingoism and we felt privileged to have been born British.

In 1938, Eden had resigned in protest at Chamberlain's appeasement of Hitler and during the war became first War Secretary and then Foreign Secretary again – as he had been before the war – in Churchill's wartime administration. Churchill might have been expected to retire after the Conservative general election defeat in 1945, but he continued on as leader.

Eden did not become Prime Minister till 1955. He was a notable parliamentarian and was much respected as a politician and statesman. He also had charisma. The nation acclaimed him in spite of his lack of practical ministerial experience in a domestic office and the fact that he had never been involved in passing legislation. He wished to continue directing foreign affairs. His mistake was to appoint Harold Macmillan as his Foreign Secretary. Macmillan was to prove in no way malleable. After only a few months, and to his considerable annoyance, Eden moved him from the Foreign Office to the Treasury. Eden appointed Selwyn Lloyd in his place: 'If Lloyd was not entirely a puppet, he was very close to being one.'[1]

The tactic called Eden's judgement into question. The Foreign Office portfolio had become extremely onerous. There were problems in Egypt, Iran (where the Anglo-Iranian Oil Company had been nationalised) Libya, Kenya and Cyprus. Egypt had been causing problems to the British since 1951: the Muslim Brotherhood had been waging war on the troops who guarded the Suez Canal – by the end of the year there were 80,000 stationed there. Open warfare had broken out by January 1952, followed by days of riots and attacks on British and European property. King Farouk of Egypt dismissed his Prime Minister, leading to his fall and abdication in favour of his infant son, but on 18th June 1953, Egypt became a republic. In July 1954, the Conservative Government agreed that its troops would leave the Suez Canal in two years' time, though retaining the right to return if free passage of the canal was endangered. It was becoming increasingly obvious that Britain could not afford to maintain all the obligations of empire. America had managed to seal its influence in the Middle East with an agreement between the Saudi King and Aramco to share the profits of Saudi oil; Britain tried to reinforce its influence with the Baghdad Pact, described by Eden as 'a Middle East NATO', involving the West with Iran, Iraq, Pakistan, Jordan and Turkey. President Nasser of Egypt was opposed to the Pact, which he saw as anti-Egyptian, and he was backed by the Soviet Union. At the same time, Eden was urging President Eisenhower and John Foster Dulles, the U.S. Secretary of State, to join a Western consortium to finance the Aswan Dam for Egypt. The proposal fell apart because Washington would not honour the loan agreement having discovered that Nasser was discussing military aid with the Warsaw Pact countries.

The growing rise of Arab nationalism was demonstrated on 2nd March, 1956, by the young King Hussein's dismissal of General Sir John Bagot Glubb, 'Glubb Pasha' from the command of the Arab Legion of Jordan's Army. When Nasser heard from Egypt's Ambassador in Washington that Dulles had told him on July 19th that the U.S. would not finance the Aswan Dam without military alignment, on July 26th he announced, to a vast crowd in Alexandria, the nationalisation of the Suez Canal, military occupation and the seizure of the Suez Canal Company's property, by force. The Canal dues would finance the Aswan Dam. Nasser's assurances that the canal would remain open to international shipping appeared hollow as he had immediately banned Israeli ships. Britain and France were equally incensed at his actions.

Over two-thirds of the fuel supplies of Western Europe passed through the Suez Canal and nearly 5,000 British ships a year; three-quarters of all Canal shipping belonged to NATO countries. Britain had only six weeks' oil reserves. Britain and France believed that the oil supplies were so vital they should fight for them; the Americans were sympathetic but their interests were not so involved that they would go to war, and thought that their lack of support would deter Eden from military action. France were equally furious at Nasser's perfidy, particularly since they had been defeated in Indo-China and were faced with conflict in Algeria; they turned

---

[1] Rhodes James

to Israel for assistance, unbeknown to the British. Neither Britain nor France had recognised that their status and power in the world was changing and that America was now the dominant Western power.

Both Parliament and the Press condemned Nasser and on July 27th, the Cabinet decided 'that Her Majesty's Government should seek to secure, by the use of force if necessary, the reversal of the Egyptian Government's action to nationalise the Suez Canal Company'. On the 28th July, Britain froze Egyptian sterling assets, and on 30th July an arms embargo was imposed upon Egypt, and General Nasser was informed that he could not have the Suez Canal. Britain, France and the United States held talks on the escalating Suez Crisis on the 1st August. There was no possibility of immediate action – which might have been the best course of action and received more or less total support from the British public and merely disapproval from Washington and Moscow – because it was an unpleasant surprise to the Government to find that, ten years after the war, British military power had deteriorated drastically. There was an alarming lack of equipment and training, and any invasion fleet would have to set sail from Malta rather than Cyprus, which had no deep-water ports, if the Libyan Government was not willing to allow land invasion from its territory.

There was an emergency Commons debate on 2nd August. Gaitskell, the Leader of the Opposition Labour party, compared Nasser's conduct with that of Hitler and Mussolini. Gaitskell had previously emphasised to the Prime Minister that 'military intervention could only be justified in self-defence or in support of a United Nations resolution, Eden answered ambiguously that he doubted if military action against Egypt could be justified on those criteria.'[2] Gaitskell assumed this to mean that Eden would not contemplate any military action without a UN resolution. Britain mobilised its armed forces on that same day – 2nd August. Eden was encouraged by the talks with Dulles to believe that, although America wanted a peaceful solution, it would look the other way if force were resorted to; Dulles declared: 'Nasser must disgorge his theft.' Eden never had the relationship with America that Churchill and Macmillan had, and he did not realise that Eisenhower 'was not going to permit the United States to be involved in anything that remotely smacked of a colonialist war on behalf of the British Empire.'[3] The United States pursued a policy of extraordinary delaying tactics from the end of July through to the end of October. On 21st August Egypt said it would negotiate on the ownership of the Suez Canal Company if Britain pulled out of the Middle East completely, but this was hardly a serious starting point. America might have thought itself the champion of oppressed nations fighting colonial powers, but Egypt turned to the Soviet Union and only two days after the negotiation proposal, the U.S.S.R. announced it would send troops if Egypt were attacked. On 26th August General Nasser agreed to a five nation conference on the Suez Canal, but on the 28th he expelled two British envoys from Egypt, accusing them of spying.

A battle plan, code-named 'Musketeer' was being drawn up, and the armed forces prepared for an invasion of Egypt. 80,000 troops were to be landed at Alexandria and after an eight-day battle, both Cairo and the Suez Canal would have been captured. Eden limited the number of

[2] Hattersley / [3] Ibid

ministers and officials he kept informed, and he did not realise the extent of the doubts of the Minister of Defence, Walter Monckton and the First Sea Lord, Earl Mountbatten. Troops moved to the South Coast, and ships and aircraft to Cyprus in preparation for war.

## Suez Crisis September-October 1956

In early September, Selwyn Lloyd the Foreign Secretary urged that the dispute should be referred to the United Nations, and the Cabinet agreed that 'the possibilities of a peaceful settlement should be explored'. On the 5th September Israel joined in, condemning Egypt over the Suez Crisis. Eden had written to Dulles, trying again to gain the support of the Americans, but the reply was not supportive: Eisenhower was totally opposed to any military action. On September 9th the conference talks collapsed when Nasser refused to allow international control of the Suez Canal. Dulles suggested that the Suez Canal Company should become the Suez Canal Users' Association, responsible for free passage along the Canal and for the collection of dues; a proportion of these would go to Egypt.

There was a second emergency debate in the House of Commons on 12th October, and by then it was clear that there would be no support from America for any military action. On the same day, America, Britain and France announced their intention to impose this Association on the management of the Canal. Nasser rejected this, and the well-intentioned conciliation services of Robert Menzies, the Australian Prime Minister, and by September 14th, Egypt was in full control of the Suez Canal. By this time, with nothing happening, the troops, particularly the Reserves who had been called up, had become restive. On September 15th Soviet shipping pilots arrived to help Egypt to run the Canal. Eden had to find a solution.

From the outset, Macmillan was in favour of military action and wanted to involve the Israelis, a course of action which Eden had refused to follow; now he was forced to reconsider. The French had already been engaged in discussions with Israel. On October 7th, the Israeli Foreign Minister, Golda Meir, declared that the United Nations' failure to resolve the Suez Crisis meant that they must take military action. The French Foreign Minister, Pineau, proposed a solution to Eden on October 14th at Chequers. Unfortunately it was 'the most squalid conspiracy of twentieth-century international relations.'[4] The Anglo-Egyptian Agreement of 1954 permitted Britain to reoccupy the Suez Canal zone if there was a risk of disruption to shipping navigating the Canal – in other words, if there was a war in the area. Pineau suggested that such a war could be arranged by Israel invading Egypt for the consideration of the port of Eilat for Israel. The Israelis would attack Egypt across the Sinai; the British and French would issue an ultimatum to both sides to withdraw from the region of the Canal and when Egypt refused to do so, the British and French would occupy it. Eden did not immediately decide; initially, Selwyn Lloyd was, against the proposal. They[5] flew to Paris on 16th October to discuss it further with Pineau and Mollet, the French Prime Minister. The plan was finalised

---

[4] Hattersley / [5] Rhodes James; Hattersley says that only Lloyd went.

at a meeting at Sevres on 22nd October; Lloyd, and Moshe Dayan, the Defence Minister, persuaded Ben-Gurion, Prime Minister of Israel that it was necessary to proceed with the conspiracy forthwith, and a secret protocol was agreed on the 24th.

In Cabinet, on 25th October, Eden presented a possible scenario to Ministers:[6] that hostilities might break out between Israel and Egypt, and whether this would require France and Britain to intervene. If they did so, as France considered they should, then Eden said they 'must face the risk that we should be accused of collusion with Israel'. Rhodes James' version is that Eden told the full Cabinet of the proposed conspiracy and that the Cabinet endorsed the proposed action unanimously. 'The majority were captivated by the cleverness of it all.'[7] The Attorney-General, Sir Reginald Manningham-Buller advised Eden and the Cabinet that they should not proceed with the plan. When Eden heard that there was a protocol in existence – a record of the agreement at Sevres, he was appalled and sent officials to destroy it, so he clearly understood that this was an illegal move. The French refused and the Israelis had already taken theirs back to Tel Aviv.

The crisis had now continued for so long that the pound was coming under pressure and having to be propped up by the reserves. Macmillan, as Chancellor of the Exchequer, knew that considerable damage to the economy would ensue; he began to be less enthusiastic about the plan, but did not change his spots too obviously. He had been a hawk over Suez, but not a genuine one; he was a hawk with prey and the prey was Eden. It was always bound to end in disaster for Eden, but Macmillan could see that it would bring him the Premiership if he played his cards right. He knew that he was also the one who could repair the 'special relationship' with America – like Churchill he had an American mother – and he looked forward to Europe rather than backwards to the British Empire.

Nasser believed that the Soviet Union would come to the defence of Egypt, but the Cabinet calculated that, as ultimately America would defend Britain, then the U.S.S.R. would not defend Egypt in the event. Israel mobilised its armed forces on 28th October. There were serious problems involved in the conspiracy: Britain and France did not believe that the Israelis could move as fast as they said they could; the fleet could hardly set sail before the invasion had occurred, otherwise the story would not hold, and it would take six days for them to reach Port Said. The Israelis invaded the Sinai Peninsula on the very next day – 29th October. Britain and France issued the Anglo-French ultimatum on the 30th October. Gaitskell was given fifteen minutes' notice of this ultimatum and still knew nothing of the conspiracy; he obtained an immediate debate in the House of Commons. The Labour Opposition 'launched the most vehement assault in recent Parliamentary history.'[8]

Eisenhower first heard of the ultimatum from the Press Association, as did the British representative to the United Nations: 'If achieving surprise was the main purpose of strategy, it was wholly successful. The trouble was that those most surprised were Britain's closest allies and friends, and virtually all her Ambassadors and High Commissioners.'[9] Eisenhower's intelligence from the C.I.A. had been faulty: they had thought Israel would attack Jordan. The U.S.

[6] Hattersley  /  [7] Rhodes James  /  [8] Ibid  /  [9] Ibid

were also much concerned with the situation in Eastern Europe: there were stirrings in Poland and demonstrators on the streets of Budapest. At the United Nations, Britain and France were forced to veto the U.S.S.R.'s demand for an Israeli-Egyptian cease-fire; the Americans moved to refer the matter to the U.N. General Assembly. Britain's air force began bombing the Canal Zone on 31st October.

# Suez Crisis – November 1956-April 1957

The R.A.F. continued the bombardment of the Egyptian airfields, which had begun on the evening of 31st October until the early hours of Monday 5th November: a success from a military point of view, it was a disaster from the political one. There were protests rallies throughout the United Kingdom and the country divided: a reader to the *Daily Telegraph* wrote, 'How good it is to hear the British Lion's roar…', but a housewife wrote to the *News Chronicle*, 'After the children had left for school this morning, I couldn't help it, I wept. I wept for shame and humiliation.'[10] The feelings of the people were reflected by the uproar in the Commons; the House was suspended. The Archbishop of Canterbury, Dr Geoffrey Fisher, expressed his disapproval. At Oxford, thirty professors, two college heads and three hundred and fifty senior members of the University signed a protest opposing the Government's action.

There had been nothing said in the ultimatum of 30th October about 'bombing'. Edward Boyle resigned from the Cabinet but kept this secret for the time being, and Walter Monckton resigned on 'health and age grounds'.[11] The B.B.C. demonstrated its independence by refusing to broadcast government propaganda or allow Foreign Office censorship. The political storm was not confined to Britain but grew abroad and most particularly in America, where Eisenhower feared that the whole of the Middle East would erupt. Of the Commonwealth countries, only Australia, New Zealand and South Africa gave any degree of support to Eden. Meanwhile in Hungary, where the new Prime Minister, Nagy, had been unable to keep the promises he made to demonstrators – that elections would be held and the Russian Army depart the country – Soviet tanks opened fire in the streets of Budapest on 4th November. It seemed opportune, and enabled the U.S.S.R. to extricate itself from any obligations to Egypt. That same day Eden made a radio broadcast to the nation, warning that war in the Middle East was about to break out.

On Monday November 5th, at 7.15 a.m., British and French forces launched an airborne invasion of Egypt: the Third Battalion of the Parachute Regiment was dropped onto Gamil airfield, while French paratroops landed a couple of miles away. The U.N. ceasefire resolution, which had been finally approved on 2nd November, had expired at 7 a.m. that morning, and the U.N. debate on the creation of an international peace-keeping force was still underway.

[10] Hopkins

[11] Hattersley. Rhodes James mentions the second resignation being that of Anthony Nutting and not Monckton.

Simultaneously with the landing, the Israelis won a significant victory against the Egyptian army at Sharm el-Sheikh on the Red Sea, and moved on towards the Canal. The invasion fleet was still at sea.

The 6th November was the date of the State Opening of Parliament. At a Cabinet meeting just beforehand, Macmillan set out the economic facts of the Crisis: that the international money markets had no confidence in sterling, and that the reserves were falling at an alarming rate. The U.S. would not provide a supporting loan, and the Federal Reserve was selling sterling at a low rate. It was agreed that there was no other option than an immediate ceasefire and Eden had to telephone Paris to say that the British economy could not risk the collapse of the pound. The French wanted to postpone the ceasefire, but Eden was insistent. The General Assembly of the United Nations voted, on November 7th, for a ceasefire: that invading powers should quit Egyptian territory. Nasser accepted the UN demand for a cease-fire and accepted, in principle, a UN force. The cease-fire was acclaimed in the Commons, but humiliations were to follow. Egypt began to expel British, French and Israeli residents on 25th November. On November 29th the tripartite invasion was officially ended under pressure from the U.N., though on the 20th December, Israel announced that it was refusing to return Gaza to Egypt. British soldiers were left stranded, waiting for the U.N. Force to relieve them; the Royal Navy was not allowed to carry out the clearance of the Canal. The British and French troops were not able to leave Egypt until December 24th. The gold reserves ran down again, and a credit squeeze had to be imposed to prop up the pound. The closure of the Canal meant that tankers had to make a lengthy detour around the Cape of Good Hope, and petrol rationing returned. The special tax of 'the Suez Shilling' was imposed on petrol until April 1958. It was only in the mid-1950s that the middle classes had started to acquire their small family saloon cars.

The whole adventure had been an unmitigated disaster for Eden and Britain. Papers released thirty years later revealed that another major purpose of the operation was to remove Nasser and replace him with an alternative government; instead, Nasser's position was enhanced and consolidated, with Egypt being the victim of aggression. On January 15th he nationalised British and French banks in Egypt. The Suez Canal was unusable for the next six months, with block-ships having been sunk in it and it was not until April 19th that the first British ship paid the Egyptian toll for the use of the Suez Canal. Britain had totally lost its authority in the Middle East, with America and the Soviet Union jostling for position.

The protocol of Sevres still remained secret; Eden's reputation for integrity ensured that he was believed and not accused of deception and collusion with Israel. In his last speech to the House of Commons, Eden said that 'there were no plans to get together to attack Egypt… there was no foreknowledge that Israel would attack Egypt.' This was untrue after the Anglo-French meeting at Chequers on 14th October. He had also told his Cabinet of the plan on 6th November and this fact was revealed under the Thirty Year Rule.

In late November, 1956, due to ill-health and the advice of his doctors, Eden left for the Jamaican sun. If he had not looked so ill standing on the steps of the plane with his wife Clarissa, it would have seemed that he was flying into exile. He had left the country reflecting on the reality of Britain's position in the world power stakes and its dependence on America;

in 1945 the British Empire still ruled over six hundred million people. In the Middle East, Arab Nationalism had broken through the frontiers established after the First World War; in 1958, there would be an officers' coup in Iraq.

Suez had created disillusion in the ruling elite, and broken the confidence of Empire. One of the lessons of the Suez Crisis was that ' 'Public Opinion' was no longer made across a few dozen dinner tables and club carpets…' [12] Macmillan took the lesson to heart.

[12] Hopkins

Chapter Twenty-One

# The Nurses

Eastbourne attracted numbers of private nurses with its considerable population of the rich and retired elderly. This was the case both before and after the introduction of the National Health Service, and they would nurse patients in their own homes or were employed in the private nursing homes. Many were older state registered nurses who, perhaps, wanted to work less hours than they would have done in the hospitals, or part-time, or maybe wanted more independence than they had under the eye of hospital matrons. Some aspired to own or manage a private nursing home. A few may have had in mind the possibility of being left a legacy by a grateful patient, or of marrying a rich elderly widower. In order to obtain work, they would register with a nursing agency, such as Miss Gartley's in Eastbourne, but they also needed to know the GPs and be acceptable to them, as a GP would soon decide which nurses he preferred for his cases.

The evidence of the nurses was of paramount importance to the police: they were the closest witnesses to the methods used by Dr Adams and the manner of patients' deaths. It should also be remembered that most of them were also afraid to say too much, either from a professional point of view, or – more likely – because they might not get further nursing work from the doctors. These statements also contain a considerable amount of information regarding the behaviour of Dr Adams from a psychological point of view.

### Sister Phyllis Mary Owen

Miss Phyllis Mary Owen, a nursing sister, was considered by Detective Superintendent Hannam to be a highly intelligent woman. He started by having a talk with her, her sister and a Miss Heald, who was a close friend. Originally, Dr Adams had been their doctor, but they had changed to another GP when he misdiagnosed Miss Heald's heart trouble, saying she was suffering from nothing more than 'nerves'. 'He always believed and said that his patients were nervous cases and that sedative treatment was essential.' Sister Owen knew of many instances where Dr Adams kept patients completely under sedatives for long periods, so that they frequently could only go about in a dazed condition. She described him as being 'fantastic in his type of sedative medication'. Several qualified nursing sisters were of the opinion that 'it is because of this type of thing he administers to some of these old ladies that they return to him for similar comforting treatment'. She believed that he had great influence over his patients and the reason for this was 'because he kept them in that dazed and doped condition.' Sister Owen provided particularly important evidence in the cases of Hilda and Clara Neil Miller and Mrs Ware.

## Sister Eunice Hitch

Miss Eunice Hitch had done a lot of nursing of Dr Adams' patients before the War: 'I have always found Adams to be a good doctor but I am afraid I have not approved of all his ways and I really did not like him. I haven't approved of his ways when attending patients. I have seen him holding their hands and passing comment on their attire, which I regard as rather silly.'

She recalled nursing Sir Alexander Maguire of 'Cluna', Upper Carlisle Road, De Walden Court and the Park Lane Hotel in London. He was a chronic alcoholic. 'One night, about midnight, I answered the front door bell and found Dr Adams. It wasn't unusual for Adams to visit patients late at night. Dr Adams came just inside the front door and took from his pocket a 12oz medicine bottle, which, I found out afterwards, contained whisky. The doctor asked me to give it to Sir Alexander when he woke.' Sister Olwen Williams had also nursed this patient and confirmed that he was 'an inebriate'. The patient decided to return to London and died there eighteen months later from chronic alcoholism.

Another patient, Mrs Coats, who had a flat in Hartingdon House, was over 80 and she liked Dr Adams immensely. She was always ready to sit up and converse with him when he visited – which would be any time between 10 p.m. and 11.30 p.m. at night. Her son once requested Dr Adams to give him a detailed account of the medical bill, 'whereupon Adams became very irate'. Sister Hitch recalled a blind patient, Mrs Wilson, in St. Theresa's Nursing Home. She usually had a box of chocolates beside her bed. Each time Dr Adams left after a visit, the box was almost empty. She regarded it as a despicable thing to take advantage of an old blind lady. She had also nursed Mrs Hollobone, the mother of Lady Prendergast, in her flat at Ridgeway, Carlisle Road. Dr Adams always gave her a daily injection at 12 noon, but no nurse knew what he was injecting. The patient would sleep throughout the day and be wakeful at night. Sister Hitch concluded her statement: 'My experience of Dr Adams is that he is out for money, and all he can get.'

## Sister Agnes Stone White

Sister Agnes Stone White had done some relief work nursing Mrs Morrell [See Chapter 11] The only other case she nursed for Dr Adams was a Mrs Meyer, who lived with a widowed sister, Mrs Campbell, in Grange Road. This was between 1950 and 1953. Mrs Meyer was the rich widow of a Ceylon tea planter. She was not really ill but Dr Adams visited daily. She observed Dr Adams' behaviour as being the same as with Mrs Morrell: he made it clear to Sister White that he wished to be left alone with the patient and she remained in a room across the landing. Mrs Meyer always looked forward to his visits and she also made it clear she wanted to be alone with the Doctor. She would ask Sister White to assist her in making her look her best. The visits appeared to act as a tonic for her, but whether he gave her anything or just talked, Sister White never knew as he gave her no instructions at all. Her sister, Mrs Campbell, regarded Mrs Meyer's behaviour with the doctor as 'very foolish'. Mrs Cerise Meyer died, aged 70, on 28th March, 1951 and Dr Adams gave the causes of death as '(a) cerebral thrombosis and (b) paralysis agitens'.

Sister White gave her view of the Doctor: 'My opinion of Adams is that he is a creeper, particularly where there is plenty of money. He wouldn't visit a poor person three times a day and every day as he did when he had a rich patient.'

### Sister Grace Osgood

Sister Grace Osgood could not remember the name of one patient she had nursed for Dr Adams, although she knew that he was a paint manufacturer from East London and a visitor to the town. He was about 85 years old and very wealthy. He had suffered a heart attack and Dr Adams visited three times on the first day and twice a day for a week afterwards, then daily for the last month. Dr Adams would take tablets out of his case, but gave no prescriptions. He would leave only sufficient tablets until the next visit. Sister Osgood had asked the Doctor what the tablets were: 'He mumbled something which I was unable to understand and I would repeat the question. Again he would mumble a reply which I failed to understand. I felt it was the doctor's intention that I should not know the prescription.' It annoyed him when she told him she felt she ought to know what the prescription was in case the patient had an intolerance to it, then she could discontinue the treatment if necessary. 'I considered that Adams' treatment is most unprofessional and not in the interest of the patient. During his visits he never discussed with me the patient's condition neither did he instruct me regarding treatment in his absence.' Oddly enough, some time later, Dr Adams had told her of this patient's death, but she did not know whether or not Dr Adams was still attending him at this time.

Sister Osgood described her nursing of another patient of Dr Adams, Mrs Woolrych of Chiswick Place. The patient was suffering from an inflammation of the right eye and ear. She was visited daily by Dr Adams, who would tell her she was getting better when she was finding the pain getting considerably worse. He had looked into the patient's ear when Sister Osgood asked if she could do so. He replied 'You'll find the ear is quite alright.' She looked with the instrument into the patient's ear and found inflammation and a slough in the passage of the ear, indicating serious infection. 'When I tried to speak to Dr Adams regarding the patient, he turned his back on me and walked out of the room.' She had observed that when Dr Adams arrived each morning, he would sit and hold Mrs Woolrych's hand. 'His general attitude towards the patient was repulsive to me.'

The last patient Sister Osgood had nursed for Dr Adams was his shooting friend, Lieutenant Colonel Gwynne of Wootton Manor. She had nursed him for about ten weeks from the end of January, 1955. Colonel Gwynne had had a car accident, fracturing his tibia and fibula. The Doctor visited every morning and again in the evening for the first week and then daily for the remainder of the recovery period. Dr Adams left tablets for the patient and when she came in for night duty at 9 o'clock each evening there were two tablets on the mantelpiece in the Colonel's bedroom. Sister Osgood gave these to him by 10 p.m. each evening. 'Colonel Gwynne seemed rather frightened of these tablets. He often told me they were too strong and made him feel drowsy and muddled during the day.' She was given to understand that the butler gave the Colonel the tablets during the daytime on the instructions of Dr Adams.

The Doctor also told her not to go into the bedroom with him when he visited the Colonel. There was an occasion when the Doctor was driving her home from Wootton Manor after her night duty, and they were discussing how long the patient had had the second plaster on his leg. The Doctor had said it was a fortnight and Sister Osgood corrected him, saying the plaster had only been on for ten days. 'He glared at me, appeared very angry and snapped back at me and said, "It's two weeks".'

Sister Osgood did not mince her words to the police: 'I did not like Dr Adams before I nursed Colonel Gwynne but after nursing this patient I intended to refuse another patient of Dr Adams. I regard his conduct as unprofessional.'

### Nurse Marjorie Summerfield Savage

Marjorie Summerfield Savage had nursed two of Dr Adams' patients privately in their homes and others when she worked in the Highland Nursing Home in Carew Road and Tredegar Nursing Home in Upper Avenue, all in the 1940s. She thought there had been nothing unusual about most of these, but one particular case had struck her – she couldn't forget it and she remembered his exact words: this was at Tredegar Nursing Home when a woman patient of Dr Adams had died. After the death, Dr Adams had stood at the foot of the bed where the body lay, and said, 'The poor wee thing, I'll take the clock away with me now. Has the brandy in the bottle been opened? I'll take that too.' He collected the clock and brandy bottle and a third item which she could not remember and left the nursing home with them. Dr Adams then instructed Nurse Savage to pack the patient's things and said he would have them collected. 'I have known Dr Adams for about thirty years and, as far as his bedside manner is concerned, it was unlike that of any doctor I have ever known. His relationship with his female patients was too friendly.'

### Mrs Jessie Neale

Tredegar Nursing Home in Upper Avenue, Eastbourne, still exists. Mrs Jessie Neale was proprietress of Tredegar from 1946. As far as she was concerned nothing untoward had ever occurred in her nursing home. She recalled two patients of Dr Adams: Mrs Mortimer [see Chapter 9] when she was present at the patient's death and Dr Adams attended afterwards, examining the body, and Mrs Alice Waters. 'Dr Adams is always attentive to his patients but I have never seen him on any occasion act in a manner to which I would take exception.'

Mrs Neale said that she kept records of all drugs and medicine supplied to patients. These were, of course, those which had been prescribed by the doctor and the prescriptions collected by nursing home staff, rather than anything which came from the doctor's bag. The nursing home did not keep any stocks of dangerous drugs, and, if a patient died, then any left-over drugs were handed over to the doctor.

### Sister Mary Elinor Gartley

It was Mary Elinor Gartley, a nurse just one year older than Dr Adams, who was principal of the agency which supplied private nurses, 'Eastbourne Trained Nurses' Association'. She was a midwife, who had twenty-seven state registered nurses under her control. She herself had nursed many of Dr Adams' patients and always found him 'very congenial and easy to work for'. Those patients whom she had nursed had 'implicit faith in him', and, perhaps more tellingly, they 'couldn't seem to get on without him.' It is also likely that she got most of the work for her agency from Dr Adams.

The Doctor presumably favoured Miss Gartley and regarded her as the most reliable nurse in Eastbourne, so far as he was concerned, as it was she he asked to nurse his cousin, Florence Henry, when she had a terminal illness – cancer. She nursed this patient from 25th May 1952. Dr Adams would leave six syringes of omnopon or morphia on the mantelpiece in the bedroom. Three of these were stronger than the others and Sister Gartley had instructions to give these when Miss Henry asked for them to relieve the pain. If she requested some, Dr Adams immediately prepared them, sterilising the needles and syringes himself. 'She was a very sweet lady but extremely ill and very considerate'. Miss Gartley knew from the first day that she nursed her that it was only a question of time before she died. It was a few hours before Miss Henry died, on a Sunday, that another doctor arrived at Kent Lodge: a Dr Henry, a relative of the patient, who lived in North London. Dr Adams and Dr Henry had a consultation. 'I do remember that, after the consultation, Dr Adams gave her the last injection himself and she fell off to sleep about half an hour afterwards. She never awoke from this sleep.' Miss Henry died about 2 or 3 o'clock in the morning. Sister Gartley was able to get Dr Adams out of bed and to the patient just before she died. This is *the* case where it can be considered that the Doctor was 'easing the passing'.

### Sister Gladys Miller

Gladys Miller had nursed several cases for Dr Adams. One was Miss Harrod at Southcliff Nursing Home. She died on 23rd March, 1951 and was seventy. Sister Miller recalled that Dr Adams had given this patient injections but had never told the nurses what injections he gave. For the ten days that Sister Miller nursed her she was in a comatose state. The cause of death was certified by the Doctor as cerebral thrombosis.

She had been nursing Mr Holland, a permanent resident at the Burlington Hotel, for Dr Adams, but she resigned because he told her she must receive all her instructions through the housekeeper. Sister Miller had, however, accepted some other cases: one of these was Mrs Constance Brierley at the Grand Hotel, 'a gastric case', who 'thought a lot of Adams'. The patient died, aged 80 years, on 26th December, 1953 and Dr Adams certified causes of death as 'uraemic coma and chronic nephritis and pyelitis', – kidney failure. The last patient she had nursed for Dr Adams was Mr James Priestley Downs. [See Chapter 15]

### Sister Florence Pearson

Miss Florence Pearson, aged 58 at the time of the enquiry, obviously considered herself to be a superior nurse: 'Dr Adams is one of the lesser doctors I have worked for…' She was the only nurse questioned who had nursed anyone other than the elderly for him: this was at Clover Cottage, South Cliff Avenue, where all five children had chicken pox. There were few families with five children who could afford private nursing care; most such families would have been the Doctor's 'panel' patients. Sister Pearson recalled that she had nursed Mrs Helen Soden at the Grand Hotel – she thought this was prior to 1950 – who had skin and chest complaints. This patient, according to the list of death certificates, died on 21st March 1953 and Dr Adams again certified uraemia and chronic nephritis as the cause of death. She thought that the last patient she had nursed for Dr Adams was Mrs Morrell in 1950. [See Chapter 11] She had never seen Dr Adams 'behave in any way unbecoming to his profession'.

### Sister Doreen Henagulph

Doreen Henagulph, having seen the publicity about the investigation, approached the police to pass on, in confidence, some information about four cases where she had nursed patients for Dr Adams. The first of these was Mrs Morrell, from about 1948.

Sister Henagulph also nursed Mrs Brierley at the Grand Hotel for four days and four nights about three years before she died. 'Dr Adams conveyed to me that the case was a malignant cyst of the kidneys and it was a question of doing just what we could for the comfort of the patient.' This does not exactly accord with the information on the death certificate or the fact that death occurred three years after this diagnosis – which, unusually, was related to the nurse by Dr Adams. At this time, however, Sister Henagulph got the patient out of bed and on her feet, and Mrs Brierley gave a champagne party in her room at the Grand Hotel. After the party, she mentioned to Sister Henagulph that Dr Adams had consumed a bottle of champagne. 'It was my impression that she was not over keen on Dr Adams.' She also said that Dr Adams had invited himself.

Mrs Atkinson of Pearl Court, Devonshire Place, was another patient Sister Henagulph nursed for Dr Adams. She was with the patient for about ten nights and Dr Adams left 'Adrenolin' [sic] for injection at night. Mrs Atkinson was said to be an asthmatic, but the nurse regarded her as 'neurotic' and did not give these injections. Of the Doctor, Sister Henagulph said, 'Again, he had an influential manner with this patient and his general attitude was one of familiarity.' On one occasion, Dr Adams had examined the patient with a stethoscope 'which he placed about her clothing and it impressed me that, while he was so doing, he was talking at the same time and looking into her eyes.'

The last patient Sister Henagulph nursed for Dr Adams was Mrs Avann; she lived in the Old Town, and this was early in 1953. She was with the patient for four days and the daughter-in-law was there as well. The nurse remarked that 'it wasn't the usual type of home in which persons of my capacity are called for nursing' – the patient's husband had to use her room for sleeping at night time, instead of another bedroom being available. She was told that the case was one of cancer of the liver.

Dr Adams had brought in a bottle of medicine and Nurse Henagulph was told to administer it, this being impressed upon her by the 'daily woman' who was a friend of the family. She found that the medicine, in her opinion, upset the patient, giving her abdominal pain, and the nurse stopped giving it. She told the 'daily woman' that she would not give the patient any further medicine until she had consulted the Doctor. He did not visit this patient until the fourth evening Nurse Henagulph was there. She informed him that the patient appeared better, that the diarrhoea had ceased and she was able to take nourishment; she had had one good night. She also told him that she thought it was the medicine which upset her and she had not given it on the previous two days. 'Dr Adams' anger was intense. He said that the patient must have the medicine as it was supplying a deficiency in the gastric juices. I told Dr Adams that I would not stay. Although I, of course, have no proof I had an idea at the back of my mind that the medicine might contain arsenic. I feel quite strongly that the patient was showing all the symptoms of arsenical poisoning.' Mrs Florence Avann, died, aged 66 years, on 24th March, 1953 and Dr Adams certified the cause of death as 'Carcinoma of stomach'.

Sister Henagulph added: 'From my experience of Dr Adams, he does try to endear himself to patients and I believe he has hypnotic influence over them. He sits very close to them and gazes into their eyes.'

### Nurse Helen Rose Stronach

Nurse Helen Rose Stronach, aged 62 in 1956, had been nursing for thirty-four years, and had been a private nurse from 1950. She was to be called as a witness at the Old Bailey trial as she had nursed Mrs Morrell. She first nursed a patient of Dr Adams in 1938 so she must have nursed the odd private case before 1950. This case and one other were of no moment so far as she could judge as the families were expecting the deaths. Nurse Stronach had nursed a very wealthy patient for Dr Adams, Mrs Carlyle of Dittons Road: Dr Adams had been very attentive towards her. Nothing was being prescribed but the Doctor visited twice each day and stayed with the patient for about twenty minutes each time. 'He nearly always held her hand and make quite a fuss of her. I don't know whether Mrs Carlyle liked this behaviour but I never heard her object to it.' However, after a few days at the Grand Hotel, where she had been taken ill, she moved to her daughter's home; her husband was still alive and he and her daughter attended to her affairs. Mrs Carlyle was still alive in 1956 at the time of the investigation.

Nurse Stronach had also attended to Mrs Brierley at the Grand Hotel. She had been told she had a weak heart – this was in May, 1950 – and she was a sick woman. The treatment had consisted of injections of Coramine (a heart stimulant) and Omnopon (morphia). She could only remember that she had given the injections at night-time and had continued this treatment under Dr Adams' instructions. Doctor had always been nice and attentive towards the patient and when Mrs Brierley was seriously ill he called three times daily and later reduced this to twice daily.

There was another patient at the Grand Hotel, whom Nurse Stronach had nursed: Mrs Foster, who was, she thought, around 70, and whose husband was very wealthy. This was in 1951 for about five days. 'She was a cerebral case and when I first attended her she was unconscious and remained in this condition until she died five days later.' She believed that this was the first and only time Dr Adams attended Mrs Foster as he had been called because the patient had been taken ill at the hotel. Mrs Foster died, aged 65, on 13th December, 1950 and the Doctor certified the causes of death as '(a) uraemia and cholaemia and (b) carcinoma of descending colon'. Another nurse, Sister Margaret Todd Methren, who had important evidence in the case of Mrs Kilgour [See Chapter 14] had also nursed Mrs Foster, and she described her as 'a cancer case'.

Nurse Stronach had some more observations to make about Dr Adams: she thought him a 'very good doctor, but a little more attentive to his more wealthy patients.' It was generally known amongst the nurses in Eastbourne that he had 'a most perfect bedside manner' and made a great fuss of his wealthy female patients. What she most certainly did not approve of was his not telling his nurses what injections he was giving to his patients. He was, in her experience, the only doctor who had not confided in her regarding injections given to patients for whom she was caring. She felt that 'such conduct could place a nurse in a very serious predicament', although, fortunately, it had never done so with her.

### Sister Audrey May Goodchild

A much younger nurse was Audrey May Goodchild, who was still only thirty-three years old in 1956. The first patient she had nursed for Dr Adams was Major Alfred Lincoln Chandler at the Burlington Hotel. This was in 1949, although she had thought it was 1951. Dr Adams had prescribed injections of Omnopon (morphia), but on one occasion he had mixed several drugs in the same syringe and injected the patient. She did not know what the three drugs were. On one occasion Dr Adams had asked to be left alone with the patient when he visited. Major Chandler died on the fourth day of her attendance upon him and his family were with him. This was on 2nd November, 1949 and Dr Adams certified the cause of death as 'Carcinoma of prostate'.

Sister Goodchild had also nursed two patients of Dr Adams in the Esperance Nursing Home. One incident had particularly struck her, when she had nursed an old man on one afternoon when Dr Adams visited him. He took two tablets out of his bag and gave them to the patient and when she asked him what they were, replied, 'Special Tablets'. She had also nursed Mr Hullett [See Chapter 17] Sister Goodchild's general feeling about Dr Adams was that, although '…his bedside manner was always extremely friendly, I did not like working with him as there was always a lack of co-operation and he would not explain the patients' treatment nor the names of the drugs prescribed. He supplied the drugs himself. I only asked on one occasion what the tablets were and I received such a rebuff that I never asked again.'

### Sister Marguerite Roberts

The first patient of Dr Adams whom Marguerite Roberts, a State Registered Mental Nurse, had nursed was Mrs Kilgour. [See Chapter 14] She mentions another case which she nursed for Dr Adams: Mrs Whitton – after 1950, who was living at the Wish Tower Hotel with her husband, Captain Whitton. This was a cardiac case and she had another heart attack and died. Sister Roberts had not seen Dr Adams and sleeping tablets had been left for the patient. She was then asked, by the visiting nurse, to return to the hotel to perform the 'Last Offices': she went into the bedroom and found the bed completely stripped. She looked around and 'sitting on a commode and underneath some blankets, I found the deceased.' The visiting nurse, who was still present, told her that Mrs Whitton had had a heart attack whilst sitting on the commode and Captain Whitton was in the sitting-room next door. The death certificate in this case is not listed in those found by the police searching for those signed by Dr Adams.

Although she had, of course, been totally uneasy about the death of Mrs Kilgour and the injection given to her by Dr Adams, she made this comment concerning his approach to patients: 'Dr Adams had a wonderful manner with his patients…. He is a doctor with a unique bedside manner and his patients, I was given to understand, thought the world of him.'

### Nurse Gertrude Brady

Unusually, Gertrude Brady was an unqualified nurse; she had seven years' experience. She recalled a 'special' she had been asked to do at the Esperance Nursing Home in August 1950. Lady Lindsay-Hogg, was in her 90s, 'senile', and Dr Adams attended once a week. The following quotations are verbatim from Gertrude Brady's statement: 'A very charming lady…There were times, of course, when she was confused and she was the type of woman who knew her own mind and would not be dictated to.' In the early summer of 1951, Sir Anthony Lindsay-Hogg and his legal advisor, Mr Guthrie James, came to the Esperance in order to get a document signed. 'On this particular day her Ladyship was in rather a difficult mood and refused to sign the document, whereupon Sir Anthony asked me if I could persuade her to sign. Shortly afterwards, by gentle persuasion, I got Lady Lindsay-Hogg to sign. I then handed it to Sir Lindsay [sic] and Mr Guthrie James was present. Dr Adams, who had just arrived to see the patient, was asked by Sir Lindsay to witness grandmother's signature. Dr Adams signed and I did likewise.' Gertrude makes it clear in her statement that Lady Lindsay-Hogg was 'senile' and 'confused' and not capable of signing legal documents: in fact not willing to sign either. Dr Adams must, presumably, have known this as well. Gertrude Brady ceased nursing at the end of July 1951 and went abroad. Lady Lindsay-Hogg remained at the Esperance, and died, aged 96 years on 23rd August, 1952. Dr Adams certified the cause of death as 'Scirrhus carcinoma of the breast'.

In the January of 1950, Gertrude Brady benefited under the will of a Mr Montague Hutton, whom she nursed at the Grand Hotel for about eighteen months. He left her £13,000. This was not one of Dr Adams' patients.

### Sister Minnie Shepherdess Carey

A nurse with the extraordinary name of Miss Minnie Shepherdess Carey was a state registered nurse who worked in Eastbourne from 1945 to 1954. She had first been employed at the Olinda Nursing Home in Grassington Road, and later joined Miss Gartley's Trained Nurses' Association. She had kept a record in a small note book which she loaned to the police, asking for its return in due course.

Sister Carey, after joining the Association, approached Dr Adams for work. 'Nearly all my friends started with his cases…' This could have been because he had more older and richer patients needing nursing care, or that he was more likely to keep his private patients at home rather than in nursing homes or hospitals. Sister Carey had no useful detailed information about her cases and, indeed, had given up seeking any when she was nursing Dr Adams' patients: 'The only thing I noticed was his habit of administering sedatives or injections. He was generally inclined to give injections or drugs without disclosing what it was he was giving the patient. This was his general practice, it was not a case of his doing it with any particular patient. His attitude seemed to be that it was his concern what he was giving the patient, not a matter to concern the nurse. He seemed to keep things very much in his own hands and I know I was not the only nurse that felt that way. With some doctors one would feel quite in order in asking them what they had given the patient, but I felt I could not do it with Dr Adams. Because it was his general practice and manner I never took any particular notice of any one occasion or patient.' The normal practice was for Sister Carey to remain in the room when the Doctor first came in, for two or three minutes while he first examined the patient, then 'because he was also as much a friend as a doctor to many of his patients, I would leave the room.'

This statement of Sister Carey is of some importance because it makes it quite clear that Dr Adams was in the habit of taking drugs from his own bag for injections and oral administration to patients. If drugs had been on prescription, either collected by someone in the house or delivered to the house by the chemists, then nurses would have known what was being given to patients. What was on the chemists' registers as prescribed for the patients was, by no means, all the drugs administered to the patients, so it would never be possible for the police to discover exactly what drugs had been given to one of Dr Adams' patients, and no nurses' notebooks would be reliable. Conveniently, Dr Adams kept no medical records for his private patients.

### Miss Edith Grace Easter

Dr Adams sent many of his patients to the Olinda Nursing Home. This was run from 1937 to 1953 by Edith Grace Easter, who had since retired to Priory Farm House at Wilmington, a village near to the prehistoric 'Long Man' cut out of the chalk of the South Downs. Olinda was at first in Silverdale Road, then during the War evacuated to Hurst Green in Surrey, returning in 1945 to 12 Grassington Road. Edith Easter had originally been a hospital almoner, but she employed five state registered nurses and one relief nurse at Olinda. When she returned to Eastbourne in 1945 she contacted Dr Adams and told him that she was re-establishing her nursing home and he immediately started sending his patients to her.

Miss Easter recalled one patient of Dr Adams: Miss Ida Eatough 'She had cancer and died on 25th November, 1952.' She did not remember the treatment. The date of death was correct; the lady's age was only fifty-five, but Dr Adams certified the causes of death as '(a) myocardial failure and (b) Cholaemia'. Presumably Miss Easter did not remember the case too well. She was anxious to inform the police of the strict control she had over drugs in her nursing home. Drugs were not in stock and these had to be prescribed by the doctor; the nursing sisters in the home were to give injections on the instructions of the doctor. If a patient died, then any drugs left over would be locked away and if the doctor asked for them they would be returned to him. Otherwise they would remain in the cupboard but only to be used in emergency on the doctor's instructions. All the drugs for Miss Eatough – the cancer patient – were used up; Dr Adams visited her at least once a day and 'I feel sure that I was present when she died.'

Having been in contact with Dr Adams for so many years, Miss Easter could say that 'his medical attention to his patients at my nursing home was always beyond reproach. He was most attentive, most kind and his one aim was always to get them well and more often than not he succeeded.' No less than thirty-three of Dr Adams' patients died at the Olinda nursing home during the period 1946-1954 according to the list of death certificates signed by him. In March 1952, three of his patients died in one seven-day period at Olinda and each of these deaths was attributed to the same causes: cerebral haemorrhage and cardio-vascular degeneration. On some of these is the address '12 Grassington Road' instead of 'Olinda Nursing Home' and this address is given as a home address for the deceased.

Miss Easter continued gushingly: 'I would say that Dr Adams was one on his own, …when we had a difficult case he seemed to be able to soothe the patient. He gave the nurses every co-operation in every way. He never asked me or any nurse to leave the room of the patient whilst he was visiting, he welcomed the presence of the nursing sisters, but it was etiquette to leave the room… in case the patient wished to complain about the nursing staff or the home.'

## Sister Kathleen Mary May

Sister Kathleen Mary May was another nurse who recalled Miss Ida Eatough being a cancer patient of Dr Adams, and she, herself, was one of his patients. Sister May had, in fact, gone with her to the London Clinic where she was operated on by 'Mr McCullock' (sic) Dr Adams was present but took no part in the operation. Sister May remained with her at the Clinic and Dr Adams used to visit her each morning and was usually there when she went off duty at 8 a.m. Sometimes Miss Eatough would ask her to leave the room when he was there. 'The only medicine he prescribed was an aperient and another for her water.' Miss Eatough was quite a pretty woman but 'she never appeared affected emotionally by the Doctor's presence'; he did not behave any differently than he did with other patients. 'I have often seen him sitting at bed-sides and sometimes I have seen him holding the patient's hand but that appears to be his normal manner.' Dr Adams had visited Miss Eatough socially about three times whilst she was at the London Clinic. She returned to the London Clinic at a later date, and then some time after that Sister May had read in the newspaper that she had died: 'The news of her death came as a shock to me as I had seen her walking about the town with her sister.' Sister May knew that she was fairly wealthy and related to a firm of shoe manufacturers in Nottingham.

### Nurse Blanche Lucy Goacher

Mrs Blanche Lucy Goacher, a State Registered Nurse, was forty-four years old when she spoke to the police in 1956. She had nursed seven of Dr Adams' patients. The first of these, in August 1953, was Mr Cowder, who occupied a whole suite on the first floor of the Burlington Hotel. He was 70 years old and a cardiac case. He was 'allergic to whisky' according to Nurse Goacher, but he used to drink 'a white spirit which was supplied to people allergic to spirits', and he had several bottles of this in his suite. Nurse Goacher nursed him at nights and, on the first night, she went on duty at 9 p.m.; Dr Adams came in at around 9.30 p.m. The Doctor told her that Mr Cowder was a cardiac case and he handed her a full 2 c.c. syringe and instructed her to give the patient an injection with it. As she had not seen the Doctor fill it, she refused to do so. Dr Adams was annoyed at the fact that she would not give the injection but he emptied the syringe in the sink and then he refilled it with one third of a grain of omnopon (morphia) after she had first seen the ampoule. She later gave Mr Cowder the injection.

Mr Cowder became unconscious that night – Nurse Goacher had thought he seemed in a deteriorating state – and he did not recover. The following night she went on duty again at 9 p.m. and the patient was still in the same condition. The Doctor did not visit that night and Mr Cowder died about 10.30 p.m. She did not inform the Doctor until about 7 a.m. the next morning and he came shortly afterwards and 'certified death, giving the cause as heart failure'. Mr Cowder's son and daughter-in-law were in the hotel but not in the room at the time of death. After Mr Cowder's death, Nurse Goacher was talking to the hotel housekeeper and she told her that 'he was worth half a million pounds'. After Dr Adams had certified the death, he said to Nurse Goacher: 'Don't worry about your fee, you want to charge, there is plenty of money there.'

This death is not recorded in the list of death certificates collected by the police yet the nurse's evidence in her sworn statement indicates that he did sign this certificate. This also means that there would have been no check on the will to see if Dr Adams was a legatee.

The next patient Nurse Goacher nursed for Dr Adams was an old lady [perhaps Mrs Atkinson] who lived with her husband in a first floor flat in Pearl Court. This was in September 1953 and the patient was 'neurotic… The Doctor told me that there was nothing wrong with her and again told me "There's plenty of money there".' The patient told her that she thought the Doctor was 'a charming man', and said that he was the only reason she stayed in Eastbourne. 'In the time I nursed her I saw no medicine at all and I did not see the Doctor administering anything to her.'

Nurse Goacher had nursed some other patients of Dr Adams in the Highland Lodge Nursing Home: she mentions two women suffering from terminal cancer, including a Mrs Tierney aged 50. The only treatment given was morphia, given by the nursing staff. The Doctor visited and left instructions for the treatment to be continued. 'He never administered anything to them in my presence.' She added: 'My experience of Dr Adams is that he did not trust nurses with drugs, he would hand me only the sufficient dose necessary.' If it is accurate, that Mrs Tierney died in the nursing home, attended by Dr Adams, then, again, the death certificate is not on the police list of certificates signed by Dr Adams.

Nurse Elizabeth Horn, another state-registered nurse, had nursed only one patient of Dr Adams, and this was because she had fallen foul of him. It was 'an aged lady' in Pearl Court, whom she had nursed. The Doctor visited the patient every day and each time he called he would shake hands with Nurse Horn when he arrived and again when he left. He brought in bunches of grapes, which, he said, came from his own greenhouse, and gave them to the patient. This patient adored Dr Adams and spoke about him several times a day to the nurse.

Nurse Horn was on day duty and Sister Henagulph did night duty. 'One day the patient asked me what I thought of Dr Adams and I told her that I thought he was "full of baloney".' It appears that the patient told the Doctor, he told Miss Gartley (proprietress of the Eastbourne Trained Nurses' Association), whom he met in the street and instructed her to take me away from this case. All I did was to expose my opinion of Dr Adams which he apparently did not like.' She added that she knew very little of 'this doctor' to be able to assess his capabilities as a medical man.

## Sister Helen McSweeney

Miss Helen McSweeney had been a state-registered nurse for forty-six years, thirty of these she had spent nursing in Eastbourne. Unusually, most of the cases she had nursed for Dr Adams were 'baby cases' – whether Sister McSweeney meant maternity nursing is not clear, but there is evidence to suggest that Dr Adams did not care for this sort of patient. Sister McSweeney had nursed Miss Gregory, the housekeeper at Holywell Mount [see chapter 17] for ten days in 1945: it was a stroke and she had been found in the bedroom by one of the maids. She died in a coma on 1st January 1946 and Sister McSweeney thought that there had been no treatment. The cause of death was certified by Dr Adams as 'cerebral thrombosis.'

Another more interesting case was that of Admiral Prendergast of Meads House, who was 85 years of age and 'senile'. There were three nurses on duty. Sister McSweeney was quite definite in her view of Dr Adams' treatment of this patient: 'I feel sure that this patient was given injections to keep him quiet. These were mostly given by the nurses on Doctor's instructions and consisted of morphia, one sixth or one eighth of a grain.' She had nursed him up until his death. Dr Adams was not only their doctor, but a great friend of the Admiral and his wife. He had been most attentive to both of them and had always been ready to come out any time of night or day to attend his patients.

Dr Adams was Sister McSweeney's GP and she was charmed by him. She described him as 'the kindest man I have ever met.' She had always found him to be 'most co-operative' with her as a nurse.

### Sister Lily Sayer

Lily Sayer had been a nurse at the London Hospital, Whitechapel, for twenty-five years. She had then retired to France in 1928, running a hotel for English-speaking people. She had to return to England in 1939 when the War began and had then worked at the Connaught Nursing Home and done some private nursing. Unfortunately, the hotel in France had been destroyed in 1942.

Sister Sayer had also nursed Admiral Prendergast, who was suffering from 'a very bad bladder complaint'. Dr Adams 'visited each evening to pass the catheter'. He gave the patient injections and sleeping tablets, and the Admiral was often delirious. 'Dr Adams appeared to be quite friendly with Lady Prendergast and often had a drink with her before leaving.'

### Nurse Anne Masters

One of the other nurses Admiral Prendergast had attending him was Anne Masters, who had retired as early as 1945; this was the only patient she had nursed for Dr Adams. He had 'bladder trouble' and was senile. Dr Adams had visited every day about 9 a.m. and again at 7 or 8 o'clock in the evening. The patient was 'troublesome' both during the day and night and he was given morphia. 'Sir Prendergast (sic) was a dying man.' When Sister Masters came on duty at 9 a.m. one morning he was comatose and never came out of the coma. He died at 7.30 in the evening and she was the only person present. She added: 'I am quite convinced that the injections of morphia hastened Sir Prendergast's death. I cannot say what the strength of the injections was because I never gave any. Dr Adams never gave any injections in my presence. I am reasonably sure they were all given by Sister McSweeney.'

Sister Masters continued: 'After this patient died, her Ladyship was naturally upset. She was put to bed by Dr Adams who, I believe, gave her something to put her to sleep. I saw Dr Adams in his shirt sleeves moving Lady Prendergast's bed to another room. I was not allowed to see her after I had completed the Last Offices. I was amazed to see a doctor moving furniture about. I had never experienced such a thing before. Dr Adams was particularly kind to his patients; I have little faith in him as a medical practitioner.'

Sir Robert Prendergast was 81 years old when he died on 14th May, 1946 and Dr Adams certified the causes of death as '(a) Uraemia and (b) chronic nephritis'.

Sister Sayer also recalled nursing an old man, about 80 years of age, at a small hotel on the seafront. The patient was a guest at the hotel and she had been on night duty. She saw Dr Adams on one occasion when he paid an early morning visit before she went off duty at 9 a.m. Sister Sayer had thought his attitude most casual: 'Dr Adams did not ask me for a report, in spite of the fact that I had been there all night.'

Sister Sayer had also nursed Dr Adams' cousin, Miss Henry, at Kent Lodge. She confirmed that the patient was very seriously ill with cancer and that Dr Adams would leave six prepared syringes before he went out. He was, however, 'not very approachable. He had a reputation for giving his own injections and he never discussed treatment with me.' She had taken over the case from an elderly relative from Ireland, who was referred to by the patient as 'Aunty'. Sister Sayer thought, however, that the patient resented the change and took a dislike to her, and, as a result, she resigned from nursing her after about ten days, and Miss Gartley took over.

### Sister Idina Ruby Penny

Mrs Idina Ruby Penny had been a state-registered nurse for thirty years and had been on call as a 'special nurse' for the Highland Nursing Home. On 23rd December, 1955, she received a call from Mrs Wentworth, the Matron to ask her to come and nurse a heart case, Mr Swift. When she arrived, Dr Adams came and attended the patient and gave him an injection and, afterwards, two tablets. Sister Penny had no idea what the injection or the tablets were: 'I did not ask the doctor and he did not tell me.' She was given to understand that Dr Adams always liked giving injections to the patients himself. This injection seemed to quieten the patient and he went to sleep. Between 5 and 6 a.m. on Christmas Eve, 24th December, the patient had severe rigor. Dr Adams was sent for and gave the patient an injection. Sister Penny remembered picking up the empty ampoule from the table and she gave it to Matron so that she could see what had been given in this injection. Mr Swift recovered slightly and slept.

Sister Penny went off duty at 8 a.m., and arrived back at 9 p.m. that same evening, 24th December. Matron gave her a report that Mr Swift was a little better and had taken some food. Soon after, his condition changed: he had another severe rigor and Dr Adams was sent for. He attended very quickly and he gave the patient an injection. She could not recall what the injection was, nor that the patient had received any kind of drink, but Dr Adams definitely left two tablets and a capsule. Matron gave the capsule to the patient that evening and Sister Penny gave the two tablets back to the Doctor after the patient had died.

Mr Swift was in distress with his breathing. He was sitting up and supported by pillows. Sister Penny continued: 'The Doctor, to my astonishment, removed several of the pillows and laid the patient in a recumbent position on his left side. This treatment was seemingly inconsistent with the patient's condition. Mr Swift remained in this position until he passed away about 2 a.m. on Christmas morning.' The Doctor was again called before the patient passed away but he arrived a little too late. It was at this point that Sister Penny was to be even more amazed at his conduct: 'When Dr Adams entered the bedroom he seemed annoyed that he had not been called sooner. I pointed out to the Doctor that the deceased had not moved from the position that he, the Doctor, had put him in. He made no comment. It struck me at the time that Dr Adams was annoyed because he had not arrived before the patient had died. There was no occasion for Dr Adams to be put out, but he certainly was so. I do not know why and I cannot express my thoughts more clearly but Dr Adams gave me the impression that he wanted to see and speak to Mr Swift before he died.'

Sister Penny described Dr Adams as 'an old-fashioned type of doctor and very attentive towards his patient.' She felt very strongly though 'that a nurse is entitled to know what injections or tablets are given to the patient, particularly when the Doctor gives the injections himself.'


## Matron Kate Wentworth

Mrs Kate Wentworth was the Matron of Highland Nursing Home in Carew Road; she was a state-registered nurse and she and her husband owned the home, which they had opened in July 1950. She employed six nurses, three of whom were fully-trained. From July 1950 up to the summer of 1956 they had had nearly four hundred patients, utilising eleven beds.

It was on the 23rd December, 1955 that Dr Adams had rung her up and asked her to reserve a place for Mr Lionel Swift, aged 78 years, a retired solicitor. He was an acute heart case and admitted the same day: his condition was very serious and Dr Adams visited at 4.30 p.m. No treatment was given on this occasion except whisky and soda: this was strictly on the Doctor's instructions.

At 9.30 p.m. that evening, Dr Adams visited the patient and Sister Penny was in attendance as the special night nurse. Matron had received a report from Sister Penny noting that the Doctor had given the patient a sedative, an injection and tablets, but he had not told her what these were, so the report could not contain this vital information. The patient had a restless night and at five past six the next morning, Christmas Eve, he had a severe rigor – severe and prolonged shivering – suggesting that he might have pneumonia or some internal inflammation. Dr Adams was sent for and he arrived at 7.15 a.m. Dr Adams did not convey to Matron what treatment he gave and so this information, again, was not in Matron's report, but Sister Penny had given an injection of 1 c.c. of coramine as the patient's pulse was extremely weak. At 8 a.m. the patient appeared somewhat better and was then sleeping quietly and this was when Sister Penny went off duty and the day staff came in.

When Matron saw Mr Swift at 8 a.m. he was still very seriously ill but towards the afternoon, after 2 p.m., his condition gradually improved and by 6 p.m. he was able to take a little nourishment. Dr Adams visited during the afternoon and Matron's reports, which she was consulting, showed that he gave the patient an intra-muscular injection of chrystomycin 500,000 units twice that day. At 9 p.m. on 24th December, Sister Penny came on duty again and at 9.45 p.m. Mr Swift had another rigor. Dr Adams attended and the patient was given brandy and 1 c.c. of coramine. The Doctor left two sedative tablets of some kind and both were given to the patient at 10.10 p.m. Dr Adams also left two more tablets with the instructions that they were to be given at hourly intervals if the patient was restless. At 11 p.m. the patient was sleeping quietly, but his pulse and respirations were increasing. By 1 a.m. on Christmas Day, the patient was sleeping heavily and appeared to be unconscious. Shortly before 2 a.m., Matron was very worried about the patient's condition and sent for Dr Adams. At 2.05 a.m. Mr Swift died and the Doctor arrived soon afterwards.

During the nursing of Mr Swift, one thing had disturbed Mrs Wentworth, the Matron, considerably; it was at 10 p.m. on 24th December: Dr Adams was present at the nursing home and the patient was rather restless. He was propped up and in a sitting position – which was usual in heart cases. 'The Doctor then said he would like to make the patient more comfortable and immediately removed three pillows from the bed and threw them on the floor. To my amazement the removal of these pillows allowed the patient to lay rather flat in the bed and in my opinion this was the wrong position for the patient in view of his complaint. Sister Randall and Sister Penny who were present, were in agreement with my feelings about the patient being left in the position described. Mr Swift died in this position four hours later.'

### Matron Nellie Spencer

Miss Nellie Spencer was Matron of the Southfields Nursing Home from 1941. This nursing home had been owned by the Rev. H.A. Plaisted of Medenham Vicarage in Buckinghamshire since 1937. Miss Spencer was much more exact about her patients: since 1945 only twelve of Dr Adams' patients had been admitted to Southfields, and, of these, three had died whilst in the nursing home. If she was correct, however, the police list of death certificates has some inaccuracies about the place of death or, alternatively, the place of death is incorrect on the death certificates. The first of the patients Miss Spencer referred to was Mr Thomas Allen, admitted on 7th August, 1955, a permanent resident of the Cumberland Hotel, who had had a stroke and was paralysed down the left side, almost losing his power of speech. The only treatment had been 'brandy, glucose and lemon which was given by the doctor himself.' The patient gradually got worse and died on 22nd August. Dr Adams gave the causes of death as '(a) syncope (loss of consciousness due to low blood pressure) and (b) cerebral thrombosis'.

The next patient was 'Miss Ingham' who is named on the certificate list as 'Edith Maud Inman'. She had been governess to friends of Lady Prendergast and lived at Meads House, the home of the Prendergasts. She, in fact, died on the very same day as Mr Allen, 22nd August, 1955 – Miss Spencer said of carcinoma of the stomach, but the causes certified by Dr Adams were '(a) anaemia and asthenia (b) carcinoma of ovary.' The only treatment given to this patient, as far as she knew, was 2 c.c. of coramine which she had administered on the morning she died.

The third patient Miss Spencer mentioned was Mrs Mary Wheale, admitted on 29th September, 1955, suffering from pernicious anaemia. The patient told Matron that she had been to Eastbourne on holiday and had consulted Dr Adams. After returning to her home in Swanage, Dorset, she became unwell and returned to Eastbourne so that Dr Adams could attend her. He had suggested that she should enter a nursing home and she had accepted his advice and been referred to Southfields. Mrs Wheale had chiefly a fluid diet and Dr Adams prescribed tablets to be taken before food and at night, and a Medinal tablet to induce sleep. Matron had not seen any injections given and her health gradually deteriorated; she died on 6th October, 1955, only a week after she was admitted. Miss Spencer thought the cause of death must be pernicious anaemia but she had not seen the death certificate. This patient was only 52 years old when she died and the cause of death given by Dr Adams was actually 'coronary thrombosis' This death certificate is only listed on the handwritten list by police and is omitted from the typewritten list.

Miss Spencer must have forgotten a couple of other deaths of patients of Dr Adams in her nursing home: that of Mrs Emily Ada Dawson who died, aged 78, on 24th November, 1955. The Doctor gave the causes of death as '(a) uraemia and (b) renal degeneration'. This was the fourth death of one of his patients at Southfields Nursing Home in slightly over three months. There was also an earlier death, that of Mrs Gladys Fawcus, aged 62 on 2nd July, 1949. The cause was given by Dr Adams as 'carcinoma of the liver'.

Yes, Miss Spencer had always found Dr Adams to be kind and attentive to the patients, and he never hesitated to come out when called at night. She was at pains to point out that he had tried to send many more patients to her but that on most occasions when he had telephoned she had no spare beds and was unable to accept them. She also made it clear that she kept no stocks of dangerous drugs: all drugs were supplied on doctor's prescription or were from the doctor's bag, and any drugs left over after death were returned to the doctor.

### Sister Annie Bell Sweeney

Annie Bell Sweeney was one of the few younger nurses who had nursed Dr Adams' patients, being only 34 in 1956. The first of these patients was Mrs Edith Bowdler who was in the Berrow Nursing Home in Carew Road. She was 91 years of age and had gangrene in her right foot; Sister Sweeney nursed her for about a month. Dr Snowball, the surgeon, came to see the patient and discuss with Dr Adams the possibility of amputating the foot, but they decided against it due to the patient's great age; naturally, she died. Sister Sweeney said that the only treatment 'consisted of dressing the leg regularly. I saw Dr Adams give no injections' – despite the painful condition, – and no antibiotics. 'She (Mrs Bowdler) had two daughters who worked for a living and I think they were quite poor.' Mrs Bowdler died on 9th October, 1950 and Dr Adams certified the causes of death as '(a) myocardial failure and (b) toxaemia-gangrene of right foot.'

A more usual type of patient for Sister Sweeney was Mr John Goulston, who lived at the Chatsworth Hotel with his wife. He had advanced cancer and 'I gave this patient injections of omnopon (morphia) and, on the instructions of Dr Adams, I gave these injections when they were required. The Doctor visited each day and after I had nursed him for about twelve days, the patient died. He had a wife and family who were present when he died.' This was on 5th December, 1950 and Dr Adams certified the causes of death as '(a) uraemia and (b) carcinoma of prostate.'

### Sister Phyllis Turner

Miss Phyllis Turner, a 'private nursing nurse' had an interesting tale to tell about one of the cases she had nursed for Dr Adams. The patient was a Mrs Chasey, who lived first at the Seaview Hotel and later at the Landsdowne Hotel. This was in 1947 and Sister Turner had nursed her 'on and off' for about eighteen months to two years. The patient suffered from bronchitis and had an arthritic hip; she was about 67 years old, a widow and 'reasonably well off'. The only treatment Dr Adams gave was 'tablets'. Mr Chasey had died in 1945, and Sister Turner did not know what had been wrong with him – this death was out of the scope of the police enquiry. Mrs Chasey had told Sister Turner that her husband and Dr Adams had been 'great friends' and that they used to discuss stocks and shares. She also told the nurse that 'the Doctor was very good at helping her with her stocks and shares after her husband had died.' Mrs Chasey also told her that she had left the Doctor £31,000 in her will.

Sister Turner continued: 'At this time Mrs Chasey had a gentleman friend who detested Dr Adams and I was given to understand by this friend, whose name I cannot recall and who is now dead, that he had persuaded Mrs Chasey to remake her Will. He did not tell me he did this to exclude the Doctor from the Will but I do know that that was his intention.' Later, Mrs Chasey told Sister Turner that she had made a fresh will and had remembered her. 'She did not say to what extent and I was taken by surprise.' The date was now January 1949 and Sister Chasey discovered that she had tuberculosis of one lung and had to go to a sanatorium in Robertsbridge in Sussex: it was a lengthy stay and she was there until January of 1953. Mrs Chasey often wrote to her whilst she was at the sanatorium, but in the meantime had moved to a hotel in Haywards Heath and later to a nursing home there, where she died in the latter part of 1949. Sister Turner read in a newspaper that Mrs Chasey left £17,000, bequeathing most of this to relatives but £2,000 to her 'gentleman friend', although he had died before the estate was settled and it went to his two sons. Sister Turner received a legacy of £200, but she was certain that Dr Adams received nothing under the will.

Sister Turner considered that Dr Adams was 'pleasant and attentive to his patients' but found that 'I could not work happily with Dr Adams because I could not get sufficient detail of the treatment given to patients and there was not always that happy co-operation between nurse and doctor.'

### Sister Olwen Williams

Sister Olwen Williams nursed only two of Dr Adams' patients as she concurred with Sister Turner's assessment of the Doctor: 'I did not like working for Dr Adams as there was no co-operation between doctor and nurse. He used to give his own treatment and would not let the nurse in the room whilst he visited his patient.'

Detective Superintendent Hannam and his team had taken statements from forty state-registered nurses. They had also imparted information other than that they wished to include in their sworn statements, but, unfortunately, this is not recorded unless Hannam mentions it in his report. He notes that, while the nurses were reluctant to criticise a doctor from a professional point of view, the majority said that Dr Adams was extremely familiar with his patients; that in some cases 'he knelt beside their beds, held their hands and, indeed, prayed with them' and was much more attentive than was normal in the nurses' experience, or professionally correct. Some had remarked on 'the stupidity of medication by giving sleeping draft [sic], injection or tablets at midday so that the patient slept during the day and had wakeful nights.' The majority of the nurses had said that Dr Adams was difficult to work with as he was unco-operative and refused to tell them what he was administering, particularly in regard to any injections. They had told the police that this was very embarrassing for them, and, also particularly mentioned that Dr Adams preferred nurses to be out of the room when he was conducting examinations of patients, which was the opposite of normal practice.

Hannam particularly referred to the evidence of Phyllis Owen, which is outlined at the beginning of this chapter, regarding Dr Adams' excessive use of sedative medication. Another nurse emphasised to the police that Dr Adams was dispensing heroin to a patient and that, on three occasions she implored him to stop it because it was making the patient ill, but he insisted on continuing. 'On her own initiative she stopped it and the patient recovered immediately.' Hannam also comments on Dr Adams' treatment of Mr Swift when he pulled the pillows away from him, that it was improper and the nurses had emphasised that this treatment had, at the least, hastened Mr Swift's death. He also notes in the report, other cases where patients' conditions remain untreated in order to prolong the need for the Doctor's attendance.

Chapter Twenty-Two

# General Practice

It was the 1911 National Insurance Act of Lloyd-George which ensured that the general practitioner became an established and enduring part of British Society. The Act provided general medical care for uninsured workers – though not for their families. There were also, by 1911, six to seven million people provided for by contracts with practices, at less than five shillings per person through the Friendly Societies. This still left the GP doing much work for little or no payment, and sometimes payment in kind. Those registered with a doctor under the National Insurance Act were his 'panel' patients or 'Lloyd George breadwinners', and this did ensure him a better income than previously, but still there remained large numbers of doctors who were poor and treating only poor patients.

As far as can be estimated, about two-thirds of doctors had a mixed general practice, with poor patients as well as wealthier ones who were private patients. 15% of well-off patients in a practice might be contributing over 50% of its income, thus enabling the doctor to charge his poorer patients very little. Many doctors though built their reputations by starting in industrial areas with poor patients. This is well-described in some of the novels of A.J. Cronin, himself a doctor.

There was a major crisis among doctors in 1914, with the advent of the First World War, particularly in the medical schools. Students not only had to qualify, but also face service in the War; 9% of all the men under 45 were killed. It was also true that even becoming a medical student had its hazards: whereas in the 1870s and 1880s it was typhus, by the early 20th Century, it was septicaemia and TB. The medical syllabus had remained much the same as it was from the late 19th Century, certainly until the late 1920s. A GP who retired in 1935 had been taught at medical school by a professor who had himself been taught by a surgeon who had learned his techniques during the Crimean War, and did not believe in using anaesthetics for fractures: that GP had continued the practice.

Much of the dispensing was done in the doctors' practices rather than in chemists' shops and I still recall this being done in my own doctor's surgery as late as the 1950s. What did they dispense? Dr Stane explains:

'Well, you used your placebos. We had a lot. White aspirins, green aspirins and blue ones. We had a mixture of lactose, you know, milk sugar which was dissolved. Some we put some stuff in it to give it a horrible taste, some we didn't. In fact we used no end of stuff, you know. We had long lectures on Materia Medica. You don't get these things nowadays [1984]. We had every drug from every plant and every weed that grew… We made them in the surgery – your mixtures, your concoctions, your infusions… For neurotics we had a mixture of potassium bromide and valerian. The smell rather reminded you of a cat on the ground. I always felt you must be feeling pretty bad to drink that stuff. Did any of those linctuses help? Strychnine in the tonic? I don't know… Old Sir John Craven always said to us – "Remember, 90% of your patients will get better whether you treat them or not. Never give them anything that may be likely to harm them; 7% or 8% will require a little attention and some skill; 2 per cent are going to die anyway. But the healing force of nature is the one thing you've got to remember."'[1]

I remember our doctor's wife, Mrs Whiting, dispensing only two kinds of medicine: cloudy white or opaque brown, through the hatch in the waiting room – she was never seen full-length by a patient. Alternatively, Dr Whiting would rummage through a heap of samples on his roll-top desk in the surgery, peer through his pebble-lensed glasses and proffer it, saying, 'I wonder you don't try this. Tell me if it works.' He had probably qualified in the early 1900s. The waiting-room too was probably fairly typical of many in the first half of the twentieth century: brown linoleum on the floor, brown leather benches around the room, brown paintwork and a Victorian fireplace in which a coal fire was lit in the winter. On the walls were long photographs, hung from the picture rails, of the Doctor, arms folded, wearing striped jersey, in his University rugby fifteen. The magazines on the table for the waiting patients to read were pre-War 'Punch's and Country Life of the 1930s, with sales notices from Knight, Frank and Rutley advertising Elizabethan manor houses and estates, priced at £25,000. The Doctor never did take down the government notice from Aneurin Bevan announcing the inauguration of the National Health Service.

The Cottage hospital system developed during the first half of the 20th century, with patients being dealt with locally in rural areas and the GPs able to perform surgery. Dr Stane explained how they anaesthetised patients:

'Chloroform was the safest one from that point of view – but it was deadly stuff you know. After a big operation they were vomiting for days afterwards and half of them died from liver poisoning. Of course, people wouldn't accept that but half of them vomited their way out. You gave them a quarter grain of morphine and some atropine to knock them out, and then you gave them the chloroform. And in the process of going from the conscious to the unconscious, they became violent as they were on the table, especially with an alcoholic. Actually, the patients never knew this, we actually tied them down, with a broad belt. If you didn't they would have thrown themselves off.'

[1] Gathorne-Hardy

Another doctor, Dr Chathill, recalled:

> 'There was a gauze mask on a metal frame and you dropped the ether on to it. It was quite an art actually, to get someone under. They used to fight like blazes because they thought they were suffocating. Later I was taught to give ether through a machine without pentothal. You had to get exactly the right balance of ether and oxygen so that it put them out quickly with a lot of ether, and then lifted the ether and put in the oxygen before they suffocated themselves. I never killed anybody.'[2]

The general practice system which existed before the National Health Service, encouraged patient-poaching – which was an activity indulged in by Dr Adams almost as soon as he arrived in Eastbourne, intent on being a 'fashionable' doctor for Eastbourne society. The 'poached' patients were both the richest and the most neurotic: they required regular visits and many prescriptions, and paid well for them. Some practices depended upon their neurotic patients. In the depression years of the 1930s, there was also a great deal of poverty, and patients found real difficulty in finding the money for subscriptions and medicines. The maximum relief available was 2 shillings a week and the cost of feeding a child more than twice this amount. As a result, the state of health of the unemployed and their families rapidly worsened. The poorer private patients often could not pay their bills, but doctors did not refuse to treat them; by the time the National Health Service came into being in 1948, most practices had enormous debts and the general practitioners needed the NHS as much as the patients did.

In 1948 the GPs became independent operators under contract to the State, leaving them still to choose or not choose their patients. This was an immediate relief in financial terms, but no one knew what to expect, or seemed to have predicted what would happen. There was a great flood of demand due to the backlog with some conditions. Many women, for example, had been waiting, in great distress for twenty years to have prolapse repairs done. With the development, during and after the Second World War, of many new drugs, there was also the growing awareness that, at last, doctors could do something about many conditions. Disease had dropped through the 1920s and 30s – as it had since the age of great municipal enterprise in the late Victorian period – with improvements in public health and living conditions, but then came the drug revolution. Many still remember how streptomycin was hailed as manna from heaven when it saved so many lives from the scourge of TB in crowded cities such as Glasgow. The GPs set about prescribing pills; some at an alarming rate.

In general, GPs in the 'fifties seem to have come under increasing strain, and they did many more visits in those days – thirty odd a day was not unusual in an urban area. In some practices there were GPs who 'worked the system' by seeing private patients and leaving their colleagues to do the NHS work; and Dr Adams was not the only one who prescribed for private patients using NHS prescriptions. It was never permitted for GPs to treat patients privately and also to have them on their NHS lists; private patients had to pay for their drugs privately.

[2] Ibid

It was not uncommon, however, for a patient to be on one GP's list as a private patient and on another's as an NHS patient, thereby receiving their drugs on the NHS on a 'second opinion' basis. This type of collusion was not illegal but prescribing for a private patient on an NHS prescription without the consent of the NHS doctor was, of course, fraudulent.

It was the system of payment for GPs that caused the near-collapse of NHS general practice in the later 1950s. When the NHS was set up the method of payment was a capitation system with some 'items of service' payments. There was a pool fund on a yearly basis which had to be shared between 21,000 or more GPs. Sometimes the pool dried up and sometimes there was a little left and this would be divided up with each GP getting just a few pounds extra. The doctors did not get paid more if they did more patient care and, in order to make sufficient income, some GPs would take the maximum number of patients – then 4,000 – which was an almost impossible amount to service adequately. Doctors could get vastly different incomes, depending on where they were in the country and if they had the opportunity for some private patients and the odd hospital appointment. Being a doctor to hotels provided a substantial income. Dr Adams, with his 800 NHS patients, the rest of his list private patients, two hospital appointments, and as doctor to several of the larger hotels, would have been one of the highest paid GPs in Britain.

The goodwill of the GPs towards the National Health Service was running out by 1956, and in February 1957, just a few weeks prior to Dr Adams' trial, amidst much controversy, the new Macmillan Government appointed a Royal Commission to consider the remuneration system for doctors and dentists and make comparisons, to decide upon the proper levels and provide for regular reviews of payment. This was followed in 1958 by the setting-up of a Medical Services Review Committee under the chairmanship of Sir Arthur Porritt [called in by Dr Adams to see Mr Hullett]. This Committee was 'to review the provision of medical services to the public, and the organisation, in the light of ten years' experience of the NHS and to make recommendations'. Any collapse of the National Health Service was totally unthinkable and would have brought down any government: despite its youth it had quickly become one of the most cherished possessions of the British people.

—•—

A. J. Cronin's Dr Cameron, so memorably portrayed by the late Andrew Cruikshank, is our picture of the ideal and traditional GP: eccentric, kindly, clad in Harris tweed, enjoying his dram of whisky, the Scottish accent – it is all so comforting to the patient. The GP is set somewhat apart in the community by his profession and, in what the French historian Phillipe Ariés has dubbed 'The Age of the Medical Death', he has gradually been usurping the place of the vicar or minister. The last rites for the soul replaced by the last rites for the body. As power was wielded by the priest before his congregation were literate or could read the scriptures in the vernacular, so the doctor has power over his patients when they have little or no medical knowledge. In addition to the doctor's 'apartness' there is a formality in the doctor-patient relationship and a certain distance is expected. If that thin line is crossed then certain assumptions may be made. Very little might mean a lot in a more inhibited age when emotions were not usually exhibited.

For at least a hundred years, dating from the Apothecaries Act of 1858, the aim of the medical schools was to turn out a doctor who would be able to cope with any situation: from measles or the difficult childbirth to an outbreak of cholera or an emergency operation on the kitchen table. It has given Britain this vision of the ideal and heroic family doctor. No wonder we're all annoyed at the GP who doesn't want to turn out for a home visit at night! The medical student was trained by doctors from various branches of medicine to produce this universal doctor. But the specialties increased and became considered more important than general practice. It was not realised that general practice was fundamentally different from specialised branches of medicine and that, therefore, the students recruited for general practice would need different qualities. It has been suggested that high rates of suicide, alcoholism and stress found amongst general practitioners may be partially attributable to some being chosen for a profession to which they are quite unsuited.

Perhaps today we are more willing to acknowledge the considerable emotional damage that can be caused by sudden death of a family member or similar suffering at the age of eighteen or nineteen. Perhaps we are also more willing to acknowledge that the traditional initiation of the medical student – i.e. the dissection of a corpse – while quite deliberate and intended to 'toughen-up' the aspiring doctor could also cause some emotional trauma. John Bodkin Adams' father died when he was 15, two years before he dissected his first cadaver. His brother died while he was still at medical school.

# Matters Medical

## The BMA, The Government and Scotland Yard

Early in the police investigation, on 24th August, 1956, the Secretary of the Eastbourne Division of the British Medical Association had sent a circular to all doctors in the area. This letter was headed 'Professional Secrecy' and reminded doctors that if they were approached by the police for interviews that confidentiality of information on patients was paramount and that the State had no right to demand information. The Secretary referred to a resolution of the BMA of 1952, 'when a suggestion was made that in certain exceptional circumstances it might be a doctor's moral or social duty, for the protection of innocent persons, to disclose information, without the patient's consent, to an interested party. This suggestion was rejected…'

It was only 'by statutory sanction', i.e., in a court of law, that they could disclose such information. The letter did not mention information on dead patients, who could hardly consent or otherwise, but the effect was that, even without their natural inclination to close ranks, nearly all the GPs in Eastbourne felt that the BMA had effectively banned them from talking to the police.

The Attorney-General wrote to Sir Theobald Mathew, Director of Public Prosecutions [DPP's archive] on 9th November saying that he had seen Dr Macrae, Secretary of the BMA on the previous day and, as a result, Dr Macrae had gone to Birmingham to see the Chairman of his Association. Dr Macrae returned the following morning to see the Attorney-General at his office stating that he would do what he could 'to persuade the two doctors to give all the information in their possession to the police.' The Director was asked to let the Attorney-General have the names and addresses of the two doctors and these would be passed to Dr Macrae so that he could call them in and 'discuss the matter with them and will let me know what they have decided to do'. If they were prepared to give information then Hannam should go and see them. The Attorney-General regarded it as 'essential that if he does so his visit should not be attended by any publicity.'

The names written on this letter are those of Dr Philip Mathew, Dr Harry Estcourt, MBE, and a third, Dr Victor Williams, who had left Eastbourne eight or nine years previously and was then living in Reading, and these names and addresses were sent to the Attorney-General on the same day.

Dr Mathew of the White House practice in Eastbourne – very near to the Red House practice of which Dr Adams was a partner – was one of the two doctors in Eastbourne, the other being his partner, Dr Estcort, who was willing to talk to the police. There is no doubt that this took great courage, but he obviously felt that this was his moral duty, that he should take this opportunity to protect elderly patients in Eastbourne from a doctor whom he considered to be dangerous.

Correspondence between Dr Mathew and the British Medical Association, which he handed over to Detective Superintendent Hannam was at the beginning of a Scotland Yard file, marked 'Secret'. The first of these was a letter dated 15th November, 1956 from Dr A. Macrae, the Secretary of the BMA read with some surprise by the recipient, Dr Mathew:

> 'I have been informed by the authorities concerned that you have been approached about a matter concerning Dr J. Bodkin Adams of Eastbourne and I have been given to understand that you find yourself in some difficulty because of a ruling of the British Medical Association. It seems to me that in a matter of this kind the decision as to what you ought to do must rest with yourself. If, however, you should feel that it might be helpful in any way to talk the matter over with me in strict confidence I should, of course, be very glad to see you…'

Dr Mathew hastily scribbled a reply, crossing out the heading on his notepaper, which revealed that he was once the Honorary Secretary of the BMA's 'Local Medical War Committee':

> '…I am very puzzled at the contents of the letter, and cannot understand who the "authorities concerned" are. I would like to be enlightened on this point by you. I am not personally feeling in any difficulty because of any ruling of the B.M.A. that I am aware of. Consequently I do not feel that it is necessary for me to come and see you, though I appreciate your offer…'

A response came from Dr Macrae, dated 21st November:

> '…I recently had an off-the-record conversation with the Attorney-General, Sir Reginald Manningham-Buller, at his invitation. He told me that it had been reported to him that you were in a position to supply information which might be helpful to the police in an investigation which they had been conducting but that you found yourself in some difficulty because of the B.M.A. policy on the subject of professional secrecy. I gather from your letter that this is not the position and I am very sorry to find that I have troubled you unnecessarily.'

Dr Mathew scribbled an even hastier reply on the reverse of the letter:

'…I now understand the position perfectly, but I was quite at a loss about your first letter. The matter to which you allude is not of course an ethical matter, but obviously a police matter. In this case, were I asked, I should act on my own judgement, and would give a statement in accordance with the facts known to me.'

Still, another letter arrived from Dr Macrae:

'…When I saw the Attorney General I gathered that he was reluctant to trouble you to no useful purpose and I think it was his intention that the police should make no approach to you unless I was able to inform him that you had no objection to being approached and that you were prepared to give information. In view of this, I should be glad to know whether I may inform the Attorney General that you are prepared to make a statement in accordance with the facts known to you.'

What is quite extraordinary is the lengths to which the Attorney General (in fact the Government) went to ensure that the medical profession's feathers were not ruffled by the police enquiry.

Dr Mathew responded wearily:

'…I have subsequently had the opportunity of a conversation with Det. Supt. Hannam on the matter. I have made it clear to him that he is at liberty at any time to ask me any questions should he wish to do so…'

He has crossed out in his draft letter:

'He [Hannam] told me that the police do not propose to ask me to make a statement at the present time.'

Hannam, in his first report, makes it clear that Dr Mathew's information was very instructive as to method but that the cases he had mentioned were not recent enough for witnesses to be produced to provide evidence.

Dr Macrae wrote to the Attorney-General on 22nd November (DPP's archive) saying that Dr Victor Williams had been to see him that morning and that they had had 'a frank "off-the-record" talk' in which he had stated that he had no objection to the Attorney-General being 'informed in confidence that he has a strong personal dislike of the professional colleague in whose activities you happen to be interested'.

However, he had no information which would be of assistance to the police and Dr Macrae considered that 'no useful purpose could be served by a further approach being made to Dr Williams'. The BMA seem to have overruled the police. Nothing had been heard from Dr Estcourt at this stage.

On Wednesday, 28th November, notice was given in the House of Commons of two

Questions addressed for the Attorney General to answer on the following Monday, December 3rd. These were:-

> Mr Swingler: To ask Mr Attorney General what recent communications he has sent to the General Medical Council.
> Mr Delargy: To ask Mr Attorney General what reports he has sent to the General Medical Council of the British Medical Association during the past six months.

Sir Reginald Manningham-Buller was disturbed to see these questions and wrote on 14th December to Sir John Nott-Bower, the Commissioner at Scotland Yard to tell him that 'they were obviously directed to my communication with the Secretary of the British Medical Association in regard to the Adams case at Eastbourne. Knowledge of this, which was a highly confidential matter, had been confined only to those immediately concerned with my enquiries into this case and the appearance of these Questions indicated that there must have been a leakage.' He had spoken to the two Members concerned and had been told that the source of their information was 'a highly reputable Fleet Street journalist'. The Attorney General sought information on the journalist's source through the two Members of Parliament. In the meantime he gave a written answer to the Questions through the Solicitor General:

> 'My right hon. and learned Friend has had no communications with the General Medical Council within the last six months. He has communicated with an officer of the Council about a criminal case which is now sub judice.'

The Attorney General mentioned that he had been unable to answer the questions orally because he was engaged in opening the case for the prosecution in the Armstrong case at Winchester Assizes. This was also a poisoning case [the Attorney General had to prosecute in these cases] but the prosecution was successful when John Armstrong was found guilty of the murder of his five-month old son by giving him seconal (a barbiturate) and sentenced to death, though later reprieved,

A response came from the journalist through one of the Members of Parliament, disclosing his source as 'Scotland Yard'. This news caused the Attorney General 'considerable concern' for the fact that he had had discussions with the Secretary of the British Medical Association, Dr Macrae, was known 'only to a very limited circle'. He wanted a thorough enquiry at Scotland Yard to ascertain whether this was the source of the leakage.

Sir John Nott-Bower responded, on 21st December, by asking Sir Reginald the name of the M.P. so that one of his 'trusted senior officers' could interview him and obtain the name of the journalist, for without this he did not see that he could discover the source of the leakage, although he could not, of course, 'accept that Scotland Yard was in any way involved in the matter'.

This response was not at all acceptable to the Attorney General who did not see what useful purpose such an interview would serve and would deprecate such a move. As the information could only have been known to a very few at the Yard, enquiries should be pursued there.

He had been told, in strictest confidence, the name of the journalist and knew him personally: 'I am sure he would tell the truth… and there is no reason to doubt his word.' It seems likely that this was Rodney Hallworth of the *Daily Mail*. He would be glad to hear that the internal enquiry was taking place.

The reply to the Attorney General from the Commissioner was drafted and then amended by Hannam as both are in his handwriting. This was a report on an internal enquiry at Scotland Yard and this made it clear that what had, in fact, happened was that Hannam's Report on the Adams' case had actually been sent – this word was crossed out and 'loaned' entered – to the BMA. Those at the Yard who knew this were Mr Jackson the Assistant Commissioner and Hannam 'who were informed by the Director's Office', [Director of Public Prosecutions] and later Commander Hatherill and Mr Jackson's personal secretary, Mr Tyler. The Commissioner was 'satisfied that none of these gentlemen has disclosed this information to anyone else'. In the circumstances he was afraid that he could not 'carry the enquiry any further'.

He thought that the journalist had acted 'not only indiscreetly, but most unfairly to Scotland Yard' by giving a pledge of secrecy and then passing information to an M.P. 'It is difficult to understand why he did so since it can hardly have been in the public interest to disclose the facts'. And then, whilst not disclosing the name of his informant, he implicated Scotland Yard: 'It would be difficult to imagine a meaner course of action'.

The Commissioner then mentions that Hannam had informed him that 'doctors in Eastbourne' had shown him letters received from the BMA 'each of which referred to an approach made to the Association by yourself' and said that this information was a matter of 'common knowledge among the doctors in Eastbourne'.

The sting was in the tail of the letter: '…in view of the Home Secretary's special responsibility in regard to documents for which he claims privilege [police reports] I have thought it right to inform him of the facts of this matter.'

This letter was actually sent to the Attorney-General on 1st January, 1957, although it seems to have been drafted earlier.

A letter of 27th December from George Hatherill (Commander 'C') to the Commissioner throws further light on what occurred. He had seen the Deputy Commander of 'C' Department and the Chief Superintendent of Criminal Investigation (Findlay) and discovered that they had known nothing of the leak until after the Commissioner had received the letter of 14th December from the Attorney General. Prior to this only the Assistant Chief Commissioner and Hannam had known that Hannam's Report had been sent by the Attorney General to the BMA. The Police Report on the investigation into Dr Adams' activities had been sent to Dr Adams' trade union, the BMA, by the Attorney General who was to prosecute the case! Hannam had been 'most emphatic' that he had never discussed the matter with anyone, not even DS Hewett as 'he considered it too dangerous a matter to talk about'. Commander Hatherill had held the same view and he had not even discussed it with the Deputy Commanders or the Chief Superintendent C.I.

The Commissioner then wrote to Sir Frank Newsam at the Home Office on 1st January, 1957 informing him of the travels of Hannam's Report on Dr Adams:

'…On 16th October, 1956, Detective Superintendent Hannam submitted his report and on 25th October Jackson sent the papers to the Director of Public Prosecutions. The report is a document of 187 pages containing inter alia many facts about the doctor's activities over a long period and the background of the case generally.

In view of the Home Secretary's responsibility for the privilege attaching to police reports I think it right to inform you that the Attorney-General left a copy of this report with the Secretary of the B.M.A. whom he saw in connection with the case. I am also informed that the document has been copied and supplied to the medical experts in the case.' [Doctors Douthwaite and Ashby for the prosecution]

The letter the Commissioner had sent to the Attorney General on 1st January, drew a response dated 4th January:

'It is not the case that Hannam's report was taken to the British Medical Association. I am not concerned to defend the journalist who is the subject of your animadversions but I am at a loss to know why it is assumed that he obtained the information from someone under a pledge of secrecy. I can understand a journalist not wishing to get further involved in this matter. I suspect that the disclosure to the two Members of Parliament was prompted by the erroneous belief that communication had been made with a view to disciplinary proceedings being taken by the profession against Dr Adams. If that had been done, it would, of course have been highly irregular. It is to me most puzzling that the journalist in question should have asserted to a Member of Parliament with whom he communicated that the source of his information was Scotland Yard.

As enquiries at Scotland Yard can throw no further light on the matter, and as enquiries of the Members of Parliament will not do so, I agree that no useful purpose will be served by pursuing the matter further. I am surprised to hear that any communication to a doctor at Eastbourne specifically referred to me. I have been informed of the contents of one of the letters. There was no reference to me and I am assured no reference to a report. You will note that one of the two questions tabled specifically refers to a report.

I am not aware that any claim of Crown Privilege can possibly arise unless and until it is sought to produce Hannam's report in evidence.'

Here in the archive an 'Extract' intervenes as a note to the Chief Superintendent from Hannam and Findlay, merely setting out that the only press conference held in the case was the one in Eastbourne on the 17th August, 1956. This Extract is dated 4th January, 1957.

The next letter received by Sir Reginald Manningham-Buller, dated 7th January, cannot have pleased him; it was from the Home Secretary, Gwilym Lloyd-George:

'I have just heard from the Commissioner of Police that a copy of Detective Superintendent Hannam's report in the case of Dr Adams has been given to the Secretary of the British Medical Association.

The disclosure of this document is likely to cause me considerable embarrassment. As you know, police reports have always been treated as highly confidential documents and it has been the invariable practice to refuse to disclose their contents to Parliament or to individual Members. Indeed I should have no hesitation in claiming privilege if their production were required in a court of law. Moreover I am far from happy that police reports should be shown indiscriminately to expert witnesses.

I can only hope that no harm will result.'

The Attorney-General wrote on 9th January:

'My dear Gwilym'
'…it would not seem that you have been either fully or accurately informed [by the Commissioner of Police] I am certainly not aware of police reports being 'shown indiscriminately to expert witnesses'. I should be grateful if you would inform me who are these alleged expert witnesses… As I shall probably be conducting the case for the Crown, I think it is important that I should be told…

In his letter of the 1st January the Commissioner of Police asserted quite inaccurately that Hannam's report had been taken to the British Medical Association.

I think you should know the full facts. Hannam's report stated that there were some doctors at Eastbourne who had informed him that but for the ruling circulated to them by the British Medical Association they would have been able to give him information sufficient to warrant the preferment of the most serious charges.

After discussion with the Director of Public Prosecutions I decided to see Dr Macrae who is a responsible individual in order to try to get him to remove the ban and so enable the Crown, in the interests of justice, to get possession of this apparently most important information.

It is true I showed Dr Macrae the passages in question. He said that he would go to Birmingham to see the President of the British Medical Association. I allowed him to take the Report with him. Having regard to the status and character of Dr Macrae and the President of the British Medical Association I felt I could safely do so in the strictest confidence.

Dr Macrae did not feel he could approach the doctors at Eastbourne without his President's approval. The report was returned to me the next day.

Dr Macrae then approached the doctors in question and it soon became apparent that Hannam's report was entirely misleading in that they had no information which would justify the preferment of such charges.

All this occurred last November. The report was not 'given' to the Secretary of the British Medical Association. He had it in his possession for a few hours.

That this occurred was known to certain persons at Scotland Yard last November. It is not without significance that it is only now that the Commissioner should have written to you about it.'

The question which had been asked in the House by Swingler referred to 'reports' sent to the General Medical Council of the British Medical Association, so the Attorney General had inferred some leakage from Scotland Yard.

> 'I really cannot conceive that what has happened in connection with Hannam's report is likely to cause you any embarrassment at all. Indeed, I doubt whether you would have been troubled by it at all were it not for the fact that a leakage occurred and the journalist in question, who is known to you but who will not agree to his identity being divulged, asserted that the leakage came from Scotland Yard.
> Yours ever,
> Reggie.'

Hannam's first report was handed to the Director of Public Prosecutions on 25th October, 1956. The second report of 5th December made it clear that, by this time the police had all the evidence they required from doctors. The relevant paragraph of Hannam's report is this:

> 'Two doctors told us that in giving information to us patients would necessarily be involved and this prevented them from doing so. Then added that if the BMA or the G.M.C. approached them direct they would then give sufficient facts about Dr Adams to justify the most serious charges against him. We seriously believe that with perhaps two exceptions, all doctors in Eastbourne are most anxious to see "the menace in their midst" removed.'

It was always obvious that there would be no direct evidence from doctors in Eastbourne: how could they have such evidence? Only nurses would have this. The BMA circular to the GPs also did not ban doctors from assisting the police because the assistance required was regarding patients who were dead. Hannam mentions in his report, Dr Mathew and Dr Estcort as being prepared to assist in any case, but that they do not have direct evidence. Dr Snowball, the surgeon partner of Dr Adams is mentioned with regard to operations on various patients, and Dr Barkworth a junior partner of Dr Adams, who gave a statement to police with regard to the witnessing of the will of James Priestley Downs. Other doctors gave statements in respect of forgery of NHS prescriptions and cremation form statements by Dr Adams. The only doctor able to give any direct evidence regarding Dr Adams' clinical practice was Dr Harris, Dr Adams' junior partner, who had to make a statement in the case of Mrs Hullett and who was a witness both at the Hullett inquest and at the Old Bailey. The police did not, in fact, come across problems in getting statements required from doctors in Eastbourne. Paragraph 14 of Hannam's report is the only one which relates to general evidence of doctors.

Not only did the Attorney General give the report to the British Medical Association – and not 'loan' it, which is pure semantics – but he must have given it for a different reason to the one he gave the Home Secretary. The British Medical Association has always been the professional association of doctors since it was founded in 1885. Although it only officially became a trade union in 1974 (Trade Union and Labour Relations Act 1974) it always represented the interests of the medical profession and not the interests of patients. The General Medical Council is an entirely different organisation which has a duty to represent the interests of patients, although it is questionable whether it has always or even now manages to do so adequately.

What the Attorney General had, in fact, done was to allow the British Medical Association to make a copy of Hannam's confidential report for the Prosecution and present it to the Defence team for Dr Adams. Dr Macrae's duty as Secretary of the British Medical Association was to do anything in his power to protect his members. It cannot be imagined that the Attorney General, a lawyer just one place below the rank of the Lord Chancellor of the realm could 'loan' a police report of such importance for Dr Macrae to take it to his President and expect that only one particular paragraph would be read by them or that they would make no copy of the report. There is no evidence of any response from the BMA to any request from the Attorney General for assistance. It is clear, as Hannam obviously decided, that the Attorney General had most deliberately presented the Defence team with the police report and was seeking to deflect his action by concentrating on the leak and looking for a scapegoat.

Sir Frank Newsam sent copies of the Home Secretary's letter and the Attorney General's reply to the Commissioner on 14th January: 'The Home Secretary would be glad of your observations and in particular he would like to know who are the medical experts referred to…' In the meantime Hannam had borrowed Dr Mathew's correspondence with the BMA and sent this to Commander Hatherill on 17th January.

The Commissioner replied to Sir Frank Newsam on 24th January, saying that the expert witnesses, Dr Douthwaite and Dr Ashby, had been supplied with copies of the report by the Director of Public Prosecutions 'on the instructions of Counsel after a conference with the Attorney General.' He continued:

> '…the Attorney General states that I am wrong in saying that the report had been taken to the British Medical Association… however, he makes it clear that not only did he show the passages from the report to Dr Macrae but left the whole report with him to take to Birmingham to show to the President of the Association. It seems to me that this is a distinction without a difference.'

The following few communications in the file make it obvious that Hannam had been trying to force the cat out of the bag, and that he had the backing of the Commissioner and Scotland Yard seems in no doubt. Parallel with this saga was that of the nurses' notebooks.[see the Morrell case.]

Hannam was now given what amounted to an official 'carpeting' about the leak. On 8th March the Commissioner saw Hannam in the presence of Jackson (Assistant Commissioner C Department) and Mr Hawkyard. Hannam was told that Hawkyard had completed his enquiry into the leak and had failed to get any first-hand evidence that Hannam had made 'any improper disclosures to the press at his meeting with them in the Duncannon Public House.'

The Commissioner told Hannam that the Attorney General had authorised him to tell him that 'so far as his position as investigating officer and witness in the Bodkin Adams case is concerned, the matter was still as it had been in the past and that he retained the Attorney General's confidence.' Hannam had apparently admitted that he had had a meeting with press representatives, and the Commissioner was 'far from happy about it' but did not intend to pursue the matter, at least until the proceedings against Dr Adams were completed. He gave a direct order to Hannam to refrain, as far as possible, from having any contact with the press: 'Mr Hannam said he quite understood and would carry out my instructions loyally.'

The note of this meeting was sent the same day to the Attorney General, accompanied by a letter from the Commissioner:

'…I decided that this was as far as I could go. You will remember that you took the view that the circumstantial evidence might well be sufficient to bring home a discipline charge against Hannam. I think this would be the case if all the information disclosed in Hawkyard's report were available at disciplinary proceedings but the fact of the matter is that practically nothing would be available. None of the people concerned would be likely to be willing to appear before a discipline tribunal and we could not compel them to do so… Hannam would be entitled to have back his own statement given to Hawkyard and it could not be used in evidence, nor should I be entitled to use what Hannam admitted to me when I first acquainted him of the allegations that had been made…

…I should like to repeat how very much I regret that one of my senior officers should have behaved in this manner.'

Commander Hawkyard's report is not in the file, but the Attorney General refers to it in his reply to the Commissioner of 8th March, saying that he 'cannot agree with his conclusion that the complaint against the Detective Superintendent is not substantiated.' There was no direct evidence, but the circumstantial evidence was 'very strong indeed'. He wished to show the report to the other two barristers for the prosecution, Melford Stevenson and Morris for this reason:

'The steps taken by the Defence in having Hannam watched do make it likely that they may deliver a powerful attack on Hannam and I should like to consider our attitude with them. I should also like to speak to the Director about the matter referred to on page 8 at paragraph (b). I hope you have no objection.'

This last reference is not available as Hawkyard's report seems likely to have been destroyed, not being in the file. The reference to this in the Commissioner's reply to the Attorney General of 11th March is oblique when he agrees with the Attorney General's request. The Attorney General responded again on 12th March:

'I think that what you said to Hannam is excellent and that you certainly went as far as it was wise to go at the present time. Whether any further action is required after the trial is over is, of course, a matter for you and not one in which I am concerned.

I too regret very much that this has happened but these things cannot be helped and I hope we shall not have any further trouble.'

Having deflected the matter of the police report and the BMA from himself most satisfactorily, the Attorney General seems to reflect that he must ensure that nothing is raised again about this matter, which might well happen if any action is taken against Hannam. He sent a letter to the Commissioner on House of Commons notepaper in his own handwriting on 21st March:

'I have been considering the report you so kindly let me see and while I have no doubt that on the occasion in question, Hannam was guilty of a serious indiscretion, and perhaps has been on other occasions, I cannot help feeling on reflection that the enquiry and discovery must have shaken him a great deal.

He has done and is doing very good work on the Adams case. I fear he will be a long time in the witness box and I expect he will be cross-examined about associations with the Press.

It is not on account of the trial that I am writing to you but because on reflection I feel that perhaps I took too hard a view of what was an indiscretion. Against that I do feel one should have regard to the strain he has been carrying and in the circumstances I wonder whether it would just suffice to tell him off and to take no further action of any kind. If you felt this would do, it would no doubt ease his mind if he could be told this soon.

Forgive me for writing to you on a matter which is solely your concern.'

The last letter of this sequence was sent from the Attorney General to the Commissioner, Sir John Nott-Bower on 28th March. He had apparently received a letter in response to his of the 21st, which must have expressed agreement to his suggestion.

'…I am sure you will be glad to know that Hannam and Hewitt [sic] from Scotland Yard gave it [their evidence] excellently and indeed so well that after yesterday's hearing I personally expressed to them and Detective Inspector Pugh my feeling that they had given their evidence both very fairly and very well.

I hope you did not mind my troubling you with my last letter, but I am frankly becoming more and more of the opinion that Hannam has had a real shock and that there is really very little probability of the error being repeated.'

# The Search

## 24 November 1956

Hannam's original handwritten notebook is in the file, written up after the first police visit to Dr Adams' house, Kent Lodge on 24th November, 1956. It begins:

'8.30 p.m. entd. house. Pugh gained entrance and admitted us. J.B.A. coming downstairs in evening wear – dinner jacket –

H: 'Good evening Dr you know who I am?'
JBA: 'Oh, yes Mr Hannam'
H: 'May we go into a private room, I have something to say to you.'
JBA: 'There is no question of a statement for I have been told not to make one.'
Took us into surgery, large well apptd. Rear right G. floor. Cautioned.
H: There is one other thing I must tell you immediately. I have here a warrant issued by a mag. directing D.I. P[ugh] to search the house under the D.D.A. [Dangerous Drugs Act]. I will read it.'

Read search warrant.

JBA: 'There are no D.Ds. here what do you mean by D.Ds.?' Whilst saying this he walked to built in cupboard in right hand recess. 3 compartments. 3 keys in locks. Opened middle. [sketch of cupboards]
JBA 'I have quite a bit of barbiturates here, is that what you mean?'
H: 'D.I.P's quest is for D.D.s'
JBA: 'What do you mean by D.Ds, poisons?'
H: 'Morphine, Heroin, Pethidine and the like.'
JBA: 'Oh, that group. You will find none here. I haven't any. I very seldom ever use them. I think I have perhaps one little phial of tablets in my bag but no more.'

I sent D.I. P. to check blinds = front of house – Press and see what staff were up to. Press cameras outside.

H: 'May I have your D.D.s Reg[ister] please or your D.B[ook] = which drugs are dealt with?'

JBA: 'I don't know what you mean. I keep no register.'

H.: 'Whenever you obtain for your use a D.D. your acquisition of such must be entered in a proper D.D. Register, it is that I want.'

JBA: 'I never knew that. I don't keep any record.'

[There is a half page gap and notes start again on next double page]

JBA: 'I am quite at a loss, I have no register and I never keep any record of those things.'

H.: 'We will wait until Mr Pugh retns. for he is the officer directed to make a search.'

Took from my briefcase statement of clerk of Brownes: list of medication for Mrs Morrell.

H: 'Doctor, look at this list of your prescriptions for Mrs Morrell. There are a lot of D.D.s here.'

Dr A. raised his hands and stopped me.

JBA: 'Now all these I left prescriptions for either at the chemists or the house. She had nurses day and night.'

H: 'Who administered the drugs?'

JBA: 'I did nearly all. Perhaps the nurses gave some but mostly me.'

H: 'Were any left over when she died?'

JBA: 'No none, all was given to the patient.'

Turned to last days of prescriptions = clerk's statement. Showed JBA Between 30.IX.50 and 12.XI.50.

H: 'Doctor, you prescribed for her 75 – ⅙ grs. Heroin tablets the day before she died.'

JBA 'Poor soul, she was in terrible agony. It was all used. I used them myself.'

H: 'I have no medical training myself, but surely, the quantity of D.Ds obtained for Mrs Morrell during the last week of her life alone would be fatal and is pain usual with a cerebral vascular accident?'

JBA: 'Let me look at that list.'

I gave list to him and he looked at important part. He read it. I ran my finger over prescriptions Nos. 87 to 91.

JBA: 'There might have been a couple of those final tablets left over but I cannot remember. If there were I would take them and destroy them. I am not dishonest with drugs. Mrs Morrell had all those because I gave the injections. Do you think it is too much?'

H: 'That is not a matter for me Doctor. I simply want to get at the truth. Were those drugs taken to the house by you?'

JBA: 'No, the chauffeur collected them and I got them from the nurses.'

H: 'Have you any record yourself here of what you prescribed for Mrs Morrell. Have you a patient's clinical card?'

JBA: 'I do not keep any records of what I prescribe for patients. I only record visits and perhaps not that for private patients. Even my card is destroyed a year after a patient dies.'

I made no reply to this. Detective Insp. Pugh returned. He had been about a quarter of an hour or perhaps a little more. JBA flopped into chair and held his head in his hands. Told Pugh to proceed with search. JBA moved when we commenced and again opened cupboard on R. side. I was beside it.

JBA: 'there are a number of barbiturates there but no drugs.'

This cupboard very untidy – Lot of bottles on top and lying on each other. Boxes of chocolates – slabs stuck – butter, margarine, sugar, very dirty. I took out: –

    1 bottle containing 12 cachets bearing on label, 'Mrs Hullett'.
    7 empty bottles, 'Mrs Hullett' – ink on labels.
    1 bottle, contg. 22 tabs. with 'Mrs Hullett' on label.

There were jars etc. which appeared to contain phenobarbitone, but not a great deal. JBA walked slowly to opposite cupboard. D.I. Pugh nodded. He opened centre compartment, bunch of keys fell to side on chain to... There was a key in each lock.? Put hand inside, centre shelf, took out two objects and put same in his L jacket pocket. Closed door.

H: 'What did you take from that cupboard Dr?'
JBA: 'Nothing I only opened it for you.'
H: 'You put something into your pocket.'
JBA: 'No, I've got nothing.'
I moved towards him and said sternly: 'What was it Dr?'
JBA took from his L. pocket small bottle morphine (intact) and carton containing ditto. Initialled all. Gave to I.Pugh envelope 'A'.
H: 'Dr, please do not do silly things like that, it is against your own interests.'
JBA: 'I know it was silly. I didn't want you to find it in there.'
H: 'What is it and where did it come from?'
JBA: 'One of those I got for Mr Soden who died at the Grand Hotel and the other was for Mrs Sharpe who died before I used it.'
Made J.B.A. sit on chair in centre of surgery. Put my hand in his left pocket – empty. Solicitor James arrived 9.10 p.m. D.I. Pugh continued search. I told James outline of charges and what we were doing.
H: 'Have you any other D.D.s in another bag?'
JBA: 'Yes, I have a bag in my car. It is unlocked and is in the front of the seat at the back.'
Directed DS Hewett to fetch same. James declined offer to accompany him. DS Hewett returned with other bag. Gave it to I. Pugh.
H: 'Dr please pick out for the Inspector all the dangerous drugs.'
JBA took out item – which was on top – gave it to D.I. Pugh and said: 'There are a few very old ones in there and there is no more.' [Half page gap lower left page]

I then searched records cabinet and desk. J.B.A. opened it for me.

H: 'Have you any record card or records of any kind for Mrs Morrell?'

[half line wiped out here and 2.5' gap in notebook]

JBA: 'No, I do not appear to have, I expect I destroyed them after they [sic] died.'

[Lower third of page blank] [On the next double page there is one para in middle of left hand page] Then with D.I. Pugh and J.B.A. looked in every room of house. Dining room saw carved chest of silver – J.B.A. said 'That is the famous Morrell piece.' He got key. Double carved doors – inner eight thin drawers full of silver, some still wrapped in tissue paper. bottom drawer – silver trays etc. [Photocopies of photos in Yard archive of cabinet open and closed] [The next double page is blank with line towards bottom and then date]

25.XI.56

10.15 a.m. (meet planned by James and J.B.A.)

To surgery 6, College Road, Eastbourne. Adams opened door. He asked D.I.Pugh to park car away from house because of Press.

J.B.A. gave me two old D.Drugs Registers and said:-

JBA: 'These are two Ds. Registers we used to keep before the N.Health came in. You see there is nothing since 1949. I now realise I should have kept a register, but I haven't since these, when our dispenser used to keep it. [Like many surgeries they had a dispensary at the surgery before the NHS] We have had no dispenser since 1949. Mr James told me to say nothing else again.'

Searched two very small surgeries – nothing of interest.

26.XI.56

10.30 a.m. Magistrates Court. Chairman: D.G. Honeysett, M.M. Esq. Adjourned Thursday 20.XII.56. Self (J.B.A.) £1,000 and like surety and surrender passport. 10.45 a.m. approx. DS Sellars told J.B.A. he wanted official photograph. Willing and said:-

J.B.A.: 'I would like to have one word with you.'

H: 'I will see you in a moment or two.'

11 a.m. Entered photographic room on 2nd floor of Police H.Q. DS Sellars waited outside.


JBA: 'You told Mr James there might be other charges. I am very worried, what are they?'

H: 'That is not quite accurate. I told him he must not automatically assume the charges preferred were final.'

JBA 'Well what else is there?'

H: 'Hiding that morphine on Saturday night is a serious offence and I am still enquiring into the deaths of some of your rich patients. I do not think they were all natural.'

JBA: 'Which?'

H: 'Mrs Morrell is certainly one.'

JBA: 'Easing the passing of a dying person isn't all that wicked. She wanted to die. That can't be murder. It is impossible to accuse a doctor.'

The next double page in the notebook begins with references to Dr Adams' passport, although the first phrase seems out of context so something is missing:

'above refunded on 27.VI.49.

Ditto – £100 on 3.VI.55. Passport No. 916134. all above travellers (cheques) cashed at Midland Bank, E. as not used. American visa 1458646 on 25.IV.55. No exit or entrance stamps and other visas in passport. Passport sent to Clive House.'

There is a gap and then Hannam's notes on the arrest begin at the bottom of the page:

'11.45 a.m. 19.XII.56. D.I. Pugh and DS Hewett entered Kent Lodge. Found patients in surgery were in fact photographer and reporter from *Paris Match*. 11.50 a.m. Adams to lounge. 'We will go into your surgery and talk.' Asked reporters to leave.

H: 'Dr Adams on 13th Nov. 50 a patient of yours a Mrs Edith Alice Morrell died at Marden Ash, Beachy Head Road and you certified the cause of death to be cerebral thrombosis. I am now going to arrest you and take [you] to the local police Headquarters where you will be charged with the murder of Mrs Morrell.' Cautioned.

JBA: 'Murder – – – murder – Can you prove it was murder?'

H: 'You are now charged with murdering her.'

JBA: 'I didn't think you could prove murder. She was dying in any event.'

Long pause whilst I was searching him.

JBA: 'Will there be any more charges of murder?'

H: 'I cannot discuss that with you now.'

[Blank bottom half of left-hand page and blank top half of right hand page]

Pause.

JBA 'Can I ring Mr James.'

H: 'We are going immediately to the police station and I will inform him then.'

In hall gripped hand of receptionist and said -

JBA: 'I will see you in heaven.'

Eastbourne H.Q.

12.20 p.m.

Telephoned Mr James 12.25 p.m.

Charged 12.30 p.m.

Cautioned:-

JBA: 'It is better to say nothing.'

Searched again. Property listed by D.I. Pugh and Hewett.'

On the last two pages of this notebook Hannam has noted discrepancies in the lists from the chemists' registers of prescriptions for Mrs Morrell which require to be checked against the prescriptions.

Chapter Twenty-Five

The Arrest

On the 18th December 1956, a conference was held in HM Attorney General's room at the House of Commons, and at its conclusion, Hannam was instructed by the Director of Public Prosecutions 'to proceed to Eastbourne, re-arrest Dr Adams, and charge him with the murder in November, 1950, of Edith Alice Morrell, a lady of 81 years'. The time of arrest was discussed at the conference and as it was late when it finished, 'no one at Scotland Yard was aware of the impending development'. Hannam telephoned Chief Superintendent Findlay at his home and reported to him in a manner which was pre-arranged so that nobody listening would understand what was to happen. Neither the Chief Constable of Eastbourne nor any member of his staff were informed. Hannam then spoke to DI Pugh and arranged for him to come to Eastbourne Station at 10.10 a.m. on the 19th December.

At 8.30 next morning, Hannam met DS Hewett at Victoria Station and, to his dismay, found there three reporters. They were from the *Daily Mail*, the *Daily Express* and the *Daily Mirror*. 'Each was unkempt. Then they spoke to me, saying that I had at last turned up, and that they had been keeping observation there the evening before and all night long.' It must have been obvious to them that Hannam would have to travel to Eastbourne on the 19th because Adams was due to appear before the Magistrates at Eastbourne on the 20th December, on the earlier charges, and over twenty witnesses had already been warned to attend that hearing. The press reporters travelled down with Hannam and Hewett to Eastbourne, and they were told that no new development was likely to take place.

When they arrived at Eastbourne on the morning of the 20th, Hannam gave DI Pugh directions to drive all around Eastbourne to see if they could pick up Dr Adams whilst he was visiting some patients, 'and therefore completely hoodwink the press'. This effort was unsuccessful and, as he normally returned to Kent Lodge to see private patients at about 11.45 a.m., they went there, leaving the police car some yards away from the house. There was no-one outside.

They entered and had to wait in the lounge for some minutes as his receptionist said he was seeing a patient; there were six or seven patients in the waiting room. Of course when they entered the surgery they found there the photographer and reporter from *Paris Match*: they had called at Eastbourne Police headquarters earlier that morning, which was why DI Pugh knew who they were. They had asked the time of the Magistrates Court proceedings on the following day. It was obvious to Hannam that they had been invited in by Dr Adams, and he attached a copy of *Paris Match* of 29th December with his memorandum. 'It will be seen from it, as we have maintained for some weeks, when comment has been made about the publicity in this case, that Dr Adams delights in it. Not only does it show that he posed for two photographs in his own surgery, but also indicates that before his arrest he had been giving the reporters his own exemplary life history, and it is even reported in that publication that prior to our arrival he had been explaining to the reporters *that he had always been interested in anaesthesia* (my italics). We have said before that Adams is a loquacious man and delights in talking about himself.'

The arrival of the C.I.D. team was 'an accidental piece of excellent fortune, for the *Paris Match* reporters.' Hannam ordered them out of the house, but when they left after twenty minutes, they were, of course, waiting outside to take photographs. Also outside was a photographer from the *Daily Mail* who had been informed by the *Paris Match* men.

Hannam noted that the *Daily Sketch* had its own colourful account of the police arrival at Kent Lodge: as they entered 'Dr Adams was in the breakfast room having coffee, and he stopped to have a second cup of coffee before he went into the hall to see me', and further adds that, 'I saw him in a green walled, plainly furnished room where I read the charge, that he was offered a chair and accepted it, and sat down'. The *Daily Mail* recorded that 'Sergeant Hewett left the house carrying a suitcase containing Dr Adams' pyjamas. Detective Inspector Pugh came out of the house and stood at the top of six white stone steps'. Hannam observed that there were, in fact, ten.

Chapter Twenty-six

---

# The Memoranda

## End December 1956

---

### The 'Charges' Memorandum

Before the end of December Hannam was having to deal with a complaint from Defence Counsel, Mr Edward Clarke. He was called to Commander Hatherill's office at Scotland Yard on Friday, 28th December, where he saw Sir Theobald Mathew, the Director of Public Prosecutions, who informed him that he had received this complaint. Writing a Memorandum to the Chief Superintendent on 29th December, Hannam notes that it was alleged that he had seen Mr James and told him that he expected two further capital charges to be preferred against Dr Adams. Mr Clarke had complained that he had to wait until 14th January for any information about the Morrell murder charge and now there were two more pending.

Hannam explained in his memorandum exactly what had happened over Christmas carrying on with enquiries resulting mainly from the recent exhumations of the bodies of Julia Bradnum and Clara Neil-Miller. Several matters required further investigation in the Neil Miller case: 'She died in very suspicious circumstances on 22nd February, 1954' having made gifts to Dr Adams and the landlady, Mrs Sharpe, eleven days previously and he and DI Pugh had been investigating various bank accounts. Hannam explained Mr James' involvement in the case. He had been 'the Solicitor acting for Adams, who was the sole executor of Miss Clara Neil Miller's will, and he has supplied us with considerable information in our various enquiries about the wills with which he dealt on behalf of Adams.' Adams had instructed him to supply the police with any information they needed in respect of wills and Mr James was able to supply the necessary information with regard to the Neil Miller cheques.

Mr James had asked Hannam what the further enquiries about Clara Neil Miller meant, 'adding "Not another capital charge."' I told him that I had not the slightest idea and that I had merely the duty to tie up these outstanding matters. He asked the result of the post-mortem examinations on Bradnum and Neil Miller and I told him I had no idea for the report of the pathologist was not to hand.' At no time had any mention been made of two capital charges and Hannam thought there was insufficient evidence in these other cases. He ended the memorandum: 'The defence in this case are well aware that we did not carry out two exhumations for our amusement, and this may well be a typical Edward Clarke probing move.' Sir Theobald Mathew received a copy of Hannam's confidential report and that seems to have been the end of this matter.

But not the end of complaints, however. On the 4th January, 1957, Hannam was responding to another complaint, this time from an obscure solicitor, George E. Hughes of Collins & Hughes of 15 Gay Street, Bath, who had written to Mr Walker, the Chief Constable of Eastbourne. Again, Hannam's memorandum is addressed to the Chief Superintendent.

Mr Hughes had made 'an emphatic protest' at the circumstances – as reported in the national press – surrounding the arrest of Dr Adams, stating that it was quite clear that someone in the Police Force must have disclosed the impending arrest to the press. He set out five specific points which led him to such a conclusion, saying that the matter called for 'instant and searching enquiry into the methods adopted by the Police' and that the episode 'lends colour to the suggestion that someone in the Police Force had been bribed to give advance information, thus facilitating a press "stunt".' He deprecated 'such American methods'.

Hannam comments that the police had adopted 'unusually surreptitious methods' and that the Chief Constable of Eastbourne was not told that Dr Adams was to be arrested on 24th November until 5 p.m. on the previous day. When he and DS Hewett had travelled down by train to Eastbourne, they had even been met at Lewes by DI Pugh who drove them to Eastbourne by car. The journalists had been lying in wait at Eastbourne Station all day, 'anticipating some action'. When this arrest was made, the press were caught unawares and 'only one photographer happened to be alert, and he was merely leafing outside the Police Headquarters when we entered'.

As a result of this failure of the press, editors of national newspapers 'gave directions for constant surveillance' and the press speculated on exhumations and the possibility of a capital charge for some days.

## The 'Homosexuality' Memorandum

The following note was in the Scotland Yard archive:

> 'A highly confidential and dangerous memorandum belonging to a reporter of the *Daily Mail* fell into the hands of the police tonight at Eastbourne. Among other suggestions it contained one relating to rumours about homosexuality between a police officer, a magistrate, and a doctor in Eastbourne. They were named.
>
> It contained also phrases such as 'H—m told me' together with a lot of off the record information about enquiries in Eastbourne.
>
> Another suggestion I understand was that the Chief Constable of Eastbourne had mishandled the original enquiries into the suicide of Mrs Hullett and suggesting that H—m had no confidence in him. The police know that this memorandum was the

property of the *Daily Mail* reporter. The *Daily Mail* reporter was tonight summoned to Eastbourne Police station and faced with H—m, the Chief Constable and the officer against whom homosexuality had been suggested.

I understand from the *Daily Mail* reporter that the Chief Constable mentioned 'criminal libel' and a possible approach to the Home Secretary. I understand also from the *Daily Mail* reporter that instead of claiming full responsibility for the memo, he denied that he was the author and the typist. He implied that it was the work of more brains than his. As a result the Chief Constable told him that he wished to see all the national newspaper reporters working on the story at 9.30 a.m. tomorrow (Wednesday).

No direct invitation to this effect has been made to me. The *Daily Mail* reporter tonight returned to London to seek advice from his office.'

Chapter Twenty-Seven

# The 'Mistresses'

Detective Superintendent Hannam, in his First Report, states that there are 'three women who have been mistresses of Dr Adams: a Miss Betty Cradock of East Dean – he visits her weekly and presents her with flowers. From 14th September 1956 to 29th September 1956, she was in Scotland with Dr Adams and Lieutenant-Colonel Roland Gwynne, Chairman of the Magistrates, on a shooting holiday.'

'Second: Miss Norah O'Hara, 4, Pashley Road, to whom Mr Adams was engaged and broke off the betrothal a few days before the wedding when the house and furniture had been acquired.'

'Third: Miss Ella Leach of 30 Vicarage Drive – similarly 'turned over' by Dr Adams and he [sic] acquired 30 Vicarage Drive as a peace offering.' Hannam added: 'We are not out to further scandal unless a useful issue is likely to result so that no enquiry has been made of these persons.'

Hannam does, however, comment further on in his First Report on Mr Percy Cradock, who died aged seventy-three years on 27th September, 1946 at his home Little Hill in East Dean. The Will of Mr Cradock was made on 10th August, 1942 and the witnesses were officials of Barclays Bank and 'it was engrossed by a reputable solicitor'. On the same day there was also a codicil prepared which was witnessed by Dr Adams and a male nurse who was in attendance at the time. He was a man of considerable wealth, with an estate of over £100,000 and he left his motor cars and the residue of his estate 'which we have reason to believe totalled over £30,000 to his niece Elizabeth Beecroft Cradock.' Hannam refers to the previous information from Mrs Muddell, and adds: 'We also have correspondence from Cheshire Constabulary which confirms the general opinion in Eastbourne that Miss Cradock is the mistress of Dr Adams. He visits her frequently and makes presents to her and during the recent holiday he took in Scotland, …Miss Cradock went with him.'

Chapter Twenty-Eight

# Macmillan Becomes Prime Minister

When Eden flew back from Bermuda on 14th December, 1956, he had believed that he would continue as Prime Minister; it was soon made clear to him that he would not. Rab Butler was the acting Prime Minister and he and Macmillan had been having discussions with Eisenhower whilst Eden had been away. He had lost the support of the country and his closest colleagues and he still had health problems. Eden held his last Cabinet meeting on Wednesday, January 9th 1957 at 5 p.m., and on the same day he resigned. He had told Macmillan of his decision only at 3 o'clock that afternoon; the only others who knew were Salisbury and Butler.

> 'Eden spoke shortly, and with great dignity. The doctors' decision was irrevocable. He must resign. Salisbury spoke – with great emotion, almost in tears – of his lifelong friendship. Butler spoke next – very appropriately. I said a few words. Then it was all over. It was a dramatic end to an extraordinary, and in many ways, unique career…
>
> '…after the Cabinet, I went back to No. 11, and spent the evening alone there, working and reading. Butler, I have no doubt went back to his house. Meanwhile, Salisbury and Kilmuir asked all the members of the Cabinet to see them – one by one. This took place in the Lord President's rooms. I heard afterwards that the opinion was practically unanimous in favour of me, and not Butler.'[1]

The Press, in particular, had predicted that Butler would succeed him but Conservative MPs voted for Macmillan. Although Macmillan was known to have helped persuade Eden into war over the Suez Canal, and then to have withdrawn his support as soon as it started, Butler was known as a supporter of Neville Chamberlain's position as an appeaser of Hitler, when he was Under-Secretary for Foreign Affairs to Lord Halifax. He had also privately expressed doubts about Eden's policy over Suez but had then voted for it in Cabinet. Gossip put the choice of Macmillan down to Lord Salisbury's influence with the Queen, and the fact that they had both married into the Devonshire family, but there seems no doubt that he was the better man for the job.

Macmillan noted in his diaries that he was called to the Palace at about 12.55 p.m. on the

---

[1] Harold Macmillan's *Diaries*

next day, Thursday, 10th January, and kissed hands as Prime Minister, accepting the Queen's charge, remarking to her that he could not guarantee that his Government would last six weeks: 'The Queen was gracious – but brief.' He described his thoughts as he drove back to No. 11 Downing Street:

> '…I thought chiefly of my poor mother. The first little note wh[ich] I got later in the afternoon was from my sister-in-law [Mary, Dowager Duchess of Devonshire] with the same thought. She understood and had a great affection for my mother.'

Macmillan noted that it was Butler he had to placate, that he was 'the key figure'. He should have the pick of the offices available, although he wished to retain Selwyn Lloyd as Foreign Secretary. He thought that Butler, however, did not really want the F.O. 'in today's circumstances' – there were far too many problem areas, prominent among them the Middle East and Cyprus. Rab returned the next day, to say that he had decided to take the Home Office.

> 'I at once agreed, altho' it meant a rather sad parting with Gwilym LG… …LG (who is to become Viscount Tenby) is so old and shrewd a politician that, as soon as he knew that Butler was to succeed him, he realised that I had no option.'[2]

He had decided that he wanted Duncan Sandys as Minister of Defence and, as he thought that Lord Hailsham would oppose this, moved him from the Admiralty to Education. Macmillan thought that he would be

> '…a first-class Minister of Education. Anyway, he is one of the cleverest, if not always the wisest, men in the country today.'

Macmillan recorded that it took ten days to form the whole administration: 'a most difficult and exhausting task', and that he could not have done it without the help of Edward Heath, the Chief Whip, who was 'quite admirable'. It had 'gone well' and he had seen nearly a hundred people, 'trying to say the right thing to each'.

> 'In the circumstances, many considerations had to be borne in mind – the right, centre, and left of the party; the extreme 'Suez' group; the extreme opposition to Suez; the loyal centre – and last, but not least, U and non-U (to use the jargon that Nancy Mitford has popularised) that is, Eton, Winchester, etc. on the one hand; Board School and grammar school on the other.'

It was not particularly noticeable to the electorate that he had formed a less 'Establishment' Government, except for the inclusion of Ernest Marples, educated at an elementary school, as

---

[2] Ibid

Postmaster General. He had, however, described Reginald Maudling as having 'no background', Selwyn Lloyd as 'a middle-class lawyer', and Lord Hailsham as 'a temporary gentleman'.[3] Perhaps the most interesting description of Macmillan himself was that given by the late Duke of Devonshire:

> '…Uncle Harold would like to have been thought of as a Trollopian character whereas in fact he was straight out of Galsworthy.'[4]

On becoming Prime Minister, Macmillan's priority was reconciliation with America; his wartime friend Eisenhower seemed willing to be friendly and on 22nd January a conference between them in Bermuda in March was arranged. Without the support of the USA, Britain could not get a loan and there would be no oil and the prospect of a cold winter and the return of rationing. His next concern was the economy – he had to do something to gain some popularity in the country after the Suez debacle – and the plan was to win the next General Election on a rising tide of prosperity. He was sure that if his Government could survive until the Summer Recess of Parliament in 1957, then he could go on to win. 'Macmillan expected all to submit themselves to the greater good of short-term survival; there was no room for "principle", to rock the boat was little better than treachery.'[5]

[3] Thorpe  /  [4] Devonshire  /  [5] Ball

Chapter Twenty-Nine

# Committal and Custody

## 14 January 1957

### Committal

The Committal proceedings began on 14th January, 1957 in Eastbourne, before the examining magistrates. This was to determine whether Dr Adams had any case to answer. In France such a decision would be made by the *juge d'instruction*, in Scotland by the procurator-fiscal, after examining all the evidence collected. In England and Wales it is made by the Justices of the Peace sitting as 'examining magistrates'. These proceedings could have been heard in private (since the Magistrates Courts Act 1952) but the Eastbourne magistrates chose to have the hearing in public – an unwise decision considering the vast press interest in the case, but it had been their invariable habit to do so.

The morning of 14th January was a bitterly cold one when Dr Adams arrived at the courtroom in Eastbourne Town Hall from custody in Brixton Prison. There were crowds waiting outside and inside were both local people – some his patients – and pressmen, police and lawyers. There were seventy seats reserved for the press alone, so the queues for seats had begun before dawn. Dr Adams appeared cheerful and waved to friends as he entered and faced the magistrates, nearly all of whom he knew.

The Chairman was not the usual one – his close friend, Lieutenant-Colonel Roland Gwynne – but Mr David Honeysett, a local pub manager. Gwynne had not been permitted to preside over this hearing. The other magistrates on the bench were Mrs Mary Bradford, a local coal merchant's wife, Mrs Eileen Corner, the daughter of a local hotelier, Mr Lionel Turner, the Chairman of the local newspaper, and Colonel Leonard C. Stevens, local preparatory school owner and Chairman of Eastbourne Cricket and Football Clubs. Colonel Stevens did have an interesting connection – his acquaintance with the Home Secretary who had been displaced by Rab Butler only four days previously in Macmillan's new Government – Gwilym Lloyd-George.

It was for the Crown to put their case to the magistrates; the accused and his legal representatives could be present but were not required to take part in the proceedings. The evidence of all prosecution witnesses is heard: they are examined on statements which they have already made to police. The defence is entitled to cross-examine witnesses, but the purpose of the Committal hearing is only for the Crown to try to prove that there is a case to be tried. For the defence to try to prove their case would just be to 'show their hand', so they would usually not do so, thus giving the accused the advantage.

Dr Adams could only be charged with one murder in an indictment, as this was the law in 1957. The Crown alleged, however, that he had also murdered Mr and Mrs Hullett in similar circumstances. The Attorney General was trying to prove 'system' in doing so in order to secure the committal, although it is difficult to understand why he used these cases in preference to others, particularly that of Mr Hullett. There has to be convincing similarity in a series of cases to offer convincing proof of 'system'.

Unusually, both parties were represented by Counsel: Mr Melford Stevenson QC and Mr Malcolm Morris for the Crown, instructed by the Director of Public Prosecutions, and Mr Geoffrey Lawrence QC and Mr Edward Clarke [the nephew of Sir Edward Clarke, the prosecuting counsel in the trial of Oscar Wilde and defence counsel for Adelaide Bartlett]. The transcript of the Committal hearing is missing from the archives, but the cases put are clearly outlined in Lord Devlin's account in his book *Easing the Passing* and he must have had a transcript before him when he wrote his account. What was in the archives was evidence which could have been used to prove method, similarities, in the cases and which was not used, and would have told a different story. The Attorney General had chosen the route.

After the charges had been read and Dr Adams had replied 'Not Guilty', Mr Lawrence made a submission to the Magistrates and asked that the court should be cleared while he did this. The Chairman, Mr Honeysett, replied that he would have to make this submission in open court. Mr Lawrence pointed out that his application was for certain evidence not to be disclosed. The Bench, after some discussion, decide that Mr Stevenson should proceed with the prosecution case and stop when he came to this point in the evidence when they would consider the application.

Mr Melford Stevenson outlined the evidence for the Crown concerning the death of Mrs Morrell: that she had died, not of cerebral thrombosis as Dr Adams had certified, but because he had poisoned her with drugs: heroin and morphine. He had benefited under her will, receiving a chest of Georgian silver and a Rolls Royce car. Mr Stevenson went on to give details of Mrs Morrell's illness, pointing out that she had never been in any severe pain which might have justified the use of such powerful drugs. The two sources concerning the treatment which Mrs Morrell received were the nurses who attended her and the prescription lists of drugs prescribed for her. There would also be expert medical evidence from authorities on these drugs which would prove that such administration must be fatal:

> 'Death would result from it without any sort of doubt, and no doctor of experience could
> fail to know that death would result, and you will bear in mind that Dr Adams held the

diploma of anaesthetics and you may be satisfied that he knew all there was to know about the action and properties both of morphine and heroin.'

Mr Stevenson continued, describing at length the death of Mrs Morrell, her will and the police interviews with Dr Adams. When he was ready to begin the Hullett evidence, he advised the court that he would pause for Mr Lawrence's submission. Mr Lawrence objected that the evidence to prove system might be deemed inadmissible if the case went to the High Court, and therefore it should be heard in private before the magistrates alone because otherwise it would influence any jury which heard the Morrell charge:

> 'Is it humanly possible, that a jury could not already have been in some way influenced by the publicity given to evidence which they might be instructed not to consider at all?'

Mr Stevenson gave a response which seemed almost intended to confuse:

> 'My position is that while I cannot consent to Mr Lawrence's request I do not intend to oppose it.'

Lord Devlin expressed the view that he should have agreed, because the lay magistrates 'had no idea what to do'. They therefore, rather pointlessly opted to hear the evidence in private first and then decide whether it should be heard again in public. Mr Stevenson then outlined the evidence he would call in relation to the Hullett cases in closed court; the magistrates decided that it should be heard in open court; Mr Lawrence had failed in his submission.

Mr Melford Stevenson rose:

> 'Now it is my duty to deal with the deaths of two other patients of Dr Adams, who died in circumstances which the Crown says exhibit similarity to the death of Mrs Morrell so closely that it is essential that the facts surrounding their deaths should be given in evidence upon the charge of murdering Mrs Morrell.'

Mr Stevenson began with the case of Mr Hullett who had died on the 14th March, 1956, aged seventy-one, the death certified by Dr Adams as being from cerebral haemorrhage [see Chapter 17]:

> 'Dr Adams received under Mr Hullett's will the sum of £500, although as Dr Adams later said to Superintendent Hannam, he thought it would be more. The points of similarity between the deaths of Mr Hullett and Mrs Morrell are many. Like Mrs Morrell, Mr Hullett was an elderly patient. Like Mrs Morrell, he was an invalid whose death might occur without exciting very much curiosity. Mr Hullett, like Mrs Morrell, finally died following a substantial injection of morphine, but above all else, Mr Hullett, like

Mrs Morrell, was rich, and again before he died Dr Adams knew, as he thought was the case with Mrs Morrell, that he would benefit under the will. Again, in the case of Mrs Morrell, Dr Adams gave a false answer to Question Four on the cremation certificate. When being asked if he had any financial interest in the death of the deceased he replied 'No'. The result was that the body of Mr Hullett, like Mrs Morrell's, was burned, and any evidence that there might have been of drugs in the body, and more particularly drugs causing his death in his case, was consumed.'

Mr Stevenson gave the history of Mr Hullett's illness and operation; his having a heart attack, Dr Adams coming to the house, the injection given to him, taken from what Nurse Miller had recognised as a small brown bottle of morphia, deep sleep with stertorous [noisy] breathing; his awakening at 6 a.m., speaking with the nurse and death half an hour later. The Crown alleged that Dr Adams had given his patient a lethal injection:

'It appears to have been morphia in a very concentrated form and it is material that shortly after Mr Hullett's death, probably on March 14th, 1956, Dr Adams called on Messrs. Temples, chemists in Mead Street, Eastbourne, and he there asked for five grains of morphia in the form of 10 cubic centimetres of hypodermic morphine solution to be sent to his house, and to be sent to his house upon a prescription of A.J. Hullett, who was already dead, a prescription dated the 13th March, 1956. He specially requested that it should be delivered to his house, and it was done in circumstances which clearly implied that it was to take the place of morphine which he had already injected into and used on that patient, and the 10 c.c. solution in that prescription contains 5 grains of morphine.

We say that that prescription was designed to take the place of the morphine which Dr Adams injected into Mr Hullett on the evening of the 13th March…'

Dr Douthwaite was called as an expert medical witness and he estimated that, to produce the deep sleep and breathing described by the nurse, would have required an injection of ½ to 1½ grains of morphia when the correct amount should have been ¼ grain. The Crown further demonstrated that Dr Adams had taken the morphia from his bag, but on the day after Mr Hullett's death went to Browne's the Chemist with a prescription for Mr Hullett of 5 grains of hyperduric morphia to be delivered to Kent Lodge and charged to Mr Hullett. This left two possibilities: either the Doctor had injected 5 grains or he was stockpiling dangerous drugs.

Mr Lawrence, cross-examining Dr Douthwaite asked whether it was possible that Mr Hullett could have awakened at 6 a.m. and had the conversation if he had been injected with the 5 grains of morphia, and the answer was that it was impossible, and when further questioned, agreed that the dose was unlikely to have been lethal.

It was only on 25th January that DI Pugh interviewed the cardiologist who had been called in by Dr Adams to examine Mr Hullett: Dr Roy Kemball Price and a note of this interview, stating what Dr Price would say in evidence is in the Scotland Yard archive. Dr Price had already been seen by the Defence. It was his evidence that made the Crown rely on the testimony concerning the injections alone because he had examined Mr Hullett on 9th March, 1956, five days before he died:

> 'He was suffering from aortic sterosis a condition from which he had suffered for many years and it appears he had suffered from some type of heart trouble since childhood. These symptoms would become apparent and develop between the age of 50 and 60 years from when onwards the patient's condition would deteriorate rapidly. I would not condemn the walking of Mr Hullett upstairs in one complete operation [as witnessess had condemned Dr Adams for doing] I would say that by doing it by this means there would be less labour on the heart than by taking the patient upstairs and making pauses. There is a possibility that life could have been measured in months and the patient would be likely to die suddenly at any time.'

This case was always quite hopeless for the Crown to rely upon; why would it be pursued when there were others that could have been utilised?

The fact that there had been a verdict of suicide at the inquest on the death of Mrs Hullett made it difficult for Mr Stevenson now to show that this was a case of murder by Dr Adams; the inquest should have been adjourned, but Hannam's instructions had been otherwise. The Crown had also decided that the Doctor's motive for murder in each case was to benefit from the wills of the victims. In the case of Mrs Hullett, she had not made the will by which he was bequeathed the Rolls Royce until 14th July, 1956, and she wrote the £1,000 cheque on 17th July and she consumed the fatal dose on 19th July.

Mr Stevenson put the case that Dr Adams had murdered Mrs Hullett 'whether she herself administered the fatal dose or whether she did not'. It was not remotely likely that Dr Adams had 'administered' the barbiturate tablets which comprised the overdose. It was likely that he had assisted her in committing suicide, both before and after the overdose was taken. As Lord Devlin remarked 'Not the warmest advocate of euthanasia would condone its performance under the superintendence of a doctor whose fee was a legacy of a Rolls-Royce and a cheque for £1,000' The total value of this was around £4,000 – a vast sum in 1956.

Mr Stevenson 'recited the long list of barbiturate prescriptions given between 1 May 1956 and the fatal dose on 19th July'; there were also the barbiturates prescribed for Mr Hullett which Dr Adams did not retrieve after his death. The amount of barbiturates taken in overdose by Mrs Hullett was about ten days' supply. There were other questions for Dr Adams to answer which he had not satisfactorily answered at the inquest: why did he have the cheque specially cleared so that it was in his account by the 19th? Why did he not suspect suicide when she had so often threatened it? Why did he not inform Dr Harris and Dr Shera that he had been prescribing barbiturates and was in a depressed state? Mr Stevenson recalled Dr Adams' telephone call to the Coroner after Mrs Hullett's death: 'That was something far odder than the other things that had occurred.' At the close of his address, Mr Stevenson explained the 'system' in the three deaths:

'The same pattern repeats itself. A rich patient, heavy drugging over a period of months ending up with a fatal dose. A patient obviously under the influence of the Doctor; a patient under whose will Dr Adams benefited. You get the impatience, the same desire for money, evidenced by the special clearance of that cheque for £1,000. In this case [Mrs Hullett] there was no false cremation certificate because the circumstances deprived the Doctor of the opportunity of disguising the cause of death, as he had in the case of Mrs Morrell and Mr Hullett.'

Mr Stevenson then called forty witnesses for the Crown; Mr Lawrence only chose to examine some of them. At this stage he dealt gently and politely with the nurses, reserving his devastating cross-examination to a later stage. Dr Douthwaite also had no inkling of what would occur at the Old Bailey. But things did not go so smoothly with Detective Superintendent Hannam, particularly on the subject of his notebook, which Mr Lawrence wished to be an exhibit, but Hannam objected as it contained 'other matters' and it was needed for further enquiries. Mr Lawrence pressed:

'I am entitled to see the book. It would be a manifest denial of justice if I am not. It is a vital document, but how vital I do not know.'

Superintendent Hannam responded:

'If it is decided to retain the book in the custody of the court I ask that it should not be examined except in my presence.'

He moved to return the book to his pocket:

'What are you putting that book in your pocket for?'
'Sorry, sir?'
'Might I enquire, what the object is of seeking to prevent the examination of the book except in your presence?'
'I want to see exactly what happens to that book whenever it is examined by anybody connected with the defence. Never before in my experience has a book been retained as an exhibit. On many occasions courts have decided that a book should be examined only in my presence.'
'I am not sure we are very interested in your experience.'
'It affects me very much in the answers I give to you.'
'Do you desire to be present when the book is examined by the defence?'
'I do.'
'It would follow reciprocally that the defence should be present whenever you want to examine that book during the same period, would it not?'
'If you made that request, of course the court would consider it.'

'I am asking you.'

'That is for the court, not for me.'

'Is that the best answer you can give?'

'I think it is the proper answer for me to give.'

On the ninth day – the final day of the Committal hearing, Mr Lawrence submitted that there was no case to answer, that the bench should dismiss the case. The magistrates' deliberations took only five minutes, and Dr Adams was committed for trial.

The outstanding question is: why was there other evidence in the case of Mrs Hullett which was not used or further investigated at this stage? Leslie Henson and his wife Harriet were friends of Mr Hullett and his first wife, and then of 'Bobbie' Hullett, his second wife. Mrs Henson made a statement to Scotland Yard's Detective Sergeant Grieves at their London home in Kingsgate Avenue, N.3. She describes visiting Mrs Hullett after her husband's death at Holywell Mount in April 1956: '…at this time the Doctor [Adams] was giving her injections and on occasions she gave herself injections.' The Italian maid, Teresa Yogna:

'told me she wanted to tell the police that Mrs Hullett was being drugged by Dr Adams. She said the morning Mr Hullett died the Doctor gave her drugs and had continued to do so. She said the cook, Kathleen, was willing to go to the police with her but Mary, the parlour maid, said they would be made to do so because she thought the injections were being given to Mrs Hullett in place of food and would tell the police so. The maid Therese [sic] asked me to help Mrs Hullett and I did try to dissuade her from taking [barbiturate] tablets on one occasion but she insisted on doing so and got bad tempered.

The last time I saw Mrs Hullett was on 25th June 1956. It was about 12 o'clock midday when I left. Doctor Adams had just attended Mrs Hullett and after he had gone she came out to say 'goodbye' to me. She looked very bright and stimulated. She usually looked like this after the Doctor had visited her. She asked me to forgive her for shouting – she shouted 'goodbye' to me – and said she always felt as though she was a long way off and her head felt like cotton wool after the Doctor's visit. I cannot add anything further except that it was common gossip in Eastbourne that Mrs Hullett was being drugged.'

The other witnesses from the staff at Holywell Mount had not, of course, been asked to make statements about what they knew about the previous treatment of Mrs Hullett – all had been concentrated on the inquest into the death. Mrs Henson made her statement voluntarily. She was not called as a witness. The expert witnesses did not criticise the drugs given to Mrs Hullett because they only had evidence of barbiturates being prescribed, and they knew nothing about injections which would have been from Dr Adams' own stocks – barbiturates are not drugs which are injected.

Yet this case, with the injections being given as well as the barbiturates, begins to look more like the case of Mrs Morrell. Missing evidence and a witness from the Morrell case makes the two look more alike, but the Crown could not prove the Hullett evidence admissible in the Morrell case. The Committal hearing had lasted nine days and the Crown had convinced the examining magistrates that Dr Adams should be sent for trial on the charge of murdering Mrs Morrell.

# Custody

Dr Adams had been taken into custody on the murder charge on 19th November and was taken to Brixton Prison after he had been charged at Eastbourne Police Headquarters. He was brought back to Eastbourne on the 14th January 1957 for the Committal hearing and held in a cell at Eastbourne Police Headquarters. Eastbourne Police kept the 'Constable's Notebook' for the period from 14th to 31st January recording details of his stay in Eastbourne. He was watched by a Police Constable at all times during the day and night and the station sergeants on duty would also make supervisory visits, taking great care of their celebrity prisoner.

The notebook records Dr Adams' arrival at 5 p.m. on 14th January and he was almost immediately visited by his local solicitor, Mr James, who had brought various papers for him, for five minutes, and his defence barrister arrived ten minutes later. He wanted to see his receptionist, Miss Lawrence, his housekeeper and chauffeur, but Constable Spicer had instructions from Detective Superintendent Hannam that only 'legal advisers' were allowed to visit. The Doctor occupied himself reading 'pamphlets, a magazine and letters' and P.C. Haddon came to see him to announce the recovery of the 'name plate stolen from the gate pillar of Kent Lodge' from a souvenir-hunter. He requested two books from his personal property: *Daily Readings* by F. B. Myers and *Lone Horseman*, and also that he should have a change of laundry: fresh underwear and a suit. This was duly arranged with his housekeeper and the books arrived.

Seemingly anxious for his comfort, P.C. Wilshaw brought him 'a telephone message from a well wisher'. Blankets and pillows were provided but he 'stated he was used to sheets'. He was also provided with an 'Alophen' pill (laxative), and had brought with him a supply of chocolate. He read his Bible, knelt by the bed to say his prayers, wrote notes and read in bed. He was able to sleep soundly for eight hours each night and organise and fill his time.

On 15th January, the first day of the Committal hearing, he had to be awakened at 7.45 a.m. by Station Sergeant Huddleston. He 'transferred various papers, chocolate and charm' (this seems odd for one of his religious persuasion) from the pockets of one jacket to another and then washed and shaved. He cut his middle finger whilst cleaning the razor after shaving; still they trusted him with a razor as they were watching so closely. He was not the man, however, to commit suicide whilst there was hope. His wound was dressed and he was given '4 teaspoonfuls of liquid paraffin' and then breakfast. Writing the notes on this particular shift, PC20 Leckenby was assiduous, so we know exactly what he was wearing for his court appearance as a parcel of clothing had just arrived from Kent Lodge: 'blue suit (jacket, waistcoat and trousers), blue striped shirt, blue tie, woollen vest, woollen trunks, blue socks, white stiff collar and white handkerchief.' There were more collars and 'red, white and pink striped pyjamas' in the parcel.

Dr Adams read the Bible, prayed and read his magazine and personal papers; his soiled laundry was collected and his own bed linen and blanket from Kent Lodge delivered. Mr Taylor, the Defence Counsel arrived for a brief conversation before Dr Adams was taken from the cell to Court at 10.20 a.m. and into Court at 10.30. Whilst he was away the cell was cleaned and washed by 'cleaner Bartholomew' under supervision. He returned for lunch, and spent the rest of the time praying and writing notes until he was taken back to Court. He had again been taking notes in Court and had a further visit from Mr James, and this time by his leading Defence Counsel, Mr Lawrence as well as Mr Taylor. Apart from these visits from his legal advisers and the supervisory visits from the Station sergeants, things continued in much the same routine: praying, reading of the Bible and devotional books such as *Our Daily Walk*, magazines, making notes and eating the three meals a day and the cup of Bovril before bedtime. At night the Sergeant on duty removed Dr Adams' tie, collar, braces and shoelaces from his cell. Some of the constables made a note every time he changed position in his sleep: 'Doctor sleeping on left side', 'Doctor lying on his back asleep'. Their vigils were all very meticulous.

Dr Adams, although 'locquacious' with Hannam made little conversation with the constables on duty: he was probably under instructions from Counsel to say nothing which concerned the case, but he was not, in any case, a man to chat with those he considered to be of a more lowly social station than himself. He confined himself to requests and complaints: 'Remarked that the pipes in his cell were 'dead cold' – he wore his overcoat while he was sitting in the cell.

On Wednesday, 16th January he asked if Mr Gray, his friend the dentist who was his closest friend from the Plymouth Brethren, and Mr Atfield could come and see him. PC Burnage records that Mr Atfield was a 'lay minister for the Friends Meeting House', but as the Quakers have no ministers, he may have been a preacher with the Brethren. By the morning of Thursday, 17th, being awakened by PC29, who in time-honoured police manner wrote down the following:

> 'He remarked that his sleep was disturbed at about 6 a.m. by noise. I informed him that there is always a certain amount of added activity when reliefs are changing over. He appeared to accept this, and then made a request for his suitcase containing fresh clothing to be brought in to him. This was done and upon examining the articles herein, he alleged that a new plastic collar, for which he had made a special request, was missing. I informred Sgt. 1 Brett who stated that he will make an enquiry.'

The Doctor was asked by Sergeant Brett if he required exercise. He declined but requested that he be allowed to examine two parcels of books 'as he did not wish to take them all back to London with him'. One way or the other he was not expecting a long stay in Brixton. The books were brought in and, 'after taking out four volumes of *Countryman* and the *Practitioner*, together with a box of Players cigarettes and a box of chocolates, he requested that the remainder be placed in his suitcase for subsequent return to Kent Lodge'. He wrote notes and then underlined words in a printed book, taking the notes with him when he went to Court that morning. After Court that afternoon he was visited by Mr James and by a cousin, Mr Hogg, who stayed on after Mr James left. After tea, he 'had his hair cut in the charge room by Mr Prescott of Thwaits' and the evening went on in the usual manner followed by another good night's sleep.

The routine continued on Friday 18th January. Dr Adams asked PC 29 Leckenby if the plastic collar about which he had enquired the previous day had arrived: 'Informed him that a new collar of this type arrived yesterday'. Could he borrow a pair of scissors to trim his finger nails? 'Complied with'. The Constable remained in the cell with him while he used them. He asked for his suitcase and parcels of books and personal papers as 'he wished to sort them as he did not intend taking them all with him should he be returning to London for the weekend'. It all sounded so normal. What he did not wish to take was put in the suitcase and the remainder were wrapped in 'two separate brown paper parcels'. After breakfast he remarked to PC Leckenby: 'they didn't bring me any sugar but I survived.' The Constable said he would notify the station sergeant of this complaint. Dr Adams busied himself making notes and then meditating with *Our Daily Walk*. When Mr James visited following the afternoon Court session, Dr Adams gave him several letters to deliver; a member of the Defence team made a short visit and he was taken in a police car back to Brixton for the weekend.

On Monday morning at ten past ten, Dr Adams arrived back at Eastbourne Police Headquarters and Defence Counsel visited almost immediately. By 10.30 he was in Court. When he returned at lunchtime a basket of fruit had been delivered, and after lunch he ate two bananas and an orange. He wrote notes and checked them in time for his return to Court. Mr James came again after Court at 5.30 for another five-minute visit, followed by Defence Counsel. The Doctor gave him what appeared to the Constable to be letters. He spent much of the evening 'reclining on the bed reading magazines', rounded off by a 'cup of Bovril administered to the prisoner by PC21' accompanied by chocolate biscuits, with prayers and reading as usual until he slept at 11.30.

Tuesday 22nd January – when he had washed and dressed, he sat on the bed and read *Our Daily Walk*. The Station Sergeant arrived with his clean shirt and underwear, and some parcels, the contents of which he proceeded to sort out. He enquired regarding a pack of some kind of cards, but it is not discernable what kind of cards these were and they are not mentioned again. He parcelled up the dirty laundry in blue paper and a constable took it away. Just before he went to the court that morning, a solicitor from Hempsons, his London solicitors arrived to see him briefly, and he catnapped before going into Court. When he returned for lunch he wrote a letter, then made notes. And, the only time it is ever mentioned, he smoked a cigarette, before praying and returning to Court. Mr James made a quarter of an hour visit at 5.25, followed by a much longer visit from Mr Lawrence. The rest of the evening was enlivened only by the Sergeant delivering six clean collars. But unusually, during the early hours of Wednesday 23rd, he woke up and got out of bed to make notes on three occasions. After his usual routine next morning, he was making copious notes on toilet paper – the shiny kind – and when asked if he required exercise replied 'No, thank you. I am far too busy.' Both Mr Lawrence and Mr Clarke called to see him before Court that morning.

Before lunch the duty Sergeant delivered a package to Dr Adams – how easily it could have been one of his guns! He even had his prescription pad with him and wrote out a 'prescription for ointment to be obtained from Brownes Chemist' which he gave to PC82 to take to the Sergeant – this actually turned out to be a prescription for suppositories. Whether prescriptions he wrote for himself were checked to find out what they contained is not known. There were further visits just before tea from Mr James, Mr Lawrence and Mr Clarke, followed by Mr Gray, the dental surgeon by permission of DI Pugh… They 'engaged in conversation and prayer' for forty minutes.

On the following morning, Thursday 24th January, he was engaged in much meditation, studying 'texts in Bible, *Our Daily Walk* and another small book – set in conjunction with one another', and prayer before leaving for Court. When he returned to the cell at lunchtime, a weary PC57 noted:

'1.5 p.m. Whistled 'Abide with Me' over and over.

1.12 p.m. Sat down at table and looked through books and papers.

Still whistling 'Abide with Me'

1.17 p.m. Commenced meal.

1.25 p.m. Finished meal and commenced looking through letters and papers.

Resumed whistling 'Abide with Me'

Commenced eating cake.'

One can only assume that he was whistling this hymn in cheerful fashion as the court hearing was not affecting his appetite.

Following the afternoon session, the court was adjourned. Dr Adams was visited by Mr James, accompanied by Sergeant Maxted and he sorted out the belongings that he was not taking with him to Brixton, which were checked by them, and, after a visit by Defence Counsel, he left Police Headquarters for London.

It was not until the following Thursday, 31st January, that he was returned to Eastbourne with Prison escort. He had with him an *Argosy* magazine to read – this publication was one of adventure stories, both fact and fiction, some by well-known writers such as Edgar Rice Burroughs. A basket of fruit, a package and a letter had been delivered to the Police Station and were brought to him by the Station Sergeant. Mr James came along bringing his briefcase and producing from it books and papers for the Doctor. Dr Adams was taken to Court for just fifteen minutes for the Court's decision. Mr Lawrence arrived with his Junior, and Mr James returned later with a suitcase of clothing, and left with the dirty linen.

Although the Doctor had just learned that he was committed for trial on a capital charge to the Old Bailey, he washed his hands, requested nail scissors and proceeded to cut his finger and toe nails. He read his *Argosy* magazine until lunch arrived; ate the lunch and some fruit from the basket. And resumed reading the *Argosy* until the prison officer arrived to take him back to Brixton to await trial at the Old Bailey on the charge of murdering Mrs Morrell.

# Chapter Thirty

## Poetic Injustice?

### February 1957

On 22nd February, Superintendent R.C. Lewis of Scotland Yard had been instructed by Mr F. Donal Barry, Assistant Director of Public Prosecutions to make enquiries in Eastbourne and the surrounding area concerning a complaint received by the Director of Public Prosecutions 'about certain verses which could imply that Dr Bodkin Adams, a man at present committed for trial for murder, was guilty of that offence'. Mr Barry had explained that, when enquiries were complete, consideration would be given on whether or not to prosecute 'in respect of the reading of certain verses – a kind of poem – which had been read by a Mr Johnson, Manager of the Cavendish Hotel, Eastbourne, at a meeting of the Eastbourne Hoteliers Association on 13th February, 1957'. Superintendent Lewis reported back on 4th March to Mr Barry.

The meeting to which Mr Barry had referred had been held at the Burlington Hotel on Eastbourne seafront – the Cavendish was also located on the seafront, and both hotels are still in existence. There were up to 150 members of the Association present and Dr Adams' solicitors, Messrs. Hempsons had sent the letter to the Director of Public Prosecutions suggesting that Mr Johnson's action was in contempt of Court.

Mr Barry had asked Superintendent Lewis to obtain evidence in the usual way to show whether any offence had been committed and to see if there were any similar verses being widely circulated, 'with an object of trying to ascertain the author or source of the verses'. Superintendent Lewis set off to catch the train from Victoria Station for Eastbourne, in company with his assistant, Detective Sergeant Grout. Around the corner from Eastbourne Station they had made an appointment to see Mr Mayo of Messrs. Mayo & Perkins, solicitors. They were acting for Mr Johnson and Mr Mayo was also the Deputy Coroner for Eastbourne. With some reluctance, Mr Mayo agreed that they could see Mr Johnson 'as there appeared to be ample evidence available that Mr Johnson had read certain verses which could relate to Dr Adams'. Mr Mayo asked Superintendent Lewis to promise him that he would try to find evidence that 'the poetry alleged to have been read by Mr Johnson was well known in Eastbourne and that many typewritten copies were known to pass from hand to hand and were well circulated throughout the district'. An appointment was made for Lewis to see Mr Johnson at his hotel at 3 p.m. that afternoon.

Superintendent Lewis and Sergeant Grout met with Mr Edward Johnson at the Cavendish Hotel which was, and still is, one of the larger and superior hotels in Eastbourne: west of the pier and overlooking the Carpet Gardens which were created in 1904. The name of Cavendish is the surname of the Dukes of Devonshire, and next to the hotel is the statue of the 7th Duke, whose architect designed Eastbourne. The seafront is still protected by covenants of the estate of the Duke of Devonshire, so that it is not despoiled by shops of any kind. Mr Johnson 'quite openly admitted' that he had read verses out at the Hoteliers' Association meeting and made a statement. Dr Adams was an infrequent visitor to his hotel, and when the case against the Doctor first became known, Mr Johnson heard that 'odd funny stories had been told in the hotel bars about the case', and he said that these were similar 'to those published in the past concerning the 'Bishop of Birmingham' and the 'Rector of Stiffkey' but none of these alleged jokes as far as he knew had been treated seriously'. A copy of the verses had been handed to Mr Johnson by a customer a few days before the meeting; he had read them and thought them funny, so he borrowed the verses and made a copy for himself.

It was quite by chance that Mr Johnson had the verses in his pocket whilst he was chairing the Hoteliers' meeting, and, towards the end of the evening, 'when things were becoming rather out of hand he thought it would be amusing to read the poem to the assembly'. He had a word with Mr Ellis, the past Chairman and Proprietor of the Lathom House Hotel, who was sitting next to him: Ellis had laughed and 'intimated that he thought it would be a bright idea to wind up the meeting'. Johnson told Superintendent Lewis that he stood up and, after passing some remarks about the new Town Guide for holiday-makers, 'said a bird had told him that the town's publicity officer was going to take out the picture from the front page of the Guide and instead insert a poem about Eastbourne'. He proceeded to read the poem but was unable to finish it because there was so much laughter.

Lewis reported that there was no doubt at all that Mr Johnson much regretted his indiscretion as he now agreed that it was something which could be detrimental to Dr Adams but he 'did not stop to consider that it might be an offence or have the slightest bearing on anything such as a law case.' He had added that he would not have been 'such a clot' as to say anything which would injure Dr Adams or himself for that matter. He apologised most sincerely and 'emphasised that what was done was without any grain of malice or unpleasant feeling in his mind towards anybody'; he had just thought it a joke. Mr Johnson could not produce a copy of the verses because he had destroyed his copy. Several people had told him that they had heard the poem before and thought it very amusing, but he himself had no idea who the author was.

Edward Johnson was, of course, a very worried man; if any action were taken against him he might well lose his job as Manager of the Cavendish Hotel. He had been there for two years, the business had improved and he felt that managers of other hotels were jealous of him and were 'taking advantage of his predicament'.

Superintendent Lewis and Sergeant Grout went around to the Lathom House Hotel to see its proprietor, Mr Albert Ellis: the man who had been sitting next to Johnson and encouraged him to read the poem. He agreed that he had seen the poem and remembered it 'as referring to "a needle and a bodkin",' and had told Johnson that it was a good idea to read it. He remembered that Mr Johnson had prefaced his reading by saying 'something to the effect that what he was about to read was not for the Press'. It had certainly ended their meeting 'in a bright way'. Mr Ellis did not see it as detrimental to Dr Adams or likely to prejudice his case in any way: he and Johnson, like any other sensible person, had 'a completely open mind about the case'. The reading of the poem had not influenced him; it was just a 'humorous incident'. Ellis had heard that other poems and limericks were being circulated in Eastbourne and it was 'all part of the Englishman's sense of humour'. Superintendent Lewis noted that 'He identified the copy in my possession of verses headed 'Adams and Eves' and said that these are similar to what were read by Mr Johnson.' Mr Ellis also gave his opinion that articles which had appeared in *Time* and other American periodicals contained far more serious accusations against Dr Adams than the verse read by Mr Johnson.

Next stop in the enquiry was the Hydro Hotel and its Assistant Manager, Mr John Halifax. The Hydro Hotel is still one of the best hotels in Eastbourne and the nearest to Beachy Head, high on the west cliffs, with its terrace where guests can partake of their cream teas overlooking the hotel's croquet lawn, the cliff gardens – where the herring gulls await naive picnickers – and the English Channel. Mr Halifax recalled two lines of the poem, which were about 'odd kin' and 'needle and bodkin'. Lewis noted that 'He easily identified the poem with the Dr Adams who was charged with the murder' and considered it clever and amusing, but in 'bad taste'. But Johnson had not meant it maliciously, just as light relief for the meeting. Halifax had already seen a printed copy of the verses, not just the typewritten one shown to him; it was a visitor to his hotel who had shown him this, but he could not recall which one.

The two policemen retraced their steps along the seafront to the Cumberland Hotel, which is just west of the pier – another large hotel, fronted by the Carpet Gardens and just around the corner from the main shopping centre of the town. They had a talk with Mr Myles Evelyn Trollope, the Manager: he had thought it in very bad taste of Mr Johnson to read the verses. Mr Trollope had known Dr Adams for some years because he was the doctor for the residents of his hotel.

Mr Barry, when he had referred the whole matter to Superintendent Lewis, had handed him a letter from Coles & James, Dr Adams' solicitors in Eastbourne. Apparently, a Mr Tyrer had called to see Mr H.V. James, the senior partner, and told him that he had seen a copy of the verses in a bar in the Sussex Hotel. Mr Tyrer was a private enquiry agent employed by Messrs. Burr & Wyatt of 4, Clements Inn, London who were carrying out investigations on behalf of Hempsons, Dr Adams' London solicitors. Mr Tyrer was somewhat elusive and Superintendent Lewis was unable to locate him. As he had been staying at the Sussex Hotel, Lewis went to see Mr Douglas Raeburn, the proprietor of the Sussex. Mr Raeburn had not seen any verses about Dr Adams and they had not been circulated in his hotel to his knowledge, but Mr Tyrer had certainly stayed there on 16th February.

Lewis and Grout went round to the offices of Coles & James, a few doors away from Kent Lodge, Dr Adams' residence. They took statements from Mr H.V. James and Mr Cheeseborough. The verses first came to the notice of Mr Cheeseborough when he had attended a meeting at the Town Hall and Mr Petch of Polegate Motors produced a typewritten copy – which copy was, in fact, the one which had been given to Superintendent Lewis. Petch had got the copy at a party held at the Cavendish Hotel on 9th February from a 'half-intoxicated' man. It was on the 16th February that it had come to Mr Cheeseborough's knowledge that the verses had been read out at the Hoteliers' meeting. The verses appeared to have been circulating on a fairly wide scale in Eastbourne and also in Hastings. Mr James had had a conversation with Mr Johnson about his reading of the verses, and told him that they were libellous, and probably in contempt of court, advising him to consult his own solicitor. Superintendent Lewis found Mr James very helpful and 'invited his suggestions' on whom he should interview in the enquiry.

The Superintendent in his efforts to find out how widely the verses had circulated, visited several bars at some of the 'better class hotels' and chatted to the barmen and customers about the Adams case, 'without disclosing his identity'. He found that 'almost everyone' he spoke to knew about the verses, but when he tried to discover the sources 'people were not very anxious to involve other people'. It was, by now, well known that Mr Johnson had got himself into trouble over reading out the verses.

'Underlying the insistence of Mr H.V. James that something should be done about the publication of the verses', Superintendent Lewis discovered that 'there was something of a controversy' between the various hotel proprietors in Eastbourne. Mr Johnson, the Manager of the Cavendish Hotel was somewhat of an outsider, having just held his post for two years, and having little knowledge of Eastbourne and the staff and owners of the other hotels. His boast to Lewis had been that he had increased the turnover of the Cavendish by 'thousands', to the detriment of other hotels, such as the Hydro and the Cumberland. 'Other sources' also informed him that there was particular rivalry between these three hotels. Lewis was convinced, however, that the success of the Cavendish was due to the 'industry and ability' of Mr Johnson.

At first glance this 'rivalry' might seem irrelevant in the context of Superintendent Lewis' investigation, but he discovered that Mr H.V. James, Dr Adams' solicitor and personal friend, was also the Chairman of the Board of Directors of the Hydro Hotel, and that Mr Trollope, the Manager of the Cumberland Hotel, was employed by Miss Chattey, the proprietress, who was also a personal friend of Dr Adams – mentioned by the Doctor's chauffeur in his statement to police. It was also believed, Lewis found out, that Miss Chattey 'is assisting in providing funds for the Doctor's defence'.

It occurred to Superintendent Lewis that 'Mr Johnson is not popular with those persons controlling the Hydro and Cumberland Hotels and that Mr James and his associates might like something to happen which would cause Mr Johnson to be relieved of the power to take business away from certain other hotels in Eastbourne.

He had 'sensed' when interviewing both Mr Trollope of the Cumberland and Mr Halifax of the Hydro that 'they were somewhat anti-Johnson'. They were also the only two persons who considered Mr Johnson's reading of the verses to be in 'bad taste'.

Superintendent Lewis summarised matters in his interim report: there was clear evidence to show that Johnson had read 'verses similar to those sent to the Director by Messrs. Hempsons'; there was no doubt at all that 'the offending poem' was widely circulating in Eastbourne and district, but he had not yet been able to identify the author. Enquiries were continuing. Mr Donal Barry confirmed that the Superintendent should endeavour to obtain a copy of the printed verses, identify the printer and the author and obtain the necessary evidence.

Lewis reported back again on 14th March, 1957, having been back to Eastbourne with Detective Sergeant Juckes to assist him. They arrived in the town on 5th March and went straight to see Mr Herbert Victor James, Dr Adams' solicitor. They were greeted with the words: 'Well, it looks as if your visit had had the desired effect. I understand people are now rushing to destroy their copies. You might have difficulty now in getting hold of any'. He added that Lewis' previous visit to Eastbourne 'had been widely discussed amongst people in the hotel business.' During this second enquiry, Superintendent Lewis saw Mr James several times, and upon each occasion he pressed him for any useful information: he had reminded him that, in his letter to Hempsons, he had implied that the author of the verses was 'a medical man not well disposed towards Adams'. Mr James replied that he had 'no idea' who was the author of the verses. Why then had he suggested it might be a doctor, Lewis asked. It was just his opinion as he thought that the author of the verses probably had some medical knowledge. Superintendent Lewis could not agree that this was so, and told Mr James that he had heard 'from varying sources in general conversation' that the poem was first introduced to Eastbourne by journalists during the committal hearing in Eastbourne.

Lewis and Juckes went off to see Mr Stanley Love, proprietor of the Pevensey Bay Hotel, as they had heard that the printed verses had been seen there. Mr Love said that he had heard people talking in his saloon bar about the poetry about Dr Adams, but insisted that he had never seen his customers with any printed versions.

Later that day, they asked Detective Inspector Longhurst, the Senior C.I.D. Officer at Hastings, to make enquiries in his area, particularly to see whether the verses were being printed in that district. The Superintendent and his sergeant also visited 'several of the Hastings licensed premises', but obtained no evidence of any large circulation of the verses, and then only typewritten copies. DI Longhurst reported back that he could get no information on any printed copies having been seen in Hastings.

The following day, 6th March, Mr John Cheeseborough of Coles & James was able to provide some information that 'a man named Freeborn, alleged to be a reporter on the 'Eastbourne Gazette', was in possession of a printed copy of the verses entitled 'Adams & Eves'.' The Gazette's offices were then in Pevensey Road, and Lewis and Juckes saw Mr Alfred Coggan, a director of T.R. Beckett Ltd the owners of the newspaper. Mr Coggan said that John Freeborn was his Works Manager, and a man of 'exemplary character'; he handed over a printed copy of the verses. This copy had been obtained by Mr Freeborn and was the only printed version he had seen. Except for a couple of words, it was identical with the typewritten copy.

Following the trail, Lewis and Juckes interviewed Mr Freeborn and he made a statement: one of the doctors in Eastbourne, whom he knew well, had asked him if he had seen a copy of the verses concerning Dr Adams. He had not attached much importance to this at the time and just assumed that he was being asked as he was in the printing industry. He managed to get a copy from a friend: he was satisfied that this friend was not involved in printing the verses but did not wish to disclose his name. Freeborn thought that the print indicated that the verses had been produced on a hand printing machine and that the paper, being water-marked, was writing paper rather than printing paper. The Superintendent asked him if the type had been set automatically on a linotype or monotype machine and Freeborn agreed that it could have been, and a block so made possibly taken away to reproduce the printed material privately.

Superintendent Lewis and Sergeant Juckes visited several of the larger printing firms and consulted printers. The type was identified as 'Tenpoint Times Roman' and the heading in capitals as 'Centaur Italic'. The 'Times Roman' print was common to most printers but the ornamental mark underneath the title and repeated at the end of the verses was not normally stocked at that time. The expert printers were generally agreed that a monotype machine had been used and a block made by the compositor and, perhaps, then taken home and duplicated on a printing machine, perhaps an 'Adana'. Lewis and Juckes set about visiting the premises of all the larger printers in Eastbourne, trying to identify the type and the paper upon which the verses were printed. They also visited anyone known to have an 'Adana' printing machine.

On the 7th March the two policemen interviewed Mr Derek Platt, the Secretary of Sussex Printers Ltd in South Street, – which was owned by the same company which owned the local newspaper – together with his Manager Mr Randolph MacInnes. Mr MacInnes examined the Superintendent's copy of the verses and said he thought the type was 'ninepoint' and not 'ten', and he identified the paper as one known in the trade as 'Baynard Bond', a kind of paper used for printing bill heads and letter headings. The ornament in the printing, he could not recognise, but as for the paper, his firm used this. If it was 'ninepoint' type, however, this could not have been printed at Sussex Printers.

Later the same day, Mr Platt contacted the Superintendent to say that, after they had left his works, Mr MacInnes had realised that he had made a mistake and it was indeed 'tenpoint' and not 'ninepoint' type. Back they went to Sussex Printers to investigate further: eventually they saw Gordon Vallins and Superintendent Lewis told him that 'he had reason to believe' that the printed copy of the verses had been made at the premises of Sussex Printers. He replied 'Yes, I may as well tell you right away that this was a joke that's gone sour. I don't want to hide anything. I'll tell you anything you want to know.' Lewis cautioned him and he dictated a statement: he had obtained a typewritten copy of the verses from 'his young lady friend'. He had taken this to work and showed it to his workmates, who, like him 'appreciated the humour of it'. They had the verses set on a monotype keyboard and case on a monotype caster from which they 'pulled' about twenty-five copies. A hand-press was used and when the copies were made they were passed around the works – really just meant for the amusement of the employees. The type was put 'in the melting pot', which was the custom with type when it had served its purpose.

Vallins himself had taken home two copies, one for his father and one for himself. His father 'whilst admitting that the verses were amusing' had said: 'These might be serious son, let's burn them'. After 'further advice' from his father, he had gone to work on the following Monday and asked his colleagues to destroy their copies; most had agreed to do so. When Gordon Vallins had had time to think, he realised that 'the joke had gone far enough'; he had not meant that any copies should leave the workshop and was now very sorry that he had got involved in the incident.

Later, Mr Coggan, who was present when Vallins made his statement, told Superintendent Lewis that he knew Gordon Vallins and his father very well. Young Vallins had followed his father into the printing trade and joined them as an apprentice. He described him as 'an excellent craftsman, of a respectable family'. Mr Coggan also made a statement: he was very disturbed about the whole matter and would 'take steps to see that such a thing does not happen again'. The printing shop was normally 'very well-supervised' but there had been 'a period of re-organization in the management'. The antics of printing shop apprentices were, of course, traditional and have been documented since the late 18th Century – the time of the great expansion of the printing industry, at least. [Robert Darnton – *The Great Cat Massacre*]

The next day, 8th March, saw Superintendent Lewis and Sergeant Juckes again at the works of Sussex Printers, this time to see the Deputy Manager, Mr Anthony Ezra Taylor. He gave a statement after examining the printed verses: the paper was 'Baynard Bond', similar to that which the firm used for letter headings. Offcuts of the paper had been used, and the type was 'Tenpoint Monotype Times New Roman'. He was satisfied that the verses were mechanically set; the italic heading was in 'Blado', also a type used by his firm, but he did not recognise the ornament as one in stock. He thought that Vallins could have had some assistance with the printing, but he did think that the intention was to print the verses for their own amusement. Superintendent Lewis decided that 'no useful purpose would be served in disrupting the printing going on in the works to question the men named by Taylor particularly as this firm has been so helpful to me.'

Later that day Lewis and Juckes saw Charles Hobden, an experienced mechanical compositor and charge hand. He made a statement in which he said that a typed copy of the verses was brought to him by Vallins and he had made a copy on a monotype keyboard, which produced a spool for passing to the casting department. He gave the copy to the casting man and asked if it could be cast off for him. He just 'did it because he wanted to do the boys a favour'. The heading and decoration were not done by him. When he had set the verses 'it was definitely understood that they should only have a copy of the verses for themselves in the works and not for outside publication.' He thought that there were only sufficient printed for them to have one copy each. Hobden had certainly never intended the printed verses to be circulating around Eastbourne. The irony of the whole incident was that Sussex Printers' printing shop was just a few yards away from Eastbourne Police Headquarters.

Superintendent Lewis and his Sergeant had, at the same time, continued their quest for the author of the verses, visiting hotel bars and public houses. But Lewis reported: 'We were quite unsuccessful, however, in getting any lead as to their origin'. It was the general opinion that they had been composed by a London journalist and planted in Eastbourne during the period of the Committal Hearing at the Magistrates Court. At one of the places they visited, the

American Bar at the Clifton Hotel, they saw several men and women 'apparently deriving enjoyment from reading a typewritten copy of the verses which was passed from hand to hand'. In police parlance: 'Observation was kept on these people until the bar closed, but no information was disclosed by anybody about the source of the verses. The persons who were reading the copy of the verses had been drinking and I decided it would be unwise for us to disclose our identity to them.'

When the bar closed, the Superintendent saw the Manager, Mr M.J. Barrie, and made it clear to him what he thought of 'the way in which the bar was being conducted', warning him of the possible consequences. Mr Barrie promised to take 'immediate steps' to rectify these 'irregularities'. It was at this hotel, the Clifton, [and not the Sussex Hotel] that Mr Tyrer, the private eye, had seen the copy of the typewritten verses circulating. Lewis and Juckes had not managed to interview Mr Tyrer but the Sergeant had spoken to him on the 'phone. When he saw the verses at the Clifton Hotel, it was a woman 'whose name he believed was 'Dora' who had them. Lewis reported 'From the description given of Dora to Police we identified that woman as one of the party in the bar at the Clifton Hotel when the verses were produced'.

Superintendent Lewis and Sergeant Juckes had again met with Mr Johnson, the Manager of the Cavendish Hotel, as they assiduously visited the bars of Eastbourne. He had not been able to assist them any further, but, like Mr James, he had noticed that the copies of the verses had been fast disappearing from the town.

Superintendent Lewis' report, together with statements, blank specimens of paper from Sussex Printers, and 'two printed copies of the verses in question', were sent to the Director of Public Prosecutions. The copies of these verses have not been kept in the archives!

### Adams and Eves

*In Eastbourne it is healthy*
*And the residents are wealthy*
*It's a miracle that anybody dies;*
*Yet this pearl of English lidos*
*Is a slaughter house of widows –*
*If their bank rolls are above the normal size.*
*If they're lucky in addition*
*In their choice of a physician*
*And remember him when making out their wills*
*And bequeath their Rolls Royces*
*Then they soon hear angel voices*
*And are quickly freed from all their earthly ills.*
*If they're nervous or afraid of*
*What a heroine is made of*
*Their mentality will soon be reconditioned*

*So they needn't feel neglected*
*They will shortly be injected*
*With the heroin in which they are deficient.*
*As we witnessed the deceased borne*
*From the stately homes of Eastbourne*
*We are calm, for it may safely be assumed*
*That each lady that we bury*
*In the local cemetery*
*Will re-surface – when the body is exhumed.*
*It's the mortuary chapel*
*If they touch an Adam's apple*
*After parting with a Bentley as a fee*
*So to liquidate your odd kin*
*By the needle of the bodkin*
*Send them down to sunny Eastbourne by the sea.*

*Anon.*

Chapter Thirty-One

Preparations for the Trial

17 December 1956 – March 1957

Murder is a crime which is triable only on indictment, and it has to take place in a Crown Court, but this has to be preceded by preliminary proceedings in a magistrates' court. The function of these proceedings is to decide whether the evidence put before these examining justices is sufficient so that a reasonable jury could convict the accused. This does not mean that the magistrates consider that they might convict on such evidence – the standard of proof required for committal is quite low – but that they consider that there is a case to answer.

Dr Adams had been charged with the murder of Mrs Morrell on the 13th December, 1956, so the Director of Public Prosecutions had been proceeding with arrangements for the case some time before, and had, presumably, been in communication with Scotland Yard from an early stage. The conduct of the case, from the time when Detective Superintendent Hannam's reports were presented to the Office of the Director of Public Prosecutions, was very much in the hands of Melford Stevenson QC, Counsel appointed to support the Attorney-General.

A conference was held in the afternoon of 17th December, 1956 at Melford Stevenson's Chambers in London. Malcolm Morris, his junior, was present, together with Dr Francis Camps, the Home Office pathologist, Superintendent Hannam and Mr Leck from the DPP's Office. The medical evidence was discussed and some conclusions reached about this: 'that there was no medical justification for prescribing drugs in such quantities; that the reason for so prescribing was to kill the patient.' In mitigation it might be said that Dr Adams was committing euthanasia, but this was not likely in so many cases.

Dr Ashby and Dr Douthwaite must have already been recommended as expert witnesses at this stage, and presumably Dr Camps would have had some hand in this and known them. The minutes of the conference record that it would be 'necessary to obtain corroboration of Dr M. Ashby.' and that 'Dr A.H. Douthwaite must be given sufficient time to study the facts'. With regard to the proof of administration of drugs, it was concluded that this was incomplete, but that the chemists' dangerous drugs register would be evidence. Hannam was instructed to make further enquiries.

The evidence required for the hearing on 20th December, 1956 was discussed and advice was given by counsel on this, and on witnesses. Three further charges under the Dangerous Drugs Act, 1951 were to be preferred, and these related to the search carried out at Dr Adams' home and were for 'obstructing' and 'concealing' the bottles of morphine, and for failing to keep a register of dangerous drugs. Superintendent Hannam was given instructions to deal with these charges.

The minutes of the conference refer to 'Preferment of murder charge at this stage' – which presumably meant the Bill of Indictment as Dr Adams had already been charged with the murder of Mrs Morrell. It was concluded that 'such a charge must await completion of the other proceedings before the Justices' because, obviously, they had to decide whether to commit the accused for trial at a Crown Court. It was also decided that the enquiries into the evidence of administration of drugs was incomplete and that there was a lack of corroboration of Dr Ashby's report, and 'insufficient evidence adduced at this stage to justify the preferment of such a charge.' At this time there was about a month left before the committal hearing and it could be inferred that those present at this meeting did not expect him to be committed.

Following this conference Mr Barry [DPP's Office] took Dr Ashby's report on the papers to Dr Douthwaite in Harley Street at 5 o'clock, and Dr Camps arrived, at his invitation, an hour later. A rather different picture of Dr Douthwaite emerges from Barry's minute of this meeting, than the one presented at the trial. Douthwaite did not agree entirely with his colleague Ashby's views, particularly with regard to addiction. Discussion ensued for one and a half hours, and Dr Douthwaite 'seemed to think that on this case alone it would be very dangerous to charge murder as there were many loopholes in the symptoms exhibited by Mrs Morrell'. He drew a distinction between 'pain and irritability': Mrs Morrell might not have been in actual pain but could have been mentally and physically very irritable, and the administration of morphine and heroin might have been justified in this instance.

Dr Douthwaite suggested that 'if he were in Adams' position he would defend this case by saying that he had this elderly patient who really had nothing to live for and in his opinion it was his duty to keep her in as little pain as possible by administering drugs even to the extent of running certain risks and that was why he did give her the quantities he apparently did. At the end she would have been in a state of great irritability if she had come out of her coma and therefore he 'stepped up' the drugs to be sure that she would remain in the coma – knowing very well that in doing so he was probably hastening her end.' Dr Douthwaite said that, of course, he was confining his reasoning to this one case, and that if there were a number of similar cases where it could be shown that Dr Adams had benefited from the patient's decease, then this was a different matter.

On the following day, 18th December, 1956, another conference was held: this time at the Attorney-General's Room at the House of Commons in the later afternoon. Present at this were: the Attorney-General, Sir Theobald Mathew, Director of Public Prosecutions; Melford Stevenson QC; Malcolm Morris; FD Barr; JE Leck; Drs. Douthwaite; Ashby and Camps; Detective Superintendent Hannam and Detective Sergeant Hewett. The brief note of this says that Dr Ashby's report was discussed and that both Dr Douthwaite and Dr Ashby were 'both of the opinion that Mrs E.A. Morrell died as a result of overdosing of drugs.' The evidence for this administration was considered and the Attorney-General 'instructed that Adams be charged with the murder of Mrs E.A. Morrell'. Amongst other cases discussed were those of Mr and Mrs Hullett, Mrs Bradnum, and the Neil Miller sisters.

Dr Ashby's original report is not in any of the archives but he prepared another, dated 28th December, 1956, after the Attorney-General had requested that he review all the evidence for two purposes: to see whether there were any further cases 'definite enough to warrant a capital charge' and to see if there was any evidence of 'system'. He found that many of the features of the Morrell case did conform to a pattern and that Dr Adams 'has over the years developed a very effective system' for bringing himself tax-free income. He thought that Dr Adams' actions could be 'better interpreted in the light of a psychological study of his actions and efforts, whether successful or not', and had tried to answer 'The problems as to whether Dr Adams is careful or haphazard; simple or crafty; greedy or selfless; truthful or the reverse'. He thought that his study answered these questions, and whether such answers were relevant to the Morrell case and others. It has to be said that Dr Ashby was not a psychologist and that, in the 1950s, he did not have the benefit of extensive literature and studies of serial killers, and that, therefore, his interpretation of various actions was that of his time.

Dr Ashby thought that there had been 'a considerable measure of selection' by Dr Adams in choosing the patients on which 'to devote such time and attention, in order to obtain power over their affairs and considerable proportions of their wealth and possessions, both before and after their deaths':

> 'Extreme old age, considerable wealth, and the absence of children, who would natural-ly be strong and perhaps watchful competitors, seem to have been criteria from which he hardly deviated.'

Dr Ashby had looked at twenty-three cases and the average age of the patients was 80½ years, but when he selected from these the nine which had caused him 'the greatest concern', the average age of these was 84.4 years: Mrs Mouat – 89, Mrs Mortimer – 75, Mrs Morrell – 81, Mrs Kilgour – 89, Mrs Bradnum – 85, Mrs Norton-Dowding – 79, Miss C. Neil Miller – 87, James Priestley-Downs – 88, and Miss Hatton – 87. He thought that it was 'well-known' that, although many of advanced years had their full faculties, many had not; that the majority would have lost nearly all their friends, and would be 'notoriously liable to become very attached to anyone befriending them, and then to change their wills for the benefit of those recent friends'. The evidence confirmed that many of these patients were 'typical of this latter group'.

Dr Adams' motive and object was obvious to Dr Ashby:

> 'The evidence that the main driving force in Dr Adams' life and actions was to obtain as much money and goods from his patients as possible seems to abundant to need spe-cial detailing.'

Dr Ashby was trying to look at the whole matter from a scientific point of view in order to make his analysis. At the same time he was clearly horrified to find a brother doctor behaving in such a way and disgracing his profession.

Dr Adams had frequently 'resorted to dishonest means' to gain his ends, and he also had 'another revealing and perhaps fatal characteristic… his undoubted impatience to acquire, rather than be content to await the natural course of events'. He considered the 'most distressing example' was the taking of Mrs Thomas' new typewriter the day before her death, and 'the most disturbing act of impatience' the obtaining and clearing of the £1,000 cheque from Mrs Hullett just before her taking of the fatal dose. Then there was the obtaining of the £500 cheque from Miss Clara Neil Miller eleven days before her death. Dr Ashby continued:

> 'If repeated acts of petty pilfering and dishonesty are admissible in considering a system, examples of them abound in these cases.'

He mentioned the testimony of Mrs Mawhood: placing items on his patient's account in a shop, and 'to a fellow doctor, the disturbing episode of the gold pencil'. Dr Ashby admitted that the following comment might 'indicate prejudice':

> 'Whether charging on the basis of 22 visits at 3 guineas a time during a patient's last 8 days is dishonest or just plain extortion is a matter of opinion.'

The 'picking up of one or two things from a dead patient's room' indicated to Ashby 'a pathological degree of acquisitiveness'. But when such circumstances were considered in the light of Dr Adams' habit of excluding friends, relatives and nurses, there were 'strong grounds for concluding that Dr Adams was systematic rather than haphazard in his handling of patients and their property'. He thought that the taking of chocolates from an old lady who was blind was evidence of Dr Adams' standards, and:

> '…as an illustration of Dr Adams' attitude of mind nothing perhaps could be clearer than his suggestion to Mrs Galloway, "Whatever the bill is make it out for double, she has plenty of money."'

Dr Ashby hoped – in vain as it turned out – that 'this vital insight into Dr Adams' character as a doctor' would be placed before a jury.

He had noted some major attempts to defraud, such as the case of Mrs Harris and the cheque for £1,900, which, in Counsel's opinion had been 'a clear case of fraud', and that of Mrs Mouat and the attempt to get her to sign a blank sheet of paper only two days before her death.

These were 'psychological aspects of Dr Adams' system of treating the patient 'as a whole', and Dr Ashby proposed to analyse his clinical methods, although 'it might be more accurate to use this word in the singular' as it appeared that 'sedation with addicting hypnotics was the lynchpin of Dr Adams' therapy'. The evidence for this was abundant. Sedative treatment was, of

*The Grand Parade Band Enclosure, Eastbourne*

*Royal Parade and Pier, Eastbourne*

*Three Promenades, Grand Parade, Eastbourne*

*Lt. Col. Sir Roland Gwynne, DSO* (Towner Gallery)

*The family grave*

*The crack shot; Dr John Bodkin Adams*

course, widely used by doctors 'in the harassing times in which we all now live' [This now seems a strange way to describe 1950s' Britain!] It was necessary to consider whether this treatment was being 'given judiciously' or used in unsuitable cases and 'in a negligent degree'. Here he mentions that he has discussed 'more serious misuses' in another document on the case of Mrs Morrell.

Dr Ashby thought that it was 'of inestimable value' that they had 'not only the reports of the nursing sisters of long experience, but also two clear cases of the most flagrant and improper use of sedatives described by doctors who have taken over cases from Dr Adams'; in both cases the doctors stopped the sedatives and which there were 'almost miraculous' recoveries. He understood from Superintendent Hannam that he had now obtained information on two further such cases. The original two cases were of Mrs Pike – reported by Dr Mathew – and that of Mrs Oddy, described by Dr Estcort. These two examples were, Dr Ashby thought, very important in considering 'system' in relation to the treatment of Mrs Morrell and the 'far more serious treatment with hypnotics' of that patient.

He also thought that more detailed statements should be taken from many nurses who had commented on 'Dr Adams' mid-day doping' of patients and that this was more possible 'now a capital charge has been made.' He mentioned Sister Owen in particular, and the case of Mr Cockhead, from whom Dr Adams had received a legacy. Dr Adams had been giving this patient 'a rising dosage of Pethidine, a very powerful drug used against pain, with strong addicting qualities, to a total of 600 tablets', the last 100 being dispensed only 17 days before death.

Dr Ashby considered that injections were 'the subject of the greatest difficulty in assessing their value as evidence'. Nurses in hospitals had to show what they were injecting, for the dose and label to be checked, but a doctor had 'no such check placed upon him'. They knew that Dr Adams was prescribing and giving morphia, heroin, and other hypnotics to his patients, and that some should not have been receiving them. There was also clear evidence that he often took these drugs 'from his own ample store'; some of the supplies for these drugs were shown 'in the enclosed documents' – prescription lists and the lists of the drugs which were in his medical bags – 'including 5,000 phenobarbitone tablets purchased 3rd January 1952'. Dr Ashby notes that 'He denied purchasing these or having them during his talk with Detective Inspector Pugh on 24th November, 1956'. [Some parts of this report of Hannam's regarding this visit were excised, presumably by the DPP or Counsel.]

There were several incidents where there were 'grounds for suspecting that Dr Adams gave a large terminal injection, following which the patient never regained consciousness'. However, it was 'a matter of conjecture' as to whether these injections were lethal dosages of dangerous drugs or not, although in view of the supporting evidence, Dr Ashby regarded them as 'sinister', especially so 'when at first hand we have heard from Dr Mathew of Dr Adams giving an injection to a patient already deeply sedated'.

Dr Ashby quoted several instances where he believed that Dr Adams had given lethal injections: Mrs Kilgour, who had lapsed into coma after his injection and where he had 'abstained from any remedial treatment'; Mrs Bradnum, where Dr Adams had given her an injection and then made a comment containing 'a remarkable prophesy'; Mrs Norton Dowding who had been given an injection when she was in a 'drowsy' state and who then did not regain consciousness again; and Mr Hullett. Dr Ashby expressed surprise that Mr Hullett had been hurried upstairs after a heart attack, and commented 'Why Dr Adams had to give an injection of highly concentrated morphia, drawn up into the syringe in a darkened corner of the room, it is not possible to say.' Then that 'Dr Adams diagnosed cerebral haemorrhage without looking at the body. This is the act of a charlatan.'

Dr Ashby had considered Dr Adams' 'techniques with patients' wills' and the 'remarkable lengths' and 'assiduity' with which he had pursued 'this aspect of his activities' with the intention of acquiring as much of the patients' wealth and goods for himself as possible. Dr Ashby was much struck by Dr Adams' moral and professional standards. On the deathbed attempt to get Mr Mawhood to alter his will in the doctor's favour, he comments:

'A more brazen betrayal of our code of professional honour could scarcely be imagined.'

It seemed to have been 'an incentive rather than a deterrent' for Dr Adams if the patients were confused, and it had taken the threat of High Court action by Miss Hatton's relatives to make him withdraw from his actions. Dr Ashby thought that Dr Adams' explanation of the affair of Mrs Hughes' codicil just before her 'sinister' deterioration 'in the box would be illuminating'. There had been similar cases of attempts to get power of attorney over Major Christie's and Mrs Movat's affairs, and his success in the case of Mrs Whitton – a 'doping case' – where he had obtained well over half the patient's fortune.

However, his review of 'Dr Adams' methods' had 'failed to show any other case at all comparable with that of Mrs Morrell.' Dr Ashby concluded his report:

'Many patients have been severely and improperly doped and their money has been obtained by the most flagrant abuse of Dr Adams' professional relationship with them. He may well have killed some of them with his terminal injections. It can be said, however, with assurance that Dr Adams did have what in my opinion was a system, but it was a system for extortion rather than a system for murder.'

Dr Ashby was a Consultant Neurologist. He had considered the police reports and the statements which had been taken in the course of the police investigation, so he had only reviewed the actions and motivations of Dr Adams which were apparent from that information. It certainly could not be said that his report was, in any way, a psychological study. He knew nothing of his background or his beliefs, and was so little of a psychologist, that he saw no reason to look into them. He saw the power and domination over patients as a tool of the sin of greed. And he saw murder as incidental to the desire for acquisition.

There follows in the file a letter dated 2nd January, 1957 from Dr Francis Camps to FD Barry in the Director of Public Prosecutions' Office. Dr Camps had been involved in the whole matter from the beginning as he had carried out a post-mortem on Mrs Hullett's body. He was a Home Office pathologist and therefore was much closer to the police than the doctors retained as 'expert witnesses' on the case. The letter states that there is enclosed 'some further notes and opinion upon the case of Morrell', but this was not in the archive. Apparently, Dr Camps, had tried to point out 'loopholes' in the case, and suggested that a table be prepared 'to show the times of employment of the various nurses and this tabulated against the prescriptions and drugs administered by them'. The question is: how would he have known what drugs were administered by the nurses? It is possible to infer from this sentence that he had seen the notebooks. Again in the following paragraph of his letter, there would appear to be a reference to the 'special injections', as well as a caveat about the whole case:

> 'I still foresee the difficulty of saying that a doctor is not entitled to employ such drugs as he thinks to relieve symptoms. This does not, of course, mean an overdose. I can see no possible reason for a doctor not to tell nurse what he is giving except a deliberate concealment for some motive.'

As a pathologist, Dr Camps also points out that some of the cases should have been reported to the Coroner, 'as unexpected deaths or possibly due to accident', including those of Mrs Bradnum and Mrs Morrell. He did not, of course, know about the most blatant example: that of the Tenth Duke of Devonshire.

The Director of Public Prosecutions listed 'Observations' for Counsel, dated 19th February, 1957, to inform him that various statements had been taken 'since the papers in this case were last with Counsel'. This date was after the committal to the Central Criminal Court, but they included: a statement from Dr Roy Kemball Price relating to his examination of Mr Hullett on 9th March, 1956; three statements regarding the case of Mrs Pike; additional statements from Dr Harris on the cases of Mrs Hullett and Mrs Morrell; and the statement of Superintendent Hannam relating to his interview of Lieutenant Colonel Sir Roland Gwynne. Counsel was also informed that Hannam had interviewed Lady Taylor, the wife of Eastbourne's M.P., 'but the result of the interview was negative'. As the result of a request from the solicitor representing Dr Adams, he had been informed 'of the names and addresses of all persons not called as witnesses in the cases of Mrs EA Morrell, AJ Hullett and Mrs GJ Hullett, with the exception of Celia Mary Mayo' as she had been too ill to attend the preliminary hearing. He had also been sent copies of the exhumation reports on Miss Clara Neil Miller and Mrs Julia Bradnum.

A letter from Dr Ashby to the Director of Public Prosecutions, dated 13th March, refers to a recent conference, when the Attorney-General had expressed his concern 'as to whether there was any material disagreement between the two consultant physicians' and, in particular, whether there was any point 'where serious attempts could be made to drive a wedge' between himself and Dr Douthwaite. According to Dr Ashby it was merely a matter of semantics: where Dr Douthwaite had used the word 'negligible' in regard to tolerance, and he, himself, had used the word 'appreciable' – in the witness-box at Eastbourne. He trusted it would be clear that they were both correct and neither needed to retract from their stands. Summarising:

> 'Dr Douthwaite is correct that the protection afforded by tolerance was 'negligible' to the enormous doses of the last five days. I was equally correct in saying that of course

after nine months of morphia there would be some 'appreciable' measure of tolerance, but not of course adequate to protect against more than a moderate increase in dose.'

Dr Ashby threw in that he had 'thought at the time that Mr Lawrence was very wise in abstaining from trying to drive home a wedge which would crumble in his hands.'

There follows in the archive Dr Douthwaite's 'Comments on Evidence', but these are undated. They were certainly written before he appeared in the witness-box. He begins by making some general comments: firstly, about the 'stress laid on the great detail given by Dr Adams on the cremation certificate.' This was of no importance because the body had been disposed of about 36 hours after death. The confirmatory certificate given by Dr Fox was 'just routine' and was 'really absolutely useless from the point of view of security as all that an external examination can do is to show that death is not due to any violence'. It would be impossible from such an examination to show that death was due to 'cerebral thrombosis, drug poisoning or anything else'.

Dr Douthwaite thought that Dr Camps' suggestion that it should be 'brought out', when he was in the witness-box, that he had been in general practice for four and a half years from 1924 to '28, was a good idea, particularly as he was in practice in Worthing, Sussex, with its elderly population and 'vast number of old women'. He also suggested another consultant witness who had been a GP for many years, should be called – Dr Harwood Stevenson. [If the trial had already started this would not have been possible, but it is likely that Dr Douthwaite did not know this.]

There is then a heading 'Nurses treatment books' and Dr Douthwaite comments that a GP would not normally want to keep these after a patient's death, although it was true that a nurse would offer them to him. The exception would be when it was a case of outstanding medical interest and he might want to write a paper on it. In this case he might keep the books. If he habitually kept such books then his house would be full of such records. Dr Adams had made a statement [to the police] that he did not keep treatment notes, only a card recording visits to patients, which he destroyed a year after death, and this showed that he was not keeping case records for scientific purposes. Dr Douthwaite had done some research and there were no references to scientific communications by Dr Adams in the Medical Directory. Dr Douthwaite mentions that this statement of Dr Adams was 'not yet in evidence'.

Dr Douthwaite had then looked at the drugs used on Mrs Morrell: the medication fell into three periods: from July 1948 to late in 1950, when there was 'continuous adminstration of barbiturates in doses suitable for sedation, plus what has been termed 'routine injections' nightly of morphine grain ¼ and heroin grain ⅓.' In the second period, from September 1950, the morphine was increased by the addition of Omnopon and some hyperduric morphine; and in the third period, from 10th November, there had been a 'startling increase' of heroin and the use of paraldehyde on the 12th.

He enumerated the effects to be expected from these drugs: addiction within the first month to morphine and heroin, and a tolerance to the depressant or sedative action but not to the stimulant one on the spinal cord. At a level dose, the tolerance would not increase further because tolerance development was slow and minimal with 'a constant, small and adequately spaced dosage'; it would be maximal if the dosage steadily increased and was more often repeated. The craving for the drugs would not be satisfied if the dosage were not stepped up and would make a patient 'irritable, bad-tempered, emotionally unstable and difficult to deal with'. An increase to a higher level would relieve these symptoms until a higher degree of tolerance had been acquired, and then the symptoms would recur. If the drug were withheld for even a few hours, the patient would become 'violently excited, abusive, shivery, cold, sometimes collapsed and might have running at the nose and sneezings'. Also characteristic of addiction were poor appetite, constipation and sleeplessness.

Although cerebral arteriosclerosis was often associated with bad temper and unreasonable behaviour, this disease was characterised by progressive deterioration, and not with the intervals of comparatively good health which Mrs Morrell had even in the latter part of her life. Her variability of state was more consistent with drug-related illness rather than arterial disease. Dr Douthwaite also mentioned that if a doctor thought that his treatment might have resulted in his patient becoming addicted, then the usual procedure was to call in a second opinion in order to protect himself.

Morphia, and particularly heroin, powerfully depressed the nerve centre of the brain which controlled breathing, and this would result in slowing the breathing from the normal 18 to 20 respirations per minute down to 10 or even less (Cheyne Stokes breathing). This was particularly dangerous to old people. Depression of respiration was liable to lead to lung collapse and pneumonia. 'Any such complication or heart failure would result in rapid breathing in spite of heroin action on the respiratory centre'; therefore rapid respiration was 'no argument that the patient was not under the effect of heroin or morphine'.

The spinal cord would have been irritable, and this would be caused even by $\frac{1}{3}$ grain of heroin daily, and mental excitability would result. In larger doses 'twitching of the limbs or even face may appear from time to time… especially if the depressant effect of barbiturates is not being exerted at that time':

> 'The doses of heroin on November 10th, 11th and 12th would have caused the jerks and convulsions. There can be no other explanation of these.'

The weak state of the patient would also have caused slower excretion of the drugs, and therefore accumulation of them in the body. This would apply also to the morphia, particularly with the hyperduric type. The convulsions confirmed that high level of heroin in the body:

> 'The terminal convulsions were in a semi-conscious patient, if not actually comatose. It only needed the two injections of paraldehyde (each of 4 c.c.) to ensure death. Mrs Morrell died of poisoning from heroin, morphine and paraldehyde. Cerebral thrombosis could not have produced such a picture.'

Dr Douthwaite saw no justification for a daily dose of morphia or heroin except for severe pain –

in which case one or other might be used – or of using both together as heroin was an alternative to morphine. It had been suggested that the drugs were given 'to relieve excitability in an old cerebral arteriosclerotic. The drugs for this, as indeed was shown, are absolutely contraindicated because of the danger.' Nurse Randall had suggested that the dose was increased on November 9th and 10th because the patient had become 'chesty', but 'this would be the worst possible treatment'. He concluded:

> 'It is outstandingly clear that they [the drugs] were administered during the first two years for the production and maintenance of addiction and thus complete dependence on the doctor. To this extent he was successful.
>
> The drugs administered on and after November 10th 1950 were given in order to terminate life and in this he was also successful.'

Dr Douthwaite must have produced this document during the course of the trial and after he had heard the evidence of the nurses.

He wrote a further letter to the Director of Public Prosecutions during the trial, on 6th April; this time it concerned Dr Harman's evidence. Dr Douthwaite considered that Dr Harman's admission 'that morphine was not fully excreted under five days' endorsed his 'so-called "theory of accumulation".' Additionally, the excretion rate which was 'set out in text books' was based on research on healthy 'or relatively healthy subjects' and not on those 'at the extremes of life'.

# PART III

# The Trial – Days 1–4

## 18 – 21 March 1957

The Old Bailey is London's Central Criminal Court and it has a long history. Its location, about 200 yards northwest of St. Paul's Cathedral, just outside the western wall of the City of London, gave it the name, as 'bailey' referred to the outer wall of a fortification. The mediaeval courthouse was destroyed in the Great Fire of London in 1666 and, since then, it has been reconstructed several times, the last being in the early 1900s. It has been extended to provide additional courtrooms, but Court Number One is still as it was early in the 20th century, with its original furniture and the dock which leads down to the cells below. It stands on the site of the old ancient and infamous Newgate Prison and in 1957 it was recalled that, only about ninety years previously, the last public hanging had taken place at Newgate. A prison warder conducting Dr Adams to his cell – Number 23 – at Brixton Prison, had said to him as he sat down: 'I have been here with many famous prisoners… Christie sat where you are sitting now… And Haigh sat there too.'

Courtroom No. 1 is about 50 feet square and oak-panelled. It seats about 200 people, including the judge and jury, but very few were able to hear what was happening as it was designed for only a few to do so. The Judge and the accused faced each other above the well of the court, counsel for the prosecution and the defence sat below them in the well. It was difficult for the jury to even see the witnesses properly while they testified and more so for the press and the public to hear and see everything.

Three knocks on the door, signifying that the judge, Mr Justice Devlin, was ready to enter, opened Dr Adams' trial. He wore the red robes of his office and carried the traditional white gloves, and, more sinisterly, the black cap he might have to don when passing sentence upon the prisoner. Sir Patrick Arthur Devlin was, at fifty-one, one of the youngest and most able judges in England. His handsome, deep-lined face was grim as he sat down, his chair pushed into place by his clerk. The court was silent as the accused appeared in the dock in the middle of the courtroom: heavy, stolid, in his blue Savile Row suit.

During the whole of that 17 day trial, the longest murder trial ever held in Courtroom No. 1

at that time, Dr Adams had sat immobile as the Lord Buddha, seldom glancing at the participants, expressing no emotion.

# The Trial

There was some discussion during the committal proceedings about where the trial should take place; in the normal way it would have been at Lewes Crown Court in Sussex. Not only was it unlikely that, with all the publicity and the nature of the case, Dr Adams could have had a fair trial in Sussex, but the court was small, and the case was likely to be a long one, so it was decided that the case should be tried at the Old Bailey, the Central Criminal Court in London. The Lord Chief Justice, Lord Goddard, thought of presiding over such an important case himself, but he decided to nominate Lord Devlin. It is interesting that Lord Devlin mentions in his book that the case was 'a very important one for the medical profession, which was naturally worried by the thought that the prescription of drugs might lead to a charge of murder'. The Attorney General, Sir Reginald Manningham-Buller was to prosecute for the Crown, with Melford Stevenson QC as his No. 2. The Attorney-General 'Reggie' as Lord Devlin says everyone called him, was not only the 'son of a Northamptonshire baronet' and a member of the Conservative Government, but he was a member of the Cavendish family – the Dukes of Devonshire – and a first cousin four times removed of Lady Dorothy Macmillan. The press liked to call him 'Sir Bullying Manner' but Lord Devlin did not agree that this was so: he *was* a bully, but not obviously so:

> 'He could be downright rude but he did not shout or bluster. Yet his disagreeableness was so pervasive, his persistence so interminable, the obstructions he manned so far flung, his objectives apparently so insignificant, that sooner or later you would be tempted to ask yourself whether the game was worth the candle: if you asked yourself that, you were finished.'

He was a large and imposing man, who had strong inner convictions which, according to Lord Devlin, were invariably wrong and therefore led to unacceptable results: he was a 'do-badder'. Maybe this is a clue to what occurred in and before this trial. The character of Widmerpool in Anthony Powell's *A Dance to the Music of Time* is partly based on 'Reggie'. Manningham-Buller had concentrated on his political career to the neglect of his legal practice, but this had benefited him as vacancies in legal appointments occurred and he became Solicitor-General in 1951 and Attorney-General in 1954. Lord Devlin says that 'Reggie' was industrious and he obviously had no high opinion of his intelligence and judgement. He had a much higher opinion of Melford Stevenson. The junior counsel for the Crown was Malcolm Morris.

Hempsons, the solicitors of the Medical Defence Union ['We have defended the medical profession from Bodkin Adams to Shipman'] had engaged Geoffrey Lawrence QC This was odd because his practice was in local government cases and not even in criminal work: he had no experience in medico-legal cases. He was far from being a criminal defence lawyer in the Marshall-Hall mode of dramatic eloquence, but he was used to digesting boring technicalities. Lawrence was to surprise everybody. His No. 2 was Edward Clarke, the great-nephew of the famous criminal barrister, Sir Edward Clarke, and Mr Heritage, the junior.

When the Attorney-General went to see Lord Devlin to fix the date for the trial, he announced that he had decided not to use the Hullett evidence to prove 'system'. He also said that he intended to apply to the Lord Chief Justice for leave to file an indictment for the murder of Mrs Hullett, and if there was an acquittal on the Morrell indictment then he would request that the Hullett indictment should follow immediately. He was undecided what he would do if there was a conviction on the Morrell charge and there was a political reason for this.

There had been considerable debate throughout the fifties about capital punishment, and there had been some very controversial hangings: Derek Bentley, Timothy Evans, Ruth Ellis. The current Lord Chancellor, Lord Kilmuir (David Maxwell Fyfe) had refused the reprieve for Bentley, and the Home Secretary, Gwilym Lloyd-George had refused to reprieve Ruth Ellis. The electorate were divided but there was a majority in Parliament for abolition. As a compromise and stepping-stone to abolition [which came about in 1965] the Homicide Act of 1957 differentiated between capital and non-capital murder: the murder of a policeman, for example, was still a murder punishable by hanging. From time immemorial, premeditated murder and particularly by poison, had been considered a most heinous crime, but this was now a non-capital murder. However, to allow for this general feeling, those who had been convicted of a second murder were still to be executed.

The Homicide Bill became law on 21st March, 1957, which was the fourth day of the trial of Dr Adams, but only applied to indictments signed from that date. If Dr Adams had been convicted, the sentence would have been the death penalty. Lord Devlin thought that he would have been given a reprieve in this instance as 'the Home Secretary could not have allowed death to turn on a date of commencement'. But if he had been convicted on the second indictment as well then it 'would have looked like a guarantee of immunity for double poisoners under the new law'. He wonders 'whether one of Reggie's objects in pressing the second indictment was the death of Dr Adams'. This seems most unlikely as it would have been political dynamite and what can be inferred from the archives shows quite a different objective on the part of the Attorney General and the Government.

The Attorney-General had been to see Lord Devlin on 21st February, but it was not until the 26th February that Geoffrey Lawrence called upon him. Lord Devlin noted in his memorandum to the Lord Chief Justice on 4th March:

> 'When I saw Lawrence, he was extremely reserved. It is clear that he feels very bitterly about the conduct of the prosecution to date; …he said he thought a fair trial was now impossible anyway.'

Lord Devlin was:

'taken aback by Lawrence's vigour which in any other man I should have thought to be slightly paranoiac. What he would say when he heard that the Crown was abandoning the evidence to which he had unsuccessfully objected [at the committal hearing] I hardly cared to imagine.'

Lord Devlin's impression was that he was 'deeply disturbed'.

All of this suggests that, at this stage, he did not have the nurses' notebooks in his possession and did not know about them. This is completely at variance with Dr Adams' statements about the notebooks after the trial, but fits with the evidence in the archives. Lord Devlin believed that Geoffrey Lawrence had in mind that he would appeal, if there were to be a conviction, on the grounds that the jury had been prejudiced due to the excessive and damaging publicity.

# The First Day*

THE CLERK OF THE COURT: John Bodkin Adams, is that your name?
THE PRISONER: Yes, sir.
THE CLERK OF THE COURT: You are charged that on the 13th day of November, 1950, you murdered Edith Alice Morrell. Are you guilty or not guilty?
THE PRISONER: I am not guilty, my Lord.

Eight words – the only words that Dr Adams would utter during the whole fifteen days of the trial. No one was supposed to know that; everyone acted as though he were going to give evidence on his own behalf.

The jury having been sworn in, the Attorney-General rose to make his opening speech. He urged them to forget anything they might have read in the press; it would have been impossible that they had heard nothing about Dr Adams, and nearly all of it was detrimental. It seems that Lord Devlin was almost alone in the land in having read nothing concerning Dr Adams. The Crown submitted that Dr Adams, 'by the administration of drugs to Mrs Morrell, drugs given by him and given upon his instructions, killed her... that those drugs were given to her with the intention of killing her.' The Attorney General mentioned Dr Adams' medical qualifications: a Doctor of Medicine, a Bachelor of Surgery, that he had a Diploma in Public Health and a Diploma in Anaesthetics and held an appointment as Anaesthetist at the Princess Alice Memorial Hospital in Eastbourne. He therefore knew a good deal about dangerous drugs and their effects.

The Attorney-General briefly spoke of Mrs Morrell's death, her stroke, and of the nurses: Sister Randall, the night sister, who attended the patient from January 1949 until her death on

---

* The copy of the trial transcript in the Scotland Yard archives has some underlinings and annotations made by Detective Superintendent Hannam; these usually indicate answers from witnesses which he considered particularly important and enlightening.

13th November, 1950, Sister Mason-Ellis who nursed Mrs Morrell for the fourteen months preceding her death, Nurse Stronach, the relief nurse and Nurse Hughes who was a day nurse for about two months before Mrs Morrell's death. These four nurses he intended to call as witnesses to testify that Mrs Morrell had been in no pain.

The Crown was dealing with a period from the beginning of January 1950 until 13th November, 1950, and during this ten and a half months, Dr Adams had prescribed for his patient: 1,629½ grains of barbiturates (sedatives); 1,928 grains of Sedormid (sedative); 164 $^{11}/_{12}$ths grains of morphia; and 139½ grains of heroin. The Attorney General described the effects of these drugs, including the fact that morphia and heroin had a depressant effect upon the central nervous system and were dangerous and addictive drugs which caused dependence upon the person providing them. He emphasised that Mrs Morrell had been in no pain which would have warranted their use. Dr Ashby and Dr Douthwaite, Harley Street doctors, would be called to provide his expertise on these points.

The Attorney-General turned to the question of motive: this had not changed since the beginning of the whole investigation into Dr Adams' activities: 'Perhaps… the answer lies in the changes made by Mrs Morrell in her will after she had been taking these drugs.' He explained what evidence Mr Sogno, Mrs Morrell's solicitor would give about how Dr Adams involved himself with her will to an extraordinary extent.

The Attorney General asked the jury to look at the graphs of prescriptions prepared by Dr Ashby: Exhibit No. 36A, to give an indication of the size of the prescriptions of morphia, heroin and omnopon (50% morphia) and their frequency; and the rising amounts over the days and months. The culmination was the six days from 7th to 12th November when Dr Adams had prescribed 40½ grains of morphia and 39 grains of heroin – in fact a little more as Dr Ashby had allowed for a tablet or two left over after Mrs Morrell died. Dr Ashby would say that, 'She could not have survived if she had been given all the heroin alone.' Exhibit 37A was a further graph of the daily dosage of drugs, which was made up on the presumption that one prescription would follow when the previous one had been entirely used up. The Crown was relying on the fact that Dr Adams had told Detective Superintendent Hannam that all that was prescribed was used on Mrs Morrell, apart from a tablet or so.

The Attorney-General went on to relate what the nurses would say in their evidence: the injections Dr Adams gave without telling the nurses what they were; that those injections were out of his bag and not from the prescription stock; that in the last few days of her life Mrs Morrell was comatose and had 'jerky' spasms; Dr Douthwaite would attest that these were due to the large doses of morphia and heroin. Sir Reginald came to the last injections prepared by Dr Adams with a larger, 5 c.c. syringe, instead of a 1 c.c. or 2 c.c. syringe, and presenting these to Sister Randall to inject. 'Why have these two large injections been made into an unconscious patient?' …'we submit it was murder by Dr Adams giving these lethal prescriptions in that period, the 8th to the 12th November… he killed her, and killed her deliberately and intentionally.'

The prosecution case did not stop there: Dr Adams had filled in the cremation form that same day of her death, and he had answered the question 'Have you as far as you are aware any pecuniary interest in the death of the deceased' – to which he had answered 'Not as far as I am aware', and the very same day the body of Mrs Morrell was cremated and her ashes scattered on the English Channel. 'So there was no post-mortem, no possibility of exhumation – all avoided by a false answer given by Dr Adams to a question on the cremation form.'

The Attorney-General now turned to the evidence which Hannam would give of his interviews with Dr Adams and the words which Dr Adams used in answering his questions on these occasions; words which certainly indicated that he had expected to benefit from Mrs Morrell's will, not to mention that he liked cremations to go off smoothly for the 'dear relatives'. 'Well, members of the jury, the cremation did go off smoothly... But for his false answer on that form there might not have been cremation and the prosecution might have been in a position to tell you how much morphia and heroin was in the body of Mrs Morrell at the time of her death.' Dr Adams had said he had no dangerous drugs and that he 'very, very seldom ever used them'. And the drugs he prescribed for Mrs Morrell? 'Poor soul! She was in terrible agony. It was all used. I used them all myself.' Yet, 'the nurses will tell you that she had been comatose for days and not suffering pain.' Dr Douthwaite would say that the drugs prescribed in the last days – on the 8th, 9th, 10th and 11th – would definitely have killed her.

The prosecution would establish four facts which were indisputable: that Mrs Morrell died on 13th November after two injections had been given her on Dr Adams' instructions; that she was then in a coma suffering from spasms due to heroin and morphia; that Dr Adams told Hannam that there were no drugs left over except for a couple of tablets from the final prescription because he gave them all to her. Here the Attorney-General was very specific about the maximum quantity of heroin and morphia which should be prescribed, relying on his medical witnesses.

He came to the 26th November, 1956, when Dr Adams had asked to see Superintendent Hannam, and, with reference to Mrs Morrell, had said: 'Easing the passing of a dying person is not all that wicked. She wanted to die. That cannot be murder. It is impossible to accuse a doctor.' That phrase, Sir Reginald submitted, '...must refer, must it not, to something that Doctor Adams did shortly before her death?' Her condition was brought about by Dr Adams and she was not in pain: 'Doctors are not entitled to kill people even if they say they want to die.' When Dr Adams was arrested on 19th December, he had been cautioned by Superintendent Hannam and had then said: 'Murder', then he had paused: 'Murder. Can you prove it was murder?'... 'I did not think you could prove murder. She was dying in any event.' On leaving the house, he had grasped his receptionist's hand and said to her: 'I will see you in heaven'. The Attorney-General addressed the jury: 'Is that what you would expect an innocent man to say when he is charged with murder, or is it what a man might say if he had committed a murder but thought he had done it so cleverly that his guilt could not be proved?' The Crown would prove conclusively that 'this old lady was murdered by Dr Adams.'

The evidence of Robert Clegg, (Exhibit 1) the Group Secretary to the Eastbourne Hospital Management Committee was read, attesting to Dr Adams' medical qualifications, and particularly that he had been practising as an anaesthetist at the Princess Alice Hospital in Eastbourne two days a week and at St. Mary's Hospital one day per week.

Mr Morris examined Alfred Spenceley, the former manager of Browne's, the chemist's shop just around the corner from Dr Adams' home, Kent Lodge, from where he had the great majority of his prescriptions dispensed [all that now remains of this shop is the tessellated name on the paving outside – it is now an interior design shop]. The point of the examination was to establish the procedure for prescriptions of dangerous drugs, entries in the register and the records kept, and how the list of prescriptions, Exhibit 4A, (a slightly altered list and now exhibited as a replacement for Exhibit 4) of those dispensed for Mrs Morrell, had been checked.

Mr Lawrence cross-examined Mr Spenceley, establishing that the original prescriptions signed by Dr Adams had all been destroyed and he had had to rely upon the prescription book kept by the shop, and that prescriptions nos. 67 and 71 were written by Dr Harris when Dr Adams had been on holiday. Mr Lawrence also displayed, for the first time, his skill at eliciting 'yes' or 'no' responses, getting witnesses step by step, little by little, to places where they had not intended to go. This is the adversarial system: it does not aim to find out the truth, but to play a game of chess. Mr Lawrence continued his concentration on the fact that Dr Harris had prescribed barbiturates and omnopon for the patient, then, having asked for one of the chemists' registers, he directed attention to various items other than dangerous drugs which Dr Adams had prescribed. He threw in the odd question that had nothing to do with Mr Spenceley's evidence: 'Benzedrine and methedrine are tablets for brightening people up, stimulating them, are not they?' His way of asking questions seems idiosyncratic, archaic. 'Seconal is a sedative, is not it?' 'A sedative' replied Mr Spenceley. He was not questioned about possible side-effects or contra-indications – what should not be taken with certain drugs. In this way relevant information is withheld from juries.

A supplemental list of prescriptions dispensed for Mrs Morrell: those not included in Exhibit 4A, was added as Exhibit 4B; this was a list of prescriptions other than dangerous drugs. Mr Lawrence began reading some of these out: imaginative and varied 'bottles of physic', ointment for irritation and sores, eye drops and ointment, lozenges, an odd prescription for caffeine capsules. Mr Spenceley described how these were made at the chemist's shop making little cylinders from hard gelatine, and the mixing of a medicine: emulsion of magnesium hydroxide, syrup of peppermint, syrup of Virginian prune... how much more fascinating it seems than today's pharmacies of boxes and bottles of *prêt-à-porter* branded drugs. Mr Lawrence then, seemingly innocuously, asked: 'Your firm were making up prescriptions for Mrs Morrell on Dr Adams' instructions before the beginning of 1950?' Mr Spenceley replied: 'I believe so.' A modulation led to asking about prescriptions for 1949 and part of 1948. Having a list of these would give 'the complete picture'. No, there was no list but they were in the prescription book so it was possible to supply such a list. Then a carefully structured question from Mr Lawrence:

'Has anybody ever asked you <u>on behalf of the Police</u> to get out a list so that it can be seen what Doctor Adams was prescribing before January 1950 for this lady?'
'No, Sir.'

Mr Justice Devlin intervened asking for information concerning the dates in the prescription books and how they compared with the dates of the original prescriptions. Despite some difficulty and misunderstanding it was established that the date on list 4A would be the dispensing date and this would normally be the same.

The assistant at Browne's Chemists for the last 40 years, Mr Arthur Butler, was the next witness. He attested, on examination by Mr Malcolm Morris, that he had checked Exhibit 4A, the list of prescriptions, with the registers to ensure that it was correct. Mr Lawrence didn't want to ask about the document, but about the system of recording prescriptions in the shop: the time difference between when the prescription was handed in and when it was entered in the book; trying to see how far he could stretch the interval. Mr Butler would not allow it: the entry was always on the same day, invariably. Mr Morris returned to re-examine, to establish that a number was given to each prescription when it was dispensed, that this number would be in the register and that the numbers proceeded serially.

Mr Arthur Young was the pharmacist at Browne's from October, 1949 to January 1951. He also confirmed to Mr Morris that Exhibit 4A was correct and the procedures for dispensing in the shop. Mr Lawrence went through the procedures again in his cross-examination, and asked about a particular prescription (No. 54) for 6 capsules of seconal, a restricted drug, a ready-made drug. It would still be 'dispensed', and not just handed over the counter, the capsules would go into a bottle and be labelled with a reference number on the label.

Then the expert pharmaceutical witness, Mr Thomas Reid, who had held senior management positions with Savory & Moore Ltd and John Bell & Croyden of Wigmore Street, and now had his own shop in Haselmere, Surrey. He had prepared Exhibit 4A from Browne's registers of all prescriptions of restricted drugs supplied for Mrs Morrell; all were prescribed by Dr Adams, except for two by Dr Harris. He explained to Mr Morris that 'restricted drugs' were those coming under the Dangerous Drugs Regulations: morphia, omnopon, heroin, all barbiturates, sedormid, benzedrines, methedrin and atropine.

Exhibit 4B included also all the other prescriptions by Dr Adams for the year 1950 – all quite simple preparations such as mild tonics. He had also prepared from 4A a list showing the monthly totals of barbiturates, sedormid, morphine, omnopon and heroin – this was now marked Exhibit 35A. (Omnopon was calculated as being 50% morphine and only the morphine content calculated.) The totals for the period January to 12th November were: 1,629½ grains of barbiturates, 1,928 grains of sedormid, 164$^{11}\!/_{12}$th grains of morphine, and 139½ grains of heroin.

Mr Reid was asked to produce syringes: 1 c.c., 2 c.c., and 5 c.c., now marked Exhibit 47. – this was in connection with the last two injections which Mrs Morrell had been given. Mr Reid explained that they had capacity above the stated one, and that heroin tablets being very soluble would allow 12½ grains in a 5 c.c. syringe. If it were three-quarters full then the grainage of heroin possible would be 10. Morphia, he said, was less soluble and 3 grains would be the limit in 4 c.c. of water; using hyperduric morphine (a mucate salt of morphine) 8 grains in 4 c.c. A hypodermic tablet, Mr Reid explained, was a tablet designed to dissolve rapidly in a hypodermic (under the skin) syringe. 'Hyperduric' was a patent name coined by a manufacturer (Allen & Hanbury's) of this slower-acting morphine with a longer time spread; additionally, it came ready-prepared and not in tablet form to be dissolved in water.

Mr Lawrence reverted to confirming that a 5 c.c. syringe could contain 12½ grains of heroin. He did not get the 'yes' he expected.

> 'That is in tablet form. If it were in salt form it would be considerably more.'
> 'Have you tested that yourself?'

Mr Reid was every bit a match for Mr Lawrence:

> 'I have. I have confirmed with the manufacturers themselves and with that data confirmed my own findings.'
> 'This evidence is the result of your own findings?'
> 'Undoubtedly.'

Mr Lawrence tried another tack: asking Mr Reid about his late enlistment as an expert witness. It was after the committal proceedings, about a month previously. He was cross-examined about how he had prepared the lists of drugs: from the prescriptions register and the earlier ones had been prepared from the accounts. His lists were perfectly accurate: Exhibits 4A and 35A. There were some prescriptions which had appeared in Browne's accounts but were not in the prescription register. Mr Lawrence moved quickly away from this curious discrepancy – drugs charged to Mrs Morrell's account yet not in the prescription register – to enquire what barbiturates were included in the barbiturate column of 35A: phenobarbitone, sodiumbarbitone, allonal, phenobarbitone solution or sodium phenobarbitone. He made the mistake of suggesting that amounts were allocated 'arbitrarily to the calendar months' 'Not arbitrarily, sir, actually to the calendar month as shown in the prescription register.' Mr Lawrence turned to the sedormid column and questioned Mr Reid as to its nature:

> 'It is a non-barbiturate with barbiturate-like properties– a shade milder, but it is today restricted in the same manner as phenobarbitone or barbiturates of other sorts.'
> 'It is not now a barbiturate; is that right?'
> 'It is not a barbiturate but it has all the characteristics of a barbiturate.'

This witness clearly knew exactly what he was talking about. Mr Lawrence asked about the morphia column and the inclusion of omnopon:

> 'And I understand from you that you say that omnopon is made up as to half its total contents –'
> 'It is the total alkaloids of opium standardized to be half morphia.'

Mr Reid had been more than fair and taking only the morphine content as 50% of the omnopon. And the heroin was 'a straightforward interpretation of the heroin ordered'.

Mr Lawrence now began asking about the prescription books prior to 1950. Mr Reid was aware that there were many prescriptions for Mrs Morrell for earlier dates, one even going back to 1937. What Mr Lawrence was 'anxious to get at the earliest possible stage... a complete list of prescriptions of whatever kind of the medical treatment that was prescribed by Dr Adams for this lady...' The whole picture would be found in such a list? 'Undoubtedly' replied Mr Reid, and he agreed to find it for Mr Lawrence if the Court ordered this. Mr Lawrence, however, had already had the list extracted from the registers, although not by a 'qualified chemist of the distinction that you enjoy'. He asked the Judge if Mr Reid could be instructed to make a list of prescriptions for Mrs Morrell 'at least from July 1948'.

The Attorney General said that the Defence had not previously made a request for such a list, otherwise the Crown would have prepared it; it could take some time to compile. He was not complaining, but it was unfortunate. Mr Reid made the last point: 'I must not be hurried over this because the list must be correct...'

Mr Malcolm Morris re-examined Mr Reid to clarify a few points: if hyperduric morphine were used instead of dissolving tablets in sterile water, then a greater quantity of morphine could be injected, i.e. half a grain per c.c. The items in Exhibit 4 A which had been paid for on Mrs Morrell's account and were not in the prescription register:

'From that it looks as if the prescription register may not be quite complete.'
'That was my assumption.'

Mr Morris confused the follow-up question so much that it was incomprehensible, as Mr Reid found it. Mr Morris did not pursue it, yet the question that remains is: why were any prescriptions for a patient by Dr Adams, which should have been entered in the register, omitted? Was it the only case in which this occurred?

The next witness was Nurse Helen Rose Stronach, and Mr Melford Stevenson examined her. She had been nursing since 1920, mainly privately but had also done war and hospital service. She was the relief nurse and had been nursing Mrs Morrell at her home, 'Marden Ash'; the last period she was there was in October 1950 until November 2nd. Mrs Morrell had been 'of a very neurotic disposition' and very weak then. She had given her a quarter grain of morphia hypodermic injection each night, and Dr Adams would come in late and prepare his own injection, although she had not been allowed in Mrs Morrell's bedroom to see the injection given. Nurse Stronach had no idea what the injections were as Dr Adams never told her.

It was now late in the afternoon, and Mr Justice Devlin instructed and warned the jury not to discuss the case and not to remind themselves of anything which had occurred at the committal hearing as the evidence given there might not coincide with the evidence at the trial.

# The Second Day

Mr Stevenson continued his examination of Nurse Stronach, asking her to speak up so that the court could hear her. She had done a fortnight of night duty, relieving Sister Randall and a fortnight of day duty relieving Sister Bartlett (now Mrs Hughes). Mr Stevenson asked her again about the injections: Dr Adams came in around 11 o'clock at night and got the injections out of his bag. She had to fetch a glass of water for him. Mrs Morrell would be 'very dopey' as Nurse Stronach had already given her an injection. On the last day she was with the patient, 2nd November, she was 'in an almost semi-conscious condition and rambling'. No, she had not seen any real signs of Mrs Morrell being in pain; she had mentioned it upon occasion but Nurse Stronach had considered it to be 'neurotic'.

The Judge asked if the witness could say what happened to drugs when they arrived from Browne's the chemist: where they were put and whether they were locked up. The following two questions and answers have a line drawn beside the text to emphasise their importance:

> 'Mr Stevenson: 'When the drugs had been either delivered by Browne's or fetched by Price [the chauffeur], do you know what was done with them or where they were kept? Do not tell us if you do not, but if you do know tell us now?
> Nurse Stronach: They were kept in a drawer to the best of my knowledge in the dining room.
> Mr Stevenson: Do you know whether it was locked or not?
> Nurse Stronach: I think so.'

Mr Lawrence began his cross-examination with the usual sort of question intended to make the witness relax or not be on her guard: she had nursed many patients since Mrs Morrell had died; Mrs Morrell had had a stroke – he showed his appreciation of Nurse Stronach's medical knowledge. The 'irritability' she displayed, was it due to 'the injury to the arteries of the brain?' 'Not only that' said Nurse Stronach. The following is underlined and marked in the margin by Hannam.

> 'What else?'
> 'I should say that it was due a great deal to the amount of drugs she was having.'

The first time Nurse Stronach had been asked to remember the case of Mrs Morrell was the previous September, 1956, nearly six years afterwards; Mr Pugh had visited her and she had made a statement about various cases she had nursed for Dr Adams. She had had three or four visits from the police between September and January, and had made three statements. Nurse Stronach admitted that she had discussed the case with two other nurses, Randall and Mason-Ellis before giving evidence at the committal hearing.

Mr Lawrence moved on to the injections: Nurse Stronach had said she gave Mrs Morrell ¼ grain injections of morphia when she was on night duty, only morphia, and that the Doctor came later and gave another injection. He seemingly casually mentioned that Nurse Mason-Ellis had mentioned, giving evidence at the committal hearing, that they had noted the injections they gave in a book which was passed on to the next nurse. 'Yes, that was quite correct' said Nurse Stronach, 'We wrote down every injection we gave.' Quite the usual and proper thing to do.

'Well, all experienced and trained nurses do it, do they not?'
'Yes, they do.'

Now she and the other nurses were being totally hooked and tied.

'And whatever you wrote in that book would be accurate, would it not?'
'Yes.'
'Because it was done right at that very moment?'
'Yes.'
'That is the usual nursing practice?'
'Yes.'
'And I suppose – I just want to find out about the practice, you see –
'Yes.'
'In the case of these books, I suppose everything that happened of significance in the patient's illness would also go down in the book by the nurse?'
'Yes.'
'By the nurse?'

Nurse Stronach, oblivious to what was to come, responded:

'Yes, we reported everything.'
'Reported everything that was of any importance?'
'Oh yes, a proper report is written down.'
'And that would be a full report, would it not?'
'Yes.'
'Not only injections, I suppose, but medicines and all that sort of thing?'
'Yes, that is so.'
'Doctor's visits?'

Further into the mire:

'Well, we would just put down that the doctor visited and the time, usually.'
'And, as distinct from memory six years later, of course, these reports would be absolutely accurate, would they not, I mean yours would, at any rate?'
'Oh yes, they would be accurate for each one of us.'

Mr Lawrence went in for the kill:

'So that if only we had got those reports now we could see the truth of exactly what happened night by night and day by day that you were there, could we not?'
'Yes, but you have our word for it.'

This was perhaps the most dramatic moment of the trial:

'I want you to look at that book please. [It was handed to the witness.]
Would you look at the day report for the 4th June 1950?'

Mr Justice Devlin asked Mr Lawrence if this was one of the Exhibits. It was not – the Defence are permitted to withhold exhibits even if they exist before the trial – it would be a new one in due course. Mr Lawrence was engaged, however, in an attempt to authenticate this notebook immediately. The Judge intervened to ask the court might know what the book was.

'Yes, my Lord.' Mr Lawrence asked the witness:

'That is one of the books in which the nurses made their day and night reports that you have just been talking about in relation to Mrs Morrell's case, isn't it?'
'Yes' replied Nurse Stronach.
'Would you look at the 5th [June, 1950], night report; is that in your handwriting?'
'Yes.'
'Is that your signature?'
'Yes.'

Mr Lawrence, triumphantly:

'There is no doubt about it, is there Miss Stronach, that is the very book of daily and nightly records kept by nurses when you started your first spell of duty in June 1950?'
'Yes, that is so…'

She could not remember the odd dates when she had come in on duty, 'That is impossible.' Mr Lawrence jumped at this opening:

'Of course one cannot remember things after six years, I am not suggesting you can. In view of what you said, if we look at this book we can see what happened as recorded by you.'

He authenticated with her entries signed by herself and Mrs Mason-Ellis and also the note-book which followed on from the first book.

The Attorney-General asked to see the books but Mr Lawrence continued, with the Judge's agreement, to produce the other books for Nurse Stronach to identify. Then he addressed Lord Justice Devlin to say that the Defence had the whole of the nursing reports from June 1949 until 13th November, 1950, eight books in all. Nurse Stronach had identified handwriting in three of these and the other five could be presented to her in the same way. Accurate copies had been made and checked for the jury and the Prosecution.

The Attorney-General said that he had 'not had an opportunity of seeing any of these alleged nursing reports', then said that 'this witness can speak as to the entries she made in the books herself'. She could say whether she recognised the handwriting of other nurses, but was not in a position to give evidence as to what the other books were. He would not consent, at this stage, to the admissibility of the books in evidence without even seeing them.

Lord Justice Devlin asked Mr Lawrence for copies of the books for the Prosecution and himself; Mr Lawrence should put questions to the witness and he would then hear the Attorney-General on whether they should go to the jury or not.

Mr Lawrence replied that 'There can be no question… that those three books have been properly proved in evidence,' and wished to cross-examine the witness on the contents of those books. He would provide copies to the Prosecution and wanted copies to be put before the witness. The Attorney-General objected: the entries were not evidence apart from the fact that Nurse Stronach could refresh her memory from them: Mr Lawrence had 'changed his ground' from the original three books in which she had made entries, to the other five books as well. He had not seen them at all, and it was only the witness' own entries which could be evidence. Mr Lawrence professed astonishment at the submission and the Judge would not rule at this stage but thought that the Attorney-General had a right to object: 'Had they been shown to the Prosecution earlier, it might have been possible for steps to have been taken which would have enabled them to go straight to the jury…'

Mr Lawrence provided the Judge with a copy of the books and copies for the Crown. Mr Justice Devlin then asked Mr Lawrence how he suggested 'they could most conveniently be marked'; Mr Lawrence replied that they had been numbered 1 to 8 on the outside. The Judge then took the seemingly odd step of asking Mr Lawrence: 'Would it be convenient if they were marked Exhibit 48, 1 to 8?' 'Yes, my Lord. I am obliged.' said a grateful Mr Lawrence. The notebooks seemed duly accepted as evidence, and the Attorney-General made no objection.

Mr Lawrence went straight into the attack, with the first entry Nurse Stronach had made when she came on night duty on 4th June, 1950 at 9 p.m. The day nurse had already given the injection of ¼ grain of morphia and ⅓ of heroin, so she had not given it herself that night; there was also no record of the Doctor visiting. It was simple to show that her previous evidence was contradicted by this report. When she responded that she had not given the injection because it had already been done earlier, Lawrence admonished her in headmasterly tone:

> 'You are going to listen to the questions and not argue with me, are not you?'
> 'Yes, certainly.'
> 'You did not give any injection, nor did the doctor visit. That is right, is it not?'
> 'Not according to this.'
> 'You say "not according to this", but you have already said that that is what you wrote down at the time of the happenings and that you wrote them down accurately…'

Mr Lawrence here successfully prevented any chance of the truth being told: none of the nurses would now be able to admit that their notebooks were other than absolutely accurate records. To agree to anything less would be to allow themselves unprofessional and negligent before the world. Of course, nurses' notebooks were not a total record of all that had occurred; of course they were not always filled in just after something was done or happened. They would usually enter what they thought the next nurse should know: that was their purpose. It was quite clear that Dr Adams' visits were frequently not entered: he did not tell them what he injected into the patient or what he thought of her condition, so there was no point in entering something which conveyed absolutely nothing to the next nurse on duty.

Mr Lawrence continued through the entries made by Nurse Stronach. These showed that Mrs Morrell was wont to be irritable and irrational and had bouts of temper. She had called Nurse Stronach 'a nasty common woman', and she could be depressed and weeping. In addition to the drugs he prescribed, Dr Adams allowed the patient to have milk with 2 or 3 drams of brandy, when she wanted it, 'as much as she liked' on a regular basis, combined with a Sedormid tablet. Mr Lawrence repeatedly referred to there being no reference to a Doctor's visit. Nurse Stronach pointed out:

> 'It is no proof that he did not call that night because I did not put it down here.'
> 'You realise that before you saw this book you told me that everything of importance, including the doctor's visit if there was one, would have been put down by you, as a trained nurse, in your contemporary record made at the time, did not you?'
> 'Yes.'
> 'And that was the truth, was it not?'
> 'Yes, as far as I knew it...'

The truth but not the whole truth: only what was of importance to the next nurse on duty.

Mr Lawrence continued reading through the entries in the notebooks. One from Nurse Randall to Nurse Stronach detailed minutely, Mrs Morrell's preferred routine in the mornings. One notable point, which never emerged as of any importance, was that Mrs Morrell could not bear to have the curtains drawn and any daylight to enter into her bedroom. Mr Lawrence concentrated on the fact that Nurse Stronach had not, from 4th to 24th June, 1950, recorded either herself giving injections to Mrs Morrell or the Doctor having visited and given them. Just taking these particular entries in isolation did not, of course, give a full picture of the medication over 24 hours. Nurse Stronach agreed that she would have put down in the book, injections if she had given them, but she was reluctant to agree that she would have entered all Dr Adams' visits. Mr Lawrence pressed her to give the answer he wanted: if she had entered every dram of brandy, surely she would enter a doctor's visit, surely a state-registered nurse would not omit to do this? Eventually, she did not 'think' she would have done. Such 'evidence' had no value in the search for the truth, but was invaluable in putting that element of doubt in the minds of the jury.

The third notebook beginning on 12th October was given to Nurse Stronach: Mr Lawrence referred to the day report entry by the witness. The following exchange was quite extraordinary and unwarranted:

> 'Is this in your writing: 'Hypo injection omnopon $\frac{2}{3}$rd given at 4.30 p.m.'?'

'Yes.'

'…but do you remember telling me earlier this morning, before you saw these contemporary records, that you had never given Mrs Morrell any injection except morphia?'

'Well, I believe that to be true.'

'Well, this entry show that your memory was playing you a trick, does it not?'

'Apparently so.'

'Obviously so. Miss Stronach, may I ask you to face this squarely. Obviously your memory played you a trick, did it not, when you said you had never injected anything but morphia?'

But Omnopon is at least 50% morphia – her memory was quite accurate.

In the same report, for 12th October, Mr Lawrence asked a question about an interesting note in the record. Nurse Stronach had noted: 'Passed urine, large quantity, dark coloured.'

'Did Mrs Morrell have kidney trouble, do you remember?'

'I do not think I remember.'

He had, however, asked the wrong question, though Nurse Stronach would have been unlikely to supply the answer. He needed to ask one of the medical experts – or Dr Adams.

Mr Lawrence pounced on another entry for 12th October: '7.30 p.m. Visited by Dr Adams. Hypodermic injection morphia gr. ¼, heroin gr. ⅓, omnopon gr. ⅓.' On this occasion it had been 'quite clear' that she knew what the injection was. The same occurred in the night report for the 14th/15th. It was, of course, the regular evening injection which Mrs Morrell had been having. She had been restless and talking incessantly, passed the same dark brown urine; her breathing during her sleep was 'Cheyne Stokes' – the only time this type of breathing was recorded – faint, then increasing in depth, and quiet breathing again, in cycles. She was very thirsty, excited and muddled, and chronically constipated with the drugs and supplied with laxative medicines. On the 18th October, the patient was 'stripping the bed, complaining of pain across the forehead, very restless and mind very confused'. Pressure points and sores were treated. On the 23rd Mrs Morrell was again complaining of a pain in the head and 'being afraid of something' and had iced compresses applied to her head. She had 'a small piece of superficial skin off sacrum' and her back had to be constantly treated with lotion; her right hip was inflamed and her knees were sore. She was asking for drinks and then refusing them. Mr Lawrence encouraged Nurse Stronach to agree that all the symptoms were due to 'the sort of thing that happens to those senile patients towards the end' or 'typical of people with a stroke condition'; that sores were 'typical of the last stages in this sort of case'. Nurse Stronach could not be persuaded to agree to the last proposition.

Mr Lawrence pointed out that Mrs Morrell was, in fact, eating well, his objective being to prove her continuing consciousness. On 28th October, Nurse Stronach had recorded that Dr Adams had said that the patient was to have 'big hypo. injection each night just after 9 p.m.'. On the 29th, that Dr Adams had visited in the morning and given her a 'special injection'. Did

Nurse Stronach know that Dr Adams had for some time been visiting in the mornings and giving what the nurses called 'special injections'? She did not.

On 31st October, Dr Adams had instructed that the regular evening triple injection of morphia, omnopon and heroin should now be changed to omit the morphia and omnopon and just consist of ⅚ grain of heroin at night, and ⅓ grain of heroin could be given during the day as thought necessary by the nurses. He continued giving his 'special' injection. The last day Nurse Stronach had made notes was on 1st November and she was then with her for part of the morning of the 2nd. She had noted that the patient 'has been more awake and taking interest in things. Taken well of diet…' Mr Lawrence pointed out to Nurse Stronach that she had told Mr Melford Stevenson that Mrs Morrell had been 'in a semi-conscious condition and rambling.' Nurse Stronach replied that she had been referring to 2nd November, for which day she had made no notes as she was called away during the afternoon: a patient's condition could change very quickly. Mr Lawrence began to read out Sister Mason-Ellis' notes for that morning. The Attorney-General objected to his questioning the witness on 'this alleged note made by someone else.' The Judge, however, found it admissable in cross-examination. Mr Lawrence continued by asking Nurse Stronach to read out the extract concerning what the patient had for lunch:

> 'It says she had partridge, celery, pudding, brandy and soda But, of course, I must add that would only be very, very small quantities that she would be given; she would not have much of anything.'
> 'What is the object of adding that?…'

Mr Lawrence attacked, viciously. A few questions later and Nurse Stronach realised that she had actually written the notes up to a quarter to two that day, and, in particular, this one concerning the lunch:

> 'You have written it? You have recorded the lunch of the partridge and celery and the pudding?'
> 'Yes.'
> 'Consumed by this semi-conscious woman?'
> 'Yes.'
> 'Miss Stronach, let us face this: it is another complete trick of your memory to say that on the last day when you left Mrs Morrell was either semi-conscious or rambling, is not it, now you see what you wrote at the time?'
>     (A pause.) 'Is not it?'
> 'I have nothing to say.'

Mr Lawrence eventually persuaded her to admit that it was wrong to say Mrs Morrell had been 'semi-conscious and rambling' on 2nd November: 'Apparently so.'

He directed his questioning to Nurse Stronach's evidence that after injections given by Dr

Adams, Mrs Morrell was 'very dopey and half asleep'. He pointed to the reports of 14th and 15th October: at 7.20 p.m. Sister Mason-Ellis had recorded the Doctor giving an injection of ¼ grain of morphia, ⅓ of heroin and ⅓ of omnopon; at 10.20 p.m. he visited again and gave the patient an exactly similar injection; she then continually asked for drinks and talked incessantly, so Nurse Stronach had given her a further ⅔ grains of omnopon. Mr Lawrence sat down.

The Attorney-General re-examined the witness, now utilising the notebooks, the copies of which had only been given to him that same morning in court. As he had to listen closely to the cross-examination in case he needed to make any objections, it is difficult to imagine that he had had any time to read through anything in the notebooks, yet he questioned the witness, referring to entries in them. He enquired about Nurse Stronach's recording of 'special injections' given by Dr Adams; he got the wrong answer:

'Every entry of yours in this diary, in this record, relating to your day duty, apart from the first one, has a reference to a special injection being given by Dr Adams; I think I am right in saying that?'
'Yes.'
'Did you at any time know what the special injection was?'
'I cannot remember, I am sorry. I did know but I just cannot remember what it was.'

He reverted to the question a few minutes later:

'Did Dr Adams ever tell you, so far as you can recollect – I want you to be careful about this – what that special injection contained?'
'No. If I had known, I would have written it down in the book. I have no idea.'

Mr Lawrence immediately objected that she had made a different response shortly before. The Attorney-General tried again and got the same answer as he had just received. The Judge clarified:

'Then it is right, is it, that you did not know at the time?'
'Yes, my Lord, it is right.'

Mr Lawrence asked, just before the lunchtime adjournment, that the witness should not communicate the contents of the notebooks to the other witnesses.

The Attorney-General announced, after lunch, that he had had an opportunity of considering the copies of the notebooks, but not the entries therein, so that the Crown could not say if they were entirely accurate, but there was no objection to the jury having copies, subject to their only looking at specific references when reference was made to them. They would need to examine the copies against the originals that evening. [Neither the notebooks, nor copies of them are in the police archives, but they are in the D.P.P.'s archive.]

Nurse Stronach must have been much relieved to have finished with the cross-examination, and to be the subject again of gentler interrogation. The Attorney-General returned to the injections given by Dr Adams: some were noted explicitly rather than as 'special'. These were occasions when the Doctor had actually told her what he was injecting; always the regular: morphine ¼ , heroin ⅓, omnopon ⅓ grain. He took up the point about omnopon being 50% morphia, so that this was what she would have had in mind when she said she had only injected morphia. Had Nurse Stronach ever noticed any signs that Mrs Morrell was suffering? No, not during the whole of the time she had been with her. She had been instructed from 31st November that the patient should be having heroin injections only. He proceeded with questions about the patient's irritability, reminding Nurse Stronach that she had said that this 'was due a great deal to the amount of drugs she was having'. She agreed. The other effects she attributed to large amounts of heroin and morphia were 'all kinds of jerky movements'.

Lord Justice Devlin intervened to ask how the prescriptions for Mrs Morrell came to be written and dealt with. Dr Adams would write them, either because he found the drug supply was running out or a nurse would tell him. The nurses would hand the prescriptions to the chauffeur, Price, on the same day and he would go to Browne's, and he would usually collect them on the same day, hand them to the cook, and they would be given to the nurse on duty. The following question has been underlined by Hannam:

> 'That would mean she would put them away in this cupboard in the dining room. Is that right?
> 'Yes, my Lord, that is right.'

The cupboard was locked and the nurse had the key. Nurse Stronach herself had kept the key in her pocket and passed it to the next nurse. If Dr Adams wanted drugs, he would ask for the key, but 'He usually used his own drugs… From his bag.'

Mrs Annie Mason-Ellis was the next witness. The Attorney-General began examining her; he handed her Exhibit 48, which she recognised as 'Our report books'. She had last seen them on the last day of her duty with Mrs Morrell, although this was before the day of her death. They were handed over from nurse to nurse as they came on duty. Sister Mason-Ellis had started with Mrs Morrell as a relief nurse in July or August 1949. At that time Mrs Morrell was suffering from having cerebral haemorrhage of her left side, which had no movement; she was irritable when things did not please her, but she was mentally alert and 'slowly recovering', going out in the car and to tea on some occasions. There was no real treatment and Sister Mason-Ellis discussed this with Dr Adams and, as a result, she began giving Mrs Morrell some massage.

The Attorney-General proceeded to pick out some passages in the reports which had been signed by Sister Mason-Ellis as 'H. Mason' – she was unmarried at the time. One report mentioned the patient as having been given 'Doctor's tablets':

> 'Do you know what the doctor's tablets were… If you had known at the time what they were, would you have entered up what they were?'
> 'Yes.'

On the 10th August, 1950, Sister Mason-Ellis had written in the notebook:

'Had a 'brain storm' between 3.15 p.m. & 5.20 p.m. Accused me of the 'usual things' & wished me to leave at 6 p.m. Dr Adams informed of Mrs Morrell's state of mind. Visited at 7.15 p.m. Mrs Morrell quietened down at 5.45 p.m. & has been quiet & as usual since. Special sleeping tablets given at 8.15 p.m. (asked for) and 8.30 p.m. Hypodermic injection of morphia, ¼ grain, heroin ⅓ grain at 8.40 p.m. Appears subdued and quiet.'

Her next entry on the 18th August read:

'Mrs Morrell. Very irritable and difficult between 3 p.m. and 5.30 p.m. Complained about the massage & exercise, etc… Took own sleeping Tab. 1 at 8 p.m. & 1 at 8.30 p.m. Hypodermic injection, ¼ grain morphia, & heroin ⅓ grain at 8.40.'

20th August:

Mrs Morrell. Slept from 3.10 p.m. until 5 p.m. Said she had been ringing the bell all afternoon & that I had not answered it. Seems muddled and heavy. 5.30 p.m. Has been weeping and complaining since 5 p.m.'

Sister Mason-Ellis was not on relief again until 7th September. This was in a different notebook (No. 7 of the 8) and Mr Lawrence handed this over as it had not yet been produced for authentication. She had noted in the entry for 7th September that Dr Adams had visited morning and afternoon. The Attorney-General pointed out an entry for 9th September where no visit from Dr Adams was noted – unfortunately, because none of the nurse witnesses could now admit that there were any omissions in their notes. When Dr Adams came to see Mrs Morrell were the nurses present in the room, Sister Mason-Ellis was asked. The reply was that he was alone with Mrs Morrell. 'Yes. They had been asked to leave.'

Dr Adams would draw up the hypodermic injections himself. In order to make an entry about the content of one of the injections, she either had to see what he did precisely or he had to tell her what he did. She could not say where he got the drugs from. The drugs in the nurses' possession were 'kept on a tray' in the dining room, and the nurses would not leave them unguarded for 'any length of time'. She could not remember ever having seen Dr Adams prepare an injection.

It is clear from the Attorney-General's preamble to his next question that he is relying on Mr Melford Stevenson and Mr Morris to read the notebooks and point out to him the relevant entries:

'The next one, my learned friends tell me, is 5th October…'

On the 14th October, Sister Mason-Ellis had noted:

> '11.20 p.m. Dr Adams visited. Hypodermic injection of morphia.' [given by Dr Adams]

By the time she returned on 20th October, she had got married. On the 2nd November, the day Nurse Stronach left, her entry was of considerable interest:

> '10.30 a.m. visited by Dr Adams – patient asleep and not disturbed.
> Dr Adams ordered one sedormid (due at 10.45) to be given on waking and no more until Mr Morrell's son's [Claude] visit at 5.30, as Dr Adams wished Mrs Morrell to be clear mentally. 4 p.m. Has not slept. Appears rather depressed and sullen… 5.30. Has been very lachrymose since 5 p.m. Does not want to see Mr Morrell… 6.20 sedormid i [one] given. Malvern water. 6.30. Patient became hysterical. Said I was trying to kill her, etc… 7.30 Phoned Dr Adams. ½ grain of heroin prescribed. Patient asleep on return to room. Injection given eventually at 8.15.

The next entry by Sister Mason-Ellis was on the 11th November, and there was another on 12th November. This was very near the end of Mrs Morrell's life The Attorney-General attempted to find out Mrs Morrell's condition on these two days: at one point Sister Mason-Ellis said she was not conscious, but then more or less withdrew this answer by saying: 'Please don't ask me these questions I can't tell you.'

Mr Lawrence started gently with his cross-examination: Mrs Morrell had brought about changes of nurses through her 'own bad temper'; she was 'a very difficult person to nurse', but of course she had had a stroke about the middle of 1948. She was also old, with paralysis down her left side, and had to be lifted in and out of her bed and wheelchair. He enquired about the 'brainstorms' – irrational outbursts of temper which were unpredictable, but she could also be 'quite charming'. There would have been a steady deterioration over the weeks and months…

> 'I suppose towards the very end the deterioration got more rapid?'
> 'I can't answer that.'

Mr Lawrence expressed surprise:

> 'You can't answer that?'
> 'No, because she was having drugs.'

He put the question to one side, but tried a different tack:

> 'And in the latter months I suppose there was no question of her being able to get out of bed and being able to walk about even with assistance?'
> 'Not when she was having drugs to the extent she was.'

He moved sideways to the question of sedation; day to day regular sedation 'for months and months' 'without any alteration'. Sister Mason-Ellis said mysteriously 'As far as the books are concerned, yes.' He picked up the notebook which included the end of August, 1949; her first day on duty was the night of 26th/27th August, 1949. The night-time injection of ⅓ grain heroin and ¼ grain morphia had already been instituted as a routine standard dose. Shortly before this injection she was given 'sedative tablets' (allonal or sedormid) 'to settle her down and soothe her' and at 2.10 a.m. two phenobarbitone tablets. On 4th September, 1949 Mrs Morrell was given 3 allonal (sedative and analgesic) tablets at 7 p.m., one phenobarbitone at 7.20 p.m., then the routine injection at 8.38 p.m. At 8.15 p.m. the notes described the patient as 'Hysterical – wanting to die – weeping'. He got Sister Mason-Ellis to agree that all this medication was essential because stroke patients with 'brain irritation' needed sleep and quiet at nights in order to prevent a further stroke. He was constantly emphasising and insinuating that all the drugs were for Mrs Morrell's well-being.

Mr Lawrence read out notes which described Mrs Morrell walking around the bedroom or being helped by the Doctor and chauffeur to walk around the garden 'bringing back... a little bit of extra movement'. He continued through Sister Mason-Ellis' reports, rather wearisomely, 'awake and restless... half a grain of phenobarbitone and some brandy' during the night. She had given these 'extras' of course, but only on Dr Adams' instructions. Oddly, he picked out a night, 2nd/3rd October 1949 when Sister Mason-Ellis had refused Mrs Morrell the phenobarbitone and had given only brandy, and she had had a good night's sleep; the night of the 3rd/4th October was the same. Mr Lawrence carried on to the entries for November, 1949, which had reverted to the previous drug regime, giving the phenobarbitone as well through the night. But the day report for 10th November had the entry: '2 doctor's tablets at 7.15 p.m.' He enquired as to what these were and she replied, 'We did not know what those tablets were.'

This means that they must have come out of Dr Adams' bag – the nurses had all the supplies dispensed by Browne's on prescription, so it cannot have been from these and they were obviously not recognised by the nurses. Another nurse had described them as 'special tablets' – a term commonly used by Dr Adams when anyone asked what he was giving a patient.

Mr Lawrence pointed out an entry mentioning that Mrs Morrell had 'an ounce of port wine left on the bedside table'. He came to 24th November, 1949 and another notebook for Mrs Mason-Ellis to identify. She asked the Judge if she might sit down, and was permitted to do so. Mr Lawrence enquired about 'ordinary Veganin, Codeine [an alkaloid obtained from opium)] or Aspirin tablets' which were available to Mrs Morrell. Sister Mason-Ellis agreed that there were 'some tablets in her drawer' but did not know what they were and had never used them. The routine continued and 'we have not reached any variation in the amount [of drugs] at all, have we?' 'No.' He read an odd entry for 22nd December, 1949:

'Mrs Morrell. Very disturbed this afternoon re. Dr Adams & Miss Keenan.' [one of the nurses who seems to have done a few shifts during 1949]
'Do you remember what that was about?'
'Yes, I do vaguely.'

'Vaguely?'
'Yes.'

The report continued 'Shouting & quite hysterical for about 1 hr.'

'That means Mrs Morrell, does it not?'
'Yes.'
'Not Miss Keenan?'
'No.'

Mr Lawrence presumably thought better of pursuing this matter: it seems likely that Mrs Morrell may have been jealous of Miss Keenan for some reason.

# Third Day

Mrs Mason-Ellis was to be in the witness box for much of this day being cross-examined and re-examined, but Mr Lawrence began by asking if she had been talking to Nurse Stronach and Nurse Randall in the hall of the Old Bailey after she had left the witness box. She agreed. He asked if they had also travelled together in the same railway carriage on the 6.45 from Victoria to Eastbourne with the evening papers in front of them and discussing the reports in them. Yes. And had they travelled together on the 8.40 train from Eastbourne to Victoria that very morning? Yes.

'At one point were you discussing the cupboard or cabinet in which the drugs were kept in the dining room at Mrs Morrell's house?'
'That was discussed, I think.'

He repeated the answer as a question. 'Yes.'

'Did one or other of you – I am not in a position to put it to you which one it was – say this, or something like it, about that drug cabinet, or something to do with it: 'Don't you say that or you will get me into trouble'?'
'That I cannot – no, I cannot answer that one.'

She could not say which one it had been.

'Was it you?'
'No. Oh! no, because I did not know anything about it.'
'Then it was either Nurse Stronach, who has already given evidence, or it was Nurse Randall, who has not yet given evidence. That is right, is it?'

'Yes, it must be so.'
'Which one of those two was it?'

There was a pause.

'Must I answer that, Sir?'

Mr Justice Devlin replied 'Yes'.

'Then it was Miss Randall.'

She had spoken to both of them: Nurse Stronach and herself; she couldn't really remember what was said as she was 'not terribly interested'. This could hardly have been more helpful to Mr Lawrence:

'...I am not asking you to remember something which happened six years ago, like the learned Attorney-General did yesterday; I am asking you to remember something which happened in the train this morning. What was she talking about when she said: "Don't you say that or you'll get me into trouble?"'
'About the drugs.' 'And what was it that you were not to say?'

She paused:

'There has been a little confusion about it, I think, Sir. You see, the drugs were kept in a drawer, not in a cupboard, and there was no key attached to them.'

Nurse Stronach had, of course, on the previous day told the Judge that the drugs had been kept in a locked cupboard to which the nurses kept a key and would produce this if the Doctor wanted to go to the cupboard. Sister Mason-Ellis knew of no cupboard and no key. The whole thing was untrue and 'that is why we were discussing it'. She only knew about the wrong evidence upon reading it in the newspapers. Mr Lawrence continued his attack:

'Just tell me this: after you three were sitting in the hall of this building last night and before you left to catch your train together, were you told by Superintendent Hannam that you were not to talk to each other?'
'Yes, Sir.'

Apparently Superintendent Hannam had been sent for when someone noticed the nurses talking together in the hall. It has been suggested that it was an unnamed civil servant who had overheard the nurses on the train talking, but it seems much more likely that the Defence had sent either a private detective or an employee to listen to the nurses. Whoever it was had positioned themselves to listen to them on two journeys. *The Empire News* reported, after the trial, that 'At one time nine private detectives, some of them former Yard men, were searching for evidence that might be useful for the defence. They even kept an eye on the movements of Det. Supt. Hannam and other Scotland Yard officers engaged on the case.'

Mr Lawrence enquired whether the nurses had discussed the notebooks. They had talked about them but not about the contents. Sister Mason-Ellis remarked that she 'was glad they had been procured'; Nurse Randall had not replied. This was an opening not to be missed:

> 'You are glad they have been found, are you not —for this reason; that those are the notebooks that tell the truth?'
> 'Yes.'

He continued with notebook No. 3 on 5th January, 1950, and back to the 'routine' administration of drugs and alcohol. On the 12th, a septic sore on the patient's right ear was noted, otherwise nothing untoward, and on to the next notebook, No. 4. By the 1st February, the sleeping tablets had been increased: 'Allonal tablets 3, 8 p.m., sodium barbitone tablet 1, 8.30 p.m. Left two for patient – may be repeated s.o.s. [in case of need]' On 23rd February, a 'special tablet' had been left by Dr Adams for the patient to take at 8.30 in the evening. Mr Lawrence, asked the witness to confirm that this 'would be like the usual sedormid or whatever it was that was given half an hour after the first?' [3 tablets]

She would not agree:

> 'No, that would be a tablet left by Doctor Adams.'

Mr Lawrence approached from another angle: 'You see, I am going to suggest to you how easy it is to guess and how wrong you can be in these matters…'

He extracted from a day report of Nurse Keenan's the sentences: 'Please reduce by half the P.C. [after meal] mixture. I think she should have cascara [laxative] p.m.'

He suggested that both these instructions were the nurse's own, 'Nothing to do with the instructions on the bottle at all?' He concluded that 'That is another instance, isn't it, where we find we can only get at the truth by looking at these contemporary reports?'

Mr Lawrence continued: Sunday afternoon, 12th March, 1950. '4.45 p.m. Mrs Morrell visited by Dr Adams who administered dose of P.C. [after meal] mixture on arrival and gave injection of Cytamin'. This was a vitamin and the first time Sister Mason-Ellis had recorded such an injection. Nurse Keenan had recorded 'Cysamine' being given as an intra-muscular injection by Dr Adams on the following three days. 'Cysamine' was a misspelling [Cysmine also appears] – Nurse Keenan cannot have heard the word clearly. Mr Lawrence asked the witness:

> 'There is no doubt what these morning injections by Dr Adams were, is there?

Sister Mason-Ellis said darkly: 'There is no doubt when they are written down.'

On 3rd April, codeine tablets were being administered to Mrs Morrell after the allonal tablets and prior to the routine injection of morphia and heroin.

Mr Lawrence picked up notebook No. 5, which began around 7th April, 1950, and then reverted to a report for 6th May by Nurse Keenan [who never appears at the trial]: it indicated that Mrs Morrell had had an intra-muscular vitamin injection, given by Dr Harris, acting as locum for Dr Adams. Sister Mason-Ellis mentioned that Dr Adams sometimes went up to London and Dr Harris would come in his stead on these occasions; it transpired that he had been on holiday as Dr Harris came in on five days. Mr Lawrence drew attention to the fact that it was Dr Harris who had given a vitamin injection and not Dr Adams. On 11th May, Mrs Morrell accused Sister Mason-Ellis 'of leaving her alone the whole afternoon to die' and told her 'that I should be dismissed when Dr Adams returned'. Mr Lawrence read on: 'Said I refused to look after her etc.etc. and that I did nothing but sit down when I was on duty. Wished she was dead and that she knew a doctor who would "put her to sleep for ever".' Then some, seemingly odd, questions were put to the witness:

'Here she was wishing that she knew a doctor – who apparently she did not – who fulfilled the qualifications she wanted. That is right, is not it?'
'Well, I don't know whom she was alluding to.'
'No, but that is what she said, and the only doctors you knew of were Dr Harris or Dr Adams?'
'Yes.'
'Then she apologised. Do you see that evening? I just want you to look at this carefully and see whether my copy is right. At eight o'clock 2 allonal, 8.30 p.m. one codeia [codeine], 8.40 p.m. morphia, grains what?'
'A quarter.'
'And heroin, grains what?'
'A sixth.'
'That is half the usual dose?'
'It had been reduced, yes.'

Reduced by Dr Harris. After another visit by Dr Harris the next day, the heroin was back at one-third grains. The next notebook, No. 6 was handed to the witness. By 15th June, the evening codeine had been replaced by sedormid. Mr Lawrence confirmed with Sister Mason-Ellis that Mrs Morrell had 'many, many good days' in addition the 'outbursts' which occurred from time to time and that June 1950 was 'two years after her original stroke' and on 22nd June had 'A good day. Visited by Dr Adams at 3.30 p.m. Walked round the bed several times'. And this on the 'regular evening treatment of sedation under Dr Adams.'

The 13th July, however, was a very bad day: Mrs Morrell had an 'outburst' – Sister Mason-Ellis explained that this was the same thing as a 'brainstorm'. Her note in the book read: '…when I was making the bed, called me a 'slum woman & a brute', when I asked her to allow me to make the bed tidy & comfortable & not to worry, etc. Has been very argumentative over everything since… 3 p.m. Has been very hysterical re. Bessie & the sugar ration, throwing off bedclothes & beating the bed in anger.' An extra sedative, Luminal (phenobarbitone) one grain, was given to the patient at 6.30 p.m.; on 27th July two sedormid (instead of one) were being given with the allonal at 8 p.m.; by 3rd August, in addition to the allonal, there were 2 'doctor's tablets'. On 10th August another 'brainstorm' was recorded and Mrs Morrell wished Sister Mason-Ellis 'to leave at 6 p.m.'. Sister informed Dr Adams of 'Mrs Morrell's state of mind.' and he visited at 7.15 p.m. Mr Lawrence again confirmed with Sister Mason-Ellis that these 'brainstorms' were due to 'the uneven flow of the blood to the brain' and 'some pressure'. That evening 'special sleeping tablets given at 8.15 and 8.30 p.m.' before the usual injection. Mr Lawrence suggested:

'She was beginning obviously, to go downhill by this time, was not she?'
'Yes; yes.'
'It would be right to say, would it not, as a trained nurse, that the end was very nearly if not quite in sight by that time?'
'It would be rather difficult to answer that in that light.'

Not once did the Attorney-General rise to complain that the witness was being led.

Mr Lawrence went on to notebook No. 8 and the 7th September: 'Usual day… Seen by Dr Adams morning and afternoon.' There was an odd report on 9th September: 'Day Report. Mrs Morrell. Insisted on having 2 opium tablets put in bedside drawer at 4.45 p.m.'

By the 14th September Dr Adams was away on a shooting holiday in Scotland, and Dr Harris was acting as locum for his patients. (See Chapter 38 file as to what Mrs Morrell thought he was up to.) Mr Lawrence noted the Omnopon tablet given to the patient at 2 p.m. by Sister Bartlett 'no doubt… to give the sleep to give refreshment?' and the result: 'Enjoyed her supper and ate well.'?' 'Yes, Sir.' Mr Lawrence read an entry for Saturday, 16th September that mentioned 'Electrical treatment given'; he asked Mrs Mason-Ellis if the doctor had given the treatment. 'No. We had someone in to give it.' This was a masseur, Mr Hode, who was blind. He persisted in suggesting that Dr Adams did it himself. 'That I can't remember.' Dr Adams must have informed his Defence Counsel that he had done so.

On the Sunday, Dr Adams had returned from his holiday 'to see Mrs Morrell at her insistence' and, after a day or two, went back to Scotland, and Dr Harris took over again. When he visited on the 21st September, Dr Harris reduced the dose of heroin with the ¼ grain of morphia, and also directed that an Omnopon tablet could be given in the night in case of need. Mr Lawrence pointed out that Mrs Mason-Ellis had noted on 24th September that the patient's breathing was 'rapid at times 34' and that morphia and heroin tended to slow the breathing rate. This and 'incontinence of urine' were signs of 'senile decay'. The witness replied that it was a sign of this.

Mr Lawrence recounted the notes for 28th September:

'"(Urine) Dark in colour… Dr Adams visited 7.15 p.m. and administered hypodermic injection morphia ¼ grain, heroin ⅓ grain" and that is what she had been having for months and months?'

'Yes.' [He did not point out that the Doctor had increased the dosage again after Dr Harris had reduced it.]

'And then there is the addition of ⅓ grain omnopon at 7.30 p.m.?'
'Yes.'

Mr Lawrence emphasised that Mrs Mason-Ellis had recorded here the visit made by Dr Adams and the exact content of the injection. He moved rapidly on after her reply:

'On this occasion I must have asked Dr Adams and he must have told me. Otherwise I could not have recorded it.'

The omnopon tablets had been increased to 2 to be given at 9.30 p.m., as well as the ⅓ grain omnopon added in injection form.

'Did you know that the omnopon had been introduced into her sedation by Dr Harris a fortnight or so before, when Dr Adams was away?'
'I could not remember that.'

But Dr Harris had, of course, reduced the amount of heroin, and this had been increased to the original amount, *and* the omnopon had been retained. This point was quite obscured.

'Outside the contents of these books and your entries in them you would not pledge your recollection to anything, would you?'
'No.'

Mr Lawrence reiterated this point in question and answer a couple more times: anything other than what was written in the notebooks could be utterly dismissed; the nurses' own memories could not be accurate, were, so to speak, inadmissible as evidence. He got to the 26th October and read out a passage:

'"Pressure areas given special attention with compericum and lotion of Calamine." Now, that is an indication that senile deterioration in the pressure points or bed sores were getting almost beyond control at this stage?'

This proved to be a mistake as Sister Mason-Ellis could not agree that Mrs Morrell had been suffering from bed sores: they had been preventing them and it was not usual if the patient was properly cared for. In fact, the condition was something different, as recorded in the note-books:

'Skin on knees and back very red and delicate, skin on sacrum slightly broken.'

He returned to the note on the injection, which indicated: 'morphia a quarter grain, heroin one-third of a grain, plus omnopon two-thirds of a grain'. There had been one-third of a grain increase of the omnopon.

Sister Mason-Ellis' notes for 2nd November, eleven days before her death, indicated that Mrs Morrell was still able to get out of bed to use the commode and was 'very talkative'. At 10.30 a.m. on 3rd November, Dr Adams visited and found the patient asleep. He did not disturb her but 'ordered 1 sedormid (due at 10.45 a.m.) to be given on waking, and no more until after Mr Morrell's [her son, Claude Morrell] visit at 5.30 p.m. as Dr Adams wished Mrs Morrell to be clear mentally.' Then she had been 'very lachrymose since 5 p.m. Does not want to see Mr Morrell. Cried most of his visit with occasional bright moments.' After the visit 'Patient becoming hysterical. Said I was trying to kill her, etc.' Sister Mason-Ellis decided to call the Doctor and he prescribed ½ grain of heroin for the hysteria, which was given to the patient at 8.15 p.m. after she had been sleeping. She was 'very restless, but quieter'; Dr Adams said he was to be called 'if not sleeping in one hour's time', but at 9 p.m. she was asleep.

Sister Mason-Ellis was next on duty on 7th November and the extra ½ grain of heroin which had been added to the medication was given to the patient at 4.30 p.m. At 4.50 p.m. an injection of morphia ¼ grain, heroin ½ grain and atropine 1/100 grain was administered, together with ½ oz. of brandy with soda. Dr Adams had given the same injection earlier in the day at 10.45 a.m. and left instructions to repeat it as necessary during the day. On the 8th November, five days before she died, Mrs Morrell was able to sit out in a chair for eight minutes; the next day, Thursday, 9th November, she was able to get up and to ask for a sherry with her lunch. Dr Adams visited at 6.30 p.m. and gave her an injection of half a grain of heroin, saying he would call 'last thing' at night. At 8.20 p.m. she had 'three yellow tablets' – an indication that Sister Mason-Ellis had received them from the Doctor and did not know what they were. [Although both Allonal and Dexedrine tablets were also yellow, she was used to administering these.]

Sister Mason-Ellis next came on duty on Saturday November 11th in the afternoon at 4.45. Mrs Morrell was awake, 'Quiet until 4.30 p.m. then restless and becoming excited.' She was given a half grain of morphia and a half grain of heroin, and at five past five three drams of brandy with milk. This was the end of Sister Mason-Ellis' entry for that day. It was clear that Mrs Morrell was not in a coma at that stage. The witness' entry for the following day, Sunday 12th, began at 5.30 p.m.: 'Awake. But quiet. Half a glass of milk and brandy, three drams, taken. Hypodermic injection repeated at 5.25 p.m.'

'…on the 12th November Mrs Morrell could not have been in a coma?'
'Not according to my report…'

Mr Lawrence had a few more questions on other matters. He ascertained from Sister Mason-Ellis that the drugs were kept in the dining room in a drawer in the sideboard and not locked up because there was no key. There was a 'hypodermic tray' with a syringe, sterile water, swabs and liquid to clean the skin, which was 'covered with a towel, and we would carry that with us if we were giving frequent injections.' The drugs the nurses were about to use were on that tray; the tray was kept in the dining room usually. The drugs were phials of morphia, heroin and omnopon.

Had Dr Adams not used the drugs in the tray? 'Dr Adams had his own syringe which he usually used and his own tablets (hypodermic).' Oddly, on 9th November, he had 'left 1 tube of ½ gr. Sulp: Morph: Tabs: & 1 tube of ¼ gr. Heroin tabs: for future use only, and wishes Mrs Morrell to continue with ½ gr. Heroin Tabs:'. These would have been from his bag because the chauffeur collected the prescriptions and delivered the regular drugs to the nurses.

Mr Lawrence asked Sister Mason-Ellis:

'As to the doctor seeing Mrs Morrell by himself without the nurse in the room, that was by Mrs Morrell's own wish, was not it?'
'That I don't know.'

It was the practice but she did not know how it originated.

Mr Claude Morrell had sent Mrs Mason-Ellis a gift of £50, as his mother had wished it, and thanked her for what she had done.

Mr Lawrence wanted to know about the police visits which she had had. The first was when Detective Superintendent Hannam called about the 30th July, 1956, and he had called on one other occasion, in August. After that, 'Inspector Pugh called with Mr Sellars.' Then she had had a visit from 'a gentleman on the Defence'. He ended his cross-examination by referring to Dr Adams discussing with her 'exercises and massage' for the patient.

The Attorney-General began his re-examination of the witness, surprisingly by confirming that she 'would not leave out anything important' from the note-books. He asked upon what information she had based the details of any injections given by Dr Adams as recorded in the note-books: seeing what injection he made up, or by his telling her what he was giving. It might have been either, she replied. The books themselves were kept in Mrs Morrell's bedroom, so that the nurses could write the reports whilst they were with her; they could not leave her.

Sister Mason-Ellis agreed that she had made no entry in the books of Mrs Morrell suffering from any severe pain, and she had never appeared to her to have any severe pain. She had been nursing since 1918 and she could not recall any other doctor instructing her to give injections of 'heroin and morphia mixed'. Morphia and omnopon were given 'quite often as a pre-medication' before an operation. The Attorney-General pointed out that there was no record of temperature taken, was it ever taken? 'Yes, it was from time to time, but it was usually sub-normal.' The nurses had charts but these were not kept. 'They were always the same.'

When Dr Harris had attended when Dr Adams was in Scotland, he had reduced the dose of heroin, but why was this? 'It did not seem to agree with her, the heroin.' The night nurse had mentioned to her that this was the reason. The Attorney-General turned to the day of Mr Claude Morrell's visit when Dr Adams had ordered that no more sedormid was to be given to Mrs Morrell until after the visit as he wished her 'to be clear mentally'.

'…So the administration of drugs might affect the state of her mind, as to whether it was clear or not?'

'Yes, it would.'

The 'routine' injection had been changed from September to a mixture of morphia, heroin and omnopon, had Sister Mason-Ellis in her long experience as a nurse 'ever administered that as a routine injection to be given every evening?' 'Never.' And never morphia and heroin together either. The Attorney-General asked her to look at her entry in the book for Sunday, November 12th [entered as the 11th incorrectly]:

> 'Now I want to ask you this. Can you say why when this lady had in the day-time had this injection at 2.35 of half a grain of morphine and half a grain of heroin, at 5.25, when she was awake and quiet, you gave her another injection of the same quantity?'
> 'I must have been ordered to do so.'
> 'What?'
> 'I must have been ordered to do so by the doctor. We do not give injections without the doctor's instructions. He must have left instructions for me to give that.'

Sister Mason-Ellis confirmed that it was not a routine injection so soon after the other:

> 'It must have been ordered by the doctor.'

Mr Justice Devlin asked Mrs Mason-Ellis how she would have known what the Doctor injected if he had not told her. She explained that this would only happen if he arrived when she was about to give an injection and he offered to do it himself because it would please Mrs Morrell; he would have made it up but she would have known as the nurses counted all the tablets and kept a record under the Dangerous Drugs Act:

> '…on a special paper, which we used to paste on as time wore on and the paper was fin-
> ished – do you follow me, my Lord?'
> 'Yes, I think so.'
> '…and we kept that for our own personal use. The report books also are for our personal
> use, to keep each other *au fait* with what is going on. If Dr Adams gave the injection as
> stated, then he gave it as I have put it down, and he must have either told me or I knew
> from what he took from the tray. The "special" injections must, therefore, have all come
> from his own bag.'

The Judge asked what had happened to 'these bits of paper'.

> 'Well, usually, my Lord, after the case is over the last nurse on the case asks the doctor
> if he wants any of the references, charts or any other papers connected with it, and we

hand them over to him if he wants them with the drugs that are left, and they are checked up. We are most scrupulous about this, because it is a very important matter for the nursing profession. I was not the last nurse there, so that does not come into my province, you see.'

He ascertained how the system worked: when, for example, a bottle of tablets was received then the tablets would be counted and put on the 'credit' side and as a nurse took a tablet out to inject into the patient, then this would be deducted and the amount left written down so that the nurses knew how many tablets had been used. This meant that they would have known if the doctor had taken any from their tubes of drugs. Dr Adams had 'his own drugs' and had never asked Sister Mason-Ellis for any; she had always carried the nurses' tray with her. She would never have had to enter any of the doctor's injections, only her own on the pieces of paper. What can be inferred from this information is that the nurses did not need to enter any of the Doctor's injections into their note-books as a routine: the drugs did not come from their supply and usually they did not know what he was injecting.

The tubes which the heroin and morphia were in were 'very, very thin, like a straw that one drinks from'; the tablets were tiny and were dissolved in a spoon with a very small amount of water over heat, or in boiling water. When a tube was nearly finished the nurses would notify Dr Adams and he would write another prescription and it would be sent to Browne's the Chemists, and the drugs delivered to kitchen and the cook or a maid would bring it to the nurse on duty. The nurses would have one tube each of morphia, heroin, sedormid, omnopon and atropine. The tray would be kept with a nurse and before she went off duty she would put it in the drawer in the dining room, which was also the nurses' sitting room. The Attorney-General produced a tube of 25 omnopon tablets and handed them to the Judge, and some of morphine and heroin; he put them into a little box and Mr Justice Devlin agreed that they should be marked as an exhibit. [No exhibit number was given at this stage.]

Sister Mason-Ellis now withdrew and Mr Melford Stevenson asked that Dr Walker, the medical referee of the Downs Crematorium at Brighton, who was elderly and had heart trouble, should be the next witness in order to save him from making daily journeys from Brighton. His testimony related to the statutory forms which had to be completed for cremation. Exhibit 2 was the Cremation Form which had been completed before the body of Mrs Morrell could be cremated. Part B of the form had been filled in by Dr Adams: Question No. 4 read: 'Have you, so far as you are aware, any pecuniary interest in the death of the deceased?' And Dr Adams had answered: 'Not as far as I am aware'. He had been the 'ordinary medical attendant of the deceased' for 'about 5 years'; attended her during her last illness for 'two years four months'; he had last seen her alive at '10 p.m.' on the 12th November, four hours previous to death; he had seen the body '8½ hours after' death and made a 'general' examination; the 'immediate cause' of death was 'cerebral thrombosis'. The space in which the medical practitioner was required to 'state to what the cerebral thrombosis is due' was left blank and the space for 'Other morbid contitions… contributing to death' was also left blank. The 'mode of death', Dr Adams had filled in as 'Coma' and its duration: 'About 2 hours'. The doctor was required to say how far the answers to the last two questions were a result of his own observations or were based on the statements made by others, and this was answered by 'Both' and the other person identified as Nurse Randall. To the question: 'By whom was the deceased nursed during his or her last illness?', Dr Adams had written: 'Firstly in Esperance Nursing Home… Later at Olinda Nursing Home, after that in her own home until death. Had three nurses on duty in 24 hours. Often changed. Nurse Randall – Night Duty – 19 months, Nurse Mason – day – 14 months, Nurse Bartlett – day – 3 months.' 'Present at moment of death: Nurse Randall'. Dr Adams had had no 'reason to suspect that the death of the deceased was due, directly or indirectly, to (a) Violence, (b) Poison (c) Privation or neglect.' The confirmatory medical certificate was signed by Doctor E. Owen Fox.

Mr Lawrence cross-examined Dr Walker: the date of the certificate was the 13th November, 1950, the day of death; Dr Walker had signed it on the 15th, which was the day of the cremation. He repeated all the questions and answers on the form to demonstrate how scrupulous Dr Adams had been in supplying every detail required. He asked the witness to observe the last portion of the form: 'Additional information regarding either of the certificates may be given here if necessary' Dr Adams had entered here the addresses of the three nurses. Mr Lawrence drew attention to Form 'C', the Confirmatory Medical Certificate of an independent doctor of 'not less than 5 years' standing'. This read:

> 'I, being neither a relative of the deceased, nor a relative or partner of the medical practitioner who has given the foregoing medical certificate, have examined it and have made personal inquiry as stated in my answers to the questions below.'

Dr E. Owen Fox who had signed this form, had seen Mrs Morrell's body and 'carefully examined the body externally'; had seen and questioned Dr Adams, and had seen and questioned Nurse Bartlett – although it was Nurse Randall who had been in attendance at Mrs Morrell's death. The fee for the signing of Form C on the cremation certificate has generally been known to doctors as 'ash cash'.

Caroline Sylvia Randall was now sworn in as the next witness. She had nursed Mrs Morrell for one year and ten months up to the time of her death. The Attorney-General asked her if she had made notes in the 'exercise books' which they now had 'the advantage of having'. Her reply was: 'I did when there were three trained nurses on the case'. He referred to an entry for 22nd June, 1949 when one injection of morphia gr. ¼ Heroin gr. ⅙ was given at 7.15 p.m., and another of 'Heroin gr. ⅙ and Morphia gr. ⅙ was given at 10.50 p.m.; on 25th June, the heroin in the injection had increased to ⅓ grain. The Attorney-General turned to an entry for 27th September, 1950; Dr Adams had visited twice and on each occasion had given a 'special injection'. What had Sister Randall understood by this term?

> 'I understood that Dr Adams was giving special vitamin injections to Mrs Morrell at one time.'
> 'A special injection at 7 p.m. Did you know what that was?'
> 'No, I did not.'

The day report for the 28th September revealed that Dr Adams had visited at 7 p.m. 'special injection given'. Allonal iii (3 tablets) at 7 p.m. Hypodermic injection Morphia ¼ grains with Heroin ⅓ grains & Omnopon ⅓ grains given at 7.30 p.m. Sister Randall then recorded that Dr Adams visited at 9.45 p.m. and gave 'Hypo: Injection Omnopon 2: no effect'. He returned at 11.30 p.m. and gave another injection of 'Omnopon ⅓. Between 11.45 p.m. and 12.45 a.m., Mrs Morrell became 'restless and rather collapsed cold perspiration: TDS brandy given twice, complained of feeling very hot, body and limbs cold'. Dr Adams made another visit at 1.15 when Sister Randall called him that night. She told Dr Adams that she did not think the heroin 'suited' Mrs Morrell. He replied that he 'did not think it was anything to do with the heroin', and gave an injection of coramine, a heart stimulant. The following day, 29th, Dr Adams gave a 'special injection' at 7 p.m., Nurse Bartlett gave the morphia, heroin and omnopon injection at 7.30 p.m., Sister Randall gave an omnopon ⅔ grain injection at 9.30 p.m., and another at 10.15 p.m., milk with brandy and sedormid at 10.25 p.m.; Dr Adams visited at 10.40 p.m. and prepared a hypodermic injection which was given at 11.15 p.m. The Attorney-General asked:

'When Dr Adams came at 10.40 that evening did you have any discussion with him about the patient's condition that night and the previous night?'
'I expect I did, yes.'
'About the restlessness?'
'Yes.'

Mr Lawrence intervened: 'Please do not lead her.' Mr Justice Devlin allowed the Attorney-General to continue, and then the Judge asked Sister Randall whether she remembered any particular discussion she had had with Dr Adams:

'I do know that I said that I did not think that heroin suited her.'

Sister Randall had described Mrs Morrell that night at 11.45 p.m. as being 'in a cold sweat, legs and body very cold and clammy, but voice strong & eyes very wild looking.' Later the patient seemed 'more normal and said "The brain storm has passed".'

The Attorney-General enquired whether she had ever injected either a mixture of morphia, heroin and omnopon or a mixture of morphia and heroin 'on the instructions of any other doctor than Dr Adams'. She had not. He now asked her to look at her night report of October 27th, 1950: 'Mrs Morrell slept heavily until 3.15 a.m.; then began to fidget a little, yawned loudly & frequently but still seemed in a semi-comatose condition, did not answer when spoken to or open her eyes.' The instructions were now to give the patient the injection of morphia, heroin and omnopon 'S.O.S.' – repeated when necessary.

Turning to the day report of 6th November, 1950, this showed: 'special injection given by Dr @ 11 a.m. Has been very confused and depressed this evening – continuously pulled blankets on to floor etc. & has been crying. Sedormid 1 given @ 10. 30 a.m. – 6 p.m. Allonal iii given 7 p.m.,

Hypodermic injection gr. ½ given @ 7.30 p.m. – May have Heroin gr. ½ repeated S.O.S.' Sister Randall's night report read: 'Hypodermic injection heroin gr. ½ – 1 a.m., H.I. Heroin gr. ½ – 1.55 a.m., (Dr's orders) H.I. Heroin gr. ½ – 7.55 a.m.' Sister Randall told the Attorney-General that she must have had a specific order from the Doctor for the injection at 1 a.m. because 'it was so close on top of the other injection'. She certainly recalled that Mrs Morrell had never suffered from any severe pain, more 'occasional pains, perhaps from stiffness'. On the night of the 7th November, hypodermic injections of heroin ½ grain, morphia ¼ grain and atropine $\frac{1}{100}$th grain were given at 3.35 a.m. and repeated at 5.45 a.m. 'by Dr's orders' and at 7.25 p.m. On the night of the 8th November, the same injection was given at 1.30 a.m., 3.30 a.m. and 8.30 a.m.

The Attorney-General drew Sister Randall's attention to her night report for November 9th and 10th: '10.15 p.m. visited by Dr Adams. Hypodermic injection of heroin and morphia, 1 grain, at 10.20.' Underneath that there was written 'To have heroin gr. 1 given S.O.S.' Mrs Morrell was given 1 grain of heroin at 4.15 a.m., brandy and phenobarbitone (1 tablet) at 5.20 a.m.; at 6.30 a.m. a further 1 grain of heroin and at 8 a.m. Dr Adams gave her a hypodermic injection of ½ grain of hyperduric morphia. Sister Randall supposed that the heroin and morphia were increased because the patient was 'getting chesty'.

The following night, that of 10th and 11th, Dr Adams visited at 10.30 p.m. and gave an injection of hyperduric morphia. Sister Randall's report read: '10.45 p.m. sleeping. Awake 3.45 a.m. Very alert and wild eyed. 4.50 a.m. Heroin gr. 1 (gives a sharp cry at every touch or movement... twitchings more pronounced... 6 a.m. Heroin gr. 1 given. 7.30 a.m. Very restless and confused. 8.15 a.m. Visited by Dr Adams Injection of hyperduric morphia given.' The Attorney-General asked her why she had not noted the amount of the morphia injection. She thought that this would be because the doctor had given the injection; she could not recall the nurses ever having had any hyperduric morphia and the only reason she could have had the information was 'Dr Adams must have told me'. She had not entered the amount for the 8.15 a.m. injection for the same reason.

Sister Randall's report for the next night, 11th and 12th November recorded a visit by Dr Adams at 10.45 p.m. when he gave 'a hypodermic injection of morphia half a grain and heroin half a grain'. At 1 a.m. she had given an injection of 'heroin one grain with hyperduric morphia half a grain'. By 2 a.m. Mrs Morrell was 'more wakeful, crying out at times' and was given another half grain of heroin and half a grain of hyperduric morphia. '3 a.m. Still chattering, more wakeful & jerky. 3.40 a.m. Heroin gr. i given'. '8 a.m. Visited by Dr Adams'. the Attorney-General asked Sister Randall whether she could describe the kind of jerks which had occurred:

'Well, just involuntary jerks; just sort of hit out at you;' she demonstrated: 'sort of hit
out like *that*'
'With her arms?'
'Yes, her arms, and her legs would come up.'

The next report of Sister Randall's was, of course, the last night of Mrs Morrell's life: 'Mrs Morrell Awake. Restless. 10.30 p.m. Paraldehyde 5 c.c. given i.m. (intra-muscular) by Dr

Adams. 11.30 p.m. Very restless, no sleep. 12.30 a.m. Restless and talkative & very shaky. 12.45 a.m. Seems a little quieter, appears asleep. Respiration 50. 2 a.m. Passed away quietly.'

Had Sister Randall 'perceived any jerks that night?' Yes, they were very bad and she had been afraid to leave Mrs Morrell. 'They almost jerked her out of bed'. She had never seen any spasms like that in another patient. When Dr Adams had given the injection at 10.30 p.m. Mrs Morrell 'had not been conscious. She might have been semi-conscious'. Sister Randall thought that Dr Adams was trying to do something to prevent the 'jerkiness' [convulsions] and make Mrs Morrell quiet for the night. The syringe must have been from the Doctor's bag and he had prepared it. He also prepared another injection for Sister Randall to give the patient. She now thought that she had given the first of these large injections on Dr Adams' orders and he refilled the syringe and gave it to her 'to keep in case the patient was very restless in the night... He didn't say any time'. During the night, before she gave that second 5 c.c. injection, she had tried to get in touch with Dr Adams by 'phone at about 11.30, she thought. 'I didn't want to give another injection, you see.'

> 'Why?'
> 'Not yet awhile. It was too soon I thought.'
> 'Too soon after the one he had given?'
> 'Yes.'
> 'Did you give that other injection?'
> 'I did.'
> 'What was the effect of that injection?'
> 'She became quieter, and when she became quieter I called Sister Bartlett, because I could see that she was passing out.'

The Attorney-General asked whether Mrs Morrell had been in a coma before her death. Yes.

> 'How long had she been in a coma before her death?'
> 'Well, she would be in a coma and then come out gradually and then perhaps go in again. When we had to attend to her she might rouse up a little, and then she would go into a heavy coma again.'

The last three words have been underlined by Hannam in the transcript.

The Attorney-General asked for how long Mrs Morrell had been going in and out of coma.

> 'Oh, I should think quite two or three days she was in and out of that sort of heavy sort of coma.'

Mr Justice Devlin decided that it was time to adjourn, and he warned Sister Randall that she should avoid the company of the other nurses who had given evidence and that he wanted no repetition of what had occurred the day before.

# Fourth Day

The Attorney-General resumed his examination of Sister Randall, asking her about the last two injections when she had used the 5 c.c. syringe: how full was it? She would say 'about 4 c.cs.' The Doctor must have brought the paraldehyde and told her what it was. Yes, paraldehyde had a very distinctive smell. The Attorney-General pointed out that there was an entry in the notebook for the first injection at 10.30 p.m. but not for the later injection. She had written 'very shaky' and underlined this twice, but as the patient died at 2 a.m. she had not made any further entry, the purpose of the notes being to inform the next nurse on duty, but Sister Randall just said that she 'couldn't think why' she had not entered the other injection. With regard to the increase in the heroin injections to one grain when necessary on the 10th November, she had never had such an instruction before – and not since, as she had previously said she had not used it upon a patient since Mrs Morrell's case. Dr Adams had not told her why he was increasing the heroin dosage.

The Attorney-General turned his attention to what had happened to the nurses' notebooks. Sister Randall said that, after the death of a patient, she usually took them, kept them for a while and then destroyed them. 'We do not let the patients see them, I mean the relatives see them as a rule.' She did not know what had happened to the notebooks in Mrs Morrell's case as she 'waited until 10 o'clock [a.m.] and he [Dr Adams] didn't arrive, so I left.' She had left Sister Bartlett there. Sometimes Dr Adams would look at the books. Sister Randall confirmed that the drugs tray held a small methylated spirit heater for water to dissolve the drugs tablets, the injections to be used and a spoon; and that the record of tablets used and left was written down on a piece of paper. She could not recall what drugs had been left over after Mrs Morrell's death.

The Attorney-General then referred to Book 6, 26th August where something had been cut out of the page. The notes said that Mrs Morrell was 'Very worried over tablets in bottle in drawer beside her bed. When Mrs Morrell thought I was not in the room I watched her hold bottle in left hand and unscrew top, she said she was going to take them so that they would not be taken away. She would not let me have them to put in drawer. Mrs Morrell was so muddled at times she did not seem to know what she wanted to do; uncovering herself frequently & trying to lift herself up; position changed frequently from one side to the other with difficulty, she was very heavy indeed to lift or turn over.'

> 'Then: "7 a.m. Bottle of sleeping tablets not in drawer, found loose in bed. Mrs Morrell more heavy. Dr Adams called. Hypo gr. ½ Caffein". Does that appear?'
> 'Yes.'
> 'Then 'treatment given'. Does that appear?'
> 'No.'

Sister Randall is looking at the original notebook where the extract is in her own handwriting. The Attorney-General is looking at a copy, but must have examined the original.

'That does not appear?'

'No. That is cut out.'

'Let me just look at that. (Handed). Will you look at this again? Someone has written this in. I do not know whether it was you. "Hypo gr. ½ Caffein".'

'In green ink, is it not?'

'Yes.'

'And the rest is written in blue ink?'

'Yes.'

'And whoever has made this excision has cut through the word 'called' and cut through the word 'treatment'. You can see half the word. Then there is the entry '9.30 a.m.', with the beginning of another piece of handwriting, and that is cut out and then there is nothing on the opposite page?'

'Yes.'

'Is that green ink your handwriting?'

'No, Sir.'

Mr Justice Devlin then examined the book.

The Attorney-General concluded his examination of Sister Randall by asking her whether she had been present in the room on the night of 11th/12th November when Dr Adams had given an injection at 10.45 p.m. and another at 8 a.m. She had not.

Mr Geoffrey Lawrence began his cross-examination: Sister Randall had been in private nursing since she qualified in 1925, both in patients' homes and nursing homes. She had come across all the drugs mentioned in that time, including paraldehyde, which, she agreed, had a distinctive and pungent smell. Mr Lawrence asked whether the notes were 'first of all so that the doctor in charge of the case can see exactly what has happened' Sister Randall answered 'Yes. He doesn't always look. He relies on the nurse.' 'Another purpose' was to inform the next nurse on duty of what had happened during the preceding duty period. Then, edging forward, he ascertained that it would be the duty of the nurse to write down any instruction she had received from the doctor.

The nurses' notes were so important that they had to be accurate 'to include everything of importance that happens' and they 'must not leave anything out' and any 'conscientious' nurse would have fulfilled these obligations – the inference to be drawn was that the nurses' notebooks contained everything and were perfectly accurate, and Sister Randall had agreed at every step in the cross-examination, precluding any possibility of her saying that she might have omitted anything.

Sister Randall had first nursed Mrs Morrell in February 1949 at the Cumberland Hotel; the first of the notebooks began on 21 June, 1949 when there were regular shifts of nurses on duty. Sister Randall thought she had been having morphia injections to begin with. Mr Lawrence, with cross-examination, positioned Mrs Morrell as an elderly invalid, with history of stroke, outbursts of irritability, 'brainstorms', with hardening of the arteries, restlessness at nights and unable to walk without assistance.

'Now, I dare say you knew, as the nurse there all the time, that the object of Dr Adams' treatment was to give her, if he could, rest and sleep at night?'

'Yes.'

'That is quite right?'

'Yes, sir, yes.'

'Because, as a nurse of experience, you knew that if that elderly lady with this brain trouble, and so forth, had been robbed of any sleep at night it would not have gone on very long without trouble, could it?'

'No.'

'And the treatment was therefore designed to give her, and secure, if you [sic] could, the rest and sleep that she needed?'

'Yes.'

There was no intervention from the Attorney-General concerning the leading of the witness, yet how could a nurse know what Dr Adams' treatment was designed for?

Mr Lawrence diverted into questions about where Sister Randall had nursed since Mrs Morrell's death, how Mrs Morrell's illness was a 'downhill story', and then on to police visits to Sister Randall and the statements she had made. Then to the notebooks: the blue book, July 1st, 1949: '8.40 p.m. hypo injection, morphia gr. ¼, with heroin ⅓ given. Seems rather depressed. Complains of pains in the left leg.' On the 8th and 9th July, the same injection and 'complains of pain in the left foot'. Sister Randall said that these were not severe pains, but Mr Lawrence was indicating the drug dosage for July, 1949 when the morphia and heroin were already being given together and that this and 'sedatives' were being given on a regular basis: On 12th/13th July there was this injection plus '3 Allonal. + Phenbarb gr. i repeat S.O.S.' – (Allonal-aprobarbital, anti-anxiety and sedative drug).

Mr Justice Devlin intervened:

'Mr Lawrence, this is in order to establish that the standard injections remained up to the end of September [1950]. This witness seems to doubt it, but by now the books must have been examined by the Prosecution.'

The Attorney-General accepted this, but pointed out that the witness had said that before the books started the injection was only of morphia.

Mr Lawrence referred to 17th January, 1950: 'Special tablet P.C. [after food]' which would have been given in the morning. The day before there had been another 'Special tablet 1 Mane [morning]':

'You probably don't remember what that tablet was?'

'I know she had a Dexadrine in the morning.'

'Did you know at this time in January 1950, on the 16th January, 1950 there is a prescription by Doctor Adams for Benzadrine?'

'No.'
'Later she had Dexadrine in the morning.'
'Yes.'

Apparently Mr Lawrence thought these drugs quite innocuous. Dexadrine is an amphetamine, a controlled substance and Benzadrine a related, and more potent drug. They both work by suppressing all spontaneous or self-generated behaviour, such as exploration, socializing and curiosity and there is an increase in obsessive-compulsive behaviours. Side effects that occur include: addiction, irritability, insomnia, dry mouth, headaches, nausea, behaviour distur-bances, thought disorder, tics, exacerbation of motor skills, restlessness and Tourette's Syndrome – which might explain the regular verbal abuse of the nurses. At this period these drugs were often used as an appetite suppressant.

> '"7th March, 1950. The last three lines: 'Special yellow tablet: I given
> at 8.20 a.m. (Dexidrine) [sic]" . There it is.'
> 'Yes.'
> 'Three lines above: "Complained of Wheezyness. [sic] Dover's tablets 1 given warm
> drink." '

Dover's tablets are opium.

On 7th May, 1950 (book 5) there was an entry 'Not complained of any pain or discomfort' yet at 10.50 p.m. a codeine [obtained from opium or prepared from morphine] tablet was given and another at 1.40 a.m. '4.15 to 4.45 restless.' 'At intervals throughout this case that is the word isn't it that you used often?' 'Yes.' But not surprisingly.

3rd September, 1950: the injection is exactly the same but at 2 p.m. Mrs Morrell had half a grain of Luminal (phenobarbitone – an anti-convulsant and sedative); at 10 p.m. Sedormid (aprobarbital – sedative). On the 4th September, Dr Harris gave her an injection of omnopon (50% morphia) at 10.40 p.m. and Sister Randall gave a Dover's tablet 'for wheeziness' accord-ing to Mr Lawrence, at 4.10 a.m. He remarked on 'one rather strange feature' of the notes for the night of 8th September:

> '"Mrs Morrell has had a fair night, disturbed frequently by mice", and that is underlined
> three times?"'
> 'Yes.'
> 'Does that mean real mice or Mrs Morrell's imaginary mice?'
> 'No, real mice.'
> 'Real mice?'
> 'Yes.'

The 11th September, 1950 and Dr Harris had taken over whilst Dr Adams was on holiday in Scotland: the 'usual' injection was given in the evening but he also added omnopon and left omnopon tablets 'to be repeated S.O.S.'. It is not possible to know the difference between the medication given by Dr Harris and that previously given by Dr Adams due to 'special injections' and 'special tablets given by Dr Adams", he never kept records of what he prescribed for private patients or, indeed, clinical records for them. Mr Lawrence concentrated on the addition of omnopon to the regime but it seems likely that some other drugs were missing during Dr Adams' absence. By the 16th December Mrs Morrell had become very 'nervy and irritable' and it was on the 17th that Dr Adams came in to see her, having been summoned down from Scotland, at 3.45 p.m. and again that night. The morphia in the regular injection was increased to ½ grain from ¼ .

By the 20th September, Dr Adams had returned to Scotland to resume his holiday and Dr Harris was in again. The morphia was back to the 'normal quarter grain', reduced by Dr Harris. The day report for the 23rd September noted that Dr Harris had reduced the heroin content of the injection to ⅙ grain. Despite having omnopon at 9.50 p.m. after this reduction, Mrs Morrell was awake and restless and Dr Harris was called for at 11.40 p.m. and gave her an injection of ⅔ grain omnopon, and then she slept until 6.40 a.m., when she awoke 'very confused and irritable. Complained of feeling very queer.' Dr Harris continued the same injection of morphia ¼ grain, heroin ⅙ grain and omnopon ⅓ grain the following night. Still confused and irritable, Mrs Morrell got through the night with just two phenobarbitone tablets during the night – she had the usual 3 Allonal at 7 p.m.

The next day September 25th, Dr Adams had returned and 'special capsule and injection given 10.45 a.m.', the 3 Allonal at 7 p.m. and the heroin in the injection was back to ⅓ grain from Dr Harris' ⅙ and the omnopon content was continued. Dr Adams had told Sister Randall that Mrs Morrell had 'pancreaitis' [sic] but after the injection she had a quiet night and there was 'no need for additional medication', although the Doctor had issued the instruction 'May have two tablets of omnopon by injection if necessary'. On the following day, Mrs Morrell watched television and listened to the radio; she was 'brighter & talkative'. Mr Lawrence constantly referred to the drugs as being necessary for 'restlessness and the absence of sleep'; to the patient becoming 'senile' and 'going downhill'. Sister Randall agreed with him each time. She was not, after all, as a nurse, able to form or give a medical opinion. After the usual injection, Sister Randall gave another of '2 omnopon' and when Dr Adams called at 11 p.m. on 27th September he gave the patient another ⅓ omnopon and 'she slept soundly until 8.15 the next morning'.

After the adjournment for lunch, Mr Lawrence drew Sister Randall's attention to the fact that although she had said that she had not injected a mixture of morphia, heroin and omnopon on the instructions of any other doctor than Dr Adams, she had in fact done so on Dr Harris' instructions. This demonstrated that it was better to rely upon notes than upon her memory. Doubtless she was thinking that it had not happened in any other case other than that of Mrs Morrell. Mr Lawrence reverted to the night of 28th September, after Mrs Morrell had had one grain of omnopon (50% morphia) in addition to the 'usual injection' of morphia, heroin and omnopon. Sister Randall had to call Dr Adams that night because Mrs Morrell became restless and was 'Rather collapsed, cold perspiration, complained of feeling very hot, body and limbs cold'; Sister Randall administered brandy. Dr Adams came at 1.15 a.m. and gave her an injection of 1 c.c. Coramine. [a circulatory stimulant] The symptoms noted could indicate morphine overdose, although this was not mentioned and Mr Lawrence concentrated on confirming that the amount of heroin which had been injected had remained stable as Sister Randall had actually questioned the suitability of *heroin* for the patient with Dr Adams as she thought that the symptoms were those of *heroin overdose* and seemed not to have noticed that the increase was in the amount of morphia. It enabled Mr Lawrence to demonstrate the unreliability of Sister Randall's memory and evidence.

The events of the night of 28th September did not deter Dr Adams from giving the instructions: 'If awake please give injection: omnopon 2 tablets at 9.30 p.m.' If Mrs Morrell was not sleeping at 11 p.m, he 'will come up again and wishes to be called'. At 9.30 p.m. Sister Randall noted 'awake, depressed and perspiring freely, very weepy' and she gave her 'warm milk and brandy' and at 10 p.m. gave the omnopon injection. At 10.45 she was still in the same condition 'and became quite agitated when I said we would let Dr Adams know she had not slept. She seemed to think that everybody was against her. She telephoned Dr Adams herself to tell him she was all right'. She 'rang her bell at 11.45 p.m., ...was in a cold sweat, legs and body very cold and clammy, but voice strong and eyes very wild looking.' At midnight Sister Randall gave her more milk and brandy, a sedormid tablet and a pain (codeine?) tablet and at 12.30 p.m. a coramine injection.

On the evening of the 29th September, a 'special injection' was given to the patient by Dr Adams at 7 p.m. followed by 'the usual compound injection' was given at 7.30 p.m. and '2/3 of omnopon by injection at 10.15 p.m.' She 'perspired profusely' after the injection and at 10.40 p.m. she was visited by Dr Adams who prepared a hypodermic injection which he left with Sister Randall who gave it to Mrs Morrell at 11.15 p.m. Complaining of 'giddiness' she was given a sedormid tablet at 12.30 a.m. (30th September). There was no extra omnopon on the following evening and Mrs Morrell 'had a very good night and has not been confused'. On October 1st she was 'sitting out in the chair for two and a half hours with no ill-effects'. 2nd October and the extra omnopon injection was given at 11.40 p.m. In the morning when Dr Adams visited he gave a 'special capsule' and a 'special injection'. That night Mrs Morrell was complaining to Sister Randall 'frequently, of extreme weakness' and seemed 'very shaky' the next morning – the extra omnopon had not been given on the previous evening. The allonal (3) and sedormid (2) continued. Dr Adams came in the morning and again gave the 'special' capsule and injection, and again the next morning. Mr Lawrence asked:

'She was getting very shaky at this time, was she not?'
'Yes.'

He observed that Sister Mason-Ellis had noted on 5th October that Mrs Morrell had 'Prolonged twitching of the left shoulder', '...when there has been no increase of the Heroin of ⅓ grain every day for months and months'. After six hours sleep that night – which seems a good amount for her age, Mrs Morrell was given an injection of ⅔ grains of omnopon 'solely for the purpose of giving her sleep' on Dr Adams' instructions. Unsurprisingly, she was 'very drowsy until 3.30 p.m.' [this is underlined by Hannam on the transcript] on 6th October. She appeared 'very ill and weak' at lunch time and Dr Adams was called and gave the 'special' capsule and injection. After the combined injection and Doctor's visit at 10 p.m., she 'slept heavily until 4.30 a.m.' and was given ⅔ omnopon at 5.15. Mr Lawrence suggested that this was because she was getting 'wheezy', 'a common characteristic of senile old people in their last weeks or days?' Yes, said Sister Randall. Altogether Mrs Morrell slept for about 9½ hours. During the early morning of 7th October, she had a Dover and an aspirin tablet, the ⅔ omnopon injection and sedormid at 5.15 and 9.30 a.m. 'Very drowsy'. The following morning (8th October) Sister Randall noted that the patient was 'very muddled, but complained of much pain over right ear' and eau-de-cologne compresses were applied 'with relief' and that there was a 'small inflamed patch on the left shoulder'. Then Mr Lawrence read from Sister Bartlett's day report

> '"Seen by Doctor this morning. Special capsule and injection given." Pausing there; we have seen, haven't we, day after day that it is recorded by the day sister that a special capsule and injection have been given and the patient takes the diet well?'
> 'Yes.'

Sister Bartlett had then recorded 'Patient became very drowsy at 11 a.m. and went into deep sleep and could not be wakened. Was in semi-comatose condition. Lower lip very blue – brandy given with no effect at 1.30 p.m. Patient eventually awoke at 4.30 p.m. ? Stroke.' This last question in the notes was of great assistance to Mr Lawrence. 'Has taken supper and breakfast but no lunch. Patient appears more normal this p.m. but has slight difficulty with speech.' Sister Bartlett rang Dr Adams 'again at 7 p.m.', but 'he will not visit again this evening'. This does not suggest that he thought that Mrs Morrell had had another stroke. And, after the usual injection, she 'slept well up to 5.30 a.m., dozed on and off until 5.45 a.m. Muddled but quite happy between 6 and 7 a.m. Warm milk and brandy and Sedormid given at 5.45 a.m… slept again from 7.15 to 8.30 a.m. Asked for waking up tablet. Sedormid i given [!] at 9.15 a.m. [9th October].' Dr Adams came in the morning and continued with the 'special' capsule and injection. There was 'bowel trouble' but 'We needn't go into that'. The patient slept for 4 hours in the afternoon and for four or five hours at night; 'restless and muddled yet still drowsy', she was given the extra sedormid and omnopon. By 5.15 a.m., she was 'unable to make herself understood'. Mr Lawrence asked one of his almost rhetorical questions:

> 'She was going rapidly downhill at this stage, wasn't she?'
> 'Yes, Sir, she was.'

The 'special' morning injection and capsule followed. Mrs Morrell was 'Drowsy most of the morning. Awoke at 1.30 p.m. Very confused, continuously rang the bell and pulled bed-clothes etc. on to the floor'; at 3.15 in the afternoon Sister Bartlett gave her an injection of ⅔ grain omnopon – on Dr Adams' instructions and the first omnopon injection during the daytime. The

Doctor visited again in the afternoon and 'Became very confused again this evening – could not remember me [Sister Bartlett].' Although on 12th October, Mrs Morrell 'slept quite heavily until 3.15 a.m.', she was given sedormid and ⅔ omnopon. She slept most of the morning 'Doctor will visit patient between 7 and 7.30 p.m. and will give her an injection'; by 4 p.m. she was 'restless and picking bedclothes' and was given ⅔ omnopon. After Dr Adams' injection and the usual one, she 'Slept until 4.30 a.m.' and was given more omnopon at 5 a.m. Bad incontinence ensued. Dr Adams gave her 'an injection' in the morning [13th October] and there was an afternoon injection of omnopon, the usual evening triple injection and, this triple injection was repeated at 1 a.m. on 14th October. Sister Randall, when asked, said that 'The doctor must have given me permission to give it if I thought necessary'. Mrs Morrell was still restless and ⅔ omnopon was given at 2.20 a.m. *plus* ⅓ grain of heroin 'on Doctor Adam's orders' and sedormid in between. 'Restless until 3.45', then sleeping and at 7 a.m. 'Very restless again'.

Sister Randall had a couple of weeks off duty and returned again on the night of the 27th October. She came back to find that the drug regime was similar but that the omnopon in the triple injection had increased to ⅔ grain. This injection could be given 'S.O.S.' as necessary. The 'special' injection and capsule were still being given by Dr Adams in the morning. Sister Randall had written in her night report for the 26th/27th October: 'Mrs Morrell slept heavily until 3.15 a.m.: then began to fidget a little, yawned loudly & frequently but still seemed in a semi-comatosed condition, did not answer when spoken to or open her eyes… had to be roused to be changed. Back looking very bad & right hip & between knees & heels very inflamed. Hypo. injection prepared but patient had fallen asleep again and slept until 8.45 a.m., then was very drowsy'. Mr Lawrence suggested to Sister Randall that there had been no drugs given on the previous day which could have caused a 'semi-comatosed condition'. 'No' she replied. He 'worked still further back' to the 'last recorded injection of these drugs', the 'special' capsule:

'I am not armed with the full list of prescriptions at the moment, but that was that special capsule. I do not know whether you know it, because you are only the night nurse. That was a caffeine capsule, was it not, a stimulant?'

The Attorney-General was moved to object:

'How can my learned friend put that to this witness when she does not know and was not there? My friend is really seeking to give evidence about this matter when he says: "Let us look back to see if there is any injection before". I thought it right to draw his attention to it. She says she does not know what this is, in effect.'

Mr Lawrence apologised, then cunningly and immediately asked Sister Randall:

'…was it you or one of the other nurses who told me that these morning injections were vitamin injections?'
'Yes, that is right. I said yesterday I understood they were special vitamin injections.'

There was only one possible witness who could know.

Mr Lawrence returned to the 'semi-comatosed condition' which Sister Randall had noted on the night of the 27th. The last recorded injection before that night was more than two days before on the evening of the 25th at 7.30 p.m. – which seems likely to have been an omission on the part of other nurses, otherwise there would have been significant withdrawal symptoms at least from 24 hours after that.

Mr Justice Devlin intervened: 'Mr Lawrence, is it not merely comment on what is recorded in the report?'

Mr Lawrence went on to the night of 28th October, when Sister Randall had administered a triple injection of heroin ⅓, morphia ¼ and omnopon ⅔ at ten past two in the morning when Mrs Morrell became restless. The next day Nurse Stronach had written the Doctor's instruction: 'To have big Hypo Injection each night just after 9 p.m.'. Sister Randall had given the triple injection at 9.30 p.m. and when the patient began 'to be restless, throwing the clothes off' she gave an injection of ⅔ omnopon at 11.15. Nurse Stronach had noted in the morning 'Special injection given by Dr Adams'; Sister Randall had given the same injections on the night of 30th October as on the previous night. Mrs Morrell was much more confused and restless on the night of 31st October 'continually stripping the bed, and repeating same words over and over again'. She had two injections of omnopon at 4.15 a.m. and 5.15 a.m. and had seven hours sleep altogether.

> '…You see, during those nights up to this point, using your judgment to deal with Mrs Morrell's condition, there had undoubtedly been an increase in the administration of these drugs, had not there?'
> 'Yes.'

The responsibility for this was put squarely upon the shoulders of Sister Randall.

> 'And here is the doctor on the 31st October ordering the omission of two of them [morphia and omnopon] and limiting it to one-half grain – that is ³/₆ths?'
> 'Yes.'
> 'And ⅓ if required, S.O.S., during the day. That is an obvious change in the routine, is it not?'
> 'Yes.'

So Mrs Morrell had ½ grain of heroin and on the night of 1st November 'Slept well from 9.30 pm. until 6.15 a.m.' and she was given another ½ grain of heroin at 9.15 a.m. Dr Adams visited and gave his 'special injection' at 10.45 and instructed that the 'heroin only' regime should continue. Mrs Morrell seemed 'more awake and taking interest in things' and seem 'bright… and not confused'. On 2nd November, indeed, she had a good breakfast and the notable lunch of 'partridge, celery, pudding and brandy and soda'. At 9.30 p.m. on 2nd November, Sister Randall injected ½ grain of heroin and she was 'talkative' till midnight. With a couple of sedormid tablets and 'some Allenburys and brandy' the patient slept well, but upon waking at 7 a.m. was 'rather weary and muddled'. The 3rd November was the Saturday of Mr Morrell's visit when Dr Adams wanted her to be mentally clear, and which ended with 'a restless hysterical attack'; Mr Lawrence proceeded to the night of the 4th November, when, having had the now 'usual' injection of ½ grain of heroin at 9.30 p.m., Sister Randall gave her another ⅓ heroin at 1 a.m. She then slept till 7 in the morning, but was 'very confused at times' and her 'speech indistinct'.

No injection during the day of November 4th had been recorded, Mr Lawrence pointed out, but Sister Randall had given two additional injections of heroin that night: ⅓ grain at 3.30 a.m. and another ⅙ grain at 4.15, and 'at six o'clock in the morning you gave her another one-third of heroin'. He went on to Sister Bartlett's administration of ½ grain of heroin at 7.30 p.m. on 5th November and the instruction in the notebook 'May have ½ grain heroin repeated S.O.S.', when necessary. That night Sister Randall gave three ½ grain heroin injections to Mrs Morrell at 1 a.m., 1.55 a.m. and 7.50 a.m. The patient had seven hours sleep but 'mucous very troublesome in throat'.

> '…That is the first occasion we have seen a record of that trouble?'
> 'Yes.'
> 'That came on her towards the end, did not it?'
> 'Yes.'

The patient was 'very aggressive' when she awoke, then, of course, another ½ grain of heroin had been injected and, during the day, 'an injection of Caffeine'.

When Mrs Morrell refused to take the regular Allonal tablets, Dr Adams was telephoned and at 7.30 p.m., on his instructions, an injection of ¼ grain morphia, ½ grain of heroin and ¹⁄₁₀₀th grain of atropine given. [atropine – an alkaloid, probably intended to dry the mouth] This injection could be repeated and

> 'on the night of the 7th – we are getting towards the end now – you did give that injection at 3.35 in the morning, did you?'
> 'Yes.'

At 5.30 a.m. the injection was repeated, and, again during the daytime at 4.50 p.m. Dr Adams visited at 7.40 p.m. and increased the morphia content of the injection to ½ grain 'same may be repeated during the night', then, 'if patient does not sleep after 2 hours, the injection may be repeated again.'

> 'The injections are getting more frequent?'
> 'Yes.'
> 'But it is quite clear that the object is to produce sleep for this unfortunate woman, is not it?'
> 'Yes.'

Sister Randall gave an injection at 1.30 a.m. on the night of the 8th November, then at 3.30 a.m. At 6 a.m., Mrs Morrell was 'very chatty, but confused. Asked for sherry'. By 8.30 she was 'getting irritable and aggressive' and Sister Randall gave another injection 'no sound sleep since 1 a.m.'. She slept during the day and at 4.30 p.m. she managed to sit in a chair for eight minutes. '…there is no record of any injection having been given until the evening?' It hardly seemed a question, but Sister Randall retorted:

'Because she had it at 8.30 in the morning.'

Mr Lawrence moved his chess-piece back.

Mrs Morrell was 'alert and talkative' that evening. At 7.40 p.m. she was visited by Dr Adams and given a hypodermic injection of 'hyperduric [longer-acting] morphia half grain, with heroin a half grain'. Mr Lawrence confirmed with Sister Randall that this hyperduric morphia always came in ampoules. No, it could come in bottles, but not in tablets which had to be dissolved in water. 'May have the same injection repeated S.O.S.' Sister Randall's report for the night of the 9th noted that the patient had slept until 1 a.m. when she was 'wide awake, alert & fidgety',

'Quite the opposite of anything like a coma, is not it?' enquired Mr Lawrence.
'Yes.'

At 1.40 a.m. Sister Randall gave an injection of half grain morphia, half grain heroin and $\frac{1}{100}$th of atropine; at 4.30 a.m. she noted: 'Cough troublesome & patient very talkative' and at 4.45 gave her half a grain of morphia and half a grain of heroin. In the morning Mrs Morrell was 'Very chatty but muddled in mind'. Sister Bartlett's day report described great confusion 'Wanted to dress and go out – dressed in fur coat & hat – Patient sat out in chair for nearly an hour'. At 2 p.m. 'Visited by Dr again – special injection given – Asleep 2.10 p.m… he will call this evening.' At 2.30 p.m. Mrs Morrell was 'wide awake'. This was the day that Sister Mason-Ellis had recorded 'the chicken soup and queen pudding with ice cream, and Dr Adams leaving the tablets for future use'.

When Sister Randall came on duty that evening of 9th November, Mrs Morrell was 'awake, confused and talkative' and visited at 10.15 p.m. by Dr Adams, who gave an injection of hyperduric morphia.

'Then', said Mr Lawrence, 'he evidently gave you the direction that she was to have a grain of heroin S.O.S.?'
'Yes.'

Mrs Morrell then slept for 6½ hours and at 4.15 a.m. on the 10th, Sister Randall gave an injection of one grain of heroin. By 5.15, she was awake and given 'milk, brandy and phenobarbitone; dozed quietly, occasionally opening eyes wide and staring round the room' and at 6.30

a.m. Sister Randall administered another injection of one grain of heroin. Phenobarbitone at 7.40 and Dr Adams came at 8 a.m. and injected '½ grain hyperduric morphia' and the patient was asleep again. She was still 'confused but has appeared restful [sic]'

Mr Lawrence wanted to make the point that the direction from Dr Adams was that the patient was not to have the injections 'in any event' but only 'if necessary' or 'S.O.S.'

10th November and by 8.15 p.m. Mrs Morrell had become 'very restless' and was given another grain of heroin. Dr Adams visited at 10.30 p.m. and gave her an injection of hyperduric morphia. She slept well, but then was awake from 3.45 a.m. [11th November] 'very alert and wild-eyed' and Sister Randall gave her one grain of heroin at 4.50 a.m. 'She gives a sharp cry at every touch or movements, twitchings very pronounced', read Mr Lawrence. At 6 a.m. Sister Randall gave another injection of a grain of heroin; 7.30 a.m. and the patient was 'restless and confused'. Dr Adams arrived at 8.15 a.m. and he gave her some more hyperduric morphia, following which, she slept until 12.30 p.m. The Doctor called again 'Patient may have hypodermic injection morphia ½ plus heroin ½, hourly if necessary'. There followed an injection at 1 p.m., another at 2.40 p.m. Mrs Morrell was still awake, 'quiet until 4.30 p.m., then restless and becoming excited' and was given another injection. At 7.15 p.m. Dr Adams visited, giving her 'A grain of morphia and a grain of heroin'.

Mr Lawrence came to Sister Randall's report for the night of 11th/12th November: Dr Adams called at 10.45 and gave an injection of half grain of morphia and heroin. Mrs Morrell was awake at 12.30 a.m. and became 'fidgety and talkative' by one o'clock.

> 'That is not a coma, is it?'
> 'No, sir.'
> 'Or anything like it?'
> 'No.'

At 2 a.m. the patient was not sleeping, 'more wakeful, crying out at times' and Sister Randall gave her half a grain of morphia and half a grain of heroin. At 3 o'clock, she was 'still chattering, more wakeful and jerky' and at 3.40 Sister Randall injected another grain of heroin. By 6 a.m. she was 'quieter. Dozing and whispering to herself'. She became 'violently agitated if asked to have a drink…' There was no coma. Mr Lawrence became aggressive:

> 'What do you say? Do you agree with me or do you not?'
> 'I do agree, yes.'
> 'That is the night of 11th/12th. And the movements that you are describing or are described – just follow this – by the use of the word 'jerky' at 3 o'clock in the morning; you see?'
> 'Yes.'
> 'And that is the whole time when the word 'jerky' is used throughout the whole night; do you see that?'
> 'Yes.'

The Attorney-General could not hear, 'If she could keep her voice up, it would be easier.'
Mr Justice Devlin was more sympathetic:

'Will you try and keep your voice up. I expect you are getting very tired, Miss Randall – '

Mr Lawrence was on to the day report for the 12th November, the last full day of Mrs Morrell's life. She awoke at 9 a.m., and Dr Adams visited at 11.15 p.m, giving a 'special' injection. At 2.35 p.m. 'hyperduric morphia, half a grain of heroin and morphia each, quiet but not asleep'. He delicately alluded to 'H.N.P.U', suggesting that the patient's kidneys were no longer working and that 'what follows is characteristic of the last stages of senile deterioration'. Sister Randall agreed. At 5.35 p.m. Sister Mason-Ellis gave a repeat injection. At 7.30 Dr Adams came and '2 c.c. of Paraldehyde is recorded as having been given intramuscularly with no effect'. At 8 p.m. Mrs Morrell was awake. The Doctor was to visit again at 10.30 p.m.

Mr Justice Devlin asked Sister Randall:

'What is the normal dose of paraldehyde, do you know?'
'It depends how you give it, your highness. [sic]'
She thought 'four or five c.c.' would be a very large dose' and 2 c.c. 'quite small'.
'Is it a dangerous drug, Paraldehyde?'
'No, It is given to help make people sleep often'.
(Now used rarely, usually for epilepsy as it is an anti-convulsant; many drugs and alcohol contra-indicated with it.)

Mr Lawrence, of course, challenged her answers and knowledge. She admitted she had been confused – she had not seen it since Mrs Morrell's case.

'You have not what?'
'I have not seen it since Mrs Morrell's case.'
'You have not had any experience of it?'
'No.'

He pointed out that the British Parmacoepia full dose, whether given by mouth or intra-muscular injection was 120 minims or 8 c.c.

'Do you know that?'
'No.'
'Of course not. Well, you cannot be expected to know these things. There is only 2 c.c. recorded as having been given, you see?'
'Yes.'

Mr Justice Devlin adjourned the court.

# The Homicide Act 1957

The first move towards the abolition of the death penalty in England was in 1808 when Samuel Romilly introduced reforms to abolish hanging for some of the two hundred offences under the 'Bloody Code'. Between 1770 and 1830 around 35,000 people were condemned to death in England and Wales; most were reprieved by the royal prerogative of mercy, but even so, some 7,000 were hanged.[1] The beginnings were modest and the pressure for reform was a result of the 18th Century Enlightenment philosophers' consideration of the criminal codes and punishment in Europe and America. The Code of England was thought particularly brutal. By the early years of the 19th Century, there was considerable reluctance to prosecute people for petty crimes which would result in a death sentence and if they were prosecuted the juries displayed reluctance to convict. Changes in the law followed on what was happening in practice. This increasing sensibility and squeamishness of the middle classes resulted in the abolition of the spectacle of public execution in 1868.

The abolition of public execution almost inevitably meant that the abolition of the death penalty itself would follow. 'What we now construe as meaningless cruelty was integral to the symbolic display of the sovereign's might.'[2] The sovereign's power was also expressed in the role of the 'King in Council' considering whether to exercise the prerogative of the 'King's Mercy' in cases where convicted prisoners had been sentenced to death. The inexorable progress towards abolition and changing sensibilities became very apparent in the behaviour of King George IV (also Prince Regent) when he agonised and pleaded with his Council for reprieves for many of those sentenced to be executed. He would send for his Home Secretary, Sir Robert Peel in the middle of the night, in floods of tears over particular cases. As capital crimes reduced so the role of the 'King in Council' gradually fell into desuetude – also with the powers of the monarchy reverting to the Government, in the person of the Home Secretary. Before Queen Victoria came to the throne, the mercy of the monarch was purely symbolic. Equally, there was no longer the necessity to demonstrate the power and justice exercised by the monarchy.

Attitudes in Britain were changed by the Second World War, particularly by the Holocaust of Nazi Germany, although the move towards abolition had begun earlier when a Commons

[1] Gatrell  /  [2] Ibid

vote in 1938 called for legislation to abolish hanging in peacetime for a five-year experimental period. In April 1948 the House of Commons voted in favour of Labour M.P. Sidney Silverman's Bill to suspend the death penalty for five years. The Labour Home Secretary, James Chuter-Ede, announced that he would reprieve all murderers until the future of the Bill was resolved, which resulted in twenty-six reprieves by 2nd December 1948. The House of Lords rejected the Bill late that year and the Government set up a Royal Commission to examine all aspects of capital punishment. This Report, published in 1953, led to some slight improvements in procedure, including compulsory psychiatric examination and electro-encephelograph of the brain of all persons accused and convicted of murder.[3] It made little difference, except to those being hanged.

Nevertheless, there were a surprisingly large number of murderers hanged in the ten years following the end of the War: 151, including five women. There was a great deal of press interest in murder trials in the 1940s and 1950s, and in much more detail than is usual today. Naturally, there was more drama involved because of the death penalty, and considerable speculation as to whether there would be a reprieve. There were petitions for reprieve in many of these cases. Three cases in particular caused enormous concern, with the public as well as in Parliament. Timothy Evans was hanged on 9th March, 1950 for the murder of his daughter; he was also charged with the murder of his wife. Two years later, it was discovered that John Christie, his landlord, had murdered four more women, whose bodies were discovered in the same house, 10, Rillington Place, Notting Hill and it was clear that an innocent man had been hanged. The second case was that of Derek Bentley, aged nineteen, who had learning difficulties; he was hanged January, 1953. I, aged ten, and practically the whole nation, saw this as totally unjust as he not only had not killed the policeman, but was under arrest at the time. The murder was committed by Christopher Craig, who was only sixteen, and could only be detained 'During Her Majesty's Pleasure'. Nobody understood why the Home Secretary, Sir David Maxwell-Fyfe did not reprieve Bentley and how he managed to live with that decision. This execution, more than any other, swayed public opinion against capital punishment. The third case, two years later, was that of Ruth Ellis, sentenced to death for the murder of her boyfriend. There were mitigating circumstances which did not come to light at the time, but she was also only twenty-eight, blonde, attractive, and a mother of two children. It was a crime of passion, which in France would only have attracted a minimal prison sentence, but she went to the gallows on July 13th, 1955, the last woman to be hanged in Britain. Anyone who remembers it will know that the public did not want it to happen or to have any more executions. Gwilym Lloyd-George, the Home Secretary, would not reprieve her.

In November, 1955 Sidney Silverman introduced the Death Penalty (Abolition) Bill and it was passed by the House of Commons in February 1956. During its passage the Home Secretary, Gwilym Lloyd-George reprieved all those condemned: forty-nine people. The House

---

[3] Haigh had a 'brain test', done at the Maudsley institute in 1949 and also three psychiatric reports, as did other prisoners, so it was nothing new; the Home Secretary, Chuter-Ede, saw those done on Haigh.

of Lords again blocked the passage of the Bill. There were no executions between the 10th August, 1955 and the 23rd July 1957.

The Homicide Bill was already before the House of Commons when Macmillan became Prime Minister on 9th January, 1957. The Homicide Act 1957 was compromise legislation, which distinguished between different categories of murder. It limited the death penalty to five types of murder: murder committed in the course of, or for the furtherance of theft; murder by shooting or causing explosions; murder in the course of or for the purpose of resisting, avoiding or preventing lawful arrest, or in the course of effecting or assisting an escape from lawful custody; murder of a police officer in the execution of his duty or of assisting him; murder by a prisoner of a prison officer in the execution of his duty or of a person assisting him. The death penalty was also retained for a person who committed a second separate murder on a different occasion from the first.

It was a very unsatisfactory Act because the Government had not sought to find philosophical answers to the questions which were being debated. Did society have the right to take life? Did the system of reprieve distinguish between the degrees of wickedness in the crime? What was the purpose of capital punishment? Should the Home Secretary and faceless officials at the Home Office hold the power of life and death in their hands? There were also the concerns that innocent people might be hanged, and whether it was a humane method of execution. It had always been known that capital punishment was no deterrent to murder yet the Act clearly sought to deter specific types of murderers. These were not those traditionally and culturally thought of as the worst sort – those who committed murder in cold blood with malice aforethought, particularly poisoners.

If Dr Adams had been convicted of the murder of Mrs. Morrell and then of Mrs. Hullett's murder, then he would have fallen into one of the categories of murderer for whom the death penalty was retained under the new Homicide Act. If he had been convicted of the murder of Mrs. Morrell then he would have been liable to the death penalty under existing legislation because the Homicide Act 1957 had not come into operation at the date of his indictment on that charge. If he had been executed, his would have been the first execution since that of Ruth Ellis. The first person to hang under the provisions of the Homicide Act, 1957 was John Vickers on the 23rd July, 1957 – the first anniversary of the death of Mrs. Hullett.

# The Trial – Days 5–8

## 22 – 28 March 1957

## Fifth Day

The cross-examination of Sister Randall by Defence Counsel, Mr Geoffrey Lawrence, continued. He began by again referring to the instruction 'S.O.S' in the nurses' notebooks: the Latin words were *si opus sit*, translated as 'if there be need.' It was 'very much like' the other phrase which nurses used, *pro re nata*.

Mr Lawrence had reached the last night of the record, 12th/13th November, Sunday and Monday: Sister Randall's first entry read: 'Mrs Morrell. Awake, restless' and this was made at around 9 p.m. The next entry at 10.30 p.m. was 'Paraldehyde 5 c.c. given IM [intra-muscular] by Dr Adams'; 11.30 p.m. Very restless no sleep. ; 12.30 a.m. Restless and talkative and very shaky ' – the last two words were underlined twice. At 12.45 a.m. Sister Randall had written: 'Seems a little quieter, appears asleep. Resp. [respirations] 50'. And the very last entry was: '2 a.m. Passed away quietly', followed by Sister Randall's initials.

Mr Lawrence wanted to ask Sister Randall 'about the evidence that you gave about this jerkiness'; she had used the word 'twitchings' in her report of 10th/11th November. Surely, whatever word she had written in her report was the word that best suited the condition of the patient as she saw it at the time? 'Yes, at that time.' It was in the report for the night of 11th/12th November that she had written, after giving Mrs Morrell an injection at 2.10 a.m., at 3 a.m. 'Still chattering, more wakeful and jerky' – the first time Sister Randall had used the word. Then at 3.40 a.m. she had administered another injection of heroin, and noted at 6 o'clock: 'Has been quieter'. Mr Lawrence turned to her report of the last night:

'There is no mention there, is there, from start to finish in your writing of any twitching or jerkiness at all?'
'No, sir, not here.'
'What you told the Attorney-General when he examined you in-chief was, in substance,

this, was not it, that the words 'very shaky' at 12.30 a.m. were meant to include the jerk-
iness?'
'Yes.'
'Do you still say that?'
'I do.'

He pointed out that she had only used the word 'jerky' twice – and both on the night of
11th/12th November – in the whole of the notebooks, but she had not thought it appropriate
when she wrote the notes up just after the patient had died, to use the word, so now if she would
care to look at her record for the night of 26th December, 1949 (Book 3), this showed that she
had written 'Very shaky this a.m.', but this was not underlined, so there was no reference to any
'jerkiness'. 'No, sir.' So 'very shaky' meant exactly what it said? Yes. Mr Lawrence had the report
for 3rd October, 1950 (Book 7) handed to the witness. Again, Sister Randall had written 'Seems
very shaky this a.m.' Earlier in the same report she had noted that the patient 'complained frequently of extreme weakness'. Therefore this description had 'got nothing whatever to do with
twitchings or jerkiness'. The report she had made on 5th October contained the same phrase.
The only difference in the report for the last night, 12th/13th November, was that the words
'very shaky' were underlined. Sister Randall insisted on the difference.

> 'Are you standing there in face of this record made on the last night by you, are you
> standing there and saying, as a trained nurse with 25 or more years' experience, that
> when you wrote those words 'very shaky' and underlined them on the last night report
> they were intended to mean something quite different from what they had meant when
> you had used those very words in your earlier reports?'
> 'Yes, I do. They were more intense.'

The start of a battle: shakiness and jerkiness were 'quite different'; she supposed she had just
written the notes down quickly before she left the house that morning.

> 'You suppose you just wrote it! Let me suggest the reason why you used the same words
> and underlined them. The reason was that you then, six years ago, were describing the
> same condition of shakiness that you had described months before but that it was
> greater in degree but still the same kind of thing. That is the reason, is not it?'
> 'I can only remember how very dreadful they were, the jerks.'

After further contretemps between Defence Counsel and witness, Mr Justice Devlin intervened:

> 'Have you got now, apart from what is written down in the book, a clear recollection in
> your mind of her being jerky an hour and a half before she died?'
> 'I have. I never want to see anything like it again.'

Mr Lawrence turned his attention to the matter of coma:

> 'It is quite obvious on these reports made by you during these last three or four nights
> that Mrs Morrell was not in a coma, is not it?'
> 'She would be in a coma or in a heavy sleep after the injections for a time. Almost like
> a coma.'
> 'A heavy sleep and a coma are not the same thing – '
> 'No.'
> '– from a nursing point of view, are they?'
> 'No.'

If a patient was 'properly described as talkative' she was hardly in a coma; if Sister Randall had described the patient as being 'Not sleeping, seems more wakeful', she surely did not intend to record that she was in a coma. 'No, sir.' But she had told the Attorney-General when he was examining her that Mrs Morrell was 'in and out of a heavy coma'. She had probably meant a 'heavy sleep'. Mr Lawrence pounced: there was 'all the difference in the world between a heavy sleep and a coma from a nursing or medical point of view'. He read out what she had given in evidence on the third day of the trial, when she had the notebooks available in front of her: 'Oh, I should think quite two or three days she was in and out of that sort of heavy sort of coma.' and 'Well, she would be in a coma and then come out gradually and then perhaps go in again. When we had to attend to her she might rouse up a little, and then she would go into a heavy coma again.' Sister Randall said again that she 'must have meant a heavy sleep…' There was a further exchange when Sister Randall retorted:

> '…But having so many drugs she would be so heavily asleep it would be like a coma.'
> 'Did you think I had asked you any question to which that is an answer?'
> 'No, sir.'

Mr Lawrence pointed out that Sister Randall had noted 'Now and again will suck on a swab on forceps' which indicated that she was not in a coma. Sister Randall agreed that this was a sign that there was no coma.

Mr Justice Devlin intervened in a kindly manner:

> 'Well, as I understand your evidence, Nurse Randall, you are saying now that you do not
> think she was in a coma but that she was in a sleep like a coma?'
> 'Yes, my Lord.'

Mr Lawrence did not refer back to the cremation certificate upon which Dr Adams had stated that Mrs Morrell had been in a coma for 2 hours prior to her death, and that he must have discussed the matter with Sister Randall and checked her notes.

Now Mr Lawrence took up the matter of the last injections: Sister Randall had noted that at 10.30 p.m. Dr Adams had given Mrs Morrell an intramuscular injection of 5 c.c. of par-aldehyde. There was no further injection recorded by her. And yet, he flattered her, she had always kept the records 'in meticulous detail'.

'And if this second injection which is not recorded here was given by you – '
'It was.'
'Will you allow me to finish my question – '
'I am sorry.'
' – before you interrupt? If that last injection which is not recorded here was given by you it was the last injection before her death?'
'Yes, sir.'
'And according to your evidence it was an injection with 5 c.c.?'
'Yes.'
'And it was given by you on your own responsibility as a nurse, having failed, if your evidence is right, to get in touch with the doctor?'
'Yes, sir.'

She had given it, but it had been left ready prepared by Dr Adams.

'And within an hour of your giving that injection the patient was dead.'
'She passed away, yes.'

Mr Lawrence suggested that it was hardly conceivable that she would have left such an important injection out of the record, but Sister Randall was not to be moved: it should have been put down but she had to do many things that night. He questioned her memory, but she was adamant that she had given that second injection as Dr Adams had instructed her to do.

Mr Lawrence then asked about her experience of paraldehyde; she had 'very little experience of it'. She knew, however, that it had a very distinctive smell. But, did she know, or did she know now that 'that Sunday, Dr Adams prescribed at the chemists's some paraldehyde for Mrs Morrell?' She had not known but she did now. Paraldehyde was the drug recorded, not only by herself at 10.30 p.m. but also by Sister Bartlett at 7.30 p.m. 'towards the end of the preceding day'. Could she now say that that was not paraldehyde injected. She could not say.

Mr Justice Devlin clarified the matter:

'I have not quite understood that. If Paraldehyde has this distinctive smell, quite apart from what Doctor Adams told you about what he put into the syringe, would you have had any doubt about it at the time?'
'No, I think I would have known. I am sure, I would have known because of the smell.'

Mr Lawrence ascertained that Sister Randall had left the house the following morning at 10 o'clock, having waited an extra hour after her duty time finished for Dr Adams, and when he was not there by that time, she left. As far as the last injection was concerned, she would have waited about three hours before giving it, that is 1.30 a.m. Mr Lawrence told her that she had noted that the patient was asleep at 12.45 a.m. so did she not agree that she must have given the injection before that time? She did. So it was more likely little more than two hours after Dr Adams had given the 10.30 p.m. injection – yes. She thought it was about 11.30 p.m. when she had tried to 'phone Dr Adams, after the patient became 'very, very restless and jerky'. Mr Lawrence said that she had described the patient's condition at that time as 'Very restless. No sleep', not 'jerky'. No, but Sister Randall knew she was, even if she had not put it down in the notebook.

Mr Lawrence now read out evidence that Sister Randall had given on the third day of the trial when examined by the Attorney-General. First of all she had said that Dr Adams had prepared and injected the 5 c.c. syringe at 10.30 p.m. and then, when further questioned, she had said that she had given 'one injection of a 5 c.c. syringe and I took it back to the dining room to the doctor', 'on his instructions' and given the syringe back to him; he had 'refilled it' and 'gave it to me to keep in case the patient was very restless in the night'. Her memory was hardly trustworthy, was it? – 'It appears not to be.' 'But the book is quite clear, isn't it?'

Mr Lawrence asked Sister Randall whether she remembered what drugs had been left over; she couldn't. Nor could she remember about the last strip of paper recording what drugs had been used and what remained; she was just sure it would have been kept with the notebooks.

Now the matter of what was said on that train journey with the other nurses. Sister Mason-Ellis had said that it was Sister Randall who had said 'Don't you say that or you will get me into trouble' – with regard to there being no key to lock the drugs away. She could not think it was her that Sister Mason-Ellis meant and she could not remember saying it; she did not remember whether she said it or not.

Her memory of events was again considered questionable. She could only possibly have said 'alluding to the key, that I would have got into trouble for not keeping a key for the drugs'. But she was saying that Sister Mason-Ellis was wrong and she had no idea why her colleague had said that.

Mr Lawrence now went back to 23rd August, 1950, which was where Sister Randall had recorded that Mrs Morrell was 'very worried over tablets in bottle in drawer beside her bed'; she had watched her unscrew the top of the bottle; very muddled, 'she said she was going to take them so that they would not be taken away'. At 7 a.m. Sister Randall had found them 'loose in bed'. She had not known what the tablets were. Why hadn't she, the night nurse responsible for the patient, taken them away when she first saw them?

'I could not find them, I remember looking for them. But I dare not disturb her.'

Sister Randall had called Dr Adams at 7 a.m. 'because you thought she might have taken some of those [tablets] in the night' – she had.

'When Dr Adams arrived he was very angry with you, was not he, and there was a row with you?'

'No. I never remember that. I have never known Dr Adams to be angry with me. I never remember it.'

Mr Lawrence suggested that the Doctor would have had every reason to be angry – and it can be inferred that Dr Adams had told Mr Lawrence that this 'row' had occurred.

'No, I suppose not, but Dr Adams would not have been.'

There is evidence that Mrs Morrell was a very difficult patient and that some nurses had felt unable to continue nursing her. If there had been a 'row' Dr Adams would probably have had to try and persuade another nurse to come to 'Marden Ash'.

Dr Adams had given Mrs Morrell ½ grain caffein injection when he came 'as a stimulant', said Mr Lawrence, 'to counteract the influence of any extra tablets she had taken. That is the truth, is it not?' Sister Randall supposed so.

This was the same page of the notebook which had had a strip cut out of it. Sister Randall had said to the Attorney-General that she would not cut anything out of a record 'unless I had spelt it wrongly, perhaps, or it was not necessary to put it in.' She really could not account for it being cut out – the straight question as to whether she knew who cut it out was not put to her.

The final matter which Mr Lawrence put to Sister Randall concerned the time when Dr Adams had gone away on holiday, then interrupted it to come back and see Mrs Morrell. Had Mrs Morrell told her that she was going to alter her will and cut Dr Adams out of it?

'Yes, sir, but she was very angry at the time.'

What had actually been said and occurred was not made clear during the trial.

And 'just one other thing', had Sister Randall not received a legacy from Mrs Morrell? Sister Randall had got £300.

The Attorney-General rose to his feet to re-examine the witness. Firstly, he just confirmed with Sister Randall that Mrs Morrell had told her that she was going to cut Dr Adams out of her will before his return from Scotland. He then asked about the entry for the 23rd August where the piece had been cut out of the report: the words 'Treatment given' were 'cut right through' – yes. These words had been in her handwriting? Yes. Sister Randall had gone off duty at 9.30 a.m. and this entry was on the bottom left hand corner of that page; just opposite the '9.30' a piece was cut out.

'You said that writing in green in that – just look at it – was Dr Adams's handwriting?'
'So I have been told.'

She did not remember having seen him make that entry – which was 'rather squashed in' with the piece cut out below it.

The Attorney-General asked whether the reports were for the use of the nurses who were following on from the previous duty. She agreed that they were. So if the patient died, there would be much to do and no nurse following on. 'Well, yes.' He asked what normally happened to 'these exercise books' on the death of a patient. She replied, as before, that they were only for the nurses and that the relatives should not see them as 'it is rather distressing for them'; she might herself keep such notebooks for a while and then destroy them but often they might be 'even torn up the same night'. Sister Randall had made the entries for the last night after the patient's death in this case.

Now Defence Counsel, when he had been asking Sister Randall about September, 1950 and the patient's 'restlessness', put it to her that this was caused by 'the brain lesion from which this poor woman has been suffering as a result of her stroke' and she had answered 'Yes.' But the stroke was in June, 1948; did Sister Randall know whether or not heroin could produce this same condition. She was sure of it, it could also produce 'sweating, a cold sweat, and a slow pulse, and the patient feels ill, even with linctus heroin they do.' And repeated injections of morphia, could they lead to irritability and brain storms? Yes.

The Attorney General now embarked on a rather unfruitful line of enquiry: as to whether occasional incontinence could result from taking drugs because when Mr Lawrence had continually suggested that such symptoms showed that the patient was getting 'senile' and 'going downhill'. She thought very heavy sleep might cause it. Did she know the 'characteristics of the last stages of a person's life when life is drawing to an end due to excessive injections of morphia and heroin?' She did not quite 'get' him. Then she said that they needed 'more injections and just get more heavier sleep and get excited if they do not have it'. She did not really know.

The next attempt by the Attorney-General, to find out why Sister Randall had, in her note for the night of 14th September, written: 'Visited by Dr Harris last p.m. 10.30 p.m. omnopon i [here 'given' was written and crossed out] and H.I. [hypodermic injection]? given'.

'Does this entry indicate that something was given and you did not know what it was…'

Mr Lawrence got to his feet and objected to the way the question had been put; the Attorney-General countered this and continued. Sister Randall replied:

'It is a query whether it was given.'

But she expected it was given.

The Attorney-General now reminded Sister Randall that Defence Counsel had drawn her attention to the fact that she had said that she had only ever given routine injections of heroin and morphia to a patient on Dr Adams' instructions, and then she had had to agree that she had done so on Dr Harris' instructions also. However, did a doctor's partner, acting as locum, usually change a patient's medication?

'Not as a rule unless there is some very definite reason for it.'

Unfortunately, when she was then asked if she could recollect having any other doctor's instructions to administer routine injections of morphia and heroin, she decided she really could not remember.

The Attorney-General marched on: the 28th September, 1950, when Sister Randall had recorded Mrs Morrell having become restless and 'rather collapsed, cold perspiration...' after an injection at 11.30. When he had asked her about it earlier, she said that she had thought it was a 'heroin collapse'. Did she form the opinion that heroin 'did or did not agree with her'?

'Well, I did not think at that time it agreed with her.'
'Why not?'
'Because of this cold perspiration. I had seen it before in patients that had heroin, feeling ill and cold when awakened.'

Had she spoken to Dr Adams about it? She had, but knew that 'he thought I was just not right'. She remembered the conversation but not the night upon which it had occurred. This sort of 'opinion' she would just tell the other nurses rather than enter it in the notebook.

The Attorney-General referred to Defence Counsel's questions and Sister Randall's answers regarding the 'object' of the drug treatment: that this was to keep the patient 'as quiet as you could'. It was. He asked:

'Is that one result of drugging?'
'If she is not kept quiet she would become excited and irritable'.

Neither the question or answer seemed to bear any relationship to each other or the aforegoing. He asked whether the injections had been given to stop the restlessness or for some other reason. Yes, Sir. To stop the restlessness? Yes, Sir.

In Sister Bartlett's report of 9th October, she had noted that the patient was in a 'semi-comatose condition. Lower lip very blue' and she had questioned the possibility of a stroke. The Attorney-General asked Sister Randall her opinion as to what was the difference between 'a heavy drugged sleep' and 'a semi-comatose condition'. She considered it 'very much the same really' but in a semi-comatose condition the patient would 'be able to suck on a swab, but she is unable to swallow.' The sucking would be automatic, though not in a complete coma. There would be no reflexes to light in a comatose condition, nor if the patient were in a deep, drugged sleep. A 'slight difficulty with speech' for a while could be a result of a stroke or of drugging, and Sister Randall agreed that her report for the following night indicated that there was no further such difficulty, and that her report of Mrs Morrell being 'muddled and very heavy to move' was equally consistent with drugging.

The Attorney-General clarified with Sister Randall that, when she gave injections to the patient, these were given on the instructions of Dr Adams; although it was left to her judgement when the instruction was 'S.O.S.', when necessary, the only thing left to her own initiative was in deciding that the patient had reached the stage when the Doctor had said it would be necessary to administer the injection, which was when the patient was restless. He asked Sister Randall whether the very severe constipation which the patient had suffered had been a cause of her restlessness. 'It could be' was the answer, but, surprisingly, he did not relate this to the drugs and abdominal pain.

In Sister Randall's report of 27th October, she had noted that the patient 'still seemed in semi-comatose condition', what had she noticed? Mrs Morrell 'had not reacted to light or anything'. The Attorney-General said that Mr Lawrence had suggested to Sister Randall that the patient 'had not had any heroin during the previous two days', but in fact, had she not noted an injection of morphia, heroin and omnopon was to be given 'after 11.30 p.m. S.O.S.'. She had. He asked Sister Randall whether she had ever had any other doctor, other than Dr Adams or Dr Harris, give her instructions to administer 'heroin or morphia just when you considered it necessary in your own judgement'. Yes, she had. He cannot have expected the answer he received to his next question:

> 'Have you ever had instructions from a doctor, other than Dr Adams and Dr Harris, to administer dangerous drugs such as heroin and morphia when necessary when the patient has not been suffering pain?'
> 'It might be if they are very excitable or to keep them quiet.'

He retreated to 'indistinct speech' in her note for 4th November, but with no better result:

> 'I think you can take it from me (and perhaps my learned friends will) that the only previous entry prior to that of speech being indistinct was the entry to which I drew your attention on the 9th October.'
> 'Yes.'
> 'Would it appear to you, with your experience of strokes, unusual to have indistinctiveness of speech appearing only at such long intervals if there had been a stroke or not?'
> 'No, you do get it.'

Mr Lawrence intervened to say that he had 'turned up the night report of the 24th October, which is in Nurse Stronach's time, and at 5.30 a.m. appears: 'Lay awake very restless and speaking indistinctly'.' The Attorney-General was 'obliged to his learned friend'.

There was the matter of the injections during the last few days of Mrs Morrell's life: Sister Randall had agreed with Defence Counsel that they were 'getting more frequent'. On the night of 9th/10th November, Dr Adams had given a hypodermic injection of hyperduric morphia 1 grain at 10.20p.m., five minutes after he arrived and left instructions 'to have heroin 1 grain S.O.S.'; then Mrs Morrell slept for 6½ hours until 4.10 a.m. Sister Randall thought that 'it must have been a heavy sleep or I would have reported otherwise'. Five minutes after the patient awoke, she had been injected with one grain of heroin, after a 'long period of sleep'. The next entry was at 5.15 a.m. Sister Randall did not really know whether Mrs Morrell had been awake or asleep during this period. The Attorney-General read the report from 5.15 a.m. when the patient was 'Not sleeping, but quiet at times', then: 'Dozed quietly... 6.30 a.m. Hypodermic injection heroin 1 grain given. Dozed for one hour'. Then at 8 o'clock: 'Visited by Dr Adams. Hypodermic injection given, one ½ hyperduric morphia'.

> 'Do you notice there that you have made no entry, in the course of that night when she slept 6½ hours, of any restlessness?'
> 'No. It was doctor's orders to keep her from getting restless, <u>to keep her under as much as we could then at that stage</u>.'
> [The underlining is Hannam's – in manuscript – and 'then at that stage' is doubly highlighted.]

The Attorney-General repeated the last phrase as a question, to emphasise it. When did Dr Adams tell her to do this? 'Probably that night'. What did Sister Randall understand him to mean? Why did she use those words? Mr Lawrence told him not to cross-examine; he said he was not.

> 'What do you mean when you say "keep her under?"'
> <u>'So that she did not come right out from the drug and did not get restless again.'</u>
> [Hannam's underlining]

Sister Randall was asked what exactly she had meant when she had written in the night report for the 10th/11th November, the night before Mrs Morrell died: 'Very alert and wild eyed. 4.50 a.m. H.I. injection heroin gr.i. Gives sharp cry at every touch or movement, twitchings more pronounced'. In particular, the word 'twitchings'.

> 'She would give sudden sharp movements.'
> 'What kind of movements?'
> 'Well, jerky movements.'
> 'You also said in answer to my learned friend about the night of 12th/13th that you could only remember how dreadful they were?'
> 'Yes.'
> 'Had you ever seen anything like that before with any other patient?'
> 'Never, sir.'

Sister Randall had attended many patients who had died as a result of strokes and many who had died of senile decay, but she had never seen such symptoms in any other patient.

Now the Attorney-General had come to the last injection in the 5.c.c. syringe. His 'learned friend' had suggested that it was given on Sister Randall's own responsibility. Mr Lawrence corrected him: he had put it to her that 'it was never done, because her record does not show it, if it was given then it must have been on her responsibility'; that was how he had put it. The Attorney-General asked her directly. She replied:

'It was given to me to give to her if she did not get quiet. I rang up the doctor to find out if it was too soon to give it, and as she was so very restless, the spasms were so intense, I gave it. Mrs Morrell told me that Dr Adams had promised her he wouldn't let her suffer at the end.'

The last sentence was an unexpected bonus.

'I did not ask you that last bit, Miss Randall. If you have any doubt at all as to what happened that night, as to what you did, you will say so. Have you any doubt about that?'
'No, I gave it.'

The Attorney-General had finished his re-examination, and sat down. Mr Justice Devlin now had a few questions for the witness. He attempted to clarify whether there were any rules laid down by the doctor when he instructed that drugs should be given 'S.O.S.' – it was just 'when necessary'. Had Dr Adams ever discussed with Sister Randall what he was giving Mrs Morrell morphia and heroin for?

'Well, we all knew that she was so restless and such an excitable patient that we had to give her something to keep her quiet.'

It was definitely something 'we all knew' – this reason for giving the drugs. Therefore they would just look for the signs of 'restlessness and so on' and then 'exercise their discretion' in giving the drugs.

'But you would not in those circumstances say to yourself, would you, "Well, I don't think heroin is any good for restlessness so I'm not going to give it at all?"'
'No.'
'That was a matter for the doctor's decision?'
'Yes. my Lord.'

Mr Justice Devlin addressed the Attorney-General: was he going to 'invite the jury to say that these last two – or one, whichever, it was – injections of 5 c.c. were given or caused to be given by Dr Adams with intent to cause the death of Mrs Morrell?' The Attorney-General did 'submit that they were given deliberately by Dr Adams and that they accelerated the death of the patient.' He would not elaborate further but his medical evidence would indicate why he had said this.

Mr Justice Devlin reminded Sister Randall that he had already asked her if she knew that these injections were paraldehyde and she had said that she did, but did she remember them also because of the distinctive smell? She did not remember this drug having a distinctive smell at the time. But she must have remembered either because the Doctor told her it was paraldehyde or because she recognised the smell. (She had never seen where it came from or a label) She said she would only have written down the name of the drug if she had been told by the doctor it was paraldehyde. Was the smell of paraldehyde so strong that this would tell her at once it was this drug? Oh, yes. Would she have noticed the absence of the smell? Sister Randall thought it would not smell so strongly if it were in the syringe, but then she would have thought the syringe would have smelt of it. However, there was nothing in her mind to suggest that it was not paradehyde? 'No, my Lord.' She did not think that a dose of 5 c.c. of paraldehyde would be a dangerous dose for anyone 'that had so much sedation'. No-one seems to have thought about the interreaction of drugs. Sister Randall had not remembered what the drug was at all; it was only when she saw the book. Mr Lawrence asked the Judge if he could put a final question: did she know that paraldehyde had this distinctive smell in 1950, 'at the material time'. Yes, she did.

Sister Randall must have been very relieved to withdraw.

The last of the nurse witnesses now took the stand, to be examined by Mr Melford Stevenson: Brenda Doreen Hughes, now married and living in another seaside town, Brixham in Devon – in 1950, Sister Bartlett. She was by far the youngest of the nurses and had only been nursing for fourteen years in 1956.

Sister Hughes had started nursing Mrs Morrell on 22nd August, 1950. She seemed to her, at the time, 'a very ill woman'. On that first day she had recorded that the patient was seen by Dr Adams at 10.30 a.m. 'special injection given' – a regular feature in her reports. Had Dr Adams told her what the injection was? 'No, he did not, Sir.' She had, on one occasion asked him:

> 'I think it was either the second or the third day I was there I saw Dr Adams give an injection in the garden and I did ask doctor then what injection he had given after he left Mrs Morrell and he said "It is" – either a pick-me-up or a pep-me-up, and I cannot remember which.'
> 'In your experience as a nurse, is it usual or unusual for the doctor to tell the nurse what it is that he is injecting into the patient?'
> 'Oh, it is usual.'

Mr Melford Stevenson asked Sister Hughes if Mrs Morrell had ever complained to her of severe pain:

> 'I cannot ever remember her doing so, certainly not severe pains.'

She was, of course, familiar with nursing patients with painful cancer.

Sister Hughes recalled the 23rd September, 1950, which was the time when Dr Adams was on holiday and Dr Harris visited, and Mrs Morrell's reaction:

> 'So far as I can remember, she did not know Dr Adams was going until the day he went and Mrs Morrell was very angry and very upset about it, and in the evening she asked

me to get through to Scotland to Dr Adams for her, and I presume she spoke to Dr Adams. However, she sent me out of the room when I got through to Scotland.'

This nurse is rather more direct with her answers than the other nurses: she is quite sure if she does not remember something, and this makes her replies when she does remember, more valuable. She has no idea of why Dr Harris added omnopon to the injections and no idea what Dr Adams was injecting with his 'special injections'. She had not 'applied her mind to the question of why Mrs Morrell was drowsy during the day' because she 'probably put it down to the fact she had had drugs during the night.'

Sister Hughes was asked about her report of 9th October when she had written that the patient was 'in a semi-comatose condition', and her 'lower lip very blue'. She thought that this was the only time she had seen this particular condition, and she had written '? stroke':

'I should think myself if I put "? stroke", Dr Adams might have suggested that when I rang him. I would not have made that diagnosis on my own.'
'You think he suggested it?'
'He must have done.'

Mr Melford Stevenson turned to the day report for the 9th November when Mrs Morrell had been 'very troublesome and confused. Continually trying to get out of bed'. Then the Doctor had called at 11.30 a.m. 'special injection given by the doctor with no effect'. Sister Hughes jumped in before the question:

'That meant to say that she had the injection but it didn't have any effect on her at all.'

The following question and answer are marked by Hannam.

'It didn't do what?'
'I suppose the doctor gave her an injection to settle her.'

Mr Lawrence got to his feet to object that this was 'a very unusual form of examination-in-chief' and asked his 'learned friend to refrain from any kind of cross-examination' which he had done by putting 'another form of question when not satisfied with the complete answer that has been given.'

Mr Justice Devlin ruled Mr Melford Stevenson's question as admissible.

Mr Melford Stevenson continued with the day report of 10th November, where Sister Hughes had recorded the 'morning special injection' and that the patient was sleeping, then woke up at 6.10 a.m., followed by an injection of one grain of heroin at 6.30. She would only have given this injection on the instructions of the doctor. As to why it was that 'this old lady, being very quiet at 6.10 was given a grain of heroin at 6.30', Sister Hughes could not remember 'I wish I could, sir. I cannot.' Mr Stevenson drew her attention to another injection of a grain of heroin at 8.15 after Mrs Morrell became restless. She could recall nothing about the instruction she had to give this.

After a break during the afternoon of the 12th November, Sister Hughes had come on duty again at 7.30 p.m. and recorded a visit by Dr Adams and 'the administration of 2 c.c. paraldehyde, with no apparent effect'. She could 'vaguely remember something about Mrs Morrell having paraldehyde, but I think the doctor gave this injection.'. Mr Stevenson asked her to carry her mind back to the last two or three days of Mrs Morrell's life; how would she describe her 'condition in relation to this drowsiness; was it more or less drowsy' than her previous condition.

> 'To the best of my knowledge, for the last two or three days of her life she was sort of semi-comatosed. I cannot explain it any other way.'

As to what she attributed this condition to:

> 'Well, I thought myself that she was having a lot of drugs.'

And the patient's movements in those days:

> 'In the last two days of her life – I suppose it was about two days – she had twitching spasms. As far as I can remember, it was about two days; but it is so long ago.'

Sister Hughes said that Dr Adams knew about these spasms as he visited 'in the mornings and evenings, etc.'. On the 12th November:

> 'As far as I remember, Sister Randall 'phoned the doctor, and he came about 10 to half-past, or something like that, and he went to see Mrs Morrell, and then the doctor came out of the dining room and drew an injection which he gave to Sister Randall.'
> 'Can you now recollect what that injection was?'
> 'No, I cannot. I did not ever know what it was.'

She remembered seeing the syringe and thought it was a 5 c.c. syringe. Dr Adams had handed that syringe to Sister Randall, who 'left the room with the syringe'. Sister Hughes did not remember 'anything apart from that' because she was then off duty. She did not recall Sister Randall coming back again, and had then gone to bed. As she had been in the room shortly before Mrs Morrell died, Mr Stevenson asked her whether the 'spasms' had stopped or not:

> 'Well, of course, they stopped a little while before she died, but she did actually have the twitches when I went into the room.'

This was about five or ten minutes before death.

Sister Hughes had stayed in the house until Dr Adams arrived. Mr Stevenson asked if Sister Randall had handed anything to her when she left:

> 'She handed me some drugs which were left over, and, as far as I can remember, it was a phial of morphia and one of heroin or omnopon, <u>but I am not sure about that.</u>'
> [The underlining is Hannam's and the left-hand margin is marked here.]

She had given the two phials to Dr Adams. As for the record of drugs, this was kept in the sideboard drawer with the drugs and she thought it possible that she had torn the last piece of paper up, but could not remember.

> 'Can you tell us what happened to the report books? Do you know?'
> 'No, I cannot.'
> 'When did you last see them?'
> 'I last saw this report book when Doctor called on the morning of Mrs Morrell's death, and Doctor read the report, naturally. I don't remember seeing the report books after that.'

Mr Geoffrey Lawrence rose to cross-examine the witness with, at first, some unexpected results. He reminded her that she had given evidence before the Eastbourne Magistrates, but had not seen the report books then from the time that Mrs Morrell had died. She had become aware that they had survived when she 'read it in the newspapers' this very week. Was she 'like Sister Mason-Ellis' glad to know that they had survived? She did not know that she had really thought about it. Mr Lawrence had to go on small step by small step till she eventually agreed that utilising the note-books was better than relying upon memory.

Sister Hughes had 'arrived in the closing stages' of Mrs Morrell's illness. She sometimes shared the day duty with Sister Mason-Ellis and she knew Sisters Randall and Stronach, and also recalled another nurse who had come in for a few days: 'I think her name was Methlen, or something like that'. [Methren – there is a general statement from this nurse in the file of statements and see case of Mrs Kilgour]. Mr Lawrence asked if Sister Hughes had ever had experience of one of Mrs Morrell's 'brainstorms'. She had not, but 'she used to be irritable and depressed' and 'very bad-tempered'; she would get herself into one of these 'states' for very little reason and the nurses were 'sometimes the victims of her complaints'.

> 'In fact, these angers and this excitability and irritability and temper was so much that, even during the short time that you were there, on two occasions you had to tell her that you would not go on nursing her, did not you?'
> 'That is true.'

Mrs Morrell had got Sister Mason-Ellis to apologise to Sister Hughes for what she had said and asked her to stay.

Very soon after Sister Hughes had arrived at Marden Ash, Mrs Morrell had said to her: 'I never allow the nurses in the room when the doctor visits me'. Mr Lawrence pressed his point: that it was Mrs Morrell who would say 'You may go' when Dr Adams arrived. Had she asked the Doctor for guidance? Sister Hughes agreed that she had and that Dr Adams had told her that Mrs Morrell was a very difficult patient and that 'it was quite alright'. Was Mrs Morrell 'an autocratic person'? He had to repeat and add 'wanted her own way?' 'Oh, she had a terrific will of her own, yes.', replied Sister Hughes. Mr Lawrence kept attempting to confirm with Sister Hughes that Mrs Morrell had got into 'these states of temper', that the treatment for 'cerebral irritation' was to keep her 'as quiet as possible' and to avoid such states. Sister Hughes had some difficulty with the complicated structure of his questions, but did agree.

Book 7 of the notebooks was handed to the witness, and Mr Lawrence started going through her reports. He pointed out 'special morning capsule discontinued' in the report of 23rd August, the second day of her duty: could she remember what this was? She could not, of course, because she never knew, but the objective was to demonstrate that Dr Adams kept a watch on the drug regime and did not always just add drugs to it. The next report Mr Lawrence referred to, 24th August, Sister Hughes said was not hers, but that of Nurse White [Agnes Stone White – see Chapter 21]; she vaguely remembered that she had come one afternoon and that 'Mrs Morrell more or less dismissed her the same day'. This, however, was not accurate. (It is of interest that this is a nurse who said in her statement that Dr Adams had told her he wished to be alone with the patient. She had other experience of nursing his patients and referred to him as 'a creeper' where rich patients were concerned.)

At this point, Sister Hughes asked if it was permissible for her to take her hat off because she couldn't hear properly with it on. Mr Lawrence asked Mr Justice Devlin, who replied:

'Oh, yes, certainly; and if at an time you find yourself getting tired and want to sit down do so, but as long as you can stand I think your voice carries better.'

Those were the days when it was proper for a lady to wear a hat in court.

Sister Hughes' report for the 25th August began by saying 'A fairly good day on the whole. Seen by Dr Adams this morning and this afternoon. Walked the stairs with Dr Adams and Price. (the chauffeur)' – Just under three months before her death, Mrs Morrell could still manage the stairs with assistance. On 27th and 28th August she was again in the garden. The evening injection at this stage was ¼ grain of morphia and ⅓ grain of heroin. Sister Hughes said she was finding it difficult to recall this period although she remembered the end of Mrs Morrell's illness clearly. On 31st August Nurse White was back again. 3rd September and half a grain of Luminal (phenobarbital) had been added at 2 p.m. The following four days saw the patient walking out in the garden. It was on 8th September that she was very unwell and Dr Adams came and she had '2 Special Tablets given – may have 2 more if diarrhoea persists' and at 12 midday when she was 'very cold and faint' she was given brandy and put to bed. Dr Adams gave her an injection in the evening and she seemed better. By 10th September Mrs Morrell was out in the garden again.

Mr Lawrence asked Sister Hughes to speak up as he was 'a little deaf' and it would be 'all the better for the ladies and gentlemen of the jury'. He had got to the point where Dr Adams had gone on his holiday to Scotland and Dr Harris came in morning and evening on 10th September. Dr Harris gave Mrs Morrell an injection of 1 c.c. Coramine [heart stimulant] at 5.30 p.m. She had had the 'special capsule' at 11 a.m., one tablet of Luminol at 11.30 a.m. and half a Dover's tablet [opium] for 'abdominal discomfort' at 6 p.m., and then the 'usual' injection at 8.30 p.m. In her report for 12th September, Sister Hughes had recorded 'opium pill' and Mr Lawrence questioned her about this: it was probably the Dover's tablet she had meant. He then suggested that any 'special tablet' could be traced back through the notes in this way and identified from a previous report! Or that it could be matched to a contemporary prescription from the chemist's registers; trying to remove suspicion from the mysterious 'special' injections and 'special' capsules and tablets.

Mr Lawrence again wandered into the mire with Sister Hughes, having asked about a 'special injection and amp. i': it did not say what the ampule was.

'No, but she appeared to be having them all the time, each morning.'
'This is in the morning, certainly – '
'I see she has been having them each morning since I arrived.'
'…Well, your note does not record what was in the container, does it?'
'…Well, if I have not got it down, Doctor did not tell me it.'

Mr Lawrence tried to get a word in edgeways, but Sister Hughes was not to be stopped:

'If you will excuse me, sir, I think I have made a mistake. I think that should be capsule or tablet. I would not put 'Special injection and ampul i given'; it would either be a capsule or a tablet. It is a mistake; I feel sure of that.'

He decided to ask her about Dr Adams mentioning to her that these injections were either 'a pick-me-up or a pep-me-up', did she know from the other nurses that they 'were in fact some sort of vitamin injections'?

She answered unhelpfully:

'No, I cannot honestly say I did.'

Mr Lawrence pointed out that Dr Harris had also, according to her notes, given a 'special injection', that is, an injection that she did not know the content of. That was true and that also was 'unusual'. It was 'usual' for a doctor to inform the nurse of the content of an injection. He went on confirming the entries which Sister Hughes had made.

Mr Justice Devlin intervened: could matters be shortened by 'treating all these entries as being in' so that Mr Lawrence need only refer to 'those which he particularly wants to single out'. Mr Melford Stevenson thought that this 'would be an excellent course'. Mr Lawrence asked if he might take it that all the notebooks were now 'in'. Mr Justice Devlin agreed that this was so.

Mr Lawrence now referred to Dr Harris having given ⅔ Omnopon by injection on 23rd September, and Dr Adams being back from holiday on 24th September and having given the instruction on 25th that the patient should have 'two tablets of Omnopon by injection if necessary'. Sister Hughes agreed that this was the same as 'S.O.S.'. Then to her report of Sunday, 1st October: that Mrs Morrell 'May get up and dress more'. Yes, this would be at the doctor's suggestion. On 3rd and 4th October, she was still sitting up, but became 'very tired'. 'The utmost efforts' were being made 'under Dr Adams' authority to keep Mrs Morrell as mobile and active as she possibly could be'. It seemed so.

On to Book 8, the last notebook, and Sister Hughes' report of 7th October: did she think that the 'special capsule' she had noted might be caffeine to counteract the patient's drowsiness? She could not 'honestly remember'. Then the day of 9th October 'which has attracted some attention in this case':

'"Special capsule and injection given."'

Mr Lawrence continued, with rather obvious intention and somewhat untruthfully,

'That is the usual formula isn't it, that we saw right back to Dr Harris's time?'
'Yes, that is right.'
'…You see "? Stroke?" You say that was the result of something he [Dr Adams] suggested to you on the telephone?'
[The last is heavily underlined by Hannam]
'It is very likely, Sir.'
'You cannot actually remember, can you?'
'No, I cannot, but I don't think I would have put "? Stroke" on my own.'
[This last answer is also underlined by Hannam]

Mr Lawrence continued asking Sister Hughes about strokes and their degrees of severity, difficulty of speech and Mrs Morrell's 'going downhill' and signs of 'restlessness', so that on the 11th and 13th October, she had given some extra injections of ⅔ grain omnopon for this 'restlessness'. She had done so. The Doctor had instructed her on 15th October, not to give the routine injection whilst the patient was asleep, but to wait for her to wake up. This was true. It enabled Mr Lawrence to point to some days where Sister Hughes as 'day nurse' had not given any injection as the injection had not been given during the day. There were some slight improvements and some indications of what overtook 'old people towards the end of a senile illness' – not just those on morphia and heroin. Sister Hughes agreed with it all.

Sister Hughes had had a few days off and returned on 4th November when she found that the injections were now ½ grain heroin; she gave one of these at 8.40 p.m. On 6th November, she recorded Mrs Morrell as being 'very confused and depressed this evening – continuously pulled blankets onto floor etc. and has been crying' and that Dr Adams' instructions were 'May have heroin ½ grain repeated S.O.S.'. She had also recorded the content of an injection given by Dr Adams: Caffeine and Atropine. Mr Lawrence made much of this unusual occurrence.

Mr Justice Devlin here adjourned the trial, for the weekend, until Monday, 25th March.

# Sixth Day

Mr Justice Devlin began by asking Sister Hughes if she would try and speak as loudly as she could and also turn round towards the jury.

Mr Lawrence continued with the day report for 6th November, which now proved to have been mistakenly dated '7th'. She had recorded this injection of caffeine and atropine at 10.50 a.m.; he asked about the way in which atropine was supplied. Sister Hughes had only seen it in little tablets in a tiny glass phial, similar to the heroin and morphine. Later that day, when the patient was very restless, sleepless, and 'refusing Allonal' [analgesic sedative and hypnotic], she had 'phoned Dr Adams and been instructed to give an injection of ¼ grain morphia, ½ grain of heroin and $\frac{1}{100}$th of atropine, which could be repeated 'S.O.S.'. Mr Lawrence went on to the reports of the next day, again with the purpose of emphasising the atropine content of injections. [Atropine is an alkaloid found in nightshade *Atropa belladonna*, synthesized in the laboratory. It is used to help restore or control heart function as it would cause increase in heart rate, and, in combination with other drugs, to treat other health problems, including diarrhoea and excessive salivation. It may cause amnesia, confusion and excitability in the elderly. It is used as a pre-med. in anaesthesia.]

'So that was two more atropine. That brings us to eight tablets. Do you see at 8.30 a.m. she [Nurse Randall] has put down, 'Getting irritable and aggressive'?'
'Yes.'
'Well, of course, that was exactly the state of the patient which the policy was to avoid if possible, was not it?'
'Yes.'

By the 8th November, the regular evening injections given by the nurses was increased to ½ grain morphia, ½ grain heroin and $\frac{1}{100}$th grain of atropine. There was linctus heroin for the patient's cough. By that evening the hyperduric [longer-action] morphia ½ grain is injected by the Doctor, and ½ grain heroin at 7.40 p.m., which was to be 'repeated as last night S.O.S.'. 'With good effect' meant that it had a 'good sedative effect' on Mrs Morrell, which was the policy? Yes. At 1.40 a.m. on 9th November the last of the morphia, heroin and atropine injections was recorded – the tenth by Sister Randall – Mr Lawrence asked Sister Hughes to 'take it from him' that this was correct.

When Sister Hughes came on duty on the morning of Thursday, November 9th, Mrs Morrell was 'troublesome and confused, continuously trying to get out of bed'. This was the day on which she had recorded that, after the doctor came and gave a 'special injection', Mrs Morrell 'dressed in fur coat and hat' and sat out in a chair for nearly an hour. Mr Lawrence asked if 'this sort of thing' often happened with patients who were 'senile' and had 'brain lesions as a result of a stroke'. Of course, that was so.

Sister Hughes had come on duty again on the morning of November 10th when Mrs Morrell was asleep from 9 a.m. to 1.40 p.m. The Doctor had visited in the morning and left the 'special injection' ready for her to give to the patient, and she had administered it at 1.45 p.m. Her instructions from Dr Adams were also that 'patient may have heroin gr. 1 hourly if necessary'. At 6.10 p.m. Mrs Morrell was 'wide awake but very quiet' and at 6.30 p.m. Sister Hughes gave her a grain of heroin. Then 'Patient has been awake. She has had slight jerkiness of the body and has given out a cry each time'. At 8.15 when the onset of restlessness was recorded, Sister Hughes injected a further ½ grain of heroin.

On the 11th November, after some confusion with the copies of the notebooks, Sister Hughes confirmed that, in the original, she had recorded: 'Doctor called this a.m. Patient may have hypodermic injection of morphia gr. ½ with heroin gr. ½ hourly, if necessary' and that at 1 p.m. she had 'resorted to that injection' and again at 2.40 p.m. Sister Mason-Ellis relieved her at 4.45 p.m. and she gave another injection. Sister Hughes was back at 6.30 p.m. and noted that the Doctor visited at 7.15 p.m. and gave an injection of 'a grain of morphia and a grain of heroin'. By 7.30, the patient was asleep. Then Mr Lawrence makes what is clearly a mistake when he says: 'There we are on the 11th. There is plainly no injection of any kind recorded on that day, is there?' – with automatic agreement this time by Sister Hughes.

Mr Lawrence passed on to the next day's report, that of Sunday, November 12th, the last day of Mrs Morrell's life. Sister Hughes had come on duty at 9 a.m., after an early morning visit by the Doctor. The patient was awake, the Doctor visited again at 11.15 a.m., gave a 'special injection' and Mrs Morrell went to sleep for two hours from 11.30 a.m. and, when she awoke, was 'restless and talkative'. At 2.35 p.m. Sister Hughes gave her an injection of ½ grain of hyperduric morphine and ½ grain of heroin and she was then quiet but not asleep. Sister Mason-Ellis came in at 5.30 p.m. as day relief nurse and administered the usual milk and brandy and a repeat injection of the hyperduric morphine and heroin. Mr Lawrence pointed out that there was no mention of any coma up to this time and did Sister Hughes observe that neither nurse had 'made any record on that day of any twitchings or jerkyness'? She did.

When Sister Hughes came back on duty that day at 7.30 p.m., her first record was 'Visited by Doctor. Paraldehyde 2 c.cs. given I.M. (intramuscular)'. Mr Lawrence asked, almost rhetorically:

'It [paraldehyde][1] is an old fashioned well established remedy for sleeplessness, isn't it?'
'Yes.'
'And it is generally regarded as one of the safest soporifics to use?'
'Yes, it certainly hasn't an effect like morphia or any of those.'

Mrs Morrell had been still awake when Sister Hughes went off duty at 9 p.m. 'That is right.' Did Sister Hughes ever think that the 2 c.c. injection was not Paraldehyde?

'I am being quite honest, I do not remember this Paraldehyde being given.'

But if she had put it down in the report, then the Doctor must have given it. Mr Lawrence returned to her reply to Mr Melford Stevenson when she had said: 'I can vaguely remember something about Mrs Morrell having Paraldehyde, but I think the doctor gave this injection.'

'Oh, did I, Sir?'

Mr Lawrence asked Sister Hughes about Dr Adams' visit at 10.30 that evening: her recollection was not too clear about that? Oh, but it was, she was 'quite clear about the doctor coming'. She had not been on duty, but as she was sleeping at the house, she was in the dining room – which was really the nurses' sitting room – and as she had said in her evidence on the previous Friday 'The doctor went to see Mrs Morrell, and then the doctor came out of the dining room and drew an injection which he gave to Sister Randall'. It was a few minutes after 9 o'clock when she went off duty, after 'doing the patient' together with Sister Randall. She had not gone back into the 'sick room' until five or ten minutes before the patient died, and she had been present at the death.

The next morning, after Mrs Morrell's death, Sister Randall had left the house before Dr Adams arrived, so Sister Hughes had been left in charge. She had handed over to Dr Adams two phials, one of morphia and the other was heroin or omnopon. She was sure about that. Mr Lawrence wanted to know what had happened to the atropine: he suggested that as Browne's the chemist had dispensed a prescription for 20 tablets of $\frac{1}{100}$th grain of atropine on 6th November, there must have been ten of these tablets left over. Where were they? If they had been with the nurses' drugs, then 'any drugs left over are handed back to the doctor.' Sister Hughes had no recollection of them.

> 'I dare say, but we are interested to know what happened on this particular occasion in this particular case.'
> 'Yes, but I don't remember about the atropine.'

The atropine had actually been dispensed on 6th November and that same morning at 10.50 a.m. Dr Adams had injected some atropine into the patient. As he lived just around the corner from Browne's the Chemist, he often collected drugs from them himself and it seems likely that

---

[1] *Black's Medical Dictionary* – clear, colourless liquid with a penetrating ethereal odour, it may be given by mouth, rectally, or occasionally in intramuscular injection. The drug's prime use is as an hypnotic in mentally unstable patients and has been used in the treatment of alcoholism. It is also indicated as an anticonvulsant in epilepsy and tetanus. Other sources (USA): indications are for sedation, seizures. It *adds* to the effects of alcohol and central nervous system depressants, e.g. narcotics, barbiturates. Toxicity: disagreeable taste and odour, local irritation, pulmonary oedema, haemorrhage, hypertension. It has now mainly been replaced by safer medicines. Maximum dose (1995) was 5 c.c.; in 1957 it was 8 c.c.

he did this on this occasion as he was calling on Mrs Morrell. The drugs would, in that case, have been kept in his bag.

Mr Lawrence pressed his case: Sister Hughes had said that 'it was quite possible' that she had torn up the piece of paper with the record of the drugs which the nurses kept. It was possible but she did not remember. She had stayed on at the house and left on the afternoon that Mrs Morrell's body was cremated, on 15th November, and she had seen Mrs Morrell's son when he came down. She remembered Dr Adams coming on the Monday morning, the 13th, and Dr Fox arriving. Sister Hughes had been the nurse they interviewed about the circumstances of death.

Mr Lawrence was 'sorry to have troubled you so much, Mrs Hughes' and thanked her.

Mr Melford Stevenson began his re-examination of the witness. Sister Hughes had been asked 'a number of questions about the policy in regard to Mrs Morrell'. She had some difficulty understanding the question, and after a couple of attempts, he managed to put the question more clearly: did Dr Adams ever tell her the reason why he was administering the various drugs to Mrs Morrell?

> 'Well, I cannot remember the doctor sort of telling me. (After a pause:-)
> Why she should have these drugs?'
> 'Yes.'
> 'Because Mrs Morrell was so very highly-strung and aggressive and – oh dear! I don't seem to be able to find words. May I have a glass of water?'
> 'Yes.'
> ' – and so very difficult, etc.; that is why she was having the drugs, to keep her quiet.'

Mr Justice Devlin tried to elucidate the matter: Sister Hughes could not actually remember Dr Adams expressing that idea to her, but it was 'the understanding'. Mr Stevenson asked her about her nursing experience 'quite outside this case': had she ever been required to administer a mixture of heroin and morphia together, to a patient who was not suffering pain? No she had not.

Sister Hughes was asked about the 'special injection' which the Doctor had left for her on Friday, 10th November, as Mrs Morrell was asleep when he called; she had injected this at 1.45 p.m. She had said previously that, on only one occasion, had she asked Dr Adams what a special injection was, but he had just said it was a 'pick-me-up' or 'pep-me-up'. Yes, on only one occasion; she did not remember enquiring on the 10th November, neither did she recall what kind of syringe it was in as she didn't remember giving it at all.

> 'Why, in fact, did you give that injection at 1.45 p.m.?'
> 'Well, the only thing I can think, sir, is that there was an instruction left from the doctor which I omitted to put in the report.'

Mr Stevenson sat down, and Mr Justice Devlin questioned the witness on behalf of the Court. Could Sister Hughes remember giving Dr Adams the syringe when she gave back the drugs left over. She could not, but she might have done. When the doctor injected drugs himself, where had he got the supply from?

> 'I know he did not get them from the supply on the tray, sir, because I used to wait in the dining room for Doctor to come out again.'
> 'And the tray would be with you?'
> 'Well, the sideboard drawer was in the dining room and I used to sit in the dining room so that I could see Doctor come out of the patient's room, so that I know Doctor didn't get it from the dining room, from the drawer.'

Mr Justice Devlin made sure that the matter was made doubly clear by asking twice more. Sister Hughes replied:

> 'I have never seen Doctor use that tray to my knowledge. Doctor had his own, as far as I can remember – his own equipment.'

How had the supply of drugs arrived for the nurses' tray: they were given to her by the chauffeur. Did they keep any reserve supplies of drugs? No they did not; the procedure was to ask the doctor for a new prescription when a phial was 'going down'.

A final question:

> 'On these occasions when Mrs Morrell sent you out of the room, about how long did the doctor stay in the room with her alone?'
> 'Usually the doctor was there about a quarter of an hour each morning.'

Sister Hughes withdrew, and Mr Malcolm Morris asked if the evidence of Harry Gibson could be read; he had been 'conditionally bound over', to be called if necessary. The Clerk of the Court read his deposition. Harry Gibson was the van driver employed by Browne's the Chemist. During the months of January to November 1950 he had made deliveries to Marden Ash, 'three or four times a week' and handed the parcels of various kinds on behalf of his firm, to 'female members of staff' at the house. He also stated (relating to the Hullett case) that he had delivered similar parcels to Kent Lodge, 'addressed to the accused or to members of his staff' between March and July, 1956. Cross-examined, Mr Gibson said that it was a full-time job to deliver to premises all over Eastbourne and 'had been for years'. However, his job was 'simply to deliver the goods'.

Mr Morris now asked for the evidence of Ethel Julia Dockerill to be read. Mrs Dockerill had been employed as a 'daily domestic help' by Mrs Morrell for about three years. Her duties included the cleaning of Mrs Morrell's bedroom. She remembered when Mrs Morrell had returned home from the nursing home and stated that 'from that time onwards the accused called in the mornings.' She was not on duty during the afternoons. From 'time to time' she talked to Mrs Morrell and she 'did not at any time complain to me of suffering pain'. 'On the day before Mrs Morrell died I went into her bedroom and saw her. She laid there with no movement at all. Two days before that occasion I saw Mrs Morrell. This would be on the Wednesday. I spoke to her and she was able to talk to me.' When she had helped to lift Mrs Morrell with the nurses she had not noticed anything wrong with her arms at all and 'she used to put her arm round me when being lifted.'

The next witness to be called was Mr Thomas Price, who had been Mrs Morrell's chauffeur for three years and seven months before her death. He had driven her 1938-39 Rolls Royce, '25 horse-power'; strangely, he did not know the name of the model. Mr Price had taken Mrs Morrell from the nursing home to the Cumberland Hotel in Eastbourne and then to her house, 'Marden Ash', where she had lived until her death. He knew that Dr Adams had called 'every day except when he was on holiday'.

Mr Morris asked Mr Price whether Mrs Morrell 'got up, at any time'. 'More or less every day'; he had assisted her in 'getting about'. In the summer, when the weather was nice, she would go into the garden: 'I would take her in her wheeled chair in the garden and then I would walk around with her on the lawn; or indoors I would take her in the lounge and we would prob-ably walk around three or four times.' He meant by this that when she walked, he would 'take hold of the right-hand side, the right arm, sir, and the doctor would be on the left.'

As to the prescriptions, the nurses would give them to him and he would take them down to H.R. Browne's the chemists, and usually he would collect the medicines later, bring them back and give them to the nurse on duty. He would do this about two or three times a week. Mr Price had last seen Mrs Morrell about ten days before her death; at the time 'She was very agitated'. Mr Morris asked what had happened to 'her Rolls Royce motor-car after her death': Price had taken it to Dr Adams himself. 'Dr Adams came out and we looked at it, sir, and I left it there'.

Mr Lawrence began his cross-examination of Mr Price by asking how long he had stayed at Marden Ash after Mrs Morrell's death; it was about six months, so he had actually started as her chauffeur in about November, 1947. Price recalled going to the Esperance Nursing Home, where she was when she came back from Cheshire after her stroke, and that she had then moved to Miss Easter's nursing home in Grassington Road [Olinda]. He had not helped to move her there, but from the 'Olinda' to the Cumberland Hotel. He used to visit her at the 'Olinda' nursing home. Mr Lawrence asked how much assistance Mrs Morrell had required, 'a great deal'? Yes, definitely: she had to be 'assisted out' of her wheelchair in order to walk.

Mr Lawrence again wished to demonstrate that Mrs Morrell's stroke had been a serious one and also that Dr Adams had attempted to improve her condition. Had Price taken her for drives? 'On three occasions, sir.' One of these was the launching of the local life-boat in the summer of 1949. He had 'practically bodily lifted her – well as best as possible', out of the car. Mr Lawrence went quickly from subject to subject: the prescriptions were handed to Price by the day nurse? Yes. When he had described Mrs Morrell as 'agitated', did he mean 'excited'. Yes. Might it have been a few days either side of the ten days he mentioned when he had last seen Mrs Morrell? Yes. The Rolls Royce car, was the body of it 'the Landolette type'. It was a 'seven-seater. Two occasional seats in it.' Was it 'one of those things with a black leather back that sort of open up and went down at the back?' No. It was a 'Limousine, sir, all metal' and black in colour.

Mr Lawrence concluded by asking how much Mrs Morrell had left him under her will; it was £1,000 and a cheque had been handed to him by Mr Claude Morrell.

(Leaving bequests to permanent household staff was a usual practice in those days and was considered to be in lieu of a pension fund, so such bequests were entirely different in nature from others.)

Mr Morris asked that the evidence of Ronald Norman Islip be read to the court. Mr Islip was employed as a funeral assistant by Haines, the Eastbourne funeral directors. His evidence stated that 'On 13th November 1950 I received instructions from the accused to arrange the cremation of Mrs Morrell'. He had removed the body on the 15th November, 'first to a Church in Eastbourne and thereafter to a Crematorium at Brighton'. He had collected the ashes and delivered these to her son, Mr Claude Morrell. Mr Islip identified Dr Adams' signature on Exhibit 2, forms B, C and F of the application for Cremation. Cross-examined, Mr Islip confirmed that Form A had to be signed by either the Executor, or the nearest surviving relative of the deceased and the form had to be completed before a Commissioner for Oaths or a Justice of the Peace. This had been done by Mr Claude Morrell, who was also the Executor of Mrs Morrell's estate.

Mr Morris further asked the Judge if the evidence of Albert Harry Crowhurst could be read. This was very brief: Mr Crowhurst was the foreman furnaceman at the Downs Crematorium, Brighton. He had received the coffin with the name of Edith Alice Morrell on the name plate from Messrs Haines and the cremation was carried out under his supervision and the ashes handed to Haines' representative.

The next witness to take the stand was Mr Richard Steers. He was employed as a removals foreman by John Pring & Co. of Eastbourne. In 1951 he had removed from 'Marden Ash' 'a carved oak cabinet with a pair of carved doors on the front. Inside was the shelves with the silver all lying on them'; he 'took it down to Doctor Adams' House at Kent Lodge, Trinity Trees.' Mr Lawrence had no questions.

Detective Inspector Brynley Pugh was sworn as the next witness. Mr Lawrence addressed the Judge, saying that 'his appearance in the witness box at this stage is something of an embarrassment to me'. He was not expecting him 'for some time' and after the medical evidence. The Attorney-General stated that he had 'furnished his learned friend' with a provisional list of witnesses although he had been 'under no obligation to do so'. He had been going to call Mr Sogno next, but Mr Lawrence had known the order would be changed. Mr Lawrence had not received the information and was not ready for DI Pugh; the Attorney-General did not 'desire to call the doctors' until he had recalled Mr Reid, who was not yet ready. Mr Justice Devlin asked Mr Lawrence if his problem was that he was not ready for police evidence or he wished to cross-examine the principal police witness first. It was both, and he was 'embarrassed' by the 'sudden appearance of this Police Officer in the box today'. The Attorney-General again said that there was 'no obligation on the Prosecution to give the defence any indication of the order in which the witnesses are going to be called'; Dr Harris was not available. However, he was prepared to be helpful to Mr Lawrence, so that he could reserve his cross-examination and let DI Pugh given his evidence-in-chief and perhaps put Mr Sogno in the box after this. Mr Lawrence felt that would help and was 'obliged'.

DI Pugh was with the Eastbourne Borough Police Force, and had his notebook with him which contained notes made after various interviews with Dr Adams. He had gone, with Superintendent Hannam and Detective Sergeant Hewett of the Metropolitan Force, to 'Kent Lodge' on 24th November, 1956; the door was opened by the receptionist and Dr Adams 'came from a room on the first floor, down the stairs into the hall'. Superintendent Hannam greeted him and the Doctor said: 'Yes, Mr Hannam?' The Superintendent then 'asked the accused if we could go into the surgery where we could talk in private' and 'the accused made a remark then before we went into the surgery. He said: "There is no question of a statement, for I have been told not to make one."' They then went into the surgery and 'there was a conversation between the accused and Superintendent Hannam, and then the Superintendent said to the accused: "There is something I must tell you immediately. I have here a warrant issued by a Magistrate directing Detective Inspector Pugh to search this house under the Dangerous Drugs Act."' The warrant was then 'read over to the accused'.

The warrant, marked 'Exhibit 50' was then read out in court by the Attorney-General. The magistrate who signed it was 'E.M. Collis'. After the warrant had been read out by Hannam, the accused had said 'There are no dangerous drugs here. What do you mean by "dangerous drugs?"' The Superintendent had made no comment. 'I then saw the accused walk up to a built-in cupboard on the right-hand side of the fireplace and he opened one of the cabinets there, turned round to the Superintendent, and said: 'I have quite a bit of barbiturate here. Is that what you mean?' The Superintendent replied: – '

Mr Geoffrey Lawrence interrupted; he wanted to make a submission to the Judge, and without the jury present.

Mr Justice Devlin addressed the jury: this was clearly on the admissibility of evidence and they should retire to the custody of the bailiff during the discussion.

He asked Mr Lawrence if he wanted the witness to be present. He did not, and the witness left the box.

Mr Lawrence submitted that the evidence of DI Pugh concerning the warrant and the police visit to Dr Adams' house on 24th November, 1956, which would also be in the evidence of Superintendent Hannam and DS Hewett, concerned another charge relating to the keeping of a Dangerous Drugs Register, and not with the charge of the murder of Mrs Morrell and was therefore inadmissible 'until this particular officer says that he was given an instruction to perform other duties outside the surgery' and there was 'a further matter' which concerned all the evidence of DI Pugh until his going to Kent Lodge on 19th December when Dr Adams was arrested on the charge of the murder of Mrs Morrell. The other evidence was 'of a prejudicial nature' and should be excluded in order to 'secure that there should be a fair trial on this indictment'. There had 'been enough and more than enough, if I may say so, in the past' of 'extraneous matters' which were prejudicial to his client.

The search warrant and what DI Pugh had done with it, were events which occurred in

November of 1956, relating to the failure to keep a register and complying with the Dangerous Drugs Act at that date, without any reference to the alleged crime of murder in 1950, which could neither prove or disprove that alleged crime, not being related to Mrs Morrell in any way. There was evidence about what was in his client's medical bags in 1956, six years after Mrs Morrell had died. There was some evidence in Superintendent Hannam's statement which was 'in a different category altogether' because it related directly to Mrs Morrell and took place in the absence of DI Pugh; Mr Lawrence mentioned this because it 'pointed out the contrast' in evidence. He said that, 'in his submission this is peculiarly a case in which evidence should be admissible only if there is no doubt whatever about its relevance'. In the case of this particular evidence 'its prejudicial effect may quite outweigh the tiny and... negligible quality of admissibility'.

The Attorney-General 'reminded his Lordship' that when he had opened the proceedings he had referred to the police search of 24th November and the evidence which related to Dr Adams responding to the caution by saying 'There are no dangerous drugs here. What do you mean by dangerous drugs', and going to the cupboard, opening it and saying 'I have quite a lot of barbiturates here. Is that what you mean?'. And when he was told 'Morphine, heroin, pethedine and the like', he had then said 'Oh, that group. You will find none here. I haven't any. I very, very seldom use them', and then 'I think I have perhaps one little phial of tablets in my bag but no more.' Then the Attorney-General said that he had gone on to say, later, that two bottles of hyperduric morphia had been found in his possession. The evidence he proposed to call from the police officers would be confined to those two matters, and was relevant; he would not go into 'the circumstances in which the two bottles of hyperduric morphia' had been found. The Doctor saying that he had 'very seldom' used such drugs as morphia and heroin, when the Prosecution was alleging that these very drugs were amongst those responsible for Mrs Morrell's death, was very relevant.

Mr Justice Devlin thought that the Attorney-General had met Mr Lawrence's objection, but Mr Lawrence still considered that the Doctor had responded to the question about drugs in the present tense and, therefore, this related only to 1956 and not to 1950. 'Questions had already been asked about the usual practice in these matters', the Judge responded; the nurses had been asked if there had been other occasions where doctors had prescribed 'drugs of this sort and in this quantity'. He was still expecting Dr Adams to be called as a witness in his own defence because he added that the prosecution would be entitled to pursue that line of questioning with him and that he might say: 'Oh, yes, there was nothing at all exceptional about Mrs Morrell's treatment; I frequently used these sort of drugs'. In this case the evidence of what he said on 24th November, 1956, would be entirely relevant.

Mr Lawrence replied that the test was whether the evidence in question was admissible now, and not whether it might be 'on a certain hypothesis'. He must already have decided at this stage, if not well before, that he would not be calling Dr Adams to given evidence. Mr Justice Devlin thought his objection very 'technical', that whether this evidence came out 'from the mouth of Dr Adams or through someone else' was a 'matter of machinery'. Mr Lawrence would not commit himself 'with regard to the future course that this case may take' – that is, whether Dr Adams would give evidence or not. Mr Justice Devlin ruled that the evidence in question was relevant and that he would allow the Attorney-General to question witnesses on the matter.

'If your Lordship pleases.' said Mr Lawrence.

The Attorney-General now offered to help 'his learned friend' by putting Mr Sogno in the witness box – as he had now arrived – and defer his examination-in-chief of DI Pugh.

Mr Hubert Sogno, Solicitor and Senior Partner of Lawson Lewis & Co., Solicitors in Eastbourne, was now sworn in. He had been in practice since 1930 and the late Mrs Morrell had been a client of his. He described his procedure with regard to the making of notes: each morning his 'shorthand typist' would bring him his book containing the names of clients he had seen or spoken to on the telephone the previous day, and he would 'dictate to him notes of those interviews', which would be typed out. There would also be a 'letter book' containing copies of letters written on the preceding day. He had brought these records with him.

Mr Sogno had first been consulted by Mrs Morrell early in 1947, and prepared a will which had been executed by her on 27th February, 1947. She had executed further wills on 25th October, 1947 and 8th October, 1949 and added a codicil on 19th March, 1949. Dr Adams had not benefited under any of these wills or the codicil. The Attorney-General asked Mr Sogno if he had ever had 'a telephone conversation with the accused'. He had – on 28th April, 1949. He did not know Dr Adams well, although he had 'often met him in and about the town'. Dr Adams had said 'that he was telephoning on behalf of Mrs Morrell, that she was extremely anxious about the contents of her will, and she desired to see me urgently that day.' Mr Sogno had called on Mrs Morrell that day, and received instructions from her to prepare a draft will. The will was executed on 9th June, 1949 and that will left a bequest to Dr Adams.

Here Mr Lawrence intervened: the contents of earlier wills had to be proved before they could be evidence; it could not be done by merely asking a witness. The Attorney-General agreed that he should have asked the witness to produce the will but would do so later.

The Attorney-General proceeded: Did Dr Adams call at Mr Sogno's office on 8th March, 1950? He did, at ten minutes to one; the time was material as it was just before his going to lunch and someone 'said it was very urgent'. Dr Adams had told him that 'Mrs Morrell had promised him many months ago that she would give him her Rolls Royce car in her will, and she now remembered that she had forgotten to do this. She now wanted to give the car to him and also the contents of a certain case in a locked box at the bank.' Mr Sogno was asked about the contents of this case: 'He [Dr Adams] told me he didn't know precisely what they were'. He went on to say that, although Mrs Morrell was very ill 'her mind was perfectly clear, and he had no doubt she was in a fit condition to make a codicil or a new will.'. Mr Sogno had asked him again about the contents of the case at the bank and 'he said it contained some article or articles of jewellery, and it was to be supposed the two gifts together were of considerable value'. Mr Sogno had reminded him that Mrs Morrell had made some gifts by cheque some months previously, ('not in favour of Dr Adams') and had come to regret them, and suggested that the matter should be left until her son visited at the end of the week.

Dr Adams had responded to this suggestion by saying that 'Mrs Morrell was very uneasy and wanted to get the matter off her mind'. 'I suggested if that were so he might ease her mind by pretending to receive the case and hand it to the nurse in the other room to be preserved for her.' But Dr Adams had then stated 'that Mrs Morrell seriously wished him to enjoy the gift'. He then suggested to Mr Sogno that he should prepare a codicil, 'that it should be executed and later destroyed if it didn't meet with the approval of Mrs Morrell.' Mr Sogno had told him that that was 'quite impossible' and said he would call on his client later that day.

Mr Sogno had called on Mrs Morrell and a codicil was prepared and executed on 19th July, 1950. He had then prepared a further will which was completed on 5th August, 1950, and on 24th August, 1950, there was yet another will. It was this last will that was admitted to probate. Mr Sogno produced Exhibit 7, a copy of the will and probate of Mrs Morrell. In this last will there was a bequest to Dr Adams of 'the Oak Chest containing silver in my drawing room at Marden Ash together with all the silver articles usually kept in it'. In addition, in the event of her son predeceasing her, then Dr Adams would inherit her 'Rolls Royce Motor Car and the Elizabethan court cupboard in the lounge at Marden Ash'.

Mr Lawrence began his cross-examination by ascertaining that Mrs Morrell's previous solicitors were Messrs. Coles & James; Mr Sogno knew this because he had been given an earlier will which bore the signatures of Mr H.V. James and one of his clerks as witnesses. On each occasion when Dr Adams had conveyed to him that Mrs Morrell wanted to see him urgently was it not because 'she was in an excited state of mind about her will'. Mr Sogno said that she 'certainly wanted everything done without delay' but whether she was in 'an excited state' he did not know.

> 'Was it a point, at any rate, made by Dr Adams to you on both of these occasions that he wanted, as her doctor, that you should go without delay and deal with the matter so that her mind could be put at rest?'
> 'He certainly asked me to go and see her without delay, and I am quite willing to assume that that was his reason. I cannot remember now that he told me so.'

Dr Adams had told Mr Sogno on the second occasion he had visited him, that Mrs Morrell wished to leave him her Rolls Royce car and that she had forgotten to put this in her will. Did this not also apply to the locked box at the bank? The case at the bank was 'to be given to Dr Adams then'. Was Mr Sogno quite sure of this:

> 'I am not relying on my recollection. I am relying on the note which I have of the interview with Mrs Morrell.'
> 'The note of your interview which you had with Mrs Morrell or with Dr Adams?'
> 'Both together.'
> 'I am asking you about your interview with Dr Adams. Do you see?'
> 'Well, as far as the interview with Dr Adams was concerned, it was in several respects, in my experience, unique, and, although it is a long time ago, I can remember some of it.'

Mr Sogno did not remember that Dr Adams had told him that Mrs Morrell 'was in a terrible state of mind and he, as her doctor, wanted her agitation quietened'; Mr Sogno said that it was, indeed, he who had suggested to Dr Adams that, in order to relieve her mind, he should only appear to take the jewel box. Mr Lawrence again suggested that 'the case in the locked box at the bank' was 'to be a matter of testamentary disposition', but Mr Sogno was adamant that it was not and that the proposal had been that he should get instructions from Mrs Morrell to take it from the bank so that she might give it to Dr Adams. The box was at Martin's Bank in Eastbourne. Mr Lawrence asked if Dr Adams had not, in fact, told Mr Sogno that he had checked at the bank and reassured Mrs Morrell that the box was there and had then come straight to see him? Mr Sogno could not remember that, but was 'prepared to accept it that he did'. [Mrs Morrell's son was a director of Martin's Bank.] Mr Lawrence tried again: Dr Adams had suggested that the Rolls Royce should be dealt with by way of a codicil which could be destroyed if it did not meet with the approval of Mr Claude Morrell. Yes. And the case in the bank? No. Dr Adams had not wanted to go behind Mr Claude Morrell's back, had he? Mr Sogno pointed out that he had 'already suggested to Dr Adams that the whole thing should stand over until Mr Morrell's visit, which was in a few days.'

> 'I agree, and his answer to that was, in effect: "That will not do, because she is very uneasy in her mind and it cannot be left over."'
> 'That was so with regard to the case of jewellery, yes.'

Mr Lawrence retreated back to the codicil which had been completed on 19th July, and then immediately asked whether Mr Sogno had not been sent for by Mrs Morrell on 12th September, 1950. Yes, Mrs Morrell had telephoned him and he went to see her that day. Dr Adams was on holiday in Scotland and she was very angry with him and gave Mr Sogno further instructions; as a result he had returned the next day, having prepared a codicil to the will of 24th August, and she executed the codicil. Mr Lawrence asked Mr Sogno to produce the codicil. He had it but: 'The codicil, I would say, is all in small pieces.'

The codicil was 'to cut out Dr Adams wholly from any benefit whatever under her will'. It was. Was she capable, mentally, on that day?

> 'She was quite capable, although I tried to dissuade her from doing it.'

But was Mr Sogno not of the opinion that 'the codicil cutting Dr Adams out of the will was never validly revoked before she died'? His view was that the codicil was 'validly revoked' but that 'It was not an effective way of reviving the gifts in favour of Dr Adams which had been contained in the will'. That was how he had advised Mrs Morrell. Mr Lawrence asked if Mr Sogno remembered that he had asked that same question 'before the magistrates' [at the Committal hearing].

> 'The question you asked me before the magistrates was – and I remember it well –: "Did

Mrs Morrell subsequently execute any testamentary document which had the effect of putting back the gifts to Dr Adams?" You asked me whether she had executed a document, not whether she had revoked a codicil.'

'I beg your pardon. She never did, did she?'

'No.'

When Mrs Morrell died, Dr Adams was not a beneficiary under the will. The codicil which was torn up in pieces was sent to Mr Sogno in an envelope by Mr Claude Morrell, and was received by Mr Sogno on 23rd October; he had told Mr Morrell that this did not reinstate Dr Adams in the will and nothing further was done. The will was admitted to probate, including the bequest of the oak chest and its contents to Dr Adams, because only Mr Morrell could have objected to it and 'the will was allowed to be proved as it stood'. The Probate Registrar was informed 'and that was the view he took'. Mr Lawrence clarified the matter:

> 'So really it shortly comes to this, does not it: that Dr Adams was put back into the will after Mrs Morrell's death, really by the favour of Mr Claude Morrell the residuary legatee?'
>
> 'Well, he could not be put back into the will, but Mr Morrell said, "By all means he shall have this gift because it was my mother's wish."'
>
> 'Was this not equally true of the Rolls Royce?'
>
> 'Well, of course, I didn't know about that. I have since learned that it was so from Mr Morrell.'

Copies of the will (Exhibit 7) were then handed to the jury. The final gross value of Mrs Morrell's estate was £175,000 (net £157,000 after deduction of Death Duties). Mr Lawrence drew Mr Sogno's attention to Clause 3, 'I desire that my body shall be cremated'. Mr Sogno knew that this had been in the will of 1947 prepared by Messrs. Coles & James. [Dr Adams' solicitors], though this was not mentioned Mr Lawrence trawled through the bequests in the will to demonstrate that there were quite a few 'four of £1,000 and one of £500 before we reach Dr Adams at all.' The Georgian chest of silver had been 'valued by Messrs. Horn of Eastbourne at £276:5s.' This was the probate value. There were legacies to staff and then some to charities, 'one to somebody in America, a number of dollars', and the residuary estate to Mr Arthur Claude Morrell in Clause 7 of the will. The provisions of Clause 8 would only have come into effect if Mrs Morrell's son had pre-deceased her, and these included the bequest of the Rolls Royce motor car and an Elizabethan court cupboard to Dr Adams. This meant that the Rolls Royce was given to Dr Adams by Mr Claude Morrell and not by his mother.

The Attorney-General submitted that, as Mr Lawrence had asked Mr Sogno about earlier wills regarding the request for cremation, including one made before Mrs Morrell was his client, then he was entitled in his re-examination of this witness to ask about the contents of these wills. Mr Lawrence objected as he had only asked 'whether it was always her wish that she should be cremated'; it was only the witness who had referred to previous wills. The

Attorney-General asked for 'his Lordship's ruling' on the matter; he did not object to further cross-examination by Mr Lawrence subsequently. Mr Justice Devlin ruled that the re-examination should be restricted to the subject of cremation.

The Attorney-General first asked Mr Sogno about the case of jewellery: what had been said to him to indicate 'that it was a case of jewellery'? Dr Adams had told him that 'it contained an article or articles of jewellery', but not about how long it had been at the bank, and he could not recall whether Dr Adams had told him 'about Mrs Morrell not knowing where the box was'. The Doctor had expressed an opinion 'about her capacity to make a codicil or a new will on that day'. With regard to the torn up codicil, it was given by him, in one piece, to Mr Morrell on 14th September so that he could put it with Mrs Morrell's will and other documents in the bank, and the next time he saw it was on 23rd October when it was in small pieces. The Codicil dated 13th September, 1950 was marked 'Exhibit 51'.

The Attorney-General had finished his re-examination of Mr Sogno but had made no mention of the matter of cremation. Detective Inspector Pugh was recalled for the Attorney-General to continue his examination concerning the police visit to Dr Adams' house, Kent Lodge, on the evening of 24th October, 1950. DI Pugh had produced the warrant and Superintendent Hannam had read this out to the accused. He had just responded by saying 'There are no dangerous drugs here. What do you mean by dangerous drugs?'. He then went to the cupboard to the right of the fireplace in the surgery, turned to Hannam and said 'I have quite a bit of Barbiturate here – is that what you mean?' Superintendent Hannam replied 'Inspector Pugh's quest is for dangerous drugs.' He asked: 'What do you mean by dangerous drugs? Poisons?' Pugh had heard Superintendent Hannam mention morphine, heroin and pethedine, and Dr Adams had said, 'Oh, that group. You will find none here. I very, very seldom use them. There might be a little phial of tablets in my bag but no more.' Inspector Pugh said that he had then left the surgery on Superintendent Hannam's instructions.

The Attorney-General asked if Inspector Pugh had then returned to the surgery. He had: Superintendent Hannam and Sergeant Hewett were still there and they had looked in the cupboards in the surgery and found 'two small bottles of morphia. One was in a cardboard carton.' These were produced as Exhibit 26. The label on the bottles was 'hyperduric morphine'. While they were in the surgery Mr James the solicitor had come in. Had Inspector Pugh picked up any bag then? He had.

> 'I asked the accused if he had any more dangerous drugs. He said "Only those in my bag, the black one there," and then he pointed to a black bag which was on the floor with two others near the door. I picked that bag up, placed it on a couch and opened it and the accused said to me "I very, very seldom use dangerous drugs. There might be a little in that bag but nowhere else."'

The Attorney-General asked if Inspector Pugh, Superintendent Hannam and Sergeant Hewett had gone back to Kent Lodge. They had done so on 19th December at about 11.45 a.m. and were shown into the lounge. About five minutes after, Dr Adams came in. Superintendent

Hannam had asked him if they could talk somewhere privately and the Doctor took them into the surgery. There were two men there. Inspector Pugh knew that they were French, one a press reporter and the other a press photographer. 'They were told to leave and they left at once.' Superintendent Hannam had told Dr Adams that he would be arrested and taken to the police station and charged with the murder of Mrs Morrell; then 'The accused made as if to speak and the Superintendent stopped him by raising his hand' and cautioned him.

> 'The accused said "Murder?" He paused and appeared to look more intently at the superintendent and repeated "Murder? Can you prove it is murder?" and the superintendent then said "You are now charged with murdering her." The accused then said "I did not think you could prove murder. She was dying in any case."'

The Attorney-General asked whether anything had happened while they were standing in the hall:

> 'Yes, sir. The accused had just put his overcoat on, the receptionist had given him his hat and I saw that they grasped each other's hands and the superintendent went forward at the same time as I did. The superintendent looked at the accused's hands and as the accused turned away I heard him mumble something which I am afraid I failed to catch, but as he turned towards me I heard the words "See you in heaven."'

Inspector Pugh had been present when the accused was charged with murder and cautioned once more. He had then replied: 'It is better to say nothing.'

Mr Lawrence again asking 'the indulgence of the court' wished to postpone his cross-examination of Detective Inspector Pugh, and the Attorney-General called his next witness, Superintendent Hannam, who was sworn in.

The Attorney-General commenced by asking whether he had met the accused on the evening of 1st October, 1956: had this been a 'chance meeting' or had he gone deliberately to see Dr Adams? It was a chance meeting; the Superintendent had seen him closing the doors of his garage in Lismore Road, behind Kent Lodge.

The Attorney-General stopped and told the Judge that 'his learned friend' had an objection to the questioning that would follow and whether it would be best to hear that objection forthwith. Mr Lawrence wished to do this in the absence of the jury and Mr Justice Devlin agreed that they should withdraw, and also Superintendent Hannam.

Mr Lawrence submitted that the only evidence which Superintendent Hannam should present about this meeting was that which related to Mrs Morrell and the issue in this case, and that therefore there were some lines in his statement which were admissible and some which were not. The Attorney-General agreed to exclude one of the passages to which Mr Lawrence objected, but Mr Lawrence submitted that several more were prejudicial to his client. The Attorney-General did not agree that these passages should be excluded, still seeming to suppose that Dr Adams might admit or dispute such evidence himself. Mr Justice Devlin ruled that 'the part to which Mr Lawrence objects is irrelevant and therefore inadmissible, and the part which is relevant and is admissible can be separated from it.'

The Jury and Detective Superintendent Hannam returned to the Court and the Attorney-General resumed his examination, directing his attention to the part of the conversation between Superintendent Hannam and Dr Adams which related to Mrs Morrell. They had discussed the chest of old silver, and Dr Adams had said 'that Mrs Morrell was a very dear patient. She insisted a long time before she died that I should have that in her memory and I didn't want it. I am a bachelor. I never use it. I knew she was going to leave it to me and her Rolls Royce car. She told me she had put it in her will. Oh, yes, and another cabinet.' 'Had Superintendent Hannam referred to Mrs Morrell's cremation certificate form?' He had:

> 'I said: "Doctor, I have examined the cremation certificate form you filled in in your own handwriting for Mrs Morrell and you have said on it that you were not or that you were not aware that you were a beneficiary under the will."'

What was the reply:

> 'He said: "Oh, that was not done wickedly. God knows it was not. We always want cremations to go off smoothly for the dear relatives. If I said I knew I was getting money under the will, they might get suspicious, and I like cremations and burials to go smoothly. There was nothing suspicious really. It was not deceitful."'

Superintendent Hannam had told Dr Adams that he hoped to 'finish all these enquiries soon and we will probably have another talk.' The Doctor had replied: 'Don't hurry. Please be thorough. It is in my interests. Goodnight, and thank you very much for your kindness' and they shook hands.

The Attorney-General turned to the visit of Superintendent Hannam, DI Pugh and DS Hewett to Kent Lodge on 24th November, 1956 at 8.30 p.m. As they went in Dr Adams had come down the stairs and Superintendent Hannam had said to him 'Good evening, Doctor. You know who I am?' and he had replied 'Oh, yes, Mr Hannam.'

Hannam had asked if they could go into a private room as he had something to say to Dr Adams, and he had replied: 'There is no question of a statement, for I have been told not to make one.' He took them into his surgery on the ground floor and there Superintendent Hannam had told him of the warrant and read it to him, and cautioned him. Dr Adams had said in response 'There are no dangerous drugs here. What do you mean by dangerous drugs?'

What did he say then: 'There are no dangerous drugs here. What do you mean by 'dangerous drugs'?' and walked over to the recess on the right-hand of the chimney-breast to a built-in cupboard and opened the centre compartment, saying 'I have quite a bit of barbiturates here. Is that what you mean?' Hannam had said 'Detective Inspector Pugh's quest is for dangerous drugs.' Dr Adams said: 'What do you mean by 'dangerous drugs' – poisons?' 'Morphine, heroin, pethedine, and the like,' Hannam had replied. The Doctor's answer was:

'Oh, that group. You will find none here. I haven't any. I very very seldom ever use them. I think I have perhaps one little phial of tablets in my bag, but no more.'

Superintendent Hannam had then given DI Pugh instructions to go out and make certain that all the blinds in the front of the house were secure. Whilst DI Pugh was out of the room, Hannam showed Dr Adams Exhibit No. 25 – the statement from Browne's the Chemist of medication prescribed for Mrs Morrell by him. [The corrected list was Exhibit 4A]; the Attorney-General asked Superintendent Hannam to read out the alterations. Showing the list to Dr Adams, Superintendent Hannam had said, 'Doctor, look at this list of your prescriptions for Mrs Morrell. There are a lot of dangerous drugs here'. He had replied: 'Now all these I left prescriptions for, either at the chemists or at the house. She had nurses day and night.' Hannam had asked who had administered the drugs and Dr Adams had replied: 'I did, nearly all. Perhaps the nurses gave some, but mostly me.' He was then asked if there were any left over when she died, and the Doctor said, 'No, none. All was given to the patient.' The Attorney-General asked what had happened when Superintendent Hannam had turned to the page which carried prescriptions 70-91, those for the period which covered 21st September to 12th November, 1950:

'I said: "Doctor, you prescribed for her 75 one-sixth grains heroin tablets the day before she died." He said: "Poor soul, she was in terrible agony. It was all used. I used them myself." I said to him: "I have no medical training myself, but surely the quantity of dangerous drugs obtained for Mrs Morrell during the last week of her life alone would be fatal, and is pain usual with a cerebral vascular accident?"'

Dr Adams had asked to look at the list and Superintendent Hannam handed it to him and turned it over to page 5 and he took it in his and was looking at it while Hannam ran his fingers over the prescriptions nos. 87 to 91 [those for 11th and 12th November] while he was looking at it. He looked for a second or two and then said: 'There might have been a couple of those final tablets left over, but I cannot remember. If there were, I would take them and destroy them. I am not dishonest with drugs. Mrs Morrell had all those because I gave the injections. Do you think it was too much?' Hannam had told him that it was not a matter for him; that he just wanted to 'get at the truth'. Had the Doctor taken the drugs to the house? He answered: 'No. The chauffeur collected them, and I got them from the nurses.' The Superintendent had then enquired whether Dr Adams had any record himself of what he had prescribed for Mrs Morrell or a clinical card, and the answer was 'I do not keep any records of what I prescribe for patients. I only record visits, and perhaps not that for private patients. Even my card is destroyed a year after a patient dies.'

After this, the conversation turned to other matters [inadmissible] and then Detective Inspector Pugh came back into the surgery and started the search. During this search, two bottles of hyperduric morphine were 'found in his pocket, and small quantities in his bag of tablets.' The Attorney-General asked if the Superintendent had looked through the records cabinet beside the desk. The accused had opened it for him and Hannam had said: 'have you any record card or records of any kind for Mrs Morrell?'

'Did you look at the 'M' index?'
'Yes, we went through it together.'
'What did he say?'
'He said: "No, I do not appear to have. I expect I destroyed them after she died."'

The Attorney-General asked if Superintendent Hannam had looked in other rooms in the house. Yes. The dining room? Yes. Had the accused said anything to him? Yes. He had pointed to a carved chest and said: 'That is the famous Morrell piece.' Dr Adams got the key and they opened it together: 'inside were eight drawers which contained silver, quite a portion of it was still in tissue paper. There were eight trays containing silver articles and drawers at the bottom.'

Mr Justice Devlin adjourned until the following day.

# Seventh Day

The Attorney-General continued his examination of Superintendent Hannam by asking him if he had seen Dr Adams on 26th November, 1956. Dr Adams had asked to see him and they had spoken together in the photographic room of police headquarters in Eastbourne. Dr Adams had said to him: 'You told Mr James there might be other charges. I am very worried. What are they?' Hannam had replied, 'that is not quite accurate. I told him he must not automatically assume the charges preferred were final.'. The Doctor had then said: 'What else is there', and the Superintendent had said: 'Mrs Morrell is certainly one.' Dr Adams had replied:

> 'Easing the passing of a dying person is not all that wicked. She wanted to die. That cannot be murder. It is impossible to accuse a doctor.'

The Attorney-General then went through the police visit of 19th December to Kent Lodge when Superintendent Hannam had arrested Dr Adams on the charge of murdering Mrs Morrell. Hannam's evidence corroborated that of DI Pugh, but he had heard clearly what Dr Adams had said to his receptionist, which was: 'I will see you in heaven.' At half past twelve that day Dr Adams was formally charged at police headquarters.

Superintendent Hannam produced Exhibit 27, the death certificate of Mrs Morrell and he also confirmed that the writing on the Cremation Form Exhibit 2 was that of Dr Adams, and the portion filled in by Dr Walker was his handwriting.

Mr Lawrence began his cross-examination: was Superintendent Hannam in charge of the case? He was, and Sergeant Hewett was a senior sergeant from Scotland Yard and his immediate assistant. Detective Inspector Pugh was the senior C.I.D. officer of Eastbourne Borough Police. The meeting which had taken place between the Superintendent and Dr Adams was supposed to be 'an unplanned, casual meeting' and Mr Lawrence questioned this assiduously and rather surprisingly. It was not at all unlikely that this was a chance meeting as both Dr Adams' house and the Police Headquarters were in the town centre and not too far apart. Mr Lawrence concluded this line of questioning:

> 'It was a rather remarkable coincidence if that was an entirely unplanned and chance meeting, wasn't it?'
> 'I don't think so, Sir.'
> 'The truth of the matter is that you were waylaying him, weren't you?'
> 'Indeed I was not.'

Mr Lawrence went on: there was a discussion about 'this chest of silver' – the Superintendent asked for Exhibit 33, the notes he wrote of the interview. Mr Justice Devlin asked if Mr Lawrence had any objection:

> 'My Lord, no. I want to be quite fair. If the Superintendent thinks he is unable to answer my questions without his notes, by all means.'

Hannam responded sharply:

> 'That is quite improper. I want to be accurate.'

The Attorney-General intervened, Lord Justice Devlin rebuked Hannam and at the same time allowed him to have his notes and Mr Lawrence asked if the remark had been directed at him – no, at his question. The Judge told Mr Lawrence to continue.

Mr Lawrence returned to the chest of silver, unused silver; Hannam presumed that it was unused. Mr Lawrence put it to the Superintendent that Dr Adams had made no reference at all to the Rolls Royce car or the other cabinet. [Elizabethan court-cupboard], saying that he knew that Mrs Morrell was going to leave these to him.

> 'Oh yes, Sir, indeed he did.'

Mr Lawrence asked whether Superintendent Hannam had already taken evidence from Mr Sogno, whether he knew what the legal position was regarding the legacies. Hannam said that he had been in Court during the committal proceedings in Eastbourne and had seen Mr Sogno previously. He had known that the reason Dr Adams had the chest of silver was 'by favour of Mr Claude Morrell' and that he had given the Rolls Royce to the Doctor, and that he had never had the other cabinet at all.

Superintendent Hannam agreed that he had introduced the topic of the cremation certificate, where Dr Adams had stated that he was not aware that he was a beneficiary under the will. Mr Lawrence asked him if he had realised at that time that 'the essence on that form is not the fact of being a beneficiary but whether or not he knew that he was?'

'Absolutely. I know the state of mind is the important feature.'

He had known what Dr Adams had put on the form and he had known that Dr Adams was not actually a beneficiary under the will, but had been cut out of it.

'What he said, according to you is this: 'I knew she was going to leave it [the chest of silver] to me and her Rolls Royce car. She told me she had put them in the will. Oh yes, and another cabinet'. '
'That is what he said.'
'That may be a matter of argument, but that is not saying to you that he had received all those goods under the will, was it?'
'No, Sir, but it was dealing with what you were referring to before, his state of mind about it.'

Mr Lawrence kept on asking why the Superintendent had not asked if Dr Adams knew that he had not inherited these items under Mrs Morrell's will. Hannam pointed out more than once that this had been a conversation and not an interrogation; Dr Adams had asked him questions and 'I had merely directed his mind to the matters upon which I was interested.'

'Then you say the accused said to you: "Oh, that wasn't done wickedly. God knows it wasn't. We always want cremations to go off smoothly for the dear relatives. If I said I knew I was getting money under the Will, they might get suspicious and I like crema-tions and burials to go smoothly. There was nothing suspicious really. I wasn't deceit-ful." Again, I want you to understand what I am putting to you quite clearly, that those matters that I have just read from your evidence <u>are not things that Dr Adams said at all, but that they are the reflection of things that you were saying and putting to him and to which he was making no reply</u>.'
[The underlining is is Hannam's in manuscript upon the transcript, and marked in the margin].
'That is quite untrue. These were his actual words, and I recorded them accurately.'

Mr Lawrence moved on to the police visit to Kent Lodge on 24th November, and questions concerned the warrant being made out to Detective Inspector Pugh: under what authority had Superintendent Hannam entered Dr Adams' house that night? He 'went in to supervise Mr Pugh's search'; it was 'a matter purely of law': the warrant authorised Pugh to enter and he and Hewett had gone with him. Mr Lawrence produced the warrant for the search under the Dangerous Drugs Act 1951. He read it out and asked a few more questions. Mr Justice Devlin intervened:

'Mr Lawrence, I think you are right, that this witness was a trespasser. But does it mat-ter to any issue in this case that he was?'

So the Superintendent was supervising Pugh; what was Hewett doing?

> 'He was assisting Pugh. This was a complicated search for drugs. An officer never goes
> to a house to search for drugs alone, never.'

The matter had been at his direction. Dr Adams had been about to leave the house when they arrived, and Mr Lawrence suggested that he had said to the police: 'If it is a question of making a statement, I will only make one if my lawyer is present'.

> 'No, sir. He did not.'

Well, he had gone into his surgery and tried to ring Mr James, his solicitor. The Superintendent said that he had asked him if he might do so and that he had given him permission.

> 'You, a trespasser in his house, giving him permission to ring up his own Solicitor? Is
> that what you are saying?'

Mr Justice Devlin intervened:

> 'He has not admitted that he was a trespasser.'
> 'My Lord, perhaps I put it too high' admitted Mr Lawrence.

Hannam said that Dr Adams had asked his permission, then made three telephone calls. He was unable to speak to Mr James, but spoke to his son, asking him to get his father to come round as soon as he could. Mr James arrived at 9.10 p.m., forty minutes later, and they had proceeded with the search.

Mr Lawrence clarified the lay-out of Kent Lodge with Superintendent Hannam: it was a double-fronted house with four main rooms on the ground floor and staff rooms at the back; 'as you go in through the central front door, the room immediately on the right is the dining room and behind that is the surgery, and on the left-hand side as you go in is, first of all the lounge and behind that the waiting room.' Dr Adams had stood beside the desk in the surgery, 'phoning.

Dr Adams had been told that the search was for dangerous drugs and he had asked what was meant by that. Mr Lawrence contended that there was a very long list of dangerous drugs, but Hannam had referred to 'morphine, heroin, pethedine and the like' because 'There are many obscure dangerous drugs. These are the common, well known ones.'. Mr Lawrence protested that Dr Adams had said 'there' – meaning the cupboard, when he said 'Oh, that group. You will find none there'.

> 'He said, "You will find none here."'

They had not even got to the cupboard at that stage; they were talking about the house.

'That is where I am venturing to put something different to you, you see, that the reference was to the cupboard and not to the house?'

'I disagree, sir.'

[Hannam has marked this question and response in the margin]

'And I put it to you that he did not say, "I haven't any"?'

'Oh, he did. I was very amazed at the time.'

'And that he did not say, "I think I have perhaps one little phial of tablets in my bag but no more", but that he did say words to this effect: "Whatever I have is in my bag"?'

'The answer to the first part of your question is "He did say it", and to the last part of your question "No, he did not say that".'

Mr Lawrence had presented Dr Adams' alternative version of what he said; he questioned the Superintendent on his sending DI Pugh out of the room, again emphasising that the warrant was in Pugh's name. So, then there had been the conversation 'you say had with Dr Adams about Mrs Morrell, the prescriptions and the amount of drugs that she had'. Mr Lawrence suddenly felt he had to virtually apologise to the Superintendent, who was clearly such an upright man:

'And you understand that I have to put to you what we suggest happened – '

'I fully appreciate that.'

' – at this part of the proceedings?'

Mr Lawrence suggested that Dr Adams was, at this point, standing opposite to Hannam, by the hand basin, but Hannam disagreed: he had been standing on his right hand side. Then the Superintendent had opened his brief case and had taken out 'one small quantity of papers, Exhibit 25'. He had told Dr Adams that they were a list of drugs he had prescribed for Mrs Morrell. Mr Lawrence said that he had 'to put the best of Dr Adams's recollection', and this was that when the Superintendent had asked if they were all given to her, the Doctor had actually said that he could not remember.

'No, sir, that is quite untrue. He was most emphatic about it.'

Mr Lawrence asked if it were not the case that Dr Adams had maintained that 'he could not possibly remember the details and he would not discuss it with you'.

'That is quite untrue, the whole thing. He was most loquacious, and always has been since I have known him.'

Mr Lawrence tried again, and again the answer was:

'He did not. He was dogmatic at once.'

Dr Adams had still refused to discuss it when the Superintendent had referred to the last amounts prescribed for Mrs Morrell: quite untrue. He did not reply when asked about what was left over: yes, he did. He did not say that he was not dishonest with drugs: he did say that. Superintendent Hannam disagreed 'with your substance of the account, sir'.

Mr Lawrence asked if the Superintendent had 'taken a statement from any doctor in this matter of Mrs Morrell'. Hannam said that the would have to check his notes; he could not be sure. (Presumably this could only be Dr Harris.) There had been some conversation with Dr Adams concerning clinical cards and visits? Yes, the Superintendent had asked for 'his record or clinical card' both before Pugh came back and after. Mr Lawrence suggested that what Hannam had asked Dr Adams was a general question 'as to how he kept his patients' clinical records and it had nothing to do specifically with Mrs Morrell. It had been afterwards, when Mr James was present that the conversation regarding his general records had taken place, and the earlier conversation was certainly specific to Mrs Morrell's records. Had Dr Adams not told him that 'he kept a card index system containing the clinical notes and the drugs prescribed'?

'No. He told me he kept no record of drugs prescribed.'

Mr Lawrence suggested that Dr Adams had made it clear that he kept two records; the clinical cards and the visiting lists which were 'transferred to a card index system kept by the book-keeper who sends out the accounts'; Hannam disagreed. Inspector Pugh had then returned and commenced the drugs search; he had been out of the surgery for about 15 minutes. Mr James arrived at ten past nine and was there for the rest of the time the police officers were on the premises, and they eventually left at 10.25 p.m.

Mr Lawrence moved on to the 26th November when Dr Adams was in Eastbourne Court in connection with other charges. He had been in the dock and the magistrates had granted bail, but before he could be released certain formalities had to be completed. There was then a considerable amount of questions and answers as to what had happened next: Dr Adams' movements from the court and to the police station because the version given to Mr Lawrence by Dr Adams was quite different to that of Hannam. It concerned where a conversation between them had taken place. As this also involved DS Sellars of Eastbourne Police Force and he was in court, he was asked to withdraw.

Superintendent Hannam had heard a conversation between Sellars and Dr Adams 'in the open court… outside the dock', when Sellars had asked if the Doctor was willing to have his photograph taken for police records. Mr Lawrence suggested that this had happened in the charge-room. It might have been repeated, said Hannam but he had heard this conversation as he had recounted.

It was also not accurate that he had 'put his head into the photographic room' whilst Dr Adams was being photographed; he went into the photographic room and nobody else except the Doctor was there. It was not true that Dr Adams, after the photograph was taken, went to the charge-room, met his solicitor and went straight home:

'I sent an officer with him for a particular reason, to comply with the direction of the magistrates. It is not true.'
'And in fact, superintendent, that [sic] he had no conversation with you at all that day?'
'I did. He did.'

Mr Lawrence proceeded to deal with the police visit on the 19th December, 1956: there had first been a meeting in the lounge, then the Superintendent had suggested going to the surgery to talk, crossing the ground floor diagonally to the back room on the right-hand side, Dr Adams had led the way, followed by Hannam. In the surgery were 'the two French gentlemen'. Was it Dr Adams who had said 'That will be all now. You go.'? Hannam said that he had ordered them to leave; he had not asked Pugh who they were as 'it was easy to see… without asking'. He had then stated that he had come to arrest the Doctor for the murder of Mrs Morrell and cautioned him. Then Dr Adams had said 'Murder', paused 'and the rest of it'? Yes.

'The inflexion of the voice on that word "Murder", was interrogative, wasn't it?'
'Now, Sir, I think it is only fair to say this; Doctor Adams was a very, very shaken man indeed, and I am not going to suggest there was any inflexion of any kind. I think he was very distressed.'

Superintendent Hannam said that Dr Adams had been standing with his back to the bookcase, which was on the passage wall, his desk being on his right and the window on his left, and 'stayed in that position the whole time' with his hands at his sides. He had then told the Doctor he was going to search him and took the contents of his pockets out; these were laid out on his 'reclining couch' by Sergeant Hewett, and they afterwards used his waste paper basket as a container for these. When they went into the hall, Dr Adams had stood in the centre, facing the street door and Hannam had had his back to the surgery door, 'so therefore I would be left inclined towards Doctor Adams'. Miss Lawrence, his receptionist had gone upstairs to fetch some books and for his warm overcoat; when she came down 'she grasped his hand and turned away from him'. Mr Lawrence reached the crux of the matter:

'I put it to you quite plainly that he never said the words: "I will see you in Heaven", or anything like it?'
'He did; they were very staggering words to me, Sir, and I recall them quite plainly.'

Miss Lawrence had been 'crying when he said those words'. However, the Superintendent's view was that Miss Lawrence had been unable to hear these words, 'Firstly, she was turned away from him and he was talking quietly, and secondly, she was crying and was herself very distressed, and I don't think she heard it.' Hannam had said to her 'If anyone comes to the door, say nothing to anybody'; he had given her 'quite a bit of advice before I left'. 'Unhappily' a patient was entering as they went out.

The Attorney-General re-examined briefly on a couple of points and confirmed with

Superintendent Hannam that the information for the warrant under the Dangerous Drugs Act had been sworn by him. He had, in fact, 'typed that warrant myself in London and named the local Detective Inspector in it in conformity with the Statute and showed it to the Justice of the Peace'. The matter was rather simply clarified. It had also been suggested to the Superintendent that his first meeting on 1st October with Dr Adams 'was not a casual, unplanned interview', but on other occasions when he met the Doctor he had been accompanied by other police officers. Yes, he was.

Detective Inspector Pugh was recalled to be cross-examined by Mr Lawrence, who suggested, as he had to Superintendent Hannam, that Dr Adams' words and movements had not been as reported in his evidence. Pugh refuted what Mr Lawrence had been told by his client as surely as Hannam had: Dr Adams had said 'There is no question of a statement'; the warrant was read over to him by the Superintendent. The Doctor had not said 'I haven't any' with reference to dangerous drugs.

> 'Well, the inference to me – it conveyed to me that he did not have any. That is why
> I could not understand that, because I would expect to find dangerous drugs in the
> surgery'.

Mr Lawrence repeatedly made the point that Hannam had been conducting the search and the conversation, and the fact that Pugh had been out of the room for over fifteen minutes, and sent out by Hannam, and obeyed him 'without question'. The search for dangerous drugs had begun when he returned to the surgery and this was about half an hour after they had arrived at the house. Mr Lawrence mentioned the 'two little bottles of hyperduric morphia' which had been found, and moved on to the day of the arrest. DI Pugh knew who the two press reporters were 'because I had seen them before'. Again Mr Lawrence asked about the way in which Dr Adams had responded when he was charged with murder:

> 'Well, when he said on the first occasion "Murder?", he was looking at the Superinten-
> dent. The Superintendent was standing just in front of him. Then there was a pause
> and, …he appeared to look more intently at the Superintendent before he said on the
> second occasion "Murder?" It was as though he was – soliloquising.'
> 'We have been told by the Superintendent that he was shocked, shaken, by this
> announcement of murder.'
> 'I would say that he was in a way stunned, or he appeared to be stunned.'

Before they had left the house with Dr Adams, he and his receptionist had 'appeared to be gripping each other's hands' and:

> 'As I remember it, when the Superintendent stepped forward their grip parted and the
> Superintendent looked at the doctor's hands and he appeared satisfied, and – I think
> it was the movement – the doctor turned with that, and I do know I recall the recep-

tionist – as the doctor turned it appeared that she realised that we were going to take him away, and she turned and put her hands up to her face or to her eyes, and it was as the doctor was turning that I heard him mumble something and then as he came round I heard three words: "See you in heaven".'

The Attorney-General re-examined Detective Inspector Pugh: when had he made his notes of what had occurred on 24th November? He had made 'a few of them in the surgery whilst the accused was being searched, and the remainder outside the surgery in the dining room shortly afterwards.' The Attorney-General asked him to refer to his notes. When Dr Adams had said 'There are no dangerous drugs here', Pugh said there was no indication that he was referring to the contents of the cupboard. The Doctor had referred to barbiturates in the cupboard afterwards, and then he had definitely said, in answer to the Superintendent's question about 'morphine, heroin and pethedine and the like': 'Oh that group. You will find none here. I very, very seldom use them. I think I have one little phial of tablets in my bag, but no more.'

Detective Sergeant Hewett was sworn, and examined by Mr Melford Stevenson, who went through the police visit to Kent Lodge on 24th November. DS Hewett's replies to his questions on conversation and movements matched those of Hannam: he had been with the Superintendent throughout the conversation with Dr Adams concerning Mrs Morrell, the prescriptions for drugs and clinical cards. Hewett had then continued the search for dangerous drugs with Inspector Pugh: Dr Adams had said that the only other dangerous drugs he had were 'those in my bag, the black one over there', and he had pointed towards the door where 'there were three cases'. Inspector Pugh had opened it on the couch and he and Hewett had gone through it together. There was a point where a tin was found. Mr Melford Stevenson asked whether anything was said by the Doctor 'as to his general practice in regard to drugs'. Mr Lawrence objected to this as irrelevant; Mr Stevenson thought that this had already 'been the subject of consideration. Your Lordship sees the next matter in the depositions'. This was additional evidence which had been notified. Mr Lawrence apologised and said that he had been mistaken. The evidence in question was that Dr Adams had said, when the bag was picked up: 'I very seldom use any dangerous drugs. There might be a bottle in that bag, but nowhere else.'

Mr Stevenson went on to the day of the arrest, 19th December, and, again, the evidence of Sergeant Hewett matched that of his colleagues. He had heard Dr Adams say to the receptionist as he parted from her: 'I will see you in heaven.'

Mr Lawrence cross-examined the witness: the Sergeant had not given evidence before the magistrates in Eastbourne at the committal hearing, and his evidence had been the subject of a notice of additional evidence served on the defence: there was no deposition of evidence in that case, but he made a statement and this was transmitted to the defence. This was taken from a statement that he had made on 26th November 'and quite a lot of it was taken out, of course.' Hewett thought that the statement was compiled on the 20th December, and again confirmed that Dr Adams had said 'I will see you in heaven' to his receptionist. To his receptionist? Somewhat cheekily, Hewett replied: 'It would not be to me, sir, would it?' Mr Lawrence ignored this and was on to something else.

Mr Lawrence now ascertained from Hewett that he had not himself made any notes of the conversation in the surgery between Superintendent Hannam and Dr Adams: 'I have adopted Superintendent Hannam's notebook'. He had made notes on the arrest on the 19th, and the search with Inspector Pugh for drugs in the bags.

> 'And is this really right, that all the time you were giving your evidence Superintendent
> Hannam's notes were open in front of you in that witness box?'
> 'I was reading them, sir.'

Hewett hoped that his evidence was 'word for word the same' as Superintendent Hannam's, otherwise he would be misreading it. He had first seen the notebook at midnight on the night of 24th/25th November and had, in fact, watched the Superintendent write it. Mr Justice Devlin asked if Hewett had taken any part in the writing of the notes:

> 'Yes, sir, on his [Hannam's] directions; it was done that way, and he said if I disagreed
> with him I was to tell him.'

Had Sergeant Hewett felt 'emboldened at any stage, to differ from what Mr Hannam was putting down'? He certainly had, and what was done was perfectly usual practice to make a composite record in this way. Mr Lawrence challenged the record of 'this vital interview' in the surgery. Hewett said that he had not known that the Superintendent would refer to the case of Mrs Morrell; he was 'just there to assist Mr Hannam, Sir. I never made any inquiry or investigation of this case at all'. Mr Lawrence went through the beginning of the conversation about Mrs Morrell and the drugs prescribed. In answer to Hannam's question of whether all the drugs were given to her:

> 'Then did Doctor Adams say in effect he couldn't remember the details of them?'
> 'No, Sir. I remember very, very clearly he said they were all given. It was such a surprise
> to me I remember it very distinctly.'

Sergeant Hewett firmly contradicted all Mr Lawrence's suggestions that Dr Adams had not made all these definite statements about the drugs. He understood the 'version' that Mr Lawrence was putting to him, but it was totally untrue. Mr Lawrence gave the impression throughout that he found it embarrassing to relate his client's version of events and conversations.

Hewett was asked where the notes on this visit and search were made: this had been done in Superintendent Hannam's bedroom at the New Inn public house where they had both been staying. He had made an independent record as well: 'I went through and recorded the whole of the things that were found and little bits of conversation that was said as Doctor Adams was saying it, but the rest of it was left to Mr Hannam, and we did it when we got back.'

Mr Lawrence sat down and the Attorney-General just asked whether Sergeant Hewett had signed Superintendent Hannam's notes of what took place on 24th November: they had both signed the notebook.

The Attorney-General now asked the Judge whether Sister Randall could be recalled 'on one matter'; this was agreed. He asked Sister Randall whether, after giving evidence, she had recollected something and contacted the police: she had 'phoned Eastbourne Police Station. She had remembered that she had rung Dr Adams on the morning after Mrs Morrell died and spoken to him. She had told him 'the time Mrs Morrell passed away and the time the injection was given': this was the last injection that she gave. He had said to her: 'I'll be round presently'. She did not say what the last injection was 'because I didn't know'. She made no record of what he told her to do.

Mr Lawrence cross-examined Sister Randall, trying to ascertain why she had suddenly remembered this when she had been asked to remember the events of 13th November, 1950 so often before: was it memory or just because it was obvious that she must have informed the Doctor about a death at which she was present? She explained that she did remember, but not the time she had 'phoned; she had told Dr Adams she had given the injection. She had not made a note of the call because nurses notes 'were of no use' after the patient's death, 'they would be just torn up… The notes belonged to the nurses, they were our books and should have been torn up if we had no more use for them.' Mr Lawrence asked what had been done with the syringe she had used for the injection: 'It was left for Doctor Adams'. She definitely remembered that, and the syringe belonged to Dr Adams; she had boiled it up and left it. Mr Lawrence argued with Sister Randall that, although she had written in the note-book: 2 a.m. passed away quietly', she had not entered the injection left by Dr Adams which she said she had given, and not the morning telephone call: he thought it very important that there should be doubt as to whether that last 5 c.c. injection had been given.

Mr Reid, the expert pharmaceutical witness was recalled for further examination by Mr Malcolm Morris. Mr Reid now produced a list of prescriptions recorded at Browne's the Chemist as having been prescribed for Mrs Morrell during 1948 and 1949; he had checked the records at Browne's against the list prepared by the Defence. The additional list was marked as Exhibit 52.

The new list began on 7th July, 1948; the first prescription for hyperduric morphine was on 9th July, and on the 21st there were two prescriptions for hypodermic tablets of heroin and of morphia. These were repeated 'for example' on 31st August and again on 2nd October. Mr Reid felt that it would be helpful if he could divide the list to show where the patient was in a nursing home and when in her own home: she had arrived from Cheshire at the Esperance Nursing Home early in July 1948 and stayed there until the middle of October, 1948; then she was in the Olinda Nursing Home in Grassington Road until around 7th January, 1949 when she moved to the Cumberland Hotel, and she returned home to 'Marden Ash' at the end of March, 1949. Mr Morris informed the Judge that Dr Ashby had made another graph of prescriptions of morphia and heroin to cover 1948 and 1949, similar to that which he had made for 1950.

Mr Morris asked Mr Reid about the comment he had put on his list about prescriptions 95 and 97: 'Repeat now shown in Prescription Register. Entered in Accounts Register'. Serial numbers 122, 125 and 126 were again entered in the accounts register but not in the prescriptions register. This had happened also with the list for 1950. The original prescriptions had been destroyed so they could not be consulted.

Mr Reid had also noted some arithmetical errors in the calculation of grainage in entries for prescriptions signed by Dr Harris on 13th June, 1949, but the entries of them in the dangerous drugs register were correct. These were the only prescriptions where there was an instruction by the doctor; 'Please label' followed by details to label in a certain way. Mr Reid had also prepared monthly totals of drugs prescribed, which he produced as Exhibit 53. Additional drugs in this exhibit were veramon tablets and pethedine, which did not appear in the previous list for 1950.

Mr Morris asked Mr Reid if he had carried out an experiment with a 5 c.c. syringe filled with paraldehyde:

> 'I took the paraldehyde syringe and, using a large needle – which is used for intra-muscular injections, a larger type of needle than for a hypodermic injection – I drew up the 5 c.c.s of paraldehyde into the syringe; I then placed a cotton wool swab over the neck of the needle and placed that syringe on an instrument tray, such as would be done in a hospital or by a nurse; I then covered the tray with a towel and left it for one hour, and at all times there was a quite unmistakable odour of paraldehyde pervading the same room, which was not a too small room, where that was done, and particularly around the syringe. It is an unmistakable smell, paraldehyde, and I had no difficulty in feeling that the smell of the paraldehyde must be there if paraldehyde had been used in the syringe. Similarly when I concluded the experiment and then cleansed the syringe in the appropriate manner, it was quite obvious that the smell would be even stronger, then, particularly if one used warm water, which is the usual thing at that point.'

When preparing a syringe, Mr Reid explained, the air would normally be expelled by holding the syringe upwards and just expelling the air, and with that some liquid must come out also; in cleaning it afterwards, the nurse would always disassemble it and clean it either with a solution or by boiling for sterilization.

Mr Reid had examined the nurses notebooks and prepared from them a summary of the injections which appeared in it as having been given to Mrs Morrell, going back to 20th June, 1949; he now produced this as Exhibit 54. What emerged was that by June, 1949, the 'routine' evening injection was ¼ grain morphine and ⅓ grain of heroin. He had found a couple of odd injections interposed: one of Scopolamine (hyoscine) ¹⁄₁₅₀th with heroin ⅙th (a combination which causes hallucinations, paranoia and agitation) on 20th November, 1949 and the first injection which included omnopon was on 21st November: morphine ¼, heroin ⅓rd and omnopon ⅓rd. There was 'no supply of prescription to tie up' with the omnopon. (It had been said earlier in the trial that Dr Harris had initiated the use of omnopon for Mrs Morrell, but this shows that it was, in fact, Dr Adams.) Omnopon appears in injections additional to the routine ¼ morphine and ⅓ of heroin, again in January 1950 and March 1950.

In being questioned about the 'special injections', Mr Reid said that he had been 'particularly careful in going through the books to see if I could ascertain what this special injection might be', but he had been unsuccessful in identifying them. He had also produced a summary showing a 'daily contrast' – the difference between the drugs shown as injected in the nurses' records (Exhibit 48) and the drugs shown as prescribed in the list Exhibit 4A. The summary was now Exhibit 55. This showed that there were 30½ grains of morphia and 21 and $^{11}/_{12}$ths grains of heroin prescribed but not accounted for.

Mr Lawrence rose to cross-examine Mr Reid: Mrs Morrell had been, more or less, on a regular dosage of drugs until the latter part of September? It was from the 23rd replied Mr Reid. Mr Lawrence referred to the omnopon having been given on 21st November, 1949, and the Attorney-General intervened to point out that this should be corrected and it was actually given with the heroin and scopolamine on the 20th November. Mr Reid corrected him: it was a day when only omnopon and scopolamine [omnopon -(50% morphine) and scopolamine: the effect of these together is a state known as 'twilight sleep', a combination formerly used in obstetrics but which is now considered too dangerous] were given instead of morphia and heroin.

Mr Lawrence focussed on the Citamin injections, some of which were identified by this correct spelling and by similar spellings. Mr Reid explained that he had not included these as they were 'a very, very mild type of medicament' and 'not medication in the strict sense'. Mr Reid explained that Citamin was a 'non-specific tonic which is normally only given for a short period, not given for a very, very long time.' Mr Lawrence again insinuated that the 'special injections' were Citamin: '…it appears only as a special injection then it crops up in your document?' Mr Reid was not a man to be led in this way:

> '…I have copied, as it were, the wording, [in the notebooks] and 'X' being the unknown quantity of the special injection, I felt it should be entered here.'

Mr Reid admitted that it could 'possibly' be that the 'special injections' were Citamin, but pointed out that on many days 'special injection' appeared twice, so one of these could not be Citamin. Mr Lawrence suggested that the nurses just 'dropped' writing 'Citamin' and put 'the sort of shorthand words 'special injection' for it'.

The Attorney-General objected at this point, saying that this was not borne out either by the reports or the nurses' evidence. Mr Justice Devlin stopped Mr Lawrence, telling him that it was only 'how the table was actually made up' that concerned this witness, 'Not how it ought to have been made up'.

Mr Lawrence continued: there had been regular prescriptions of heroin and morphia for Mrs Morrell from the date of her arrival in Eastbourne? Oh, yes. There were some ampuls [sic] of Vitamin B1 in December 1948 – Mr Reid said that these were 'Minerva', a proprietary name for Vitamin B1. Mr Lawrence went on to a time in June 1949 when Dr Adams must have been away on holiday and Dr Harris was acting as locum; again, to emphasise that Dr Harris had prescribed morphia and heroin for Mrs Morrell, and also phenobarbitone and sedormid.

Mr Reid was reminded by Mr Lawrence that he had asked for a list for 1950 which included the non-restricted drugs prescribed for Mrs Morrell, which was Exhibit 4B. He referred to repeat prescriptions for 'bottles of physic', and amongst their ingredients was a tincture of nuxvomica, 'a tonic'. Mr Reid agreed that it was a 'bitter tonic' containing a 'very small strychnine content'. Had Mr Reid investigated the prescriptions for Mrs Morrell with another chemist, F.W. Temple? He had a list of them with him: the only restricted item in these 'some 40 items' was some phenobarbitone tablets, one grain, prescribed by Dr Harris. Mr Lawrence directed Mr Reid's attention to a prescription for Dexedrine tablets and some repeats for this, which 'went on for some little time'. The Jury were hearing about this variety of medication prescribed – even the liquid paraffin with Phenolphthalein added. Mr Lawrence sat down.

The next witness was Dr Ronald Vincent Harris MD, BSc., M.R.C.S., L.R.P.: to be examined by Mr Melford Stevenson. Dr Harris had been in practice in Eastbourne since 1937, except for the war years. He stated that Dr Adams would just ask a member of the partnership to look after a patient if he were away, and he had agreed to visit Mrs Morrell; he had seen her on 12th June 1949, and on 6th, 8th, 10th, 12th, 15th, 17th and 19th May, 1950. Dr Adams 'would usually instruct one to carry on whatever treatment had been given to the patient'. When he gave directions to the chemist to label drugs, this was for the benefit of the nurses.

The other period when Dr Harris had acted as locum for Dr Adams was from 12th September, 1950. Mr Stevenson asked him why he had given the direction increasing the morphia and heroin and 'may have omnopon gs. ⅓ if necessary'. He recalled that 'Mrs Morrell was in an extremely irritable state over the fact of Dr Adams being away' and that was why he had increased 'the sedative' she was already having. As to the 'special injections', he thought 'she was having vitamin injections' but he might have given small doses of atropine, which was 'sometimes given to counteract any effect of pulmonary congestion that morphia might give'.

Mr Stevenson asked about Dr Harris' own professional practice: did he every prescribe morphia and heroin together for a patient suffering from cerebral thrombosis? He could not remember 'prescribing that for any of my own patients', nor 'such a thing as a matter of routine'.

Mr Lawrence then cross-examined Dr Harris, commencing by explaining that there was no intention to criticise him in any way. His visits to Mrs Morrell amounted to one in 1949, seven in May of 1950, and two on 11th September, 1950, four on 12th September, two on 13th September, 2 on 14th September, two on 15th September, one on 16th, none on the 17th and 18th, one on the 19th, one on the 20th, one on the 21st, two on the 22nd and two on the 23rd, which amounted to 20 visits. Having established this, Mr Lawrence questioned Dr Harris about the need for preventing attacks of 'cerebral irritation' in the patient, keeping her quiet by providing sedation and using drugs to achieve this. He agreed with all the questions. It was a question of the doctor concerned choosing suitable drugs, then? Yes. In Dr Adams' case he had decided to use morphia and heroin in combination:

'Yes, it was his line of treatment that he thought was necessary.'

Then, in cases like that of Mrs Morrell, the patient improved for a while, then went 'downhill'. 'It would be impossible to make a definite prognosis.' Dr Harris said that he had 'merely repeated what she already had been given at the request of the nurses' in June, 1950 – which led Mr Lawrence to May of 1950 and the nurses' reports, which he then went through. On the 10th, Dr Harris had given an intra-muscular injection: was this Citamin? He presumed it was. Was there 'any particular magic about giving a vitamin injection in the morning and not in the evening?' No. He felt certain that the 'special injections' he had given were not more morphia and heroin. Then on to the September reports. The 11th: Dr Harris visited twice. He couldn't remember what the 'special capsule' was. Caffeine? It might have been. 'Special injections'? One would have been Coramine, probably; another might have been a small dose of atropine. Dr Harris would not have given another additional sedative as there was one already recorded.

> 'As far as I was concerned it was increasing something that she was already on, and it was necessary.'

Mr Lawrence asked about pain: Dr Harris had a 'vague memory' that she did have 'a certain amount of pain'. He had added omnopon on 12th September, giving her 'extra sedation'. Dr Harris pointed out that the oral tablets he had prescribed contained $\frac{1}{12}$th grain of morphia 'a very small quantity'. The cause of Mrs Morrell's disturbance, said Mr Lawrence, may have been 'her anger or distress at Dr Adams' going away for his holiday', but nevertheless Dr Harris had to deal with it, no matter what the cause, in order to avoid the 'possible consequences'. So, stepping up the sedative drugs, then reducing to normal level later was the method? Yes.

The trial was adjourned until the following day, Wednesday, 27th March.

# Eighth Day

Mr Lawrence continued with his cross-examination, going through the nurses' notes during September, 1950 in the same vein: 'special injections' must be vitamin injections in the mornings, atropine in the evenings – 'It certainly wouldn't be another injection of Morphia or Heroin or Morphia and Heroin combined, would it?' Dr Harris could not imagine that it would have been, no. Dr Adams had come back from his holiday on the 17th and 18th September, and Dr Harris came in again on the 19th: the capsule and injection he gave, would these be 'the Caffeine capsule and vitamin injection?' Dr Harris didn't see that they could have been anything else, no. By the question regarding the next day, he was 'pretty sure about that'.

On the 20th September, Dr Harris had brought forward the 'routine injection' by one hour, which he imagined would have been to get the patient to sleep earlier in the evening. That her respirations were increased that evening, might be due to pulmonary congestion. He went on giving his opinion on the symptoms described in the reports; it seemed apparent that he did not actually remember what had happened, but his answers agreeing to 'reasonable conclusions' and it being 'not uncommon' were all useful to Mr Lawrence. Dr Harris had left an instruction to give an extra injection of $\frac{1}{6}$ morphia and $\frac{1}{6}$ heroin on the night of 21 September and on 23rd September reduced the 7.30 p.m. injection from $\frac{1}{3}$rd heroin down to one sixth.

That same night he had to visit Mrs Morrell at 11.40 p.m. and give her an injection of ⅓rd Omnopon. Mr Lawrence drew the inference that Dr Harris 'had increased the sedation', when, in fact he had reduced the morphia and heroin earlier and now put back only the morphia content to its normal level of ⅓rd. Dr Harris agreed with Mr Lawrence!

It was on the evening of the 23rd September that the first combined injection of morphia ¼, omnopon ⅓ and heroin ⅙ had appeared. Dr Harris replied that heroin was reduced but the omnopon had been added. He must have been trying to reduce the heroin and adding to the sedative effect of the injection. The next day Dr Adams returned. Dr Harris agreed with Mr Lawrence that Mrs Morrell must have been going through 'a phase of deterioration'.

Mr Lawrence wound up with a few general questions. Dr Harris qualified in 1933 and had been in 'hospital work and general practice', and he came back from the war in 1946. There was a quick reference to the day report of 5th October, 1950 and Mr Lawrence asked if the 'prolonged twitching of the left shoulder' noted by a nurse was the same kind mentioned in a report for a night when he had attended Mrs Morrell – yes, it could reasonably be said to be so. And a quick confirmation that 'special injections' were probably vitamin or atropine. Mr Lawrence must have felt that Dr Harris was a most helpful witness for the defence, but Dr Harris must also have felt that he was, in a way, defending himself.

Mr Melford Stevenson re-examined: he asked if Dr Harris had ever seen 'the kind of movements' which resulted from morphia or heroin addiction. He could not honestly say he had. Had he made any note of Dr Adams' instructions with regard to this patient? Dr Adams might have given him a piece of paper telling him 'to carry on with whatever treatment she had been having', but he would have destroyed it. Mr Stevenson asked him to look at the day report for 8th May, 1950 and see if his visit that day was recorded: although Dr Harris had recorded it, the nurse had not done so. Again, his record for 15th May showed that he visited Mrs Morrell, but the nurses' notebook did not; the same applied for 17th May and for the 19th May. All these had been Nurse Keenan's reports, but the one for 21st September which Dr Harris had a record of had been omitted by Sister Mason-Ellis. For the 12th September, Dr Harris had recorded paying four visits to Mrs Morrell and only three were recorded by Sister Bartlett (now Hughes).

Mr Justice Devlin questioned Dr Harris about the drugs he would 'have had in mind from which the selection' for the patient would have been made. Dr Harris pointed out that the selection would have been different in 1950 and his list was:

'The barbitones, phenobarbitone drugs, bromides, sometimes Valerian, sometimes paraldehyde; that is the main group of drugs that would be used.'
'And what about morphia and heroin then?'
'Well, I can only speak from my own experience, that I have had to use morphia in this type of case over a short period of time. That has just been my experience.'

Dr Harris thought that his list 'would probably be the first choice' except if the patient had a bad phase of acute cerebral irritation, then he 'might have to use stronger drugs to cover that period.' By 'stronger drugs' he meant morphia. Heroin was stronger than morphia?

'Yes. I have not used it myself very much actually so I cannot speak from great experience. One has used it, particularly for pain.'

The Judge asked if perhaps he were mindful of the long-term effects of such drugs. Dr Harris said he would always have to consider this: the length of time they would have to be used. A case of 'severe pain' was the 'usual indication for the use of those drugs.' He did think that, in 1950, morphia might have had to be used 'in a case of acute restlessness'. Mr Justice Devlin wondered whether he had in mind a short period of treatment with morphia in such a case?

'Well, I can only speak from my own experience, that I have never had to use morphia for a long period of restlessness.'

As to taking on the patient of another doctor for a short period, the Judge understood that Dr Harris would not make a new diagnosis and prescribe new and different treatment? He would not change the treatment when he was attending only for a few days, he had to continue with the current treatment; if he had started withdrawing the morphia and heroin from Mrs Morrell it might have made her 'extremely ill'. Mr Justice Devlin asked Dr Harris if he would have 'done something' about the treatment if he had thought it was shortening her life or just thought that it was none of his business. Dr Harris considered that if he was only seeing the patient for a few days and it was 'not doing the patient harm over that short period of time, one would not change the treatment, with the instructions one has been given.' But ten days in September 1950 was not so short a time, suggested the Judge, suppose he had formed the view that the treatment was harmful and shortening the patient's life, would he have spoken to Dr Adams about it? The answer was startling:

'It is a very difficult question to answer, my Lord, because Dr Adams had definite ideas of treatment which were not necessarily my own, and I do not think I would have felt I was in a position to have said anything to him.'

Dr Harris was forty-six or forty-seven years of age in 1956, and a very experienced doctor. He could not remember ever discussing the case with Dr Adams. Mr Justice Devlin finally asked Dr Harris if he had felt that Mrs Morrell was just 'going through a phase' and was likely to get better, or was it the beginning of final deterioration. Unsurprisingly Dr Harris was unable to answer either way, although he felt that 'these patients do vary so much in the course of an illness like this.'

The first of the expert medical witnesses was now called, to be examined by the Attorney-General: Dr Arthur Henry Douthwaite, MD, BS, FRC., MRCS, who lived and practiced at 49, Harley Street in London. Dr Douthwaite was editor of Hale-White's text book *Materia Medica*, senior physician to Guy's Hospital in London, a consultant physician to the Royal Hospital and Home for Incurables and to Horsham Hospital, and a Fellow of the Medical Society of London; from 1924 to 1928 he had been a general practitioner in Worthing, Sussex.

The Attorney-General asked Dr Douthwaite what were the causes of a stroke: these were, he said, a haemorrhage of the brain, cerebral haemorrhage, where a blood vessel bursts; cerebral thrombosis, which meant a clot occurring in an artery of the brain, cutting off blood supply; and 'so-called' cerebral embolism where a clot is carried from the brain to another part of the body. Cerebral thrombosis was 'usually gradual' whereas cerebral haemorrhage 'frequently began with a headache, but not invariably'. Severe cerebral haemorrhage 'is almost always followed by death within three or four days, whereas with cerebral thrombosis the majority do not die as a direct result of it and gradually improve over the next few days, and in fact, over several months.' Life could last 'for many years' after cerebral thrombosis.

Dr Douthwaite's conclusion as to the cause of stroke from which Mrs Morrell suffered in 1948, was that it was 'in all probability a cerebral thrombosis'. One effect, said the Attorney-General, was paralysis of the left side, what would the other symptoms be? Dr Douthwaite indicated depression, irritability and tearfulness, which would be natural. His treatment would be within a few days 'to mobilise the patient, encourage movement of the body and indeed, encourage her to try to move the paralysed part. Massage, exercises and so forth.' The Attorney-General asked Dr Douthwaite to look at the first prescriptions for Mrs Morrell, dating from July, 21st, 1948 (Exhibit 52): these were 'Hypodermic tablets of heroin ⅙ grain, 40' and '40 tablets Hypodermic morphine sulphate ⅙'. Did he think there was any justification for injecting these drugs after a stroke?

> 'It is wrong. In all circumstances it would be wrong to inject Heroin and Morphia.'
> 'What about Morphia alone?'
> 'Morphia alone should not be given to someone who has had a stroke unless there was an episode of acute mania, then that would be justified as a single injection.'
> [The last question and answer are heavily marked in the margin by Hannam.]

The Attorney-General went through Exhibit 52, the prescription list, pointing out the numerous prescriptions for heroin and morphia while Mrs Morrell was in the Nursing Homes and after she returned to 'Marden Ash'; he asked what the effect of the administration of the drugs would be:

> 'These drugs, especially in the early stages, before any appreciable craving is developed or if the dose… was kept approximately the same, will result in a general feeling of ill-health, interspersed at times with a feeling of good health or even pleasure, especially soon after the injection. The administration of drugs as set out in these prescriptions would inevitably produce severe addiction both to morphia and to heroin.'

This drug regime would seriously interfere with resumption of normal life: 'It would take away all the co-operation, the desire to move…' Sedation for ensuring sleep at night was 'quite reasonable', but would 'completely exclude' morphia and heroin. Keeping a stroke patient very quiet during the day would increase the risk of another stroke; it was necessary for the patient to move and not to rest and be sedated during the daytime. Heroin and morphia slowed respiration and there would be a danger of chest complications. Morphia was also 'powerfully constipating' , which would cause distress and restlessness.

The Attorney-General questioned Dr Douthwaite about 'cerebral irritation': he would expect this to be a short-term effect, but the patient was almost certainly suffering from some degree of cerebral arterio sclerosis (hardening of the arteries of the brain) and would be 'very likely to be irritable'. Morphia was 'a completely contrary indication' in this case. Bromide, barbitone and 'lots of the barbiturates' were available in 1950 and safer. In the short term morphia and heroin would have caused 'drowsiness and sleep, but on recovery from that, on awakening, the person would feel ill and irritable.' They might feel nausea and vomit. Irritability could only be made worse. Morphia depressed the brain and produced drowsiness and sleep and depressed 'an appreciation of pain'; it had 'a powerful depressing effect on respiration', but was likely to stimulate the spinal cord slightly. The immediate effect of administration in 90% of people would be to give a feeling of pleasure. Would Dr Douthwaite say something about addiction?

> 'It is a drug which is very liable to produce addiction and if it is given daily the individual is likely to have become addicted within a fortnight and certainly within three weeks.'

He had no doubt that Mrs Morrell would have been addicted by the end of July, 1948. The patient's normal reaction to the doctor supplying the drug would be 'one of dependence on the doctor. He, naturally, if this medication be continued, obtains a complete ascendancy over that patient once that patient is addicted.' The only reason for administration of the drug over several months would be 'for a severe pain which cannot be quelled by drugs which are less dangerous.' Normal dosage would be ¼ grain, once four-hourly for bad pain, but for agonising pain hourly, 'but the *British Pharmacopoeia* of 1948 gives the maximum as ⅓$^{rd}$ of a grain.'

The Attorney-General asked how heroin differed from morphia. Dr Douthwaite replied that heroin was stronger: it was powerfully depressant on the respiratory centre in the brain by 'three or four times'. One sixth of a grain was the maximum recommended dosage; perhaps it might be given at intervals of six hours, but more frequently 'in the face of terrible pain'. Heroin was only mildly sedative 'and loses that effect if repeated frequently'; it removed pain. The administration of heroin would induce a feeling 'Of intense pleasure with repeated doses; …often excitability, not necessarily unpleasant from their point of view'. Could 'twitchings of the limbs' be occasioned by heroin? Oh, yes. But barbiturates given with the heroin would tend to prevent the twitchings. Heroin 'stimulates the spinal cord much more constantly and violently than does morphine'. It would give rise to 'jerky movements, twitchings, convulsions'.

How long would it take to acquire 'tolerance' to morphia and heroin, asked the Attorney-General. Dr Douthwaite considered that it could be 'within a fortnight to three weeks'. 'Tolerance' meant that 'a larger dose of a drug has to be given in order to secure the initial effect': the effect lasted for a shorter time. Of the symptoms as the effects of the drug wore off:

> 'The most striking and constant symptom is craving, but that may be associated with signs such as sneezing, running at the nose, excitability, bad temper, or weeping; and, dependent on how long they are kept without a fresh injection, there may be vomiting, pains in the limbs…'

The Attorney-General wanted to know what the effect these drugs would have on the appetite of a patient: they would suffer a loss of appetite, 'the whole body nourishment is interfered with and the weight is likely to fall'. The only ways to deal with the tolerance were to stop the drug or to increase the drug; if the drug were increased then a fresh tolerance would be acquired for the larger dose. The withdrawal symptoms which would occur if the drugs were stopped, or even if too long an interval were allowed between injections would be for the patient to become 'wildly excited… they get pain in the limbs, sweating, sneezing, they may get collapse – a whole host of symptoms.' The symptoms would 'become maximal if the drugs have been withheld for about two days'. Keeping the patient on approximately the same level of drugs for months would keep her 'in a state of almost constant craving for more drugs and thus ensure that she would be excitable, bad-tempered, impossible to live with'.

Dr Douthwaite was asked by the Attorney-General if paraldehyde was a sedative: it was and its smell and taste were 'revolting'; it was a depressant of the central nervous system, which could be used 'in an endeavour to stop twitchings' (an anti-convulsant). What would the effects be if it were superimposed on heroin or heroin and morphia?

> 'That would be likely to produce death.'

In reply to Mr Justice Devlin, Dr Douthwaite said that it was not 'of itself a dangerous drug', but it would deepen coma or heavy, drugged sleep.

Exhibit 54 (summary of routine and additional injections taken from the nurses' reports) was handed to Dr Douthwaite, and he was first asked 'what could be the medical object' of giving routine injections of morphia and heroin? 'There is not one', he responded firmly. In his opinion, Mrs Morrell was 'an addicted patient' by 20th June, 1949. There were five months of routine injections of ¼ morphia and ⅓ heroin from 23rd June, 1949 to 19th November, 1949: was there, the Attorney-General queried, 'any sufficient increase to counteract acquired tolerance during those five months?' 'No.'

There were odd occasions, such as 10th December, 1949, when there was a sudden reduction in drugs: they were reduced by one half, and the report for the night following this indicated withdrawal symptoms. The same had occurred on 22nd December when the heroin was cut by one half, and Mrs Morrell was 'shouting and hysterical' about Dr Adams and Miss Keenan.

On 19th July, 1950 the heroin and morphia were reduced to one half for that day, and it was noted in the night report: 'Said she was dying and would like to see Dr Adams to say goodbye'. Dr Douthwaite called this 'an unsatisfied craving', and there were other instances of behaviour which was consistent with craving for drugs when the dosage was reduced for one day. No reason could be ascertained for these occasional and sudden reductions in the drugs; only Dr Adams had the answer.

The Attorney-General asked what would happen if the dosage of the two drugs was suddenly increased: if this were rapid, then 'the individual would go into a deep sleep or coma'. If the heroin alone were increased, said Dr Douthwaite, then there would be more jerky movements or possibly even convulsions. He was asked to look at the entry for 29th September, 1950, when it was noted that Mrs Morrell had ¾ morphia, ⅓ heroin and 1 grain of omnopon, an injection of coramine and two special injections. Following the last 'special injection' at 11.15 p.m., she was 'restless, giddy, and perspiring freely, and her legs and body were feeling cold'. Dr Douthwaite felt that these symptoms were 'a result of a fairly large dose of Morphia or Heroin'. On 9th October the nurse's notes had reported the incident when, after a 'special capsule and injection', the patient went into a 'a deep sleep and could not be wakened. Was in a semi comatose condition. Lower lip very blue' and '? stroke' Dr Douthwaite stated that this was 'in fact suggestive of a large dose of one or the other' (heroin or morphia), and he confirmed that 'drowsiness' was inconsistent with a vitamin or stimulating injection.

On the 14th October, it was listed in Exhibit 54, that Mrs Morrell had, on that day, ¾ grain of morphine, 1⅓ grains of heroin and 2⅓ grains of omnopon – this was the largest quantity she had so far had on one day? Yes. There was also a special injection 'but we do not know what it was'. The night report which followed recorded that Mrs Morrell was 'very thirsty and talking incessantly' After another injection at 4.15 a.m. on 15th October, she was restless and 'very muddled, does not know where she is. During sleep breathing was Cheyne Stokes…' Dr Douthwaite attributed the Cheyne Stokes breathing 'to the drugs she was given'; if it had been due to senile decay then it would have occurred again. Turning to the entry for 1st November, the Attorney-General read out 'Special injection given: continue with Heroin injections only'. Could Dr Douthwaite account for this:

'No, I do not know why it was done.'

Dropping the morphia and omnopon, would be dropping the chief sedative element in the routine injection.

The day report of the 3rd November: this was a day when Mrs Morrell was asleep when Dr Adams visited; he did not disturb her and ordered 'a Sedormid to be given on waking, and no more until after Mr Morrell's visit at 5.30 p.m. as Dr Adams wished Mrs Morrell to be clear mentally'. One Sedormid, said Dr Douthwaite, would have been unlikely to affect the clearness of her mind. Then the nurse had made a note at 5.30: 'Has been very lachrymose since 5 p.m. Does not want to see Mr Morrell. Cried most of his visit…' Dr Douthwaite was of the opinion that 'it was certainly consistent with her unsatisfied craving for drugs to which she had become accustomed'. By 6.30 p.m. she had become 'hysterical' and said that the nurse 'was trying to kill her'. There was 'excessive nose-running during the crying periods'. Dr Adams was 'phoned and he prescribed ½ grain of heroin to be given, which was done at 8.15. This was all consistent with drug addiction and the withholding of the heroin and morphia.

It was in the day report of the 5th November, that the instruction appeared in the notebook 'May have heroin grs. ½ repeated S.O.S.' and on that day Mrs Morrell was given 1½ grains of heroin; on 6th November she had 2½ grains of heroin and morphia had reappeared with ¼ grain. And on the 7th November, 1½ grains of morphia and 2½ grains of heroin was administered, and the instruction was altered to 'H.I. morphia gs. ½ and Heroin gs. ½ – same may be repeated during the night with Atropine gs. ¹⁄₁₀₀ if necessary – if patient does not sleep after 2 hours, the injection may be repeated again.' Dr Douthwaite regarded this as 'a heavy dosage' and the two hour interval 'dangerously short'. The Attorney-General asked:

> 'I think that there is an entry that she is to have 1 grain of heroin hourly if necessary. I think that appears from the night report of the 9th/10th. "10.15 Visited by Dr Adams." That is 10.15 on the 9th. "H.I. of H. Morphia gr. 1 at 10.20. (To have heroin gr. i given S.O.S.)" How would you describe that dosage?'
> 'It is a high dosage and an astonishing instruction.'

Dr Douthwaite explained that if a doctor felt it necessary to prescribe six times the normal dose of heroin, 'S.O.S.' would not be 'a satisfactory indication to give to the nurse. The precise reason for giving it should and would normally be written down.'

After the adjournment for lunch, the Attorney-General asked if Dr Douthwaite had found any entry in the notebooks 'not consistent either with the effect of the morphia and heroin wearing off or with an overdose of either morphia or heroin' – he had not. He returned to the night report of the 10th November, when Dr Adams had visited at 10.15 p.m. and gave an injection of one grain of hyperduric morphia and left the instruction to have 'heroin 1 gr.' when necessary. Mrs Morrell had slept for 6½ hours and was given one grain of heroin at 4.15 a.m. and another at 6.30 a.m. At 8 a.m. Dr Adams visited and gave ½ grain of hyperduric morphia. She had been peaceful, confused but not restless, and not eating. This was when the instruction was given for 'heroin 1 gr. hourly if necessary'. The patient had 'slight jerkings of the body', then became restless at 8.15 p.m. and was given 1 grain of heroin at 8.20.

The Attorney-General reminded Dr Douthwaite that Sister Randall had given evidence about this night report when she said she had been 'instructed to 'keep Mrs Morrell under' – was the information consistent with that? 'Yes, indeed.' What did all this indicate to Dr Douthwaite?

> 'It seems to me that the only reason why this was given was in order to keep her under. There was no indication that I can see for the therapeutic administration of heroin on those dates in those quantities.'
> 'When you say "keep her under", what exactly do you mean by that?'
> 'Well, to put it in simple language, to keep her thoroughly doped or drugged.'

The Attorney-General came to 11th November, when Mrs Morrell had been given 'a total in those 24 hours of 3½ grains of morphine and 5 grains of heroin'; the morphine had gone up by 2½ grains and the heroin by another grain. The day report for the Saturday 11th, recorded:

'Doctor called this morning. Patient may have hypodermic injection of morphia 1.2 gr., heroin ½ gr. hourly if necessary', increasing the hourly injection 'from a half a grain of heroin by half a grain of morphia'. The Attorney-General asked Dr Douthwaite to look at the dosage from the 8th November:

> '…seeing the rise from 2 of morphia and 2 of heroin on the 8th, 2 of morphia and 1½ of heroin on the 9th, and then on the 10th November to 4 of heroin and 1 of morphia, then on the next day, the 11th, 3½ and 5 respectively, and on the 12th 2 and 3½ – looking at those dosages of heroin that she had leading up to the time of her death on the 13th, making all allowances for acquired tolerance, what in your opinion was bound to be the effect of that dosage of heroin as administered to her as shown in the nurses' reports?'
>
> 'I believe that it would have produced jerking spasms or convulsions, and ultimately death.'

Dr Douthwaite could find no evidence to justify this: of her suffering severe pain. Severe pain following a stroke, 'thalamic syndrome' occurred 'very rarely'. In this condition, there would be bouts of agonizing pain recurring frequently and was associated, sometimes, with violent outbursts of rage. He could see no indication at all in the reports that Mrs Morrell had suffered from this syndrome.

The Attorney-General now had some questions about prescriptions (Exhibit 4A): in particular the prescriptions for November, 1950. If those prescriptions exceeded the amounts shown in the nurses' reports and 'the difference was in fact administered to Mrs Morrell in that period' what would have been the effect?

> 'They would have killed her.'

There was a difference of 30½ grains of morphia and 21½ grains of heroin between the amounts shown as administered and the amounts shown as prescribed. The police evidence was that 'Dr Adams said that he had administered 75 one sixth grains of heroin on the last day, the 12th'; this would equal 12½ grains, plus the 3½ shown as administered on the nurses' reports – quite enough to kill, even if the amounts supposedly left over of one phial of morphia and one of heroin or omnopon were deducted. As for the 'symptoms of jerkiness' described by Sister Randall, these had to be a result of the heroin, 'no other explanation was possible'. 'The whole picture created by Nurse Randall and the other nurses' evidence of Mrs Morrell's condition in those last few days' could not be ascribed to cerebral thrombosis.

Dr Douthwaite found that 'there was no justification' for the daily treatment given to Mrs Morrell; the 'certain consequence was addiction' and as for the dosage administered to her in the last few days of her life:

> 'The only conclusion that I can come to was that the intention was to terminate her life.'

Mr Justice Devlin asked him to state which days in particular had led him to that conclusion:

> 'If we start on November 8th, and from the 8th to the 12th inclusive, those figures justify, in my opinion, the conclusion I have given.'

The rise in the dosage of heroin meant 'increasing danger'. The paraldehyde's effect would be to 'make the heroin more lethal'. The paraldehyde injections 'would make death more certain than it already was' and would probably have made the patient unconscious, or deepen an already existing coma.

The Attorney-General asked Dr Douthwaite about the cause of death, as recorded on the cremation form by Dr Adams: 'cerebral thrombosis'. Were there any signs in the nurses' reports to justify this conclusion? No. Dr Fox had also certified this cause after an external examination of the body, could a doctor tell whether a person had died of cerebral thrombosis by external examination? 'No, you cannot.'

Would Dr Douthwaite prescribe heroin for the elderly? No, 'over the age of 70, it is almost axiomatic that it should not be given', unless they were dying from some 'terribly painful and incurable disease' and if the pain could be controlled by no other drug. He could think of no legitimate reason for the amounts of drugs prescribed from 8th November, 1950 onwards. Were these sufficient to cause death? Yes.

The Attorney-General had finished his examination and Mr Lawrence asked for 'the indulgence of the court': the defence had only received some additional evidence the day before and he asked leave to postpone his cross-examination of Dr Douthwaite until the following morning. The Crown had no objections and Mr Justice Devlin granted the application. The Attorney-General suggested that Detective Sergeant Sellars should now give evidence.

Detective Sergeant Leslie Sellars of Eastbourne County Borough Police was sworn, and examined by Mr Melford Stevenson, who asked him if he had been in Eastbourne Magistrates' Court on the 26th November, 1956 when Dr Adams had been before that Court. DS Sellars said that he had been: Dr Adams had been granted bail and he had taken charge of the accused. After the Magistrates had made the order granting bail, Dr Adams had left the dock and then went 'to the well of the Court.' Sellars said that he had asked the Doctor whether 'he would mind having his photograph taken', and he had said: 'I am quite willing'. He had then said: 'I would like a word with Superintendent Hannam first.' The Superintendent had been standing also in the well of the Court, but was 'some little distance away from us'.

Detective Sergeant Sellars then called to Superintendent Hannam to come to him. 'Mr James, the Solicitor, was standing with Doctor Adams and myself.' Then Dr Adams had said to Superintendent Hannam: 'I would like one word with you' and the Superintendent had replied: 'I am busy for the moment. I will see you later.' At this stage the bail formalities had been completed before Dr Adams had left the dock. Sellars had said to the Doctor 'If you would like to avoid the press and the crowds, I will take you down underneath the dock to the Police Station' – which was in order to reach the photographic studio in the Police Station next door. Dr Adams had agreed with him that this would be the best thing to do, and DS Sellars took him that way and up to the studio on the second floor. Detective Constable Barnes, the photographer, was already there; this was about 11 o'clock in the morning.

Detective Sergeant Sellars explained to Mr Stevenson that D.C. Barnes left the studio to load his camera, and 'whilst he was gone Detective Superintendent Hannam came to the door. He said 'The Doctor wants to see me. You had better leave the room for a moment.' DS Sellars had done so and Superintendent Hannam had only been in the room 'for not more than a minute' and came out again. Sellars had been present when Dr Adams was photographed. As a result of further instructions, he had gone with Dr Adams to his home to obtain his passport: they had gone down to the ground floor of the police station, met with Mr James and they all went together to Kent Lodge.

Mr Lawrence cross-examined the witness in a somewhat vain attempt to shake his evidence: Sellars agreed that the Court that day was 'packed with people', but the bail formalities had been completed in the Court and not in the Police charge room; 'Mr Gray, a dentist, (fellow member of the Plymouth Brethren) stood surety for him and he went into the box for that purpose, Sir.' The Station Sergeant had been in charge of the signing of the bail form and the Warrant Officer was 'in charge of the Court, Sir, but not of the Doctor.' Mr Lawrence asked more than once if Hannam had been in the well of the Court:

'He was perhaps five yards away, Sir, immediately underneath the Bench, Sir, which is half the width of the Court. The dock is in the centre of the Court, then comes the Solicitors' benches and a large table, the Magistrates' Clerk, and the Magistrates. Mr Hannam was nearer to the Magistrates than to the dock.'

Superintendent Hannam would have been 'within speaking distance' of Dr Adams 'if there had not been so many people about'. Sellars had taken Dr Adams back into the dock and down the steps that led from the dock to the 'underneath', then through the Police Charge Room and out into the little hall, up the stairs and into the photographic room. It was prior to the photograph being taken that the Superintendent arrived. D.C. Barnes had to go to the dark room to put new plates into the camera, then return to the studio, fix the lights and take the pictures. Superintendent Hannam had asked him to leave the room. Barnes had come back while the Superintendent was speaking to Dr Adams. After that the three photographs were taken: one standing up and the others sitting down. Again Mr Lawrence suggested that Mr James had already left the Police Station when Sellars and Dr Adams came down:

'He was standing in the vestibule when I came down to the ground floor.'

Mr Justice Devlin adjourned the Court until the following morning.

# Chapter Thirty-Five

———

# The Trial – Days 9–12

## 1–4 April 1957

———

## Ninth Day

The Attorney-General had one or two points which he had omitted to put to Dr Douthwaite. The first was regarding barbiturates; what would be the effect of combining these with heroin and morphia? They would increase any depressant effect. And how would Dr Douthwaite describe the degree of drugging? This, he considered 'heavy'. A general practitioner would have knowledge of all the main drugs and the main occasions upon which these should be used, but the holder of a diploma in anaesthetics would have more knowledge of morphia and heroin and barbitones, and had to make a special study of 'drugs of this sort in order to achieve their speciality'.

Mr Lawrence rose to cross-examine Dr Douthwaite. He went immediately for the jugular:

> 'I think it follows from what you said to my Lord yesterday that that murderous intent in your view was present in his mind from and including the 8th November onwards to the end?'
> 'Yes.'

When he had given evidence at the preliminary hearing, Dr Douthwaite had not known about the medication given to Mrs Morrell prior to January, 1950, and he had also believed that she had been in a continuous coma for the last three or four days of her life. This was so. But the evidence which he had given in Court on the previous day was now founded on the treatment by Dr Adams of Mrs Morrell before January, 1950? Yes, Dr Douthwaite said that he had always thought 'it would be interesting' to know what treatment she had before she came under the care of Dr Adams, particularly in relation to 'any question of addiction', but it was not material to his 'final conclusion'. Mr Lawrence demanded to know why he had not asked to be furnished with the information if he had thought it relevant. Dr Douthwaite had been told it was not available 'at one of the conferences with counsel for the Crown'. He had known that Mrs

– 393 –

Morrell was staying in Cheshire with her son when she had the stroke. He did agree with Mr Lawrence that 'it might throw a great light upon the treatment that he [Dr Adams] adopted at the Eastbourne nursing home in July of 1948'.

Mr Lawrence now produced the nurses' notes from Neston Cottage Hospital in Cheshire from the beginning of Mrs Morrell's illness, which could be proved 'if it is ever necessary to prove this by one of the nurses and the doctor who were at the hospital' [this has been underlined by Hannam and there are two exclamation marks in the margin]. They began on 25th June, 1948, when the day report began: 'Mrs Morrell. Haemaplegia [sic]. Paralyzed [sic] left side. To have Luminal 2 gr.' Dr Douthwaite agreed that luminal was a synthetic barbiturate sedative. On 27th June, the notes recorded that: 'Patient very distressed and complaining of severe pain'. She had been given Veramon tablets, which Dr Douthwaite confirmed were pain-killing tablets. She was unable to swallow them and 'Dr Turner informed. Morphia gr. ¼ given at 11.30 a.m. Has slept since.' The direction 'Repeat morphia S.O.S.' had been put on the day report, and morphia was given at 1.30 a.m. On 28th June, the patient had been injected with 'Benerva, 1 ampul', which Dr Douthwaite said was vitamin B1. She was reported as being 'very ill'. She was still having morphia injections of ¼ grain to help her sleep up to 5th July, and taking diet and fluids. The last night she was in the cottage hospital was 5th July and she was then discharged.

Mr Lawrence pointed out that Mrs Morrell had been in the cottage hospital for some ten days, that, at first, she was under the care of a consultant, Dr Pemberton and then under Dr Turner; that she was 'a very ill woman', that she complained of severe pain on 27th June, 1948, and that they had had to resort to morphia for sedation. Dr Douthwaite tried to answer one of the questions, but failed; Mr Lawrence was in full flow. The Attorney-General intervened to mention that the Doctor was trying to answer. He wanted to say that it was important to point out that they were trying Luminol, phenobarbitone for sedation. But two grains was rather a lot? Yes. Then morphia had to be used. And hadn't Mr Morris, for the Crown, suggested that this was a slight stroke? He had but he withdrew and it was never suggested by medical witnesses that she had a slight stroke.

Mr Lawrence asked if Dr Douthwaite had not said yesterday that no doctor should give morphia to a patient with a stroke, unless the patient had 'acute mania' and then only one injection, neither had she suffered from the rare thalamic syndrome. Dr Douthwaite stood by his statement. Then there were three doctors: Turner, Harris and Adams, two of whom 'were not in the dock on a charge of murder' who had given injections of morphia to this patient. Mr Lawrence asked him if he condemned the use of morphia in the case of Mrs Morrell:

> 'I do in the latter part, not for the pain. On the occasion of the 28th June, when I see her pulse was 116, it may well be that they thought that she was showing signs of heart failure, she might have been dying, then Morphine might have been given because of the impending heart failure, but that would not be giving Morphine simply on account of the stroke.'
>
> [This answer is underlined by Hannam and marked in the margins.]

Would Mrs Morrell have become addicted to morphia over the nine days of injections in the hospital – to any degree by the time she had left hospital? Dr Douthwaite thought it 'improbable' and Mr Lawrence reminded him of his answer to the Attorney-General that a person could become addicted 'within a fortnight and certainly within three weeks', but would it not depend upon the individual?

> 'Yes. I would qualify that. All individuals will become addicted if given drugs of addiction regularly but at variable lengths of time.'

It was possible that addiction could occur 'in less time than a fortnight'. Dr Douthwaite 'did not think we ought to' forget his answer, as Mr Lawrence suggested 'we' should, that someone could be addicted to morphia within 'a fortnight to three weeks'.

Mr Lawrence now considered the expectation of life which Mrs Morrell had at the time of the stroke, the prognosis 'at that time' was bad? Yes. [Hannam has marked this in the margin, 'journey to Eastbourne' – presumably meaning, that if it were so bad, why was she subjected to a long journey by ambulance or able to survive it.] Dr Douthwaite agreed that a reasonable prognosis would have been 6-12 months.

Mr Lawrence moved on to the prescription list (Exhibit 52) and Mrs Morrell's stay at the Esperance Nursing Home in Eastbourne which started on 5th July, 1948, highlighting just some of the numerous prescriptions: a 'tonic' containing tincture nuxvomica, 'rather old-fashioned'. Yes, said Dr Douthwaite, but still used, 'it contains strychnine'. And sodium barbitone 5 grains? Yes. Mr Lawrence added the other innocuous ingredients 'chloroform water, syrup'. Two days later there was the 'first prescription for morphia', but 'hyperduric morphia'; he emphasised 'slow sort of drug'. Yes, it was to spread it over a longer period. 'of sleep?' 'If it was given for that purpose, yes', said the Doctor. The Veramon tablets continued, 'pain-killing tablets' (phenobarbitone), and prescription No. 26 was labelled 'when pain is severe'. [Here Hannam has marked this and written 'why morphine' – these tablets were for the severe pain, so what was the continuing hyperduric morphia for?] There were also other 'sedative mixtures' in the prescriptions, containing morphia.

No. 38 of the prescriptions was for 'ampules of Vitamin B'; the Veramon tablets continued and by prescription No. 62, 'Tablets Pethidine 50 mg. four-hourly for pain' had appeared. Allonal was added on 21st April, 1949 – a barbiturate with amido-pyrine, a pain-killer? Yes. Mr Lawrence was getting to the point: that by June, 1949 Mrs Morrell had survived the stroke by 12 months, the best prognosis – Yes. Had not Dr Douthwaite considered the prescriptions for veramon 'for severe pain' and those for pethedine before? Yes, he had and he agreed that for some months Mrs Morrell had probably suffered from pain somewhere.

> 'If and when he [Dr Adams] got her back to Eastbourne he continued with a daily injection of morphia, he was only continuing what had already been done by the hospital doctor in Cheshire, was not he?'
> 'Yes.'

'Now it looks as if – and we know from the later nurses' books, you see, because there is a gap in the historical record from July, 1948 until June, 1949, when these things (Exhibit 48) began – the prescriptions look as if there was a course of medication, both by morphia and heroin, from July onwards in Eastbourne?' [Heavily marked in margin with query by Hannam.]
'Yes.'

Brushing over the matter of the addition of heroin, Mr Lawrence asked if it had some 'slight sedative quality' as well as being 'notably a pain killer', and leaving the patient 'with a sense of well-being'. Yes. But was the object not, asked Mr Lawrence to make the patient's life 'as bearable as it could be to her, and as bearable as it could be to those who had to look after her?' The first object, said Dr Douthwaite, would be 'to try to restore her health if possible'; for the general practitioner to 'do his reasonable best', but as far as those who looked after her were concerned 'that is a side consideration'. Mr Lawrence put the point that 'nurses, in 1950, after the war, were pretty scarce, were not they?' The Doctor answered 'yes', though private nurses do not seem to have been scarce in Eastbourne; the town attracted them.

The questions moved to the objectives being to 'keep her up and about as much as possible in the day-time' and 'to see that she had sleep at night'. These seemed reasonable objectives to Dr Douthwaite. Mr Lawrence had got over the hump of the matter fairly easily: 'she was having a regular routine injection at 8.30 of a quarter of morphia and one-third of heroin, and during that period she was being assisted further to sleep by slight additional doses of barbiturates when necessary?' 'Yes.'

After some carefully structured questions regarding Dr Douthwaite's answers to questions put by the Attorney-General on thrombosis, cerebral and otherwise, which restricted Dr Douthwaite's ability to respond adequately, Mr Lawrence asked him about 'cerebral irritation', which Dr Douthwaite preferred to refer to as 'irritability'. Yet again Mr Lawrence asked him:

'You see, you never saw Mrs Morrell, did you?'
'No.'
'Neither did I – '
'No.'

It was possible to have a complete personality change after a stroke? Yes. There was another witness in Dr Harris, of Mrs Morrell's bad temper; she had outbursts of 'vulgar abuse' and this 'From a woman who was a rich woman and probably gently nurtured, for all we know?' Yes. There was good evidence of 'cerebral irritation' and Dr Douthwaite was called as 'a medical witness who is invited to give an opinion derived solely from his own inferences from the facts?' Yes, he was. Then it was necessary to look at 'the picture of his [Dr Adams's] treatment of Mrs Morrell as a whole right from the start'.

Mr Lawrence wanted Dr Douthwaite, first of all, to go through with him, various points from the nurses' notebook entries from 24th June, 1949 when 'Dr Adams came at 10.30 and interviewed representative from Jones's with reference to boots'. Mrs Morrell had been fitted with new boots and she had also used a crutch. It was 'quite obvious he was still doing his best to keep her mobile?' 'Yes, I quite agree.' She was walking by 4th July, round the bed and on the 14th July 'she had gone out in the car to the launching of a lifeboat with the doctor'. Mr Lawrence threw in that she had 'left quite a sum of money to the Lifeboat Institution', did Dr Douthwaite know that? He did not know that he had heard it. However, if it would help Mr Lawrence:

> 'Signs of this activity go on for several months, I do realise that.'

He accepted this till the end of 1949, and 'possibly further'. Mr Lawrence mentioned as far as 9th August, 1950 'Walked the length of the tennis lawn twice' and August 18th 'Walked upstairs with much less effort.' Dr Douthwaite agreed that there was 'ample evidence' that Dr Adams was keeping her 'up and about and interested' up to August, 1950.

Mr Lawrence asked Dr Douthwaite to look at the case from the point of view of a general practitioner who 'inherited the morphia addiction'. He could not accept that she was addicted after a short stay in hospital, the chances of this were 'really negligible'; well, that 'he has inherited a patient that another doctor has found could be beneficially treated with morphia'. He agreed; and that there was some 'substantial degree of pain' at that time.

> 'It is pretty clear that he continued the Morphia injections that the hospital were giving,
> and after a little while, a very little while, added Heroin?'
> 'Yes.'

Hannam has underlined the question mark after 'Heroin' and put in the margin '= doubling morphine = adding heroin'. Douthwaite also missed that she had been given the morphia in hospital because she could not swallow the Veramon tablets at the time, and the Veramon tablets had been added back by Dr Adams and he had not taken away the morphia, but even added heroin as well – not to mention other drugs.

To Mr Lawrence it was simple: 'ignoring any adjustments of pheno barbitone here and there or any reduction [!] or addition to the regular routine dose, the picture is this, is it not, the adherence every evening at the same time of the day to the routine injection of the two drugs' the patient had been 'on an even keel' and no 'disturbances were recorded' until Dr Harris was in 'locum tenens' whilst Dr Adams was on holiday in September, 1950. Yes, Dr Douthwaite agreed. Dr Harris had been confronted with, what he thought was 'a marked degree of cerebral irritation?' Yes. Dr Harris dealt with it with additional morphia, by 'introducing Omnopon?' [It had actually been introduced earlier by Dr Adams.] Yes. However, Dr Douthwaite was saying that 'by that time Mrs Morrell was addicted to both those drugs' and had acquired a tolerance to both.

He was. Mr Lawrence returned to Dr Douthwaite's answers to questions put by the Attorney-General, then he put it to Dr Douthwaite that some people went on 'day after day without any increase' in the dose of drugs, the taking of these doses 'has become part of their ordinary lives. He mentioned 'professional people' and 'labouring people in Eastern countries'. Then he moved the case on:

> 'Of course, if you are dealing with a case not of a Morphine addict such as I have just put to you, but dealing with a case where you are administering Morphia either to deal with pain or to deal with some physical degenerative condition, [the last underlined by Hannam] the time will come when you will not be able to deal with what you are trying to deal with by means of a level dosage, won't it?'
> 'I agree.'
> 'So by just stopping a drug like Morphia or Heroin after a long period would cause illness and suffering; it might very well cause a collapse'.
> 'Yes, If it were stopped suddenly, certainly.' [Circled by Hannam.]

The other course would be to give her more, which Dr Harris did. Crucially, Mr Lawrence now got Dr Douthwaite to agree that Mrs Morrell 'was in fact physically going downhill from September onwards' and 'reaching… the terminal stages of her illness' and then, quite inaccurately, stating in a question that a doctor 'in the terminal stages' of her illness:

> '…would be faced with the dilemma that you have mentioned: either having to stop the drug, with a risk of collapse and death, or going on with it in increasing doses?'

Dr Douthwaite had already explained that collapse would be risked only if the drugs were stopped suddenly, [Hannam marks this in the margin] but he replied 'Yes.'

There were some instances, drawn to Dr Douthwaite's attention by the Attorney-General where he had said that certain events when drugs were reduced 'were consistent with withdrawal symptoms', but Mr Lawrence found one on 14th June, 1950 where the heroin had been reduced by one half [temporarily] and the following day had been 'good'. Then a limited question:

> 'There is no indication of any withdrawal at this moment?'
> 'No.'

This was 'to be balanced' against evidence Dr Douthwaite had given on the previous day; Dr Douthwaite pointed out that he had not picked out the instances upon which he had given answers. Mr Lawrence asked if he had realised that 'it was not fair' to pick out 'instances'. The Doctor did not think it was 'his duty to point out whether it was fair or not.'

> 'You agreed yesterday with the expression of opinion that my client intended to kill her and killed her?'
> 'Yes, I did, and I expressed that view in relation to the last few days in November.'
> [The last answer heavily sidelined by Hannam.]

Mr Lawrence asked Dr Douthwaite if he might now disregard his evidence on 'selected instances' on withdrawal symptoms. He was not prepared to say that. Perhaps he would look at one of the instances, the 19th July, 1950, when there was a reduction of heroin from ⅓ to ⅙ grain, but firstly, the withdrawal symptoms and the craving would come after the drugs had worn off, then 'maximal' after being withheld for about two days? Yes. In this case Dr Douthwaite had attributed a 'withdrawal symptom' to a symptom which occurred one hour and twenty minutes after the injection. But the symptoms would 'come on rather before the next dose is due and not after it?' Yes, but in this case the dose of heroin had been reduced and she was unsatisfied with the lower amount: 'She was unsatisfied, in other words.' Mr Lawrence went on to show that on the 20th July, the same injection had been given but there was no resultant 'mental distress' which Dr Douthwaite had postulated was the result of 'craving'; this 'old woman' after a severe stroke was quite likely to suffer mental distress which could be 'cerebral irritation'.

Now the 22nd August when Dr Adams had ordered three-quarters of the usual injection to be given at 8.40 p.m. (temporarily): Dr Douthwaite had attributed the episode when Mrs Morrell was saying, with reference to a bottle of tablets that 'she was going to take them so that they would not be taken away' as 'craving'. Surely she would know that it was an injection she wanted if this symptom was 'craving'? Yes, she would, of course.

In another instance on the 23rd September, Dr Harris had visited at 5 p.m., ordered a reduced dose of heroin with ¼ morphia to be given at 7.30 p.m. and Dr Douthwaite had attributed the symptoms of confusion and irritability during the night as being attributable to craving. Mr Lawrence asked if it could have been possible that there was 'craving' if at 5 p.m., Mrs Morrell had been noted as having 'slight improvement in condition' – the reason why Dr Harris had reduced the dosage. Dr Douthwaite did not think this gave 'one any direct information'. Dr Harris' evidence had not given his views on the matter. But, said Mr Lawrence, the lack of sleep after the drugs were given could not indicate 'craving'; 'Perhaps a better word would be "inadequate dose."' Dr Douthwaite thought.

The Attorney-General was moved to intervene to protest that Mr Lawrence was putting things out of context in referring to previous answers given by the witness. Mr Lawrence put it that 'both these doctors' were 'experimenting' with reductions and, if Dr Douthwaite was right, going back to the 'routine' dosage again. It was all 'the dilemma' they had discussed. The Court adjourned for lunch.

Mr Lawrence returned to the addiction symptoms: would Dr Douthwaite not expect any such symptoms to both continue and perhaps increase up to the time of the next injection and not to disappear beforehand? He would. Yet this was what had happened in instances he had referred to that very morning. Dr Douthwaite accepted his statement. Therefore there had to be a 'time element' and for them to be 'manifested with regularity' and for them to be similar to define them as 'true withdrawal symptoms'. The 'proper inference' was that these symptoms were not withdrawal symptoms at all. Dr Douthwaite demurred: that was 'going a little too far.' They could be due to 'the patient's disease accompanied by senility' as Mr Lawrence put it, but:

'They would also be fully consistent with a patient feeling ill as a result of days and weeks and months of drugs such as morphia and heroin.'

[This answer is underlined and marked in the margins by Hannam.]

Mr Lawrence understood that Dr Douthwaite had definite objections to morphia and heroin because a patient was liable to become addicted to them. The gravest objection? Dr Douthwaite objected to them almost equally because 'they were both dangerous drugs for an old person.' There was the danger of using them from the point of view 'of the physical condition' and of 'certain addiction'. Mr Lawrence, taking the addiction argument, supposed that the shorter the prognosis, the more likely a doctor would be to choose morphia and heroin, whereas he might choose differently if the expectation of life were in years. The Doctor agreed: but if the prognosis were doubtful or more than 'a month or two' then the matter of addiction should be borne in mind. Now, proposed Mr Lawrence, a 'a lot more is known, I suppose now, in 1957, about drugs… than thirty or forty years ago, when Dr Adams qualified… in the early 1920s.' Morphine and heroin were commonly used as hypnotics. Dr Douthwaite agreed that morphine was, but 'heroin not commonly' as its dangers were known. Mr Lawrence made the point that 'fairly recently, there have been great public debates about heroin'. Very recently, yes. There was no mention that Dr Adams was a practising anaesthetist who had to be very up-to-date with drugs. Mr Justice Devlin asked for an explanation of the word 'hypnotics', which Dr Douthwaite defined as drugs 'designed to produce sleep'.

Still, it was the hospital doctor who had first given Mrs Morrell morphia and he must have known that she was over seventy. Dr Douthwaite said he was speaking of heroin which should not be used except in cases of severe pain; dangerous drugs were beneficial if used properly. Mr Lawrence asked if Dr Douthwaite had not himself led a deputation to the Home Office 'asking that there should be no ban placed on the manufacture of Heroin in this country'. Indeed he had taken 'a leading part'. Had he not also edited the latest edition 'of the well-known medical book Hale-Whites Materia Medica' where, in dealing with opiates, he had listed contra-indications – cases where they should not be used, and these did not include an age limit of 70? Dr Douthwaite again pointed out that he had only referred to heroin in previous answers, and the Attorney-General confirmed this, endorsed by the Judge.

Mr Lawrence returned to the addition of Omnopon by Dr Harris, and this 'finding its way into the regular evening injection' being carried on by Dr Adams: this was 'resolving the dilemma on the side of increasing the dose rather than cutting her off altogether'? Dr Douthwaite agreed with this presumption. Extra Omnopon was given during the nights which followed then to 'avoid restlessness and promote sleep' and this was because of 'some level of tolerance being acquired over the years'? Dr Douthwaite thought this seemed likely. Clearly Mr Lawrence was accepting that Mrs Morrell had become a drug addict.

In the nurses' notes for the night of 14th/15th October there had been the one reference to the 'Cheyne Stokes breathing' – ' intermittent breathing: at one time heavy and stertorous and then quiet and shallow'; Mr Lawrence suggested that this was the sign of a failing heart. Dr Douthwaite replied that it might be, but, in such a case, it would usually tend to recur and this had not happened. Mr Lawrence asked about the nurse's note on the 9th October '? stroke' and if it were not reasonable for a 'general practitioner' to diagnose this when the nurse had also noted 'slight difficulty with speech'. It would be 'compatible' said Dr Douthwaite. This was, of course, a 'diagnosis' made over the telephone by Dr Adams, but this was not mentioned by Mr Lawrence.

Mr Lawrence asked Dr Douthwaite if he were 'making any suggestion' that the 'special injections' recorded were morphia or heroin. The Attorney-General objected as such 'suggestions' should come from the prosecution and not the defence. After a few more questions, Mr Justice Devlin intervened to tell him that he was 'entrenching' on 'what is the Attorney-General's province', and that the witness had said only that 'some of the injections to which his attention was drawn are, in his view, not vitamins or stimulants, but probably morphine injections'; he should deal with individual instances.

Mr Lawrence suggested to Dr Douthwaite that it was 'not at all unusual' for nurses to write down, when a patient was on regular injections of vitamins, the words 'special injection':

> 'Yes, I should have thought that was unusual. It is one of the things that has puzzled me, this use of the words 'special injection'.'
> [The last two words are heavily underlined by Hannam.]

Had Dr Douthwaite tried to check the 'special capsules' mentioned against the prescriptions? No, he had not: 'special' was an inexplicable term. He was referred to the Cheshire Hospital notes where 'special sleeping tablets' were recorded: at least this gave 'some idea' of what they were. Mr Lawrence pressed him on his lack of interest in 'special' capsules and injections, particularly as he had committed himself to stating 'Dr Adams' murderous intention at a given time'. Dr Douthwaite countered that he had been asked if he 'could think of any conceivable reason for giving certain doses of heroin and morphia' during the last days of Mrs Morrell's life.

Mr Lawrence wondered whether Dr Douthwaite 'would take it from him' that the 'special capsule' was 'contemporaneous with the prescriptions of Brownes for Caffeine capsules specially made up'? He would certainly do so. Was caffeine a stimulant? Yes, 'in certain doses'. And an antidote to morphia?

> 'A feeble one. It has some slight antidotal properties. Yes, I will grant you that.'

Mr Lawrence was suggesting that if the 'special capsule' were caffeine, then it would 'make sense' to suppose that the 'special injection' was a vitamin injection. Then choose an instance where the patient was 'bright and talkative' afterwards...

> 'It does not look as if that was a morphine or heroin injection, does it?'
> 'No, it does not.'

All this enabled Mr Lawrence to extract the admission from Dr Douthwaite, that the 'special injections' and 'special capsules' had played no part in his conclusions and could therefore be discounted.

They were back to 'acquired tolerance', the doctor's dilemma and the 'awful restlessness' which 'Dr Harris' had regarded as 'manifestations of cerebral irritation'. Then 'as time went on' said Mr Lawrence, 'it was left with the nurses to increase the dosage'. 'To repeat', that was the point replied Dr Douthwaite. Well, the effect of repeating the dosage was to increase it. Then there would be 'increased tolerance'. Mr Lawrence put it to Dr Douthwaite that the reports 'showed quite clearly the degeneration and the terminal stages of the patient's illness'; indeed that he had said so. Dr Douthwaite did not agree; he had 'not said that they showed clearly that the terminal stages of the illness were due to senile degeneration'. 'By and large' the symptoms were consistent with this view, but not entirely. Well, said Mr Lawrence, suppose the nurses were right, the attacks were 'cerebral irritation' as 'Dr Harris thought':

> '…The doctor is trying to deal with it in the only way that he has got at that stage, is
> not he, by increasing the dose of the drug to which she is accustomed?'
> 'At that stage, yes.'
> [This question and answer have been underlined by Hannam.]

Mr Lawrence asked if Dr Douthwaite was suggesting 'murderous intent' either in the Neston Cottage Hospital or when Mrs Morrell was in the Esperance Nursing Home. [In the Esperance, Dr Adams was in charge of medication.]. He was not. Then the nurses were given discretion to give additional doses of morphia and heroin and did so. Yes. Then to 31st October, 1950 'the time when Dr Adams… has stopped the morphia and put the patient on heroin only':

> 'One of the things that a general practitioner would do or try to do in the dilemma that
> he gets in and the choice he has to make of increasing the drug rather than cutting her
> off is the variation of drug, is it not? To see if a variation will do the trick rather than a
> level increase?'

This did not work:

> 'It is withdrawing the component of the usual injection which is most likely to help
> sleep.'
> 'But it was "a variation"… to see what happens?'
> 'I do not know what was in his mind, whether it was to see what happened, but…'

Mr Lawrence cut him off.

They continued going through the reports: from the day report of 31st October where the morphia and omnopon were omitted and the heroin only was introduced during the early hours of 1st November, for Mr Lawrence to show that 'up to the 4th – it would not have appeared to the general practitioner that that variation of drugs was too bad in its results'. It was that day 'the occasion of Mr Morrell's visit' – when, of course, drugs had been withheld [not mentioned] – that 'she became hysterical' and 'Dr Adams resorted to the half grain of heroin', and, Mr Lawrence said 'Dr Adams' concern was to get the patient to sleep'. Yes, Dr Douthwaite agreed. There was further restlessness on the night of the 5th, so the half grains of heroin were 'his attempt to deal with further outbreaks of restlessness?' It looked like it.

On the night of the 6th November 'notwithstanding those injections, she was very restless and aggressive' and on the following day 'she gets ¼ of morphia, ½ of heroin and ¹⁄₁₀₀ atropine at 7.25. So you see the morphia has now come back again?'

'Yes, the morphia has now come back again.'

And added to the increased amount of heroin on 6th November; Dr Douthwaite was, of course, tied to his date of the 8th as the date of 'murderous intent'. Mr Lawrence proceeded relentlessly through the nurses' notes: the nurses finding it necessary to give the extra injections at night; on the 7th Dr Adams giving instructions that these injections could be repeated during the day, and by that evening the injection was ½ grain morphia [he did not mention this had been doubled] and half grain of heroin – also to be repeated as necessary. And it was 'the nurse, with the patient under her care, in the room under her very eyes' who 'exercises her discretion to give injections'. That night Mrs Morrell had been given injections at 1.30 a.m., 3.50 a.m. and 8.30 a.m., and Dr Adams visited that morning, the 8th November at 11.20 and, challenged Mr Lawrence 'if you are right, formed the intention to murder her; is that right?' It was.

There was an altercation between Mr Lawrence and Dr Douthwaite about the heroin linctus prescribed for the patient's cough, which Dr Douthwaite maintained was 'useful for certain forms of cough, but not in the aged': he would 'advise against it'; Mr Lawrence thought it impossible that Dr Adams could kindly prescribe linctus to help an old lady with her cough on the same day 'when you say he had made up his mind to murder her'. 'Maybe' ventured Dr Douthwaite. Mr Lawrence was incensed:

'What do you mean, maybe? He is, is he not?'
'He is prescribing linctus, yes.'

That evening, the morphia content of the injection had changed to hyperduric morphia, the slower-acting kind, 'with good effect' for the patient slept until 1 a.m. on the 9th when the nurse gave a further injection, followed by another at 4.30 a.m. and one of Dr Adams' 'special injections' at 11.30 a.m. 'with no effect', and a later one at 2 p.m... Dr Douthwaite did not know whether he was 'out of order' but 'One wonders what effect was expected'. Mr Lawrence had asked the nurse, who had 'no recollection', however, 'whatever it was, there was no effect'. Dr Douthwaite thanked him. The 'no effect' was presumably that it did not produce sleep as both Mr Lawrence and the notes remarked on this, surely showing that this 'special injection' was a hypnotic. Now Mr Lawrence asked Dr Douthwaite:

'Now, just pausing there, look at that day, because that is the 9th; it is the second day of this murderous intention?'
'Yes.'

At 9 p.m. Sister Randall had reported that the patient was 'awake, confused and talkative' after a day 'on which there were only 20 minutes sleep'; at 10.15 p.m. Dr Adams gave her hyperduric morphia.

Would 'a man determined upon murder' use hyperduric morphia? Four questions on this type of morphia, but the next question brushed swiftly past the doubling of the heroin in the notes "To have Heroin gr. i given S.O.S.?"' 'Yes.' Mrs Morrell slept until 4.15 a.m. and the nurse, Mr Lawrence pointed out 'without reference to the doctor' gave her a grain of heroin under the S.O.S. instruction, followed by phenobarbitone at 5.20 and another grain of heroin at 6.30 a.m. Dr Adams gave ½ grain hyperduric morphia at 8 a.m. Now Mr Lawrence asked Dr Douthwaite how much of his conclusion was based on the view that Sister Randall 'had been instructed by the doctor to keep Mrs Morrell continuously under, in the sense of doped'. He had taken it into account, but he was 'not basing the whole of his view on that.' Mr Lawrence went back to Sister Randall's explanation of what she understood 'to keep her under' meant, which was 'Not to let her get to the stage of being excited and restless' and when asked again by the Attorney-General what did she mean by 'keep her under', the answer was 'So that she did not come right out from the drug and did not get restless again'. 'Restless' was the operative word, Mr Lawrence suggested.

In fact, it was the same dilemma that he had posited earlier: there was no choice at this stage but to increase the drugs already being given to the patient? Dr Douthwaite thought 'it would not be unusual if he was satisfied he was getting good results'. The injection of hyperduric morphia at 8 a.m. on 10th November, Mr Lawrence said, had the result of producing sleep at 8.15 a.m. Dr Douthwaite questioned this assumption as it was, he considered, unlikely with this sort of morphia, that the two were connected.

Mr Lawrence returned to the night report for the 8th/9th November, where the nurse had given at 1.40 a.m. an injection of morphia ½ gr., heroin ½ gr. and Atropine gr. ¹/₁₀₀ in order to refer to 'your book for what Atropine is'.

Mr Lawrence read out the passage containing: 'Atropine is an antidote to Morphine...' and more, that ¹/₁₀₀ grain of Atropine sulphate could avoid some of the 'undesirable effects of Morphine, such as vomiting and constipation...' Had Dr Douthwaite considered this? The Doctor countered, he had of course:

'Yes. Perhaps I might add that it is an extremely weak antidote to Morphine and is commonly given with Morphine. The usual reason to give it with Morphine is to reduce mucus in the throat or lungs.'

Mr Lawrence didn't mind whether it was weak or strong; it was an antidote.
The Judge adjourned the Court until the following morning.

# Tenth Day

After the usual corrections to the previous day's transcript, Dr Douthwaite enquired as to whether he could correct a piece of evidence. Mr Justice Devlin allowed him to speak: it related to the Latin term 'dol.urg.' on prescriptions for Veramon and the defence had translated this as 'if pain is severe'. As it was not an abbreviation he had used, he had accepted this, but it then struck him as 'being rather strange' in relation to this drug. He had checked it and it actually meant 'if troubled by pain'.

Mr Lawrence rose to continue his cross-examination, immediately dismissing this as unimportant. He reminded Dr Douthwaite of his answer of the previous day, where he had said that he had not analysed the nurses' notebooks as he had never been able to take them away from the Court. What analysis had he made? He had 'noted the drugs, especially morphia, heroin and paraldehyde... in cumulative quantity'. And he had tried to analyse these against 'the immediate background; the general state of the patient as recorded by the nurses'. It was clear, was it not, that the 'cumulative total' for a day as shown on Exhibit 54 was made up of 'a number of isolated injections' which varied in amount and type and were at 'irregular intervals'? It was. He returned to the record of the night of Thursday and Friday, the 9th and 10th November and went through the injections: 1 grain of hyperduric morphia given by the Doctor at 10.15 p.m., 1 grain of heroin at 4.15 a.m., 1 grain of heroin at 6.30 a.m., 8 a.m. Dr Adams visited and injected a ½ grain of hyperduric morphia. The patient then slept from 9 a.m. to 1.40 a.m., and Mr Lawrence then asked a question making an inference from the day report:

'Do you notice this: that when the doctor visited her that morning, on the 10th November, which is two days after you say that he had formed the intent to kill her, he did not give any injection at all on that visit but left it with the nurse?'
'Yes.'

The night report of Sister Randall records Dr Adams' visit at 8 a.m. when he injected the hyperduric morphia. Sister Bartlett's (Hughes) report merely says: 'Visited by Dr: this A.M. – Spec. Injection left – same given @ 1.45 p.m.'

It is not clear if this was a different visit or the 8 a.m. visit as there is no time on the note by Sister Bartlett. Why, in any case, would he make a second visit that same morning when Mrs Morrell had had a satisfactory night's sleep? Why Dr Douthwaite agreed that 'no injection was given' and that that was because 'she was asleep' is difficult to understand. Whatever the injection was, it was given at 1.45 p.m.

There had also been the instruction that 'the patient may have a grain of heroin hourly if necessary' and, said Mr Lawrence 'in fact, your analysis of these last days has shown you, has not it, that never in fact did she ever get a grain of heroin hourly?' Dr Douthwaite agreed. The next heroin injection of 1 grain was given at 6.30 p.m. and at 8.15 p.m. another when she became 'restless'; at 10.30 p.m. on 10th November, Dr Adams visited and gave an injection of hyperduric morphia (the amount is not recorded). This was followed by five hours' sleep after the report of her being 'very alert and wild eyed' at 3.45 a.m., Sister Randall gave her 1 grain of heroin at 4.15 a.m. and another at 6 a.m. At 8.15 a.m. Dr Adams visited and gave another injection of hyperduric morphia of unknown quantity. Mr Lawrence observed that 'the pattern of injections that night is precisely the same as the pattern of injections the preceding night'. Dr Douthwaite wanted to check this. The Attorney-General asked that he be given the summary (Exhibit 54) in front of him.

The point Mr Lawrence now made was that Dr Douthwaite had not distinguished between hyperduric morphia and morphia, the former being the longer-lasting kind, and that this type had been given in the evening and in the early morning by Dr Adams. Yes. And the nurses had given, on each of the two nights, two one-grain injections of heroin? Yes. Dr Douthwaite was forced to agree with Mr Lawrence that if 'the doctor wanted to give as peaceful and helpful nights as possible for this patient at this stage in her illness, he was not doing too badly so far' on the two nights in question.

On the morning of the 11th November, the reports showed that Mrs Morrell had slept from 8.45 a.m. until 12.30 p.m. after the Doctor's morning injection of hyperduric morphia; he had left instructions [it is again unclear whether he made a second visit that morning, but there would seem, again, to have been no reason for one] that the patient could have ½ grain morphia and ½ grain heroin hourly, if necessary. 'He was varying the drug?' Yes. At 1 p.m. Sister Bartlett gave one of these injections and another when the patient became 'restless' and 'excited' at 4.45 p.m. She was again 'very restless after 6.30 p.m.' and when Dr Adams visited at 7.15 p.m. he injected one grain of morphia and one grain of heroin. Mr Lawrence asked for confirmation that this was the 'largest single injection that is ever recorded as having been given?' Dr Douthwaite agreed. A quarter of an hour later, Mrs Morrell was asleep, and slept until 10 p.m.

10.45 p.m. and Dr Adams visited and gave Mrs Morrell an injection of morphia ½ grain and heroin ½ grain: 'A reduction of half of the preceding injection?' and 'Given by this murderous doctor?' Dr Douthwaite replied diplomatically: 'Given by Doctor Adams, yes.' She slept until 12.30 a.m., then was 'awake but quiet' but 'fidgety and talkative' by 1 a.m. and the nurse injected 1 grain of heroin and ½ grain of morphia, and at 2.10 a.m. when the patient was 'crying out at times' another injection of ½ grain of hyperduric morphia and ½ grain of heroin. Mrs Morrell was 'still chattering, more wakeful & jerky' at 3 a.m. and another injection, this time of 1 grain of heroin was given at 3.40 a.m. There was no sleep, on this 'the last full night of Mrs Morrell's life' was there? Like many of Mr Lawrence's questions, it could have been rhetorical.

Sunday, November 12th: the last complete day of Mrs Morrell's life. Dr Adams had visited at 8 a.m. that morning but no injection was recorded in the night nurse's notes, although there is 'No sleep up to 8.15 a.m.' At 11.15 a.m., Dr Adams visited and a 'special injection' was given, resulting in sleep from 11.30 until 1.30 p.m. Mr Lawrence wanted Dr Douthwaite 'to follow this' because this, he thought, 'was the last recorded sleep on this day'. At 2.35 p.m. an injection of ½ grain of hyperduric morphine and ½ grain of heroin was given because the patient became 'restless and talkative'. There was twice a note that she was quiet but not asleep, and the same injection was repeated at 5.25 p.m. Then at 7.30 p.m. Dr Adams called again.

Mr Lawrence thought they should 'just pause there' and 'try to take stock of the position from the aspect of the general practitioner dealing with this patient, remembering all the time the dilemma you mentioned' – it was Mr Lawrence. Was it not now obvious that the 'hypnotic value' of the two drugs 'was gone'.

'Yes, completely.'

Mr Lawrence was winning the game:

> 'Let us see what this murderous doctor who has varied the drug, who has procured sleep up to the last night, what he does when the picture changes. 'At 7.30 p.m. visited by Doctor Adams. Paraldehyde 2 c.c.s given intra muscularly.'

It was noted 'no apparent effects'. Mr Lawrence asked about paraldehyde: it was 'a well-established remedy for insomnia' – a hypnotic, 'generally one of the safest' It was, said Dr Douthwaite. 2 c.c. was a proper dose; it could go up to 8 to 10 c.c., 'cannot it?' 5 was 'quite a common dose'. Dr Adams had visited again at 10.30 p.m. and was recorded as giving an intramuscular injection of 5 c.c. of Paraldehyde. The record entry for 11.30 was 'Very restless no sleep; at 12.30 a.m. 'Restless and talkative & very shaky' and at 12.45 'Seems a little quieter, appears asleep. Respirations 50'. Was this not a very high rate? Yes. So, Mr Lawrence suggested, 'it is obvious that the end was close at hand?' Dr Douthwaite agreed.

Dealing with the last stages of the illness, a doctor would have had to use some sort of drugs for the purpose of preventing the patient from becoming restless and excited, and Mr Lawrence thought that he and Dr Douthwaite were agreed about this, he had 'implied that there was no choice left except to increase the heroin and morphine… when you said 'some other but much less dangerous drug', what had you got in mind?'

'Hyoscine.'

This was a drug 'which produces sleep, which is slightly antidotal to morphine… but the effect on the brain of hyoscine is entirely different to that of atropine, in so far as that atropine tends to excite and hyoscine tends to soothe.' Mr Lawrence put it to Dr Douthwaite that it 'would have been very dangerous' to have introduced this drug with morphine in this case. Dr Douthwaite disagreed: 'morphine and hyoscine are used frequently for what was known as 'twilight sleep' '. (Hyoscine was the drug used by Dr Crippen and Dr Adams did carry some in his bag.) Paraldehyde was also a suitable drug. He would have made 'suitable reductions of morphia and heroin'. Surely not in the last few days? Dr Douthwaite explained that as the patient was dying, 'all the natural functions were depressed. Therefore, the effect of these drugs was slowed down', causing an accumulation, therefore a lesser quantity was required in the last few days.

Mr Lawrence set out to 'summarise the troublesome road over which you and I have travelled in these last few hours', starting with the patient in hospital in Cheshire, coming to Eastbourne 'under the care of Dr Adams' and charting 'the first signs of the approaching end' appearing 'when he went away on holiday and Dr Harris began to attend her'. The policy of drugging, he suggested was 'self-consistent' and then at the end there was 'a switch to one of the safest of all the hypnotics' – paraldehyde. Dr Douthwaite was almost swept away with the barrage, but ventured that it was not accurate to suggest that the 'morphia and heroin were completely abandoned and in place Paraldehyde was tried': heroin and morphia had been injected at 5.25 p.m. on 11th November and the paraldehyde at 7.30 p.m.; that injection 'would be operative for a very long time'. But the 7.30 injection of paraldehyde was followed by a further one at 10.30 p.m. of 5 c.c. 'within the reasonable limits of the B.P. dose' responded Mr Lawrence, 'even if there was another one not recorded some time in the early hours'. It was 'getting up to a big dose for an old woman', Dr Douthwaite considered.

Mr Lawrence persisted that there was 'a possible alternative view' that 'this general practitioner' was 'following a consistent course' to 'produce the result which it was his duty to produce'. Dr Douthwaite thought that 'he produced what he wanted to produce, or the result that he wanted to produce'. Mr Lawrence meant 'sleep… and the avoidance of restlessness and excitability'. Certainly the avoidance of restlessness, and sleep.

> 'Leaving aside any Harley Street judgment on the quality of the skill of a general practitioner, going through the history, going through the details of these reports, as I have tried to indicate to you, there is no necessity at all to postulate a murderous intent at any time here, is there?'
> 'In the first place, if I may give my judgment as a physician on the staff of a hospital – because, with the greatest respect, where I live has nothing whatever to do with my opinion or knowledge –, there is, in my opinion, evidence of intent to terminate life.'
> [The last underlined by Hannam.]

Mr Lawrence said that it was not the question he had put, which was that there was no need to postulate an intent to murder:

> 'I was forced to postulate that on my views on the drugs given in the last few days of November, and therefore I felt it was needed.'

But in the 24 hours before the last visits 'there were indications' that the drugs 'were not producing the sedation and avoidance of restlessness and the positive quality of sleep that it was his duty to give'.

> 'Yes. There were indications of more than that.'
> 'I dare say, but that at least is shown, is not it?'
> 'That is shown.'

Mr Lawrence cajoled Dr Douthwaite: would he not 'at any rate… come some of the way, agreeing with me with regard to the possible alternative view I put to you?' Yes. Then it must be a matter of medical opinion? Dr Douthwaite had no doubt it depended 'largely on it'.

Then so far as 'jerkiness' was concerned – he would use the word 'convulsions', although it did not appear in the records, but was a convenient medical term: these were surely rare in heroin poisoning?

'In heroin poisoning uncommon in so far as heroin poisoning is uncommon.'

The 1950s were a very different age: Mr Lawrence thought there were 'very few recorded instances'. They were recorded in textbooks of pharmacology, but not in the experience of 'the ordinary general practitioner' – this might have been somewhat ironic, one suspects.

'Oh no, naturally not. They are not common in anybody's experience.'

Dr Douthwaite had 'seen twitchings, but not what I would call convulsions, in heroin, yes.' Had Dr Douthwaite made any research into them for the purposes of this case? He had not because he realised that 'it was an uncommon thing to meet' so that there was no point in trying. Mr Lawrence suggested that in recorded cases the 'twitchings or convulsions' were of the rigid tetanic (rigid spasm lasting for a variable time, as in tetanus) type rather than the clonic (repeated jerks). Dr Douthwaite explained that the sort of twitchings he had seen were the result of heroin.

Mr Lawrence had one other matter to deal with: the quantity of prescriptions, shown on Exhibit 4A [the corrected list]. No. 83 of 8th November, 1950 was for 40 x hypodermic tablets of heroin each ⅙ grain – 6⅔rds grains of heroin; 85 was for hypodermic tablets of morphine sulphate ¼ grain – 10 grains, the next: hypodermic tablets of ¼ grain heroin 25 (6¼ grains) and ½ grain morphine tablets, 25 on the 9th. If those quantities had been administered on the 8th, would Mrs Morrell not have died before the 13th November? Dr Douthwaite agreed: he thought he had said that at the hearing in Eastbourne. The same would be true of the prescriptions for the 9th: 6¼ grains of heroin and 12½ grains of morphine.

If any of the daily totals had been administered on the day, would they have resulted in her death? Dr Douthwaite gave a proviso: that 'you are referring to a single injection of both drugs at the same time'. It was not at all the same if they were given over the course of 24 hours, some would have been eliminated. These could have been significant amounts, he maintained. Mr Lawrence found in the Committal hearing transcript what Dr Douthwaite had said: that if the morphia and heroin prescriptions of the 8th had been administered to Mrs Morrell, then they would have caused death before the morning of 13th, and not later than the 9th, and that the same was true of the prescription for the 9th; and of the prescription for 6¼ grains of heroin on the 10th, 'given as one dose would probably have been fatal'. Dr Douthwaite agreed with that.

Mr Lawrence continued to read another confusing answer: that 'if the drugs prescribed on 8th, 9th and 10th November had been administered on 11th November', then the patient 'must have been dead'; followed by: the prescriptions for the 11th administered on that day would have killed the patient. Dr Douthwaite had made only one mention of the drugs being given as 'one dose', and Mr Lawrence was able to say, very truthfully, that what he had read was 'far from clear', but Dr Douthwaite agreed that he had said it.

Finally, the doses recorded in the nurses' notebooks did not get 'anywhere near the totals of these prescriptions?' No, they did not. Mr Lawrence apologised for taking so long, and was obliged to the Doctor. Very obliged.

The Attorney-General re-examined the witness. He asked why prescriptions of dangerous drugs were written 'by Doctors for particular patients':

'In order that they shall be administered.'

Looking at the list of prescriptions and assuming that what was prescribed for each day from 8th November to 12th was not used on the day; that 'all but a little' were administered, what would have been the consequence?

'It would have produced death.'
'And if the "major part of what was prescribed between the 8th and 12th" had been administered?'
'The same.'

The Attorney-General went back to the beginning, to Mrs Morrell's stroke and her stay in the cottage hospital; he assumed the stroke was suffered on 24th June, 1948, then what would happen? Dr Douthwaite said that 'the process in the brain would have settled down or be settling down'; at the first onset what would happen would be unpredictable, but two or three days later it would be clearer. On 27th June, 1948, morphia was 'a possible course of treatment'. On the next day report, there was a complaint 'of severe pain in the region of the heart': would this be 'a consequence of the stroke'? No. As 'brandy was given with relief': a pain on the left, was commonly due to flatulence and could be 'quite unpleasant'; brandy would not give relief if the pain were due to heart disease. As to the morphia, he could not see why it was continued in the hospital.

The Attorney-General asked whether Dr Douthwaite confirmed that the prognosis after the stroke was, as he had agreed with Mr Lawrence, 6 to 12 months; then when Mrs Morrell had eventually returned home, would he 'be able to form a fresh estimate of her expectation of life'. He though he would.

'It is not the case of someone having exceeded the expectation of life and therefore having a bonus, as it were, is it?'
'No, I agree that would not be the way to look at it.'

Were there grounds to suppose her expectation of life would have been 'materially shortened' by the stroke, say, in July, 1949:

'No. Really, her expectation of life then would be the expectation of life of a woman of eighty or eighty-one, possibly slightly affected by the fact that she had had a stroke, but very very slightly.'

The Attorney-General turned his attention to the prescriptions: on the list (Exhibit 52) No. 2 was for 'Ampules Hyperduric Morphia grains ½':

'In hyperduric, is that double the quantity administered in the nursing home as recorded in the nurses' reports in Cheshire?'
'Yes, it is.'
'Is it correct to describe the doubling of the quantity as merely carrying on the medication of the hospital?'
'No, it is not.'
[These last two questions and answers are underlined in the transcript by Hannam.]

Dr Douthwaite was asked if there was any reason to add morphia injections to the Veramon for prevention of pain. No. [The hospital did this because, at the time, Mrs Morrell could not swallow the tablets; afterwards Dr Adams prescribed both, but the Attorney-General did not seem to notice this point.]

What kinds of pain might occur following strokes?

'They are what people loosely call rheumatic pains. When lying with a paralysed side the joints are apt to get painful, the sort of pain which could be relieved by mild so-called pain-killers, such as veramon, which is quite mild.'

The Attorney-General queried whether it was possible to distinguish between 'cerebral irritation' and 'manifestations of irritability'. Dr Douthwaite wished to emphasise that the conduct was indistinguishable. Arterio-sclerosis of the brain was apt to make old people irritable. Was it justifiable to administer 'routine' morphia and heroin for such irritation or irritability? It was not. Would a doctor taking over the case from the hospital, have considered what the consequences of continuing morphia might be? Yes.

'What consequence would follow if morphia injections were continued?'
'Well, addiction.'

Dr Adams had doubled the quantity of morphia when Mrs Morrell went back to Eastbourne, and then 'after the 12 days following the 9th of July, (1948) Dr Adams prescribed for her not only morphia but also heroin?' Yes.

'Could the addition of heroin to the morphia, the morphia having been doubled by DrAdams, be properly regarded as merely following on the medication in Cheshire?'
'No, it could not.'

Would Dr Douthwaite expect 'any degree of addiction' following the nine days at ¼ grain of morphia in the hospital?

'It is a very short time indeed to develop addiction. No.'
But then if that were followed by, say, twelve days on ½ 2rain of morphia?
'Then it is highly probable, yes.'

It would have caused no suffering to the patient if she had been weaned off it then. The Attorney-General repeated a question of Mr Lawrence's: '…that he continued the morphia injections that the hospital were giving', was this correct?

'He continued giving morphia, but he did not give the same quantities and then added heroin.'

Mr Lawrence protested that the only evidence for this was in the prescriptions: that the ampules were ½ grain ones. The Attorney-General asked Dr Douthwaite to look at the prescription list: 9th July, 1948 – 6 grains of hyperduric morphia were dispensed and then on 21st July, there was the next entry for morphia. If all the grains prescribed on 9th July were used at the rate of ½ grain a day, the supply would have run out on 21st July? 'Twelve days, yes.' agreed Dr Douthwaite. There was also written on the prescription by Dr Adams 'Repeat twice at 6 days intervals', would this indicate the rate at which they were to be used? It would indicate 'that it was in the prescriber's mind' that they should be used at the rate of one grain per day. The Attorney-General asked if there was any 'physical degenerative condition' unaccompanied by severe pain 'which would justify' routine injections of morphia and heroin. Dr Douthwaite considered that morphia was sometimes used for a short period for 'some forms of heart failure', but otherwise, no.

The Attorney-General referred to questions put by the Defence concerning stopping morphia and heroin being likely to cause a collapse and Dr Douthwaite replying that that would only be so if the drugs were stopped suddenly. Was this necessary and were there methods of stopping addiction? It was not necessary to stop 'suddenly' and he would use 'the slow withdrawal method, which would take about ten days', substituting methadone in smaller quantities 'to overcome the withdrawal symptoms', and then there would be no risk of collapse. This could still have been done as late as the autumn of 1950.

An interesting point, which had not previously emerged, was raised by the Attorney-General:

'What is the effect of administering barbiturates on withdrawal symptoms?'
'It tends to reduce them, to mitigate them.'

In other words, the barbiturates given to Mrs Morrell would have masked withdrawal symptoms.

Had Dr Douthwaite found any symptoms mentioned in the nurses' notebooks which were inconsistent 'with a symptom which would follow from drugging by morphia and heroin?' He had not. 'In considering whether or not she was going downhill because of senile decay in September and October of 1950' it was not possible to 'leave out of account' the effects of the drugging.

The Attorney-General brought up the matter of qualifying in anaesthetics: a doctor normally took the Diploma later, 'after special experience of anaesthetics', and, being an anaesthetist at two hospitals as Dr Adams was would 'normally mean' that he would be up-to-date with modern treatment. Indeed, he would be.

Was it significant that the 'Cheyne Stokes' breathing had occurred only once? Dr Douthwaite had told the Defence that it might occur with a failing heart; he now told the Attorney-General that it would recur frequently if this were the case, and, there being no record of it in November, 1950, meant that this was not the cause. The Attorney-General pursued more matters raised by the Defence for which Dr Douthwaite had not been allowed to give adequate answers: did the words 'special injection' indicate that there was only one ingredient in the injection: 'special injection' conveyed absolutely no information at all. When the Defence had mentioned that it was left 'up to the discretion of the nurses' to increase dosage, had Dr Douthwaite wished to make a point:

'Well, it is very unlikely that any discretion would be left to a nurse to increase the dose without a more specific instruction as to exactly why and to how much.'

But when there was the instruction 'S.O.S.' given by the Doctor, then 'with that direction alone', he had left the nurse discretion as to when to inject the dangerous drugs.

The Attorney-General asked Dr Douthwaite to look at the instruction given by Dr Adams on 9th November, 1950 to the nurses to give 'one grain of heroin hourly if necessary', which 'would contemplate a maximum of 24 grains of heroin in the day'.

'What is your view of that kind of dosage?'
'It can only be described as colossal.'

The Defence had asked 'a great many questions as to the necessity at all costs of securing for this lady sleep', suggesting drugging during the day, and Dr Douthwaite had agreed that 'she should be helped to sleep at night'. The Attorney-General proposed to go through the notebooks from 30th October, 1950 to ascertain 'the reason for trying to keep her under throughout the day as well', by checking the amount of sleep she had at nights: the 31st October was described as a 'poor night, slept only about five and a half hours'.

'What would you normally expect to be the normal sort of hours of sleep for a lady of eighty-one who is bedridden?'
'Oh, they are usually short: six, five and a half, five.'

Dr Douthwaite saw no reason for 'keeping her under' the next day. She had, in fact, slept also from 7.15 a.m. until 9 a.m. in addition. Then the rest of the day report for 31st October:

'...That is the day Dr Adams says morphia and Omnopon are to be omitted. That is the sedative part, is it not?'
'Yes.'
'And to give heroin during the day and at night?'
'Yes.'

And at 2.45p.m. the record showed that she slept 'a very deep sleep for one hour.' On the night of 1st November, 'slept well from 9.30 p.m. until 6.15 a.m.' and further from 7.30 a.m. to 9 a.m.; again at 2.50 p.m. 'sleeping soundly'. The night report for 1st/2nd November recorded: 'Slept from 11.20 till 6.45'; then 35 minutes' sleep at 3.30 p.m. On the night of 2nd/3rd November Mrs Morrell had slept from 12 to 1.30 a.m., then dozed and at 2.15 a.m. 'slept well up to 7 a.m.', which worked out at 6¼ hours' sleep that night. '3rd November 10.30 a.m. patient asleep and not disturbed' – the day of Mr Morrell's visit – 7.30 p.m. 'patient asleep'; 4th November 'Has had a very good night. Slept until 12.15 midnight – 4 hours, and again from 1.15 until 7 a.m...' The Attorney-General followed through the reports: Mrs Morrell had had plenty of sleep, there was no question about it.

Pausing at the entry for the night of 6th November, where it was noted that the patient was given a hypodermic injection of ½ grain of heroin at 7.55 a.m., after she had had adequate sleep, the Attorney-General asked Dr Douthwaite if this indicated 'a change in policy'. He thought that it did. Was there any shortage of sleep at night time 'such as would justify procuring drugged sleep at all costs in the day time? 'There was none.' The Attorney-General continued checking the amount of sleep recorded in the notes; when he reached the night report for the 9th/10th November, Mr Justice Devlin thought it might be convenient to adjourn for lunch.

When the Court resumed, the Attorney-General asked Dr Douthwaite 'to glance back' at the report for the 31st October, where Dr Adams had instructed 'Omit Morphine and Omnopon. Instead give at night ⅚ Heroin and ⅓ during the day S.O.S.' and at the report for 1st November 'Doctor visited. Continue with Heroin injections only' and tell him what would be the result of this.

'That would reduce appreciably any sedation'
'Bearing in mind that this lady had had Morphia and Heroin over a long period what effect would Heroin alone be likely to have upon her condition?'
'It would be likely to make her excitable and it would be likely to produce twitchings.'

The Attorney-General returned to calculating the amount of sleep which the patient had from the night of 9th/10th November, where the instructions from Dr Adams were now to give 'Heroin 1 grain S.O.S.' That night she had 6½ hours' sleep recorded, and in the day report that she had been asleep from 9 a.m. until 1.40 p.m. Dr Adams had visited during the morning, left a 'special injection' and given the instruction 'Patient may have one grain hourly if necessary'. Could Dr Douthwaite see any grounds for this instruction, which 'would contemplate 12 grains in the day'. He could see none whatever. The record for 10th/11th November reported about six hours' sleep, and the following morning she slept from 9 a.m. until 12.30 p.m. and again from 7.30 p.m. and was awake at 10 p.m. The night summary showed 'No sleep up to 8.15 a.m.', then on the Sunday 12th 'Slept from 11.30 a.m. to 1.30 p.m.', there being no further reference to sleep. Then was it necessary 'to keep her under' during the daytime? No, Dr Douthwaite replied.

The Defence had asked questions about the nurses' reports:

> '…Was there, in your view, looking at the whole picture, any justification for the instructions [about dosages] given as shown in this book from the 1st November onwards?'
> 'No.'

With reference to the patient's tolerance for drugs: the Attorney-General asked whether 'the restlessness at the very end of her life' indicated that 'an acquired tolerance had not been overcome by the drugs', or was there another cause? Dr Douthwaite was clear that it suggested that it had not been overcome. Looking at the totals of drugs given (Exhibit 54) as recorded in the nurses' notebooks, would the 1 grain of morphine and the 4 of heroin given on 10th November have given 'immediate tolerance'? Not as a single increase; it would take three weeks at the same level. So would there have been any tolerance for such a massive increase given on 10th November? No.

> 'The total on the 11th November is 3½ grains of Morphine and 5 of heroin, is it not?'
> 'Yes.'
> 'Would there, or would there not, be any acquired tolerance for that dosage?'
> 'No.'

Finally, the Attorney-General asked Dr Douthwaite if he had any doubts, or heard any evidence which had affected his opinion in this serious matter, or changed his opinion as to the cause of Mrs Morrell's death? No.

> 'To what do you attribute her death?'
> 'To drugs, Morphia and Heroin, possibly assisted by Paraldehyde, in the absence of Paraldehyde, in my opinion, Morphia and Heroin administered in the last few days would have killed her.'

Mr Justice Devlin now questioned Dr Douthwaite on behalf of the Court: in the circumstances of this case the jury had to be satisfied that the accused 'either administered the drugs himself intending it to kill her, or he gave directions or instructions to the nurses which he hoped and intended, if carried out, would kill the patient, Mrs Morrell.' Dr Douthwaite's evidence covered the period from November 8th to November 13th 'for this purpose'. It did. During that period Dr Adams made 17 visits to the patient, when he either administered drugs himself or left instructions to the nurses to do so. He did.

'If the case for the Crown is right then one or more of those acts amounted to murder'; the Judge proposed to take Dr Douthwaite through them in order that he should say what forced him 'to postulate that murder was being committed, or attempted'. The night report for November 7th recorded that the Doctor visited at 7.40 p.m. and gave an injection of half a grain of morphia and half a grain of heroin, an increase of a quarter of a grain of morphia. Was this, for instance, an act of murder? Not that single dose. Was he forced to postulate murder in relation to the doses which came after? Dr Douthwaite reasoned that from the 1st to the 5th November when only heroin was given:

> '…By withdrawing Morphia for five days in a woman who had been having it regularly it would have diminished any likelihood of producing a comfortable sleep after having received it for so many months…'

The tolerance she had acquired to it would have rapidly reduced over the five days; then it was returned in a small dose of ¼ grain on the 6th, on the 7th 1½ grains and on the 8th to 2 grains.

> '…I wondered what was a possible reason for stopping this Morphine, and that is why I didn't make up my mind on the probable desire to terminate life until I saw the substitution was returned on the 6th followed by a rapid increase together with large doses of heroin…'

It did not seem to be an attempt to wean her off drugs, otherwise should the heroin not have been reduced rather than the morphine: Dr Douthwaite could only think that it must have been deliberately withheld in order to reintroduce it as there was 'no attempt at substitution'. The Judge asked:

> 'Is it your view that in dropping the morphine, Dr Adams was merely changing the drugging, or is that an impossible view?'
> 'I think it is an impossible view.'

When the morphine was reintroduced at 7.25 on the 6th November, 'with heavy doses of heroin, knowing that the morphine tolerance would have been reduced in the previous 5 days, then he intended to kill.'

Dr Douthwaite believed that Dr Adams 'embarked on a wrong line of treatment from the very beginning', but did not suggest that murder was the explanation of that. He did not believe it possible 'that a medical man of his experience and qualifications' was not 'aware of the action of these two drugs'. But did he have 'rather an old-fashioned idea' about them? Dr Douthwaite conceded that it was possible that Dr Adams thought that heroin might be used for some conditions not associated with pain, but it was not possible that he did not know the effects of morphine and heroin administration; therefore the original line of treatment might not have been 'for any sinister reason'.

'Well, he did not kill as a result of that', said Mr Justice Devlin, referring to the re-introduction of the heroin; but then Dr Adams increased the dose of morphia from ¼ to ½ 'to see if that would do?' Yes. There was an instruction that the same dose might be repeated: was this 'making sure, as it were, that if the first dose did not work, then doses would be given during the night that did work?' This was the right medical inference, agreed Dr Douthwaite. He came the next morning, the 8th to see the patient, giving a 'special injection', and Dr Douthwaite was disregarding these for the purpose of his conclusion as he did not know what they were; he left directions that morning for ½ grain morphia and ½ grain of heroin, if necessary. He made the third visit of the seventeen in the evening and, as no injections were given during the day, injected ½ grain of hyperduric morphia and ½ grain of heroin, again directing for the injection to be repeated if necessary. Was the hyperduric version of the morphia of any significance? It was not, said Dr Douthwaite.

So, when Dr Adams arrived for his fourth visit at half-past eleven on the morning of the 9th, he finds 'that the patient not only has had one lethal dose, but three lethal doses, two more during the night, and that she is still alive?' 'Yes.' He gave a 'special injection' – disregarded – and came back at 2 p.m., his fifth visit, again giving a 'special injection'; came back in the evening at 6.30 p.m., the sixth visit, and injected ½ grain of heroin, dropping the morphia. Dr Douthwaite was 'forced to the conclusion' that he was carrying on his intention to murder:

> 'That is my view, my Lord. With the heroin, my Lord, she is excitable, as has been repeatedly referred to here, and everyone knows that Heroin would make her worse and jumpy, and the withdrawal of the small amount of morphia might make her more so.'

Also on the sixth visit, Dr Adams left a tube of ½ grain sulphate morphine tablets and a tube of ¼ grain heroin tablets 'for future use only, and wishes Mrs Morrell to continue with ½ grain of heroin when necessary'. The seventh visit occurred 3¾ hours later at 10.15 p.m. when he gave one grain of hyperduric morphia. This dose also 'would be intended in the circumstances to kill', agreed Dr Douthwaite, but, 'much more seriously', he left an instruction to give one grain of heroin S.O.S. One grain of heroin 'might well have been fatal', and must have been intended to be so.

The eighth visit was at 8 a.m. on the 10th, when Dr Adams had found that one grain of heroin had been given an hour and a half before, and gave an injection of half a grain of hyperduric morphia. He left a special injection and his direction that the patient should be given a grain of heroin hourly. He returned on his ninth visit at 10.30 p.m. that evening and gave an unknown quantity of hyperduric morphia. Dr Douthwaite expressed his view that there was no particular significance 'to be attached to the giving of hyperduric morphia'. This being slightly confusing, the Judge sought to clarify whether he regarded all the injections, at this stage, as being 'given with the intent to kill'. That was so: any one injection was an intent to kill.

The tenth visit in the morning of the 11th at 8.15 p.m. and, again, Dr Adams gave an unknown quantity of hyperduric morphia to the patient and then changed the instruction to the nurses from one grain of heroin into half a grain of morphia and half a grain of heroin. Dr Douthwaite saw no significance in this change. When the Judge questioned this:

'There is clearly a deliberate change, but I don't know why.'

Then he said that the combination of the two drugs was 'more lethal.' At 7.15 in the evening Dr Adams came on his twelfth visit [what has been counted as the 'eleventh' visit is not clear as there is just a record of an instruction] and increased the dosage to one grain of heroin and one grain of morphia, which was the largest injection given. He had doubled the dose and this was a lethal dose. Dr Douthwaite supposed that with this dose adding to the accumulation of drugs in the previous few days 'one could expect death within two or three days'; he was 'taking into account that the woman was clearly dying – clearly dying.' Even without administering anything more, 'she might well have died.' Indeed she could have died, 'say, 24 hours before'.

'So that the medical picture appears to show this: that he was giving her more doses than were really necessary to achieve his end?'
'Yes, my Lord.'

The Judge asked if Dr Adams might then have just waited a few days after November 10th 'to see what result it produced'. He might just as well have. But he came again that evening on the thirteenth visit at 10.45 p.m. on the evening of the 11th, giving Mrs Morrell half of morphia and half of heroin, and, on his instructions, more injections were given during the night. On the fourteenth visit in the morning he did nothing; then on the fifteenth visit gave a 'special injection'. It was on the sixteenth visit that the first injection of Paraldehyde was given:

'Is it your view, then, that Paraldehyde was given to accelerate it [death]?'
'Yes, my Lord.'
'...But again you are forced to draw the conclusion that Dr Adams gave the Paraldehyde perhaps because he was tired of waiting for the heroin to take effect, to bring about a quick and immediate result?'
'Yes, my Lord.'

Dr Douthwaite did not think that the first 2 c.c. injection of Paraldehyde would have been sufficient to make any difference. The only thing he could think of was that 'he tried to mask those convulsions... perhaps to quell that particular symptom'. He did not regard the 2 c.c. as 'in any way sinister'. But the 5 c.c.? He was 'forced to postulate' that the 5 c.c. of Paraldehyde was given to kill. Why, asked the Judge.

'Because it would necessarily – and I think a doctor must know it – it would necessarily have aided or accelerated death from this heroin depression of the respiratory centre. 2 c.c. is too small to produce that effect.'

The same applied to 3 c.c., but Dr Douthwaite agreed that '60 per cent more means murder'. Whether the second injection of 5 c.c. of paraldehyde was given or not, did not affect his view. The Judge sought to summarise Dr Douthwaite's view:

> '...that the first time the design for murder emerges from the medical pattern – because that is all you can deal with – is when he drops the morphia and concentrates on the heroin?'
> 'Yes, my Lord.'
> 'The only possible medical explanation of that being that he intends to reintroduce morphia with lethal effect?'
> 'Yes, my Lord.'

And then any one of the subsequent injections could have been lethal, and could only have been explained 'on the basis that they were intended to be lethal'; the first injection of paraldehyde could have been 'for an innocent purpose', but the larger quantity was intended to have brought about her death 'more quickly than the accumulation of morphia and heroin would have done'. Dr Douthwaite agreed with that.

The Judge wanted help on another 'quite different matter': if there had been a post-mortem would the morphia and heroin have been detected. Yes, Dr Douthwaite was quite sure of this. He did not know for certain after how long there would remain traces in the body, as he was not a pathologist.

It would have depended upon the circumstances of the burial and the surrounding soil, but it would be possible after even thousands of years under certain conditions. Dr Adams' friend, Lieutenant-Colonel Gwynne, had been more aware of this than Dr Douthwaite. (See Chapter 42)

The witness withdrew and the Attorney-General asked if he might recall Mr Reid 'for one moment'.

The Attorney-General asked Mr Reid, the pharmacist, if he had prepared and checked a graph prepared from Exhibit 54, which was of the administrations of drugs to Mrs Morrell which were recorded in the nurses' notebooks. Mr Reid produced this and it was now marked 'Exhibit 54A'. Mr Reid explained the graph, which showed heroin and morphia dosage, and the morphine content of the omnopon for each day; 'special injections' were not shown at all; heroin was shown in black, morphia 'in the hatched colour' and 'omnopon expressed as morphia' was the dotted area.

Mr Lawrence then cross-examined Mr Reid, trying to interpret the graph and check its accuracy and method: each square covered three days, divided into three equal sections, reading vertically, each square was equivalent to one grain. The graph, in fact, was merely 'a transference of Exhibit 54 into graph form' and only expressed the information derived from the nurses' notebooks. Then it was 'merely a question' from the defence point of view 'of checking its accuracy'. Yes. Mr Lawrence asked Mr Reid if he were 'an expert in drawing graphs'. He was not, but he had done his best.

The Attorney-General just clarified one point in a further re-examination and the witness withdrew.

The second expert medical witness for the Crown took the stand: Dr Michael Ashby, M.A., M.B., M.R.C.P. had a practice at 148 Harley Street: he was a surgeon, a Fellow of the Royal Society of Medicine and a Member of the Institute of British Neurologists. He had been medical registrar to that most famous of British neurologists, the aptly named Sir Russell Brain. Dr Ashby had become a consultant in 1949 and since then had been neurologist to the Whittington Hospital and five other hospitals in north-west London. The previous evidence he had given at the Magistrates' Court was based upon evidence he had heard and, of course, he had not then seen the nurses' reports and those from the Cheshire Hospital.

The Attorney-General began by asking Dr Ashby about the graphs he had prepared based on the record of prescriptions Exhibit 4A. Mr Justice Devlin did not quite follow 'what the prescriptions have to do with the case.' The Attorney-General told him:

> '...I am not accepting for one moment that all the visits that Dr Adams paid are recorded in the nurses' register, and, my Lord, I am putting my case as I opened it; I am putting it, first of all, on the quantities prescribed, and I am putting my case in this way, that on the nurses' register and the reports as well there is only one conclusion to be drawn.'

Mr Justice Devlin understood then that he was suggesting 'that all the quantities prescribed were given to Mrs Morrell'. He was relying on the police evidence that they were all used apart from a few final tablets, and the prescriptions showing the amounts the Doctor prescribed. The Judge 'had in mind' that the evidence of the nurses appeared to be that when Dr Adams had injected drugs, he had taken them from his own bag, which would not be out of the list prescriptions; if the Crown deducted these drugs from the prescriptions then there would be less to account for the recorded drugs in the nurses' notebooks. The Attorney-General insisted that there was 'a fallacy' and that he hoped to prove that some of the prescriptions went to Kent Lodge or were collected by Dr Adams himself. This was 'not the evidence so far' said the Judge.

> 'So really you put your case as to the quantity that Mrs Morrell had that it is shown at its highest, as it were, in the list of prescriptions – and at its lowest in the nurses' books?'
> 'Yes, my Lord.'
> 'I am much obliged. I did not follow that.'

The graph was now put in and marked Exhibit 36A. The Attorney-General started elucidating the graph with Dr Ashby: he had presumed that each dose of drug, when it was given, was given when the previous lot had run out. The graph showed only prescriptions: the drug, the date and the amount. The morphia prescribed from the 7th to the 10th November, 1950 was nearly double any previous prescription of morphia; the prescription of heroin on the 10th and 12th was the second largest prescription of morphia and the largest heroin prescription. Dr Ashby had also prepared another graph, an enlargement of the six day period from 7th to the 12th November, 1950. The total morphine prescribed for those days amounted to 40½ grains [½ deducted for left-over amount) and the heroin to 39½ grains, again allowing a deduction]. A further graph (Exhibit 35A) was the monthly totals of drugs prescribed.

When the Attorney-General suggested to Dr Ashby that 'it was common ground' that morphia and heroin were dangerous drugs, and he agreed, Mr Lawrence intervened to disagree; but they were under the Dangerous Drugs Act? Yes. Sir Reginald followed this up with:

> 'Are you aware of any reason for prescribing Morphia and Heroin for a patient if they
> are not intended to be used on that patient?'
> 'I can think of no legitimate reason.'

Dr Ashby had also prepared a graph based upon the Defence's record of prescriptions for the earlier period from July 1948 to January 1950. This was marked as a new Exhibit 36B. A further graph, Exhibit 37A, gave the daily dosage. The Attorney-General checked this through with Dr Ashby. He asked if the evidence of Superintendent Hannam had affected the preparation of chart 37A: Dr Ashby confirmed that he had made the graphs quite independently of that evidence. He had done his best to ensure that he did not 'insert into them conjectures' and considered them to be 'graphs of indisputable accuracy'.

Mr Justice Devlin thought it convenient to pause there and addressed Mr Lawrence: he had questioned Dr Douthwaite, not to cross-examine him, but to clear up certain 'divergencies' in his answers, particularly on the variation of drugs. When he had asked Dr Douthwaite about the dropping of the morphia, he had expressed the view that it was done so that it could be re-introduced later with lethal effect, but when Mr Lawrence had asked him his answer was that he did not know what was in the mind of Dr Adams, and in reply to another question he had agreed that it looked as if it was an attempt to deal with restlessness, and further, that a variation of drug was being tried. In view of those answers, the Judge would consider a Defence application to cross-examine further.

The Court was adjourned until the following Monday morning.

# Eleventh Day

After a few corrections to the transcript of the previous Friday, including Mr Justice Devlin noting the reference to 'Solicitor-General': '…you have been reduced in rank, Mr Attorney', Mr Lawrence made his application for leave to further cross-examine Dr Douthwaite. The Judge thought he should allow this and asked the Attorney-General's opinion: he thought it desirable that Dr Douthwaite should 'have an opportunity of dealing with that matter'. Dr Douthwaite was put back into the box.

Mr Lawrence asked if Dr Douthwaite's theory was made up of 'two limbs': firstly, that Dr Adams withdrew the morphia on 31st October in order to reduce Mrs Morrell's tolerance to it, and secondly re-introduced it on 6th November in increasing doses with heroin 'in order to bring about a fatal result'. These 'two limbs' were 'mutually interdependent', yes.

It was put to Dr Douthwaite that the level of dosage during the last five days of the patient's life was 'well within the experience of general practitioners in your profession in the terminal stages of illness without producing fatality'

> '…Five grains of heroin on the 11th – this is the total on one day – that is thirty times the normal maximum dose. Thirty times.'

Mr Lawrence was annoyed: it was 'no use taking one day in isolation'. He tried again: taking the level of dosage over those days, if the drugs had been used for inoperable cancer, the level would not have caused fatality. Dr Douthwaite wondered whether Mr Lawrence intended him to take an average level of drugs, but he had to consider individual days as well. But still, taking the level over the last fortnight, the picture was 'well within the experience of the profession?'

> 'It would have been one suggesting a desire to terminate life.'

If it led to the death of a patient suffering from pain it would be 'precisely the same thing as murder'. Then suppose it was a case, say, of a spinal carcinoma. Dr Douthwaite opined that if the drug regime over the two weeks were isolated from the previous weeks of drugs accumulating, then he would not be forced to the conclusion that it was murder.

> 'I would say that faced with a woman in terrible pain he was giving large doses of drugs and those doses of drugs as set out here would have caused death.'

Mr Justice Devlin intervened; it was a question of law:

> 'Would you say you were forced to conclude he intended to kill?'
> 'Yes, my Lord. Earlier on, when I was asked what my conclusions were from these drugs, I deliberately said my conclusions were that they were given to terminate life. I said that deliberately because I don't know, it is my business to know, whether that is synonymous with murder. I never introduced the word murder myself, but learned counsel did so, and I take it he meant that was synonymous. In fact, I thought he obviously wouldn't deceive me. I was giving that opinion on giving these drugs to an old woman who was not in agonising pain.'

The Judge thought the matter of law was too tied up with the question.

Mr Lawrence elucidated the law for Dr Douthwaite:

'Murder, Doctor Douthwaite, is killing with the intention of killing, or terminating life.'

Mr Justice Devlin pointed out that 'that if a doctor gives drugs knowing that they will shorten life but gives them because they are necessary to relieve pain, he is not committing murder.'

Mr Lawrence followed up this 'helpful' comment of the Judge: if this old woman was not in extreme pain, but nevertheless in acute distress from her condition and the general practitioner gave these doses 'to ease that distress', what would Dr Douthwaite think of that:

> 'I think I made it clear that this distress which Mrs Morrell was suffering was largely, in my opinion, especially in relation to the terrible twitchings to which Nurse Randall referred, a result of drugs. Your earlier example of someone in terrible pain is quite another matter in my mind.'

Would Dr Douthwaite not agree then that the level of dosage was justified in the case 'of the terminal stages of senile disintegration with the brain affected by a long-standing arterio sclerotic condition…' He would not:

> 'Because there is a profound difference between the acute pains of inoperable cancer and the terminal pains of arterio sclerosis [sic].'

Mr Lawrence asked about the case of a doctor who had a different ethical standpoint and treated such a woman with morphia and heroin; would he be a murderer? Dr Douthwaite said that this was not what he had said at all, but the previous drugging and the amounts had influenced his final conclusion in this particular case. But bearing in mind the accumulated problems Dr Adams had from his previous treatment of the patient, he was left with the tolerance to the drugs and had to give increasing doses. Dr Douthwaite could not still consider that 'an intention to terminate life', could he? He did, because 'large quantities of drugs were given to an individual who is saturated with drugs', unless, of course, the Doctor was completely ignorant of their action – which he found difficulty in accepting as a possibility. Mr Lawrence was 'struggling' to see the difference between this case and the hypothetical one of inoperable cancer: the sole difference then was the presence of severe pain? Yes, it was. He returned to the withdrawal of the morphia on the 31st October: now was this 'removing the shield of protection from large doses.' deliberate and with the intention of 'reintroducing the morphia with lethal effect?'

> 'So it appears.'

In that case Dr Douthwaite must mean that the 'intention to terminate life' was made on that day. Dr Douthwaite was 'not sure that that follows absolutely'. Mr Lawrence was struggling again: either it was or it was not 'part of a design to terminate life'.

> 'Yes, or it was not.'

Dr Douthwaite explained that it was very difficult to answer some of the questions 'Yes' or 'No'. He had now come to the conclusion that the withdrawal of the morphine was part of a design to terminate life, but 'I cannot say whether that design was formed on the first or second day.' – either 31st October or 1st November. He agreed with Mr Lawrence, however, that now the date had to be brought forward from the 8th November, the date he had previously designated.

Did he still consider, Mr Lawrence wanted to know, that the ¼ grain of morphine reintroduced on the 6th November was a dose with intent to kill, as he had said in his answer to the Judge: 'He reintroduced morphia in a patient, with heavy doses of heroin, knowing that the morphine tolerance would have been reduced in the previous 5 days.' Dr Douthwaite did still agree with this answer. So, 'it would not be an unfair summary' that his view was 'that with every dose, and whatever the dose and whatever the kind, there was an attempt to terminate life?' He thought that this was inaccurate: he hoped he had not given the impression that he thought 'each dose was expected in itself to kill'; it was the accumulation; he did think though that there was an intent to kill present with each injection.

> '…The whole thing was based on this mounting up of drugs in an individual who, as I said, was dying and, therefore, excreting or destroying the drugs in her body slowly.'

Mr Justice Devlin tried to clarify the matter: Dr Douthwaite was postulating that Dr Adams intended to kill and that he had knowledge of the effect of these drugs:

> 'Let me suppose that 3 grains is larger than anything that has been given and is in the nature of a lethal dose in the sense that it will produce death without anything more. What you are inferring about Dr Adams' mind is that he refrained from giving a dose that of itself would kill?'
> 'Yes, my Lord.'
> 'Perhaps because he thought: 'This is too large and may arouse suspicion?'
> 'Yes.'
> 'And what he did was to give a series of doses over a period, the combined effect of which he knew would kill?'
> 'That is exactly what I meant, my Lord.'

Mr Lawrence asked for confirmation that this theory depended on 'the medical theory of accumulation'; it did. When had Dr Douthwaite first thought of the theory that the intention to terminate life was formed at some time when the morphine was withdrawn? He was not able to remember, but 'some time when I was in this Court'. Mr Lawrence reminded him that he had said nothing of this and that the transcript of Day Nine showed that he had said then that the intention to terminate Mrs Morrell's life was formed on the 8th November – so that 'to say the least of it' was 'an incomplete answer'? He might put it that way, admitted Dr Douthwaite. Mr Lawrence read out Dr Douthwaite's previous answers to him in the first cross-examination as he would not admit that these were inconsistent with what he was now saying:

'Not a word about the drugs withheld?'
'No.'

The truth was, said Mr Lawrence, that he had made some statements in his evidence which were 'the exact opposite' of his present theory:

'Well, if I have done so, no doubt you will point them out to me.'

Mr Lawrence went through some of Dr Douthwaite's answers to questions put by the Attorney-General. His answer that he did not know why the morphia was withdrawn was 'quite true'; at the time it was a complete and truthful answer because he did not know. He had puzzled over it for some time. But why had he accepted Mr Lawrence's suggestion that it was a 'variation', the withdrawal of the morphia? Dr Douthwaite said that he had been under intense cross-examination and that he had accepted Mr Lawrence's meaning of 'variation' – which was why he had asked 'By stopping the morphia?', but a doctor would understand by the word that the drug should be changed, rather than an alteration of the dose. Then, said Mr Lawrence, he had also accepted that the re-introduction of the morphia, together with heroin and atropine was a 'variation of drugs'. Dr Douthwaite agreed that was accurate, but he had not agreed the reason for it; he had only agreed that there was 'increasing restlessness'. It was the previous Friday, in answering the Judge's questions that he had said that the idea that Dr Adams was merely trying a variation of drugging 'was an impossible view'. Mr Lawrence put it to him that both views could not be right.

'It is perfectly right to say there were variations of drugs, but I don't believe that variation was for the benefit of the patient.'

There was further altercation, by the end of which there was considerable confusion and Mr Lawrence had to ask Dr Douthwaite for his final view:

'The view that the Morphine was reintroduced with a lethal purpose. And that involves the view that it was also withdrawn for the same purpose, doesn't it?'
'Yes.'
'And that is the part of your evidence which never emerged until my Lord himself asked you questions at the end of hours and hours of examination-in-Chief, cross-examination and re-examination?'
'True.'
'In any case, Dr Douthwaite, the medical theory upon which it is based is absolute rubbish, isn't it?'

There was no answer. It was based, explained Mr Lawrence, on the theory that taking away some tolerance of the drug would make a patient more vulnerable when it was brought back.

'...it would also leave her to the mercy of the stimulating action of Heroin' responded Dr Douthwaite. What about the high cross-tolerance between heroin and morphia, both derivatives of opium?

> 'Cross-tolerance means this, that if you take Morphia and acquire a tolerance to it, you are acquiring at the same time a cross-tolerance to its chemical ally, Heroin?'

The Doctor agreed that there was a 'considerable degree' of cross-tolerance, but not that there would have been withdrawal symptoms if there had been 'any appreciable reduction of tolerance'. Without the heroin there would have been withdrawal symptoms but 'there would be an appreciable reduction in tolerance.' Mr Lawrence suggested that whether there would be fatal results from dropping of the morphia and the re-introduction would 'depend entirely on the degree of reduction of the tolerance'. Again, Dr Douthwaite did not agree, and, what was more:

> 'But I have not suggested – at least, if I have I withdraw it – that this withdrawal of morphine from the 1st to the 5th – if it had not taken place – that the woman would not have died as the result of the doses given her from the 8th to the 10th. I am merely suggesting that that was making it more certain. I hope that is clear.'

Mr Lawrence still could not see why Dr Douthwaite 'was forced' to put a sinister interpretation on the withdrawal of the morphia.

> 'Well, if not forced, the only other thing I can say is that I can see no other explanation for it, and that I said to my Lord very early on when he was questioning me.'

Then 'this business of accumulation of morphia and heroin in the body' – he had used the word 'rubbish' previously and perhaps he 'ought not to have done so', but 'that is not founded upon sound premises' and it was 'a well-known fact' that heroin and morphine were 'non-accumulative drugs'.

> 'In the normal person, yes.'

Dr Douthwaite had certainly had 'this point of accumulation in mind'; morphia was eliminated from the body partly in the urine (75%) and 5% in the faeces and it was believed that the remaining 20% was destroyed in the liver. Mr Lawrence wondered whether checking the nurses' notebooks would give an indication of whether the morphine was being eliminated 'at a normal speed'. It was a non sequitur because 'the failure to eject morphine adequately cannot be judged or checked by the amount of urine passed. When there is a retention of a drug in the body it is held in the tissues of the body.' The only possible way to prove the morphia was in the urine would be to analyse it. Dying persons 'do not excrete drugs at the end'. Mr Lawrence conjectured that this 'was all speculation'.

'That statement is not speculation. The weaker and nearer to death the patient, the more accumulation will occur. That is definite. As to the precise percentage of accumulation, I cannot say, and I will not attempt to.'

Dr Douthwaite was quite accurate, but Mr Lawrence persisted but got nowhere this time in shaking the Doctor's statement. He returned to the re-introduction of the morphia on 6th November at ¼ grain for five occasions and then going up to ½ grain. There had been then many 'variations and alterations in the last days' which would be significant or, at least, 'consistent with an innocent intent'. Dr Douthwaite conceded that.

The 'final medical matter' was that Dr Douthwaite had 'expressed the opinion that a combination of heroin and morphia was more lethal than either of these drugs separately'. That was quite right: the action of the two drugs combined was stronger than when taken separately. Mr Lawrence suggested that this was 'quite wrong' and that it was 'what is called in medical parlance synergism' – 'that is to say that certain drugs when you mix them are more effective in combination than if you give them separately'. Dr Douthwaite agreed, but with morphia and heroin:

'...it is not what one would call synergism. Or put it this way: one would not say, I quite agree, morphia and heroin are synergistic as an example of striking synergism, but if you do give those two drugs together their action is more pronounced than if you give them separately.'

But 'the combination of morphia and hyosin [sic] is a very clear and well known case of synergism' and 'more lethal than either of them separately' and Dr Douthwaite had even suggested hyoscine himself. He had also said, though, 'with a considerable reduction of morphine', and 'a simple example' of synergism was the action of Phenacitin and Aspirin, which were more powerful together than given separately.

Mr Lawrence put 'the picture' of a doctor who began the medication of his patient 'in a totally wrong way', due not to any intention to kill but 'to ignorance or stupidity, or something of that kind?' Dr Douthwaite was on the defensive:

'Have I said that? I must start thinking again.'

It was clear though, that Mrs Morrell was 'in the terminal stages of her life in this last fortnight'. Dr Douthwaite agreed that she was dying then. Mr Justice Devlin wanted to get a date if possible; did Dr Douthwaite mean that she was dying before the 1st November? He did. Mr Lawrence saw his opportunity: if the day report of 9th October was right 'where the nurse rang up Dr Adams and he diagnosed a possible further stroke' [over the telephone] – if there had been a further stroke 'that would certainly bring the final end of her life nearer'. If she had had a second stroke, 'it would make the prognosis worse.' With a few further references to the 'variation' in drugs, Mr Lawrence wound up:

'The truth of all this matter is this, Dr Douthwaite, that you first of all gave evidence on one basis to support a charge of murder and then thought of something else after you had started?'
'That is quite likely. In fact, I think it is probable. I had been turning it over in my mind but at what time it crystallised and became clear I do not know.'

And Dr Douthwaite could conceive of a medical opinion contrary to his own?

'Certainly. I have always agreed that a contrary medical opinion I am expecting.'

The Attorney-General re-examined his witness. He wished Dr Douthwaite to look at the relationship between the doses of morphia and heroin given to the patient with the 'normal dose' and with the maximum dose according to the *British Pharmacopoeia*: for instance on 7th November, the normal dose had been given four times in that day 'and the final dose of morphia was twice the normal dose'; each dose of heroin was three times the normal. This meant that on that day 'the total of morphia was six times the normal and the total of the heroin was 15 times the maximum'. On the 6th November the daily total for the heroin was '15 times the maximum' as well.

'And each date from 6th November, each injection of heroin itself, three times the maximum daily dose?'
'Yes.'

On that same date, 6th November, there was half a grain of heroin injected at 1 a.m. and another half a grain at 1.55 a.m. Would the effect of the former injection of three times the maximum dose have worn off by the time of the next injection?

'No, that is quite impossible.'

The Attorney-General turned to the 8th November, and on that day, Mrs Morrell had been given 'twelve times the maximum dose of heroin' as well as 'eight times the normal dose of morphia'. On the 9th the total dropped a little with the morphia total being 'eight times the normal' and the heroin 'nine times the maximum'; 10th November and the morphia daily total 'four times the normal' and 'each of the four injections of heroin were six times the maximum'.

'And the daily total of heroin is consequently 24 times the maximum?'
'24 times, yes.'

Amazingly, the next day, 11th November:

'…the total administered in the day of heroin being 30 times the maximum?'

'Yes, 30 times the maximum.'
'Plus 14 times the normal dose of morphia?'
'Yes.'

The 12th November, and the morphia dose was 'eight times the normal' and the heroin '21 times the maximum'. The Attorney-General asked Dr Douthwaite if he had taken days in isolation or formed his opinion of the cause of death, having regard to all those days. He had certainly taken into account the dosage on all those days.

The Attorney-General asked if Dr Douthwaite had ever come across cases of inoperable cancer where injections of morphia and heroin had been administered together in the same injection:

'The answer is almost certainly no.'

Not in his experience of almost thirty years. Morphia and heroin were pain-killers for severe pain; he had seen many cases of cerebral arteriosclerosis but, in his opinion, there was no need, even in the terminal stages, for heroin or morphia as it was not normally a painful disease.

The Attorney-General asked Dr Douthwaite if had changed his opinion at all as 'to the intention of these final doses': he had not. Could he summarise the main factors that led him to that conclusion:

'The main factors were that he had a very old and sick lady who had been heavily drugged and was a drug addict. That is the sort of background. He also had a woman who was not, so far as I can tell, in severe pain. Therefore, the administration of very large doses of these drugs could not, as far as I could see, be justified, and that is why I was driven to the conclusion that their administration was in order to terminate life.'

When Dr Douthwaite 'had considered further Exhibit 54 [prescription list] and the nurses' reports', was this 'for the first time on the cessation of the Morphia?'. It was, but his opinion on the cause of death of Mrs Morrell had not altered at all. With the withdrawal of the morphia and the increase of heroin, 'what consequences in the patient's condition' would he expect? Dr Douthwaite considered that there would be an increase in restlessness and 'especially some increase of twitching', but whether it would have made her 'more excitable or slightly quieter, I just don't know. It varies.' As to heroin having any sedative effect, this was 'very unlikely'. He could not consider that the doses in the last few days of Mrs Morrell's life, including 31st October, was 'consistent with an innocent intent'. She was 'almost certainly dying' on the 1st November and 'the prolonged use of drugs would have contributed' to that condition, although 'to what extent, of course, that is quite impossible to say.'

Mr Justice Devlin now questioned Dr Douthwaite again:

'Doctor Douthwaite, on that last question. Do you see anything in the medical treat-

ment before the 1st November or the dropping of the Morphia, which would indicate
to you as a medical man an intent to kill?'
'No, my Lord.'

No single injection, by itself, had been large enough to postulate that there was an intent to kill
by that one injection, and none of the instructions to the nurses had driven Dr Douthwaite to
that conclusion either.

> 'Whether the intent to kill was formulated first at the end of October or the beginning
> of November or whether it was formulated first on the 8th November, it depends on
> what has been called the accumulation theory?'
> 'The production of death.'
> 'Your inference that there was an intent to kill depends on the attribution by you to
> Doctor Adams of the knowledge that a single drug, not dangerous in itself, would be
> lethal because of the accumulation of drugs already in the body?'
> 'Yes, my Lord.'

Dr Douthwaite explained that he had answered Mr Lawrence, saying that he accepted the possibility of a medical view contrary to his own as doctors frequently disagreed on various points,
but he 'would be astonished' if another doctor disagreed with his views on accumulation. He
attributed the knowledge about accumulation to Dr Adams, excluded 'error, ignorance and
incompetence', and postulated an intent to kill:

> 'Because my Lord, I think I said before, I could not conceive of a man with Doctor
> Adams's qualifications and special knowledge of drugs having this ignorance, or being
> ignorant of drugs of this sort.'

He believed that 'if Dr Adams or any other doctor with Doctor Adam's qualifications went into
the witness box and said that he had no knowledge of the accumulation theory, then he would
be committing perjury.'

There was another matter, Mr Justice Devlin said, on which he would like Dr Douthwaite's
help: he had in mind that the Jury might have to consider the motive which Dr Adams had in
his mind, and that suggested was that 'if she lived long enough she might alter her will and
deprive him of the benefits he had, or thought he had under the will'. Considering the 'medical
picture as you see it', how far would a doctor have seen it 'worthwhile to shorten her life for a
purpose of that sort?' Dr Douthwaite thought that if he had seen her in October, he would have
expected her to live 'only for a matter of a few weeks, probably not more than two months.'

> 'If one were to take the lower estimate of that, is Doctor Adams saying to himself, "She
> can only live for let me say three weeks anyway?" He would be embarking on a course
> on the 1st November that in fact took 13 days to bring about her death, and which prob-

ably he would have estimated would take about 13 days, would he not, since he had to withdraw the morphia, reintroduce it and step it up to overcome the tolerance?'

'He might well have, my Lord.'

The Court adjourned for lunch.

Dr Ashby returned to the stand for further examination by the Attorney-General. They continued with the graphs Exhibits 35A and 37A. After Dr Ashby had explained various points, the Attorney-General asked him:

> 'In your opinion, what would be the effect on a woman of 81 years of age if given morphia and heroin in the quantities shown to have been prescribed between the 8th and the 12th of November?'
>
> 'I don't think it is possible that she could have survived those quantities, without being steadily worked up to that dosage; that is to say, a patient receiving those doses when being treated for the pains of cancer would survive them, but they would have been built up several weeks before. They would have been getting perhaps 3 or 4 grains of each. What led me to a conclusion about an inability to survive was the very sudden rise in the prescriptions as illustrated on the graph. The two situations are entirely different.'

He explained that this was the taking of morphia and heroin together. Suppose she had had the morphia alone? Dr Ashby did not think that she could have stood such a very sudden increase; there was 'no previous raising of morphia at all really right back to the 18th of August. So there was no preparation for the big dose in respect of acquired tolerance to very high doses, again differing from the usual cancer patient.' The same considerations applied to her having the heroin alone. And if she had had the major part of all the morphia and heroin prescribed? She could not have survived. There had been 'a five-fold increase of heroin' over six days: could this have built up tolerance for her for the doses of heroin from the 8th to the 10th November?

> 'I do not think a five-fold increase for six days it would be possible that she could have survived what was then more than 12 times as much. It is a difference between $\frac{1}{3}$ to $6\frac{1}{4}$, which is 18 times. The dosage was raised 18 times after only six days. I do not think it is possible that a woman of eighty could survive that.'

Dr Ashby thought that every general practitioner would be aware of all the facts in relation to morphia as it was 'a drug of almost universal use', but the same could not be said for heroin and there were family doctors 'who virtually never use it, except perhaps as a linctus'.

> 'In your experience, have you ever found heroin and morphia being used together in conditions where there is not severe pain?'
>
> 'No, I have never done it myself or seen it used by a colleague.'

The Attorney-General asked if the doses given from the 8th to the12th November have been required to overcome tolerance. Dr Ashby replied that adding another ½ grain should have been sufficient: the patient who was becoming tolerant to ¼ grains would then be put on ½ grain, or ⅔ grain. It would be 'very unusual to do more than double a dose to counteract the patient's tolerance'.

Dr Ashby's attention was now drawn to the Neston Cottage Hospital nurses' reports. He attributed the 'severe pain' recorded on the 27th June, 1948 to arthritis, the pain of which could develop quickly when an elderly person was immobilised; he agreed with Dr Douthwaite that the 'severe pain in the region of the heart' on the 28th was 'probably dispeptic [sic]' and brandy frequently did give relief from this. As to the morphia given in hospital, it was not 'rational to say that there is no measure of addiction after nine days', if assuming it is reduced after three weeks, but it would be 'very slight' and not require any weaning process. In a very neurotic patient, prone to addiction, even one or two injections could 'sow the fatal seeds of desire to continue with the drug', but he did not think this applicable in this case. When she was discharged to be taken to Eastbourne, she must have greatly improved for this to have been agreed. Dr Ashby thought that any general practitioner then 'would be thinking in terms of how much further it was right or proper' to be continuing the morphia injections. It was quite justifiable for the hospital doctors to put Mrs Morrell on morphia for the first days after the stroke when there was pain and the expectation of life poor for those few days.

The Attorney-General asked what the patient's expectation of life would have been on discharge from the hospital. Dr Ashby replied that 'there would be an immense change in the prognosis' after the first few days: no evidence that the haemorrhage or thrombosis was spreading, no pneumonia: 'by that tenth day (she) could have been expected to live from six months to several years'.

'Now we have got her back to Eastbourne', said the Attorney-General: leaving Cheshire on 5th July, 1948 and making the journey, presumably in one day. The first prescription by Dr Adams was two days later on the 7th July for a mixture containing sodium phenobarbitone, and the second on the 9th July for:

> '...Ampules hyperduric morphia grains half, 12. Total morphia grains 6. Repeat twice at six days interval'. Assuming that was given, half a grain for the twelve days, that would be twice the dose in the hospital, would not it?'
> 'It would, yes.'
> 'Does the sentence "Repeat twice at six days interval" have any significance to you?'
> 'That, I think, envisages the possibility of multiplying it by doubling it yet again.'

In Dr Ashby's view the morphia should have been withdrawn: if there had been any pain then other powerful analgesics could and should have been used: 'those considerations of addiction' were now paramount and overrode any benefit of morphia. There was no record of pain since the 28th June in the hospital and there was no justification for injecting Mrs Morrell each evening with hyperduric morphia to secure sleep – the 'hyperduric' part had no significance as it really meant 'a spreading out'. One of the barbiturates should have been used to promote sleep. On the 21st July, heroin was added to the morphine injection, what could be the reason for this:

> 'I can think of no justification and I think it enormously increased the already present danger of addiction, because heroin is the most dangerous drug of addiction known to man.'

Heroin, he explained was more effective than morphia in producing 'euphoria – that is the tranquillity of mind unjustified by circumstances'; it was less effective in respect of restlessness and sleep and much more dangerous in respect of addiction. Heroin was a poor sedative and barbiturates were 'infinitely better' except in cases of severe pain. Barbiturates were 'short-acting', making a patient go to sleep in half and hour and would be 'used up by the body after eight hours', giving deep sleep at night and be 'relatively lively by day'. Would Mrs Morrell, in his opinion, have been addicted when she left the nursing home in October 1948?

> 'After three months I would have said firmly addicted; in no sense unweanable, but firmly addicted.'

There were many prescriptions for Veramon on the list and Dr Ashby explained that they had an action similar to barbiturates, containing amido-pyrine as a pain-killer and barbiturate to produce sleep. Shorter-acting barbiturates, such as amital [sic] and nembutal were also available in 1948.

Mrs Morrell returned home to Marden Ash on 30th March, 1949 and Dr Ashby considered that, at this time, she 'could reasonably be expected to live several years', although it was 'impossible to forecast these matters'. He agreed with Dr Douthwaite that such a patient should be 'got up and about as soon as possible and kept active in body and mind and physiotherapy given and training to reduce the disability of the stroke to a minimum'. It was not necessary to keep a stroke patient as quiet as possible, they must move. Morphia and heroin would 'impair the chances' of rehabilitation 'by reason of their sedative action'.

What would be the doctor's duties regarding the addiction, asked the Attorney-General:

> 'I think it would be obligatory upon him to wean her of this addiction because it is a matter of universal knowledge that drug addiction is something which is highly undesirable. Much legislation has been devoted to it.'

The information as to how to wean a patient off drug addiction was available in the Pharmacopoeia, known as 'Martindale' [a synthesis of standard books], which 'would be on the shelf of most doctors and every hospital, including that at Eastbourne'. Dr Ashby was asked to read from this book a paragraph relating to morphine addiction:

> 'Withdrawal symptoms vary in intensity with the individual, the degree of addiction and the rapidity with which the drug is withdrawn. They begin within 24 hours, become

severe within 48 hours, reach their acme within 72 hours and then gradually subside. They include violent pains and muscular twitchings, headache, weakness, insomnia, irritability, severe digestive disturbances, nausea, vomiting, loss of weight, diarrhoea and vasometer disturbances. [flushings and attacks of perspiration]'

He was then asked about heroin dosage recommended in the book: this was one-twelfth to one-sixth per day in Britain, and it also included the daily dosage regarded as the maximum in Germany, Switzerland and Denmark as ¼ grain, and, in France, ⅓ grain. Mr Justice Devlin asked Dr Ashby about the reference in the book to drug addicts in Assam who were taking 'doses of opium ranging from 45 to 250 grains daily' and had been successfully treated. He agreed that doses 'enormously exceeding' those given to the patient in this case had been known to be taken. The Attorney-General asked what the effect would be on the doctor-patient relationship of 'prolonged drugging' by the doctor:

> 'The patient would become progressively more dependent upon the source of supply. If it is a doctor who is the source of supply, the patient would become very dependent upon that doctor. The doctor, would, I think it is fair to say, become an almost essential part of the patient's happiness and well-being.'

On reading through the nurses' notebooks, Dr Ashby felt that, up until the Spring of 1950, Mrs Morrell was 'pretty well' and certainly 'well enough to be weaned' off the drugs, yet there was 'nothing which I should call a serious effort to wean'.

The Attorney-General turned to the prescription lists and graphs again, particularly looking at the period from 28th August to 7th September:

> 'Is it right, therefore, to conclude that the nurses' injections at that period were less than the amounts of prescriptions?'
> 'Yes. It seems that the nurses' injections were one-quarter against two-thirds, and in respect of heroin one-third against three-quarters, I make it.'

Was it also right that there was a big difference from the 8th November onwards, between the amounts shown in the nurses' reports as having been injected and the prescriptions?

> 'Yes. A quick glance suggests about twice as much was prescribed in respect of heroin, and I should have said, looking at it visually, about three times more of morphia.'
> 'So if that dosage or the major part of it was in fact administered to Mrs Morrell, it is not recorded in the nurses' books?'
> 'That seems certain.'

Sister Randall had mentioned that every time Dr Adams came 'he wanted a glass of hot water when he saw Mrs Morrell alone'; what would this have been for? This would obviously be to rinse out a syringe for an injection – it could not have been used for any other purpose. The Attorney-General came to the omission by Dr Adams of the morphia and omnopon on 31st October: this had not crossed Dr Ashby's mind as 'a very strange event' and he had not regarded it 'as being a matter highly prejudicial to the patient'. He did agree that it would produce 'some more irritation' but it was not significant 'with regard to the cardinal issue at stake'; and not as 'an act calculated to cause the death of the patient'.

The Attorney-General asked what, in Dr Ashby's opinion, would have been the effect of the injections of morphia and heroin given from the week beginning on 6th November on the patient:

> 'I think, my Lord, that those injections in a woman of 80, who was, to judge by the books, in a very weak state at that time, would hurt her survival, she could not have survived that set of doses as a whole because the increase on the one hand was very sudden over what she was getting only a few days before, and on the other there was the matter of her age and her very weak state. I don't say a young adult would not have survived; I wouldn't say that for a moment.'

Dr Ashby stated that the 'jerky spasms and twitchings' were 'a very rare phenomenon', but he had no alternative but to come to the conclusion that 'they were attributable to the heroin'. The very high level of heroin, to which Mrs Morrell had no tolerance, was 'by far the most likely explanation' of them. The Attorney-General asked:

> 'In your opinion, was the administration of heroin and morphia on that scale in any way justified?'
> 'Well, I don't see the justification really. The patient, we were told, had some superficial abrasions, though they hardly reached the stage of being regarded as serious bed sores. It is very difficult. I think it must be borne in mind, my Lord, that there are no doctor's reports, nothing that I am used to in the way of doctor's notes about the condition of the patient at the time, and in the absence of accurate description it is very difficult for me to say whether something which I think must have been at least easing her passing was justified at the time or not. I really don't think it is possible to do more than say that I can see on the evidence no real justification for it in respect of either pain or – really I think pain is the only justification, pain or the most dreadful discomfort, which would make a doctor feel that he should ease the patient past that stage.'
> [The last part of this paragraph is underlined and heavily marked in the margin by Hannam.]

What did Dr Ashby think of the policy of 'keeping the patient under'? He considered that keeping a patient in a very low state of consciousness was hazardous as very serious complications could occur, such as pneumonia; a doctor would have to consider the inevitable consequences. If the patient had incurable and painful cancer, it would be a doctor's 'bounden duty' to keep them in such a state and 'the fact that their death from an apparently natural cause will come a little sooner is not something which in my opinion should really influence him from that merciful act.'

Dr Ashby had thought long and hard about the drug therapy given by Dr Adams in the last two or three weeks of Mrs Morrell's life, and he had come to the conclusion, even without proper doctor's notes, that 'there was still a faint chance during the first week of November' of weaning her off her addiction; he could not believe 'that the patient could not stand an attempt at weaning… even at that stage. What was there to be lost?' Yet there had been 'nothing which I should call a serious attempt at weaning'. There could have been, at the time the morphia was withdrawn, 'a sufficient increase in the barbiturates' in order 'to drown the withdrawal symptoms', and no increase in the heroin, but this was not what Dr Adams chose to do.

> 'From what you have seen and heard, what would you say was the cause of her death?'
> 'I think that is very complicated, the factors causing her death. The immediate factors, of course, would be the combination of what we refer to as terminal natural causes, like terminal pneumonia, which in its turn would have been fairly directly caused by her being kept under for the last few days. Then I think another very important factor – probably the larger factor – was this very heavy pressure of opiate therapy. Thirdly, the patient's age cannot be ignored. I don't for the moment think of anything else. It is not possible without a post-mortem examination, my Lord, to say with any certainty what the actual final closing act was which ended life in the majority of patients.'
> [This question and answer have heavy underlining and sidelining by Hannam and an arrow in the margin pointing to 'the actual closing final act'.]

The Attorney-General questioned Dr Ashby about what he thought had been the effect of the Paraldehyde injections:

> 'I think the injection was given to suppress the spasms. As a neurologist I frequently use this drug, and that dosage, to suppress rather analogous conditions of epilepsy. From these records, and on an unbiased view, that is probably the reason they were given. I think their effect undoubtedly would have been, in so far as they were also inevitably powerfully sedative, to have antedated the inevitable tipping of the scales, but I cannot say for how long; I should not have thought for many hours.'
> 'By that do you mean accelerating death?'
> 'Yes.'

In saying by not many hours, he 'was taking into consideration the very big doses of heroin and morphia she was carrying on the 12th' – what she had had that day and on the two previous days. Did he mean there was an accumulation, asked the Attorney-General:

> 'I think I would agree with Dr Douthwaite that in the really terminal stages of a patient the kidneys probably were not fully excreting these doses before the next one arrived. In

many of these days there were five at least. (I am going by the nurses' books alone). There were five or six injections. There were six administrations on the 11th, four on the 10th and five on the 12th. I think there must have been some overlapping, without doubt, but its precise extent, as I think was made clear this morning, is quite impossible to say – that is that there was an overlap of one dose or two doses.'

The Attorney-General now asked Dr Ashby about the time after the first week in November, when the last opportunity for weaning had passed, which was by the 8th November.

'Doctor, were the drugs then administered after that in any degree a cause of death or not?'
'Very largely.'

At this stage the drugs given were not given 'to improve the health of the patient' because the patient was dying, and not being given for inoperable cancer; it was a question of 'dealing with someone who had become a drug addict'. In this case, he felt that the patient 'could have been kept completely somnolent and comfortable with barbiturates'. It could be argued that there would have been withdrawal symptoms, but 'the right course would have been to carry on with what may have been the necessary doses of the previous week and keep the patient in an hypnotic state with hypnotic drugs, the barbiturates.'

The Attorney-General examined the nurses' notebooks with Dr Ashby, from the day report of 5th November to see at which point it became obvious that Mrs Morrell could not recover. The 5th and 6th seemed normal, and the day report of the 7th indicated that she was 'in a pretty low state' but not that death was inevitable. Dr Ashby remarked that the nurses' notebooks were not clinical records and that 'they do not really tell us how she was'. He could not see 'a very clear reason for giving Morphia' on the morning of the 7th.

At this point Mr Justice Devlin adjourned the Court until the following morning.

# Twelfth Day

The Attorney-General went through the notebooks again with Dr Ashby, this time to look at the last administration of barbiturates or Sedormid; to see if there was any shortage of sleep; to find out when the records showed the policy of keeping the patient under being in operation and the indication that she was a dying woman. On the 5th November barbiturates were given; on the night of 5th/6th she had seven hours' sleep, being given at 1 a.m. ½ grain of heroin, another ½ at 1.55 a.m. and a further ½ at 7.50 a.m.- about 1½ grains in seven hours. There had been no previous comparable dose of heroin. No barbiturates were given after 7 p.m. on that night. After five hours sleep on the night of 6th/7th there was another early morning injection of heroin. Dr Ashby thought it 'rather remarkable' for heroin injections now to be given in the mornings as they had been given in the evening for 'two years or more'.

The day of the 6th November was the last entry 'recording any attempt to administer any barbiturate and any administration of Sedormid'. What would be the effect of terminating the barbiturates and Sedormid?

> 'Well, I think the only consequence could be a reduction of that part of her sedation which was derived from her Barbiturate therapy, and there could be only two consequences of that, either that she would become more restless or a greater pressure of the more dangerous opiate therapy would have to be given. I don't see, for the moment, any other possible conclusion.'

Dr Ashby thought that they would have had a considerable influence on the symptoms of 'those twitchings', and yet they had been removed, and this would unmask those symptoms.

The night of the 7th showed no shortage of sleep, but Dr Ashby would have used barbiturates if necessary during the day, but these were not used. Dr Adams had given morphia, heroin and atropine during the day as well as at night. There was not so much sleep on the night of 7th/8th as 'she had a considerable part of her ration of sleep by day'. She had also sat out in a chair on the day of the 8th which, Dr Ashby, thought was not 'a good indication of inevitably impending death'. She had been 'alert and talkative' that day and even asked for particular foods and enjoyed them: 'life still seemed to hold some pleasure'. The night of the 8th/9th there was 'no shortage of sleep as necessitated drugging throughout the day'. It was on this day that she had sat out in a chair for an hour:

> 'Yes. I think patients' expressions of their wishes, particularly if they are confused, can be much in excess of their powers, but nevertheless, very objectively, being able to sit out in a chair for nearly an hour, I feel that is not really a matter of opinion, but a matter of fact, that she was well enough to sit in a chair for an hour and then had to be persuaded back to bed.'
> 'And she only had 3 more days to live?'
> 'Yes.'
> 'Any sign in that report that she was at that time what you might call, a dying woman with death imminent?'
> 'I think the chair episode is strongly suggestive that that view is incorrect.'

On the 9th at 8.20 p.m. Mrs Morrell was given barbiturates again, but between the 6th and that administration, there was no record of any given. The night of the 9th/10th was 'a very good night'. It was during the day of the 10th that Dr Adams had visited in the morning and left a 'special injection' to be given, which was injected by the nurse at 1.45 p.m. and then one grain of heroin at 6.30 p.m... Was this consistent with the policy of keeping her under, asked the Attorney-General?

> 'Yes, but I think much the most significant sentence on that page is the instruction

which appears to have been given late that morning, after the best night she had had for some time, that she should then be put on a regime of heroin grains 1 up to hourly intervals, that is to say as frequently as hourly intervals if necessary.'

Dr Ashby thought it unlikely that the 'slight jerkings', mentioned by Sister Randall, were painful; it was more likely that they gave an 'unpleasant sensation'. These 'jerkings' and the restlessness were 'quite consistent' with the heavy dosage of heroin. There seemed to be no indication that death was imminent, but Mrs Morrell was much more heavily sedated and quieter. There was still no lack of sleep during the night of the 10th/11th. The Attorney-General asked Dr Ashby his opinion on 'the sedation on that day'.

> 'In respect of morphia and heroin it seems to be very heavy indeed. I think that is the heaviest day. With the exception of the heroin on the 10th and the morphia on the 9th, I think that day contains doses of double any previous day; approximately double, in any case.'

What were the implications of such heavy sedation?

> '…Well, it does seem to bear out what I understood Nurse Randall to have implied, that her instructions were to keep Mrs Morrell under, and the implication I think I made clear yesterday: that when an old person is kept in a state of fairly deep sedation, unless they are protected from getting a terminal pneumonia with antibiotics they are very likely to die within a few days of being kept so heavily sedated as that pressure of opiate therapy suggests.'

The Attorney-General now read the description of the night of 11th/12th given in the nurses' notes: 'Mrs Morrell has not had a very good night. No sleep up to 8.15 a.m. She has been talkative and very jerky. Taken no nourishment. Becomes violently agitated if asked to have a drink or if given, now and again will suck a swab on forceps.' What 'picture' did this present to Dr Ashby's mind?

> 'I think the irritative effects of the heroin on the spinal cord are responsible for the jerkiness. Then we know that for some months at least she had been liable to become very agitated and upset, and with that pressure of sedation she would be liable to confusion. I think the three combined would probably be the most likely explanation of her episodes of becoming violently agitated.'

As to evidence of her being 'a dying woman', there was little in that report – if it were shown to 'someone with the doses blocked out they wouldn't take a particularly grave view.' Someone could suck on a swab and be in a 'fairly dim state of consciousness' because it was a primitive reflex.

The Attorney-General read through the very last day report, that of the 12th November. Even on this page Dr Ashby 'did not know' that there was any 'direct evidence' that the patient was dying. The policy of keeping her under was 'fairly clearly shown'.

'Is there any evidence in these reports at that time of what might be called terrible or dreadful discomfort being suffered by this old lady?'
'Not really of discomfort of such a degree as to render the doctor obliged to give priority to relieving the discomfort over the chances of survival.'

The Attorney-General asked about the possibility of Mrs Morrell surviving the dosages recorded in the notebooks and in the prescripton list. The answer got somewhat confused and Mr Justice Devlin rephrased the question; this time Dr Ashby's answer was clear:

'What I was trying to say was I personally do not think she could have survived the pressure of sedation given in the books. I am certain beyond any shred of doubt that she could not have survived the doses prescribed.'

He explained further that the dosage in the books had 'to be judged not just from the figures but in relationship to the fact that she was 80 and a pretty sick woman, but I think the graph [amounts prescribed] would apply to any person.' The Attorney-General wanted it made crystal clear:

' – have you any doubt in your mind as to whether or not the four grains of heroin on the 10th, the five on the 11th and the three and a half on the 12th, with the morphia on top of that, whether the patient could have survived that administration, in your opinion?'
'I do not think it is possible, really, that she could have done, really. This is largely bound up with the fact of the policy of keeping her under. That really, to my mind, is the most important feature; keeping a sick woman of eighty-one in that condition would be, I would have thought, would inevitably have caused death, with the high rate of heroin prescribed, which does suppress, strongly suppresses the vital process of respiration.'

Dr Ashby was asked about drugs: how dangerous were heroin and morphia? They were technically dangerous but in the hands of a doctor they were 'only potentially dangerous… neither more dangerous nor less dangerous than a large sharp knife'. It all depended on how they were used, on whom and when. Barbiturates also were dangerous, but much less so than morphia and heroin. Patients often committed suicide with them, but they had to take '20 or 30 tablets'; with morphia and heroin the margin was much less. Whether barbiturates were addictive or not to a patient, very much depended on the psychology of the patient: 'if a patient is given them because they are a psychological subject and need the barbiturates for their peace of mind, that is the type of person who may become addicted to them.'

The Attorney-General asked if Dr Ashby could divide the history of Mrs Morrell's illness from the time of her stroke until her death into 'chapters or periods'. Dr Ashby's view was that the first phase began 'with her stroke and the early administration of morphia and heroin, which I felt obliged to criticise in respect of the morphia and heroin, because I feel by giving those drugs the patient was made an addict of those drugs.' This was time when it was 'the duty of any doctor' to wean her off those drugs. The dosage given was 'not an even pressure of dosage'. There was 'not the faintest doubt from comparing the sheets of 1948 with that of the sheet beginning March 1949'; it seemed to him that the dosage was 'at least double', demonstrating how addicted the patient was. An even pressure of drugs would have made the addiction far less problematical.

When the accused had made his telephone call to Mr Sogno, Mrs Morrell's solicitor in April, 1949, would she then have been addicted? Dr Ashby said she would be 'very firmly addicted' at over nine months after the stroke. There was a direct relationship between addiction and dependence:

> 'They become quite dependent on the source of supply, and if it is someone to whom they have to pay money they will be prepared to use up all their worldly goods to obtain these, and if the source is a Doctor then it is not possible to deny the patient would become just as dependent on that doctor in respect at least of their enjoyment of life.'

In March 1950 when the accused went to Mr Sogno's office and had a conversation with him, the addiction would have been much more firmly established: the prescription rate 'appears to have been at least doubled' and the dependency in the same proportion. Dr Ashby was asked about the effect which weaning would have on the relationship of patient and doctor: if this was at the patient's instigation, then there would be no problem, but if it were at the doctor's suggestion then 'there would be a catastrophic reaction'. He explained this clearly:

> 'From reading about Mrs Morrell, and particularly her attitude when Doctor Adams went on holiday, I personally am not in the least doubt at all that had, for the purpose of argument, the decision to wean Mrs Morrell taken place at that time, Mrs Morrell would have been far more angry and upset. Still her pleasure and comfort was considerably derived, as it usually is, from the pleasures of addiction, and I personally think she would have been very angry with Doctor Adams indeed. I think that really is the essential basis in my own view why Doctor Harris was unable to intervene.'

The second phase of Dr Ashby's 'arbitrary history' began in the Summer of 1950 'when it was clear that the pressure of sedation' was being further increased, and 'because it had to be'. He thought that it was a time when it was 'vital' to wean the patient from her addiction because of 'very considerably mounting requirements'. She was getting irritable because she was not getting as much morphia and heroin as she needed; they were 'in a spiral and a dilemma, but a solution of that dilemma instead of being desirable became obligatory, as a disaster could only otherwise result'.

Dr Ashby's history (taken from his graph 37A) correlated with the prescription record: the Attorney-General confirmed again that there was no 'legitimate reason' for prescribing drugs for a patient that were not for use on that patient. From August 18th, 1950 there was a rise of heroin and a further rise on 28th August; on 6th September the heroin fell back again but the morphia increased, and the morphia increased again on 16th September. The Attorney-General checked with Dr Ashby the injections shown in the nurses' notebooks against the prescription levels – although, having to leave out of consideration the 'special injections'.

> 'So the injection shown in the nurses' books do not show the increase of injections which
> the prescriptions for that period would appear to warrant?'
> 'No, they certainly do not.'

Taking the information from the nurses' books, that is the lower level of dosage, the Attorney-General asked what effect would that have had on the patient's condition during the summer of 1950? Dr Ashby thought it likely, at her age, and with the considerable amounts of 'long-acting barbiturates' that general effect upon her health, activity and well-being 'would be deleterious'. This meant that by the September the dose would need to be raised or there would be 'great discomfort' and 'it would be bound to shorten her expectation of life'. No experienced doctor could have been ignorant of the position.

The third phase, was, according to Dr Ashby, 'the time when there was virtually no hope of the patient recovering from the effects of the previous circumstances'. He had to look at this both on the basis of the prescriptions and then of the nurses' reports:

> 'On the basis of the prescriptions there seems no doubt that on the 2nd November heroin was increased five-fold, and, as I said the other day, only six days later it was multiplied again, I think another four-fold on top – about twenty times in six days. And morphia much the same. Well, any possible justification for that is, I think, very difficult to see from the pages we have turned this morning.'

According to the nurses' reports, the third phase:

> '...is represented by days 10, 11 and 12. I may be wrong; it may be some days earlier. It could conceivably be just the 11th and 12th, but I don't really think that by the 11th the patient, having been put under the regime of being kept under, could have survived, and I think that must be regarded as being a different chapter from the previous one where weaning was obligatory.'

Was there any evidence that Dr Ashby could see, asked the Attorney-General, that any of Mrs Morrell's symptoms: confusion, irritability, abusiveness, one instance of Cheyne Stokes breathing, discomfort, or restlessness, were due to anything other than 'this deliberate prolonged drugging'? Dr Ashby attributed 'the major portion of her irritability' to drugs, and it was clear from the reports that it 'tended to be greater on an average in the afternoons... when the level of opiates were lowest in her body'.

Could Mrs Morrell, in Dr Ashby's opinion, have survived the injections of four grains of heroin on the 10th, five grains on the 11th, three and a half on the 12th, plus the morphia and paraldehyde? He did not see how she could have done 'particularly in view of this instruction to keep her under. I don't think it is possible to divorce the purely numerical considerations from the consideration of that instruction; the two are inseparably linked.' The Attorney-General asked:

'...Can you see any reason why this lady of her age should have died on the 13th November if the heroin and morphia had not been administered to her?'
'I don't think she would have died. I can see no reason from these reports to have expected her to die. She was sitting up in a chair talking quite brightly only a few days before.'

She 'could not possibly have survived' the prescriptions from the 8th to the 12th November. Another matter: the 'blank space' on Exhibit 54A for the days of 26th and 27th October, which was a break in the routine administration of drugs. Dr Ashby would have expected the patient to have 'rather acute' withdrawal symptoms, at least on the second of those two days. It was reported in the nurses' notebooks that a 'special injection and capsule' were given on the morning of the 26th by Dr Adams; then the patient slept from 11.30 to 1 and was 'very confused on waking' and then on the night of the 26th/27th she 'slept heavily until 3.15 a.m.' and later 'still seemed in semi-comatose condition'. The next morning, the 27th, Dr Adams again gave a 'special injection and capsule', and she went to sleep again, was then 'alert and talkative', sleeping in the afternoon and did not need an injection of morphia and heroin until 2.10 a.m. on the 28th.

'Having looked at these three days, do you see there the withdrawal symptoms that you would expect to see if the injections of morphia and heroin had been terminated on the 25th?'
'No, I do not. And I think if a doctor was given a dozen pages each side I don't think he could pick out that 48 hours as a 48 hours of the complete withdrawal of those drugs.'
'But there is no record in the books of those drugs being administered on the 26th and 27th?'
'None that I can see.'
'There is a record of the administration by Dr Adams of special injections?'
'Yes.'

The Attorney-General must have felt some degree of satisfaction when he sat down.

Mr Lawrence began his cross-examination: it was quite impossible to say whether Mrs Morrell would have lived longer than 13th November, 1950 if she had not had 'the whole pattern of treatment and medication'. Dr Ashby was nothing if not scrupulously fair: he did not think that 'the earlier treatment had any great influence on the length of her life'. Mr Lawrence was not one to miss the slightest opportunity: either it was material or it was not, the earlier period. Dr Ashby explained that, up to about June or July, 1950, when the level of drug therapy was low, it was probable that her life-expectation was not altered by it. On the evidence available there was no other cause for her dying during the last period, except 'a very heavy pressure of morphia, heroin and natural causes combining.' Mr Lawrence asked if it were not 'unsafe to be dogmatic'; there were 'limits to the powers of divination of doctors', and that medicine had 'still many uncharted deserts'. Dr Ashby did not think it was for him to say what was murder; he had done his best to guide the Court. What he did feel certain about was that 'the instruction to keep her under' and the high dosage of morphia and heroin in the last days would have brought about 'certain effects' but he was not prepared to say 'whether they were instructions of a murderous nature.'

Mr Justice Devlin asked Dr Ashby:

> 'I think you are quite right to leave the word 'murder' out of it, but were they instructions which, in your view, a general practitioner with Dr Adams' qualifications would have known would accelerate death?'
> 'The instruction to keep her under could not fail to have – I should not say could not fail, but would be almost certain to accelerate death.'
> 'And that is a conclusion which a doctor with Dr Adams' qualifications would have reached?'
> 'Yes. I think an anaesthetist is particularly conversant with the dangers of a patient being unconscious or semiconscious.'

Dr Ashby had fixed upon the instruction of the 9th November as being the point when Dr Adams had decided to 'accelerate death'. Mr Lawrence now fixed his attention on the record made by Sister Randall in the notebook and her evidence in Court: it was 'vitally important' to be absolutely accurate about what those instructions were, and in what circumstances they were given. He looked back at the evidence Sister Randall had given in her examination-in-chief by the Attorney-General: she had said: 'It was doctor's orders to keep her from getting restless, to keep her under as much as we could then at that stage'. Had she not, asked Mr Lawrence, expressed the purpose of the instruction before stating it? Dr Ashby thought it was 'one interpretation' and 'a fair one', but he did not think 'it completely was that'.

The Attorney-General had then asked Sister Randall what she understood by the instruction 'to keep her under as much as you could', and she had replied, 'Not to let her get to the stage of being excited and restless'. Then, to the next question: 'Keep her under what?', she had replied 'Keep her peaceful.', and to: 'What do you mean when you say 'keep her under'?', the answer was, 'So that she did not come right out from the drug and did not get restless again.' It was to be supposed that the nurses would be justified in giving an injection in order to prevent anticipated 'undesirable restlessness', and the vast majority of the doses were given by the nurses. Dr Ashby did not see any difference between injections given directly by Dr

Adams and those given by the nurses under his instructions. He agreed that there might 'well be circumstances in the situation of the patient which justifies the doctor putting the comfort of a patient before the longest possible survival date.'

Mr Lawrence trawled through 'certain broad matters' from the time of Mrs Morrell's stroke, through her time in the nursing homes, the hotel, her return home, the Summer of 1950 when 'she was going downhill', Dr Adams' absence on holiday at the end of September and to 'a very vital entry and date', the 9th October. This was an entry which had 'no parallel': after a visit by Dr Adams, who gave a 'special capsule and injection', the patient became 'very drowsy at 11a.m. and went into a deep sleep and could not be wakened. Was in a semi-comatose condition. Lower lip very blue. Brandy given with no effect at 1.30 p.m. Patient eventually awoke at 4.30 p.m. (Doctor informed of patient's condition at 1.15 p.m.) ? Stroke.', which was diagnosed over the 'phone by Dr Adams, and there was a slight difficulty of speech the next morning. Was all this not consistent with another stroke?

> 'Well, the clinical deductions to draw from this rather slim information are, I think, two. I think this episode is compatible with a cerebral vascular accident, but I feel obliged to say it is equally compatible with a rather heavy injection of Morphia and Heroin at that time. I think exactly the same set of circumstances would follow for the next 12 hours or so. The deep sleep, the semi-comatose condition, the patient's depressed respiration and blueness, improvement with brandy, eventually waking; and it is well known after a patient has had a heavy dose of barbiturates or opiates they can have some transient difficulty with speech. I am not saying that happened, but this single set of recorded circumstances are explainable on either ground, and I do not think I should care to say which was the more likely. As a scientist I must say a certain set of phenomena can have one, two or three different explanations.'

The circumstance he did not take into account in this answer was that Dr Adams did not visit the patient after the telephone call from the nurse, which he surely would have done if he had thought she had had a stroke. Dr Ashby then agreed with Mr Lawrence that a patient who had a first stroke was more likely to die of a second stroke than heart failure.

Mr Lawrence was able to talk almost conversationally with Dr Ashby about the symptoms of increased restlessness, confusion and physical deterioration and whether these might be due to lesion in the brain due to a further stroke or to hardening of the arteries and shortage of blood in the brain. Any observer would certainly see this as distressing, even if it was uncertain as to whether the patient were suffering or not? Dr Ashby concurred.

'This point of no return' – Mr Lawrence sought to confirm the date by which Dr Ashby considered it to be impossible for Mrs Morrell to be weaned from the drugs. The 8th November was the date he had given to the Attorney-General, and he thought this 'a fair answer'. Mr Lawrence tried to push the date back to the beginning of November when Dr Douthwaite had concluded that 'all was lost', but Dr Ashby did not think an attempt on the 8th would have been 'pointless', as doctors often had to 'try to rescue people from circumstances where we think there is no hope of success'. Nevertheless, he agreed with Mr Lawrence that 'by about the 8th or 9th' Mrs Morrell was a dying woman.

Mr Lawrence drew Dr Ashby's attention to an answer he had given on the previous day to the Attorney-General in respect of a question about the heavy drugging on the 10th and 11th November, that he saw no justification for it as he could see no evidence of 'pain or the most dreadful discomfort, which would make a doctor feel that he should ease the patient past that stage'. So if he could see that evidence, he would have found the justification for it? Certainly. And the justification was 'closely bound up with "the point of no return?"'

> 'Yes; the oncoming march of death.'
> 'In those circumstances, Dr Ashby, it may well be, may it not, that whatever drugs were given to this patient from and after the 8th November were given with the sole object of promoting her comfort?'
> 'I think that is a possible interpretation, certainly.'
> 'Well, you would assent to it.'
> 'Yes, as one interpretation, certainly.'

That, was apparently, all Mr Lawrence was asking of him, and his attention was now drawn to the contents of the *British Pharmacopoeia 1948*. There was no such thing as the 'maximum dose' in respect of these drugs? In giving figures, the textbook was not trying to indicate a maximum dose, but were intended for general guidance. It was for the medical practitioner to 'exercise his own judgment and act on his own responsibility' on the amount and frequency of administration. It was the duty of the pharmacist or dispenser to 'satisfy himself of the prescriber's intention' when he came across an unusually large dose which had been prescribed. If it was unusual to administer the drug other than orally, then the single dose suitable for that method of administration was mentioned. Mr Lawrence's point was that it was 'extraordinarily difficult… if not impossible to talk about fatal doses in the case of opiate drugs' and it all depended upon the condition of the patient. Dr Ashby agreed.

Mr Lawrence asked if Dr Ashby had researched recorded instances of survival of various dosages of morphia and heroin. He had not 'on freak dosage and survival'. Mr Lawrence put a couple to him, but it was not clear whether they were authenticated or not. Dr Ashby did accept that there was 'the principle of outstanding variability' in non-tolerant people. With tolerant people there should be a record of response to dosage. Mr Lawrence wanted to somehow differentiate between the nomenclature 'addict' in 'popular parlance' and type of addict which Mrs Morrell had become as a patient 'under continuous treatment from her doctor'.

> 'Not the sort of addict who, not under the medical profession, is going into every hole and corner to get hold of the desired drug?'
> 'I agree. A very different set of circumstances.'

Both seemed to miss the irony of the inference which could have been drawn.

Mr Lawrence went on to get Dr Ashby's agreement that a patient could remain at a steady level of dosage for a long time, and then did proceed to the subject of the dependence of an addicted patient upon the doctor. There were addicts who had to depend upon illicit sources, but there were also addicts registered with the Home Office who could be provided with drugs by doctors legitimately. He put it to Dr Ashby that before dependence upon a doctor could arise, then the patient would have to realise their dependence upon a drug. Dr Ashby did not consider that to be true. Then they would have to realise that the doctor might or was likely to withhold it? No, he did not think that a threat was 'necessary for a feeling of dependence'. But Mr Lawrence did not follow, how the patient who was getting the necessary dosage, with no 'indication of any cessation of supply', could be dependent. Dr Ashby embarked upon an explanation, but was interrupted by Mr Lawrence telling him it was 'a different thing'. The Attorney-General asked that his witness be allowed to finish:

> 'I do not think a threat to withdraw those drugs is necessary in order to bring a craving for them into the mind of the patient. A feeling of malaise during the afternoon, that restlessness I should have thought was some measure of evidence suggesting a craving for the drug and a looking forward to the next injection. I am not drawing that just from this case. I am drawing that partly from a knowledge of the usual results of long medication with Morphine and Heroin. It is difficult to divide what I know about one case and other cases.'

Mr Lawrence wanted evidence from the case of Mrs Morrell of craving:

> 'I think it is fair to say, what doubtless you have noticed, that she never once asked for an injection as reported in the book.'
> 'When we are trying to think clearly over these things, another thing that a patient would have to realise before there was any dependence on her doctor, would be a realisation if it be the fact, that she could not get it from any other doctor?'
> 'Yes. I had not thought of that one. I don't know that it would have crossed her mind about that sort of problem. I think she would just think of the medicine as she was getting it from the doctor, not necessarily a named doctor.'

There was evidence that Mrs Morrell had exhibited 'extreme bad temper', shouting, abuse, and 'sometimes violence'. It was quite likely then, that when she first came to Eastbourne, she would have been 'even more bad tempered and difficult and generally impossible'. Mr Lawrence's theory, or that of his expert medical adviser, was that the morphia was used by Dr Adams for sleep at nights and the heroin in order to make her 'more tractable and peaceful during the day'; she would then be more co-operative and recover more quickly. Dr Ashby agreed to all.

For the theory to have this outcome, Mr Lawrence's proposition was for drugs to be synergistic, because Dr Adams had combined them into one injection. Logically, it is difficult to see why they would not have been separated into two injections in this case, and there was still the missing element of the 'special injections'.

The disadvantages of giving these drugs were those of addiction? Dr Ashby responded to Mr Lawrence by saying that, 'at that stage' (presumably early) that was the only disadvantage and that 'heavy barbiturates also, if they had been necessary' might also have produced a deleterious effect. Dr Adams had, in fact, prescribed considerable amounts of barbiturates and Veramon for Mrs Morrell as the lists showed, and the notebooks recorded the administration of them. Mr Lawrence continued his interrogation as though they had never been used, and Dr Ashby seemed to be caught in a web, agreeing to Mr Lawrence's every suggestion, even when the queried stroke of 9th October was asserted as fact.

Dr Adams had also been caught in a 'spiral' which, according to Mr Lawrence, began with Dr Harris in September; Dr Ashby could not agree a date to this. The dilemma for the Doctor was to cope with the situation by keeping the raising of the drugs' level as slow as possible, or to wean the patient from the drugs. He then might have thought that 'death would overtake the spiral'; when he reached 'the point of no return', then he had to 'ease the distress of the inevitable'. All this was 'a possible view of the evidence in this case'.

> 'Will you look at the last report of all by the night nurse, beginning with the Paraldehyde recorded at 10.30 p.m.; then very restless an hour afterwards, an hour afterwards restless and talkative and very shaky, but at 12.45 "seems a little quieter, appears asleep. Respirations 50. 2 a.m. Passed away quietly.". On the face of that record it is not possible, is it, to rule out the hypothesis that when the end came in that way at that time on that date, it was the result of natural causes?'
> 'That cannot be ruled out.'
> [This question and answer are heavily sidelined in the margin and the words 'On the face of that record' are heavily underlined by Hannam.]

In the circumstances the cause of death which Dr Adams had put on the cremation certificate 'cerebral thrombosis' could have been 'a quite honest entry by him'? He could well have thought that, agreed Dr Ashby. Even if there had been a post-mortem examination of the body, the pathologist would not have been able to judge the deceased's tolerance to the drugs, only the amount in the body. That was so. Lastly, Mr Lawrence asked about anaesthesia, which was the 'suppression of brain activity producing consciousness' according to Dr Ashby.

> 'That science or art has got nothing whatever to do, has it, with the use of such drugs as morphia and heroin for therapeutical purposes in prolonged treatment?'
> 'The connection is a very complicated question, because the considerations of prolonged therapy in morphia and heroin are very different in their implications from the knowledge and skill required for short term anaesthesia, but there would be a great deal of knowledge about morphia and heroin to an anaesthetist. I do not think I should suggest that that was not the case.'

But there was 'a world of difference' between inducing short-term unconsciousness and 'the science and skill of using morphine and heroin for sedative purposes over a long period as part of the treatment of the patient'. Dr Ashby fenced:

> 'I am not prepared to accept morphine and heroin as being properly used as sedatives over long periods of treatment.'

In 1950, would the holder of a Diploma in Anaesthetics know about addiction and withdrawal in relation to these drugs? Dr Ashby had checked the examination papers and there was certainly a question on 'opiates, barbiturates and anaesthetizing drugs'. Would that person's knowledge be greater than the ordinary general practitioner's?

> 'I would have thought he would be bound to know a bit more about addiction, but I personally think that every general practitioner is aware of the problems of addiction.'[1]

Mr Lawrence asked a question to which Dr Ashby did not know the answer: whether the anaesthetics used in 1950 were not 'gas and ether… the common provincial anaesthetics' in a place like Eastbourne, though this was hardly relevant. His final point was that Dr Ashby had never been a general practitioner and therefore had never had to 'face the problems and dilemmas of the general practitioner'.

> 'Well, not as a general practitioner, but it is really our main function out of hospitals to cope, in consultation with general practitioners, with all their major problems, so I have in fact faced thousands of difficult problems with a practitioner, but I have never done so as a general practitioner.'

The Attorney-General re-examined the witness, attempting to mop up the problems caused by Mr Lawrence's cross-examination.

The picture of the last few days of Mrs Morrell's life had indicated drugging both during the daytime and at night-time? Certainly. A pathologist could ascertain from a post-mortem whether there was morphia and heroin in the body and estimate the amount with 'considerable accuracy'. Yes. He would also be able to find out if there had been a cerebral thrombosis? Most certainly.

> '…Assume for the moment that she had on the 8th November and all the subsequent days the morphia and heroin prescribed for her. In your opinion was that morphia and heroin the cause of her death, or was her death due to natural causes?'

---

[1] Dr Adams must have been aware of them since his days at medical school: his lecturers would have been well aware of widespread addiction to opiates in the nineteenth century, apart from the fact that he had a keen interest in drugs of all kinds, which is apparent from archival evidence.

'I think that would have been the cause of her death. As I said before, I don't think she could have survived that dosage... She could not have survived that dosage, but that dosage might well have killed her by an apparently, as it were, natural cause – I hope I have made that clear – such as thrombosis or terminal pneumonia.'

'That dosage might have created a condition which you called, I think, a terminal natural cause, like pneumonia or thrombosis, which might be the final closing act?'

'Yes, though I think that is more applicable to lower doses. I think the full dosage of the prescription would have caused death from direct suppression of the vital centres.'

The Attorney-General asked what the consequences would have been of the injections given on the 10th, 11th and 12th – four grains of heroin, five and three and a half, with the morphia and paraldehyde. Could she had survived that administration?

'I don't think she would have survived that administration... I think it would have certainly produced a secondary result.'

As to the 'spiral' and the 'spiral getting steeper and steeper', Dr Ashby thought it impossible to deny 'that there was some measure of a spiral of increased requirement', and that the requirement of that spiral 'was being given in the form of a heavier dosage, to judge by the balance between being comatose and restless'. And were these increased dosages on 10th, 11th and 12th required in order to overcome tolerance?

'No, I think they were steeper than that, and were given to keep the patient under, as has been clearly stated by the nurses who gave them.'

'The consequences of keeping a patient of eighty under?'

'I thought I made that clear before. I think that that would be an, as it were, terminal decision.'

The Attorney-General asked Dr Ashby about cases where substantial injections had been recorded, with the subjects surviving: could there be 'freak examples' both ways? Mr Lawrence objected to this as a leading question, but the Attorney-General pointed out that these words had been used by Dr Ashby in cross-examination, and Mr Stevenson confirmed this. Dr Ashby thought that survival of 20 grains of heroin was 'extraordinary' and the other of 120 grains 'even more remarkable'; if the last were authenticated no doubt it was 'someone who had built up over years in Assam to that dose'.

It had been put to Dr Ashby that Dr Harris 'was giving more than had been given by Dr Adams', increasing the dose on 12th September by one-eighth of morphine and one-third of heroin, so 'that he was giving more according to the nurses' books'; would he check his graph:

'No, there is no recorded increase on this graph from the 3rd to the 16th in either morphia or heroin.' [This included the omnopon]

'In fact, on the 18th, there is a drop of about a grain in the daily administration, was there not?'
'Yes.'

The Attorney-General asked about the events of the 9th October, reading part of the nurse's notes; he was interrupted by Mr Lawrence who objected that this was 'an attempt to get the doctor to alter that evidence' – which was that the symptoms recorded were consistent either with stroke or with an injection of morphia. Mr Justice Devlin allowed the question which was to find out whether one was more likely than the other. Dr Ashby clearly recalled that Mr Lawrence had not asked this question.

> 'I have read this entry several times and I must say I had regarded a heavy dose of opiates as the more likely but I cannot reject the other explanation, not by any means. I cannot say more than that I think it is rather more likely, for this reason, that this is exactly the course of events which I should have thought would follow a heavy opiate injection, whereas it is only one of many courses of events which could follow a stroke in what we call a silent area – a stroke which does not cause a paralysis. It is certainly compatible with the second.'

Mr Justice Devlin confirmed that his 'more likely explanation' was based upon the assumption that the 'special injection' was an injection of some heavy sedative. Entirely, said Dr Ashby. The '? stroke' had only been written in by the nurse after she had spoken to Dr Adams?

> 'Yes. Telephone suggestions are – the doctor is in great difficulty in making a suggestion.'

There were no entries immediately following 'to show that what she suffered on the 9th was a stroke?' None.

Mr Lawrence objected vociferously 'to the mischief of this type of re-examination'; the Attorney-General protested and a squabble ensued. Mr Justice Devlin ruled for the Attorney-General. Dr Ashby did not see that 'there was any clear pointer to a stroke'.

The Judge questioned Dr Ashby about his answers concerning the death of Mrs Morrell, when he had said that he could not rule out the possibility that death was due to natural causes in the end:

> 'So that it might be said that death is the result, in the end, of natural causes but those natural causes, or the operation of those natural causes, were themselves produced by the drugs that were administered by Dr Adams?'
> 'Certainly, yes.'
> 'And if that were so then it might be said that, looked at in the ordinary, commonsense way, the cause of death was the result of the drugs administered by Dr Adams?'
> 'Yes.'

Mr Justice Devlin wanted it to be made quite clear whether there was any possibility of her dying of natural causes:

> 'I think I can only say it in this way, that in so far as the reports do not make it completely certain that she was absolutely dying even six hours before, I do not think it is possible absolutely to rule out a sudden catastrophic intervention by some natural cause. It just is not possible to say this woman could not have had another cerebral haemorrhage at 1 o'clock that morning. There is just no evidence to say that that is impossible.
>
> I do not think it ever is possible completely to rule out the possibility, in a patient of eighty-one, of sudden death.'

When the Judge asked Dr Ashby what he had in mind when he had said that Dr Adams 'could well have thought that cerebral thrombosis was the immediate cause of death'; did he mean the original stroke or another one?

> 'I meant a terminal cerebral thrombosis'.
>
> [Dr Adams' answer on the cremation form belies this as he specifically refers to the length of time from the original stroke.]

Mr Justice Devlin wished to know whether the 'sense of euphoria' from the heroin would have applied 'right up to the very end' in Mrs Morrell's case. He thought so: unless used in inadequate quantities and that cannot be said of the last few days.'

What would have happened if the Doctor had disclosed an interest in the will on the Cremation Form? Dr Ashby thought that the cremation certificate would be refused and that there would be a choice: either burial or referral to the Coroner. He thought that the referee doctor, whose signature was required to allow the Cremation Certificate, would have suggested a post-mortem if cremation was still desired.

The Judge offered the opportunity for Mr Lawrence to further cross-examine Dr Ashby, but he did not wish to do so.

The case for the Crown had been concluded and the Court adjourned for the day.

Chapter Thirty-Six

# The Trial – Days 13 to End

## 5 – 11 April 1957

## Thirteenth Day

The Attorney-General had consulted Halsbury's *Laws of England* regarding the matter of the Cremation Certificate which the Judge had asked Dr Ashby about on the previous day. He proposed to call Dr Francis Camps who would know what occurred in practice. Mr Justice Devlin thought that this would be useful and Mr Lawrence raised no objection.

Dr Camps was one of the most famous of Home Office forensic pathologists, reader in Forensic Medicine at the London Hospital and the London Hospital Medical College. The Attorney-General asked what would happen if the Referee doctor refused to give a cremation certificate after the forms were submitted to him. There were two possibilities, said Dr Camps: he could order a post-mortem himself or, more commonly, he would notify the Coroner 'and the post-mortem would be carried out under the Coroner's auspices.' Then the pathologist's certification of death would cancel out the previous ones and this would then be accepted by the referee. He had never met a case where burial had been carried out instead of cremation and if the deceased had 'expressed a definite desire to be cremated' in their will, then this wish would have to be carried out.

Cross-examined by Mr Lawrence, Dr Camps said that when the Medical Referee had ordered a post-mortem, this had only happened in his experience 'in cases of technical difficulty, such as the person not having been seen within the prescribed time before death.' If the Medical Referee communicated with the Coroner, the Coroner would investigate the case: statements would be taken from the various people involved; he might, or might not, order a post-mortem, but 'In cases of cremation now it is always the practice to order a post-mortem because it is the final act, and then having done that, he assesses the evidence and if he thinks it is desirable to hold an inquest, then he will hold an inquest'. He could sign the cremation certificate without the inquest.

Mr Justice Devlin asked if the relatives could ask for burial if they disliked the idea of a post-mortem. Dr Camps replied that he had never met such a situation, and the relatives could not upset the original will if the person had wanted cremation. In all cases he had met the Referee had notified the Coroner. The relatives also had to meet the fee for the post-mortem.

The witness withdrew and the Judge asked the Attorney-General to clarify the legal position. The Attorney-General did this by reading a passage out of a paragraph from Halsbury, headed 'Duties of Medical Referee', the most relevant parts of which read:

> 'Before allowing the cremation, the medical referee must examine the application and certificates and ascertain that they are such as are required by the regulations, and that the inquiry made by the persons giving the certificates has been adequate. He may make any inquiry with regard to the application and certificates that he may think necessary.
>
> He must not allow the cremation unless he is satisfied that the fact and cause of death have been definitely ascertained; and in particular, if the cause of death assigned in the medical certificates is such as, regard being had to all the circumstances, might be due to poison, to violence, to any illegal operation, or to privation or neglect, he must require a post-mortem to be held…'
>
> [It is a matter of note that it was Sister Bartlett (Hughes) who was interviewed in relation to the Cremation Certificate and not Sister Randall who was the nurse on duty and present at the time of death.]

Mr Lawrence addressed the Judge and said that he now wished to make a submission, which was a matter of law and that he wished to make it in the absence of the jury. Mr Justice Devlin replied that he did not like the jury to be absent from any part of the trial 'unless something is likely to be said which ought not to be said in their presence because it is a reference to something which may not be called in evidence.'

Mr Lawrence submitted that the Crown had not disclosed sufficient evidence to support the indictment for murder: the evidence that they had produced was not enough for any 'reasonably minded jury' to convict upon. There was no 'real case of murder' but a 'shadowy adumbration of bare possibility'. The Crown needed to show that Dr Adams had committed some 'act or acts' bringing about the death of Mrs Morrell, and that he had formed a 'deliberate intent to bring about the death'; they had not done this.

He cited the case of 'The King v. Governor of Brixton Prison: ex parte Bidwell' (reported in 1937 1 King's Bench Division of the Law Reports at page 305), which, as he said, appeared to have little relevance at first sight. This was a case brought under 'The Fugitive Offenders Act, 1881, s.5, which provided that "A fugitive when apprehended shall be brought before a magistrate… If… such evidence is produced as… raises a strong or probable presumption that the fugitive committed the offence mentioned in the warrant… the magistrate shall commit the fugitive to prison to await his return".' The judgment of the court was given by Mr Justice Swift on behalf of three judges defined the meaning as 'there must be such evidence that, if it be uncontradicted at the trial, a reasonably-minded jury may convict upon it.' This was the only 'expression of view' that Mr Lawrence had been able to find.

It was true that the present case had altered considerably since the Attorney-General had opened the trial, as 'much additional and quite different information' had emerged since and it was difficult for him to see how the Crown would now present the case to the jury. This was alleged to be a murder, by means of drugs, by a general practitioner, of a patient, an old lady of 81, and the case was one which was 'exclusively based upon medical evidence'. The real enquiry was a medical one: upon Dr Douthwaite's evidence 'the field' was the period 'from and after the 1st November to the 13th, and upon Dr Ashby's evidence some time from the 8th or the 9th'. These two medical experts had not suggested that any earlier period of medication had 'the deliberate purpose of bringing about the death of Mrs Morrell.'

It was also important to remember that both doctors agreed that, 'at the beginning of that period, whether it be the last five days or whether it be the last twelve days' Mrs Morrell was a dying woman. The logical conclusion was that if a murder was committed, it 'was committed on the body of a woman at a time when she was already dying'. Dr Douthwaite had excluded an intent to kill before the 8th November. Mr Lawrence pointed out that that date 'was the earliest date on which he, as chief doctor for the prosecution, could find any intention to kill'. Dr Ashby had not gone so far as Dr Douthwaite regarding intent to kill, but he had concentrated on the last five days of the life of Mrs Morrell.

Mr Lawrence now passed on to the question of whether there was adequate proof of an act or acts which caused the death of Mrs Morrell: the Crown were committed to proving that the administration of drugs caused her death and had to prove the link between cause and effect, and prove it beyond all reasonable doubt.

> 'Once it is conceded by the Prosecution that it is a possibility, not a fantastic possibility, but a reasonable medical possibility that the death, when it came, was not the result of the drugs she had in that sense at all, then the matter is at large, and it is impossible, in my submission, in that case for any reasonably minded Jury to find that they are satisfied beyond any reasonable doubt that the death resulted from the administration of drugs.'

Mr Lawrence read through Dr Ashby's answers, both to himself and to the Judge, concerning whether Mrs Morrell could have died from natural causes. In the end, of course, Dr Ashby had told Mr Justice Devlin that the 'natural causes were themselves produced by the drugs administered by Dr Adams.' The Judge confirmed that Dr Ashby had given 'as a cause of death, ...three drugs' (morphia, heroin and paraldehyde). Again Dr Ashby had answered, when asked what would have happened if Mrs Morrell had not been given these drugs, that he did not think that she would have died; he saw no reason for it as she had been 'sitting up in a chair talking quite brightly only a few days before'. Then in the final answers given to Mr Justice Devlin at the end of the day, Dr Ashby had said that if she had been given the amounts prescribed for her from the 8th to the 12th inclusive 'or the greater part of them', 'She could not possibly have survived those prescriptions'. Then his Lordship had asked finally whether Dr Ashby could totally rule out the possibility that Mrs Morrell had died from natural causes not brought about by the drugs and he had answered that he 'could not exclude the possibility of that [sudden death by natural causes – terminal cerebral thrombosis] beyond any shadow of doubt.'

Mr Lawrence summarised Dr Ashby's view: morphia and heroin were the cause of the death and the natural causes were a consequence of that, but he could not exclude the possibility that there was 'a sudden intervention' of ordinary natural causes independent of the drugging. He was not 'searching for a fantastic interpretation of this evidence', but trying to look at it logically. The case which had been presented by the Crown was 'not a case of any reasonable certainty at all'; there could be no certainty beyond reasonable doubt. The Jury would have to be directed most carefully and told that there was reasonable doubt. He submitted that the evidence was inadequate 'and there is no real case made out'.

Mr Justice Devlin asked Mr Lawrence if he had considered that Dr Douthwaite's evidence was positive and the jury would have to decide which doctor's evidence to accept. Mr Lawrence argued that both doctors were called by the Crown and that therefore the Crown's evidence had been made uncertain because of their differences. This also was not the whole of his submission and he wished to say something about the prescriptions and nurses' notebooks. Mr Justice Devlin said, at this point, that it was his view that he was not satisfied that there was enough evidence 'to say that the quantity prescribed was administered by Dr Adams or under his directions'. This meant that the acceptable evidence for quantities administered to the patient was that of the nurses' notebooks and the nurses.

Dr Douthwaite, Mr Lawrence reminded his Lordship, had been 'under examination for hours', and his first theory had been that the 'fatal, and intentionally fatal, dosage was given from the 8th of November onwards'. Later he had 'evolved… the theory' that Dr Adams had deliberately withdrawn morphine from the patient on 31st October with the intention of reintroducing it with fatal effect. Dr Douthwaite had been unable to say when he had thought of this. However, Mr Lawrence said that Dr Douthwaite's theory 'came down to this: that she was murdered by means of an accumulation of drugs uneliminated in the body over the last few days'; that he would not have expected the ordinary general practitioner to know about this, but that Dr Adams, because he was an anaesthetist, would have known about the accumulation of drugs in such a patient. It would follow, Mr Lawrence submitted that, if there was 'nothing in the accumulation theory' [there was] or, 'if Dr Adams was really in the position of an ordinary general practitioner', then Dr Douthwaite's case 'would disappear'.

Mr Lawrence read through a number of his questions put to Dr Douthwaite and the replies given to him, and he 'fairly' summarised the result: 'there was a need to postulate murder [because of the drugs given in the last few days], but I concede there is a possible alternative view which is quite inconsistent with murder upon those reports.' Mr Lawrence submitted that 'On the admission of a possibility contrary to what the Crown are here contending, when that possibility is once conceded there is no adequate case to go to the jury.' The case was 'dependent wholly and exclusively upon the medical evidence'; there was 'no confession of murder or murderous intent from first to last'. Medical evidence was usually 'ancillary' to the evidence of other witnesses, and, without it, there would still be 'the evidence of fact'.

Mr Lawrence returned to another aspect of Dr Ashby's evidence: where he had said that the whole matter of intent to murder 'was largely bound up with the fact of the policy of keeping her under'. He had realised that it was not just 'whether she could have survived a certain administration of drugs' but why it was being done. Therefore, what was meant by 'keeping her under' was of paramount importance, and the evidence of the nurses proved that it was 'to avoid restlessness and excitability', and so was justifiable. Dr Ashby had also considered that Dr Adams had been 'obliged to prescribe larger doses' due to the patient's tolerance. Mr Justice Devlin summarised Mr Lawrence's contention: that Dr Ashby had conceded that Dr Adams 'was caught up in a situation which he solved, wrongly in Dr Ashby's view it may be, or sought to solve wrongly but quite innocently'.

Mr Justice Devlin addressed Mr Lawrence: there were two points which seemed to present him with difficulties. The first was that, looking on Dr Douthwaite's evidence 'as a whole', it might be said that he had not conceded an alternative to that of intent to murder; the other view was that he had conceded that there was an alternative as Mr Lawrence had submitted. It was not for the Judge to 'take that determination out of the hands of the jury'. Again, suppose there was an alternative: that the effect of Dr Douthwaite's and Dr Ashby's evidence was: 'We think that this treatment was wrong. We think that a doctor with Dr Adams' qualifications ought to have known that it was wrong. We think it likely that he would, but we concede as an alternative that he might not.' Standing on its own, this might sway the jury to give Dr Adams the benefit of the doubt, but put together with evidence that he benefited financially from the death, or that he thought he would, then 'the jury, if they heard no evidence to the contrary and no explanation of that, would be entitled to infer as one possibility, and as a probability as the right conclusion, if there were no explanation given to the jury, that there was an intent to kill'.

Mr Lawrence argued that 'mere evidence of wrong treatment by a doctor', even if it were 'allied to pecuniary motive' would still not be evidence of murderous intent, particularly when this had been 'expressly limited, to the last few days' of Mrs Morrell's life. Mr Justice Devlin explained what he had meant:

> '...if the right medical view is that the administration of the drugs was wrong and unnecessary at the end, that it caused the death of Mrs Morrell, that it was administered by a doctor who benefited by the death; don't those three facts together call for an explanation?'

Mr Lawrence did not think that this was 'the way the evidence' stood. The 'broad effect' of the evidence was that, at the stage when the patient was dying, 'to continue with those drugs at that stage was not wrong. The error had occurred earlier' when there was prolonged administration of the drug regime. If Dr Adams had withdrawn the drugs when the spiral was mounting, 'the dying patient' would have suffered. The duty of the doctor was the patient's comfort, although, Mr Lawrence said, he was not suggesting that meant that he had 'to take steps to accelerate death'.

Mr Lawrence read many more of the questions he had put to Dr Ashby and the answers he had received from him, and he summarised the result as he saw it:

'My Lord, the evidence of the criticism of what had gone before, so far from being, in those circumstances, evidence that is to be considered by the Jury as against Doctor Adams, is quite the other way round, because if they are right that it was the wrong treatment but innocent treatment, and that is not to be gainsaid, if it is the wrong treatment but innocent treatment, then he cannot be criticised in terms of murder for the fact that the irreversible condition was reached on or about the 8th November.'

Therefore, he argued, no drugs after that date could have been said to have been given with the intent to murder. 'The dilemma had been forced upon the doctor by reason of what had gone before'. If this had been a case of inoperable cancer and extreme pain, then there would have been no criticism of Dr Adams at all. Who was to say that 'a general practitioner is not entitled to ease it [Mrs Morrell's condition] with sedation'.

Mr Justice Devlin thought that his last point raised some difficult questions. In the end the question was 'whether a doctor is entitled to shorten life, whether in the case of severe pain or whether in the case of acute discomfort'; but this question was not to be settled by doctors, or by the jury: 'It must be a question of law, must it not?'

Mr Lawrence thought that he had not made his position clear: he had not been suggesting 'that this was a case in which drugging in either case was entered into and carried out with the intention of shortening life'. If a doctor administered these drugs 'with the intention of giving easement and comfort to the suffering patient', then there was no intent to shorten life.

The Judge pursued his point: if it was assumed that a doctor had 'no corrupt motive', no one would suggest that he intended to shorten life or wished to do so. Intention and wish were distinguishable in law, so if a doctor gave drugs which he knew would 'have the effect of shortening life', then that was the equivalent of intention. Presumably Mr Lawrence's point was 'that any drugs given by Dr Adams were given merely as part of the medical process of caring for a person in the last stages of illness and were not such as could have been anticipated would have shortened life, not in the sense of minutes or hours, because no one would deal with minutes or hours?' He asked Mr Lawrence if this was right.

It was the interpretation, Mr Lawrence said, that he had put to Dr Ashby, and Dr Ashby had followed him 'all the way without qualification, without dissent' in the proposition that, after the point of no return, then all the drugs might well have been given with the sole object of ensuring the patient's comfort and well-being. Therefore it followed that, in a case depending wholly upon medical evidence, there was not 'a sufficiently strong case to merit consideration by the jury so as to put this man in any further peril.' Mr Lawrence was about to move on to the police evidence when he was stopped in mid-sentence by Mr Justice Devlin, who did not believe that a dissection of the police evidence would alter his mind:

'…I have considered most carefully your submission on the medical evidence, and I have of course listened to it most carefully as it emerged, but my conclusion is that it does give rise to questions that can only properly be determined by the verdict of the jury, and I think that I ought to leave the case to them…'

The Court was adjourned for lunch.

As the jury had listened to his submission, Mr Lawrence did not think it necessary to make an opening speech for the Defence, but what he had to say next may well have come as a shock – at least to the Jury, and perhaps the press.

'My Lord, my first witness will be Dr Harman. I think that I should tell your Lordship – and it is right that I should tell your Lordship – that the defence have decided in the circumstances of this case not to call Dr Adams. I call Dr Harman.'

Dr John Bishop Harman MD, F.R.C.P, F.R.C.S. had a Harley Street practice in London and was also Physician to St. Thomas' Hospital, London, and to the Royal Marsden Hospital, which specialised in the treatment of cancer.

Mr Lawrence began by asking Dr Harman about 'the nature and degree' of the stroke Mrs Morrell had suffered in June of 1948. He considered that this was 'severe' and characteristic of arterio sclerosis. She had complained in the Cheshire hospital of 'severe pain'; pain did accompany a stroke 'but not usually'. There was no record of what sort of pain she had had. Dr Harman assumed that the morphine was given, at least partly for the pain, but 'one does occasionally have to use morphine as a sedative in restless people who have had strokes'.

Mr Lawrence confirmed the gap in the nursing records from the time Mrs Morrell left the Cheshire Hospital until June of 1949. [There was only the prescription list for that period and there is no evidence that any search was made for the records of the Esperance Hospital or the Olinda Nursing Home.] However, the prescription lists, which, he pointed out, 'were produced at our request', showed that morphia had been first prescribed by Dr Adams on the 9th July, 1948 and there were periodical prescriptions for both morphia and heroin 'subsequently and up to the beginning of 1950'. He assumed that they were used on the patient because 'we know from the records in 1949 that they were used'. Mr Lawrence asked 'about the use of morphia and heroin on this old lady'. Dr Harman replied:

'Well, I would first say this: that when a doctor takes over a patient from another doctor, even though he has known her before her stroke, and even though he did visit her up in Cheshire, the usual thing to do would be to continue, for a time at any rate, with the treatment that the other doctor had found necessary. That is clearly because the new doctor or the taking over doctor, is not aware on his own experience of what is necessary.'
[This is underlined from 'even' to 'Cheshire' and the last half heavily sidelined in the margin by Hannam]

'That would apply to the morphia', said Mr Lawrence, and he took the opportunity to ask about 'hyperduric morphia'. Dr Harman had not found a reference to it so early as 1948, but he found it in 'the Martindale of 1952'. [This suggests that this was a new version of morphia when Dr Adams used it in 1948. If this were so, then this would demonstrate that Dr Adams kept himself up-to-date with drugs and their actions.]

What did Dr Harman 'say to the introduction of heroin at that stage, July of 1948, into the treatment of Mrs Morrell?' He regarded it as 'unusual' because it was not a drug commonly used, and he could only guess at the reason for its use: it was usually given for pain. It was less sophorific than morphia but had a calming action. He saw nothing sinister about its introduction or continued use. As for Veramon this had 'a slight hypnotic action' but was mostly used for the relief of pain, and pethidine was 'almost entirely' used for relieving pain and was 'to some extent' a substitute for morphine.

When Mrs Morrell had just come out of hospital in Cheshire, then, Dr Harman agreed with Dr Douthwaite, that 'a reasonable prognosis was about six to twelve months'. By April of 1950, she had recovered to some extent but was a partial invalid, but there were 'no signs of anything further about to happen'. As for the drug regime, Dr Harman described this as having been 'going on for nine months', referring to the particular doses of ¼ morphia and ⅓ of heroin, [from July 1948, it was 1 year and 8 months, so this related only to the beginning of the nurses' notes] and, to his mind, there was 'no evidence that it was producing any harm'. It would certainly have had to continue as by then, the patient was addicted, and, if it had been discontinued, there would have been withdrawal symptoms. In this case, other drugs would have had to be prescribed.

It did not necessarily follow, Dr Harman said, that every addict would need the dose of morphia increased: if it were given for pain it would have to be or if the addict were a 'psychopath' or an 'inadequate sort of person' and took it for pleasure, then it would have to be increased. But if it were one of the 'several hundreds' of doctors, 'usually a doctor because they have access to these drugs', who started by giving it to himself 'for pain' and then found it impossible to stop, then they could 'and do continue throughout their whole working life taking the same steady dose… Their only abnormality is that they can only exist with morphine'. These doctors were 'essentially normal mentally but merely accidentally addicted to morphine'.

Mr Lawrence asked what the regular administration of heroin and morphine would be calculated to do to the patient. Dr Harman felt that it depended upon the state, the type of patient. Morphia would be bad for the 'apathetic' patient as it was a sedative drug, but for the 'bad-tempered and irritable' patient, these drugs might have been helpful. The general idea was to bring the patient to a state of normality. And, yes, he had used heroin himself for cases other than those of severe pain.

Late summer of 1950 to the beginning of November: this was the spiral described by Dr Ashby. Dr Harman agreed with the concept. When Dr Harris had attended 'the amount was stepped up by reason of the introduction of Omnopon', stated Mr Lawrence: what did this indicate? Dr Harman presumed that more sedative was needed due to tolerance, and that this was 'entirely reasonable'.

Dr Harman was asked to comment on the nurses' notes for the 9th October – the day Dr Adams had diagnosed a possible stroke over the telephone – he considered that, although the symptoms described were compatible with heavy sedation by morphia or heroin, they were also compatible with a stroke, and on balance he was 'more in favour of a stroke'. The incident of Cheyne Stokes breathing recorded on the 14th/15th was 'a characteristic of mild heart failure' and also could have been due to morphine. The fact that it was a single instance did not help 'one way or the other in making a diagnosis.'

Mr Lawrence had now come to the third phase: from the beginning of November or 31st October, when Dr Adams had omitted the morphia and omnopon. Dr Harman agreed with Dr Ashby that Mrs Morrell was clearly dying by the 8th or 9th November; 'on the 1st it was not so obvious' and he also agreed with him that the omission of the morphia was of no particular significance. He did not concur with Mr Lawrence's assessment of this withdrawal as a 'variation'; 'this was a change'.

Would there have been any point in considering weaning Mrs Morrell off morphia at this stage? Dr Harman saw no point in it, but in his answer was his opinion of Dr Adams' treatment:

> '…If we may go back to the summer of 1948, I have already given my view that he would reasonably have continued for a time, a week or so, with the treatment that had been instituted in Cheshire. By that time she would be some way on the way to addiction. Whatever the reason for the decision was I do not know, but we are all agreed, I think, that in a few months' time she was addicted…'

As time went on it would become more difficult to see what was to be gained by putting her through the complicated and unpleasant withdrawal treatment. He thought that what had happened around the 8th November was that the morphia was not working to produce sufficient sedation, and the drugs had to be increased. As for the justification: firstly there was 'what the drugs might do', then secondly, there was the evidence in the books that the patient's symptoms were getting worse, and thirdly there was the evidence from the nurses as to 'what the drugs were being given for.' Dr Harman's conclusion was that the drugs were being given to the patient 'to stop her getting excited, to keep her peaceful, and that they were not working very effectively.' The inclusion of atropine on the 7th, 8th and 9th, he supposed must have been given to stop mucous in the throat.

Then the paraldehyde, what was Dr Harman's view on this drug? Its only effect was a sedative one; it was an hypnotic drug and chemically allied to alcohol in its actions. It was 'universally agreed' that it was the safest of the hypnotic drugs. In this type of case he would not have thought of giving less than a 6 c.c. dose; even if the last injection was given as Sister Randall had said, the dose would only have exceeded the suggested range in the *British Pharmocopaeia* by one tenth.

The death itself, Dr Harman, could not consider was a morphine death as this would have been 'death in a coma and from respiratory paralysis'. This meant that the respiratory rate would become very slow: maybe ten or six times a minute.

> 'In this case I think this is only the second occasion in which the respiratory rate is mentioned in the whole of these books. It is mentioned as having been at 50, which is remarkably high. I don't interpret 'Appears asleep. Passed away quietly' as a morphine coma. That is merely my interpretation. She was certainly unconscious.'

The time, he thought, between the respirations of 50 and death, was 'much too short for her to have died of morphine poisoning'; the cause of death was much more likely to have been coronary thrombosis. Dr Harman could see no link between the morphia and heroin injection recorded and the death, but then answered Mr Lawrence by saying that it was possible. There was no evidence 'one way or the other' to allow him to say whether the large doses of hypnotics had done her harm or good.

Mr Lawrence asked Dr Harman to comment on the 'jerkiness' and 'twitchings' described in the notebooks: he answered that it was 'the picture of twitching and jerkings of almost any slow disintegrating illness' – without drugs; it could also be produced by 'drug intoxication' or various poisons. Heroin and morphia could have caused or contributed: 'I could not have denied that.' With regard to Sister Randall's evidence in court:

> 'The first thing I should say about that is that it impressed me on that occasion that she was describing something she remembered. I have forgotten her exact words – "It was dreadful. I hope I will never see anything like that again", and as she was thinking of what she saw she was demonstrating, partly unconsciously I think, movements of this sort (indicating), of the arms backwards and forwards. Now if that was a picture of 'very shaky', as described, then I would not include that in the general tremors and shakings of low delirium, it is something else.'

He thought it 'fair to say' that any diagnosis offered was unlikely to be true. As he knew very little about morphine convulsions and 'there is very little experience of this phenomenon', he had 'searched the world medical literature dating from 1800 to 1956', covering over 10,000 references and had found descriptions of 18 cases in adults. Some of these dated back to 1840, and the convulsions described were spinal convulsions, with respiration paralysed, and the patient being bent over backwards. At this point, Dr Harman demonstrated a spinal convulsion – 'commonly seen with strychinine', as far as was possible in the witness box. He had discovered one case of a woman who had the convulsions described by Sister Randall, 'clonic movements' as opposed to 'tonic' – fixed movements. He demonstrated both of these. Dr Harman could not say that these were not morphine convulsions, and thought that they were more likely to be something else which he did not recognise.

The dosage of morphine and heroin given to Mrs Morrell was nothing 'to talk about to friends when talking medical shop', Dr Harman considered. It was within the experience of a general practitioner. Mr Lawrence enquired about the 'conception of a fatal dose' and what amount would be lethal. Dr Harman gave a long explanation about testing drugs on mice: at one end of the scale was the 100% lethal dose which killed all mice in the experiment, the 50% lethal dose and so on. What the 100% lethal dose on humans would be could not be known, but the minimum lethal dose 'or something like it' was known. Morphia and heroin were drugs of 'absolutely outstanding variability' due to acquired tolerance. The highest daily morphine injection he had discovered was 77 grains, and the highest dose of heroin, 40 grains. What would he say about the doses recorded in the nurses' books as having been given to Mrs Morrell?

'The whole point on morphine doses is that I would not expect anything. It is much too varied and unpredictable. On this dosage I would not say that death could not occur.'

Mr Lawrence asked Dr Harman's opinion about the theory of accumulation put forward by Dr Douthwaite: Dr Harman had not agreed with it when he heard it. Dr Ashby had said that there would be accumulation from dose to dose when several doses were given in a day and he did agree that this was the case: '…it was almost certain there was an overlap from dose to dose, whatever the kidneys were like.' Dr Douthwaite had implied that there would be accumulation from day to day: so that if the doses had been discontinued on the 10th, the patient could still have died on the 13th from the accumulation; he could not agree with this, but he would 'go further than Dr Ashby'.

Mr Lawrence asked Dr Harman 'to address his mind' to the question of how much more knowledge than other general practitioners Dr Adams as a qualified anaesthetist, would have had of morphia and heroin. When he studied for the examination, which he passed in 1941, he would have had 'to have revised the pharmacological effects of morphine' which was used before anaesthetics and its immediate effects, but nothing more. This Diploma had nothing to do with morphia addiction, withdrawal and tolerance. Dr Harman saw 'no implication of that at all'. He agreed that gas and ether would have been commonly used as anaesthetics around 1950.

Dr Douthwaite had suggested that hyoscin [sic] would have been an alternative drug to morphine and heroin, and Dr Harman had been very surprised because hyoscine and morphine together were synergistic, the action of both together being much greater than the sum of each separately. This was why they were used together pre-anaesthetically, but there was a danger of respiratory failure and he would certainly not recommend hyoscin. Anaesthetists used it most often, but 'as a general rule' not in patients over 60. Barbiturates were usually used 'nowadays' as the pre-med of choice and these would also depress respiration but ether would increase respiration. Even in the past atropine would usually have been substituted for hyoscine because atropine had a slight stimulant effect on respiration.

Paraldehyde was the drug which Dr Adams 'turned to', and Dr Harman said that he would have turned to this drug as well: it was a safe drug and 'in continuous use'. Mr Lawrence asked him about 'Dexadrine' and other tablets noted as being used by Dr Adams on the patient around the Spring of 1950. Dr Harman replied that they were 'stimulants… rather like coffee but stronger'. [They were amphetamines with alarming side-effects many of which are mirrored in the nurses' notebooks] 'Cytamin', 'in frequent use as a tonic', he regarded as having no effect at all.

At this point Mr Lawrence addressed the Judge, stating that his witness from the Cheshire hospital, Dr Turner, was ill and that it was not possible for him to attend the Court; he was still in a position to prove the nurses' notes from the hospital. The Attorney-General had no objection and Mr Justice Devlin released the consultant from further attendance.

Mr Lawrence turned to his witness again for evidence concerning addiction and the dependence of a patient upon the doctor. Dr Harman said that he had 'no great experience of treating addicts'. It was true that addicts developed 'a strong emotional relationship' to the people from whom they got their drugs but this was 'an anti-fact' owing to the circumstances in which people had to get their drugs in western civilisation. 'It doesn't occur in China where opium is easily obtained.' He did not see why Mrs Morrell would have become dependent when there was no evidence that she knew she was dependent upon morphine; she would only have known if it had been withdrawn from her. She knew she could get it from Dr Adams, or Dr Harris, and he could not imagine 'any reasonable doctor refusing to give the necessary dose to an old lady who had become addicted'. Dr Harman saw no evidence of 'craving' in the nurses' notes.

Dr Douthwaite had seen 'a lot of the passing symptoms of illness or distress' as being consistent with withdrawal symptoms or overdosing. Mr Lawrence wanted to know what they were, what was 'the pattern' of these things. It was a type of hunger, Dr Harman explained, and would come on when the next dose was due. If it were not given then the symptoms would become worse for the next two or three days. It would take about ten days to complete the withdrawal, but if a dose were given then within a few minutes the person would be normal again. There was no pattern discernable in the notes of effects or withdrawal symptoms. With regular daily injections withdrawal symptoms would not occur; if they did they would occur regularly. Dr Harman then modified this by saying that he would expect the craving to be regular but he could not speak about the symptoms 'because I have never seen this symptom.'

The Judge adjourned the Court for the day.

# Fourteenth Day

Mr Lawrence had a few more questions to put to Dr Harman. Dr Douthwaite had said that heroin should never be given to old people unless they were dying from a painful disease; what was his view? Dr Harman saw no reason why heroin should not be given to elderly people: he had used them for controlling disturbed patients, restlessness and 'in states of hopeless misery in dying patients'. He had used heroin and morphine together but saw 'little point' in doing so; it was not, however, dangerous. [Heroin derives from morphine, but is much stronger; it is converted back to morphine in the brain.] Generally, these drugs were given to reduce irritability and it did so 'in the vast majority of cases', although, in the odd patient, there could be an abnormal response.

Dr Douthwaite had regarded the withdrawal of the morphia from the patient's treatment at the end of October and the beginning of November as significant and Dr Ashby had not seen it as 'strange' or 'sinister'. Dr Harman agreed with Dr Ashby's view that there would have been 'a slight reduction in the sedative effect', but no more than that. There was 'a very great deal of cross-tolerance' between morphia and heroin and addicts were able to substitute heroin for morphine. Substituting, as Dr Adams did, half grains of heroin for quarter grains of morphia, would have had no 'significant effect on the tolerance to morphine'. He could not 'conceive' that any doctor would think that reintroducing the quarter grain of morphine would possibly be likely to be fatal. Neither was giving nurses instructions to give 'morphine and heroin S.O.S.' an 'astonishing instruction'; he himself had frequently done so, assuming that the nurses would detect the symptoms he was referring to.

Mr Justice Devlin interrupted, saying that what Dr Douthwaite had referred to as 'aston-ishing' was the instruction to give one grain of heroin S.O.S. He then turned up the passage in the transcript: 'I am half right'. It was in relation to the instruction 'To have heroin one grain given S.O.S.' Dr Harman found nothing astonishing in the instruction. If he trusted the nurs-es they would know what he wanted and would give the injection when they thought fit.

The Attorney-General began his cross-examination: how long had Dr Harman spent in gen-eral practice? The answer was 'one fortnight'. He was a recognised authority on a disease known as 'Q' Fever, and he concurred that Dr Douthwaite was a recognised authority on heroin and morphia. He had first been asked to consider this particular case a fortnight before the trial opened at the Old Bailey and had started his reading on the subject during that fortnight.

The materials which Dr Harman had considered were the nurses' reports, with the back-ground of his professional knowledge, and on his study of the nurses' evidence, together with the prescription lists.

> 'Did you consider the evidence given by the police witnesses as to the statements made by Dr Adams?'
> 'No, I did not.'
> 'You disregarded those, did you?'
> 'I did not hear it.'
> 'You have had copies of the shorthand note?'
> 'No, I have not.'
> 'Did not you see the depositions of their evidence given at the magistrates' court?'
> 'I saw their depositions, yes.'
> 'Having read their depositions, did you pay any regard to those statements made by Dr Adams to them?'
> 'No. I have considered it on the basis of the evidence given in this court and I have only considered in detail the medical evidence.'

Dr Harman had not considered whether the drugs prescribed were given to the patient. He agreed that the safeguards under the Dangerous Drugs Act should be adhered to and that drugs should not be left 'lying about'. Doctors did not normally prescribe morphia and heroin for a patient 'without the intention of using them on the patient'.

The Attorney-General asked for Exhibit 36A to be handed to the witness. On sheet 4 was the graph representing the drugs prescribed from 8th November, 1950 onwards: during those five days a total of 'some 39 grains of heroin and 41 of morphia' had been prescribed. Dr Harman was, at first, unwilling to 'suggest what the effect would have been' on Mrs Morrell, 'an old lady'; then he thought it 'possible' that she would have survived, but he was not sure 'how likely' this was. Dr Harman said that he had heard of 'doses like that being prescribed for a lady of 81', then that he had not heard of 'an exactly comparable case'.

> 'It would have been a most remarkable thing if she had survived it, wouldn't it?'

'It would have been a thing worth talking about to colleagues.'
'As a remarkable thing?'
'As a remarkable thing.'
[These last two questions and answers have been underlined and sidelined heavily by
Hannam.]

The Attorney-General followed up the admission:

'You would never prescribe doses of that quantity for a lady of that age, would you?'
'I have never prescribed them.'
'Do you think you would ever prescribe doses of that magnitude.'
'I don't think I would.'
'Has anything like that ever happened in your experience?'
'No.'

Dr Harman agreed that when a doctor administered large quantities of heroin and morphia,
it was not safe to assume it was to a patient who was a 'freak' and able to cope with large quantities.

The Attorney-General asked upon what Dr Harman had based his deduction that Mrs
Morrell had a severe stroke in June of 1948, and that she had been in a 'rather difficult mental
condition'. Dr Harman replied that this was based on the nurses' reports from the Neston
Cottage Hospital and 'a proof of statement from the Neston Cottage Hospital'. He had 'forgotten' to mention this earlier when the Attorney-General had asked him what he had based
his evidence upon. Was there anything in the reports which showed that Mrs Morrell was in a
difficult mental condition? Dr Harman admitted that he had, in fact, obtained this information from the proof; there was nothing in the nursing reports 'to justify that conclusion'. It was
also the case that there was no evidence that the patient had suffered pain from 'Thalamic
Syndrome'. Arthritic pains, which were intermittent, were the more likely cause of the pain and
Dr Harman would have used codeine for these.

As Dr Adams was Mrs Morrell's regular practitioner, Dr Harman would not have been suggesting that he 'would feel compelled to follow' the medication adopted in the cottage hospital over nine days for the next two years?

'Oh, not for two years, no.'

He was merely suggesting that the treatment should be carried on for just a little while. The
Attorney-General read another of Dr Harman's answers to Mr Lawrence in which he had stated
that Dr Adams visited Mrs Morrell in Cheshire: where did he get that information from? Dr
Harman confirmed that Dr Adams had visited the hospital. He could not think from where he
had obtained this information. It might have been on 27th June? It might have been.

'Of course, it is on the 27th that she is taken off sleeping tablets and put on morphia?'

'Yes.'
'[Barbiturates are] Equally effective for the purpose of procuring sleep at night?'
'Not always. Usually more effective.'

Dr Harman had said that it was unusual to use heroin, except for severe pain. The Attorney-General asked him several questions about heroin: he disagreed with Dr Douthwaite's opinions but seemed unable to given his own.

'How many addicts have you treated?'
'Very few.'
'How many?'
'Two or three.'
'Have you ever attempted to wean an addict?'
'No.'

The last case of heroin addiction Dr Harman had treated had been 'before the war.' All the views he had expressed on heroin was 'from reading books' and what he had learned about tolerance was from papers about experiments on animals. He agreed with the Attorney-General that 'in animals large doses [of heroin] cause excitement and convulsions'. Heroin produced 'an immediate feeling of euphoria' but it was 'not likely at all' that this would make a patient 'develop a feeling of great gratitude to the doctor who is giving her such wonderful injections to make her feel so well'.

'Are you really saying that you would not expect a patient to develop a feeling of gratitude to the doctor who was keeping her feeling so well after these injections?'
'No, I wouldn't, not related to the morphine and heroin specifically.'
'Are you really saying that a doctor who succeeds for two years by the use of these drugs in making his patient feel better would not get a sense of gratitude felt by the patient towards him?'
'I think she would get a sense of gratitude from all his attention in general.'

The Attorney-General directed Dr Harman's attention to his opinion that by April of 1950, Mrs Morrell had 'recovered from her stroke as far as she is ever going to'; she was 'partially crippled', but there were no signs of anything further about to happen. Was it unreasonable to suppose she might have lived to 1954?

'That wouldn't be unreasonable.'
'She might have lived even longer, might not she?'
'She might.'

Dr Harman had told Mr Lawrence that, after nine months, the routine administration of morphia and heroin 'would certainly have to continue', but that he 'saw no evidence that it was producing harm':

> '…You do not know of any reason why it should have continued for nine months do you?'
> 'No.'

The Attorney-General, having ascertained that Dr Harman saw no reason to attempt weaning because he had 'never made such an attempt', asked:

> 'You would know, and any general practitioner would know, would he not, that the continuing with this morphia and this heroin after her return from Cheshire was bound to make her addicted?'
> 'Yes.'

*Martindale*, the authoritative medical reference book, was well-known and in the general possession of medical practitioners. Dr Harman was not quite sure, but yes it was authoritative, available and had information about the weaning persons from addiction. A contretemps followed when the Attorney-General accused Dr Harman of not mentioning that there was an alternative method of weaning apart from sudden withdrawal when he had given his evidence-in-chief. He had said that it could not be done 'without causing a clear-cut illness lasting about ten days', but he knew that this was not true.

> 'That impression, if conveyed to his Lordship and the members of the jury, would be an erroneous impression, would not it?'
> 'Yes, as the only alternative it would be.'
> 'Of course, if the doctor's medication, his weaning, did cause discomfort to a rich patient who had been made very comfortable by his administration of morphia and heroin, it might mean the loss of a rich patient, might not it?'
> 'It might.'

Dr Harman had heard of using methedone? Yes, he was aware of this method. Had he read the book *Narcotics and Narcotic Addiction* by Thomas? No, he had not, neither was it familiar to him. The Attorney-General suggested that it was 'accepted as the greatest present authority on narcotic addiction'. The book advised that patients with severe pain should be kept on narcotics, but that otherwise withdrawal was rarely contraindicated, and in admissions to the Lexington Hospital (Kentucky) it was contraindicated in 'less than one in a thousand cases'. Dr Harman's response was that the Lexington Hospital dealt 'entirely with psychopathic addicts' and therefore these patients needed to be 'broken of their addiction.'

The book also mentioned that there were few individuals (these were usually physicians) that could take a low dose of opiates for years and carry on work as normal, but these were so rare as to be almost non-existent and 'no one should contemplate the possibility of using narcotic drugs in this manner'. Eventually, Dr Harman agreed that Mrs Morrell was being given the drugs only 'to promote a feeling of wellbeing' – for the same sort of effects 'psychopaths [ordinary addicts] use them'.

Dr Harman seemed sure that it was possible to 'keep patients in a middle state', although he agreed that as tolerance was acquired, dosage had to be increased. He was adamant that it was 'proper treatment' to keep a stroke patient under the influence of drugs from the time of the stroke. Had he ever done this? Yes.

> 'What is the longest that you have kept anyone who has had a stroke under morphine and heroin?
> 'I do not recall using morphine and heroin for a patient with a stroke.'

The Attorney-General elicited from him the information that he had had hundreds of stroke patients under his care. He had heard 'talk of this sort of treatment'. Yes, it was 'medical shop', he admitted, and no, 'textbooks certainly would not recommend that [sort of treatment], not to students.' Was it good for the patient's health to be a drug addict? It was difficult to get an answer from Dr Harman. He was asked 'as a consultant', but he constantly parried the question and would not answer. Suppose he had been called in to give a second opinion on Mrs Morrell, would he have put her on morphia and heroin?

> 'Well, of that I am not sure, but I should certainly have pointed out the implications of that.'
> 'What do you mean by implications?'
> 'That she would become addicted and have to continue.'

Dr Harman had previously been asked about Dr Harris' treatment of Mrs Morrell, but, the Attorney-General asked, he surely would expect a locum to carry on the same treatment? He would, 'unless he thought it was completely wrong'. But a locum could hardly be expected to make an attempt to wean a drug addict? No. When a doctor went on holiday, would he not leave instructions about the treatment of his patients with the locum and expect him to carry them out? Unless the situation changed, yes, said Dr Harman.

> 'If the situation changes to this extent, that there is an indication for a little increase of dosage, that would be carrying on with the same treatment prescribed, wouldn't it?'
> 'Yes, it would.'

The Attorney-General focused on the strange events of 9th October, 1950: if Dr Harman had a patient who had suffered a stroke in 1948, was telephoned by the nurse and told she was in a condition of collapse, 'you suspected or said it might be a further stroke, wouldn't you go and see her straight away, or as soon as you could?'

'Yes, I think so. Yes.'

'You would expect a general practitioner to do that, wouldn't you?'

'Yes, in general.'

'Because we have heard here Doctor Adams came flying from Scotland after a telephone call in the middle of his holiday.'

'Yes.'

On the 9th October, there was no record of Dr Adams' visiting after that 'phone call?

'No.'

'Of course, if he knew he had injected an unusually large injection of Morphia and Heroin he would know, in fact, it was not a stroke, wouldn't he, this condition she was suffering from that day?'

'If that is so he would, yes.'

Dr Harman had already agreed that the condition was 'consistent with more drugs having been given' as well as with stroke.

The Attorney-General asked him to look at the report: the patient, after having been given an injection, had become drowsy and gone into a deep sleep and couldn't be woken; had he assumed that this 'was not an injection of an opiate'. Yes, he had. He had assumed that as it was a 'special injection' it must have been a vitamin or caffeine 'or something of that sort'. He thought Dr Harris might have said that. Dr Harris was not there, pointed out the Attorney-General. Dr Harman thought it was 'the usual practice… a shorthand for the one that is usually given'.

'Surely under the heading of Special Injection anything could be given, couldn't it?'

'It could be.'

'You know, do you not, that Doctor Adams's practice, according to Nurse Randall, was always to ask for a glass of hot water and, according to the nurses, always to see the patient alone?'

'Yes.'

If Dr Harman now assumed that the injection was an opiate, was Mrs Morrell's condition more consistent with drugging or a stroke? Dr Harman was most reluctant to concede that it was caused by opiates and continued to argue with the Attorney-General about the slurring of speech, which was recorded in the summary notes, saying that the patient was 'more normal this p.m.' and that there was a 'slight difficulty' of speech rather than slurring. Dr Harman eventually agreed that he could not tell if it was a stroke or caused by opiates.

The Attorney-General turned back to the night report of the 28th September: 'Rambling. Very muddled, slept from 3.30 a.m. Respiration very slow 12. Visited by Dr Adams twice.' What did Dr Harman think had happened?

'…for what it is worth that is consistent with a depressing effect from a drug, notably Morphine.'

'Visited by Dr Adams twice', the Attorney-General continued to read, 'Then an injection of omnopon given. Then further omnopon. '11.45 – 12.45 – Became restless and rather collapsed, cold perspiration'.'

> 'Are not those also and more consistent with an overdose of drugs?'
> 'No, I do not think they are, more or less. They are symptoms of illness.'

Did Dr Harman not agree that morphia 'had a very constipating effect'. Yes. Which would cause restlessness and discomfort? Not necessarily. In an old lady? It might well do. Morphia also caused loss of appetite? Yes. And weight loss? Very slight, 'in a normal person'.

> 'What about old people? Have you any knowledge of the effect upon old people?'
> 'I am not sure what that effect is with old people.'
> 'Have you any experience of it?'
> 'I have never seen a morphine addict of eighty.'
> 'When you say you are not sure, the answer really is that you do not know, is it not?'
> 'Yes.'

Then the sole incidence of Cheyne Stokes breathing on the night of 14th/15th October, which Dr Harman had said might be due to heart failure but he would have expected it to continue. Again, happening only on a single occasion when there were continuing moderate doses of morphine and heroin, it would have nothing to do with drugging either. The Attorney-General asked if Dr Harman had been aware that 'this breathing followed the day when she had been given the highest injection up to that time' and that on the following day no injection had been given.

> 'You ignored those factors before expressing your opinion?'
> 'I overlooked them, yes.'

Dr Harman was reminded by the Attorney-General that he had expressed the opinion that the morphia treatment instituted by the Cheshire hospital should only have been continued 'for a week or so', on her return to Eastbourne.

> 'With your experience of strokes, would you expect a woman with this history, being able to be moved back to Eastbourne and then taken home, to be suffering from such severe pain that it was incurable except with morphia and heroin?'
> 'No, I would not expect that.'
> 'If a general practitioner is in any difficulty [with weaning a patient] he can always call for help, cannot he?'

'Yes, he could, indeed.'
'Then I think you went on to suggest that by carrying on with these drugs he [Dr Adams] had deprived himself of their useful value later on?'
'That is the great disadvantage, that possibility.'

The Attorney-General asked Dr Harman to point out to him 'the first clear indication' he thought there was in the nurses' reports that Mrs Morrell was 'a dying woman', as he had agreed 'roughly' with the dates suggested by the other medical witnesses. Mr Lawrence objected to this question but the Judge allowed it. Dr Harman was asked to look at the report for 31st October: Mrs Morrell had slept for 5½ hours that night, and the next day Dr Adams had instructed that the morphia and omnopon should be omitted. This would be cutting out the main sedatives from her medication and 'further restlessness and excitement' would ensue, by leaving just the heroin? Yes, though Dr Harman wondered how much any sleep she had was due to the morphia and heroin 'after this length of time'.

'Of course, we know that during the middle time she was having a large quantity of barbiturates, was not she?'
'Not a large quantity.'
'A substantial quantity?'
'No, quite small.'
'You think quite small?'
'Yes.'
'Could have been increased without any risk?'
'Oh, yes.'

'This is the next day', the Attorney-General continued reading the notes for 1st November, when the patient was on heroin only. There was 'no indication of a rapid deterioration' yet, was there? Dr Harman decided that the whole matter of 'this artificial concept of dying' was nonsense and 'to my mind …meaningless.' The Attorney-General went on to another point 'Meaningless to your mind or not':

'…Then the 3rd November, the daytime, the Sedormid is withheld 'As Dr Adams wished Mrs Morrell to be clear mentally.'
'That would indicate, would it not, Dr Harman, that in Dr Adams's view part of her mental condition was due to the Sedormid and barbiturates that she was having?'
'Yes, that would indicate that.'

He went on to say that it might have been Dr Adams' view but it was not his.

'Dr Adams was seeing the patient?'
'Yes.'

'You have never seen the patient?'

'No.'

The night report of the 6th November, recorded that the patient had been given 'heroin a half at 1 a.m., heroin a half at 1.55 a.m., heroin a half at 7.50 a.m.'.

'Those are pretty big dosages, are not they, for an old lady in this condition?'

'Yes, one could call them pretty big.'

'What do you call them as a consultant?'

'Sizable I would call them.'

'And the first two given close together?'

'Yes.'

'Clearly an overlap there?'

'Oh, clearly.'

After about seven hours' sleep during the night, Mrs Morrell had been given the heroin injection at 7.55 in the morning, was this not an indication 'of a change in policy?' Dr Harman did not see it. But routine injections were always in the evening, followed by further injections for restlessness or to produce sleep, but not in the morning to produce sleep during the day. Yes, he saw that, but it was only 'possibly' a change in policy. The Attorney-General patiently pointed out that it was 'a serious matter' to keep an elderly patient asleep all day and all night 'because it might lead to pulmonary congestion'. 'Oh, yes', it was.

'The respiration might get very high, might it not?'

'It would, yes.'

Dr Harman agreed that this would be a 'normal' consequence if a patient of 80 were kept 'in a semi-comatose condition under morphia and heroin or morphia or heroin for two or three days'. The day report of 7th November showed that the patient was given Sedormid at ten o'clock and again at six o'clock and, apart from 'one more administration of Allonal at her own request.(on the 9th) …she does not appear to have been given any of her usual barbiturates (again)' The Attorney-General asked what the result of the withdrawal of the barbiturates would have been.

'It would withdraw a sedative effect in so far as it was effective then.'

Morphia had been withdrawn on the 31st October and not administered again until the evening of 6th November, and the barbiturates were withdrawn; effectively the 'sedative effect' had been reduced. Looking at the day report for the 7th, the Attorney-General had noted no shortage of sleep and there was the entry in the notebook: 'Visited by doctor at 10.45 (a.m.). Morphia, quarter grain, and heroin, half a grain, and atropine 1/100th given. May have same repeated during the day if necessary.' Did that not indicate a change of policy, 'a change to the policy of keeping her under?'

> 'Well, there is a change of the use of drugs. Presumably the policy has changed, yes.'

It was changed, the Attorney-General emphasised, by the administration of the drugs during the day-time, and, after the evening visit on the same day, the instruction was that she could have the injection repeated after two hours if she did not sleep. A sizeable injection? Yes. There were injections throughout the night of the 7th and during the daytime of the 8th the instruction was that she might have 'morphia injection of half a grain and heroin half and atropine $\frac{1}{100}$th if necessary' during the day.

> 'Does not that confirm, in your view, that the policy was one of keeping her under in the day-time then?'
> 'I object to the equivocal term 'keeping her under'. I am not sure what that means.'

It mean 'keeping her under the influence of drugs, semi-comatose'. Dr Harman concurred with the definition; that was so on the 8th. The 9th was the day that Mrs Morrell got out of bed and sat in her chair for nearly an hour: '…you would not say that that was an indication of imminence of death, would you?' He would not. Following her being out in the chair that afternoon, at 10.15 Dr Adams had issued an instruction that she was to have 'heroin 1 grain given S.O.S.' She slept for 6½ hours and upon waking up was given another injection immediately.

> 'Would that not indicate that the policy then was to give her another injection directly she woke up?'
> 'Well, I think the clearest statement of policy has come from the nurses, that it was to keep her peaceful.'
> 'Well, I am asking you about this report at this moment, not expressing your view on this case generally.'
> 'I beg your pardon. Yes, all right, she was being given an injection when she woke up.'

The Attorney-General went through the times when Mrs Morrell was recorded to have woken up, each of which was followed by an injection of a grain of heroin. After many prevarications, Dr Harman eventually agreed that the policy had been 'to give her a further injection both day and night whenever she woke up.'

It was on the 10th November that there was the first record of 'jerkiness' and it was 'slight jerking'. Dr Harman had never seen heroin jerkings or convulsions? No, he had not.

> 'And your dramatic acting of the convulsions was based upon what you have read of convulsions that follow upon heroin?'
> 'Yes.'

The kind of 'jerkings right backwards' that he had indicated would occur whether a patient was standing up or lying down? Yes.

'And convulsions of that character might well be described by a spectator as almost jerking her out of bed, might they not?'
'Yes, certainly.'

The Attorney-General reminded Dr Harman of Sister Randall's evidence that 'these convulsions almost jerked her out of bed'. The Doctor did not remember but accepted that she had said it. He would not accept that Mrs Morrell had been semi-comatose during the last two or three days of her life, rather, she had been 'waking-sleeping; confused, in... a low delirium', but he did not disagree with the nurses' descriptions of 'heavily drugged sleep' and that she was 'semi-comatose'.

The Court adjourned for lunch.

Before the Jury returned for the afternoon session, Mr Lawrence brought to the Judge's notice, a copy of a publication which had been purchased in London that morning. He had already shown this to the Attorney-General. Mr Justice Devlin thought that the matter should be left with the Attorney-General to take what action he thought fit. As far as the British press were concerned, there was no objection to the Jury reading the accounts of the trial as there had been no complaint of their reporting. This particular publication was 'described as an international news magazine' and if Mr Lawrence thought it desirable that he should warn the Jury, he would do so. Mr Lawrence wished to leave it to the Judge to decide 'the best course' ; the magazine had been published on the previous Monday, 1st April. The magazine was not named in Court and it was decided to give the Jury a general warning.

Mr Justice Devlin addressed the Jury, telling them that his attention had been drawn to this publication, which contained 'a most undesirable comment on the proceedings that have been taking place in this Court'. They should be careful only to purchase ordinary British daily newspapers while they were engaged with the trial.

Dr Harman was recalled to the stand and his cross-examination by the Attorney-General continued. Paraldehyde: was one grain equivalent to about 1 c.c.? It was one gram which was about the equivalent. Dr Harman had said earlier that he never gave 'less than six c.cs of paraldehyde'; now he said that this was in 'disturbed patients'. It was a drug he used frequently. The Attorney-General asked Dr Harman if he was familiar with *Clinical Toxicology* by Thienes Haley. He was not but he had heard of the Institute in Pasadena where Haley was Director. The Attorney-General read an extract:

'Toxic dose. Four grams of paraldehyde or 1 gram of chloral hydrate have produced serious symptoms...'

On the previous day, Dr Harman had suggested that 'anything less than 6 c.c. was quite safe' and he stood by this: 'anything less than 6 c.c. was unlikely to do any good.' The Attorney-

General put it to him 'that 4 c.c. might well have produced dangerous symptoms in this woman', particularly as she was 'almost saturated with morphia and heroin' and another hypnotic would have added to 'the depressant effect with respiration'. 'Theoretically', said Dr Harman. The Attorney-General traced through the injections of the evening of the 12th November: Dr Adams gave her the 2 c.c. of paraldehyde, then at 10.30 p.m., on his last visit, he produced a 5 c.c. syringe, giving her an injection with it three-quarters full; he left another 5 c.c. syringe with an injection which Sister Randall gave on his instructions, 'and then within a short space of giving that second (5 c.c.) injection, according to Nurse Randall, the patient dies, and she then tells Dr Adams on the telephone that she has died, after she has given the second injection.'

> 'As a consultant, Dr Harman, are you saying and do you express the positive opinion that those administrations of paraldehyde, if they took place, had nothing to do with her death?'
> 'Yes, I would, in so far as one can express an opinion on the evidence. That is my firm opinion.'

One should not 'shut one's eyes to the obvious?' He was not doing that, replied Dr Harman

> 'I thought you said this morning that if the patient was kept in a semi-comatose condition by heroin and by morphia, you would expect normally to get a pulmonary condition resulting in increased respiration after the period of a few days?'
> 'Yes.'

Dr Harman still did not accept that the patient was in a semi-comatose conditon. But the nurses had given evidence both at the Magistrates' Court and at this trial that the patient was in and out of coma, and semi-comatose, 'throwing a light upon the evidence of the books', had he not considered this? He had only concentrated on the reports. The Attorney-General said that he 'could not have it both ways', rejecting either the reports or the evidence when it suited him. He had agreed that Mrs Morrell was, at this stage, 'given a further injection directly she woke up'.

> 'If that was the system of medication, you would not be surprised if it was followed by a pulmonary congestion and increased respiration, would you?'
> 'No, I would not.'
> 'Nor would you be surprised if that led to death, would you?'
> 'No, I would not.'

The Attorney-General reverted to questioning Dr Harman about convulsions. Dr Harman argued that they were not necessarily 'very exhausting to the patient'; they might stop respirations but were not likely to make them very high. From his reading of eighteen cases in books, patients did not 'pass out in the moment of exhaustion'. He agreed that the amounts of heroin prescribed for Mrs Morrell on the 10th and 11th November were 'very heavy' for someone in her condition, and also the amounts recorded as being administered to her were very heavy 'for a lady of 81 in this condition'. Even so the amounts recorded in the notebooks were 'nothing like the amounts which were prescribed', were they? No. Dr Harman was not able to say what would have happened if 'as Dr Adams said to Superintendent Hannam' that he had given her 12½ grains of heroin on 12th November.

> 'Do you really think that she could have survived at that time 12½ grains on top of the 3½ grains of heroin administered by the nurses, or as shown by the nurses' reports?'
> 'Well, from what I know about morphine and heroin I should not have been surprised if she had.'
> 'No, but you do not know really very much, do you doctor?'
> 'No, and that is why I am less surprised.'

Dr Harman had said that this was 'not a morphine death' and he agreed with the Attorney-General that 'by far the commonest form of morphine death' was that by coma and respiratory paralysis. It was 'by no means uncommon', suggested the Attorney-General, for people 'kept under' by morphia and heroin to die from some resultant form of pulmonary congestion. Dr Harman argued that deaths from morphine and heroin poisoning were rare, and, when pushed, conceded that this was because such poisoning was, in any case, rare. He was asked to look at his answer to Mr Lawrence, in which he had stated that the morphine was taken too much earlier – 7½ hours – for it to have played any part as a cause of death:

> '...Of course, that falls to the ground if the respirations were due to pulmonary congestion set up by the morphine, does not it, that thesis?'
> 'Yes. If we are to discuss this I would draw a distinction between death from morphine poisoning and death from any remoter complication which arose from having been given too much morphine. I think that is fair, is not it?'

The Attorney-General reminded him that he had also given an answer stating that 'in old ladies of 80 who have had strokes and arterio sclerosis one does not regard it as a question so much as explaining the cause of death, one knows they just die. She might well have had a clot on the heart, a coronary thrombosis; that would be the usual thing.' The Attorney-General asked, somewhat sarcastically:

> '...She might perhaps just as equally well have been smothered by her nurse, might not she?'
> 'I don't think that would be so likely.'

Sir Reginald snapped back: 'We are not dealing with likelihoods here. We have got the record of the medication shown by the nurses' reports...'

'What you are suggesting is this, is it not: that this lady, who was a dying woman, who on top of being a dying woman had these doses which you yourself have admitted were heavy, had the remarkable coincidence that, as she was dying, and after having had these doses, she had a cerebral thrombosis or something else in no way flowing from the medication to which she had been subjected?'

'My belief is that most of her symptoms as recorded all along are symptoms of her illness and not of medication or drugging.'

'That is your answer to that question, is it?'

'Yes, if it answers it.'

'Well, I did not think it did, Dr Harman.'

For a second and then a third time, Dr Harman asserted that the morphine and heroin had neither contributed directly nor indirectly to Mrs Morrell's death.

The Attorney-General then asked Dr Harman questions about the accumulation of drugs in the body. They were agreed that while morphia or heroin remained in the body these drugs continued to have an effect. Dr Harman thought that traces of morphine could still be detected in the body for up to four days after a dose, but there would always be some unaccounted for and not passed out of the body in the urine. Was he 'familiar with the *Journal of Pharmacology and Experimental Therapeutics*, asked the Attorney-General, and in particular, a biological chemist of the United States Public Health Service called Fred Oberst? Dr Harman was familiar with the journal but not the article and when he heard that the article was dated '1940', asserted that 'the whole question changed in about 1941 or '2'. The Attorney-General painstakingly read out the salient points of the research only for Dr Harman to say: 'I don't agree with the implications of those experiments.' The Attorney-General continued:

'It is true to say, is not it, that if a patient is drugged to the extent that the circulation is slower, the whole machinery of the body is slower, then the effect of the morphia or heroin, the rate that is absorbed into the body and passed out of the body, will also be slowed down?'

'Yes. It is very difficult to know how much effect that would have, because, after all, we have patients who are poisoned, severely poisoned, with morphine or heroin in a coma, moribund, and yet their processes are working well enough for them to excrete morphine, because in fact they recover.'

'When did you last deal with such a case?'

'I haven't dealt with such a case.'

The Attorney-General moved on to the Diploma in Anaesthetics held by Dr Adams:

'Would not you expect a general practitioner who holds two posts as an anaesthetist at hospitals to keep himself up to date?'

'Well, I know some who don't.'

'That may be.'
'Therefore I would not expect all to.'

Dr Harman had commented on Dr Douthwaite's evidence about hyoscine, saying that morphine and hyoscine had a synergistic effect and that he was astonished at the suggestion that hyoscine should be used. The Attorney-General directed Dr Harman's attention to *The Pharmacological Basis of Therapeutics* by Louis S. Goodman, Professor at Vermont College of Medicine and Alfred Gillman; Dr Harman interrupted to say that he knew of their research. In that book was the statement: 'Most drugs producing the same type of response are synergistically prescribed together.' This meant that when the two drugs were used together, there would be an increased effect over using them separately? Dr Harman agreed with this. [They had been used together for decades for their analgesic properties.] He was still surprised at Dr Douthwaite's suggestion, but it was all 'a matter of opinion'.

Both Dr Douthwaite and Dr Ashby had described the quantities of drugs prescribed from the 8th November onwards as 'lethal'; did Dr Harman agree with that? He did not: although it might be that one third of a grain of an opiate was a 'minimal lethal dose', he considered that Mrs Morrell could have survived the dosage of 8⅓ grains of heroin and 10 grains of morphia administered to her on 8th November. Of the dosage on the 9th of 6⅓ grains of heroin and 12½ of morphia, Dr Harman said that she could have survived this; on the other hand she might have died from that amount.

> 'And following that, six and a third grains of heroin, and the next day, the 11th, eighteen and a half grains of morphia and six and a third of heroin?'
> 'I will say that she might have died of any or either of those doses.'

The Attorney-General asked Dr Harman several times whether with this type of case and 'with a medication of this character in four days', would he have expected the patient's death 'to have been due to coronary thrombosis?' Dr Harman persisted with his view that it was always possible to die from coronary thrombosis because there might be no symptoms of it. The Attorney-General finally asked:

> 'You told me before the matters which you considered with a view to forming the opinion which you have given in this case – the nurses' reports, etc. and one proof. Did you obtain any evidence from Dr Adams for the purpose of forming your opinion?'
> 'No.'

Mr Lawrence began the re-examination of his witness by going back to the point about death by coronary thrombosis: were there any indications that it was not this 'that carried the old lady off?' Not at all; it was 'one of the commonest modes of death after a certain age'. With lethal doses of an opiate, there was much uncertainty, when even one third of a grain of morphine had caused a death? It was the lowest amount he knew of causing a death, replied Dr Harman;

a pre-med, given by an anaesthetist before an operation. The largest dose he had found that was taken was 576 grains of morphine: 'The patient died of that.' He explained, somewhat startlingly, that when patients had a tolerance to opiates then it was necessary to form an estimate of it because certain doses would have no effect: 'If the patient does not die of a dose which you think they might have died of, then they are tolerant to that extent.' There was no inevitability in any dose having lethal results.

When Dr Harman had researched cases of heroin convulsions, he had only found 18 cases. These had been discovered by American public health medical researchers and were the only ones recorded in world medical literature, so he agreed with Dr Ashby that it was a rare phenomenon and in that case 'should be rarely diagnosed'. Mr Lawrence read out the answers Dr Douthwaite had given him about paraldehyde, then asked Dr Harman if he knew of any hypnotic which had less depressant effect upon respiration. He did not, and it was the very drug he would have used in the circumstances. Mr Lawrence took him through the nurses' notes for the night of 11th/12th and the day of 12th November: the dose of 2 c.c. of paraldehyde had been given at 7.30 p.m. on Sunday 12th and the nurse had recorded that it had 'no apparent effects', and the patient was still awake at 10.30 p.m. when another injection of 5 c.c. of paraldehyde was given. This was all in order to repeat Dr Harman's assertion that he never gave less than a 6 c.c. injection of paraldehyde – from which it could be inferred that the 5 c.c. was perfectly safe. Sister Randall's evidence for the second 5 c.c. was not mentioned.

Mr Lawrence read again the night report for 28th September with its mention of the Cheyne Stokes breathing and the very heavy drugging just before this in order for Dr Harman to state that it was because Mrs Morrell's condition had worsened that the drugs were increased to deal with it. Then the 6th November: the history of the night before was of restlessness and aggressiveness and the same in the morning, before the daytime drugging had been instituted. Was it not to deal with this condition rather than a 'change in policy'? Dr Harman had presumed that the drugs were given 'because she was worse'.

Was there any evidence in the nurses' reports, 'whatever the nurses said on their depositions or have said here', to demonstrate that Mrs Morrell was in a coma, or semi-coma? Dr Harman had seen none but said that it was consistent with 'a clouding of consciousness' and 'something short of comatose': people who could talk, eat and react but were not 'perfectly normal'. Mr Lawrence also pointed to a couple of phenobarbitone tablets which were given after the three Allonal on the 9th November, one at 5.15 a.m. on the 10th and another at 7.40 a.m. that same morning.

Mr Lawrence asked Dr Harman about the history of methadone. He thought that it dated from the end or after the war, but was certain that it was in use in 1950. (In fact it was first synthesised during the Second World War in Germany as a substitute for morphine and introduced into America in 1947. It was initially used as a pain-killer and only later for weaning opiate addicts. Dr Douthwaite probably knew of its use for this purpose by his reading of American research papers and it was unlikely to have been used in this way in Britain in 1950.) Dr Harman stated that all the 'modern experience and writing on heroin and morphine addiction' was American, where addicts were sent by the courts to mental hospitals. There was no similar problem in Britain.

It had been put to Dr Harman that heroin was four or five times as strong as morphine; Mr Lawrence asked him to describe the relationship of the drugs to one another. Dr Harman thought that he himself would only give half the amount of heroin if he were giving that instead of morphine for pain. He felt unable to comment on Dr Douthwaite's assertion that heroin was four or five times as strong, but did not deny it, and heroin caused more problems with respiration. Most of the research was based on animals and did not relate directly to humans: opiates made cats excited and put dogs to sleep. With humans: 'You do not know until you try.'

Mr Lawrence thanked his witness and sat down.

Mr Justice Devlin questioned Dr Harman about the effects of the instruction to the nurses 'to keep her under', but not the phrase, rather the way in which they carried out the instruction: giving her further injections each time she awoke. Was it his view that this was 'accelerating death' – not giving the sort of treatment which incidentally brings death a little closer, but 'a real cutting short of life, though not necessarily for a sinister purpose'? No, he did not think it had accelerated death: the patient had got to a certain stage 'in her delirium' which necessitated the drugs to control her as this state was now continuous. This policy was 'quite a common one in such cases'. Dr Ashby had said that the instruction to 'keep her under' 'would be almost certain to accelerate death', what was his view? Dr Harman replied:

> 'I would put the emphasis the other way round. I would agree that it might have done, and my opinion would be that it probably would not have done so.'

The Judge asked whether this was a point upon which there were likely to be differences of opinion amongst doctors. Dr Harman said that there would always be different views on a case.

The second witness for the Defence was Mildred Vickery, Matron of the Neston Cottage Hospital in Cheshire for 22 years. Mr Clarke examined her. She had brought with her the Day Report Book for the hospital covering the period from the 25th June, 1948 to the 5th July, 1948. (Exhibit 57) The report of 25th June referred to Mrs Morrell amongst other patients. Miss Vickery remembered her 'very vaguely'.

The first report showed that Mrs Morrell was admitted suffering from haemiplegia with paralysis on the left side. She was given luminal on that day. Then there was a night report for 26th June, signed by Nurse Evans, and an entry on the 26th signed by Nurse McIlroy, and others through to the 5th July. On the 27th June there was Matron Vickery's report that Mrs Morrell was very distressed and complaining of severe pain and was given a quarter grain of morphia at 11.30 in the morning. Dr Turner had been in charge of the case, but he was presently seriously ill after a stroke. Miss Vickery herself had been looking after Mrs Morrell on the 27th June.

Mr Clarke asked Miss Vickery if she 'at that stage' (27th June) ever seen Dr Adams at the hospital. Not that she could remember, she said. Was Mrs Morrell given morphia every night until the 5th July? According to the book, she had been.

'And, as regards Dr Adams, have you a recollection of Dr Adams coming to the Cottage Hospital at some time during Mrs Morrell being there?'

'Vaguely.'

Was this at the beginning, middle or end of her stay, Mr Clarke enquired.

'Well, I imagine that it was the week-end before she went away.'
'That would be after she had been put on morphia?'
'Yes.'

The notes had refreshed Matron's memory on one matter:

'…What sort of things, possibly as the result of the stroke, did she do that you can remember which are unusual even possibly in hospital?'
'Well, I do remember her trying to throw the reading lamp at one of the Sisters.'
'Her reading lamp?'
'The bedside lamp.'
'She tried to throw it?'
'Tried to throw it.'

Matron thought that Mrs Morrell was an 'irritable and restless' patient.

The Attorney-General had no questions, the witness withdrew, and the Court was adjourned until the following morning.

[There never was any evidence about Mrs Morrell's normal personality traits and behaviour. She was used to a household of servants and the British NHS (public) hospital of the time was run along military lines by the matron.]

# Fifteenth Day

Mr Lawrence addressed the Court to state that he had, on the previous day, concluded the evidence for the Defence, having called only two witnesses. He then began his closing speech for the Defence.

The Jury might well have thought that the witnesses for the Prosecution had made the case for the Defence, and this was the reason for shortening the Defence's case. The only charge against the accused was that he had murdered Mrs Morrell on or about the 13th November, 1950. The term 'murder' meant 'killing with malice aforethought express or implied' and 'malice aforethought' meant killing intentionally or deliberately. 'And of all murder cases that have been heard in this famous court, surely this one is one of the most extraordinary that this building has ever entertained.'

The case that had been alleged against Dr Adams was a most extraordinary one:

'…that a doctor should be accused of murdering one of his patients, an old woman of eighty-one, when she was already dying, in the last days, or, at the most, the last few weeks of her life and when, with no intervention on his part, the end was inevitable.'

The Jury had heard days of reading notes, medical debate, and 'extreme refinements of opinion', but in the end 'this case is of the simplest' and it was not necessary to be a medical expert, but to have commonsense. They had heard the submission which he had made to the Judge a couple of days previously, that there was no case for Dr Adams to answer. The Judge had ruled against him, but that only meant that the case was to be left to their judgment and verdict and the ruling was not an expression of view.

Justice could only be done by the Jury judging only upon the evidence which they had heard in Court and not upon anything they might have heard outside or read in the papers: rumour and gossip could be very wrong and nothing of that sort must influence their decision. The object to the whole system of British justice was that justice should be done to the accused. 'Those who accuse must make good their accusation by evidence, before any jury can find that that accusation is true.' The burden of proof was on the prosecution and everyone was innocent of all criminal charges 'unless and until that presumption is removed by evidence which compels a jury to say that the matter has been proved, and proved beyond all reasonable doubt.' Suspicion, probability and likelihood were not enough. In the medical evidence doctors weighed up the probabilities, but it was 'not a question of balancing probabilities.' That applied in the civil courts but not in our criminal courts. If any one of the Jury thought that Dr Adams might be innocent, then he was entitled to a verdict of 'not guilty'. This was not giving him 'the benefit of the doubt. That, as a very great Lord Chief Justice once said, is a rubbishy phrase.'

The Jury might well have been wondering why Dr Adams had not gone into the witness box to give evidence. He and his 'learned friend' stood before them as 'Dr Adams's shield', and it was for them to decide whether the accused should go into the witness box. It had been said by Lord Oaksey in a 1950 colonial appeal case, that 'that question was one of the greatest anxiety for the prisoner's legal advisers'. The Defence team had made that decision 'in the circumstances of the case' because he hoped to persuade them, the Jury, that 'the evidence does not justify, does not and cannot justify, a conviction for murder in this case.' It was only at about the beginning of the 20th Century that the law allowed the accused to go into the witness box if they wished to do so, previously they were barred, but they were still not bound to do so.

They might have thought, in any case, that there was little for Dr Adams to answer, after they had heard the evidence. It was not right to ask Dr Adams to go into the box merely for 'the entertainment of the spectators in this Court or for the edification of the Press'. Could they imagine what 'this professional man of middle years' had been living through for the last few months: in prison, awaiting trial, sitting through the evidence in Court. At the end of this 'mental suffering', would the Jury have wanted him to go through the ordeal of examination and cross-examination if it were not absolutely necessary?

Everything relating to Mrs Morrell had occurred six or more years ago: Mr Sogno, the solicitor used his notes to recall what had happened, the nurses had their notes and the police theirs. Dr Adams had none 'because they were looked for by the Superintendent in his cabinet, his clinical cabinet where he keeps his patient's records, and after six years they had been destroyed.' If Dr Adams had been asked to give evidence, there would have been 'the dreadful realisation that one failure of recollection, one inaccuracy, however innocent, would be seized upon and might well have been put before you as an indication of his guilt.'

[The underlinings which appear in the text below were made by Hannam in manuscript in the transcript and are of the utmost significance]

'Surely <u>the greatest justification</u> for that in this most extraordinary case, for which there may be no parallel, is by <u>the mercy of Heaven</u> there has been provided for you a witness that is both eloquent and unchallengeable in what he says, and that is the witness that is comprised in those <u>eight notebooks</u> made by the nurses night after night and day after day when their memory was as fresh as paint and not trying to awaken something over which six years of oblivion had fallen.'

The whole case was in those notebooks. Mr Lawrence said that he had been unable to announce the Defence decision not to call Dr Adams at an earlier stage. He hoped that the Jury would understand the reason for that decision.

He now turned to the evidence in the case: this was really just the nurses' notebooks because the alleged murder was said to be by the administration of drugs. 'That is how they say he did it: by administering drugs.' These records had been made by 'responsible women', nurses, and three of the four 'were of mature years', and the youngest had many years' experience. It had come as a surprise to them when the notebooks were produced, but 'every one of those nurses has pledged herself to the accuracy and completeness of those records.' They had not be kept 'casually', but in 'meticulous detail'. Mr Lawrence submitted that it was these records which were the real evidence in the case, giving 'a complete picture of the medication and treatment of Mrs Morrell by Dr Adams'; it was unnecessary to look elsewhere for evidence and the notebooks' evidence 'prevails over anything else and excludes anything else.'

When the Attorney-General opened the case nearly three weeks previously, he had stated that Mrs Morrell was in a coma for the last three or four days of her life, based upon the nurses' memories but when they came to look at the notebooks, they admitted that it was clear that 'whatever state Mrs Morrell was in, it was not one of coma during the last few days.' In relying on memory 'the possibility of mistake' was enormous; to make a mistake in this case the result 'might be too awful and dreadful to contemplate'.

Mr Lawrence said that he would give a clear outline and perspective of the events described in the notebooks and the Jury should bear in mind that there had been no allegation of any attempt to kill before the first days of November 1950. At the latter end of June, 1948, when she was seventy-eight or seventy-nine years of age and staying in Cheshire, Mrs Morrell had a stroke, a severe one, and was admitted to Neston Cottage Hospital after a stay of 11 or 12 days, 'and she must have been removed by ambulance all the way from Liverpool to Eastbourne, where she came under Dr Adams' treatment.'

Mr Lawrence reminded the Jury that he had asked the Prosecution to supply prescription lists for the earlier period in order to supply them with the whole picture: the beginning as well as the end. Dr Douthwaite 'had been told by someone on the Crown's side that the nurses' records at Cheshire were not available'. They were available and what they contained was 'quite remarkable': a severe stroke, a complaint of severe pain, two days of luminal [a barbiturate – these were the tablets she could not swallow] and morphia being given. He linked the Matron's evidence of Mrs Morrell trying to throw the lamp with the later evidence of irritability and restlessness: 'When we are ill and have strokes that damage the brain, we may do all kinds of things.' Mr Lawrence said that it was a 'remarkable thing' that 'before she came to Dr Adams at Eastbourne' [He was already her doctor before she went to stay with her son in Cheshire] the morphia had been started and that the Matron had given evidence that the morphia inaugurated before Dr Adams had visited Mrs Morrell in hospital. [She had actually not been able to remember when he visited.] On her return to Eastbourne, she was in the Esperance Nursing Home, then the Olinda Nursing Home, the Cumberland Hotel, and then home to Marden Ash.

The Jury were reminded that Mrs Morrell had never, throughout the times relevant to the case, been a well woman, but 'ill, aged, paralysed' and that 'permanent damage had been done to the brain, hardening of the arteries, and lack of proper circulation to the brain… Ill, aged, irritable, probably, you may think, by temperament autocratic, not helped by this stroke.' What the three doctors were agreed upon was that her expectation of life just after the stroke was 'about six to twelve months'. What was the doctor to do, but to make her life 'as bearable as possible during the daytime, to give her sleep at night and to make her co-operative with her nurses', controlling the irritability and brainstorms. So Dr Adams had put her on 'a regime of morphia and heroin with tablets for pain' [he did not mention the barbiturates]. It was 'all very well' for Dr Douthwaite and Dr Ashby to talk about 'severe pain', but this was the regime Dr Adams chose. It might have seemed that the Crown were attacking the use of heroin but this was not the issue; they were not there to judge whether Dr Adams was a good doctor or a bad one:

> '…And you have not got to decide whether what Dr Adams did then was good or bad
> from a medical point of view, because he is not charged with and it is not suggested that
> there was any murder then, or planned murder. It is only in the last days of November,
> 1950, that that intent is said to emerge.'

Mr Lawrence pointed out that Dr Adams had qualified in 1921 and suggested that 'these drugs' were used then more frequently than now, and in the absence of severe pain.

He returned to 'the picture' from June 1948 until the summer of 1950, with 'the old lady getting about' and with Dr Adams helping her to do so. There were 'ups and downs', but the Jury might think that the Doctor 'was doing his duty to the best of his ability and not doing it too badly.' Doctors Douthwaite and Ashby had said that it was wrong to give her the drugs because she became addicted, but, whilst this would be terrible in a young person, with a woman in Mrs Morrell's condition 'what does a little dependence on that drug matter? Let us be sensible.' Dr

Harman had said that it was pointless to wean her: the drugs might not have been doing her any good, 'but as she had had it, she had got to go on having it.' In medical matters, there was still much that was not yet known about causality, or the forces of nature for that matter.

He came to the summer of 1950 and focussed on Dr Harris: every locum had 'to exercise his own judgment', and he could not 'shelter behind Dr Adams'. He had done exactly what Dr Adams did and used morphia and heroin, and introduced Omnopon.

> 'If anything had been going on with Mrs Morrell that was wrong or criminal it would have been Dr Harris's duty to do something about it and to stop it. But he did not. Nobody has criticized him – nobody.'

The Jury would not do so either because he did the sensible and obvious thing.

Mr Lawrence had reached the first fortnight of November, 1950: 'The old woman dying, coming to the end of her days'; the restlessness, the brain not functioning and the distress – all these might be just as distressing as pain, and who was to judge? Was a doctor to say that he could only help with drugs if a patient had severe pain? Dr Adams had not stood back and done nothing; he had stepped up the doses 'of the very drugs that she had been having from the start'. He had tried to help her and gave the instructions to the nurses for the same reason. The Attorney-General 'for reasons best known to himself' had drawn attention to the fact that, up to the last 24 hours of Mrs Morrell's life, she had been given increasing doses of drugs, which were accompanied by sufficient amounts of sleep during the nights, 'those awful nights that come upon people, or some people, just before they are dead. He gives drugs and she has long periods of sleep.' The prosecution were saying that that treatment 'by accumulation, was the act of a murderer. That is what they say.' Mr Lawrence wondered what Mrs Morrell would have thought of such an allegation, and 'what any relative, any dear friend or relative of hers present in those last days' would have thought. [This was indeed a question that required an answer which was not provided for the jury.]

There was one small medical detail which Mr Lawrence thought might help the Jury to make up their minds: 'mixed in with the injections of heroin and morphine, were ten separate doses' of one-hundredth of a grain of atropine. He mentioned that it had 'some kind of anti-dotal effect on morphia' and that it was to dry up mucus. If Dr Adams was 'a diabolical murderer', why would he have bothered to, or have any interest in trying to ease such a symptom by giving atropine? 'It does not make sense does it?' [atropine can cause amnesia, confusion and excitation in the elderly, and tachycardia – Mr Lawrence had not mentioned adverse side-effects.] Mr Lawrence was aiding the Jury in their vital task of looking 'for evidence of what was the intention in Dr Adams's mind'. Therefore, 'these injections of atropine: utterly inconsistent with the murderer's purpose but wholly consistent and harmonious with the picture of a man who has tried everything that he knows to ease the distress in which this woman was.'

The doses of morphia and heroin given in the last twenty-four hours were 'sizeable', but the Jury should not forget 'all these variations'; that Dr Adams was trying different balances of drugs, trying one, leaving one out:

'A murderer? A murderer would have gone straight ahead with his foul purpose, would he not? – "That is the dose. No need to change it. On and on and on with it. Bigger and bigger amounts." You see, you cannot make it square, can you, on evidence like that with the suggestion that he is a murderer?'

On the evening of the 12th November, when Mrs Morrell could not sleep, Dr Adams had given paraldehyde to help her sleep, an hypnotic which was 'the safest of all'. Why would a murderer turn to the safest of drugs? And the dose he gave of 2 c.c. was 'A cautious tentative dose, well below the normal'. How could an intent to kill be inferred from that? The next dose of 5 c.c. was 'still well within the range'. Whether they believed Sister Randall when she said she had given an extra dose in the early hours of 13th November, was a matter for them, the Jury, but they might think that it did not matter anyway. Just before 2 a.m. Mrs Morrell's breathing rate increased to '50 breaths a minute', and she passed away at 2 a.m. In death by morphine poisoning the breaths became slower and slower 'This was not, as Doctor Harman says, a Morphine death at all.' It was surely likely, Mr Lawrence, suggested, that 'at that moment nature intervened' to resolve her distress and the impasse that Dr Adams and his patient were in over the use of the drugs. Dr Harman had said it was not a morphine death and Dr Ashby had said that he could not totally rule out natural causes. The Jury had to be satisfied that the death was from drugging and not from natural causes, and if they thought it even possible that she might have died from natural causes, 'then the charge of murder, in my submission, cannot be sustained.'

Mr Lawrence did not propose 'to gloss over' the 'jerkings' from which Mrs Morrell had suffered: these were well-attested, but Dr Harman's research into morphine convulsions had shown that those described by Sister Randall were of the 'clonic' type and not those which could be caused by morphine, and he had only been able to find 18 cases. There was much divergence of opinion in medical matters and there was no scientific certainty. What the cause of the 'jerkings' was would remain uncertain. The other matter that the Prosecution had relied upon was the phrase 'keeping her under', but the nurses had understood this to mean that they were to prevent her getting restless. There was no 'sinister motive' in the phrase. Dr Harman had said that it signified to him that the patient would have remained 'excited, distressed and uncontrollable' at that stage in her delirium if she had not been under the influence of drugs. Dr Douthwaite had said that these instructions did not indicate to him an intent to kill and Dr Ashby had said that the 8th November was 'the point of no return' and that the doctor's duty was then 'to promote the comfort of his patient' and that it was a 'possible interpretation' that the drugs given to Mrs Morrell on and from 8th November were given for this purpose. That was a possibility which meant that there was reasonable doubt.

Dr Douthwaite's performance in the witness-box, Mr Lawrence described as 'rather strange': he had come to give evidence upon a situation which was 'quite a different situation before these nurses notebooks came into the case'. He then had time to consider them, then after a week a copy of his additional evidence was served upon the Defence. Dr Douthwaite had then replied to the Attorney-General that he was 'driven to the conclusion' that Dr Adams had formed an intention to murder on the 8th November and then carried it out. He himself had asked the same question in cross-examining Dr Douthwaite and received the same answer. Then he had concluded his cross-examination, the Attorney-General concluded his re-examination and the Judge asked some questions. It was during the Judge's questioning that Dr Douthwaite had postulated a new theory: that 'of the withdrawal of the morphine in the early days of November so that it could be brought back again with lethal effect after about a week.' The Judge had allowed the Defence the opportunity of further cross-examination and Mr Lawrence had asked him to which theory he now adhered and he had said the second. It was 'a very strange performance' and it was 'part and parcel of the uncertainty, the medical uncertainty, about this case.'

The theory itself, in Mr Lawrence's view, did not 'hold water for one moment'. This was the theory of 'accumulation' not only had to be proved, but it had to be shown that Dr Adams knew of it. Dr Douthwaite had asserted that Dr Adams would know because of his 'precious Diploma in Anaesthetics' which enabled him to give patients 'gas and ether in Eastbourne hospitals'. Dr Ashby had said that there might be 'one or two doses' of accumulation – not days – and Dr Harman had agreed with Dr Ashby. Doctors would no doubt dispute the theory 'long after this case is over', but how could the Jury be satisfied beyond all reasonable doubt? They might also think that Dr Douthwaite's views were those 'of a man who dislikes heroin'. Dr Ashby had not thought that there was anything sinister about the withdrawal of the morphine at the end of October, and, again, Dr Harman had agreed with him. There was, in any case, cross-tolerance between morphia and heroin, which enabled them to be 'switched' – a patient with tolerance to one would have tolerance to the other.

At the end of the medical case, Mr Lawrence suggested to the Jury, that the picture was one of a doctor helping his patient: in a dilemma, increasing the drugs, and when there is no effect 'he then turns to the safest drug in the armoury, Paraldehyde. He gives her very low and cautious doses, and then, as I suggest, nature intervenes'. If that was the case, Dr Adams should be acquitted, and even if it might be the truth, the Jury should acquit. If that was 'the true position on the medical evidence there is nothing in the rest of the evidence which can alter it.'

The Prosecution had suggested that this was murder and murder for gain. 'Sordid. Sordid and sinister.' But there was no evidence for it. Dr Adams was not short of money. In the will of 24th August, 1950, the only absolute bequest to Dr Adams 'was the Elizabethan [sic] cupboard' [it had been said to be Georgian][1] and 'whether it is a genuine Elizabethan nobody knows'. The probate value was only £270 out of an estate of some £175,000. The other gift was the Rolls Royce car, 'and another cupboard of some sort' (Elizabethan court cupboard), which he had not had. These last gifts were dependent upon the son, Mr Claude Morrell, predeceasing his mother. The result of the codicil of 13th September was to cut Dr Adams completely out of the will. 'Even the bit of silver in the Elizabethan cupboard has gone. Everything.' On 23rd October, Mr Sogno, Mrs Morrell's solicitor, received the pieces of the torn-up codicil from her, demonstrating her wish to put Dr Adams back into the will, but the tearing-up of the cod-

---

[1] In fact, the cabinet was Victorian and the silver contents were Georgian.

icil had no validity in law. There never was any other will, so although Dr Adams received the chest of silver and the Rolls Royce this was because the residual legatee, Mr Claude Morrell, knew it was his mother's wish that he should receive them and he gave them to Dr Adams. Mr Lawrence mentioned that Claude Morrell had last seen his mother on 3rd November 'when, according to Dr Douthwaite, the murderous operation was in force'. The Attorney-General intervened to correct this: Dr Douthwaite had said the 8th November. This enabled Mr Lawrence to say that on Dr Douthwaite's second theory, he thought that this would mean that the murderous intent was brought forward because the morphine was withdrawn on 31st October.

Where was the matter referred to again in evidence? Superintendent Hannam, Mr Lawrence became sarcastic: 'who happened quite by chance, so he says, to be strolling down the road in which Doctor Adams lives, happened as he was strolling down the road by chance, by chance to have arrived opposite the Doctor's house when the Doctor was putting his car away.'[2] The meeting was on 1st October, 1956, and reference was made to the chest of silver. The Doctor had said to Hannam that Mrs Morrell had 'insisted a long time before she died' that he should have it in her memory, and that he had not wanted it as he was a bachelor. He had also said that he knew she was going to leave him her Rolls Royce car as well, 'and another cabinet'. Maybe, said Mr Lawrence, this meant that 'she intended to do it and didn't do it' or that 'she intended to do it and did'. Either way, how could anyone be certain of something which had happened years before. He considered that Hannam should have been 'a little more helpful' and reminded Dr Adams that the codicil had been torn up.

> 'In fact, it was I both in this Court and at Eastbourne before the Magistrates who introduced this codicil for the first time. But for that everyone might have thought that Doctor Adams got these things under the will; he never did. He never did; but for the grace and favour of the only son. You may think the only son didn't think he was a murderer, and he had seen him down at Eastbourne.'

The Jury might think that there was 'a safe beacon light which shows you what the truth is'. It was an 'utterly fantastic hypothesis' for the Crown to suggest that Dr Adams had decided to murder a dying woman for the sake of obtaining a Rolls Royce and a cabinet of silver which he could not have because the son was still alive.

> 'It is too ludicrous isn't it? But it is solemnly put before you that the Doctor had a motive. The Crown are not bound to prove motive in these cases, but they have embarked upon it and that is what they say, and that is what it all amounts to.'

The Cremation Certificate had been filled up on the same day of Mrs Morrell's death by Dr

---

[2] Hannam had not walked along Trinity Trees, the road in which Kent Lodge was situated, but along Lismore Road at the rear of Kent Lodge where the garages are at the end of the gardens; this was also along Hannam's route to New Inn where he was staying, opposite Police Headquarters.

Adams. The Jury's attention had been drawn to the question 'Have you, so far as you are aware, any pecuniary interest in the death of the deceased?'. Were they now satisfied that this was not a true statement? That on the day of her death he had made a false statement 'with the sinister motive' of having her body cremated as soon as possible. It would be 'a dreadful thing' to convict the Doctor because of 'something filled up on a form like that, and because of something said to a police officer six years later in the dark street in Eastbourne'. He had even put all the details of the nursing she had had and even the addresses of the nurses on the form. One of the nurses, Sister Bartlett (now Hughes) had been interviewed alone by Dr Owen Fox, who could have voiced any suspicions if she had had any.[3] It was only six years later that she had come into the witness-box to give evidence against Dr Adams. Sister Randall had gone off duty before Dr Adams arrived on the morning after the death. 'She got her legacy… If any of the nurses had had suspicions at the time, would they not have voiced them?'

The Court was adjourned for lunch.

Mr Lawrence continued with his theme of the nurses as witnesses to the treatment or the murder, and they had said, effectively with 'one voice' that they had understood the policy and the object of giving Mrs Morrell sleep and preventing her from becoming restless. 'They know the difference between that and murder, do not they? They must, and they must at the time.'

The son, Mr Claude Morrell, had signed the form for the cremation to go ahead; he had seen her 'very shortly' [ten days] before she had died. Mr Lawrence asked the Jury if he would have done so if he had any suspicion about his mother's death. He had allowed the Will 'to be proved as it stood' [i.e. ignoring the codicil] and allowing the gifts to go to Dr Adams. Then Mr Lawrence said something that was quite crucial, yet strange:

> 'Where is Mr Claude Morrell? You may be very sure that in the inquiries conducted by the Crown on this case they have taken a statement from Mr Claude Morrell. It is not for the Defence, as I have said before, to prove innocence or to call any witnesses. We are not bound to.
>
> 'It is for the Prosecution to lay all the facts and to be impartial. Mr Claude Morrell has not been called.'

The answer lies in the evidence not used, but which was in the archives and will be discussed in the aftermath to the trial.

Mr Lawrence reverted to the cremation certificate and Hannam's warning to Dr Adams that to make a false statement on it was a serious offence: it was a serious offence 'if the answer was untrue', and it was 'not the fact of benefit, but the knowledge of the doctor'. The Superintendent had said that he replied 'Oh, that wasn't done wickedly. God knows it wasn't. We always want cremations to go off smoothly for the dear relatives. If I said I knew I was getting money under the Will, they might get suspicious, and I like cremations and burials to go smoothly. There was nothing suspicious really. It wasn't deceitful.' Everything depended 'upon

---

[3] Sister Bartlett was not present at the instant of death, therefore Sister Randall should have been interviewed.

his state of mind from the wording of the question about the Will and what that was at the material time six years ago.'

There was another 'curious episode', Mr Lawrence said, with which he had to deal. This was on the evening of 24th November, 1956 during the search of the Doctor's house for dangerous drugs 'and that was all, strictly, that that police officer [DI Pugh] had any right to be doing.' It was when Pugh was out of the room that the Superintendent had brought up the matter of the prescriptions for Mrs Morrell. The Superintendent had asked Dr Adams to look at the list of prescriptions, saying that there were a lot of dangerous drugs on the list and the Doctor had replied to the question, 'Who administered the drugs', by saying 'I did, nearly all; perhaps the nurses gave some, but mostly me.' It was clear, said Mr Lawrence, that his recollection was wrong because the nurses' notebooks recorded that most were given by the nurses and that he was 'recorded as having given some when he visited morning and evening.' Later, the Superintendent had asked if any were left over when Mrs Morrell died, and Dr Adams had said that he had given them all to the patient. The nurses had given evidence that at least two phials were left over – which Dr Ashby estimated and deducted from the total.

The last prescription on the list, was for 75 one-sixth grain heroin tablets on the 12th November, the day before she died, and the penultimate prescription was for 4 ounces of paraldehyde. Did the Jury think it possible that any of those 75 tablets were given to Mrs Morrell? The Doctor had given a 'special injection' to the patient in the morning and another two injections were given by the nurses in the afternoon. 'It is inconceivable, is not it, that that last prescription, in the circumstances and on the evidence of the nurses' notebooks, was given to Mrs Morrell?' In replying to a further question, Dr Adams had told the Superintendent that 'there might have been a couple of those final tablets left over but I cannot remember', he was surely right that he could not remember after six years. Dr Adams was not to know that she would die so soon after the last prescription and did not know what amounts of morphia and heroin he would require.

Mr Lawrence said that his submission was 'two-fold': the written evidence of the nurses' notebooks was correct and left no room to draw an inference from the prescription list. They had all heard a great deal of expert medical evidence, but what was clear was that there was 'great uncertainty' about how much people could take of narcotic drugs and what was a lethal dose. It was quite impossible to say that the last prescription was all used; Dr Adams must have been mistaken. He just had not known how much he would require. 'Have you ever had bottles of medicine half full, left over? Of course you have.' The point in the case was what had actually been administered. And if anybody was going to say that the 'special injections' must have been morphia and heroin, then it was 'obvious what they were: vitamin injections… the nurse drops writing out "Cytamin" and writes "special injection".' Dr Harris's special injections were vitamin injections, so why should they 'assume to the contrary in the case of Dr Adams'. Dr Douthwaite had said that he had ignored these injections on arriving at his conclusions. None of this could have any relevance when there was actual factual contemporary evidence in the notebooks.

Mr Lawrence passed to Hannam's evidence when he had spoken with Dr Adams in the photographic room of the police station. The Doctor had said that he was 'very worried', and was said to have replied to a question: 'Easing the passing of a dying person is not all that wicked. She wanted to die. That can't be murder. It is impossible to accuse a doctor.' There was 'a world of difference' between giving drugs to shorten life and using them 'to give comfort and quiet at the end.' The words alleged to have been said by Dr Adams were not 'evidence of a murderous intent' and it was 'nothing of the kind if it was said'.

And then on the 19th December when he was arrested at his surgery on the charge of murder, Detective Inspector Pugh had said in evidence that Dr Adams appeared to be stunned by the charge, and 'according to police evidence, he said "Murder?", looking at the Superintendent, "Murder? Can you prove it was murder?" When the Superintendent had said "You are now charged with murdering her", he had reported the accused as replying "I did not think you could prove murder. She was dying in any case".' Mr Lawrence submitted that these were 'incredulous reactions of an innocent man' rather than 'the confessions of a guilty man'. He drew a picture for the Jury of his receptionist giving him his coat and his book, gripping his hands and saying 'something about "See you in heaven".' That was not an admission of murder in such circumstances. But none of this was relevant as it did 'not touch the matter of the medical evidence', which either proved that Mrs Morrell died a natural death or at least raised that 'as a very real possibility'. If they were not 'absolutely satisfied that Dr Adams caused the death of this woman by these drugs', that was a complete end to the case.

If they looked at the books 'if you ever want to see them again', it was clear that the patient was not unconscious or in a coma, but was 'awake, talkative and chattering' during her last days. In the end the case was totally a medical one and the experts they had heard were not in agreement and only Dr Douthwaite postulated murder. The Prosecution had attempted 'to throw some sinister light on a doctor-patient relationship'. This would mean that any professional relationship which evoked 'the gratitude of the sufferer' would be held against a doctor. The case had 'turned and twisted and inverted' a doctor's duty 'into an accusation of murder.'

This case, Mr Lawrence told the Jury, would be 'a memory which will rest with you for the rest of your lives'. He hoped it would not be one that would 'haunt your consciences'. They would hear his voice for the last time in the case, very soon:

> 'If anything that I have said to you today appeals to you, if you think I have said something that is right, if you think, as I submit to you, that there should not be a conviction, be steadfast in that belief to the end, be steadfast and see that a right verdict is reached, which, in my submission to you, can only be one, and that is a verdict of not guilty of murder.'

Mr Lawrence sat down and the Attorney-General rose to give his closing speech for the Crown:

The Prosecution also had a duty to discharge: to put before the Jury, the case as seen by them. Justice was paramount and no-one wanted to see an innocent man convicted, but, if the accused was guilty beyond all reasonable doubt, then it was the responsibility of the Jury to see that justice was done. A doctor was in a position of special trust, and this was a unique case and might also appear to be a difficult one, but he believed that the Jury would be compelled to conclude that Mrs Morrell's death 'was secured by the deliberate acts of the accused'.

It had been established that from July 1948 when Dr Adams had brought Mrs Morrell back to Eastbourne, she was having morphia and heroin. The Defence had 'made a great point of the fact that she had Morphia in the Nursing Home in Cheshire', but what had happened when she had been given morphia for severe pain at that time had no relevance and threw 'no light… on the subsequent events'. His 'learned friend' had suggested in his closing speech that Dr Douthwaite, an authority on morphia and heroin, had attacked the use of heroin, but this was quite unjustified as Dr Douthwaite had answered in his cross-examination that he agreed that opiates and their derivatives were one of the 'greatest blessings conferred on the medical profession'.

There was another similar instance: Mr Lawrence had submitted to the Jury that Dr Harman had shown conclusively that the convulsions described by Sister Randall were not due to heroin, but, in fact, Dr Harman had admitted, after his demonstration of 'jerkings' 'almost falling backwards in the witness box', that if these kind of convulsions had occurred in bed then the patient could have been 'almost jerked out of bed' by them. Just as Sister Randall had said in evidence. Dr Harman's evidence supported the conclusion that Mrs Morrell's convulsions were 'due to heroin and nothing else'.

The Attorney-General returned to 'the beginning of the history': five days after Mrs Morrell returned to Eastbourne, Dr Adams prescribed morphia for her in half grains, with a note on the prescription reading 'repeat in six days', which indicated that she was to have one grain a day 'otherwise why repeat in six days?' The next prescription was on 21st July 1948 and was for heroin and morphia. What was this for? He not only carried on with morphia but increased it and there had been no answer as to why the heroin was added and both drugs carried on from that time onwards. Dr Harman 'nearly fell backwards in his efforts to support and help the Defence, but even Dr Harman could not ascribe a reason for the administration of Heroin with Morphia at that time.' It had been suggested that he had used heroin because he had qualified in the 1920s, but why should it be assumed that he had not kept himself up-to-date particularly as he was still holding two appointments as a hospital anaesthetist? The Jury should not ignore Dr Adams' comment to Superintendent Hannam and Inspector Pugh with regard to opiates: 'I very very seldom use them.' This statement on its own disposed of the theory that he was 'an old-fashioned doctor' used to using these drugs.

There being no medical reason for making Mrs Morrell a drug addict, why did Dr Adams do it? The Attorney-General had a possible explanation. The Prosecution were not suggesting that, at that time, Dr Adams had formed a design to murder, but 'would not the springs of gratitude be likely to be opened if this rich old lady found, despite her stroke, that she was feeling daily remarkably well owing to the injections given her by her doctor, injections of heroin?' If there was no medical justification for the drugging, then what was Dr Adams' object: 'May it not have been with the intention of trying to make this elderly and rich lady, his patient, well disposed towards him with a view to his benefiting under her Will?'

There had certainly been no attempts to wean her off her addiction; even Dr Harman had admitted that if a doctor went on using these drugs, then there might come a time when they were needed and were of no use. Dr Harman had been 'evasive' and some of his answers 'wholly incredible', under cross-examination, to questions about weaning, yet even he had said that if he had been called in, when Mrs Morrell returned to Eastbourne, he would have pointed out the dangers of continuing with morphia and putting her on heroin as well. Despite the fact that Dr Harman had only 'made a special study from the books on heroin and morphia for the purpose of giving evidence in this case' and had little or no experience of treating addicts, he felt able to disagree with Dr Douthwaite, 'whom he admitted was a recognised authority on morphia and heroin'.

It was after 'month after month' of the treatment with heroin and morphia that Mr Sogno, the solicitor, gave evidence that on 28th April, 1949, 'when it may be, you may think, Mrs Morrell's feelings of gratitude had perhaps developed considerably', that Dr Adams had rung up Mr Sogno to say that she wanted to see him urgently about her will. Why was he telephoning? Mrs Morrell was capable of making calls as late as the end of September 1950 to Dr Adams on holiday. This call to Mr Sogno was before the period covered by the nurses' books. The Attorney-General commented on them:

> 'Now, it was with considerable surprise, was it not, that those books were introduced in the course of this case? This is the first time, Members of the Jury, that I have had an opportunity of making any observations to you or to my Lord upon those books. It has been said by my learned friend more than once, and I quote his actual words used today, "In these books lie the whole case."
>
> Now, Members of the Jury, that is not the submission of the Prosecution. That is not the submission of the Prosecution. It would be extraordinary, would it not, if you think of it for one moment, if the case for the Prosecution depended on documents produced in evidence by the Defence for the purpose of establishing innocence?
>
> But just let me say a few things about these books. Where did they come from? Where did they come from? They are no doubt genuine. The nurses identify their handwriting. They told you that they are usually destroyed after the patient has died. But these books have been kept from 1950 until 1957. Who kept them? Who had an interest in keeping them? There is only one person, is not there? Dr Adams. He is the only doctor who attended Mrs Morrell. Now, in 1957, Mrs Morrell having died in 1950, these books are produced by the Defence.'

Dr Adams had been asked by Superintendent Hannam whether he had any medical records for Mrs Morrell and he had said that he kept none of prescriptions, only visits, 'perhaps not that for private patients' and that even the card was destroyed after one year. So was it not 'extraordinary' that these books should have been preserved. 'Why? Might it not have been thought that at some time or other some inquiry, such as we have been engaged upon for some weeks, might arise?' Dr Adams had known that the nurses kept reports.

'Just consider one other thing. Just consider for a moment that Dr Adams knew that these reports were being kept and also formed a design for murder. If that were the case, he would take the greatest care possible, would not he, to secure that any entries put by the nurses in those books were not obviously incriminating him, not obviously showing or revealing the design which he formed? He would try, would not he, so to arrange things that the entries in the books would not look too bad?'

The Attorney-General asked why the books were 'kept until 1957 and his own records destroyed'. But the Prosecution's case did not 'depend on those books alone', the case he had opened was based upon the nurses' recollections, on the prescriptions, 'which were made out by Dr Adams and supplied' and on Dr Adams' own statements. After Sister Stronach had given evidence of what she remembered, the books were produced and it was not surprising that there were 'disparities in one or two respects', but the nurses' recollections of what had happened 'were supported by the entries they made in the books.'

The Prosecution did not challenge the entries in the books:

> 'I do not challenge either the accuracy of the entries they have made in relation to Dr Adams' prescriptions being accurate statements of what he told them that he had injected. They were never in the room when he injected them. He was always alone. He got the drugs out of his own bag. The only person in those circumstances from whom they could get information as to what he had injected was Dr Adams.'

The books were true 'as far as they go, but they do not reveal the whole truth'. They did not reveal at all what the 'special injections' were. Mr Lawrence had asked them to assume that they were all vitamin injections because some Cytamin injections were recorded, but 'a special injection was an injection of which the nurses did not know the ingredients' and all of them were not necessarily the same. 'Is not the correct view that a special injection was the entry made when the nurses were not told what had been injected?'

The main object of nurses' records was for one nurse to inform the next nurse on duty of what had been happening so far as she knew. It was known from Dr Harris' evidence that the nurses' records were not accurate because they did not recall all his visits to the patient. The Jury should remember that on each of Dr Adams' visits he had required a glass of hot water, and Dr Ashby had said that this could only indicate the use of a syringe for an injection.

The Attorney-General reminded the Jury that there was a significant difference between the doses recorded in the notebooks and the prescriptions: the graphs revealed the difference. It was clear that 'all the prescriptions given by Dr Adams to Mrs Morrell were made up'. They had all been supplied by the chemists but they did not all go to 'Marden Ash'. The paraldehyde, for instance, had been prescribed for Mrs Morrell but Dr Adams had filled the syringe from his bag: both Sister Bartlett and Sister Randall had given evidence that they had not got it in the house. When the syringe was used at 10.30 p.m. Sister Randall had to take the empty syringe back to him and he filled it again. Why would he have done that if that prescription had been delivered to the house? Some of the prescriptions must have been collected by, or delivered to Dr Adams himself. Confirming this were the prescriptions (serial numbers 86 and 87) supplied on 9th November: the day report for that day showed that these prescriptions of heroin and morphia, the exact quantities of doses, were left by Dr Adams with the nurses. This indicated that some prescriptions did go straight to Dr Adams and were the source of the drugs which came from his bag, and it could be inferred from this that the difference in amounts between what was recorded in the books and what was prescribed 'passed into Dr Adams' possession, and was the source from which he took the drugs he himself administered.'

Did this not also account for the difference in the drugs recorded as administered in the last days of November in the nurses' books and the amounts prescribed? It also confirmed what Dr Adams had told Superintendent Hannam about his having used most of the drugs when he was shown the prescription list. This statement held 'the key to account for the mysterious disappearance of drugs which were prescribed and which are not shown as administered in the day reports.'

The Attorney-General submitted that the nurses' reports should be accepted 'as true records of what the nurses themselves gave, as true records of what Dr Adams told the nurses he gave – which might be a very different thing from what he actually gave -, as a true record of Mrs Morrell's condition', but not, by any means, containing the whole truth.

He wanted to remind the Jury of what Dr Adams had said to Superintendent Hannam when he had been asked who had administered the drugs: he had said, 'I did, nearly all. Perhaps the nurses gave some, but mostly me.' If they looked at the contrast between what was recorded by the nurses from 8th November onwards, and the amounts actually prescribed, they would find that the notebooks supported Dr Adams' statement. Again, he had said: 'All was given to the patient.' and on being shown the final prescriptions: 'Mrs Morrell had all those because I gave the injections'. The evidence proved that all the prescriptions were supplied and that those not used by the nurses were used by Dr Adams on Mrs Morrell.

> 'Now, if that were so, the nurses did not know, did they, throughout the whole period the full extent of the morphia and heroin that Dr Adams was giving. They would not be able to tell Dr Harris when he took over for a short time the full extent of the heroin and morphia that Dr Adams was giving.'

Dr Harris had slightly increased what the nurses were giving, but if that were less than the actual total Mrs Morrell was getting from Dr Adams this might explain 'her getting into such a state that she rings up Dr Adams and secures his return from Scotland.'

The Attorney-General reiterated to the Jury that the Prosecution's case did not depend on the notebooks, but on 'more weighty evidence' which pointed conclusively to the guilt of the accused. The case for the Crown still rested partly, but not wholly, on the prescriptions 'which would not be given by a doctor unless he intended to use them.'

The Court was adjourned until the following Monday, 8th April.

––

# Sixteenth Day

The Attorney-General resumed his closing speech: in his review of the case, he had reached the time when the nurses' reports began, the 21st June, 1949, almost a year after Mrs Morrell's stroke. She had no use of her left arm and leg, and some degree of cerebral arterio sclerosis, but apart from that there was no evidence that she suffered from any other condition. Dr Douthwaite and Dr Ashby had agreed that her expectation of life at this point had increased to several years and Dr Harman, in dealing with the period ending in April 1950, had said there was no evidence of further deterioration, and that it was 'not unreasonable to suppose that she might have lived until 1954', yet 7½ months later, she was dead.

> 'Well now, during this period covered by the blue book, the 20th June 1949 to the 6th April 1950, she was getting barbiturates, and we can see from these reports she was getting plenty of them. She was getting not only the normal dose of Morphia, ¼ grain, but on top of that and on top of the barbiturates she was getting usually twice the normal dose of Heroin.'

Mrs Morrell had certainly been getting plenty of drugs. The Attorney-General reminded the Jury that it was on 8th March, 1950, just before the blue book started, that Dr Adams called on Mr Sogno, the solicitor, saying that Mrs Morrell was very ill, and told him that Mrs Morrell had promised him many months ago, the Rolls Royce, and now remembered that she had forgotten to put it in her Will, and that she also wanted him to have the contents of a case containing jewellery which was in a locked box in the bank. Mr Sogno had suggested that the matter wait until Mr Morrell, the son, came at the weekend, but Dr Adams said that Mrs Morrell 'was very uneasy and wanted to get the matter off her mind'. Mr Sogno had suggested that Dr Adams should pretend to take the case of jewellery and hand it back to the nurse, but he replied that she 'seriously wanted him to enjoy the gifts'.

> 'What would a bachelor want from that apart from its value? Then Doctor Adams went on to make what, in my submission to you, was an astonishing suggestion, that a codicil should be prepared and properly executed and then torn up if Mr Morrell did not approve. That shows, does it not, Members of the Jury, quite clearly that Doctor Adams was not prepared to wait for the week-end, not prepared to wait for Mr Morrell's arrival, but he wanted that done immediately.'

It was clear from the nurses' reports for August 1950, when Mrs Morrell was walking in the garden, that she was not very ill then, so if Dr Adams had told Mr Sogno the truth, then she had made 'a very considerable recovery'. The will was executed on 24th August, leaving the chest of silver, the Rolls Royce and the court cupboard to Dr Adams. 'Whether Doctor Adams hoped for more we do not know.'

In September, Dr Adams went on holiday and Dr Harris took over and it was 'quite obvious and natural that he would follow the instructions given by his partner, Doctor Adams, Mrs Morrell's regular doctor'. The Defence had attached great weight to the fact that he carried on the drug regime, as though it were 'a second opinion, if one had been called in, but a second opinion was never taken'. In the Attorney-General's submission, no weight should be attached to the fact that Dr Harris carried on with the drugs and added some Omnopon. Now he asked an interesting question:

> 'Why was Mrs Morrell so angry at Doctor Adams going on holiday? Why did she react so violently?... Mrs Morrell had had these drugs by September 1950 for a long time. Was Mrs Morrell getting the additional quantity to overcome her acquired tolerance from Doctor Adams without the nurses knowing? If she was that would account for the difference between the nurses' books and the prescriptions supplied at that time. And if that was what had happened, and Doctor Harris only carried on with what the nurses were giving, wouldn't you get the withdrawal symptoms, the craving, of which the doctors speak?'

There was no doubt that Mrs Morrell was very angry because she executed the codicil cutting Dr Adams out of her will. There was no suggestion that she was very ill as she herself telephoned to Dr Adams, and he came flying back from Scotland, certainly not because of her ill health. 'But was it to look after his own interests? In September all the nurses say that Mrs Morrell was going downhill. Why? Why?'

Dr Douthwaite had said that the regular doses of opiates would be likely to affect her health, and Dr Ashby had said that they would be bound to shorten her life and that she should be weaned. Dr Harman had said that this weaning process might well lead to the loss of a rich patient. The process was never attempted. At first he had said that the drugs were 'not necessarily bad for the patient's health', but then admitted bad side effects and eventually agreed that he had no idea what the effects of this long drugging were on old people.

The next date of importance was the 9th October, 1950, which was the day report which contained the question mark with 'stroke' written after it, and Sister Bartlett's call to Dr Adams when he had suggested that diagnosis over the 'phone. Dr Harman had expressed the opinion that the notebook entries suggested a stroke, but Mrs Morrell's collapse had followed immediately after a 'special injection'. Dr Harman had also assumed that all 'special injections' were vitamin injections. He had also said that he would have visited if he thought a patient had had a stroke. Dr Adams did not visit.

> 'Why was that? He obviously had to say something to the nurse. He could hardly be expected to tell her, could he, 'Well, I expect I gave her too much morphia and heroin'? Surely it is very surprising that she would have had a stroke immediately after a special injection, and, if he really believed that she had had a stroke, that he did not visit her?'

In the reports of 26th and 27th October, there were no injections of heroin and morphia recorded, but there were special injections. It followed logically that, if the nurses had given such injections, then they were not recorded and the records were incomplete, but if they were complete and heroin and morphia were given then they were given in the 'special injections' recorded. If the heroin and morphia had been omitted on these days, then there would have been withdrawal symptoms, but there was nothing in the reports that looked anything like a withdrawal symptom – quite the opposite: her being semi-comatosed, and confused upon waking. What was to be concluded?

> 'Surely, it must be this: either that the reports were inaccurate in not recording what the nurses did – and I would not suggest that – or that the special injections on those two days were of heroin and morphia.'

The Attorney-General had now arrived at the beginning of 'the really vital period in this case', the 31st October: the day on which Dr Adams had withdrawn the morphia and omnopon and given instructions to given three-sixths of a grain of heroin at night and one-third during the day 'S.O.S.'. 'Why was that done?' He did not suggest that the reports showed that the patient was getting better at this time, but if she was getting worse, then why stop the main sedatives? It was puzzling; it puzzled Dr Douthwaite. He had expressed the opinion that the doses from the 8th November onwards were given with the intention of terminating life: Dr Adams' instructions were to give half a grain of heroin hourly, rising to one grain of heroin hourly if necessary. Dr Douthwaite had said that 'he had done his utmost to find an innocent explanation, but that he was forced to the conclusion that those drugs were given to her with the intention of terminating life.' Dr Douthwaite had never changed his opinion as to the cause of death, but he had finally come to the conclusion that there was something significant about the stopping of the morphia and omnopon.

There was a very important entry on the 3rd November: Dr Adams gave instructions in the morning that Mrs Morrell was to have one sedormid tablet and no more until after Mr Morrell's visit at 5.30 p.m. 'as Dr Adams wished Mrs Morrell to be clear mentally'.

> 'It is clear beyond doubt, is it not, from that entry, that Dr Adams at that time, the 3rd November, only ten days before Mrs Morrell's death, thought that the drugs she was having then were the cause of her confusion, her mental confusion. It is clear beyond doubt, is not it, that so late as the 3rd November that was Dr Adams's view. If the cause of mental confusion at that time had been senile decay the confusion would not have been stopped, would it, by the withholding of sedormid and other drugs. If the drugging was the cause of her mental confusion, what a light that throws on the entries as to confusion and the conduct of Dr Adams towards Mrs Morrell.'

The Attorney-General mentioned that 'his learned friend' had complained that Mr Morrell had not been called by the Crown: if he had thought it relevant, then there was nothing to stop his calling Mr Morrell as a Defence witness. The 3rd November was the last time he had seen his mother alive 'days after she had had special treatment – the withholding of drugs for his visit 'as Dr Adams wished her to be clear mentally.' '

He had now come to the 6th November: apart from the 9th November when Mrs Morrell had asked for 'yellow tablets' and been given three Allonal, the routine administration of barbiturates had ceased.

> 'Why was that? Why was that? First the morphia and the Omnopon stopped,
> then the barbiturates.'

Normally it would be a sign of a patient's condition improving. One consequence of barbiturates was that they 'would mask the effect, the exciting effect, the restlessness, due to heroin'. On the evening of 6th November a quarter of a grain of morphia was reintroduced, and apart from this she had two injections in the daytime of half a grain of morphia each. There had been only two entries relating to daytime administration of morphia and heroin prior to this. The first of these was 20th to 22nd June, 1949, and the other given by Dr Harris on 12th September, 1950. Daytime injections were recorded on 7th and 8th November, on the 9th November there were two 'special injections' during the daytime, and on 10th November, at 8 a.m. hyperduric morphia, at 1.45 p.m. a special injection and one grain of heroin at 6.30 p.m.

The Attorney-General submitted that by the day report of 10th November it was 'quite clearly established that the policy then was to keep Mrs Morrell drugged day and night' – each time she awoke she was given another injection. Sister Randall in her re-examination had told him that the policy was then 'to keep her under'. This evidence was 'amply substantiated by the reports'. He had taken the Jury through the reports to see whether there was any shortage of sleep, which was the reason put forward by the Defence for the amount of drugs administered to her.

The Defence proposed another theory: that these drugs were given 'to ease the distress of a dying woman'. Did these reports show that Mrs Morrell was 'in terrible agony' or that death was imminent? No one would have complained of the use of these drugs in such an instance. But all the nurses had said that she did not suffer any severe pain, or even 'the most dreadful discomfort'. Even as late as the 9th November, Mrs Morrell had sat out in her chair for nearly an hour.

> 'Why, then was she drugged during the day of the 10th? …Why was it done? Why was
> she given on the 10th 1 grain of morphia and 4 of heroin, on the 11th 3½ grains of mor-
> phia and 5 of heroin, and on the 12th 2 of morphia and 3½ of heroin? And she would
> have had more – would she not? – on the accused's instructions, if those injections had
> not sufficed to keep her under.'

It had been Dr Douthwaite's and Dr Ashby's opinions that the only result could have been the death of Mrs Morrell; that she could not have survived the pressure of such drugging. Even Dr Harman had agreed that the reports showed 'a change of policy', and that half a grain of heroin was 'pretty sizable'. The only conclusion that could be drawn was 'that it was done to cause the death of Mrs Morrell'.

Sister Randall had given evidence of the convulsions that Mrs Morrell had towards the end of her life: that she 'had seen nothing like it when persons died of strokes and senile decay'. Both Dr Douthwaite and Dr Ashby had said that 'those jerky spasms were convulsions due to heroin'. There could be no doubt that they were due to large doses of heroin. 'Yet now my learned friend invites you to come to the conclusion that she died from natural causes.'

What was the evidence with regard to coma? Sister Randall had said that Mrs Morrell was 'in a coma, then would come out gradually and then perhaps go in again' and that she had been in this condition for two or three days. Later she had called it 'a sleep like a coma'. Sister Hughes (formerly Bartlett) had said that she was 'sort of semi-comatose' and thought she was having a lot of drugs. Whether the condition was described as 'coma, semicomatose' or 'heavily drugged sleep', it was really much the same condition, and what would be expected following large injections of opiates. He reminded the Jury of the evidence of Miss Dockerill, which had been read out to them: 'Mrs Morrell's maid – who swore in evidence that she was not called upon to give in this court that she saw Mrs Morrell the day before she died and that Mrs Morrell lay there with no movement at all.'

The Attorney-General came to the night of 12th/13th November:

> 'At half-past ten Dr Adams comes. It is the last time that he sees his patient alive. He brings with him a 5 c.c. syringe; he fills it three-quarters full; he gives it to Nurse Randall and she injects it; she brings it back; he fills it again three-quarters full and he gives Nurse Randall instructions as to what to do. Then, after he has gone, these terrible jerkings begin.'

He reminded the Jury of what Sister Randall had said: 'I just ran to the 'phone. I did not want to give another if I could help it. It was too soon, I thought.' Dr Adams had, curiously, left the injection, but no address for the nurse to get in touch with him. 'When she rang him at his home he was out, and she gave the injection, as she was instructed to, and shortly after that Mrs Morrell died.' She had later rung him again and told him that the patient had died after she had given her that last injection. She was due to go off duty at 9 a.m. and she waited until 10 a.m. for Dr Adams, who had not come, and so she went.

> 'He comes later. He fills in the cremation form and he says there that the immediate cause of death – the immediate cause – was cerebral thrombosis. There is no indication of that – is there? – in the nurses' reports. He says there that she was in a coma for two hours before her death. There is nothing on the form about those last injections, nothing about Nurse Randall's telephone call, about what had happened after she had given the last injection.'

Mr Lawrence had been right in telling the Jury that the burden of proof rested upon the prosecution 'but that burden of proof is not the burden of proving with absolute certainty, it is the burden of proving beyond all reasonable doubt.' In any murder case it might be said that, if the victim did not die immediately, then there was a possibility of dying from natural causes, but in this case, to ignore the large doses of opiates, the convulsions and the injections of paraldehyde just before Mrs Morrell's death would be 'to ignore the obvious. In my submission on the evidence, it is proved beyond reasonable doubt that the cause of Mrs Morrell's death was the administration of these drugs.' Dr Ashby had explained what he meant by saying that the terminal cause of death might be 'natural': that keeping an old person in bed, drugged, would cause pulmonary congestion and increased respiration: pneumonia and death.

In the Attorney-General's submission, bringing about pneumonia and death by drugging did not mean that death was due to natural causes, it meant that the cause of death was the administration of the drugs: 'morphia and heroin, accelerated by Paraldehyde'. He asked the Jury to examine the nurses' books carefully:

> 'They were put in by the Defence to aid the defence. They provided plenty of material for argument and discussion. We have seen that in this case, when carefully examined my submission is that the entries in those books support, and do not destroy the case for the Prosecution.'

The case for the Defence had changed: first it was said that the drugs were to secure sleep for Mrs Morrell and then that they were 'to ease her passing'. These were opposing theories and not consistent with each other. Were there any grounds for saying that the drugs were given 'just to ease passing'? The nurses did not speak of any terrible agony or discomfort, but of her being semi-comatose. The policy of 'keeping her under' was to be kept on until she died, presumably. After Mrs Morrell's death, Sister Bartlett had handed one phial of morphia and one of heroin to Dr Adams.

> 'We know that all Doctor Adams prescribed was supplied by the chemists. If all that was supplied by the chemists had gone to Marden Ash to the nurses, much more than one phial of morphia and one phial of heroin or omnopon would have been left over, wouldn't it? That is clear, isn't it?'

The nurses had been most careful with the dangerous drugs and kept a record of exactly what they had used. Dr Adams had used drugs from his bag. 'Did he pay for them himself? The probability is, surely, that he made out a prescription for the drugs he used himself, and either collected those drugs from the chemists or had them delivered to him.' This was confirmed by the prescription for paraldehyde on 12th November, for instance, when the nurses had none, and the two prescriptions of 9th November which had been left at the house. If the amounts prescribed had been administered, or the greater part of them, then Doctors Douthwaite and Ashby had said that she could not have survived them, and even Dr Harman thought it 'would be a remarkable thing' if she had done so.

The case for the Prosecution did not end there, said the Attorney-General. On 1st October, 1956, Superintendent Hannam saw Dr Adams. The codicil revoking the bequest to Dr Adams had been torn up, although legally this did not revive the bequest, 'but did Dr Adams know that?' He received the chest and the Rolls Royce after Mrs Morrell's death. It was inconceivable that Dr Adams would have made the statement he did: 'Mrs Morrell was a very dear patient, she insisted a long time before she died that I should have that in her memory. I don't [sic] want it. I am a bachelor. I have never used it. I knew she was going to leave it to me and her Rolls Royce car. She told me she had put them in her will. Oh yes, and another cabinet.'

> 'Surely he could not have said that if he had known that they came to him, not under the will but as gifts from Mr Morrell. Surely if he had known that that was not the kind of thing he would have been likely to forget.'

Again, his answer when he was reminded of the answer he had given on the cremation form: 'That was not done wickedly. God knows it wasn't. We always want cremations to go off smoothly for the dear relatives. If I said I knew I was getting money under the will they might get suspicious and I like cremations and burials to go smoothly. There was nothing suspicious really. It wasn't deceitful.'

> 'He could not have said that, could he, if he had known the legal position, if he had known the real effect of tearing up a codicil?'

If he did not know, then the position was that Mrs Morrell, made a drug addict by him, executed a will which benefited him 'but perhaps not as much as he had hoped….by securing her death may he have thought, if he did not know the legal effect of tearing up the codicil, that he was at least making sure of getting what she had left.' As for 'wanting the cremation to go smoothly', if he had killed her he had an obvious reason: 'no possibility of a Post Mortem or of discovering how much Heroin and Morphia there was in her body.'

The Attorney-General now came to the interview with Hannam on 24th November when the search for dangerous drugs at Kent Lodge had taken place. When the warrant was read out Dr Adams had said: 'There are no dangerous drugs here. What do you mean by dangerous drugs?' 'Surely a general practitioner would know Morphia was a dangerous drug under the Act?' Then, of 'morphine, heroin, pethedine and the like', he had said: 'Oh that group. You will find none here. I haven't any. I very seldom ever use them.' Bottles of hyperduric morphia were found in his surgery. The Attorney-General reminded the jury again that Dr Adams had said that he had administered nearly all the drugs to Mrs Morrell. According to the nurses' reports, from 8th November onwards, 10½ grains of morphia and 16 of heroin were injected and the difference between these amounts and those prescribed was considerable. Dr Adams had told Superintendent Hannam that it was all used and none was left over. Even when his attention was drawn specifically to the prescription of 12th November for 75 one-sixth grains of heroin (12½ grains), he had said: 'Poor soul, she was in terrible agony. It was all used. I used them myself.'

'An injection of 12½ grains is not shown in the records of the 12th of November, but a special injection is. One would not expect, would one, at that stage, knowing what the policy was then, that a special injection was being given at that time to wake her up?'

Then Superintendent Hannam had run his finger down the list of last prescriptions from the 8th November onwards, and Dr Adams had said: 'There might have been a couple of those final tablets left over, but I cannot remember. If there were, I would take them and destroy them. I am not dishonest with drugs. Mrs Morrell had all those because I gave the injections. Do you think it was too much?' The Defence had stressed that everything had happened six years before, but Dr Adams could have said that he did not remember, but he did not, he gave specific answers. 'Then why should Dr Adams in those circumstances make these statements if he did not remember? Why should he make them if they were not true?'

'Even if you omit the last prescription, was not there enough and more than enough to kill her prescribed since the 8th? Why did he prescribe on the 9th November more heroin and morphia if the supply procured on the 8th was not used up or almost used up? Why did he prescribe more on the 10th if the supply provided on the 8th and 9th had not been used or almost entirely used? Why again on the 11th if in the earlier days the supplies had not been used up or almost used, and why again on the 12th?'

The fact that Dr Adams did collect or have delivered to him some of the prescriptions was proved in the nurse's day report of 9th November and by the paraldehyde which he had brought with him on the 12th. The Jury could, therefore, safely conclude that all the amounts prescribed were administered to Mrs Morrell.

There had been some criticism, said the Attorney-General, about the fact that Superintendent Hannam and Sergeant Hewett had, upon occasion, used the same notebook. He referred the Jury to words used 'by the present Lord Chief Justice [Lord Goddard] in the case of Bass (37 C.A.R., p.51)' in dealing with police officers' notes, that it was 'natural and proper' that they should 'make sure they have a correct version of what was said' by writing the report together. There could be no criticism of the two officers making sure they had an accurate record.

Superintendent Hannam had given evidence of a conversation he had with Dr Adams, which the Defence had suggested had not taken place. Dr Adams had said: 'Easing the passing of a dying person isn't all that wicked. She wanted to die.' 'That is no justification, is it, for terminating a patient's life?' Then he had said: 'That can't be murder. It is impossible to accuse a doctor.'

The Attorney-General wished to refer to just one more statement of Dr Adams. This was made when he was arrested and charged with Mrs Morrell's murder, and was it, as the Defence had suggested 'the incredulous reaction of an innocent man',

'…or was it the sort of statement a shaken man might make, a shaken man who had committed a murder which he thought could not be proved? What he said was this:

"Murder. Murder. Can you prove it was murder? I didn't think you could prove murder. She was dying in any event."[4]

Members of the Jury, in my submission to you, on the evidence that has been called before you, when properly considered, on the inferences which can be properly considered, on the inferences which can properly and legitimately be draw from that evidence, murder in this case has been proved, and proved beyond all reasonable doubt; and it is for these reasons that I submit to you that the proper verdict in this case is one of "Guilty".'

The Attorney-General had finished his closing speech, but Mr Justice Devlin had a few points on his address which he wished clarified: was there any direct evidence that drugs had been collected and received by Dr Adams? The Attorney-General reiterated that the report of the 9th November showed that Dr Adams had delivered to the nurses the same amounts of drugs which he had prescribed, and he had drawn an inference regarding the paraldehyde. Was there any evidence that drugs were delivered to his house? The Attorney-General referred the judge to the evidence of Mr Gibson (Day 6, p.19), that he had delivered packages to Kent Lodge on behalf of Browne's Chemists, but no evidence of what was in the parcels. There was evidence that the paraldehyde and all the prescriptions were dispensed, and of what was left over. If all the drugs had gone to the nurses much more would have been left over than the two phials. There was also 'corroboration of the entries where those drugs must have come from the chemist into Dr Adams' possession.' There was also the probability that, as it was known that Dr Adams was using drugs out of his own bag on Mrs Morrell, that 'he would not use his own drugs if drugs prescribed were available.' The Judge did not know what the medical position was, and asked if a doctor 'was entitled to have supplies of these drugs in his possession'. If this were so, then he supposed he might 'use them on a patient and cover it by the fees that he ultimately renders.' The Attorney-General could not answer the question.

# Summing Up

Mr Justice Devlin addressed the Jury: they had had 'a long, an exceptionally long, and laborious task' and their responsibility was no light one. He would tell them, firstly, the principles of law 'which you must take from me without question and apply them', and he would then assist them to arrive 'at a just determination on the facts'. If he himself expressed any opinion, as he might well do, then this was 'for your assistance only; you can accept it or reject it just as you like, and you are not absolved from your responsibility because I express a view one way or the other. You can give it, in short, what weight you please.' [This last quotation is underlined by Hannam.] He would try and give 'the headlines' and 'the framework' of the evidence, and 'sift the essential from the inessential' for them, and then concentrate on the important points.

[4] This is reminiscent of John George Haigh's response when accused of murder: 'How can you prove murder if there is no body?'

The Judge began with the law: there were four matters of law and the first was the definition of 'murder'.

> 'Murder is an act or series of acts done by the prisoner which were intended to kill and did in fact kill the dead woman. It does not matter for this purpose that her death was inevitable and her days were numbered. If her life was cut short by weeks or months it is just as much murder as if it was cut short by years.'

They had heard a great deal of discussion about circumstances in which doctors might be justified in giving drugs which would shorten life: severe pain, helpless misery, but the law knew of 'no special defence of this character'. However, a doctor was 'entitled to do all that is proper and necessary to relieve pain and suffering, even if the measures he takes may incidentally shorten life.' That was not because there was 'any special defence for medical men; it is not because doctors are put into any different category from other citizens for this purpose. The law is the same for all.' There were cases in hospital every day where doctors were giving treatment: administering a drug or not doing so, which might prolong or shorten life 'by hours, or perhaps even longer', but 'no people of common sense would say, "Oh, that doctor caused her death", the proper medical treatment would be incidental to the illness or accident which caused her death.'

> 'But it remains the fact, members of the jury, and it remains the law, that no doctor, nor any man, no more in the case of the dying than of the healthy, has the right deliberately to cut the thread of life. That is plain, and I say it to you so that there may be no mistake.'

Mr Lawrence had been most careful not to say that Dr Adams had any such right, he had been saying that the treatment given by Dr Adams to Mrs Morrell was 'designed to promote comfort'. [The last underlined by Hannam] If that was the right treatment, then 'if it be the fact – that incidentally it shortened her life does not give any grounds for convicting him of murder. And that is so.'

The second matter of law was that it was for the Judge to say whether there was any evidence on a particular point; it was only when there was evidence then the jury would be required to determine questions of fact upon it. It was for this reason that Mr Lawrence had submitted at one point that there was no evidence at all and therefore no case to answer. Mr Justice Devlin said that he had decided that point against him. They had heard from the Attorney-General that there were 'various ways..of putting the prosecution in this case', and if there was no evidence for the jury's consideration on any one of them, it was the Judge's duty to direct them. He then gave his crucial direction:

> 'I do, therefore, direct you as a matter of law that there is no evidence upon which you could properly come to the conclusion that any drugs were administered to Mrs Morrell

over and above the injections recorded in the nurses' books; and if, therefore, the case for the prosecutor had rested solely upon the prescription lists and the suggestion that the quantity that was shown in the prescription lists had been administered to Mrs Morrell, I should not have allowed the case to go to you at all; I should have said that there was no evidence that you could properly consider and upon which you could properly return a verdict of guilty.'

The third matter of law was an obvious one, had been mentioned several times before, but was of particular importance in this trial: that they should consider only the evidence which had been put before them in the court and disregard anything else that they had read or heard. This also led Mr Justice Devlin to comment upon the desirability of committal hearings before the magistrates being heard in private rather than in public.

'There is power – there always has been power and the power was recently re-enacted by the Magistrates Courts Act of 1952 – for them to hold proceedings in private; and I should like to say this – and I say it with the approval and authority of the Lord Chief Justice, for it is not desirable that on matters of this sort judges should express what are merely their personal views – I think it would have been wiser in this case if these preliminary proceedings before the magistrates had been held in private, because when you have a case of this character, which arouses widespread discussion, it is inevitable that reports should appear in the press – and, as I reminded you at the very beginning of this case, the proceedings before the magistrates may be quite different from the proceedings as they emerge in this court – and that they should be read by people who subsequently have to serve on the jury.'

It had become an almost universal practice for preliminary hearing to be heard in public, but it should be remembered that 'these preliminary proceedings were designed, and were first laid down in the Act of 1848, for the benefit of the accused', and, that they turned out to be prejudicial, would be most unfortunate. The words from the 1848 Act which allowed privacy should always be considered '…if it appear to them that the ends of justice will be best answered by so doing'.

Mr Justice Devlin was confident that the Jury would have learned to distinguish between real evidence and mere suspicion and gossip within the three weeks that they had been engaged upon this case.

The fourth matter of law was that the burden of proof was on the prosecution: they had to prove the guilt of the prisoner beyond any reasonable doubt, and it was not for the prisoner to prove his innocence.

'The accused, as he sits there in the dock, and as he has been sitting there in the dock for three weeks, sits there as an innocent man, as innocent as anyone else in this court, and will so remain until you by your verdict have convicted him of guilt. And that has its practical application, and that is that because he is a doctor who attended his patient and is said, in the course of that attendance, to have murdered her, he has the right to be treated as any other doctor would be treated. You must look upon him in the beginning of your enquiry just as you would look upon Dr Douthwaite, Dr Ashby or Dr Harman, any of the three of them who have come into the witness box, and ask yourselves whether it is likely that a doctor would murder his patient.

Dr Adams sitting there has the right, so to speak, of the advantage of what I may call the initial incredulity which any assertion of that sort, that a doctor has murdered his patient, would give rise to in the mind of the ordinary man. He has the right to begin that way, and the prosecution, building up their case bit by bit as they have sought to do, must demolish that and must drive you to the conclusion, however unlikely it may have seemed at the beginning, that Dr Adams did in fact murder Mrs Morrell.'

And the term 'reasonable doubt' meant 'a cool, sane, reasonable doubt'; this Rule of Evidence had been designed for the benefit of the accused. Satisfaction on the balance of probabilities was insufficient, which meant that, in some cases, criminals would walk free; this was not a jury's responsibility. There might be other evidence a jury would wish to see but under the Rule of Law they could not do so. These were 'Rules which have been well settled by generations of experience' and accorded 'with our notions of how Justice should be administered… The price of making sure that the innocent are not convicted must be that the guilty will sometimes go free.'

There was one other aspect of the Rules of Evidence, upon which Mr Justice Devlin spoke: 'What is not evidence is what you might think Doctor Adams might or might not have said if he had gone into the witness box.' To return a verdict of 'guilty' they must have proof according to the Law.

There was a practical aspect of the duty of the Prosecution to prove the case beyond all reasonable doubt, and there were 'unusual features about this case' as there were not two conflicting sets of evidence 'because there has been virtually no dispute about the questions of fact'. There was not only direct evidence but indirect evidence they could use by drawing an inference and applying the 'reasonable doubt' rule. If something was 'a reasonable possibility', it followed that the Prosecution could not have satisfied them beyond a reasonable doubt. Where it was very difficult for the jury in this case was where there was a conflict of opinion between medical experts. As they, the jury, were 'not a board of medical assessors', then they had to deal with this in the same way as they would in ordinary life, that is, on their own judgment. 'You would ask yourselves which of the doctors inspired the greatest or greater confidence in you.' They might ask many questions and judge their opinions 'but in the end you would have to make up your mind as to which was the more likely to be right.' They had heard Dr Harman criticised by the Attorney-General about some of his unsatisfactory answers and Dr Douthwaite criticised by Mr Lawrence on the basis that he was a man who 'jumps to conclusions' and 'forms an opinion from which he is reluctant to part.' The clear inference was that the Jury should have most confidence in the evidence of Dr Ashby.

The Judge also pointed out that, unusually, in this case the Prosecution had 'to rely upon their medical evidence to establish the very act of murder' – in most cases medical evidence was 'only ancillary' and played a minor part in a case.

The other unusual feature of the case was 'that the accused himself has not gone into the witness-box', so there was no evidence from him. It was perhaps natural for most people, and perhaps lawyers too, 'to say: 'Well, why has not he gone into the witness-box if he was an innocent man? He was the doctor who was attending the patient throughout. He can tell us more about this than anybody else can. Why has not he gone into the witness-box, unless he thinks that it may be that questions will be put to him that he could not satisfactorily answer?' Mr Lawrence had already told them that it was on his advice that Dr Adams would not go into the witness-box. Dr Adams had the right not to do so, but it was a matter of law and it would be 'utterly wrong if you were to regard Dr Adams' silence as contributing in any way towards proof of guilt.' If a prisoner did go into the witness-box it was solely in his own defence. He was, of course, 'a potential witness for the Defence, a man who can throw light, or might be able to throw light upon the matters which you have to try', but the Prosecution were not able to call Dr Adams, not allowed to do so. The Jury were not permitted to speculate 'either in his favour or against him'.

As a practical illustration, Mr Justice Devlin alluded to the police evidence and that it had been suggested to police witnesses, in cross-examination, that words attributed to Dr Adams might not have been used by him; the jury might have expected to decide these matters after they had heard Dr Adams' evidence, but they could not now do so. They had to decide the matter without 'the potential evidence for the Defence'. If they reached the conclusion that the Prosecution had proved its case 'subject to hearing Dr Adams', then the Prosecution had proved its case. The jury were 'not entitled to invent explanations for Dr Adams which he might have given himself, but has not given.' The burden of proof was still on the Prosecution 'and it is not altered in any way by the fact that Dr Adams has not been called.'

> ' – if at the end of the Prosecution's case your attitude had been "They have proved their case provisionally, but of course we suspend judgment and keep an open mind until we have heard what Dr Adams says", then that provisional proof is now complete. That judgment that was suspended can now be final.'

The Court was adjourned for lunch.

Mr Justice Devlin said that he would set out the salient dates in the case for the jury, in chronological order: 25th June, 1948 when Mrs Morrell had her stroke, 27th June when she received ¼ grain of morphia at Neston Cottage Hospital in Cheshire, which was continued for the nine days she was there. This treatment was criticised by Dr Douthwaite but not by the other two doctors. On the 5th July, she left Cheshire for Eastbourne, arriving on 7th July at the Esperance Nursing Home. On the 9th July, in the list of prescriptions 'the first prescription of morphia'.[5] It had been suggested by the Prosecution 'that the right inference to draw from the

---

[5] Dr Adams was Mrs Morrell's doctor before her stroke, but what he had prescribed previously was never checked.

prescription list – you have no other evidence about it – is that it was an increase in the dosage of morphia.' It was on the 21st July that heroin was introduced by Dr Adams. This was criticized by both Dr Douthwaite and Dr Ashby, who also said she should have been weaned from the morphia. Dr Harman defended the treatment but the jury might think 'that he was not altogether enthusiastic about it, agreeing that heroin was unusual and that, in treating hundreds of stroke patients, he had never kept them on heroin and morphia.' Then began 'this period of addiction'.

It was important to remind the jury that Mrs Morrell had made a will on the 8th October, 1948 and that Dr Adams was not mentioned in it. On the 19th October, she had moved to the Olinda Nursing Home, and on 19th January, 1949 to the Cumberland Hotel. On the 12th February, Sister Randall came as night nurse 'in charge of the case' and remained until Mrs Morrell's death. Mrs Morrell made a codicil to her will on 19th March, but Dr Adams was not mentioned in it. Then on the 28th April, 1949, the first of two conversations between Dr Adams and Mr Sogno took place, when Dr Adams had said that Mrs Morrell wanted to deal with some alterations to her will. 'It is the first suggestion there was that we know that testamentary matters were under discussion in which Dr Adams might be concerned. It might be, you may think, quite a natural thing for a message of that sort to be conveyed through a doctor; it may signify nothing.' The Judge also reminded the jury that the Prosecution had suggested that Dr Adams had put Mrs Morrell under the influence of heroin in order to persuade her to make bequests to him but 'nine months has elapsed with Mrs Morrell under his influence during which she has attended twice to her will, once by making a will and the other time by making a codicil, and in neither of them apparently did Dr Adams' influence sufficiently extend to his being made a legatee.' On the 9th June, 1949, she had made another will, 'but I do not think we have been told what the contents of it were.'

The nurses' reports began on the 20th June, 1949, and the jury had 'that very useful exhibit, Exhibit 54', setting out the daily dosage covering each period; the routine dose of ¼ grain of morphia and ⅓ of heroin was being given 'with slight alterations' up until the autumn of 1950 – Mr Justice Devlin regarded this period as one 'when nothing significant happened'. On the 8th March, 1950, there occurred the second conversation with Mr Sogno, when Dr Adams went round to see him, and said that Mrs Morrell was upset because she had forgotten to give him the Rolls Royce, and 'there was also the question of this other case in the bank that she apparently intended or wanted to give to him outright. Nothing more happened so far as we know about that case.' The Judge pointed out that that it had been 'twenty months after the period of treatment had begun', that it was known for certain that Mrs Morrell was thinking of a legacy for Dr Adams. On the 6th May, 1950, Dr Harris had attended Mrs Morrell whilst Dr Adams was on holiday. A codicil was made to the will on the 19th July and on 24th August the will was made, which was the operative one, and amongst the exhibits, which showed precisely what Dr Adams received. She left an estate of £157,000 net, most of it to her son, and a number of legacies including 'the oak chest with silver in it, probate value £276, to Dr Adams, a monetary legacy of £300 to Nurse Randall… – and a legacy of £1,000 to Price the chauffeur.' The Judge commented that Price had been chauffeur since some time in 1947 and did not have much to do.[6] The Rolls Royce had only been left to Dr Adams as a 'purely conditional legacy', if her son predeceased her, a probability 'so remote that it is something you need not take into account.'

> 'So you may think – it is a matter for you – for a doctor who has pursued this policy of getting his patient under his influence, turned her into a drug addict so that he may make something out of her will, looked at from the point of view of what he did make it is not a very great achievement that, two years, or nearly two years, having now elapsed, what he gets is the oak chest with the silver, value £276, compared with £300 to the night nurse and £1,000 to the chauffeur.'

Dr Adams had gone on holiday on the 11th September, and Mrs Morrell had been very angry, and telephoned to Scotland to get him back. The next day, 12th September, she had sent for Mr Sogno and instructed him to draw up a codicil of 13th September, cutting Dr Adams out of her will. On the 16th September, Dr Adams came back from Scotland specially, and saw Mrs Morrell on the 16th, 17th and 18th September, and then resumed his holiday. Dr Harris had continued to look after her until the 24th September, continuing Dr Adams' treatment and introducing the Omnopon.[7]

This date, said the Judge, 'marks something in the nature of a turning point, the 24th September, when Dr Adams returned… It was the beginning of a change in the dosage.' It was also the end of what Dr Ashby had called the first of 'the three medical chapters' or phases, 'the routine dose period of addiction and the period when the patient entered…the second phase'. In Dr Ashby's view it had become 'obligatory' to wean the patient off her addiction, when the period of level dosage was ending and 'the spiral' was going to begin and the need of the patient for the drugs would increase rapidly and was 'bound to lead to disaster unless she was weaned.' The other factor confirmed by the doctors and the nurses was that 'there was a real change downhill in Mrs Morrell's condition'. Mr Justice Devlin pointed out to the Jury that 'As to what, so far as one can judge from the doses, Dr Adams does, Exhibit 54 is a useful one… because, as I say, it shows quite clearly the change in the dosage'.

> 'He continues with the routine dose, it remains the same during this period, the routine dose of morphia and heroin, but Dr Adams continues with the Omnopon which Dr Harris has introduced, and you see it there in varying amounts for each day, sometimes one grain, sometimes one and a third and sometimes more; and that is all that Dr Adams appears to do at that stage by way of changing the dose.'

---

[6] It was, however, usual for employers of domestic staff to leave a sufficient lump sum to employees for the purchase of an annuity in lieu of pension they would have paid to them if they were alive when the employee retired. Mr A. J. Hullet had done the same for his staff.

[7] Exhibit 54 shows that Dr Adams had used omnopon on three previous occasions: November 1949, January 1950 and March 1950.

[Exhibit 54 shows that the Omnopon became a regular component of the routine injection, and it also shows that a 'special injection' became a regular feature of the treatment. The Judge concentrated on the Omnopon; the content of the 'special injections was, of course, unknown and they were being set aside.]

On October 9th, during the second medical phase, Mrs Morrell had the 'incident' described by the Defence as a stroke and the Prosecution as an overdose of opiates. It was on October 21st that Mrs Morrell tore up the codicil and Mr Morrell posted the pieces to Mr Sogno, who received them on the 23rd. This signified her intention of putting Dr Adams back into her will. Dr Adams state of mind on the matter could only be derived from his conversation with Mr Sogno and from what he had said to Superintendent Hannam six years later.

'We do not, therefore, know whether he knew what Mrs Morrell was doing, although it perhaps might be a reasonable inference – it is entirely a matter for you – that Mrs Morrell, who had peremptorily summoned him back from Scotland, did not keep altogether silent about it so far as Dr Adams was concerned..'

Then Mr Justice Devlin said, rather oddly considering that he had pointed out 24th September as marking a change in dosage (see above):

'What we do know, and it is a little significant, is that in these last stages of Mrs Morrell's life, when she was getting near to the end, Dr Adams spent five or six weeks (if I may so put it) out of the will, getting nothing, and one does not see any change in his attitude that can be detected from the dosage he was giving that shows that he regarded that period, if he knew about it at all, as being different from any other period.'

But on 31st October, there was a 'marked change' in the medication: the morphia was dropped altogether and the heroin continued alone for about a week, and then on November 6th, the instructions were changed and the morphia reintroduced. At the same time there was 'a virtual dropping of the barbiturates'. It was at this time, October 31st or November 1st, that Dr Douthwaite had inferred from the medical treatment, the intent to kill. Atropine was introduced on November 2nd and Mr Lawrence had suggested that this drug was inconsistent with 'the idea that this woman was simply being drugged to death.' On the 8th November hyperduric morphia was introduced and Mr Lawrence had made the point that it was slower-acting and 'a genuine medication rather than an intent to drug to death.'

November 8th had been 'taken as the second and alternative date, in the submission of the prosecution, when Dr Adams made up his mind to kill. It is not taken as an absolute date.' Mr Justice Devlin found it 'difficult to see – any particular reason for picking out that date from among the last dates', but it was perhaps 'a central date' in a period when 'the dosage of drugs is increased at such a rate as to lead, in their view, inevitably to the end.'

On the 9th November at 10.15 p.m., Dr Adams had given instructions for one grain of heroin to be given 'S.O.S.', marking another 'stepping up' of the medication, and 'it was probably about that time' that Nurse Randall had been given the instructions which 'had been labelled – I use the word 'labelled' advisedly – labelled to 'keep under'', and Dr Ashby had considered that that marked 'not an intent to kill – he does not deal in those terms, but as marking the beginning of a course of treatment which he said would almost certainly lead to death and which he considered that a medical practitioner of Dr Adams' qualifications would have known would lead to death.' As to what Dr Adams had meant: he must have seen the nurses' notes and there was nothing to suggest that the treatment they had given on his instructions was anything he had disagreed with.

> 'You may think without quibbling about words or trying to determine exactly what is meant by 'keep under', it was that Doctor Adams had it in mind that there should be done what in fact the nurses did do.'

On the morning of November 10th, the instructions to give one grain of heroin S.O.S. were changed to one grain hourly S.O.S. Dr Ashby had denoted this day as beginning the 'third medical chapter', when it was no longer possible to wean Mrs Morrell off the drugs. The patient's condition was 'irreversible' and nothing could be done about the drug addiction. Dr Douthwaite had selected that date as marking 'the complete unavoidability of death' and had said that 'the quantity of Morphia and Heroin that by that date had been administered to her was so great she was bound to die within a day or two even though no further Morphia or Heroin had been given.'

The last recorded injection of morphia and heroin was on the 12th at 5.25 p.m. and the injections of paraldehyde followed; at 2 a.m. Mrs Morrell died. On the following day, Dr Adams had given instructions that her body was to be cremated, which were in accordance with her will. [Nothing was ever said about this being the prerogative of the executor – in this case, her son, or perhaps Mr Sogno in his absence.] Mr Justice Devlin added that there was 'nothing to suggest that Doctor Adams was in any way responsible for that wish.' He had filled in the cremation form, stating he had no pecuniary interest in the will, and on the 15th the cremation took place. [This followed unusually quickly considering that her family were in Cheshire and the family business operated from Liverpool, and also that it was certainly not normal Christian practice at that time. It would have been usual to have orders of service and memorial cards printed in such a family.] The will was proved on 13th January, 1951, and on the 8th February the chest of silver was delivered to Dr Adams, and, at about the same time, the Rolls Royce also. 'So if the object was to get Mrs Morrell under the influence so he might obtain a bequest from her and then to kill her so as to make sure of it, it had been achieved.'

The Judge then pointed out to the Jury that the 'mark of any undue influence' was that 'the influencer is able to extract something which he ought not to have got.'

> 'When you find, therefore, that the bequest so far from being something in the opinion

of the relatives which Doctor Adams should not have got, Mr Morrell thinks fit to add something to that which his mother thought fit, it may help you to decide whether this really was a case of undue influence being exercised by Doctor Adams.'

There was then a long gap of nearly six years, and, as Mr Lawrence had reminded them 'at the end of this little history there was no suspicion at all about the way in which Mrs Morrell died.' It was not until the summer of 1956 that anything further was heard, and then enquiries were made of the nurses by Superintendent Hannam and they had made the statements 'upon which no doubt these proceedings in due course were founded'. The Superintendent's enquiries had led to the four interviews with Dr Adams: October 1st was the encounter between Superintendent Hannam and Dr Adams outside his garage, in which the Doctor had made statements about the will and the cremation form. The second interview had taken place on November 24th when Kent Lodge was searched for dangerous drugs, and there was a conversation about the drugs, and the prescription list was given to Dr Adams to consider and he had made the remark about 'very, very seldom using morphia and heroin', said that all the drugs on the list were used, and 'Poor soul, she was in terrible agony'. The third interview occurred on December 19th when he was arrested and when he had said, 'Murder. Can you prove it was murder?'. The Judge emphasised that both Superintendent Hannam and Inspector Pugh had said that Dr Adams was stunned at that juncture. He directed the Jury that, with regard to the words said to his receptionist: 'I will see you in Heaven', they could not 'attach weight or importance to something of that sort which was obviously said under great emotional strain.'

Mr Justice Devlin now dealt with some 'inessential matters', which could not help them, or 'helped very little'. How did the whole period of illness leading up to the 'vital period' – the end of October, 1950 – help the jury to come to a decision? The Prosecution had suggested that Dr Adams' 'sinister plan' was in his mind from the beginning and they might think 'to some extent on the admitted facts, it is not a very pretty story'. If a doctor was 'an old family friend', then it was understandable that a legacy might be left to him; it was not desirable to try to make rules under which doctors could properly receive legacies. If a doctor was found 'angling for a legacy' or 'displaying an excessive anxiety in what he is likely to get under the will', and they might think that was 'the right inference to draw from the very curious conversation which Doctor Adams had with Mr Sogno in 1950' and the patient was also receiving drugs from that doctor and, in particular, heroin – there was a considerable body of medical opinion to say that 'heroin particularly, might put the patient under his influence' – then the question of undue influence should be considered. There were also the incidents of the Doctor being taken out of the will when he went on holiday, and then being put back again, the signing of the cremation form which they might think 'either false' or 'not genuine'. Many doctors would have considered 'that sort of conduct to be quite wrong', and that the only possible solution would have been to have nothing to do with any legacy. However, there was a great deal of difference between something that was 'not a pretty story' and murder.

If the Jury were satisfied beyond all reasonable doubt that Dr Adams had engaged in a sinister scheme throughout the period, 'in one way it weakens the case for the Prosecution'. If the

Prosecution had said that he had been treating his patient 'in a completely model way', and then gone 'completely off the rails', then there would need to be an explanation. This would have been 'stronger', than suggesting that he had begun the wrong treatment without murder on his mind. This could be countered by the Prosecution saying that the giving of the wrong treatment was with sinister intent, 'albeit not the intent to murder'.

Being satisfied with the last explanation, the Jury would 'come to the conclusion that Dr Adams was a fraudulent rogue. Indeed, rogue is too mild a word for a man who deliberately endeavours, as a doctor, to keep a patient under his influence so he can get something out of her in her will.' Suppose they did come to the conclusion that Dr Adams was a 'fraudulent rogue', how would that help them to decide if he was also a murderer? They should not allow themselves to be prejudiced because 'fraud and murder are poles apart'. Suppose they thought that the truth lay somewhere in between: that he had administered the drugs as 'the easiest way to cope with a very difficult patient', but when they came to consider whether changes in medication led to murder, then 'how the patient got into that condition really cannot help'. The Prosecution had pointed to specific dates and it was the condition of the patient on those dates which the Jury had to consider.

The second 'inessential matter' was that of the two or three doses of Paraldehyde at the very end, and whether Sister Randall really had given the second injection. On the case for the Prosecution, this was irrelevant, as this was that Dr Adams had made up his mind to murder with the morphia and heroin, at least by the 8th November. In that event, the Paraldehyde would, 'at the most' have accelerated death by a few hours. If Dr Adams had not made up his mind by the 8th November, and was not using the morphia and heroin to bring about Mrs Morrell's death, 'then no-one in their senses can suggest that because at the very end he gave two injections of Paraldehyde, which is said to be one of the safest of the hypnotic drugs, no-one in their senses could suggest that that by itself constitutes murder'.

The third matter was that they had heard, in court, some amount of criticism of the Police and, in particular, of Superintendent Hannam. It was usual for Police Officers to record statements made in interviews and summarise what had occurred; in this case Dr Adams was said to be 'a loquacious man' and the Police had to be depended upon to give the correct impression of what the accused had said. It was always relevant to consider how the Police had acted in connection with a case in order to make a judgment. In this case they had 'not got at all any competing version to put against the police version' – there being none from Dr Adams. They still had to decide how much they should rely on the police evidence. Mr Justice Devlin gave his own opinion:

> '…perhaps I may say, for what it is worth, it is my opinion, who has sat here and heard this criticism given many times, and it is not a matter binding upon you, – but I have seen nothing at all in the conduct of Superintendent Hannam in this case which appears to me to constitute anything that was unfair or oppressive.'

It had been said that Superintendent Hannam had waylaid Dr Adams on the first occasion, and the Superintendent had denied this, but: 'it would not shock me in the least if he did way-lay him'. This was a police duty. 'They cannot wait in the police station for criminals to call in.' If they waylaid the wrong man, this was not a reasonable criticism. The same applied to Superintendent Hannam interviewing Dr Adams when he went with Detective Inspector Pugh, who was the officer named on the search warrant: this was not 'unfair and oppressive conduct' and the police had not infringed the 'very stringent rules about questioning people in Dr Adams' position.'

Mr Justice Devlin agreed with the Attorney-General about the matter of two police officers compiling their record of an interview together: that it was a recognised common practice and he saw nothing wrong with it. He added further praise of police conduct:

> 'There is one thing in this case which seems to me to show that the police officers, Superintendent Hannam and Detective Inspector Pugh, were maintaining to the high-est degree the traditions of fairness that we hope govern the conduct of the police: that phrase 'Murder. Can you prove it'. It could have been twisted to have sounded very nasty, could not it? Without altering the words the impression could have been given that what Dr Adams was saying from his attitude, in effect, was: 'Well, murder; you know and I know, and we all know, that I did it, but you will not be able to prove it'.'

Instead the officers volunteered evidence which gave it a wholly different meaning and one which very much favoured the Defence: that Dr Adams had answered so as to give the impres-sion to two experienced police officers 'that murder was the last thing that he had thought he was ever going to be charged with.'

The Judge now came to 'the last of the inessentials' and that was the big discrepancy between the amount of drugs prescribed by Dr Adams and the amounts recorded as being administered in the nurses' notebooks. He had already instructed the jury that they must have regard only to the injections recorded in the nurses' notebooks. The prescriptions were not direct evidence and a link would have to be shown between these and the injections recorded in the notebooks. The Attorney-General had submitted 'in the form of a question: why do doc-tors prescribe drugs unless they intend them to be administered', and the answer was 'Well, of course, they do not'. That raised 'a presumption', but this was 'completely rebutted if you get nurses, whose business it is actually to record injections, coming and saying: 'We have record-ed the injections in writing, and these books contain all the injections that were given.' This made the presumption 'mere conjecture', and there was also no direct evidence that Dr Adams ever collected or received any of the drugs on the list. Mr Justice Devlin's next statement intro-duced yet another interesting question:

> 'I do not mean, Members of the Jury, when I say this, that you are to exclude from your calculations – and this is a matter entirely for you – any or all of those injections that are recorded in the Red Book as special injections. You have heard the evidence and the argument about that. Some of the special injections you will probably think are proved

to your satisfaction as relating quite clearly, not to morphia or heroin, but to vitamins, and so on. Others the Prosecution point to and say that the evidence and surrounding evidence, the circumstances shown in the books, show that, in relation to them, they must have been morphia and heroin. That is a matter for you. But what seems to me quite clear is that the special injections cannot possibly account for the difference between the amounts prescribed and the amounts that were actually administered.'

Mr Justice Devlin asked the Jury to look at Exhibit 55 and the record of special injections in the last five days. There were two special injections given on the 9th, one on the 10th and one on the 12th. The total difference of morphia unaccounted for was 30½ grains and 22 grains of heroin. If these amounts were spread over the four injections, this would mean injections of 12½ grains – a little less because the two phials were left over. Even if the quantity were reduced to '10, 9 or 8', that figure would still be four times as large as any other injection recorded, and if these amounts had been given 'there would be some very decisive result to be noted in the books', yet there was nothing unusual recorded. The four special injections 'were quite incapable of accounting for the discrepancy between the drugs prescribed and those administered.'

It was, of course, possible that Dr Adams could, at any time on one of his visits, have given Mrs Morrell a large injection, as he was always in the room alone with her, 'No one could say that is inconceivable'. He could have told the nurse he was giving one amount and, in fact, have given another. But this was conjecture. They had to use the medical history of the nurses' notes. Dr Douthwaite and Dr Ashby had not seen fit to suggest that there was anything in the notes which indicated 'a much larger injection':

> 'They think it right ['right' is underlined twice by Hannam and he has put two exclamation marks by the word] both of them, for the purpose of their calculations to disregard the special injections. You may think it wise to do that.'

Mr Justice Devlin now proposed a startlingly different scenario: it was also no use surmising that if all the difference had not been given, then perhaps part of it might have been because

> '…if that is the position, there is some channel existing by which drugs were being prescribed and were improperly disappearing you could not be satisfied, could you, unless you knew what that channel was – you could not be satisfied beyond conjecture as to what the quantity was which was disappearing. In other words, if there was a channel through which these drugs were disappearing, then there is nothing to show you that it did not account for the whole of the discrepancy. Was there in fact such a channel?'

The Judge told the Jury that he had come to a difficult part of the case; there were no grounds upon which they could rely:

> '…but supposing you were to think that Dr Adams had been dishonest about drugs, –

and you will remember he said in his statement 'I am not dishonest about drugs' – how much better would it be that you should unjustly suspect him of that sort of dishonesty than that you should unjustly convict him of murder.'

They had only to consider whether the discrepancy was relevant to the charge of murder. 'There must have been, must there not, carelessness or dishonesty somewhere.' At the very least there was carelessness on Dr Adams' part.

> 'One knows that dangerous drugs are things in which there is an illicit traffic, and you might think that they were disappearing in a way that they ought not to be disappearing and that someone was dealing dishonestly with them, and that someone must either have been Dr Adams himself or one of the nurses who was attending on the patient.'
> [Hannam has marked this paragraph in the margin and underlined the words 'an illicit traffic' and the last part from 'that someone' to the end. There is also other archival information indicating that he was convinced that Dr Adams was trafficking, and evidence.]

Mr Justice Devlin told the Jury that if they did begin to wonder which of the people was most likely, they would, in fairness to Dr Adams, have to consider that two of the nurses had lied about the matter in the witness-box: Sister Stronach had lied about whether the drugs were kept locked up or not, and either Sister Mason-Ellis or Sister Randall had lied about the conversation in the train concerning, again, the locking up of the drugs. He was making no accusations and invited the jury to disregard the whole matter 'as being mere speculation'. They were to have regard only to the injections 'clearly proved before you by the prosecution to have been administered by the nurses or Dr Adams and recorded in the nurses' books at the time'.

The Judge had now come to 'the essentials' in the case: there were three things that had to be proved by the prosecution. It had 'to prove an act or acts of murder'. It had to prove that 'these acts caused the death of Mrs Morrell'. It had to prove that 'at the time when those acts were committed by Dr Adams – and I of course count the giving of an instruction to act through the nurses in just the same way as the act of injection itself – Dr Adams intended to kill.'

He began with the second essential: whether the act caused the death. Mr Lawrence had contended that he could 'defeat the prosecution's case on this narrower point' that the immediate physical cause of death was not the drugs at all, but were 'merely an incident in the illness', but that natural causes intervened. The Attorney-General had been quite correct when he submitted, in his closing speech, that drugs could only kill by means of their action on the body. Dr Harman had said that the 'normal morphine death' was a slowing of respiration until breathing ceased, or there could be complications such as pulmonary congestion which would cause increased respiration and, possibly, death. This would still mean that death was caused by the drug. Mr Lawrence had submitted that there was an intervening cause such as cerebral thrombosis or '"just people dying", as Dr Harman put it'. The question for the Jury was whether an intervening natural cause could not reasonably be excluded; if the prosecution had not satisfied them on this point, then they must acquit.

They had to depend entirely upon the medical evidence. Dr Douthwaite's was 'quite clear and uncompromising'; he regarded 'the overdose of drugs – sufficient, he said, had been given by 10th November – as causing the death.' Dr Ashby had also given that as being 'the most likely of the causes', but had not excluded other possibilities. Dr Ashby was very much the key medical witness in the case as he came between the two extremes of Dr Douthwaite and Dr Harman. The Judge read out evidence given by Dr Ashby which he obviously regarded as of vital importance in helping the Jury reach their verdict:

The Attorney-General had asked (Day 11, page 56):

'From what you have seen and heard, what would you say was the cause of her death?'

Dr Ashby had answered:

'I think that is very complicated, the factors causing her death. The immediate factors, of course, would be the combination of what we refer to as terminal natural causes, like terminal pneumonia, which in its turn would have been fairly directly caused by her being kept under for the last few days.

Then I think another very important factor – probably a larger factor – was his very heavy pressure of opiate therapy.

Thirdly, the patient's age cannot be ignored. I don't for the moment think of anything else. It is not possible without a post-mortem examination to say with any certainty what the actual final closing act was which ended life in the majority of patients.'

Then, in cross-examination by Mr Lawrence, Dr Ashby had added a qualification to his answer to the Attorney-General:

'I do not think it is possible absolutely to rule out a sudden catastrophic intervention by some natural cause. It just is not possible to say this woman could not have had another cerebral haemorrhage at one o'clock that morning. There is just no evidence to say that that is impossible. I do not think it ever is possible completely to rule out the possibility in a patient of eighty-one, of sudden death.'

Mr Justice Devlin pointed out that the Jury were not 'dealing with possibilities beyond any shadow of doubt'; the Prosecution was not 'obliged and cannot be expected to prove certainties'. They must consider what Dr Ashby had said and what it meant, but if they acted on his evidence alone and disregarded that of Dr Douthwaite, then 'the prosecution could take the matter no further'. Even if they thought that what Dr Ashby had admitted was 'only a bare possibility', they had to put that with Dr Harman's evidence which was 'evidence that perhaps commends itself to the ordinary person'. The Judge read what he had said (Day 13, page 44):

'I should say in old ladies over eighty who have had strokes and arterio sclerosis one does not regard it as a question so much as explaining the cause of death. One knows they just die. She might well have had a clot on the heart, a coronary thrombosis. That would be a very usual thing… I see no necessity to link her death with the doses administered.'

However, although he had pointed to the increase in respirations on the last day and said 'That is not a morphine death', he had also conceded to the Attorney-General that increased respiration could also be 'the result of pulmonary congestion which had been led up to by coma or a semi-comatose condition.'

Mr Justice Devlin told the Jury that they must put the medical evidence of all three doctors together, and that they had to be satisfied that 'this lady did not in the end die by natural causes, and if you are not satisfied about that, the case for the prosecution ends there.'

The first and most essential part was the act or acts of murder: the prosecution had to find such an act or acts of murder. It was, 'as Mr Lawrence reminded you, a most curious situation, perhaps unique in these courts, that the act of murder has to be proved by expert evidence'. The prosecution said that it was recorded in the nurses' notebooks, but that 'without the doctor to interpret the books', they say, 'we cannot begin to put our finger on what is suggested to be the act of murder'. That act had to be proved and the line of treatment alone would not prove it; the treatment could be right or wrong, skilful or unskilful 'or even sinister', but they had to find some break or change in treatment, which 'called for an explanation' or showed a new pattern or intention. If they found this 'significant event' which was 'medically wrong in the sense that it is going to bring about a death which ought not to be brought about if the right treatment were being given', it was only then that they could find murder. Significantly, the Judge said:

'It may be that it is very much more difficult for the Crown ever to prove that a doctor murders his patient than it is to prove other acts of murder.'

The prosecution had identified three acts and the Jury had firstly to decide whether any of these were 'an act that needs explanation', for some act that was 'capable of being described as a murderous act'. The first of these was the theory of Dr Douthwaite that the withdrawal of the morphia was with the intent that it should be reintroduced with fatal effect. Mr Justice Devlin told the Jury to consider the criticisms made by Mr Lawrence of this late theory of Dr Douthwaite's and instructed them that, if there was a theory which was not supported by the other doctor for the prosecution and the doctor for the defence regarded the theory as wrong, then they might well consider it too dangerous 'to adopt the theory'.

One of the other acts was one supported by both Dr Douthwaite and Dr Ashby, although their approaches had been slightly different: they had selected 8th November as 'the central date'. The Judge added that the prosecution was 'not obliged to pinpoint a precise date', so long as they could 'show a central date in the design that they can properly label as a design for murder'. The defence had said that the treatment presented a consistent picture, however it had started, that Mrs Morrell was in condition where she was going downhill and where the increase in drugs had to be given 'and if those drugs eased the passing, in the proper sense of the term – meaning that they were properly given – and if they accelerated death, that was only incidental.' The prosecution had found a sudden change in the medication around 8th November, and said that there was no justifiable medical reason for this. If the Jury found that there was this sudden change then this gave them 'an act which is capable of being a murderous act. Can you find it?'

Dr Douthwaite's evidence seemed to the Judge to be 'quite positive and uncompromising': he had said that he could find no medical explanation for the increase in dosage at that time. 'He was not willing to credit Dr Adams even with ignorance or error. He could find no medical evidence, other than that he certainly intended to cause death.'

That was all clear enough but it was Dr Ashby's evidence that the Jury had to consider with the utmost care because it was so crucial. Mr Justice Devlin intended reading some passages of his evidence to the Jury but postponed this until the following day. The position of a doctor giving evidence for the prosecution was a peculiarly difficult one, particularly when they would not have themselves dealt with the patient or the illness in question, and had not even got the clinical reports. They could 'hardly doubt' that Dr Ashby had tried to be fair, 'to give both sides of the picture', but he had also said that 'It is not the whole picture. I have not got the doctor's reports.' This meant that there had been apparent contradictions in some of his answers. He could not read all of Dr Ashby's evidence over again, but would try to point out the 'pith of his answers'; even so, they could not go through the transcripts minutely and spend as long as they liked on reaching a verdict. This was not the way in which a conviction for murder was arrived at. They had to ask themselves whether the witnesses in the witness-box had supplied adequate evidence.

If they came to the conclusion that Dr Ashby's evidence did not convince them and was 'borderline', not leaving them 'with the clear impression beyond a reasonable doubt', then they must put it aside as it would not be safe to convict upon such evidence. The other alternative was to 'go the whole way with Dr Douthwaite'.

The trial was adjourned until the following morning.

## Seventeenth Day

Mr Justice Devlin reminded the Jury that he had been presenting them with the 'two rival versions' of the medical history and now proposed to read some extracts from Dr Ashby's evidence to them. The Attorney-General had asked Dr Ashby (Day 11, page 54) whether the administration of morphia and heroin 'on that scale' was justified, and Dr Ashby had answered: 'Well, I don't see the justification really.' The patient had some 'superficial abrasions' but these could not have caused pain. He continued:

'It is very difficult. I think it must be borne in mind, my Lord, that there are no doctor's reports, nothing that I am used to in the way of doctor's notes about the condition of the patient at the time, and in the absence of accurate description it is very difficult for me to say whether something which I think must have been at least easing her passing was justified at the time or not.'

The only justification for the dosage would have been 'pain or the most dreadful discomfort'. When Dr Ashby was asked again (Day 11, page 58) about the medical justification for the doses given after the 8th November, he had reiterated his view but considered that the right course would have been to keep the same dosage of opiates but to keep the patient in 'an hypnotic state' with barbiturates.

In answer to Mr Justice Devlin (Day 12, page 24), Dr Ashby had replied that:

'The instruction to keep her under could not fail to have – I should not say 'could not fail', but would be almost certain to accelerate death.'

The Judge had then asked him if this was 'a conclusion which a doctor with Dr Adams's qualifications would have reached', and he said:

'Yes. I think an anaesthetist is particularly conversant with the dangers of a patient being unconscious or semi-conscious.'

Then Dr Ashby had given two answers, on which Mr Lawrence had 'strongly relied' (Day 12, pages 34 and 44). Mr Lawrence had put to him an alternative explanation: that the drugs given to Mrs Morrell after the 8th November had been given to promote her comfort, and Dr Ashby had conceded that it was 'a possible interpretation'. Then Mr Lawrence had been putting much the same thing to Dr Ashby in relation to 'the spiral': that if Dr Adams had thought that she had had another stroke, he might have come to the conclusion that there was no point in doing anything but continuing with an increase of drugs to promote comfort, and in this case 'death would overtake the spiral'; that it was an 'impasse' that Dr Adams and his patient were in. Dr Ashby had answered that he thought that this was 'a possible view', whilst still holding to his own view 'as being the more probable of the two'.

The Jury could put Dr Ashby's view together with 'the certainty' of Dr Douthwaite's view but they should also consider whether they should put it together with the evidence of Dr Harman, who accepted Dr Ashby's view as 'a reasonable possibility', whilst holding another view himself. Dr Harman had said, when questioned by the Judge, that he did not think that the instructions to 'keep under' acelerated death; they signified to him that there was a change in the patient's condition where she needed the drugs to control her delirium, to keep her under control, and that this policy was 'quite a common one in such cases'. He had said that he would put the emphasis the other way round to Dr Ashby's: that such instructions might have accelerated death but that it 'probably would not have done so'.

There, said Mr Justice Devlin, the Members of the Jury, had the essential part of the medical evidence. This was the crucial part of the case upon which Mr Lawrence had made his submission, and, although he had ruled against Mr Lawrence and left the Jury to make the decision, there had been a 'strong submission' to be made on the evidence of Dr Ashby, but this was now fortified by Dr Harman's evidence.

> 'Each link in the Prosecution's chain must be strong enough to stand the strain. It does not matter how strong the other links are if it breaks down at that crucial point.'

Presumably, Mr Justice Devlin meant that if the Jury were satisfied with the evidence of Dr Ashby, then the Prosecution's case was broken and finished. He went on to say that they were just as entitled to accept Dr Douthwaite's evidence as final. If they agreed with Dr Harman that Dr Adams was merely promoting the comfort of his patient, then 'nothing in the rest of the case can alter that fact'. It was 'not a question of balancing probabilities, it is a question of being satisfied beyond reasonable doubt.' On neither of the first two points did the Judge think that evidence from Dr Adams himself would have helped the Jury because he would hardly have been giving an independent medical opinion, so that they had all they needed to make the necessary decisions.

If they, the Jury, had decided that an act of murder had been committed and that that act had caused the death of Mrs Morrell, then they had to proceed to the third point, that of intent to murder. It was on this third point, that it would have helped them to know Dr Adams' views or to have had an explanation from him. If they decided in favour of the prosecution they would have decided that Mrs Morrell 'was killed by a piece of wrong and medically unjustifiable treatment given to her by her doctor'. However, this could be due to several things: 'error, ignorance or incompetence, possibly intent'. But, in this case, it would be natural for the Jury, if they found that she had died by wrong and unjustifiable medical treatment and that her doctor had benefited by her death, to wish to hear what he had to say about it. They would now be dealing with intent to murder:

> 'Intention is something that exists in a man's mind, and apart from his own evidence it can only be proved by inferences which are to be drawn from his acts.'

If he went into the witness-box this would be 'the best evidence available of what was in his own mind'. They lacked this but, as Mr Lawrence had reminded them, until 1898 the accused was not permitted to give evidence on his own behalf, but there was a presumption 'that a man is presumed to intend the natural and probable consequences of his own acts, and… if he did them and thought… that death would follow, then he must be presumed to have intended death.' As they did not have direct evidence from Dr Adams then the prosecution still had to prove intent.

In considering the matter 'of what you would infer as to the state of mind of Dr Adams', Mr Justice Devlin said that he would point out the most relevant circumstances. Only one of these depended on the medical evidence: Dr Douthwaite had inferred an intent to kill on medical grounds alone, saying that it was impossible for a doctor with Dr Adams' qualifications to have given drugs in these quantities by 'error, or by ignorance, or by incompetence, and I am bound to see as the only explanation for it intent to kill.' But for proof of intent, there was no room for any difference of medical opinion; if one doctor – as Dr Harman had – completely disagreed with that opinion, then Dr Adams could have honestly disagreed with it, and so 'it finishes Dr Douthwaite's evidence as far as it is concerned with proving an intent to kill'.

Of the remaining circumstances, the first was motive. The Crown did not have to prove motive, but a jury would look for it in connection with intent: 'People do not normally intend things that are not going to benefit them'. Mr Justice Devlin assumed 'from the Attorney-General's opening' that the motive was one of gain, of acquiring a legacy from Mrs Morrell. Mr Lawrence had submitted that an oak chest was 'a very paltry reward for murder', but, on the other hand, Dr Adams had shown considerable interest in receiving a bequest under her will. Would it 'stimulate a doctor into committing murder'? Mr Lawrence had also pointed out that Mrs Morrell was a dying woman, and 'that the suggestion that this doctor had anticipated her death by a few days or weeks for the sake of an oak chest of silver worth £270 was ludicrous', so why, asked the Judge, would he not just have waited instead of working out an elaborate system to dispose of her? It was a strong point which required an answer:

> 'I listened carefully to the Attorney-General's speech in closing his case to you to see what the answer was. I did not hear the answer.'

The second circumstance with regard to intent was 'the false filling up of the cremation form'. The Judge said this 'advisedly' because it seemed to him that it was false as it related to what Dr Adams thought he would get under the will and he had answered 'Not so far as I am aware'. Putting this together with his answer to Superintendent Hannam, it was clear that he either knew or thought he was going to get the chest of silver and the Rolls Royce. If he thought this six years later, then the jury were entitled to think that he knew this when he filled in the cremation form.

The third circumstance was the statements made by Dr Adams to Superintendent Hannam, and some of them were 'difficult to justify on the evidence': for instance, that she was 'in terrible agony' at the end. It was clear 'that she was not in terrible agony either at the end or at any time'. The jury might have liked to hear Dr Adams' explanation of this, and for the phrase 'easing the passing' which he had used: 'a phrase that might have been used quite innocently, but, on the other hand, a phrase which might perhaps go further'. But, what had struck the Judge was, that his statements showed 'from beginning to end' that it had never crossed his mind that he would be charged with the murder of Mrs Morrell.

Mr Justice Devlin reminded the Jury of the fact that Dr Adams had been well aware that Superintendent Hannam was conducting enquiries from their very first encounter when he had said to Dr Adams: 'I hope I shall finish all these enquiries soon, and we will probably have another talk.' and Dr Adams had replied 'Don't hurry. Please be thorough. It is in my interests. Good night, and thank you very much for your kindness.' If Dr Adams had been 'the calculating murderer' he might have been expected to be very wary, but he had spoken a good deal about having the Rolls Royce and the chest of silver left to him, making it 'impossible for him to rely upon what otherwise he might well have relied upon if he had known the true legal position' that he had received these only 'through the grace and favour of Mr Morrell'. That attitude seemed for the Judge 'to pervade all these enquiries'.

At the time of the search for drugs at Kent Lodge, Dr Adams had said 'I am not dishonest about drugs' and this surely demonstrated that he thought that he was being investigated for illicit trafficking in drugs, but not for murder. Then at the last interview, he was stunned and shocked when he was charged with murder. The Jury were instructed to take into account the Doctor's attitude as it appeared from his statements when they considered the matter of intent.

There was just one further matter: that of the nurses' notebooks. The Attorney-General had made a point about this when he had asked where they were, where they had come from and where they had been, and in whose interests it was to keep them. Mr Justice Devlin said that it would have been interesting to have known how it came about that the clinical notes were destroyed and the nurses' notebooks preserved. Mr Lawrence had not anticipated the point and had not dealt with it.

He might perhaps have asked what the prosecution said that these books proved: innocence or guilt? If innocence then it did not matter where they had come from or who had been keeping them, 'if they prove innocence you must acquit'. If they proved guilt then why would Dr Adams have preserved them? Because he had not realised 'their deadly nature'? This answer would not do because the Crown said that he was aware that the doses recorded in the books would kill.

> 'That is an essential part of the case for the Crown: that he knew that at the time and therefore must have known it when he decided to preserve these books.'

He could not have preserved them in case he was confronted with 'the even more serious evidence of the prescription lists'. If that was said, then why, when Superintendent Hannam confronted him with the prescription lists, did he say he had administered it all, except for a few tablets, to Mrs Morrell? All this demonstrated the dangers of trying to find an answer about why the books were kept, and allowing this to lead them to a conclusion 'which might be unjustifiably prejudicial to the accused.'

Mr Justice Devlin came to his final summing-up: the Crown must satisfy the Jury on three points: that Mrs Morrell did not die from natural causes; that from the medical evidence there emerged an act of killing by the accused; if that succeeded then the third question was whether that act was done with intent to murder.

Mr Lawrence had said that the whole case against Dr Adams was mere suspicion, and maybe if 'this inquiry were ever to be completed' then Dr Adams would emerge as a man who had been wrongly judged, but no-one could say that the Crown were not justified in prosecuting him. He might be found on further enquiry to be a man who was 'guilty of folly, perhaps worse, but who never in his mind came within thought of murder'. It might be so but it was not the Jury's task to come to such conclusions: they did not sit 'as a court of inquiry to determine just how and why Mrs Morrell died'. They could not do that without hearing Dr Adams. The only question they had to answer was: 'Has the prosecution satisfied you beyond reasonable doubt that Dr Adams murdered Mrs Morrell?' The Judge did not criticize the fact that Dr Adams had not spoken. The law on that matter reflected

> 'the natural thought of England. So great is, and always has been, our horror at the idea that a man might be questioned, forced to speak and perhaps to condemn himself out of his own mouth that we grant everyone suspected or accused of crime at the beginning, at every stage and until the very end the right to say 'Ask me no questions. I shall answer none. Prove your case.'
>
> And so this long process that began with arrest and ends with verdict ends, too, with the question with which it began: 'Murder? Can you prove it?'

This might well be the first time that Members of the Jury had sat in a jury box, but Mr Justice Devlin had presided over many trials, and sometimes he had felt compelled to tell the jury that the case for the prosecution seemed to him to be a strong one, however:

> 'I do not think, therefore, that I ought to hesitate to tell you in this case that here the case for the defence seems to me to be manifestly a strong one and that you must not find for the Crown until after you have weighed and rejected all the arguments that have been put before you on behalf of the defence.
>
> It is the same question in the end. It is always the same. Is the case for the Crown strong enough to carry conviction in your mind? It is your answer. You have to answer it. It lies always with you, the jury. Always with you. And will you now consider what that answer shall be. You can take such time as you think fit, short or long, over your deliberations.'

The Jury retired at 11.16 a.m.
They returned at 12 noon.

# VERDICT

THE CLERK OF THE COURT –
Members of the Jury, are you agreed upon your verdict?
THE FOREMAN OF THE JURY –
We are.
THE CLERK OF THE COURT –
Do you find the prisoner John Bodkin Adams guilty or not guilty?
THE FOREMAN OF THE JURY –
Not guilty.
THE CLERK OF THE COURT –
You find him not guilty, and that is the verdict of you all?
THE FOREMAN OF THE JURY –
It is.
MR JUSTICE DEVLIN –
Mr Attorney, there is another indictment is there not?

THE ATTORNEY-GENERAL: Yes, my Lord. I have most anxiously considered what course the Crown should pursue in relation to the further indictment charging Doctor Adams with the murder of Mrs Hullett. My learned friend has referred more than once to the difficulty, owing to the reports and rumours that were current, of securing a fair trial of the case which has now terminated. As one of my distinguished predecessors said, the Attorney-General, when deciding whether a particular prosecution is to be carried on, has regard to a variety of considerations, and all of them lead to the final question, would a prosecution be in the public interest, including that phrase, in the interests of Justice?

One of the considerations I have felt it my duty to consider is that the publicity which has attended this trial would make it even more difficult to secure a fair trial of this further indictment. I have also taken into account the length of this trial, the ordeal Doctor Adams has already undergone, the fact that the case for the Prosecution on this further indictment based on evidence given before the Eastbourne Magistrates depends in part on the evidence of Doctor Ashby, and very greatly upon the inference not supported, as in Mrs Morrell's case, of any admissions. Having given the matter the best consideration I can, I have reached the conclusion that in all the circumstances the public interest does not require that Doctor Adams should undergo the ordeal of a further trial on a charge of murder, and I therefore enter a *nolle prosequi* in relation to that indictment.

Mr JUSTICE DEVLIN: Then, Mr Attorney, all further proceedings on the indictment are stayed and no further action is taken in this Court. Accordingly, John Bodkin Adams, you are now discharged.

-o0o-

The crowds had been waiting ten deep outside the Old Bailey, awaiting the verdict. As Dr Adams departed in the car supplied by the *Daily Express* to impart his life story and his wisdom to Percy Hoskins, the remainder of the press had to conjure up their own copy. A little later, he did allow *Paris Match* – who had been with him when he was arrested – to take some very good photographs on his return to Eastbourne. They also wrote, rather more imaginatively than the British press, about the case and its characters: a very French view.

Seeing him from behind – apparently the novelist's way 'to uncover what a man would like to hide', sitting there in the dock of the Old Bailey, 'his neck, scarlet and massive, his skull too round', in lumpen silhouette, he seemed passively indifferent to his fate, and very calm. So sure of the judgment; the Saint with his small black Bible just visible in his jacket pocket – as it had been throughout the trial. Every day he had politely returned the Judge's bow, then sunk his double chin into his pristine white celluloid collar.'

The Jury's bell had rung out at noon to inform the Court that they had a verdict, and 'the twelve citizens of London' returned to their seats. There were two women jurors 'wearing beige and red hats, twin-sisters of the "housewives" that one meets in the suburban trains of a David Lean film.' The accused still sat, motionless, in the dock. The Judge's seat was empty. There was a two-minutes' silence, then a small door opened and Mr Justice Devlin appeared in his scarlet robe and full-bottomed wig. He bowed to the right, to the Jury, then seated himself in his green leather chair embossed with the Royal Coat of Arms – within his reach the black cap. The accused politely returned the Judge's bow as usual. The Clerk of the Court asked the foreman of the Jury if they had reached their decision: 'Yes', was the reply. Then the verdict: 'Not guilty'. John Bodkin Adams heard the words without flinching. When the Judge ordered his discharge, his face betrayed 'neither joy nor surprise', just 'the crushing respectability of the honest doctor, who, for more than a quarter of a century, had cared until their last breath for the old maids and prosperous widows of the small town of Eastbourne.' Beyond the dock, 'stood, silent, a thin smile on his pale lips, the man who had saved him: Geoffrey Lawrence. For the first time the barrister directed at his client an indifferent look in which it would have been difficult to decipher, in the cold light of the Old Bailey, satisfaction or triumph. The curtain had fallen but the star did not bow.'

Mr Lawrence had emerged from obscurity to stardom: grey eyes behind his 'solicitor's clerk glasses', high forehead, thin lips, a black coat, Anthony Eden hat. Not a man 'to tread the boards of the great legal theatre' of the Old Bailey, but used to finding his way through the labyrinth of local authority law. Hardly the Marshall-Hall of the Fifties with that impassioned eloquence of the greatest criminal defence barristers, but a man of great persistence and even cunning. In his country home in Sussex, he was an enthusiastic amateur violinist, playing Mozart, and a gentleman farmer, winning prizes for his cows in agricultural shows.

Lawrence and Adams had neither known, nor chosen each other. Dr Adams at least would have thought their meeting providential, and that the insurance premium he had paid to the Medical Defence Union had been money well spent – £3 per annum at that time. Mr Lawrence had advised Dr Adams not to go into the witness-box. 'Sublime prudence! Supreme wisdom! To be silent. The accused, in England, is never obliged to speak. Adams, at fifty-eight, lived without opening his mouth for the seventeen pathetic days that destiny reserved for him. In his cell in Brixton prison he read the Bible. He had learned in the course of his trial, that a bill signed by the Queen limited henceforth the cases where those sentenced to death would be executed: murder by firearm or during theft. Poisoners were spared the scaffold.'

The Attorney-General, Sir Reginald Manningham-Buller, Eton and Oxford, and 'horse-lover'. He speaks with neither joy nor anger, but 'rather like a head-master reading the prize-list on prize-day.' Nurse Randall – 'one of those crabbed figures of which the English provinces have the secret… relating in a voice heavy with suspicion how Dr Adams had administered to the old lady morphine dose on morphine dose.'

The contrast between a French Court and an English one. In France 'at the assizes, the witnesses depose, the judge interrogates, the attorney summons, the counsel pleads. There are dramatic moments, turning on events, silences, murmurs, and it may happen that the president threatens to "clear the court". An onslaught is made on eloquence. The trial is midway between a contest of rhetoric and the Comédie-Francaise.' In England, the Judge is an arbiter who, from time to time, asks questions, underlines the points; he can guide the Jury to what he believes to be the truth but it is not his task to decide upon the truth.

Eastbourne itself was not spared the pen of the French journalists: '…that solid chain of insinuations and slander that a small town in the English provinces can attach to a name when it is bored and has nothing else to do. Eastbourne is less a beach than a great gilded refuge where widows in lace come to warm in the sun of the retreat, their fingers knotted by arterio-sclerosis and their old shoulders covered with pendants. They have a vice: gossip. A mortal enemy: boredom. A confidant: their doctor.'

So far as Dr Adams was concerned: 'His adventure had given him an irreplaceable experi-ence. In two weeks he seized, better than he had done in a quarter of a century, the real soul of the small town of Eastbourne. However, he will return there. Other old ladies await him, between their silver boxes and their Rolls, the man who will henceforth hesitate to do what is necessary to alleviate their last days.'

# PART IV

# Chapter Thirty-Seven

# The Aftermath

## 1957–1983

## Publicity and Questions in Parliament

Dr Adams left Brixton prison at 1.15 p.m. on the day of his acquittal. A *Daily Express* car was waiting for him in the prison yard. According to the *Express* reporter, Charles Chesworth, he sat in his solicitors' offices in London that afternoon reading the first edition of the evening newspaper, with the headline 'Dr Adams found Not Guilty'. He then telephoned two friends: one in London and the other in Eastbourne with the news, and drank some coffee. He was quoted as saying:

> 'I never had any anxiety about the result. I spent much of my time in jail keeping up with the latest medical publications. I never lost a night's sleep – they had to wake me up this morning. I had slept soundly from 10 p.m. the night before until 7 a.m. I didn't even dream.'

When asked about the time when the Jury were out, he had 'smiled – a slow gentle smile like his slow, gentle Irish voice' and said:

> 'I was reading an American medical journal. My mind, you see, was always easy because my belief in the power of prayer, my faith in God and British justice, kept me above it all right to the end. That is what I have written to the hundreds of people who have sent me letters of sympathy – I have 525 in all. This has been a triumph for British justice against vicious rumour and tittle-tattle.'

He praised the defence team who 'never spared themselves day or night' because they had been convinced of his 'innocence and sincerity from the very beginning'. He had been 'perfectly willing to go into the box' but, having been under considerable strain 'was relieved to know that it was not necessary for me to do so.' as for the future:

> 'I am going away now for a little rest – naturally. Afterwards? Well, I've had many letters from my patients looking forward to my return to Eastbourne. I shall make my plans while I am taking my holiday.'

He went to stay 'in the flat of a friend in London', – although Percy Hoskins actually took him to a hideaway in Westgate-on-Sea late that night – rather than go directly to Eastbourne. He was engaged for the next couple of weeks or so with collaborating with Percy Hoskins, writing his 'life-story' and the experiences of his arrest and trial for publication in the *Daily Express*. The last holiday he had had in the September of 1956, before the arrest and trial, was shooting in Scotland accompanied by Lieutenant-Colonel Gwynne and Miss Betty Cradock; for his post-trial holiday he went to Reids Hotel in Madeira.

*The Empire News* revealed fascinating details of Dr Adams' sojourn in Brixton Prison, having talked to some of his fellow-prisoners, presumably after their release. They had nicknamed him 'Mr Pickwick', demonstrating their 1950s' literacy. He had, at first, been given a cell to himself, but was then transferred to a hospital ward with eleven other prisoners, where he had 'chummed-up with a prisoner who acted as his "batman". Every morning his bed was made, pyjamas folded and shoes cleaned.' He had talked to the other prisoners about his religious faith, and he had remained cheerful, and remarked to one of them: 'This is only a little chore till I am free again.' He had spent time in Brixton doing jigsaw puzzles, but 'to his disappointment none of his fellow prisoners could play chess at which he excelled'. He had mostly read and answered letters but he had been permitted to have 'the current medical journals'. As his Defence had suggested that he was an old-fashioned and out-of-date doctor, it might have been a surprise to some that he had said: 'I must keep up to date, I want to be ready to take up my practice as soon as this is all over.'

Detective Superintendent Hannam wrote to the Chief Superintendent immediately after the trial with a report of what had occurred. He mentioned that, although numerous conferences had taken place between the Attorney-General, Counsel, the Director of Public Prosecutions and expert medical witnesses, the police had been asked to attend only a few of these and, even then, only for a short time. Therefore, the C.I.D. had been out of touch with the case since the committal of Dr Adams for trial at the Old Bailey. Much additional evidence had been served, mainly from the doctor witnesses but he had not even been handed copies of that evidence.

After the committal, the Attorney-General had directed an additional indictment charging Adams with the murder of Mrs Hullett, but after it had been signed, it was discovered at the Director of Public Prosecution's Office that the prosecution had no power to do this and the Attorney-General had to lodge a *nolle prosequi* at the High Courts of Justice and then apply before the Lord Chief Justice for a voluntary Bill of Indictment in the case of Mrs Hullett, and this had been granted. (What had happened is not fully explained in the DPP's archive.)

The trial of Dr Adams on the Morrell charge had lasted from 18th March and ended at 12 noon on Tuesday, 9th April. Hannam then clearly displayed his view that the Morrell case should not have been the one taken:

> 'It will be realised that the case of Mrs Morrell, which was taken independently [of the police], was one six years old, and during those six years there had been no suspicion about her death. We had no body and the cause of death was based wholly on medical opinion.'

The Crown had called Dr Douthwaite and Dr Ashby as the medical experts in the case, but Hannam said that, in the view of the Attorney-General, it was Dr Ashby who had 'let us down very badly and did not come up to his original proof of evidence', and, more seriously still, 'by no means came up to the contents of a Notice of Additional Evidence which was served during the progress of the trial.'

Even so, apparently the Attorney-General, Melford Stevenson and the Director of Public Prosecutions still thought that there was sufficient evidence to expect a verdict of 'guilty', but 'the learned Judge' had summed up the case in a way which was 'extremely detrimental to the prosecution and unusually favourable to the defence'. Hannam thought it 'right to say in this report that the Attorney-General and Mr Melford Stevenson QC were quite amazed by it and have no explanation to offer about it.' The Jury had been absent for only three-quarters of an hour 'and in conformity with his Lordship's direction, returned a verdict of "not guilty".'

Hannam then quotes the statement of the Attorney-General regarding the further indictment on the case of Mrs Hullett, when he entered a *nolle prosequi*, and the Judge informed Dr Adams that the effect of this was to stay all further proceedings, and therefore discharged him.

The police had now been informed by the Director of Public Prosecutions that he intended restoring to the cases for hearing at Eastbourne Magistrates Court, the sixteen offences with which Dr Adams had been charged in November, 1956. These comprised eight offences of forgery, all except one of these relating to National Health prescriptions, and the one of false pretences; four offences of making false statements on the Cremation forms; and three offences under the Dangerous Drugs Act, 1951. Mr Malcolm Morris was to conduct the prosecution of these cases and it was hoped that the summary hearing would begin as soon as possible. All but one of the offences were indictable, so this would mean committal to Lewes Assizes. 'Many further matters' now required police attention, and Hannam asked for the Chief Superintendent's instruction to proceed with these.

Sir Theobald Mathew, Director of Public Prosecutions wrote on April 11th to the Commissioner of Police at Scotland Yard, to endorse the commendation of Superintendent Hannam by Mr Justice Devlin: 'It is with great pleasure that I endorse this commendation. The excellence of the work done by Superintendent Hannam and Sergeant Hewett in this very difficult matter, and the fairness with which they gave their evidence, reflect the greatest credit on both officers.' He also wrote a letter to the Chief Constable of Eastbourne, endorsing the Judge's commendation of Inspector Pugh. He must also have written to Malcolm Morris on the same day as there is a handwritten response of thanks to the Director for his 'charming letter' and the 'atmosphere of mutual confidence and friendship' which would remain even 'when the details of the case have become blurred'. He referred to 'a certain dinner at the Travellers' which stood out 'as a treasured memory'.

Hannam read the 'life story' of Dr Adams which appeared in the *Daily Express* with considerable interest and compiled a notebook with quotations from it in manuscript which are annotated; some of these annotations referring to his notes of interviews with the Doctor. As the meticulous detective he was, he obviously did this and left it in the archives, for good reasons. The first annotation concerns the Doctor's mention of gossip about him starting in 1935 when he had received his 'first anonymous postcard' and then 'three or four every year', stopping during the war years and commencing again in 1945, and that the police had received anonymous phone calls about him. 1935 was notable as the year in which Dr Adams received a large legacy and was residuary legatee in the will of Mrs Matilda Whitton; a will which had been unsuccessfully contested by her relatives. Hannam thought some statements were almost exactly the same as the Doctor's words to him on that chance encounter on 1st October, 1956. In describing his feelings after the 'Jury' verdict of 'Not Guilty': 'At that moment I was perfectly calm. I felt it was all God's guidance.' The Superintendent's feelings about the verdict are indicated in his use of 'Jury' – meaning that the verdict was the Judge's direction rather than the Jury's decision.

Hannam indicates various other statements which were untrue. These includes Dr Adams' statement that he had received 'approximately £14,000' from all the wills over 35 years, and that he had 'never been a sole legatee under any Will'; that when Mrs Morrell called him back from his holiday in Scotland, she had told him about the codicil removing him from her will, and that 'at the time of her death I knew I was not legally entitled to any benefit.' The last statement, again, was diametrically opposed to what he had told the Superintendent on 1st October, 1956. Superintendent Hannam notes the difference in the account of how Dr Adams came to Eastbourne in the *Daily Express* and the one he gave him on 1st October; the influence of Professor Rendle Short had been magnified. Referring to the police visit of 24th November, Dr Adams had significantly exaggerated the time it took for Mr James to arrive at Kent Lodge.

In particular, Hannam indicates the untruthfulness of Dr Adams' accounts relating to the nurses' notebooks in this 'life story' and the discrepancy between them: on 12th April, 1957 his account read:

'The Attorney General suggested that for some sinister reason I had preserved the books, but they were not in my possession'

and on the account of the 15th April, 1957:

'About a couple of weeks after Mrs Morrell died, much to my surprise, there was delivered to my house, a brown paper parcel containing these eight now famous note books. There was a note inside which read 'These may be of some use to you'.

The note was unsigned and I do not know to this day who the sender was or who delivered them as I was out at the time.

I put them in the second drawer in the filing cabinet beside my desk. They were in view for some time. Secretary responsible for cabinet. Note books disappeared from view. Forgot about them. 24.11.56. Supt. Hannam asked for any records relating to Mrs Morrell. We examined the cabinet together and found nothing. Later that night, it was 3 o'clock in the morning. Suddenly remembered the notebooks and found them at the back of a cabinet drawer hidden by out of date records. These books were found by providential guidance.'

It can be assumed that the last note Hannam wrote on Dr Adams' 'life story' was written with ironic intent:

'My chief aim and endeavour in writing my experiences has been to prevent such a misfortune befalling any other member of my profession.'

Superintendent Hannam also kept a substantial amount of cuttings from newspapers and magazines on the case, and these he deposited in the archives.

Almost as soon as the trial had finished there were questions asked in Parliament.

Mr George Wigg, Labour Member for Dudley, demanded an inquiry into the 'preparation, organisation and conduct' of the prosecution's case – although not into the trial itself. The Attorney-General refused the request. Mr Wigg was on his feet again, asking:

'Are you quite unaware that through the whole length of the British Isles the case of Dr Adams has evoked discussion in terms which bring discredit upon the law and upon your office. And will you not therefore, in the interests of British justice, have an inquiry into this case and the circumstances in which the prosecution was brought? And also the circumstances in which you found it necessary to oppose the application of the defence that the preliminary proceedings should be held in camera?'

The Attorney-General replied that he had been totally misinformed about these matters.

Mr Anthony Greenwood, the Labour M.P. for Rossendale, asked for an assurance 'that the widespread rumours that the prosecution was launched against the advice of the Director of Public Prosecutions and the Chief Constable of Eastbourne' were unfounded.

Sir Reginald Manningham-Buller, the Attorney-General, said that he could. He was 'glad to have the opportunity of repudiating some rumours which have certainly been maliciously circulated.' There had been 'no disagreement between the Director of Public Prosecutions and myself as to the course to be pursued in this case.' [It is quite certain, of course, that the opinion of the Chief Constable of Eastbourne was never sought as the case had been totally out of his hands from the very beginning.]

Sir Lionel Heald, Conservative M.P. for Chertsey, and a former Attorney-General, said that

Mr Wigg's statement had already appeared in a publication which he 'would not dignify by naming it' – this was The *Tribune* – and he asked the Attorney-General if he was 'aware there is widespread indignation at the unfair personal attacks made upon you.'

Sir Reginald was grateful, but he had expected such attacks. However, he wanted to put an end to any criticisms of the way in which Mr Melford Stevenson had conducted the prosecution case at the preliminary hearing at Eastbourne, and repeated that he had not opposed the application for certain evidence to be held in camera.

In answer to the concerns of a former Solicitor-General, Sir Lynn Ungoed Thomas, QC, who spoke of 'deep public concerns' and 'the terrifying consequences that might have ensued if certain documents were not available at the trial', the Attorney-General appreciated this concern, but said that he 'did not accept the view as to the possible consequences if these reports had not been available, in view of the observations made by the learned judge at the trial.'

Mr Wigg gave notice that he would raise the matter again and later said that he would be writing to the Speaker of the Commons to ask for the matter to be expedited.

A Committee, under Lord Tucker, was already being appointed by R.A. Butler, the Home Secretary, to report 'with a minimum of delay' on the desirability of limiting the reporting of cases heard by magistrates before trial in a higher court.

Dr D. Johnson, M.P. asked the Home Secretary, on 18th April, 1957, about the number of inspections which had been made between 1st January 1947 and 1st January 1957 of Dr Adams' Dangerous Drugs Register, and what branch of his Department was responsible for these inspections. Mr Simon, answered on behalf of the Home Office, saying that that Inspectors of the Home Office Drugs Branch and regional medical officers of the Ministry of Health were empowered to do this: the Regional Medical Officer had visited Dr Adams on the 13th August, 1948 'and amongst other things discussed the dangerous drugs register'.

Dr Johnson ploughed on by asking the same question about the inspection of the dangerous drugs' registers of chemists in Eastbourne. Mr Simon replied that the routine inspection of chemists' drugs' registers was the responsibility of the police. Between 1st January 1947 and 1st January 1957 Eastbourne police had made 587 visits to retail chemists in the borough.

Eastbourne Police appeared to have carried out their duty satisfactorily, but a letter was sent by Mr J. Austin of the Ministry of Health on 30th April regarding a sole visit of the Regional Medical Officer, Dr Colin Mearns, by then retired, to Dr Adams. A letter had been sent to Dr Adams suggesting 'a routine visit to discuss the National Health Service', which had come into operation on 5th July, 1948. These visits were intended to be 'friendly and informal to discuss confidentially any problems or difficulties which might have arisen and to make the acquaintance of the doctors'. An official from the Ministry had recently called upon Dr Mearns, but he had 'no recollections of the visit nor does he remember discussing the doctor's Dangerous Drug Register or seeing it'. There was sent with this letter a copy of the notes of the visit, but it was mentioned that the Minister's permission would have to be given for these to be used in evidence.

An article appeared in a professional medical journal The *Medical Press* on the 24th April, edited by Sir Cecil Wakeley, a former member of the General Medical Council and former President of the Royal College of Surgeons. The article suggested that patients with terminal illnesses would suffer because doctors would be afraid of giving heavy doses of narcotics to relieve pain: 'Every one of us will be looking over his shoulder for the smiler with the knife – somebody making notes to use against us later on.' The writer commented on three aspects of Dr Adams' trial which concerned the doctor-patient relationship: firstly, there was nothing sinister about the instruction that a dying patient should be 'kept under':

'Many and many a patient has been 'kept under' at all costs to save him agony. Any doctor with normal humanitarian impulses has always felt in honour bound to reduce his patient's sufferings. Where the prognosis was hopeless he has seldom stopped to count the cost as measured in the day-to-day duration of the patient's life.'

Secondly, the writer criticised the way some of the medical evidence was given at the trial:

'Some of the statements made in open court must have made many of our readers gasp. Seldom have so many confident assertions been made on what was at the best, an ingenious hypothesis. The system whereby doctors are called to act as witnesses for the prosecution or defence should be abolished. Medical assessors giving as nearly impartial guidance to the court as possible would be better both for justice and the medical profession.'

Nearly fifty years later, no action has been taken to achieve this.

Thirdly, and with less knowledge than he required, the writer commented:

'It is not wrong or shameful for a doctor to be left money by a rich patient. The £250 cabinet of silver left to Dr Adams by Mrs Morrell and which it was alleged was part of the motive for murder, must have been trivial in comparison with the fees the doctor would have earned by keeping her alive.'

Beside the report by Chapman Pincher on this medical article, there was Dr Adams' view on these matters, with his photograph and facsimile signature, headed 'What I think':

'The articles in the *Medical Press* crystallises the position which has arisen in the medical profession as a result of my trial. What I have always tried to do is to relieve suffering, mental or physical, without shortening life or in any way endangering life.

My trial raises two queries: Where can the line between easing pain and shortening life be drawn? and – At what point does relief of pain become illegal?

Doctors will now tend to be over-cautious and it would seem that many patients, particularly elderly people, may have to endure more suffering.

I agree with the suggested appointment of medical referees. I was always under the impression that expert witnesses, even though called by the prosecution, were supposed to be neutral and their function was to express opinions and not conclusions.'

Dr Adams had, remarkably, been transformed into an authority. He had attained fame, like his revered uncle, Dr John Bodkin.

The BMA also responded to *The Medical Press* article, by issuing a statement on April 25th, saying that the trial of Dr Adams would make 'no difference whatsoever' to doctors treatment of their patients:

> 'Doctors have always been responsible for their actions in prescribing drugs and there is no reason why they should alter their professional treatment of patients as a result of the trial.'

On the 27th April, Dr Adams returned to Kent Lodge, after his stay in Westgate-on-Sea – officially, he was still said to have been in London – driving back a new Morris Minor, by way of the lanes of Surrey and Sussex. According to the *Daily Express* he stopped at a hotel in Haywards Heath for a lunch of 'consommé, roast beef, Yorkshire pudding and a strawberry ice'. At 2.55 p.m. he arrived home to find that yet another name-plate had been stolen from his gatepost. Express reporter Arthur Chesworth was there to see him sit down at the roll-top desk in his surgery: 'Piled on the desk were parcels and more mail to add to the 885 letters and 70 telegrams of sympathy, encouragement, and congratulation' he had received both before and since the trial. He was quoted as saying:

> 'It feels good to be home again – to start living again. I hope that my resuming normal life will convince everyone of my innocence. I hope now that people will leave me alone to live my life and that there will be no more rumours.
>
> As far as the immediate future is concerned I can make no decision until I see my lawyers again later this week – after the debate in Parliament on Wednesday.'

He then telephoned 'a friend' to say he was on his way for tea, 'came out of his gate past the beds of wallflowers and the neat lawn' and, watched by four passers-by, drove off in his car.

Everything was not as straightforward as he might have hoped: a letter arrived for him, dated 30th April, on the headed paper of 'The White House' practice, which included Dr Mathew, asking him to resign from the Eastbourne Medical Society because they considered all the newspaper articles by himself and his housekeeper to be against the interests of the medical profession. His reply was totally untrue:

> 'I should like to clear up what is evidently a misunderstanding. May I assure you I did my utmost to avoid publicity of any kind, and all that occurred was completely beyond my control, nor have I personally benefited from it.'[1]

He complied with their request and resigned. On the 30th June, he also resigned from the NHS. Dr Barkworth was one of the partners who asked him to leave the practice, although he was the only one to visit him in prison.[2] No doubt they all wished to distance themselves from him.

[1] Surtees / [2] Ibid

# The Adjournment Debate

There was considerable activity in the Home Office and Scotland Yard when George Wigg, the Labour M.P. for Dudley, and scourge of Government ministers and civil servants, warned the Attorney-General that, in the Adjournment debate on the Adams case on 1st May, he proposed to raise the question of the 'general practice of the police in "tipping off" journalists about points of interest in criminal investigations, with particular reference to (a) the exhumation of the bodies of two of Dr Adams' former patients; and (b) the occasion of Dr Adams' arrest when a crowd of press photographers were present.'

The Attorney-General's Office had asked the Home Office for some 'formula' for the Attorney-General's reply and the Home Office had consulted with Scotland Yard. The Commissioner of Police had already investigated an allegation that the press had been fore-warned about Dr Adams' arrest, but the Commissioner found 'that there was no justification for this allegation'. Dr Adams had already been having an interview with a reporter and photographer from *Paris Match* when he was arrested and it was 'a piece of exceptional good fortune for the press that they happened to be there' when he was arrested. As for the exhumations, the press was speculating about these before any report had been received, by the Commissioner or the Attorney-General, from Superintendent Hannam, so there had been no discussion at all on the matter. These 'disclosures' were merely the result of 'intense press publicity and speculation in Eastbourne' and it had all caused great embarrassment to the police investigation. A reply to Mr Wigg was suggested:

> 'It is well known to police officers that when investigating offences they must exercise the greatest discretion in their dealings with the press. (In the case of Dr Adams the scale and intensity of press publicity was a matter of considerable embarrassment to them, and the Secretary of State has no information to suggest that any improper disclosures were made by the police officers concerned.) If Mr Wigg has any information to support the suggestion that such disclosures were made, the Secretary of State will be glad to consider it.'

It was Mr Wigg who initiated the adjournment debate: he told the House of Commons that he was not concerned with attacking the Attorney-General or Dr Adams, but with the memory of Timothy Evans, who had died on the scaffold for a murder he did not commit. (Timothy Evans was hanged in 1950 for the murder of his daughter at a house in Notting Hill, where later the serial killings of John Christie were discovered.) This innocent man would not have died if he had been wealthy or had a great profession behind him. He immediately proceeded to tell the Attorney-General that he had written asking him for a copy of the transcript of the evidence given at the committal hearing at Eastbourne Magistrates' Court, and had been told to apply to the defence for this; he regarded this a quite improper suggestion.

The point that Mr Wigg wished to make was that which had been supported by Sir Norman Birkett, the famous criminal defence lawyer, who had said, on an independent television broadcast on April 12th, that if the defence had made an application to the magistrates for the committal hearing to be held in private, and this had been supported by the prosecution, then it would have been held in private. Mr Justice Devlin, in his summing-up, had also said this would have been preferable. Mr Wigg held the view that the Crown had opposed the application by the defence; he did not believe the letter from the Attorney-General to himself, saying that Mr Melford Stevenson had not opposed the application by the defence. In this same letter, the Attorney-General had quoted Mr Melford Stevenson as saying at the Eastbourne hearing that he did not 'for one moment concede that the admissibility of this evidence [concerning the Hulletts, to prove 'system' ] can be the subject of serious debate'. These words were 'demonstrably untrue' because this evidence was not even produced by the Crown at the Old Bailey trial. This meant that it had been prejudicial not to hear it *in camera*.

Mr Wigg now turned on the press: most national newspapers had published articles from August 22nd to the 31st, 1956, which made it impossible for any jury to be found with open minds, and these were a scandal; but they could be dealt with by the Press Council. He was concerned with how they came by their information, and suggested that it could only have come from official sources. He asked the Attorney-General, and the Home Secretary, to set up an inquiry by a Judge of the High Court because there had been 'a systematic and planned campaign over a period of 10 days to build up a picture of a monster at large who had murdered people not by the score but by the hundred and it was done in such a way as to fasten it on to a particular individual'. The handling of the whole case though, had been prejudicial to Dr Adams' chances of acquittal; it had got 'perilously near to trial by newspapers'. And the behaviour of the police also required an inquiry by a Judge.

Mr Peter Rawlinson QC, Conservative M.P. for Epsom, (who had been leading defence counsel for Alfred Whiteway who was convicted – in Hannam's renowned case – of the Teddington Towpath Murders.) said that Mr Wigg was indicting nobody but the Press, but, not only had writs of libel been issued, but what had actually happened was that it had all ended with an acquittal, which was a triumph for British justice.

Mr Reginald Paget, QC, Labour M.P. for Northampton, thought that there had been much confusion, leading to it being impossible to find a jury who had not heard something about the case, and that there should be an investigation into all the circumstances. 'In the end it was abundantly clear that the prosecution had no case at all.' When the nurses' notebooks were produced during the trial, the prosecution should have dropped its case.

Mr Marcus Lipton, Labour M.P. for Brixton – surely misunderstanding the law – considered that there had been 'a grave error of judgment' in bringing such a case as it was well-known that doctors 'made the final weeks or months of their patients' lives as comfortable as possible'. This case showed that trying to make a criminal out of a doctor who used such 'standard treatment', would be extremely difficult.

Sir Lynn Ungoed-Thomas, Labour M.P. for Leicester North-East, hoped there would be a full investigation, particularly concerning the question of preliminary hearings being held in private.

Sir Reginald Manningham-Buller, the Attorney-General and Conservative M.P. for South Northamptonshire, was much surprised not to hear a public apology from Mr Wigg for his suggestion that Counsel for the Crown had opposed an application for the evidence on the Hulletts to be held *in camera*, as copies of the transcript of the hearing had been supplied to Mr Wigg. The allegation had been made on no grounds whatsoever, and it was also made by the *Daily Express* and *The Spectator*. The *Daily Express* had had the decency to make 'a prompt, unqualified and public withdrawal', but neither Mr Wigg nor *The Spectator* had done so. The Attorney-General particularly attacked *The Spectator* for the way in which its article was written: it would be difficult to find an instance of a more deliberate perversion of truth and a more dishonest and disgraceful piece of journalism'. Copies of the relevant part of the transcript were available in the Library.

The procedure at Eastbourne was to be the subject of an investigation, over which Lord Tucker would preside. But Mr Wigg had made 'a false accusation' because the magistrates had held that there was still a case to answer even without the evidence on the two Hullett cases. After the committal proceedings were over, facts had come to light relating to Mr Hullett (from the heart consultant who had seen him shortly before his death) which had not supported the case put forward to the magistrates. But the evidence with regard to Mrs Hullett was 'clearly admissible' for proving 'system' and could have been used in the case of Mrs Morrell. However, it was 'established practice' that if such evidence was, 'in relation to the weight it bore, so prejudicial to the accused that its admission would operate to prevent him having a fair trial' it should be excluded, so he had asked leave of the Judge to prefer an indictment charging the murder of Mrs Hullett separately. (It is difficult to see how either of the Hullett cases could have been used to prove system as there were only very general similarities – such as wealth and legacies – and nothing unusual which was similar. Lord Devlin, in his book, said that he would have been 'very surprised' if the Crown had in the Morrell case 'persuaded any judge that the Hullett evidence was admissible'.) Mr Wigg had also said that he had information – about which he had revealed nothing – that there had been a conference between the Crown, the Defence and the police about the Hullett evidence and that newspaper offices had been informed privately about this. The Attorney-General said that there had never been such a conference and that there would have been no reason for it.

There had been a complaint about leakage of some detailed information to the press, but it was wrong to conclude that this must have come from the police; there had been so many journalists in Eastbourne throughout the whole investigation, and it was not a large town, and Mr Wigg had no grounds at all for his assumption. If he could produce any, there would be an investigation. Mr Wigg had also suggested that there had been some disagreement between himself and the Director of Public Prosecutions: Sir Reginald refuted this and the decision to prosecute Dr Adams on a charge of murder had been unanimous.

The Attorney-General repudiated Mr Wigg's assertion that a poor man like Timothy Evans did not get as good a defence as had Dr Adams:

> 'Counsel who defended Evans was a very able and competent junior. He was my junior in the prosecution of Dr Adams.' [Melford Stevenson]

There was loud laughter at this retort.

The Attorney-General said that he had also been asked why the Crown had not dropped the prosecution when the nurses' notebooks had been produced. He had decided to prosecute in the first instance because there was indisputable evidence that Dr Adams had prescribed very large quantities of drugs between November 8th and November 12th, and uncontradicted evidence that he had administered that quantity to Mrs Morrell. In the opinion of experts, that quantity was lethal and there was no legitimate explanation for its administration. He would have been failing in his duty not to have put such evidence before a court, and he would make the same decision now. At this there were ministerial cheers. Sir Reginald then said that he 'could not accept the imputation that the prosecution were negligent in failing to find those books. As far as he was aware they were at all material times in the possession of the defence.'

This wording is extremely ambiguous, yet it went unchallenged. He went on to say that their information had been that the notebooks had been destroyed 'just as the doctor's own notes were destroyed'. (Yet the nurses' statements had suggested that their last sighting of the notes was that they were left for Dr Adams; and he did not make clinical notes for private patients.) No evidence had been given at the trial as to where they had come from or how they came to be kept. But, the Attorney-General went on, there was evidence that the amounts of drugs recorded in the books and administered by the nurses, 'and the injections which Dr Adams said he had given because he always gave them alone in the patient's room, was lethal in its quantity and not justified in a doctor's treatment of his patient.' Ministerial cheers followed the following statement:

> 'If those books had been available to the prosecution before the proceedings were instituted I should nevertheless have decided, again without hesitation, that the evidence ought to be laid before a court of law.'

The Judge had ruled that the case, based on the notebooks, still required an answer from the defence.

Sir Lynn Ungoed-Thomas asked what the Attorney-General had meant when he said that the nurses' notebooks were only accurate 'as far as they went'. Sir Reginald replied that the prosecution had not challenged that the nurses had recorded the injections they had given, but there was good reason to suppose the notebooks were not a complete record. For instance, on one day there were no entries of any injections, yet there was 'constant daily medication', and there were the entries recorded as 'special injections' and what these were was unknown. He did not accept that the notebooks 'told the whole, complete story'. The Judge had directed that the 'special injections' be ignored. The Attorney-General also wished to point out that the defence had not challenged the evidence of Superintendent Hannam and Inspector Pugh, — who had both been commended by the Judge for their fairness — that Dr Adams had admitted to them 'that he had given Mrs Morrell the amount prescribed between November 8 and 12 — an amount considerably in excess of the amount recorded in the nurses' books.'

The Attorney-General said that he had put the record of the trial, together with some exhibits and a note of some of the proceedings of the committal hearing at the magistrates' court. He wanted to ensure 'that there was no further criticism of Mr Melford Stevenson and those who assisted him in the conduct of the case in the magistrates' court.'

Mr Ede, the Labour M.P. for South Shields, wound up the debate by saying that the House 'was under a great debt to the Attorney-General for the full and frank way he had dealt with this case'. There were loud cheers. He hoped that the Press would be very careful in future to avoid a repetition of what had occurred in this case.

Sir Frank Newsam, Home Office Minister consulted with his officials on 6th May on the report on the Adjournment Debate and a memorandum was sent to Scotland Yard on the following day: Mr Wigg had made general allegations about the police and the press and had asked for a judicial investigation. He had supported his allegations with reference to five incidents, but two of these had been dealt with by the Attorney-General in the debate, and a third was on the press conference held by police a week after Scotland Yard had taken over the case to try and ensure responsible reporting. The two outstanding incidents were: that the press were given advance warning of the visit of Superintendent Hannam and Inspector Pugh to Ocklynge Cemetery; and that the press were told in advance when the exhumations were to take place.

The Commissioner of Police passed the note to Hannam to compose the responses. Both Superintendent Hannam and Inspector Pugh denied having visited the cemetery, and stated that the photograph was faked by the press. A copy of this was sent to the Home Office. As far as the exhumations were concerned, it was known that the Press had paid the keepers of both cemeteries to inform them if the police visited them. The proceedings of the exhumations were screened from view. With regard to Mr Wigg's last point about the police and their 'efforts to stimulate the press campaign', and Scotland Yard ordering a short-hand writer to be present at the press conference, Hannam replied that the press conference was held on 23rd August, just after the inquest on Mrs Hullett, and he was only brought into the case on 17th August and was 'instructed by Commander Hatherill not to have any discussion with Press unless the Chief Constable of Eastbourne was present and a short-hand writer was present. It is true that certain statements by the Chief Constable of Eastbourne were reported in some papers on the 27th and 29th July – but this could hardly be called a press campaign.'

A meeting at the Home Office followed on 9th May, which included Sir Frank Newsam, Home Office staff, the Commissioner and Assistant Commissioner, and the question of press publicity was discussed. As a result, Chief Superintendent Spooner was instructed to 'carry out certain enquiries in Eastbourne'.

The Scotland Yard minute of this 9th May meeting records the discussion as exactly what Hannam wrote in manuscript on the original Home Office memorandum.


# A Case of Libel


Nominal fines of £50 for contempt of court were imposed by the Queen's Bench Divisonal Court on Friday, May 10th, 1957, on Rolls House Publishing Co. Ltd, publishers of the American magazine *Newsweek* and W.H. Smith and Son, who had distributed the magazine in

Britain. The motion for writs of attachment was brought by the Attorney-General, and the Lord Chief Justice, Lord Goddard, reading the judgment of the court, said that the contempt was 'of a most serious description': the magazine had contained two paragraphs of material 'highly prejudicial to the accused' and was on sale during the trial. The article in the issue of April 1st was headed 'The Doctor on Trial' and referred to Dr Adams' elderly patients 'a remarkable number of whom remembered him in their wills when they died'. Under a heading, 'Bequests' it continued: 'Eastbourne's frenzied gossip pushed Dr Adams's alleged victims as high as 400'; it then referred to Mrs Morrell and Mrs Hullett. Mr Eldon Wylie Griffiths, *Newsweek*'s chief European correspondent had told the police that the intention of the editors was to tell the story of Dr Adams' trial with accuracy and impartiality. Lord Goddard said that 'their performance was lamentably inconsistent with their intentions', but praised the swift action of W.H. Smith in taking 'every possible step they could to call in the copies', and also stopping the sale of the following week's issue, and accepted that they had not known of the offending content.

# Further Investigations

Superintendent Hannam had been in Eastbourne in connection with 'the present 16 Charges' under instructions from the Director of Public Prosecutions. He had seen all the witnesses and gone through their evidence with them. The doctors, he noted, in a memorandum from Scotland Yard to the DPP on 2nd May, 1957, had been 'more co-operative than we have experienced in the past and one tends to the view that they realise the importance of these cases succeeding in order, at the very least, Adams may be removed from the Medical Register.'

Miss Frances Abrams, a Welsh lady, 56 years of age, had been employed by Dr Adams as cook-housekeeper at Kent Lodge from June 1947 until July 1952 – she left just one month after Florence Henry, the Doctor's cousin died. In her statement of 17th October, 1956, made to DI Pugh, she had said that she had always found Dr Adams 'a very kind and generous employer' and mentioned that Miss Henry had been 'devoted to Dr Adams'. She had been 'given to understand that Dr Adams' mother adopted Miss Henry when she was three weeks old.' (This contradicts a previous account and is clearly untrue.) She knew that 'Miss Henry had a brother who was a doctor and she also had a step-brother. Her brother 'visited Miss Henry many times and was at 6, Trinity Trees shortly before she died'. (This was Dr Adams' doctor cousin in London.) She did recall that the Morrell silver had been used once whilst she was in Dr Adams' service. She had been a patient of Dr Trower's for 25 years, but he had never treated her or prescribed any medicine for her, in fact she had never been to him for treatment. Dr Adams, certainly in 1956, was issuing NHS prescriptions for her, signed 'J.B.Adams p.p. Dr Trower' on NHS forms which had Dr Barkworth's name stamped on the back. (In 1956 the Ministry of Health had issued a directive that all prescriptions should be stamped on the reverse with the name and address of the issuing doctor.)

Whilst he had been examining the entries in *Browne's Dangerous Drugs Registers*, he had discovered 18 entries showing heroin and pethidine supplied to Miss Frances Abrams, (some of the existing charges related to NHS prescriptions for her) on prescription from Dr Adams, all on the NHS, although she was not an NHS patient of Dr Adams. Hannam commented: 'This probably explains why Miss Abrams thinks the Doctor so good'. She had told Hannam and Hewett that the Defence had seen her and taken a statement and 'although adhering quite correctly to the evidence as contained in her proof, she will without doubt say that Adams was extremely kind to her and she thinks a lot of him'. The Superintendent decided against telling her of the other 18 entries he had found as 'more value' might be obtained in cross-examining her in court, and she would doubtless have informed the Defence immediately. Then, amazingly:

> 'She in fact did say that she had seen Sir Roland Gwynne within recent days to ask him
> to arrange to relieve her from the necessity of giving evidence against Dr Adams.'

Hannam was still satisfied that Miss Abrams would give evidence 'properly'. But she had told him that she 'had never had any dangerous drugs from Dr Adams but he had given her some injections for a liver condition.'

Without pursuing further enquiries, it was not possible to say that Dr Adams had not used the heroin and pethidine on Miss Abrams, but the Superintendent 'did wonder whether he had been obtaining these commodities for his own use in Miss Abrams' name as she was a member of his staff'. This would also mean that he had defrauded the NHS, and in that case these offences under the Dangerous Drugs Act would be serious ones. Hannam's enquiries led even further:

> 'I made a further search of Browne's Dangerous Drugs Registers and saw similar entries
> of heroin and pethidine for Miss Lawrence, his present receptionist, and for Miss
> Room, his present housekeeper, both of whom are patients on his National Health list.
> I observed another name, Miss Gower, who in 1950, 1951 and early 1952 was being supplied with heroin, morphine and pethidine, but this lady died late in 1952.
>
> It does seem therefore strange, to say the least, that four employees in his service
> have had these important dangerous drugs on prescription from him and, pending consideration and instructions, I have made no further enquiries about them for if the matter were pursued, it would be necessary to closely question Miss Abrams and to see
> Miss Lawrence and Miss Room and then to question the doctor himself for an explanation.'

Lists of these prescriptions were attached. And there was the very strange information that:

> 'Miss Abrams herself has changed her address and is now a housekeeper at The Manor
> Farm, Folkington, Sussex.'

She was now employed by Sir Roland Gwynne.

The enquiries into all these possibilities of drug-trafficking seem to have ceased.

Superintendent Hannam concluded his memorandum by referring to Sister Miller who was to be a witness in the case of the cremation certificate for James Priestley Downs. He had just interviewed her again and she had remembered something which had occurred whilst she was nursing Mr Priestley Downs under Dr Adams' supervision: she had said to him 'You will soon have this patient better and home again' and he had replied, 'God forbid, I thought you were a friend of mine.'

# The Trial at Lewes Crown Court

Dr Adams still had to answer thirteen criminal charges (originally sixteen) which were outstanding. These were the three drugs charges of attempting to conceal dangerous drugs, obstructing DI Pugh in his search, and failing to keep a Dangerous Drugs' Register; the other charges related to forgery of NHS prescriptions – issuing of NHS prescriptions for private patients on the NHS lists of other doctors and signing them on their behalf; and the false statements on cremation certificates.

He was tried at Lewes Crown Court on 26th July, 1957 before Mr Justice Pilcher, and pleaded guilty on all charges. He was fined a total of £2,400 and £457.17s. 8d. towards the costs of the prosecution. When the Judge mentioned that he would have to fix a term of imprisonment in default of payment, Dr Adams' Counsel informed him that the fines would be paid immediately, and so no sentence of imprisonment was fixed in default of payment. Afterwards he denied that he was guilty of these offences, particularly with regard to the cremation certificate statements, and said that he had pleaded guilty only on the advice of his barrister.[3] In the case of the will of James Priestley Downs, for instance, this had actually been read in his presence by the solicitor and then signed by Mr Downs, also in his presence.

A Notice under the Dangerous Drugs Act, 1951 was issued by the Home Secretary, RA Butler on 4th September, 1957, withdrawing authorisation from Dr Adams to supply drugs or give prescriptions for drugs under the Dangerous Drugs Regulations, 1953.

The Town Clerk of Eastbourne, Francis Busby, wrote to the Director of Public Prosecutions on 10th October, 1957, asking him why the prosecution costs had not been paid to the Borough Treasurer; he did not know whether the Defendant had paid these costs or not.

On the 27th November, Dr Adams appeared before the General Medical Council and was struck off the medical register. Nevertheless, he continued to see his private patients to have tea and cream cakes with them, or even to provide 'over the counter' medicines for them.[4]

# Sybille Bedford

An official in the War Office wrote to Mr Maurice Crump, the Deputy Director of Public

[3] Ibid / [4] Ibid

Prosecutions on 31st October, 1958, with some concern: he had noticed in the *Daily Telegraph* of 24th October a review of the book by Sybille Bedford on the trial of Dr Adams, which had stated 'she prints a skilfully abridged version of the official transcript'. The official, Mr H.E. Smith, had inferred that she had been given access to the official transcript, and he asked for information because:

> '…successive Secretaries of State have been pressed hard by Lord Russell of Liverpool
> to be given access to court-martial proceedings and, so far we have limited him to trials
> in which he, himself, appeared.'

Mr Crump asked Mr F.D. Barry for information on the matter, and his note states that 'there is no record in the Registry of the transcript of this case of Dr Adams being supplied to Sybille Bedford. I certainly gave no authority for the transcript to be passed to this woman, and I understand from Leck that he did not do so either.' He had checked with the shorthand writers for the Old Bailey and they had not supplied a transcript, and would have referred the matter to the Registrar of the Court of Criminal Appeal if they had received any application. The Court of Criminal Appeal had not received an application from Sybille Bedford for the transcript. There was also now a new Rule from 1st May, 1958 (Rule 17 of the Criminal Appeal Rules, 1958, S.I. 652) that entitled only parties to criminal cases having authority to obtain a transcript and 'other persons interested in the proceedings', but this did not apply to a person writing a book on a trial. Barry could only suggest that 'Bedford either obtained a copy of the transcript from the Defence or possibly attended the trial and made shorthand notes of what occurred; of course there is nothing to stop her doing that if she was sufficiently interested.'

The War Office was doubtless much relieved.

## The Restoration

Dr Adams was restored to the Medical Register by the General Medical Council on the 22nd November, 1961 and his authority to possess and prescribe dangerous drugs was restored by order of the Home Secretary, R.A. Butler, on 2nd July, 1962. He was allowed to prescribe all classes of dangerous drugs just as before. (This notice was in the DPP's archive and was published in the London and Edinburgh Gazettes just as the notice of withdrawal of authority was.) Many of his private patients came back to him, particularly his elderly ladies. He continued as a sole practitioner and was not restored as a partner of the 'Red House' practice. The numbers on his list were much reduced and the hotels had appointed other doctors. There is no evidence that anyone was overseeing his practice in any way for the next twenty-one years until his death in 1983, even of his prescribing of drugs or the death certificates he signed. Patients still continued to leave him money in their wills. Everything and everyone depended on his having been frightened enough by the trial to put a stop to his previous compulsive behaviour of his own volition.

# The U.S. Visa Application & Drug Trafficking

Solicitors, Messrs. William Charles Crocker of Bentinck Street, London, wrote to Mr F.D. Barry, now Deputy Director of Public Prosecutions, on 28th August, 1962. Their Mr Gordon was acting on behalf of Dr Adams, who was proposing to visit his cousin in the United States for 'two to three months early next year'. He had to apply for a visa and, because of his conviction relating to the incident when he had obstructed Detective Inspector Pugh by attempting to conceal the two bottles of morphine, the U.S. authorities required evidence showing that Dr Adams was 'neither a drug addict nor an illicit trafficker in drugs'. Mr Gordon was sure that the Deputy Director appreciated that it was 'extremely difficult to produce evidence of a negative fact' and asked for assistance. He hoped that Mr Barry could recommend to the Director that he write a letter which he could produce to the U.S. Consul 'confirming that Dr Adams has never been suspected of being a drug addict or an illicit trafficker in drugs'. Mr Barry underlined the word 'suspected'.

Maurice Crump of the DPP's Office sent a copy of the letter to the Commissioner at Scotland Yard to put the whole matter into his hands as it was only the police who could give a satisfactory answer, and informed the solicitors that he had done so. The request was passed, through Chief Superintendent Davies to Charlie Hewett, now Detective Inspector Hewett, who submitted his memorandum on 22nd September. The view of the police, even after the acquittal, is explicit in the following two paragraphs:

> 'It will be remembered that the object of the original enquiry was to endeavour to find the truth or otherwise of allegations that Dr Adams induced a number of his patients to alter their wills in his favour, after subjecting them to treatment with hypnotic drugs and other sedatives and in some cases, having achieved his aim, allowed his patients to die through lack of proper medical attention or brought about their deaths prematurely by excessive use of drugs.
>
> It was discovered during the early part of the investigation, by virtue of a search of Chemists' Dangerous Drugs Registers, that in a number of instances as the result of prescriptions issued by Dr Adams, drugs were dispensed for patients immediately before or after death. There was also evidence that some of these found their way into the possession of Dr Adams. He was in the circumstances suspected of either being a drug addict or dealing illicitly with drugs.'

They were in no doubt that Dr Adams was not a drug addict, because he had been under observation in the hospital at Brixton prison 'during which time suspicion that he may have been an addict was completely dispelled.' There had been no evidence that Dr Adams was engaged in drug-trafficking 'in the usual and accepted sense of the term'. The drugs acquired in the 'unethical' method which Hewett had already described could have been used on other patients, provided that proper entries had been made in the Dangerous Drugs Register which the Doctor was supposed to keep. But there was a proviso:

'It was also appreciated that by obtaining drugs in this manner, surreptitiously using them on patients who, by virtue of his medical treatment, had become addicts and not recording their use in his Dangerous Drugs Register, he was acting in a manner not far removed from the usual trafficking. In view of the evidence then available this aspect was regarded as not being beyond the bounds of possibility, but it was found that corroborative evidence of the actual administration was very difficult to obtain.'

The other reason for not extending this part of the enquiry was that of the twenty-three deaths they had investigated in detail, all but two of these had died prior to 31st May, 1955, and the other two – the Hulletts – had not come within the scope of that part of the enquiry.

DI Hewett related the events of 24th November, 1956 when Kent Lodge had been searched for dangerous drugs, and the Doctor had 'professed not to know what dangerous drugs were or what a Dangerous Drugs Register was'; then he had removed two bottles of hyperduric morphine from his cabinet and secreted them. His explanation had been that one had been obtained for patient, Mr Soden, who had died, and the other for Mrs Sharpe, who had died before he could use it.

'Subsequent enquiries showed that George Soden died on the 17th September, 1956, but that morphine had never been prescribed for him. It was found, however, that in respect of Mrs Sharpe, [of 'Barton' and the Neil Miller sisters' landlady – a vital witness] who died on 13th November 1956, a prescription was issued by Dr Adams for hyperduric morphine and pethedine tablets on 10th November, 1956, and these had been delivered at her address the same day.

As the result of the search a considerable quantity of dangerous drugs was taken into possession by the police. The intention was to fully enquire into the possibility that he was dealing illicitly with drugs but as the result of other evidence obtained on this occasion, on 19th December, 1956 he was arrested and charged with murder. No further enquiries were ever made into the possibility he was illicitly trafficking in drugs.'

Three charges had resulted from the search on 24th November, 1956: attempting to conceal drugs, obstructing a police officer, and failing to keep a Dangerous Drugs' Register.

Inspector Hewett pointed out that Mr Justice Devlin had, in his summing-up on the Morrell case, said that there must have been some channel of distribution to account for the difference in the amount of drugs prescribed and the amount recorded as administered; in other words, the Judge had thought it likely that Dr Adams was engaged in some sort of illegal trafficking in drugs.

When Dr Adams had pleaded guilty on the charges of forgery and false pretences of medical prescriptions, offences under the Cremation Act 1902 and the drugs offences at Lewes Assizes, he had been fined £2,400 plus costs. It was particularly significant that the Judge had fined him £500 in respect of the drugs offences, ruling that the proviso under the Statute limiting the fine to £50 if the failure to keep a Dangerous Drugs Register 'was <u>not</u> done in pursuance of the commission of any other criminal offence' did not apply, and regarding the offence as a very serious one.

DI Hewett recommended:

> 'It may be thought from the foregoing that persons other than the investigation officers had their suspicions about the way Dr Adams dealt with the drugs he unethically obtained and that the request in letter 62C should not be complied with.'

The Assistant Chief Superintendent wrote in manuscript on the memorandum to Commander 'C', advising that the police should not provide 'general information as to character' and saying that the issue of whether Dr Adams was an illicit drug trafficker was 'open to doubt'. Possibly the matter might be referred to the Home Office for consideration.

# A Terrible Misunderstanding

Dr Adams had to re-insert himself into Eastbourne society; he had been unable to contemplate rebuilding his life anywhere else or retiring into obscurity. He transformed all that had happened into 'a terrible misunderstanding'. He had the loyal patients and friends like Norah O'Hara, but it was his life-long interest in shooting which helped him the most, and he now had much more time available to pursue it.

He was still a very good shot and was President of Bisley Gun Club from 1975 to 1983, spending all of his weekends shooting and helping to organise shoots. He was a founder member of the British Clay Pigeon Shooting Society and he travelled abroad frequently for competitions, going with the English team to Belgium in 1960. He was a fine shot until almost the end of his life, when his eyesight began to fail.

In his younger days he had been a member of the Round Table, and now rejoined the '41 Club' of Rotary. The Y.M.C.A had asked him to resign from the Committee after the trial; over many years he had donated money and given time to them, but now he directed his charitable gifts to other organisations, presenting cups, supporting events, and paying for equipment and outings. In this way he was welcomed and accepted by different groups of people, often younger ones; not quite the set he had once sought out. He could often be seen in hotels and restaurants in the company of various ladies of mature years.

It was on 30th June 1983 that Dr Adams was at the Battle Abbey Hotel for a shooting meeting, and, slipping on some concrete steps, fractured his left hip. Mrs Doris Sellens, his housekeeper since 1967, related what happened after the ambulance was called:

> 'In the ambulance he asked where he was being taken, and when told Hastings he demanded, 'You turn round and take me to Eastbourne'. Mr Richards, Consultant Orthopaedic Surgeon, put a pin in on the Saturday and on the Sunday Miss O'Hara and I visited and he was bright. On the Monday he developed a bad chest, deteriorated and

died about teatime of left ventricular failure. One of his sayings was, "If I break my femur that'll be the end" – and it was.'[5]

Dr John Bodkin Adams died on 4th July, 1983. His solicitor, John Cheesbrough had arranged for the funeral to be held at Holy Trinity Church, Trinity Trees, but Dr Adams had previously asked Dr Alistair MacLeod, a Chapel Elder, to take the service, for, after all, he always remained a member of the Brethren, despite any attendances he made at Anglican churches. In the event, Dr MacLeod led prayers, and the Vicar conducted the service. The *Eastbourne Herald* reported:

> '180 friends and former patients' gathered at Holy Trinity Church on Wednesday, 20th July, 1983, to pay tribute to Dr John Bodkin Adams, the popular Eastbourne GP who was cleared of murder in a sensational Old Bailey trial in 1957.'

The journalists and photographers from home and abroad were there again in force, and the television cameras. A private cremation service was held at Langney (Eastbourne) Crematorium and his ashes taken home to Coleraine.

# The Will

Mr John Cheesbrough of Coles & James was co-executor of the Will, with Mr Harry Price. The gross value of Dr Adams' estate was £408,305.00. He had made the will on the 10th September of the previous year and, unsurprisingly, had given it a great deal of thought. He wished his body to be cremated and the ashes interred in the grave of his late Father and Mother in Coleraine Cemetery, and that the headstone and coping of the grave should be polished, the inscription renewed, and that the wording should be added:

> 'And also his Son JOHN BODKIN ADAMS MD, D.P.H., D.A.' together with the date of his death.'

He left legacies to many, 'in sincere appreciation of the loyal support the legatees have given to me in my time of trouble':

> 'To Molly Henry of Brighton, £1,000 [she must have been a cousin by marriage]
> Her daughter, Daphne Williams, £1,000
> Miss Nora Kathleen O'Hara [his former fiancée] 'in gratitude and memories of our long standing friendship any one item of furniture or personal or household or domestic use ornament or consumption belonging to me at the time of my death that she may care to select.'

[5] Ibid

This legacy was to have priority over all others in his will so that she could have the first choice of anything she wished.

Two other cousins: Eileen and Kathleen Hamilton, living in Belfast, were bequeathed £5,000 between them, and another, James Adams of Tobermore, Magherafelt in County Derry, also £5,000. Mrs Pamela Brill of Tunbridge Wells was presumably another cousin as she is set between two in the Will – received £1,000. But it was the next cousin who received the largest legacy and the items, Dr Louise Garfit-Clowes of Kingswood, Surrey, £5,000 and most of his favourite belongings: 'The Mahogany Bookcase in the Lounge, The Piecrust Table in the Lounge, The Grandfather Clock in the Waiting Room, The Cabinet in the Dining Room with the silver in it [the Morrell piece], The Antique Cabinet in the Dining Room, One Diamond Ring and The paintings of her Grandfather and Grandmother and Mrs Bodkin now in my Dining Room'. Anne Clowes, another cousin inherited £1,000 and yet another, Robert Chesney of Balligan, Co. Down, £1,000.

The other personal legacies were to many friends and supporters, to the two executors, his chauffeur, James White, to whom he left £3,000 and 'any motor car belonging to me at the date of my death', to Percy Hoskins of the *Daily Express*, £1,000, two doctors, Mr S. Jenkins F.R.C.S., £1,000, and Dr Churcher, a local GP, £2,000. There were the charitable legacies: Bisley Gun Club – £1,000, Holy Trinity Church, Trinity Trees, Eastbourne – £500, St. John's Church, Polegate – £500, The Scripture Union – £1,000, The Crusader Union – £1,000, Marine Hall, Eastbourne, belonging to the Plymouth Brethren – £500, The Medical Friend and Missionary News – £1,000, The Medical Benevolent Fund of the BMA – £1,000, The Salvation Army – £1,000. There were 47 legatees in all and the residue was to be divided between them in the same shares as the legacies bequeathed.

The oddest of all the legacies was that to Mrs Pearl Prince of £1,000 as there was a strange irony to it which was, doubtless, in the Doctor's mind when he made his Will. In the police archives is an anonymous letter which Superintendent Hannam received, dated 14th September 1956, and the story contained in it seemed to relate very closely to that of the Neil Miller sisters:

'In view of the publicity in the national press, I feel compelled to give you what information I can about a wealthy resident of Eastbourne, now deceased, and I hope that I may be forgiven by you for adding to your enormous task if my facts are irrelevant.

'Mr Sydney Herbert Prince of White Lodge, St. John's Road, Eastbourne, died in December, 1954. [Dr Adams certified the death as 'cerebral thrombosis' and received £100 under the will.] He left a wife and two daughters. His wife lives at 'Barton', St. John's Road, Eastbourne, just opposite her old home; 'Barton' so far as I can make out is a home for ageing women who are not in need of nursing attention, but who are no longer able to run their own homes.

'Mrs Prince was advised by her doctor, Dr Bodkin Adams, to take a room at his house, retaining some of her furniture for it and storing the remainder. This she did and now lives a rather solitary life in her one room. She is constantly under the "eye" of her doctor, and does nothing or goes anywhere without his knowledge and approval. He visits her at least once a week and recently, she has been suffering from nervous strain and he is, I understand, visiting her every day. She suffers from insominia [sic] and lack of appetite, pills for which have been given by the doctor. Mr Prince left an estate of something in the region of £90,000 gross, £72,000 net, (these figures may be slightly incorrect). I believe he changed his will on more than one occasion, finally leaving his wife a negligible sum. Mrs Prince seems to be kept in complete ignorance of her financial state, and merely lives from day to day, hoping that she will have sufficient money to meet her modest requirements. It is interesting to learn that the beneficiaries under the will of the late Mr Prince have been informed that their legacies will probably never be met, and to date, I believe, each has received a third, with very little hope of more to follow. The lawyer of the late Mr Prince, is a Mr Hubert Sogno of Eastbourne. Mrs Prince has been known to state that her doctor has told her that her late husband asked him "to look after her finances". As this is rather on the lines of a case reported in the press, in which a wife heard a friend discussing with her husband the matter of finance after his death, and in anger threw a stick at him at the bottom of the stairs [Mawhood], I wonder whether something of the like has occurred with Mr Prince. I am of the opinion that Mrs Prince lives in awe of her doctor and because of this will be reluctant to divulge any details of her case.'

The writer went on to mention that Mrs Prince had sisters in England, a brother in Australia, and two step-daughters, but obviously did not know them. Regret was expressed at 'the anonymous nature' of the letter. The envelope bore a 'London EC' postmark, noted Hannam in his report, so it was posted in the City. The result was that the police discussed the matter with Mr Sogno, who informed them that Mrs Prince received £15,000 under her husband's will and the residue was being held on trust for her. Mr Sogno told Superintendent Hannam that he was himself concerned about her living in one room at 'Barton' 'for he has private suspicions against Mrs Sharpe and because Adams frequently visits her, for no apparent reason.' Mr Sogno, however, did have some control over her finances and told them that he would 'watch the matter'.

When the Superintendent and DI Pugh were interviewing Mrs Sharpe on the 3rd September, they had seen Mrs Prince and talked with her. Hannam said that she had told them 'quite frankly that she regards Dr Adams as an absolutely wonderful man and would not hear a word to the contrary. If our information is true she has made a will leaving Dr Adams £10,000 and this was unknown to Mr Sogno who plans to see Mrs Prince about the suggestion at a favourable opportunity.' He saw no point in pursuing the matter as Mr Sogno would keep a watching brief. In the event Mrs Prince survived into the 1980s. Mrs Sharpe was less fortunate.

At the end of February 1984 the contents of Kent Lodge which had not been willed, were auctioned by Edgar Horn's. There were a great many items which Dr Adams had collected over the years, for the auction was a two-day one, and much local interest. Kent Lodge itself was auctioned in September of the same year: it had been neglected since the death of his mother in 1943.

# Impossible to Accuse a Doctor

Dr Adams' apparently spontaneous reaction to being accused of murder by Chief Superintendent Hannam came to characterise the strategy for the Defence. The argument was simple: medicine isn't an exact science; you can't blame the doctor if he is doing his best to treat an elderly and critically ill patient and that patient dies. To win its case, the Prosecution had to show beyond reasonable doubt that Dr Adams' purpose was to kill Mrs Morrell. In the event, the Defence's strategy proved successful; but this does not necessarily mean that Dr Adams was innocent of the charge. The Prosecution may have failed to convince judge and jury, but perhaps this had more to do with the case as it was presented than Doctor Adams' lack of guilt.

There was, for example, evidence uncovered by the police which, for procedural and other reasons, was never presented in court and which might have strengthened the case against Dr Adams. Dr Adams' behaviour can now be compared with that of known serial killers who were also doctors – a form of evidence which would not have been available to the police in 1956. Finally, the conduct of the Prosecution's case can be assessed to discover whether the case against Dr Adams might have been presented quite differently.

## Evidence from the Morrell Case which Was not Heard in Court

### Mrs Ethel Julia Dockerill

DI Pugh took a statement from Mrs Ethel Julia Dockerill on 3rd December, 1956. She was a widow and had worked as a daily help for Mrs Morrell for about three years up until about two weeks after her employer died. Mrs Dockerill's duties included the cleaning of Mrs Morrell's bedroom and taking her personal laundry home to wash for her. She was very friendly with Mrs Morrell and used to spend time with her, chatting to her in her bedroom. Mrs Dockerill related that she had 'sometimes discussed those people she was not fond of. She had a mind of her own and if she took a liking to certain people all was well, but the same applied if she didn't like them. She let them know they were not in favour.'

Dr Adams had been 'a frequent visitor' during the whole of the time Mrs Dockerill worked at 'Marden Ash': early on the visits had been 'more of a social nature' but after the stroke he had come more often, 'sometimes twice a day'. (The stroke was in June 1948, but the twice-daily visits were only regular from 22nd August, 1950.)

> 'It was during this latter period, from the way Mrs Morrell spoke, she had lost faith in the doctor, and often I heard her having high words with him. The doctor was always so placid and never raised his voice to her. It was about two weeks before she died that she said to me, "I am going to strike Doctor Adams out of my will. He shan't have a penny". She was quite rational when she said this but I never queried why she had changed so suddenly towards the Doctor and she never enlarged on why she had suddenly made such a decision. She was aware that Doctor Adams had a woman friend [Betty Cradock] and once, some weeks before she died, when Doctor hadn't called she said to me, "I expect he's gone to see his woman friend". When Dr Adams was away on one of his shooting holidays in Scotland, he would usually send Mrs Morrell a brace of pheasants.'

Mrs Dockerill had been 'very surprised' when she was told that Mrs Morrell had died. She had seen her on the Saturday, 11th November when 'she appeared to be very bright and she spoke to me'. On Sunday 12th, Nurse Mason-Ellis had told her that no-one was allowed in her room, but Mrs Dockerill thought this strange and went in without the nurse knowing. She found the curtains drawn and a screen in front of the door. She went to the foot of the bed and 'Mrs Morrell lay there and appeared unconscious.' She left the room and never saw her again.

Dr Adams had visited the house on the Monday after Mrs Morrell died. (20th November) Mrs Dockerill did not know why he had called. He had shaken hands with her and said, 'You know Mrs Morrell talked about every one, me included, but I never heard her say one cross word against you'.

Mrs Dockerill then recalled that 'on the Friday morning when Mrs Morrell was talking to me about striking the doctor out of her will, she mentioned something about candlesticks and said, "I did intend giving him the candlesticks but I am not going to let him have them now."' (This must have been two weeks before she died, so it would either have been 27th October or 3rd November.)

Mrs Morrell had never once complained to Mrs Dockerill of any pain and she personally 'never thought she was really ill enough to die so suddenly'. She had thought that perhaps it had been another stroke because she was able to speak to her properly up until two days before her death. Mrs Dockerill always used to help the duty nurse lift her and 'she had full use of both arms when the nurse and I used to lift her up in bed. She always placed her arms round nurse and myself when we lifted her.' Sometimes during the last week, she had appeared to be 'a little bit stupid and her speech was slurred', but on the Thursday before she died she had been 'perfectly all right and very bright and spoke to me quite normally.'

It must have been on 10th September that Dr Adams had gone to Scotland for his shooting holiday because Dr Harris visited Mrs Morrell on 11th, 12th, 13th, 14th and 15th

September. Dr Adams had flown back to see Mrs Morrell at her demand and visited her on the 16th, 17th and 18th September, and Dr Harris resumed visiting from 19th until Dr Adams took over again on the 26th. It seems quite likely that Mrs Morrell was so incensed because Dr Adams had taken Miss Betty Cradock with him on holiday; Hannam had discovered that he did do so.

### Mrs Myers

Detective Superintendent Hannam received this letter, from Mrs Myers, a friend of Mrs Morrell, quite early in his enquiries, and it throws some light both on the normal character of Mrs Morrell and upon what had been happening to her:

The Old Barn,
Swanage,
Dorset.
August 26th, 1956

Dear Sir,

After seeing constant appeals in the newspaper, for any information relevant to the deaths of several ladies in Eastbourne during recent years, I thought perhaps it was my duty to send you what I knew about the late Mrs Morrell of Marden Ash, prior to her death. She had been a friend of my mother (who died some years ago) and myself for many years. I had visited her quite frequently when she lived in Beaconsfield and later in Eastbourne when I lived in Wallington in Surrey – after mother's death. To me she always seemed of a placid happy disposition and was so kind and always pleased when I went to see her. The last Christmas she was alive (Christmas 1949) – I think she wrote to tell me that she would be spending it with her son and family, Mr Claude Morrell of West Kirby, and would I go and see her at Eastbourne when she returned in the New Year? I heard once or twice again after that, seemingly, she had been ill, but still wanted me to go. Eventually I wrote saying I'd call in for a short time on March 21st 1950 and if she wasn't feeling well I would only stay a short time. To my surprise I was told on arrival that she was not well enough to see me. I told the nurse that I was an old friend and that she had said in her letter how much she wanted to see me. But the nurse said that she was very ill, and very difficult, and that she had just been given either an injection or a drug (I forget which) to calm her. She also said that Mrs Morrell turned against people and might not wish to see me at all, but if I liked to go for a walk and call again in two hours – she would see how things were. I did this – but was still told it would be most inadvisable for me to see her and I had to go back to Wallington very disappointed. I never saw her again, but received a notification of her death.

That is all I can tell you and it can be of little use, I am sure, except that I had made a note of the date and was so puzzled at not being allowed even a few moments with her as I really did feel however ill she was, she would have wished it.

I hope that everything will soon be satisfactorily cleared up for you.

Yours truly,
(Signed) Lilian Myers (Widow)'

Mrs Myers remembered the concern she had felt about her friend for over six years, and it is clear from this letter that the normal character and personality of Mrs Morrell had been obscured by the evidence of the nurses' notebooks. When she was not addicted to drugs, she seems to have been able to maintain friendships over many years and was of 'a placid happy disposition' and a kind person. Mrs Myers was turned away by a nurse, but the nurse would have only been acting upon the instructions of Dr Adams, and there is evidence of this tactic of isolating patients in other cases, e.g. Mrs I'Anson Ware, Mrs Hullett. 21st March, 1950 was a day when Dr Adams visited Mrs Morrell, and March 1950 was the month when he increased his visits to twenty-six in the month, from two in January 1950 and five in February 1950. Yet it was agreed in court that her deterioration in health dated from late summer 1950.

### Sister Randall

Another statement was taken from Sister Randall, the night nurse who was present at the death of Mrs Morrell, on 15th December, 1950 when Superintendent Hannam went to see her at her home in Mayfield Place, Eastbourne. He questioned her again concerning the incident when she had found Mrs Morrell very drowsy and with a bottle of tablets in her bed. She had now recalled that these tablets were smaller than codeine tablets, and more like 'medinal or some barbiturate tablets', and she did not think that codeine tablets would have caused the condition in which she found her patient. There had never been any suggestion that Mrs Morrell should have any tablets available to her for her own use.

Sister Randall had 'never heard of Mrs Morrell taking whiskey (sic) with her lunch', but as she was the night nurse she was not present at the relevant time of day. She did know from conversation with the other nurses that Mrs Morrell was in the habit of having a glass of sherry with Dr Adams when he called in the mornings.

She had recalled something further about the last evening of Mrs Morrell's life, 12th November: she was with Nurse Bartlett when Dr Adams had prepared the syringe for the first injection (she must have meant the first intra-muscular injection in her presence, i.e. at 10.30 p.m.):

'I have no doubt in my mind it was Morphine. It is normal to use a small type hyperdermic syringe for morphine injections, but the syringe on this occasion was a 5 c.c. syringe, in other words a large type of syringe. As far as I can remember the syringe was nearly full and it was this that Doctor Adams handed to me and instructed me to inject.

I gave an intra-muscular injection into the thigh. I returned with the empty syringe to Doctor Adams who was still in the dining room and he again filled the syringe with a similar quantity, and his actual instructions to me were to inject the contents of that syringe also if the patient didn't quieten down. I was worried about this at the time because it was a lot to give. In my opinion Mrs Morrell was dying. I would in fact not have been surprised had she been dead when I came on duty that night. I have no hesitation in thinking that these excessive injections eased her passing and I have remembered since that Mrs Morrell frequently told me that Doctor Adams had promised her he would not allow her to suffer at the end.'

[As he had cut an artery on her wrist after death, it is clear that he must have made a promise to ensure that she was dead prior to cremation.]

The last part of the statement concerned another statement Sister Randall had made on the previous Tuesday, to 'a gentleman' who had said that he represented Dr Adams' solicitors. He had particularly asked about Mrs Morrell's will and she had said that Mrs Morrell mentioned that she would leave Dr Adams the chest of Georgian silver. The man had only stayed about fifteen minutes.

Nearly all of this statement had been crossed through by someone in the Director of Public Prosecution's staff; the only paragraph remaining and underlined was that concerning the final injections. Sister Randall was indicating that Sister Bartlett was still there at 10.30 p.m. with her, although she would normally have gone off duty at 9 p.m.

### Claude Morrell

Detective Superintendent Hannam took a statement from Mr (Arthur) Claude Morrell, the son of Mrs Morrell on the same day as he saw Sister Randall, 15th December, at Police Headquarters in Eastbourne. Claude Morrell then lived at 'Thors Hill', Thurstaston, Cheshire and was 62 years old. He was a Justice of the Peace, a Commander of the British Empire (C.B.E.) and a director of Martin's Bank and of Cunard [formerly the White Star Shipping Line of *Titanic* fame]. Mrs Morrell's late husband, Alfred, had died on 10th December, 1924 at the age of 59, so Mrs Morrell had been widowed for twenty-six years when she died. Between 1940 and 1944 – the war years – she was living in Canada and returned to stay with her son in November 1944 for a short while. She then 'returned to live in Eastbourne', staying at the Cumberland Hotel for a time.

It was whilst she was on a visit to 'Thors Hill' in 1948, that she had awoken on 24th June 'unwell' and the opinion was that she had had 'a mild stroke'. She had lost the use of her left arm and left leg, and the local doctor was called and had her admitted to the cottage hospital on the following day. His mother had wanted to have Dr Adams' opinion on her condition. 'My mother held at that time, and right until her death, a very high opinion of Dr Adams.' He came to Cheshire on the following evening and visited Mrs Morrell in hospital. (26th June – early in her hospital stay rather than late as Mr Lawrence assumed and it was on the following day, the

27th, when the morphia injections began.) It was his mother's wish to return to Eastbourne to a nursing home to be under the care of Dr Adams and it was thought that she could do so within a few days. 'I believe the assistance of Dr Adams was sought to this end.'

Mrs Morrell was moved to Eastbourne on Monday 5th July, 1948. Mr Morrell described the arrangements for the journey:

> 'Dr Adams had journeyed to Liverpool the day before and he accompanied my mother on the journey back to Eastbourne. He brought a nurse with him, the name of the nurse was Sister Heald. A special coach was attached to an express train from Liverpool to London and she was met at Euston by an ambulance from Eastbourne, in which she travelled the remainder of the way. On the conclusion of this journey by ambulance to Eastbourne, I am informed she was accompanied by Dr Adams and Sister Heald.'

After stays in the Esperance Nursing Home, the Olinda Nursing Home in Grassington Road, (and at the Cumberland Hotel) she had returned home to 'Marden Ash'. In her son's opinion 'her health was improving and I think that she continued to improve thereafter slowly.'

Mrs Morrell had employed a cook-housekeeper, Bessie Woodward, a housemaid, Emily Drury and Mrs Dockerill as a part-time domestic. Dr Adams had arranged for the nurses to be on duty night and day. Mr Morrell had visited his mother every two or three weeks and stayed one night on each visit, sometimes two. Her health had remained unchanged until the late summer of 1950, when he had thought 'a deterioration was becoming visible'. Until June 1949, Mrs Morrell had dealt with her own accounts and payment of staff, but this began to worry her and Dr Adams offered to pay the nurses weekly and recover this money from Mr Morrell when he visited. A special account was opened with Martins Bank, Eastbourne to deal with payments and Dr Adams had given him the receipts for the payments made and Mr Morrell reimbursed him.

Mrs Morrell had made several wills from the time of her return from Canada and then early in 1947 she had consulted Mr Hubert Sogno to make another will, and subsequently made further changes.

During his mother's illness, Mr Morrell had paid local accounts for sherry, brandy and port which were delivered to 'Marden Ash', and, occasionally, collected by him on her behalf. He could not be 'definite about any particular commodity acquired', but he was aware that 'mother was accustomed quite frequently to enjoy a glass of sherry in the morning, but I cannot detail anything further in connection with her habit of taking either whisky or brandy.'

In answer to DI Pugh's questions, Mr Morrell knew nothing of a gift of a pair of candelabra as a Christmas present to Dr Adams in 1949, nor of the purchase of a dinner set in a sale from a house called 'Corner Cottage' which was said to have been given to Dr Adams.

Mr Morrell stated that 'Until almost the close of my mother's life, she did not complain of pain, apart from the inability to use her left arm, and rheumatism. From my own observation there was no indication to me that she was in pain.' He mentioned that his mother had complained of some pain in her chest in one of her last scribbled notes. (See below) Her mental alertness had seemed to be variable: it was good up until the summer of 1950, but in the last few weeks of her life both her mental and physical abilities had showed signs of deterioration. Then he made the crucial statement: 'At no time did I ever see any signs of, or suspect that she was under the influence of drugs.'

When he had visited his mother on the 14th October, she was in bed and 'visibly poorly'; he had only been able to speak with her for a few minutes. As he had thought her in a deteriorating condition he had returned to see her on 21st October. This time, although she was in bed she was 'wonderfully clear in her mind'. During this visit, she had 'once more emphasised' to her son 'how very good Dr Adams had been to her.' Her mental alertness seemed very changeable. It was Mr Morrell's opinion that Dr Adams would have known of all his visits to his mother, either from himself in advance or from his mother. The next time he had visited her was on 4th November when he found her 'quite unwell and virtually unable to converse'. This was the last occasion on which he saw his mother alive.

On the day his mother died, 13th November, he had immediately travelled to Eastbourne, and recalled that Dr Adams had called to see him at the Cumberland Hotel late that same evening and offered his assistance. His mother's body had been cremated and her ashes scattered in the Channel, as she had wished. Dr Adams had been present at the cremation service at Brighton.

Mr Morrell had always been 'absolutely satisfied' with Dr Adams' treatment of his mother, and had himself consulted him 'on occasions this year' (1956). He had known of his mother's wish that Dr Adams should have the oak chest of silver and also the Rolls Royce. She had told him this when he saw her draft will on 19th August, 1950, and he had arranged for Dr Adams to have these items in accordance with his mother's wishes.

A further statement was made by Mr Morrell on 7th February, 1957 – after he had attended the Committal hearing at Eastbourne Magistrates Court, which was the first time he had heard medical evidence concerning his mother's treatment. This statement was with regard to medical accounts. He confirmed that he had paid a final bill submitted by Browne, the Chemist for £30:16s.3½d., which covered a period from 1st September 1950 until his mother's death.

He had received Dr Adams' account for his medical attendance upon Mrs Morrell on about the 5th December, 1950, but he had realised that the only other account he had rendered was for his two visits to Cheshire in June and July 1948, and that the account would cover a period of something over twenty-eight months. Mr Morrell had discussed the account with his co-executor, Mr Whinnersh, who had dealt with his mother's financial affairs and taxation for many years. Two or three days later, when he was in Eastbourne to deal with his mother's personal effects, he spoke to Dr Adams about the account. He thought that this was probably at the Cumberland Hotel where he was staying and 'where Dr Adams frequently had patients'. He did clearly remember that Dr Adams had said that he had paid over eleven hundred professional visits to his mother during the twenty-eight months, which included twice daily visits to the nursing homes when she was there, and later 'besides his regular daily visit having made a second visit to Marden Ash on many occasions, often late in the evening.' Mr Morrell recalled having commented to him that he was aware that he had been called back from

Scotland by his mother, and that he was entitled to be reimbursed for his expenses for that occasion. He told the Doctor that he would speak further with his co-executor and after a further conversation with Mr Whinnersh, they agreed to accept the account, believing that the eleven hundred visits was correct. Accordingly, when probate was received on 13th January, 1951, the account was paid.

Dr Adams had said that he had deferred the account because it would have worried Mrs Morrell to be presented with such a large bill. Mr Morrell confirmed that from June 1949 onwards, his mother had been very worried about the high cost of her illness. She used to worry about the cash payments to the nurses, the domestic staff and household expenses, which was the reason why, after May 1949, the cheques were prepared in Mr Sogno's office for her signature. Mr Morrell said that 'it seemed fair to add that if at any time Dr Adams had told me that he wished to submit an account for his services up to some date, but did not wish to upset the patient, I have no doubt I would have been willing in order to avoid her being worried to discharge it on her behalf.' But this had not arisen.

The police made a list of the total visits of Dr Adams and Dr Harris to Mrs Morrell from June 21st 1949 to her death in November 1950, including those 'arrived at by implication viz. 'Dr called this morning' etc.'. Using the average number of visits for June-December, 1949, the number of visits for the period July 1948 – May 1949 inclusive (i.e. before the notebooks started) was estimated at 54. So the total number of visits recorded was:

| | |
|---|---|
| 1948–1949 July–May inclusive | 54 |
| 1949 June 21st–December | 32 |
| 1950 January –November 12th | 235 |
| | ——— |
| Total visits estimated and recorded July 1948–November 12th 1950 | 321 |

Even if the number of visits from July 1948 to May 1949 had been under-estimated by 100%, this would still have brought the figure to nowhere near the 1,100 visits which Dr Adams billed the estate for.

Claude Morrell wrote two letters to Mr Hubert Sogno on 20th December, 1950 from his offices in Victoria Street, Liverpool. He appears to have called at Mr Sogno's office in Eastbourne on the previous Saturday and made a statement for Dr Adams' defence team and this letter was to modify this slightly. He had remembered that he had travelled with the Doctor, nurse and his mother in the train to London and then proceeded to Eastbourne by train, leaving Dr Adams and the nurse to accompany her in the ambulance to Eastbourne.

He had said in the statement for the defence that 'She complained that she had a pain in her chest', and felt that he had not said that he knew a little more about this, and he enclosed a copy of a letter from his mother which he had just found 'on Tuesday night' and which he had read over the telephone to Mr Sogno on 19th December. (see below) This letter, written in pencil, he was certain was written on Sunday 29th October, 1950.

Claude Morrell had also recalled that he had written several letters to Dr Adams 'dealing specially with Mother's relations with the nurses. With nurses looking after an invalid over a prolonged period some frictions and difficulties were inevitable and Dr Adams valued my opinion as to whether these frictions were or were not such as to make a change of nurse desirable.'

The second letter, written on the same day, was after Mr Sogno had telephoned him regarding an enquiry from Dr Adams' solicitors, Hempsons. This was about a chance meeting he had with Dr Adams at Victoria Station on the evening of Friday, October 13th, 1950. Mr Morrell had travelled down from Liverpool by the late train and was catching the 10.45 p.m. train from Victoria to Eastbourne. Just as he got into the train he met Dr Adams, who was wearing a dinner jacket and told him that he had been 'to a Medical affair in London'. They travelled together and talked. It was 'obvious' that he could not have told him of the tearing up of the codicil because that had not taken place until the following Saturday, October 21st. He might have told Dr Adams of this when he had settled the nurses' fees with him on Saturday, November 4th.

The letter from Mrs Morrell to her son was headed 'Marden Ash, Sunday' [29th October].

> 'Dearest Claude,
> I have felt so <u>very</u> bad again. This last few days that <u>no-one's</u> Constitution could stand out against it for <u>long</u> & the sooner my time's up the better I shall be pleased. A Doctor here committed suicide here the other day – <u>that</u> is when they have such a great advantage. They get tired of things, take a dose – & all is over but a patient must put up with untold agonies & there is no way out of it. My knee is better but the whole of the agonies I used to suffer is that seems to have transferred itself to my chest. Last night I said to the Doctor I was sure I had pleurisy – but he said it was inflammation of the nerves of the chest – the same thing that happens when you have shingles only this comes out in blisters & the other stays <u>in</u> – In the night I was in agony, I didn't turn over in <u>four hours</u> & I had a temp of 103. <u>All</u> one can hope for is that a speedy end comes to it. I shall be sorry not to have left things in better' [It ends here]

What Mrs Morrell describes as her condition in this letter bears absolutely no relation to what is in the nurses' reports for the 28th and 29th October. She is recorded as sleeping for just under 8 hours on the night of 28th/29th.

At a conference at the Law Courts on 11th March, 1957, the Attorney-General had instructed Detective Superintendent Hannam to arrange to see Claude Morrell. Hannam describes him as 'son of Mrs Morrell, the murdered woman', in his letter of 13th March to Mr Leck at the Director of Public Prosecutions Office. Mr Morrell, accompanied by Mr Sogno, the solicitor, had visited Hannam at New Scotland Yard that same day.

Superintendent Hannam mentioned in the letter that he was 'in some difficulty' because the points upon which the Attorney-General wanted clarification had already been answered in the statements or the documents. He lists these questions and it is quite apparent that the answers are already in evidence. Even a later request from the Attorney-General had already been covered in one of Mr Morrell's statements. However, he had asked Mr Morrell again whether Dr Adams had approached him concerning the Rolls Royce. Mr Morrell was still adamant that he had approached Dr Adams to comply with his mother's request and 'it was given to him solely because of the wish of his mother expressed on that date (19th August, 1950) and had no real bearing on whether or not her son predeceased her.'

Hannam had clarified one or two additional points with Mr Morrell: his mother was born on the 20th June, 1869 at Hansworth, Birmingham. He had seen her on eight occasions between July and 4th November, 1950, the last time he saw her. He felt 'quite certain' that his mother had told Dr Adams about the codicil and its effect, and he had 'no doubt at all that she also told him of its subsequent destruction'. He felt fairly sure that he also had told Dr Adams that the codicil had been destroyed. In effect, therefore, Dr Adams was expecting to receive the oak chest and the Rolls Royce.

Mr Morrell told Superintendent Hannam that his mother's speech and her general condition had improved for some eighteen months after her original stroke: her left arm and leg slowly became more mobile. He had no idea that she was receiving any medication other than 'something to induce sleep at night'. On the 4th November, he had, for the first time, seen one of the night nurses and she had commented to him that she thought that 'the medicine Mrs Morrell was having was stronger than the patient really needed'. (This was Sister Bartlett – now Hughes.) 'At no time did Mr Morrell know that his mother was being given dangerous drugs.'

With regard to Dr Adams' final account, Hannam had asked what the actual amount of the final bill was, and Mr Morrell 'knew it the moment we asked him' and produced a photostat copy of the receipted account totalling £1,674.

Mr Morrell told the Superintendent that the reason why Mr Sogno had accompanied him was that on the 12th March – the previous day – Messrs. Hempsons, Dr Adams' solicitors had communicated with him and asked to see him for the purpose of 'asking a few more questions'. He said that he would inform Hannam immediately if the defence decided to call him.

This was, by now, totally unlikely, as Hannam continues:

> 'The foregoing completes the result of our interview, apart from commenting on Mr Morrell's present opinion of Doctor Adams, and to use his own phrase it is that "I have been deceived and double-crossed". He realises, as a result of being present at the Magistrates' Court throughout the summary hearing and from enquiries he has made on his own account since the matter, that Doctor Adams is not the person he thought he was for so long.'

## Evidence from the Case for Trial for the Murder of Mrs Hullett

The Case for Trial was prepared by the Office of the Director of Public Prosecutions. It is presented below in its entirety, because it contains new information which did not come to light during the Hullett Inquest or during the Dr Adams' Trial. Of crucial importance is the evidence that Dr Adams anticipated what Mrs Hullett was going to do and that he was complicit in her suicide, firstly by ensuring that she had the means at her disposal and secondly by checking out the antidote and the dosage required with the house surgeon at Princess Alice Hospital during Thursday, 19 July, just hours before Mrs Hullett took the overdose, and then by administering a dose which was only 20% of what would have possibly saved her life. Dr Adams' preparations for her death put the fast clearance of the £1,000 cheque two days earlier in an entirely different light. It also explained why Dr Adams had not informed Dr Harris of the risk of suicide from barbiturate poisoning. The Case for Trial also addresses the fact that, during the Hullett inquest, someone removed a number of crucial exhibits, which might have been required in an eventual prosecution.

Central Criminal Court
12th March Sessions 1957

**THE QUEEN**
-against-
**JOHN BODKIN ADAMS**

———————

TAKE NOTICE THAT on the 1st day of March 1957 the Attorney-General entered a nolle prosequi to the indictment charging you with the murder of Gertrude Joyce Hullett, which was preferred against you at the February Sessions of the Central Criminal Court.

And take notice that, in accordance with Section 2(2)(b) of the Administration of Justice (Miscellaneous Provisions) Act, 1933 and Rule 3(1)(a) of the Indictments (Procedure) Rules 1933 application has been made to the Lord Chief Justice for leave to prefer a Bill of Indictment against you. On the 6th day of March 1957 such leave was granted. A copy of the Bill of Indictment, endorsed by the Lord Chief Justice is attached and marked 'A'

And take notice that this Bill of Indictment will be preferred against you at the forthcoming Sessions of the Central Criminal Court.

Dated this 6th day of March 1957

F. DONAL BARRY

Assistant Director of Public Prosecutions

The archives of the Director of Public Prosecutions contain the case prepared against Dr Adams for the charge of murdering Mrs GJ 'Bobbie' Hullett, which was to go ahead after his trial for the murder of Mrs Morrell. Counsel for the Crown was asked to advise on the evidence prepared by the DPP's Office. A copy of the 'Observations and Instructions to Advise on Evidence' was sent to the Attorney-General, but Counsel in question was Mr Melford Stevenson.

A brief outline of the case describes Mrs Hullett as 'a rich widow' who was very depressed after her husband's death. 'The accused' had been the Hullett's medical adviser and had regularly attended 'the deceased', calling every day and sometimes twice a day. Mrs Hullett had displayed suicidal tendencies, both to her friends and to the Doctor, who had been prescribing barbiturates regularly; 'the quantity so prescribed was not unreasonable for a person in her condition who was having difficulty in sleeping. However, in view of her expressed suicidal tendencies, the method of administration employed by the accused provided no safeguard against her acquiring a lethal dose with which she might commit suicide.' The Prosecution stated that she did, in fact, commit suicide by taking a fatal dose of barbiturates on 19th July, 1956 and lapsed into a coma, from which she never awoke, dying on the morning of 23rd July.

It was on Wednesday, 18th July that the accused had handed to the cashier at his bank a cheque for £1,000 dated 17th July, drawn by Mrs Hullett, and asked that it be credited to his 'No. 2 deposit account which was then £12,000 in credit', and had asked for it to be cleared 'sooner than the normal four days'; it was actually cleared on 19th July. 'This was a most extraordinary request by the accused in view of the fact that he obviously was in no urgent need of the money and the drawer of the cheque was a woman of considerable means… it would appear that he then knew the deceased might die before the 21st July, when the cheque would have normally been cleared.' (The 21st, however, was a Saturday and not a banking day, so it would not have cleared until Monday 23rd July, the day Mrs Hullett died – and in the event, before banking hours.)

Dr Adams had called at 10 a.m. on Friday, 20th July, as usual, found Mrs Hullett asleep, did not disturb her and said she should be allowed to sleep late. When he was called to the house later that day, 'in fact, he could not be found', and his partner, Dr Harris, was the first to arrive. Dr Harris had known nothing of her suicidal tendencies 'or of the possibility of her having acquired a fatal dose of barbiturates', examined her, but did not form an opinion as to the cause of her condition. Dr Adams had called later that afternoon, calling for Dr Harris, and they discussed diagnosis; Dr Harris, in fact, suggested an overdose of drugs, but 'the accused said this was not possible and failed to tell Dr Harris anything about her suicidal tendencies or her access to barbiturates.' Dr Adams had suggested cerebral haemorrhage 'and Dr Harris in his ignorance of all the facts agreed that this was a probable diagnosis.'

The Prosecution would state that 'the accused knew that the deceased had taken an overdose of barbiturates, that he deliberately withheld vital information from Dr Harris, and that he deliberately expressed a false diagnosis to Dr Harris. Acting upon the pretended diagnosis of cerebral haemorrhage, the accused deliberately denied to the deceased the proper treatment for a person in her condition.' The evidence for this was 'abundant'.

The main points of the prosecution case were:

1. The accused was supplying barbiturates to the deceased in such a way that she could easily acquire a fatal dose.
2. The accused knew that since the death of her husband, the deceased had shown suicidal tendencies.

3. His action in having the cheque specially cleared shows knowledge that the deceased might die before the 21st July.

4. His treatment of her after she had lapsed into a coma shows that he was content to let her die.

The second part of the 'Observations' are notes on the evidence in depositions already obtained from witnesses, including that of Dr Adams himself:

Mr AJ Hullett had died on Wednesday, 14th March, 1956 and Dr Adams had certified cerebral haemorrhage as the cause of death. The accused had met Mrs Hullett after the death of her first husband, Mr Tomlinson. After Mr Hullett's death he had called on Mrs Hullett each morning to give her sodium barbitone tablets, one dose at a time.

On Tuesday, 1st May, 1956: 'Accused went away for a holiday, and before he went, prescribed 36 x 7½ grn. sodium barb. tablets. During this period about 6th May, on a visit to Dublin with deceased and two other ladies gave her 8 further tablets as she had left hers behind.'

Saturday 19th May, 1956: The accused returned from holiday and again 'doled out' sleeping drugs of 2 tablets or cachets each morning, to be taken at night. He also prescribed phenobarbitone as she complained of feeling sick at meals. During this period she threatened suicide on several occasions to the accused.

Sunday, 15th July, 1956: According to the statement of the accused, Mrs Hullett was very agitated and had a 'nerve storm'. She said that she would swim out to sea and that her rotting body would come in four days after.

Thursday, 19th July, morning: There occurred a similar 'nerve storm'.

11.30 a.m. The housekeeper saw the deceased and noticed nothing abnormal about her, nor was she unwell in the afternoon.

The prosecution had evidence as to the accused's prescriptions of barbiturates for Mrs Hullett from 15th March, 1956 onwards, based upon 8 prescription forms signed by the accused. Five forms were missing, and the evidence for these had been taken from the chemist's entries in his prescription book. (H.R. Browne) There were still some discrepancies. The drugs dispensed were delivered either to the accused or the deceased.

When the police had searched Kent Lodge for dangerous drugs on 24th November, 1956, they had found nine bottles which corresponded with some of the serial numbers on the prescriptions for Mrs Hullett. [There had also been some labelled for Mr Hullett found.]

The evidence of the prescriptions and search did bear out Dr Adams' statement that he was doling out the sleeping tablets each day, with two exceptions: on 1st May when he went on holiday, and on 1st June, a prescription for 24 cachets of 7½ grams, which he could not account for.

There was also the loss of 5 prescriptions, one of which 'would probably have been returned by the chemist to the patient', but the other four could not be found by the chemist, who had handed a quantity of prescriptions to Superintendent Seekings at the end of July, 1956. Seekings had passed these to DI Pugh shortly after 23rd July and they were placed in an envelope in the file relating to the deceased, but not checked at the time. The next time DI Pugh looked at them early in January 1957, he could not find those in Exhibit 6. [Prescription forms signed by Dr Adams] This was not the only evidence in the case which disappeared.

There were two other important items of evidence relating to the period immediately preceding Mrs Hullett's fatal coma:

> Saturday, 14th July, 1956: Mrs Hullett made a will, bequeathing her Rolls-Royce car to the accused, although there was no concrete evidence that he knew of this.

> Wednesday, 18th July. The accused called at his bank, handed the cashier the £1,000 cheque dated and given to him on 17th July and made out the paying-in slip (Exhibit 12) for his No. 2 deposit account which was £12,069.6.11d. in credit and no withdrawals were made until 15th December, 1956. He had asked Mr Pill, the cashier, when the cheque would be cleared and was told by the 21st July; he was told about the procedure for special clearance so that it could be cleared by 19th July, and asked for this to be done. He had said that he 'did not wish to be advised as to the fate of the cheque'.

The £1,000 cheque was, by this time, missing and a considerable amount of secondary evidence had been gathered on the matter, which is separate from the main evidence.

The prosecution would ask 'what was the consideration for this sum of £1,000, and why did the accused have it specially cleared?' The accused had said that it was for an M.G. car which Mr Hullett had wanted him to have and had promised to pay for. There was a letter written by Mrs Hullett to Mr Handscomb and put in by the defence which corroborated this: 'Make sure Dr Adams' M.G. is paid for from Jack…' This had been crossed out and Mrs Hullett had written at the side 'Have done this 17/7/56.'

> Friday, 20th July, 1956.
> 3.30 p.m.: Dr Harris called, found Mrs Hullett in a coma, formed no opinion, and gave an injection of coramine. [a heart stimulant]
> 5 p.m. Dr Harris called again and met with the accused to discuss diagnosis. Dr Harris asked about the possibility of an overdose, and the accused said 'No' and suggested cerebral haemorrhage. He did not tell Dr Harris:

> 1. That the deceased had suicidal tendencies;
> 2. That she had been taking barbiturates for some months.

Dr Harris advised treatment in hospital, but accused disagreed and said he would arrange for nurses. Dr Harris agreed with accused's diagnosis, but he was kept in ignorance of vital facts. But, he had, on his first visit, questioned 'a lady in the house' who had told him that the accused gave the patient a sleeping cachet every night.

> 8.45 p.m. Nurse Higgins arrived: she asked the accused whether Mrs Hullett had been

in the habit of taking sedative tablets. He said that she was, but under his orders and that he regulated them, but told her that the cause of the coma was 'something cerebral'. She had seen Dr Harris give an injection, which he told her was a penicillin injection to guard against lung congestion.

Saturday, 21st July, 1956.

3 a.m. Nurse Higgins called the accused, who was sleeping at the house, because the patient was worse and a bluish colour. He gave an injection that seemed to improve her condition temporarily.

9 a.m. The accused telephoned Dr Shera, a Consultant Pathologist, and 'asked him to carry out certain investigations, spinal puncture and blood count, for his patient, Mrs Hullett at Holywell Mount, who was in a coma probably due to cerebral haemorrhage.' Prior to this Dr Harris had advised another consultant opinion and had suggested Dr Shera.

Midday Dr Shera arrived at the house and performed the spinal puncture; of the specimens two out of three were tinged with blood. Dr Shera suggested narcotic poisoning was the cause, and also recommended a gastric analysis. 'Accused neither approved nor disapproved this – no gastric analysis was taken.' He did agree that a specimen of urine should be analysed and he handed Dr Shera a specimen. The necessary form was filled in and the accused signed it. In answer to Dr Shera's question, the accused had told him that the patient had been on barbiturates, but he still favoured his diagnosis of cerebral haemorrhage.

12.45 p.m. Dr Shera took the urine specimen to Princess Alice Hospital, but did not receive the result until the 24th July, 1956.

Dr Harris arrived at the house as Dr Shera was leaving; he discussed with the accused Dr Shera's investigations, but still heard no mention of barbiturates, or that the patient had been depressed. Dr Harris advised anti-biotic injections because of the patient's pulmonary condition, and 'at the accused's request' he gave a crystamycin injection. He also suggested rectal glucose saline to give the patient fluids as she could not swallow, but the accused said that this would increase lung congestion. Dr Harris also queried the lack of a day nurse, but the accused said that Miss Reed had nursing experience and was at the house.

Afternoon. The accused called at the Princess Alice Hospital and saw the House Surgeon, Dr Cook. It is noted that the accused practised as an anaesthetist at this hospital for two days a week and at St. Mary's for one day weekly, and that, on the 19th July, he had had a conversation about Megimide, an antidote against barbiturate poisoning. But this afternoon, the Saturday, he asked Dr Cook to remind him of the name of this drug; they went to the casualty department, found none in stock but together read the notice dealing with the dosage and method of administration. They then went to the dispensary and obtained a 100 millilitre of Megimide 'in a carton which contained a pamphlet'. This notice dealt with the treatment of 'barbitone intoxication with megimide and Daptazole', which began with the words: 'It is of the utmost importance that the patient be taken to hospital without delay'. Dr Cook asked the accused if he had a case of barbiturate poisoning and the accused replied that he had. Dr Cook had asked if he had set up an intravenous infusion: he said he had not. Dr Cook then told him that if the megimide were given by intravenous injection, it should be done very slowly in doses of 10 millilitres every five minutes or so. He had not said that 10 millilitres (10 c.c.) was the dose and that if it did not work it would be no use, and the printed instructions made the dosage and administration quite clear.

9.30 p.m. Dr Harris called at the accused's request. Dr Adams arrived and said that no further anti-biotics had been given, so Dr Harris gave the patient another injection of crystamycin.

Night 21st/22nd Nurse Higgins was with the patient and the accused was in the house. At 3 a.m. on the 22nd the patient again took a turn for the worse and was bluish in the face and she called the Doctor, who gave an injection which resulted in a temporary improvement.

Sunday 22nd July 8.30 a.m. The accused telephoned the Coroner, Dr Somerville, saying that he 'wished a private post-mortem examination'. The Coroner had said 'Certainly not – you should report it to me officially.' He went on to ask when the patient had died and the accused replied that she was not dead and that he was reporting it because he was not certain of what she was going to die from. The Coroner repeated that he would deal with the matter when it was reported officially to him. 'The Coroner has never in his experience been asked whether a private post-mortem could be arranged before the patient's death.'

Morning, later: Dr Harris called and the accused was there. Dr Harris thought the patient seemed better but she still had congestive signs in the left lung and he gave a further injection of crystamycin, also advising rectal glucose saline again, and oxygen. The accused still made no mention to him of barbiturate poisoning.

Sunday evening: Dr Harris again called at the house and saw that the patient's condition was very much worse – she had developed broncho-pneumonia. The accused told him that he had given Megimide as an antidote for barbiturate poisoning, although he was still of the opinion that she was suffering from cerebral haemorrhage. The prosecution noted that, at the Inquest, the accused had said that he only gave 10 c.c. of Megimide and that he had understood from the House Surgeon that 10 c.c. was the dose and that if it didn't work, it would be of no use.

Dr Harris gave another anti-biotic injection of crystamycin, which he did on his own initiative as it had not been done by anyone else; he again stressed the importance of giving oxygen.

Monday, 23rd July
3 a.m. Nurse Higgins called the accused who gave an injection.
6.30 a.m. She again called the accused as the patient's condition was deteriorating very

obviously: Mrs Hullett was dying. The accused then said, 'We'll give her some oxygen.'

In a letter, signed by the accused and Dr Harris, the time of her death was given as 7.23 a.m.

The result of the urine test was not known until after her death.

23rd July Dr Camps carried out a post-mortem examination of the deceased.

Cause of death: broncho-pneumonia due to barbiturate poisoning.

The Metropolitan Police Laboratory analysis showed that the deceased had circulating in her body 115 grains of sodium barbitone. 50 grains was usually considered a fatal dose and the normal therapeutic dose was 5 -15 grains.

Both in his letter to the Coroner, in his statement dated 26.7.56, and in his evidence at the Inquest on 21.8.56, the accused gave his account of his treatment of the deceased.

The prosecution contended that 'the accused knew the cause of her coma, and three medical experts, Drs. Camps, Ashby and Douthwaite, will give evidence as to the proper treatment of a patient in such a coma and their comments on such treatment as was given by the accused.'

The main points for proper treatment were:

1. The sooner it starts after coma, the greater the chance of recovery.
2. Proper treatment can only be carried out in hospital or a place with comparable facilities.
3. The only way of getting rid of the poison is through the urine, therefore fluid intake has to be maintained.
4. Essential to prevent effects of lack of carbohydrate, therefore glucose is needed, either intravenously or into stomach.
5. Adequate supply of oxygen and airway kept unobstructed.
6. Continuous skilled nursing attention required.

As to the treatment given:

1. 10 c.c. megimide useless except in case of very mild poisoning.
2. Oxygen treatment only a gesture.
3. Totally inadequate nursing.
4. Lack of administration of fluids in itself would probably lead to death.

23rd July After deceased's death: The accused wrote a letter to the Coroner and there was one statement inconsistent with a previous statement he had made: 'Husband died suddenly about four months ago after a major abdominal operation.' The accused had certified the death as due to cerebral haemorrhage and the operation had taken place some months before in December, 1955.

25th July DI Pugh found in the bedroom of the deceased, articles which included 1 bottle containing 7 sodium barbitone tablets, 1 bottle containing 12¼ gr. phenobarbitone, and a box containing 62¼ grain phenobarbitone tablets. A further tablet of sodium barbitone was found in a drawer and there were a few other medicines.

26th July DI Pugh saw the accused in the presence of his solicitor and the accused dictated his statement.

The prosecution considered the sources of the tablets which Mrs Hullett had taken, which were apparent from the statement made by the accused:

Mr Hullett had every kind of sleeping draught [including sodium barbiturate].' 'I have no record of the quantity of barbiturate I prescribed for Mr Hullett before his death. I do not know if any of that supply was left over after his death.' 'I now recall that on one occasion during the period I was doling out the two cachets of sodium barbiturate, I found I did not have them with me – She said 'You need not mind, I have got some of Jack's which I can take tonight.' I said 'Don't take those, I will send you some up, and later that day I sent two cachets up by my chauffeur.' 'When I came back from my holiday on 19th May, I didn't ask Mrs Hullett if she had some of the 36 tablets of sodium barbiturate I had given her.

15th August: DI Pugh received a letter form the accused mentioning giving Mrs Hullett 2 tablets each evening during the visit to Dublin.

21st August. The accused gave evidence at the Inquest.

24th November. D.Superintendent Hannam and DI Pugh took possession of the nine bottles from the surgery cupboard.

The evidence had originally been gathered as 'evidence of system' to support the charge of murdering Mrs Morrell, and therefore certain witnesses had not been called at the Inquest who might well be called for a charge of murder in respect of Mrs Hullett. The prosecution had little evidence of her general health and Dr Adams' visits to her from 15th March to 20th July, 1956. Some other evidence was needed besides the statements made by the accused. Counsel was asked to consider whether to call some of the following persons:-

Evelyn Patricia Tomlinson – Mrs Hullett's daughter
Teresa Yogna – the Italian housemaid
Celia Mayo – parlourmaid
Percy Handscomb – great friend of Jack Hullett
Kathleen Reed – lifelong friend of Mrs Hullett

A strange omission from this list is Harriet Henson, who could have given evidence as to Mrs Hullett's condition since the death of Mr Hullett, and who had made a statement to police. This statement was not in the DPP's papers or the Sussex Police files, however, but in the Scotland Yard archive. There is no doubt that the Inquest was carefully orchestrated in its content to ensure the outcome. The indications are that Hannam's hands were tied in respect of the evidence for the Inquest.

Counsel was advised of a number of particular points 'worth mentioning':

Dr Camps had said, in his evidence, 'From the clinical evidence and that of witnesses prior to Mrs Hullett's death, there is strong suggestion that she was at times suffering from barbiturate intoxication.' It was presumed that Dr Camps was referring to evidence of Teresa Yogna, Miss Reed and Evelyn Tomlinson, but, again, there was strong evidence from Mrs Henson of this.

The Rolls Royce car bequeathed to the accused was a 1954 Silver Dawn with a probate value of £2,900, and Dodd, the executor of the will could give evidence on this point.

There was the possibility of evidence that there was no actual supervision of the actual administration of the drugs to Mrs Hullett: the accused doled out the tablets in the morning but directly to the patient rather than to, say, her daughter or a member of staff.

There should be evidence given that there was no professional nursing of Mrs Hullett in the daytime; no proper arrangements at all, in fact.

Superintendent Seekings had not been called at the Inquest as to taking unchecked prescriptions from the chemists and handing them unchecked to DI Pugh.

The list of prescriptions was not satisfactory: Dr Nickolls of the Metropolitan Police Laboratory had prepared amended lists and perhaps he should be an extra witness.

The matter of the missing cheque, which disappeared at the Inquest.

There was a discrepancy between the chemist's prescription list for the bottle of phenobarbitone tablets (⅛ grain) and the bottle corresponding to it found in the bedroom of the deceased. (¼ grain). The witness, Moss the chemist 'was mistaken' according to Dr Nickolls. His evidence on 'the sodium barbitone tablet' found in the bedroom and his prescription list was also unsatisfactory. Dr Nickolls could 'clear up' these points also.

Counsel had not yet stated which exhibits would be required in the Hullett case. Exhibits 26, 33, 34, 40 and 42 'insofar as they relate to drugs found at the accused's surgery, etc.' might be considered irrelevant. 33 and 34 were Hannam's note books, and again did not seem to have much bearing on the case. A list of the exhibits was therefore required from Counsel and an index to the depositions, together with a witness list.

Counsel were asked: to advise on the evidence and draft any notice of further evidence that was considered necessary. The DPP's representative, Mr M.J. Jardine, was dealing with this case. A copy of these Observations and Instructions was being sent to the Attorney-General, from which it can be presumed that Mr Melford Stevenson and Mr Malcolm Morris were the 'Counsel' addressed.

The following Appendix was attached to the Observations, and headed:

## The Missing Cheque

The evidence on the depositions showed that:

Mr Pill, the cashier at the Midland Bank received the cheque for £1,000 from the accused on 18.7.56

Mr Oliver, Westminster Bank, received the cheque by post on 19.7.56. He gave evidence at the Inquest but did not see the cheque and could not give any date as to when he last saw it.

Mr Kidd from Westminster Bank examined the cheque on 19.7.56, 'put it in an office tin and hasn't seen it since'.

Dr Somerville, the Coroner stated that no cheque was produced as an exhibit at the Inquest on 21.8.56

This cheque had been referred to at the Inquest in:

The Accused's evidence: when he stated that the cheque had been paid to him on Tuesday evening, the 17th June;

Mr Oliver's evidence when he described the cheque.

Mr Bull, the Coroner's Officer stated that, at the Inquest 'I saw a cheque. After its production at the Inquest, I saw this cheque circulating the legal table in Court. I'm not sure who produced it or whether it was identified by anyone in my presence.'

In his statement, Mr Bull said:

'I saw a cheque for £1,000 mentioned in the case, circulating amongst legal advisers – I have not seen it since and it did not come into my possession.'

DI Pugh was present at the Inquest and remembered Mr Oliver giving evidence:

'I saw a cheque circulating the bottom end of the solicitors' table. The cheque was never in my possession. It is customary for the Coroner to take possession of all documents produced at an Inquest.'

There was the evidence of Mr Rippon, senior partner in Hart, Read & Co., Solicitors and Executors under the Wills of Mr and Mrs Hullett:

The firm were in possession of Mrs Hullett's bank statement for the period prior to her death. Among the paid cheques that came to them from the bank was the cheque for £1,000 in favour of the accused, dated 17th July. Mr Rippon arranged with DI Pugh to deliver the cheque to Pugh during the morning of 21.8.56. At 1 p.m. he handed into Police Headquarters an envelope containing the cheque with one of his firm's compliment slips. The envelope was addressed to DI Pugh. He had not seen the cheque since and had searched his firm's files and documents and could not find it.

Superintendent Seekings stated: 'I have no knowledge of this cheque being in police possession.' He was present at the Inquest and saw a cheque being passed across the table to the accused's Counsel: 'I do not know what happened to it… I have not seen it since.'

Possible further enquiries to be considered were:

Who had received the envelope and cheque at Police H.Q. and what did he do with it?

Who was responsible for bringing documents relating to Mrs Hullett from Police H.Q. to the Inquest Court?

How did the cheque come to be on the solicitors' table?

Who was responsible for custody of police documents that were not exhibited at the Inquest?

Who in Eastbourne Police has searched for this cheque?

The Prosecution thought that difficulties might arise over questioning 'those at the solicitors' table who had among their number the accused's legal advisers' and, mysteriously:

> 'In view of suspicions as to the fate of this cheque, further enquiries may not take the matter very much further. The Director is having further enquiries made.'

There is a letter in the archives from the Chief Constable of Eastbourne, Richard Walker to the Director of Public Prosecutions, dated 5th March, 1957, and the Director's suspicion may well have fallen on him. It is marked 'Confidential':

> 'With reference to your letter of 1st March regarding further enquiries to be made with a view to tracing the missing £1,000 cheque, I enclose statements from five of my officers bearing on this matter.
>
> Mr J.S. Dodd and Mr H.V. James, both Solicitors, have been seen and statements obtained from them embodying replies to the eight questions set out in your letter.
>
> The remaining persons believed to be seated at the Solicitors' table at the Inquest on Mrs Hullett on the 21st August are living in London, and these are:- The Hon. J.R. Cummings Bruce [sic] of 5, King's Bench Walk, Temple, E.C.4.; Mr Peck, Counsel, 3 Temple Gardens, E.C.3. and representatives of Messrs. Hempson's Solicitors, of Bedford House, 33 Henrietta Street, Strand, London, and the Medical Defence Union, watching the interests of Dr Adams and Dr Harris.
>
> I am also enclosing a statement from Mrs Audrey Dodd of 41 Enys Road, Eastbourne, who speaks of seeing a cheque passing between Mr Oliver, the Bank Manager, and H.M. Coroner, whilst she attended the Inquest on Mrs Hullett on the 21st August, 1956.
>
> You will see from my Daily Order 58/57, dated the 27th February 1957 (copy enclosed) that the information supplied by Mr Rippon that he left an envelope containing a cheque for £1,000 at Police Headquarters, Eastbourne, at about 1 p.m. on the 21st August, 1956, has been circulated to all ranks, but no information has been received from any officer stating that he saw Mr Rippon or received a letter from him on the day in question.
>
> Mr Rippon is, of course, a man of the highest integrity, but you will realise that his

statement about delivery of the cheque was very vague, and I think it very probable that the envelope containing it was never, in fact, handed in here, but taken by Mr Rippon or his partner, Mr Dodd, straight into the Inquest.

I am, Sir,

Your obedient Servant,

(Sgd) R.W. Walker

Chief Constable'

In other words, Mr Walker was suggesting that Dr Somerville, the Coroner had passed the cheque to the defence team in an attempt to aid a fellow doctor. But the persons that Dr Adams had threatened to bring down with him were Lieutenant-Colonel Gwynne and Richard Walker, the Chief Constable.

There is a letter in the archive concerning another matter mentioned in the 'Observations' to Counsel: this is a letter from Hannam to Mr Jardine at the DPP's Office and dated 5th March, 1957. Hannam had gathered some information on the Rolls Royce motor car left by Mrs Hullett to Dr Adams in her Will: Mr Dodd, one of the executors had told him that the index number of the car was 'AJH532' (Mr Hullett's initials), that it was a 1954 Silver Dawn automatic and that Messrs. Caffyns had valued it for probate purposes – which would have been a low valuation – at £2,900.

Hannam thought that he would 'pursue this matter a little further' and he checked with the Borough Taxation Officer: on the 8th December, 1956, Dr Adams had visited the Taxation Office and paid the £5 fee in order to have the index number of the vehicle altered. The number was changed on 10th December to 'DJK731'.

The Superintendent believed this 'to be a common tactic of Doctor Adams with these Rolls Royce motor cars and a similar case will be observed in paragraph 102 of the Police Report in this case.' The Taxation Officer also remembered that the car had been purchased by a big firm in Leicester and on the 13th December, 1956, his complete file had been transferred to Leicestershire County Council. Dr Adams had sold the car.

The DPP's Office had requested a table to be compiled for 'The Treatment of Barbiturate Poisoning with Megimide and Daptazole in St. Mary's Hospital, Eastbourne since May 1955'. This was one of the two hospitals where Dr Adams practised as an anaesthetist: he had been on duty for one day a week here since qualifying in 1941. The first patient was treated on 22nd May, 1955 and the last patient on the list on 5th February, 1957. Six had been treated in 1956 prior to Mrs Hullett's death. There were 17 patients listed, of whom 15 had recovered, one had recovered from coma and died of cardiac failure and one had died from irreversible brain damage. All but one had been put on an intravenous drip. Several had recovered after taking larger quantities than Mrs Hullett.

This information from the hospital records confirmed that the megimide with daptazole treatment of patients with barbiturate poisoning was not a new treatment in July, 1956 and that it had regularly been used in a hospital where Dr Adams was an anaesthetist. Barbiturates were also used in anaesthesia and he utilised them in large quantities for patients as his prescriptions for his own bag testified.

New statements had been taken from some witnesses and a few of these contained new information:

Celia Mary Mayo, the house parlourmaid at Holywell Mount had been ill at the time of the Inquest and had not appeared as a witness. She had been employed at the house from October, 1950 until the end of December, 1956. She knew that the Hulletts were 'very fond of each other and nearly always together'; they went to South Africa in January, 1955 and in the September of that year, to Florida. Mr Hullett's death had come as a great shock to Mrs Hullett: Mary – the name she was always known by – had never seen anything 'abnormal' but 'there were times when she looked right through you and seemed vacant and lost.'

Mrs Hullett did not drink very often, just a glass of sherry when there were visitors. The only times the loyal Mary had ever seen her 'unsteady on her feet' were in the mornings just after she had come downstairs and 'was obviously because she had just got out of bed.' She did not recall her mistress ever spending a day in bed with illness until 20th July. It was Mrs Hullett's custom to stay in bed each day until Dr Adams had called in the mornings: Mary took up her breakfast at 9 o'clock, left it on a tray beside her bed and when she returned at 9.40, Mrs Hullett was 'up and washed and was just returning to bed to have her breakfast'. She always 'remained in bed after breakfast until Dr Adams called.'

So far as phenobarbitone tablets, Mary 'would not know one from the other', but there were occasions, after Dr Adams had called, when she had seen four tablets on the table. Mrs Hullett had once told her that she could take two when she got in the bath and one when she went to bed; the other one was if she woke up about 5 o'clock in the morning. When Dr Adams called 'he went straight up to Mrs Hullett's room. Mrs Hullett gave instructions to leave the front door unlocked for this purpose.'

Medicines had been delivered to the house by Browne's the Chemist: the delivery man called at the back door and gave the parcel to Mary or Miss Durrant and these were left on Mrs Hullett's desk in the study and she always collected the parcels herself. 'Dr Adams would never have access to these parcels before Mrs Hullett took possession of them.' Mary could 'not remember telling Teresa that Dr Adams called every day to given Mrs Hullett injections. I did not think Mrs Hullett was having injections. She did have injections immediately after Mr Hullett died. This was for a rash on her neck.'

It was on the Sunday, a week before she died, that Mrs Hullett had been unsteady on her feet: it was after she had been in the garden cutting lettuces and she had come back into the house and fallen down in the hall. She had been all right again almost immediately and got herself up.

On the evening of 19th July, 1956, Mrs Hullett had come to Mary's pantry, bringing some newspapers, and had a glass of orange juice. She had complained of a bad headache and Mary had thought it due to the thunder, and retired to bed just after ten o'clock. The next morning, she had taken up Mrs Hullett's breakfast as usual and left it; when she returned at 9.40 Mrs

Hullett was still asleep, and she just left her and carried on with her work. Dr Adams called 'as usual' at about 9.45 and Mary met him in the hall, telling him that her mistress was still asleep. She went up with him to the bedroom, opened the door and stepped into the room 'and Dr Adams stood just behind me'. Mary said 'Oh yes she is still asleep', and 'Dr Adams looked over my shoulder'. They both left the room and Dr Adams told her to let Mrs Hullett sleep, saying that he was going to a conference in Lewes. 'He put four white tablets in an envelope and put them on the hall chest and asked me to give them to Mrs Hullett.' What had happened to these she did not know. The Doctor had said he might call back but he was going to the dentist 'and it was all according to how he felt. He did not tell me to phone him if I was worried.'

Miss Reed, Mrs Hullett's friend had arrived for a few days' stay on the previous day. During the Friday morning Mary had told Miss Reed, the cook and the housemaid that Mrs Hullett was still sleeping. She did not recall telling Teresa that Dr Adams had not examined Mrs Hullett that morning 'but it is true that he did not.'

When she could not wake Mrs Hullett at 12.15 p.m., Mary fetched Miss Reed, but they had no success, so she phoned Dr Adams' house, spoke to his Secretary and found that he was out to lunch and had a conference in Lewes that afternoon; the Secretary told Mary to ring her if Mrs Hullett had not awakened by mid-afternoon. At about 3 p.m., they rang again, and the Secretary said she would get Dr Harris to call. Dr Harris arrived soon afterwards, examined Mrs Hullett, and soon left saying that he would send Dr Adams as soon as possible. It was about 4.45 when Dr Adams arrived and Mary left Miss Reed with the Doctor and Mrs Hullett.

Mary had little connection with what happened after this; she just carried on working in the staff quarters and occasionally went up to see Mrs Hullett. On the Monday morning at about 7.30 Dr Adams came to the pantry and said 'I am afraid Mrs Hullett has just passed away.' She had been very fond of Mrs Hullett and 'it came as a shock to me' when she died. Mary said that she had never heard Mrs Hullett threaten to commit suicide; upon occasion when she went out in the car and Mary had said goodbye, she replied 'Oh, what does it matter'.

Mary had become ill at Christmas of that year and left Holywell Mount to live with her sister in Reading. She had not felt well enough to work again since.

Kathleen Grace Durrant was cook to Mr and Mrs Hullett and had been working at Holywell Mount for two years. When she had first known Mrs Hullett 'she was a very happy woman', and the couple 'were devoted to each other'. After her husband died, she was depressed and lost interest in everything; she would be getting over it and 'then she would go down again'. She had given Miss Durrant instructions about meals and would not bother about her own food 'as everything tasted like cotton wool to her anyway'. Sometimes she was flustered and confused and would say 'she expected it was the dope Dr Adams was giving her'. Cook was sure she used to fight against it: 'She was often staggering about and had to hold on to furniture to help keep her feet.' Yet she was never ill, and would get about the house and go into the town.

It was in April, 1956, that Teresa Yogna, the housemaid and Kathleen had spoken to Mrs Henson when she had been staying with Mrs Hullett. They wanted Mrs Henson to take Mrs Hullett away for a holiday as they had felt that this would do her good. There were several reasons: 'She was so down I felt she needed more happiness. She was alone too much and needed to get away from doctors and forget illness. I felt that Dr Adams' treatment was doing her no good. She was not ill, she needed stimulating. All Dr Adams' treatment seemed to be doing was depressing her still more… Mrs Henson agreed with us and tried to get Mrs Hullett to go home with her but she just would not go.' They 'never believed in Dr Adams' treatment. It never did any good, it was too depressing.'

Medicine was delivered 'once or twice a week' from Browne's: the delivery man would leave the brown paper parcel, with their label, on the draining board by the back door. Mrs Hullett's instructions were that it should then be put on her desk in the study. 'I remember once a parcel was delivered by Browne's and no one was in the house. Mrs Hullett found it and was angry as she had been waiting for it.'

After Mr Hullett died, 'there were an awful lot of empty bottles and medicine jars thrown away. Even after that I am sure I saw empty medicine bottles and boxes'.

Miss Durrant mentioned that Mrs Hullett 'had some trouble with her mouth' – which was sore – and 'a nervous twitching of her face'. She had seemed quite all right on Thursday, 19th and seemed to be looking forward to the weekend and Miss Reed coming. It had been her afternoon off and she had not come back home until 10.30 p.m.

It was about 11.30 on the Friday morning that Miss Durrant had known that Mrs Hullett had not awakened and by midday, she thought it 'rather strange', and at 3 o'clock Mary had told her that she was still asleep. Later, she was told that a nurse had come. During the weekend 'we took it in turns to sit with Mrs Hullett as we had been told she was not to be left alone' and she had been alone with her at lunchtimes on Saturday and Sunday.

Finally, Miss Durrant stated that she had never heard Mrs Hullett say anything about taking her own life, nor heard any member of staff talking about such a thing.

Miss Kathleen Reed, aged 53, was a midwife, and had known Mrs Hullett since she was eight years old and they were at school together. Mrs Hullett 'was a Miss Leefe'; her mother was still alive and lived in Putney and she had a sister, Mrs Thompson, living in Helston, Cornwall and a step-sister, Miss Ivy Leefe, living in Brecon in Wales. Her friend had been 'a perfectly normal person in every way' until the death of her first husband. (This was when Dr Adams first started treating her with drugs.) All their lives they had corresponded regularly, every ten days, but since Mr Hullett's death, she had only received postcards.

Miss Reed had visited Holywell Mount at the beginning of June, 1956, stayed a week and then returned to Yorkshire; she arrived back on 19th June at about 6.30 p.m. She had thought that her friend looked 'very, very much thinner' and did not seem to be well. Sometimes she had appeared natural and at others very unhappy and depressed. They had dinner together, and it was about 10 p.m. when Mrs Hullett had said that she had a headache: 'You have had a long day's journey, you won't mind my going early to bed'. Miss Reed had gone upstairs with Mrs Hullett and Patricia and they had gone to their respective bedrooms.

Mary Mayo usually took up Mrs Hullett's breakfast and had told Miss Reed that she was still asleep and that the Doctor had called and said 'Let her sleep'. So she went out shopping and returned about 1 p.m. 'About that time I went to see Mrs Hullett in her bedroom and she was asleep and appeared as if she was drugged.' She had talked to Mary and they decided to ring Dr Adams and inform him. She had rung again mid-afternoon and asked his secretary if Dr Harris could call – which he did. Later, Dr Adams called to see her. Miss Reed was in the bedroom at this time and was present when he examined Mrs Hullett. 'When the Doctor entered the room he said, "I don't know where she got them from, and I am not touching anything", at the same time glancing round the room. He later mentioned that Mrs Hullett was suffering from some cerebral condition.' Miss Reed 'had faith in Dr Adams, which I had gained through what Mrs Hullett had told me over a number of years. I remember Doctor Adams saying on Friday evening, that he disliked the idea of her going into hospital as she had always had a horror of having treatment at a hospital.' She knew that was so.

Miss Reed stated that 'either Mr or Mrs Handscomb, one of the servants or myself, sat in Mrs Hullett's bedroom from the Friday until she died on Monday'. Very strangely, she attended a wedding at Uckfield on Saturday, 21st, being away most of the day. This also hardly fitted with the statement of Dr Adams that he knew there was a trained nurse available during the day, Miss Reed, when she was not there at all on the second day of Mrs Hullett's illness.

Mrs Hullett had 'spoken rather wildly', saying that she wished she were dead, but Miss Reed never believed that she would do anything about it. Miss Reed had spoken to Dr Adams on the Saturday and he had said nothing about the possibility of Mrs Hullett dying, though she could see it was 'in his mind'. She had seen Mrs Hullett on Sunday evening and had thought her breathing abnormal; she had been there when her friend had passed away.

Teresa Yogna, the Italian housemaid was, by March 1957 when she made her further statement to DS Sydney Gentle of Scotland Yard, Mrs Balkham, a forty-year-old housewife in Eastbourne, and a British subject by marriage. She had been employed by Mrs Hullett for three years. One of her duties had been to clean her employer's bedroom – which was on the first floor at one corner of the house, facing towards the east. On Mrs Hullett's bedside table she kept an ash tray, a little pocket mirror, telephone directory and the *Daily Light* 'which she used to read each night. It was marked with a piece of paper since Mr Hullett's death'. (The *Daily Light*, a Plymouth Brethren publication had been given to her by Dr Adams.)

Teresa described Mrs Hullett as 'a very charming person'; she got on well with her but was not her confidante. The Hulletts had been a 'a very devoted couple' and were lost without each other. After Mr Hullett's death, Mrs Hullett seemed gradually to lose her appetite and increased her smoking. She only drank 'in moderation' gin and brandy.

On the day Mr Hullett died, 14th March, 1956, Dr Adams had come to the house at about 7 a.m. and stayed there. At 9 a.m. he saw Mrs Hullett in her bedroom and Mary Mayo had told her that he had given Mrs Hullett an injection 'to counteract shock'. About three weeks after this, Mrs Hullett had told Teresa that Dr Adams had instructed that 'she must stay in bed each morning until he had visited her. Mrs Hullett was annoyed about this as she said it wasted a lot of time for her.' From the time of her husband's death, Mrs Hullett had begun to appear 'drowsy and listless'; as time went on these symptoms increased and on one occasion when she came downstairs 'she looked like a drunken person'. She had to walk by holding on to the furniture to steady herself and 'I saw her on a number of occasions leaning against the wall for support.'

At about Easter, 1956, Mrs Henson came to stay at Holywell Mount for a short time – she had previously been to see Mrs Hullett for a day on a Sunday, and it was on that day that Teresa had spoken to Mrs Henson as she had been worried about Mrs Hullett's condition. Teresa told Mrs Henson how ill her mistress was looking and her unsteadiness in the mornings; that she did not like the idea of Mrs Hullett taking drugs to make her sleep and that Cook, Kathleen Durrant was of the same opinion. Teresa had thought 'that Mrs Hullett should go away for a holiday and to stop having the treatment from Doctor Adams which I thought was doing her harm.'

Following this conversation, Mrs Henson managed to persuade her friend to stay with her for a few days. Mrs Hullett had mentioned to Teresa 'that she did not like going away for long periods as Doctor Adams did now allow her to do so.' In fact, she cut her holiday short and when she returned 'she said that the reason was because of what the Doctor had told her'.

Teresa mentioned the rash which Mrs Hullett had on her neck, which had first appeared six months after her first husband's death; she had also suffered from sores just inside her mouth. About six weeks prior to her death she had been to the dentist and had been bleeding until the following day when Dr Adams had given her something to stop the bleeding. A few days later she was complaining of 'a peculiar feeling in her gums all round her mouth and could not understand what it was.'

The staff had instructions that the front door should be left unlocked 'in order that Doctor Adams would not have to ring and wait for the door to be opened for him'; he just went straight up the stairs to Mrs Hullett's bedroom, and usually came between 10 a.m. and 10.30 a.m. each morning. Mrs Hullett would usually get up between 11 a.m. and 12 noon and only occasionally as early as 10 a.m. When Dr Adams had started to come every day, Teresa had asked Mary Mayo: 'What does he come for?', and she had replied, 'He comes to do injections to Mrs Hullett as far as I know', and mentioned that Mrs Hullett had told her that. Teresa had thought it strange that she had never found any signs of an injection bottle, carton, ampules or cotton wool, as she had when the Doctor had given injections to Mr Hullett.

During the month of June, Mrs Hullett had got steadily worse, physically, and walking about the house, she had to hold on to the furniture, particularly in the mornings; she seemed to improve after lunch, but was 'very weak on her legs'. Her mental condition had been quite normal. One morning, earlier in July, she was coming downstairs very unsteadily and had said to Teresa, 'I'm sorry I'm late, it isn't my fault, it's the Doctor's fault'. Teresa had asked her how she felt and she replied, 'Oh, I don't know' in a very tired way. Teresa then said, 'Do you think these tablets do you any good to your heart?', and Mrs Hullett said, 'Of course I don't'. She had also seemed to be more absent-minded and forgetful.

The last time Teresa had spoken to Mrs Hullett was on Thursday, 19th, when she had said, 'I have put fresh water in the vases ready for you when you do the flowers'; she had seemed 'far away' and was slow to react: 'Thank you Teresa'. It was not until the Friday when she went into the bedroom with Mary Mayo and Miss Reed that she saw Mrs Hullett next, not moving, 'she looked like a sack lying in bed. When I saw her I had a horrible thought, I was horrified, I thought it was something tragic. She didn't appear to be peacefully asleep, her breathing was not difficult but she looked very ill and her skin was loose and falling from her cheeks towards her chin.'

Teresa then went out to do some shopping, and on her return, Mary told her that Mrs Hullett was still asleep. 'Miss Patricia was present and it did not appear that she was very much worried, although she was never very expressive'. Teresa had sat with Mrs Hullett on the Friday, and then on Saturday and Sunday for about three-quarters of an hour each day, at intervals. 'I watched her closely and her colour kept changing from pale to a bluish red colour. Her face became smoother and she looked a little better. Her breathing was changing a lot and I noticed both on Saturday and Sunday it was difficult on occasions'. Her mouth became more open each day, 'and on Sunday it was wide open and she looked more like a dead person... I noticed a dark place on the left, inside her mouth and down from the corner of her mouth was a streak of dark fluid...'

Teresa thought that Mrs Hullett had committed suicide because she had no desire to live, and that she could easily have concealed sleeping tablets because nobody looked in the drawers in her bedroom. There was one occasion, about two months prior to her death, when Mrs Hullett had told her that she had not taken all the tablets the doctor had given her, but had told Dr Adams she was taking them.

DI Pugh visited the Vicarage in East Grinstead in Sussex on 24th July, 1956, the day after Mrs Hullett's death. The Rev. Harry Copsey had first met Mrs Hullett in December of 1943, when he became Vicar of Willingdon, near Eastbourne. She had then been Mrs Vaughan Tomlinson and lived in Willingdon. She was happily married to her headmaster husband until he died in 1950, and she became very unhappy and 'appeared to lose grip of herself'. Dr Adams had attended her first husband shortly before his death.

A few months after her husband's death, she accompanied the Vicar to Arosa in Switzerland, where they had stayed for about a month. It was then that Rev. Copsey had noticed that she was taking sleeping tablets and had tried to get her to give them up. It had been difficult to get her up in the mornings, and one morning, he had gone into her room, shortly after 9 a.m. 'and found that she did not appear to be sleeping normally and I found it impossible to waken her'. When she did appear at lunchtime, she seemed normal.

When they had left Arosa, 'she was wonderfully well', and soon after their return to England, she became engaged to Mr Jack Hullett. Rev. Copsey had officiated at their wedding at Putney Parish Church in London and he and his wife remained close friends with the Hulletts. They were 'an ideally happily married couple' and it was a terrible shock to Mrs Hullett when her husband died; it was then that he had learned that Dr Adams was visiting her 'at least once a day'. She had had 'the greatest confidence in her doctor and spoke in glowing terms of his care'.

On the 4th May, Mrs Hullett was to take the Vicar and his wife to Coventry for the enthronement of the Bishop. The previous evening, at dinner, he had seen Mrs Hullett take a white tablet from her handbag and swallow it. Very shortly after taking it, she 'became pale and shrunken', and said she would not be ready until 11 a.m. the following morning. They had left at this time for Coventry where they joined the Bishop's party for lunch and afterwards attended his enthronement in the Cathedral ruins. The Bishop, who knew Mrs Hullett well, had been 'distressed at her condition'.

The last time the Rev. Copsey and his wife had seen Mrs Hullett was at the wedding reception of a Miss Jill Hawkin on 7th July, when she had appeared 'very strained and unwell'. Later, when they returned to Holywell Mount for tea and she had smoked two cigarettes and had a cup of tea, she 'appeared as well as I have ever known her'.

The Vicar had met Dr Adams socially on a number of occasions and knew 'in what high esteem he is held by all his patients'. In answer to a question put by DI Pugh, he replied: 'I admit I have always had a great horror of drugs'.

One other thing that occurred to him was a remark that Mrs Hullett had made more than once on their return from Coventry: 'It is all yours if you will only put me out of the way'.

DI Pugh took a statement from Evelyn Patricia Tomlinson (known as Patricia), on 26th July, three days after her mother's death. She was 22 years of age. Her mother had been terribly unhappy since Mr Hullett's death: she had got so thin. She had sleeping tablets at night, left by Dr Adams in the morning: two small white tablets and two large ones. Sometimes she had taken very small white tablets after meals.

Patricia went out to work Monday to Friday, leaving the house about 8.30 in the mornings to go to Hailsham and getting back about 6 o'clock. It was usually just on Sunday mornings she saw her mother, who had always been bad at getting up in the mornings, but had become more so during recent months. She had said that the drug she was having 'was wonderful and gave her a good night'. Her mother had 'become rather given to occasional fits of giddiness' since Mr Hullett's death, and she had told her daughter that she felt 'as if the floor was coming up to her'.

Patricia could recollect no 'nerve storm' on the Sunday or Monday before the 19th July, though she had been told that her mother had had a fall. She had last seen her at about 10 o'clock on the Thursday evening when she had a headache and went to bed early. She had said 'Goodnight' to Patricia in the usual way.

It was only when she returned home on Friday evening at 6 p.m. and asked Mary where everybody was, that Patricia learned that her mother was not well. She went up to see her and 'she just looked as if she was asleep', though she was breathing shallowly. Dr Adams had told her when he called during the evening, that he was doing all he could, and she then realised that it was serious. It did cross her mind that 'Mummy might have done something to herself' as she had been so low and nothing anyone did seemed to help her.

On the Saturday morning, Patricia went in to work as usual; when she returned at 12.30 p.m., she found her mother in the same condition. She had asked Dr Adams on Saturday afternoon, she said to him: 'What is the matter?', and he had replied that he was not absolutely sure but he thought it was a cerebral condition – something pressing on the brain. He had never suggested having a second opinion, and nobody else suggested this. By Sunday morning, when Patricia looked at her mother, she 'saw no visible change in her facial appearance', but noticed that 'she looked very hot' and her breathing was still shallow. That evening, when she saw Dr

Adams 'he did seem reasonably pleased and perhaps satisfied', though she, herself 'didn't feel very happy about Mummy's condition'. Dr Adams 'was terribly honest to me about Mummy's condition and anything I asked he answered me right away and I think truthfully.'

Patricia had gone to bed at about half-past ten on the Sunday night, but at half past six on Monday morning she heard someone walking about and opened her bedroom door: Dr Adams was outside. He told her that her mother would 'probably only live an hour'. She realised then that she had really been expecting this since Friday. How her mother had died 'didn't make much difference to me'; she hadn't seen her afterwards, preferring to remember her as she was. So often she had asked her mother not to talk about wanting to die. It was all too much for a twenty-two year old to cope with... however, she still had 'implicit faith' in Dr Adams.

The statement taken from Dr Peter Cook was made on 17th January, 1957. He was a Doctor of Medicine, a Bachelor of Surgery, a Member of the Royal College of Surgeons and Licentiate of the Royal College of Physicians and, at the time, practising at Paddington General Hospital in London. During July 1956, he had been acting House Surgeon at the Princess Alice Hospital in Eastbourne, where the accused was employed as an Anaesthetist, so he had seen him from time to time.

Dr Cook recollected a conversation he had had with Dr Adams about 'Megimide', an antidote to barbitone poisoning. On the afternoon of Saturday, 21st July, 'about *two days after* [this would make the first conversation the day after the £1,000 cheque was given to him by Mrs Hullett and before she had taken the overdose] the conversation with him about Megimide, Dr Adams came to see Dr Cook again, asking him 'to remind him of the name of the drug I had mentioned a few days earlier and also if he could obtain any of this drug from the hospital'. Knowing there was a notice about Megimide in the Casualty Department, Dr Cook thought it might be stocked there. They went along to Casualty, where the drug was not in stock, but they read the notice concerning the drug. (Exhibit 16) The notice detailed the dosage and mode of administration precisely. Dr Cook had then gone with the accused to the Dispensary and obtained 100 millilitres of Megimide in a carton, (Exhibit 17) containing a pamphlet with complete details of dosage and administration. (Exhibit 18) Dr Cook had actually gone through the pamphlet with Dr Adams, so that he had repeated the instructions twice.

Dr Cook had then asked him if he had a patient with barbituric poisoning and 'he replied that he had'. He had asked Dr Adams if he had set up an intravenous infusion and he said that he had not done so. Dr Cook had advised that the drug was usually given in such an infusion, but that, if he was giving it by intravenous injection, it should be done very slowly in doses of 10 millilitres every five minutes or so. The accused had left with the Megimide in the carton, containing the pamphlet. 'I did not say to the accused that ten cubic centimetres was the dose and that if it did not work it would be no use.' This was quite a damning statement.

A statement was taken from the Coroner for East Sussex, Dr Angus Somerville on 18th January, 1957. He was a Member of the Royal College of Surgeons and a Licentiate of the Royal College of Physicians.

IMPOSSIBLE TO ACCUSE A DOCTOR

In the early morning of Sunday, 22nd July, 1956, he was still in bed when he receive a 'phone call from Dr Adams. Dr Somerville gathered that he was reporting a death and that he wished to have a private post-mortem examination. He said: 'Certainly not. You should report it to me officially and I will deal with the matter.' and then asked him when the patient had died. To Dr Somerville's amazement, he replied that the patient was not dead, so the Coroner asked him why he was reporting it. Adams had said that he was not certain what she was going to die from and therefore he wished to have a private post-mortem examination. Again, Dr Somerville said: 'Certainly not. You must report it to me officially and I will deal with the matter.' The accused had said 'Thank you', and the Coroner put the 'phone down.

Later, on the Tuesday morning, there had been a letter in the post (Exhibit 23), signed by Dr Adams and Dr Harris, – it was not usual to receive a letter with the signatures of two doctors – but the Coroner had already ordered a post-mortem examination. He had instructed first Dr Philps and then Dr Camps (Home Office pathologist) to make post-mortem examinations. The Inquest had taken place on 21st August, 1956. Dr Somerville had seen no cheque produced during the course of that Inquest, and no cheque was produced as an Exhibit.

Cross-examined, Dr Somerville said that he had 'known of' and 'known' the accused for some years. He recalled that Dr Adams had begun the telephone conversation by asking him if he would be in Eastbourne that day because he wanted to 'talk something over' with him. Post-mortems could sometimes take place privately at the instance of relatives, but only if the doctor is not precisely sure of the cause of death. Sometimes the results of these would be reported to the Coroner, but he would not necessarily make use of these and he would want to know why such an examination had occurred. However, if a case was reportable in law to the Coroner, then it had to be reported and the Coroner would deal with it.

The letter had been handed in to Eastbourne Police Station for him and the contents read over the telephone, and this was when he had ordered the post-mortem to be held.

Dr Shera, he knew quite well, as he was a well-known pathologist in the county. When the accused had telephoned him, 'he may have said he wanted Dr Shera' to perform the post-mortem examination.

Re-examined, Dr Somerville said that he had never before been asked whether a private post-mortem could be arranged. 'In my experience, it has never before been asked before the patient's death.'

The last of the additional statements was that of Mr Michael Clark, chemist and a Director of H. R. Browne (Chemist) Ltd, taken on 17th January, 1957. Most of the statement related to comparison of prescriptions for Mrs Hullett listed on Exhibits 5 and 6, but the particular matter of interest was the handing over of prescriptions to Superintendent Seekings by Mr Cooper in the shop.

Cross-examined, Mr Clark said that, to the best of his knowledge, the originals for the whole seventeen prescriptions were in the possession of his firm in the previous year 'including the ones which are now missing'. They must have been handed over to Superintendent Seekings at some time prior to the Inquest. He had next seen the prescriptions 'when they were shewn to me pinned together by Detective Inspector Pugh about one week ago. I have not seen the missing four since they were handed to Superintendent Seekings.' He had been unable to find them at his shop, although he and his staff had looked for them several times.

It is clear that Dr Adams' peers in Eastbourne considered him both unprofessional and unethical and perhaps even incompetent, but the *omerta* of the medical profession smothered any impulse they might have had to share their suspicions with the authorities, including the General Medical Council.

So, although the unnecessary and excessive use of drugs, the high number of patient deaths and the numerous legacies associated with Dr Adams' practice were common knowledge amongst the medical fraternity, they did nothing. Some doctors even co-operated with Dr Adams on those occasions when he required a co-signatory on cremation certificates, by routinely signing documents and collecting a fee – the notorious 'ash cash' procedure, without conducting any independent examinations. In so doing, they created the conditions for Dr Adams to flourish and became complicit in his wrong-doing. This connivance extended even to the Coroner, with whom Dr Adams had an all too cosy relationship, which permitted the undoubtedly notifiable deaths to pass unchallenged. Effectively, the disdain the profession felt for Dr Adams had atrophied into an institutionalised myopia, the doctors, the coroner and the magistrates had become like the three mythological monkeys who had chosen to hear, see and speak no evil.

The British Medical Association itself did not improve matters. On the 24 August, 1956, shortly after the Police investigation started, it took the unusual step of writing to all doctors in the Eastbourne Division, reminding them of the need for confidentiality in respect of patients, particularly those who were the responsibility of another doctor (i.e. Dr Adams). On the face of it, considering the severity of the charges, this seems an extraordinary move, almost designed to frustrate the investigation. In the event, out of all the doctors in Eastbourne, only two came forward with information and both did so casting metaphorical nervous glances over their shoulders in trepidation of sanctions.

Not that this reluctance to come forward with evidence had no previous history in the profession. Nearly 60 years before Dr Adams began practising, a certain Dr Pritchard came to trial in Scotland, accused of murdering his wife and mother-in-law by poison. A key witness for the Prosecution – a Doctor Paterson – admitted that he had suspected what was going on. Under cross-examination, he was asked:

'Then, though you saw a person suffering from what you believed to be poisoning by antimony, you did not think it worth your while to go near her again?'
'It was not my duty. I had no right to interfere in any family without being invited.'
'Dr Paterson, is it not your duty to look after a fellow-creature who you believe is being poisoned by antimony?'
'There was another doctor [i.e. the murderer] in the house. I did the best I could by apprising the registrar.' [i.e. after the death]

The Lord Justice-Clerk (John Inglis, later Lord Glencorse) in his summing-up, referred to this matter:

> '...the conduct of Dr Paterson when he formed this opinion on 24th February. He said, in answer to the questions put to him, that his meaning was – what he intended to state in the box was – that he was under the decided impression, when he saw Mrs Pritchard on these occasions, that somebody was practising upon her with poison. Now, he thought it consistent with his professional duty, and I must also add, with his duty as a citizen of this country, to keep that opinion to himself. In that I cannot say that he did right. I should be very sorry to lead you to think so. I care not for professional etiquette, or professional rule. There is a rule of life and a consideration that is far higher than these – and that is the duty that every citizen of this country – that every right-minded man owes to his neighbour, to prevent the destruction of human life in this world, and in that duty I cannot say but Dr Paterson failed.'

In fairness, the silence of Eastbourne professionals was not confined to doctors and nurses. It was clear from the Police interviews with solicitors and accountants in Eastbourne that, for many years, Dr Adams had been deeply involved in unethical practices concerned with the preparation of his patients' wills. He was actively canvassing opportunities to intervene between solicitors and their clients on the pretext of responding to his patients' concerns. In many cases, the consequence was that their wills would be rewritten, often with the effect of Dr Adams becoming the executor and a key beneficiary. On at least one occasion, witnesses reported seeing Dr Adams actually guiding the hand of a terminally ill patient to sign a new will in which Dr Adams was a beneficiary. While this activity might not have been illegal, it was most certainly unethical and would have evinced more than a simple rebuke from the GMC. The legal profession in Eastbourne was aware of Dr Adams' activities but, while individuals had voiced their disapproval to Dr Adams personally, and various practices refused to co-operate with him, nothing was actually reported to the GMC.

Thirdly, the medical profession – particularly the nurses – was aware of Dr Adams' practice of sitting with his patients alone, often for hours at a time, and that he rarely explained the treatment he was giving them, even when the drugs he was using were being administered by nurses in his absence. It was evident from witness statements that he would groom and flatter his patients during these long sessions and, depending on their state of health, would switch the conversation to their wills sooner of later. This behaviour would have been frowned on then; in modern practice, it would be totally unacceptable.

In the 1950s, doctors were held in more awe than today and perhaps the private nurses felt that they would lose their jobs if they crossed Dr Adams. Into the bargain, Dr Adams was known to have a fearful temper, which forestalled any questioning of his behaviour or treatment of patients. Whatever the reasons, Dr Adams was permitted by default to impose a regime of secrecy round his handling of patients. When he left eighty-seven-year-old Clara Neil-Miller lying naked on her bed, exposed to the cold and damp of a February night, he was able to brush off the protests of a passing visitor (reported by Dr Mathew but the person concerned, Mrs Walsh, died before the police investigation) with an angry retort; nothing was reported and no one intervened, with the result that the patient died of pneumonia, which he concealed by recording the cause of death as cerebral haemorrhage.

In this quiet, provincial, spa-like town, Dr Adams' behaviour had, over a twenty year period, fanned slow-burning speculation and rumour – perhaps the only outlet for disquiet chosen by the professionals in Eastbourne – but it was a conflagration in the making. The death of Mrs Hullett was the spark to set it off.

While none of the information connected with the Bobbie Hullett case was used in court, the case for trial which the DPP prepared with regard to her death appears much stronger in many respects than the Morrell case. Most significantly, there was a body and the telling evidence from the autopsy. In spite of the suicide verdict delivered by the Coroner's Court, there is nevertheless evidence of Dr Adam's complicity in her death and an apparent *modus operandi* emerges from a comparison between the deaths of the two women. None of this was allowed in evidence in the Old Bailey trial, which was focused solely on the death of Mrs Morrell, which had happened six years previously.

# Dr Adams' Modus Operandi

An examination of all the evidence gathered by the Police reveals Dr Adams' apparent *modus operandi* with regard to patients, which became progressively more sophisticated as the years rolled by. The pace of development and frequency of cases appears to have increased after his mother's death.

### The Early Years

Dr Adams' career as a general practitioner began in 1923. Perhaps not unnaturally, for a junior practitioner in a town like Eastbourne, there was a skew in his patient list towards the elderly, particularly widows; perhaps the partners felt that their junior would be better coping with the elderly, who required regular visits, but mainly palliative care. However, there is evidence that he was simply not keen on paediatrics or obstetrics, which suggests that his patient list was not a matter of chance or merely a whim of the partners.

The Mawhood case provides evidence that, early on, he was a sponger and became adept at finessing small gifts of money and, later on, more valuable items, from his patients. He saw nothing wrong in timing his visits to coincide with meal times so that he would be invited to have lunch, or bringing his mother and cousin so that they would be included in his rich patients' hospitality. His cousin later featured in small acts of deceit, such as being introduced as a 'masseuse' to patients requiring massage. Through this device, his cousin became quite popular with some of Dr Adams' patients and some of them left her bequests in their wills.

### 1930s

His growing ambition was evident in his decision to buy the house at Trinity Trees and set up his own practice. The purchase was part funded by a loan from a patient; on this occasion, the loan was paid back. Soon after, he made his first forays into advising his patients on the writing of their wills. He also took to advising other service providers to load their bills to his clients, saying 'There's plenty of money there.' He began his studies in anaesthetics during the '30s. There is evidence from witness statements of his elderly patients becoming increasingly dependent on him and being frequently under the influence of heavy drugs. By the end of the 1930s, there is evidence of sudden deaths amongst his patients, he was regularly receiving legacies and several firms of solicitors had refused to co-operate with him. There were reports of him filching items from the homes of the deceased whose death certificates he had just signed, claiming that the items had been promised to him. In one case, a patient, eventually (in the late 1940s) had to threaten legal action before Dr Adams would return a large sum of money which he had volunteered to 'look after' on the patient's behalf and later fraudulently claimed was payment for unpaid fees or rent.

In another case, Dr Adams persuaded a dying patient to sell him some property at a cheap price. He was constantly bargaining with the relatives of deceased patients to buy motor cars which they had inherited. He had established a practice of barring nurses from his meetings with patients under treatment in nursing homes. Nurses witnessed him on over-familiar terms with his elderly female patients, several of whom considered him to be in love with them.

### 1940s

In 1941 he qualified as an anaesthetist and started working at the hospitals. During the war, his practice suffered, because his partners departed on military service and he was not nominated as one of the twelve doctors in Eastbourne paid to tend to those injured by enemy action. The civilian population also declined and most of his private patients left Eastbourne. He nevertheless made great efforts to keep in touch with patients and there was some evidence that he was sending them drugs. His mother died in 1943.

After the war, he moved quickly to re-establish his practice, particularly as the wealthy patients returned to Eastbourne. His technique of helping patients rewrite their wills and have himself nominated as executor and beneficiary now extended to managing their funerals and cremation. The bereaved were frequently informed at the last minute and were not allowed to view the deceased, on Dr Adams' orders. When filling out cremation forms, he routinely concealed that he was a beneficiary under the will, 'We always want cremations to go off smoothly for the dear relatives' or 'If I said I knew I was getting money under the will they might get suspicious and I like cremations and burials to go smoothly.' His efficiency in this business can be judged from his handling of the funeral of Mrs Emily Mortimer. She died on Christmas Eve, 1946. He arranged for the funeral and burial to take place two days later, on Boxing Day.

At this point, it is worth examining Dr Adams' preference for cremation in those cases where he was appointed executor in his patients' wills. Nationally, the preference for cremation grew only very slowly from the time of the Cremation Act in 1902. During the 1950s, for reasons of costs and tradition, it was still a minority preference, which did not begin to increase significantly until the later 1960s and 1970s. So, up to the time of Dr Adams' trial, it was still the preference of a small minority, and this was certainly so in Eastbourne, as the archives of Haine's the Undertakers evidence. Initially, the primary reason was cost. Cremations were more expensive than burials. Also, there was often an existing family grave which could be opened at minimal expense. There was still strong resistance to the idea of cremation because it was not traditionally Christian. The doctrine of 'the resurrection of the body' mitigated against cremation, and, even if people did not realise that this was the reason, tradition is very strong in regard to funeral customs in any culture.

In the case of Eastbourne, there was no crematorium during the period 1946-56, which meant that the Downs Crematorium in Brighton had to be used. Eastbourne did have a substantial number of wealthy elderly living in retirement, far from their relatives. In these cases, cremation might be the preferred option, given the costs of removing the body to a family grave in some other region of Britain.

The resistance to cremation was gradually eroded by what Phillipe Ariés, the French historian, termed 'the age of the medical death' and the growing desire to concentrate obsequies into one short event. Churchgoing, which reached a peak in the aftermath of the Second World War in the '40s and '50s went into decline in the '60s. In the 1950s, or before, opting for cremation would have been the choice of 'modern' thinkers or even perhaps intellectuals – as a 'green' burial (or – even more recently, in Sweden – freeze drying the body to a powder which can be used to fertilise the garden) is now. It struck Hannam as significant that so many of Dr Adams' private patients should have decided upon cremation; he inferred that there had been some discussion of the cremation option, provoked by Dr Adams, at the time of the preparation of the wills.

### Late 1940s / Early 1950s

Through his shooting interests, Dr Adams had established a circle of very powerful friends in Eastbourne, including Lt. Col. Gwynne, the Chairman of the Magistrates and past mayor, the Chief of Police, a Superintendent of Police and the Coroner. At the time of the police investigation, there was a rumour of a homosexual relationship between him, Gwynne and a 'senior policeman'. There was some suggestion that Dr Adams was also involved in drug trafficking, but the police investigation had uncovered no direct evidence before it was curtailed. However, during the Police investigation, he threatened, 'If I go, I'll take a lot with me.'

It appears likely that he made a pact with one of his most long-standing and very wealthy patients – Mr Mawhood – to ease his passing and to terminate his life prematurely rather than let him suffer a painful death from bowel cancer. Such an arrangement would have been quite illegal. The *quid pro quo* was that Dr Adams would be appointed sole manager of his fortune after his death and would ensure that his widow would be provided for. Much to Dr Adams' annoyance, this deal was scotched by the patient's wife.

After this, he had a succession of very wealthy patients (starting with Mrs Morrell and ending with Bobbie Hullett) who died after having been in a coma which had been induced by heavy drugs. From these patients, he inherited large sums of money, expensive motor cars and luxury goods. Thirty years later, after his death, many of these items would be found stored and untouched in his home.

## Comparison of Dr Adams' behaviour with that of Dr Harold Shipman

In January 2000 another British doctor, Harold Shipman, a general practitioner in Hyde, Greater Manchester, was convicted of murdering fifteen of his patients and of forging the will of one. The finding of the First Shipman Inquiry Report was that Shipman had killed at least 215 of his patients over a period of 24 years. The number of deaths he certified over 12 years was 324 – a rate of 27 per year. The investigation of Dr Adams covered 10½ years and he had certified 308 deaths over that period – a rate of just over 29 per year. Given the differences in time and location, one must treat these statistics with some caution, but their patient lists were broadly similar in size and they were both skewed towards the elderly.

The police in the Adams case did not seek to compile statistics; there was little information gathered for them to do so, even if they had had the time available. They had only been concerned with finding the death certificates he had signed and the wills connected with these.

However, there are, and were, no statistics of the sort which were used to compile the Shipman Report, although even these have been found to be inadequate for the task of monitoring mortality rates in general practice. Put simply, it seems that, in an average year, there may have been slightly more deaths in Dr Adams' practice than in Dr Shipman's; in addition, the annual death rates in both practices appear high when compared to other practices. There were still significant numbers of infant and child deaths in Eastbourne in the period 1946-56 and yet only two such deaths on Dr Adams' certificate list. A considerable proportion of deaths occurred in Eastbourne hospitals, and there were few on his death certificate list likely to have been his panel or NHS patients, taking the addresses into consideration. We know what caused the high annual death rate in Dr Shipman's case. Given all the variables, there is a problem in being able to arrive at a similar conclusion in the case of Dr Adams, beyond all reasonable doubt.

However, Home Office Pathologists examined the death certificates issued by both doctors and it is interesting to compare their conclusions. When the police launched their investigation into Dr Adams, there was insufficient time to conduct a complete search of all the death certificates he had signed over the 34 years he had practised as a doctor. So the search concentrated on the period beginning on 1 January, 1946 to 31 June 1956 – only 10½ years – less than one third. A check of the nurses' statements against the list of death certificates, showed that there were at least three which were missed in the search at Somerset House.

According to the First Shipman Report, over 12 years, Dr Shipman issued 166 'highly suspicious' death certificates; according to Dr Camps, the Home Office Pathologist in 1956, Adams issued 163 'highly suspicious' death certificates in 10½ years. Dr Camps wrote:

'I have been working out a rough analysis and it seems surprising (even allowing for the average age) that of the total of 312 [4 were prior to 1946], of those over 70, 21 died of cerebral haemorrhage – 93 of cerebral thrombosis – under 70, 4 of cerebral haemorrhage and 9 of cerebral thrombosis – also 37 of uraemia. This, without other causes which might end in coma, gives a total of 163 or more than half of his cases which have died in coma which could well be due to a narcotic or barbiturate.'

Having said this, Dr Adams did not generally worry about relating the cause of death to the clinical history. He did not, in any case, keep any clinical records for private patients, only a note of visits so that accounts could be sent to them, so the only evidence available to Dr Camps about patient treatment was from the nurses who had cared for some of them.

Perhaps not surprisingly, both doctors liked to deal with their patients in private. Unlike Dr Adams, when Dr Shipman attended patients in a residential home, a member of staff would always be present; Dr Adams had the nurses and the matrons trained to accept his instructions that he should always be alone with a patient, when he would administer injections; alternatively, he would leave filled syringes to be administered by the nurses. It appears that Dr Shipman's favourite *modus operandi* was to visit his patients in their home, where he would administer a lethal injection.

Other aspects of their careers were eerily similar; Dr Adams was fined for not maintaining a Dangerous Drugs Register in 1957 and Dr Shipman was not keeping one in 1998. The police could not find 'convincing evidence of excess prescribing of diamorphine' (heroin) in Shipman's case – in other words, they never knew how he obtained the necessary amounts to kill his patients. While the evidence was that it was not difficult for Dr Adams to create a cache of dangerous drugs, the police found it difficult to conduct a full accounting of the drugs he may have had in his possession at any point in time.

Normally, he simply walked into Browne's the Chemist just around the corner from Kent Lodge and prescribed it for his 'bag' or put some extra on to a patient's account, or collected unused doses after a patient died. He could call at any chemist's shop in the town and obtain drugs as a doctor. He was also known to forge prescriptions, sometimes in the names of other doctors. The nurses' notes sometimes recorded that an injection was given, but Dr Adams had simply taken the drug from his case and not explained what was administered. In the case of Bobbie Hullett, Dr Adams was supplying her with the drugs with which she apparently committed suicide. He enquired about the antidote and the dosage the day before she took the overdose and again, a day and a half before she died; in the event, when he found her in a coma, he administered the antidote, but in too small a dosage to make any difference.

Another similarity between Dr Shipman and Dr Adams was the immense loyalty of their patients, when they were accused of murder. Even after his conviction, it was not difficult to find patients who would assert that Dr Shipman was an ideal GP: kind, always having time to talk, happy to make home visits – one of the most popular doctors in the district. Many wanted to relate stories of his kindness – just as they did of Dr Adams. Dr Adams returned to his loyal band of patients after his short period of removal from the register and practised in Eastbourne for another twenty years. Both were regarded by their patients as 'an old-fashioned doctor', treating patients in a warm and personal way, frequently visiting them without being requested to do so. As Leslie Henson left the inquest into the death of Bobbie Hullett, he was incautious enough to declare the inquest verdict a travesty and to accuse Dr Adams of her murder. He was promptly attacked by a band of elderly women wielding umbrellas who believed fervently in their dear doctor's innocence.

Dr Shipman was said to have made much of his elderly lady patients, joking and flirting with them and several nurses reported exactly the same of Dr Adams: 'They went to him for a tonic'. There was that other familiar phrase used after an old lady had been found dead: 'She thought very highly of Dr Shipman.' Neither took nurses into his confidence and both reacted badly when asked too many questions. There are many parallels between the cases but Dr Shipman was caught and convicted because of his extremely rash behaviour in forging Mrs Grundy's will, a will which left him the whole of her estate; her daughter was a solicitor. Mrs Grundy's body was exhumed reasonably soon after her death and the autopsy showed that she died from an overdose of morphine. Death often ensued after Dr Adams had given the patient an injection of an unidentified substance, which sometimes nurses realised was likely to have been morphine or heroin.

In searches of his home, Dr Shipman was found to have taken a good deal of jewellery — mainly of little worth – from his dead patients' homes. On one occasion, the deceased's brother had arrived at his sister's home to find Dr Shipman walking out with her sewing machine, saying that she had promised it to his wife. The taking of 'trophies' is a common trait among serial killers. From witness statements, it is clear that Dr Adams was also a trophy hunter. The objects concerned were normally small valuable items, such as gold pens, or the sort of objects he was interested in: clocks, cameras, typewriters, radios, on one occasion, a half-empty bottle of brandy. He liked to have clocks and antique items bequeathed to him as well as cars and money. When Kent Lodge was searched on the 24th November, 1956, Superintendent Hannam reported the following:

> 'In the basement we saw a lot of unused china and silverware. In one room there were 20 new motor car tyres still in their wrappings and several new motor car leaf springs. Wines and spirits were stored in quantity. On the second floor, one large room was given over to an armoury, for in it we saw six guns in a glass-fronted display case, several automatic pistols and many cases full of 12 bore cartridges. The Chief Constable of Eastbourne informed us that Adams had firearm certificates to cover these articles. A second room on this floor was used wholly for photographic equipment. A dozen very expensive cameras in leather cases were seen and large quantities of unused films of various types were set out in trays.'

Dr Shipman did attempt to obtain legacies from patients, but he was not very successful, receiving only the odd £250, perhaps he simply lacked rich patients or Dr Adams' polished technique. There is evidence that he tried to involve himself in patient's property and financial affairs. He also solicited money for his 'Patients' Fund' and stole cash and some valuable jewellery from the homes of his victims after killing them. He is thought to have sold most of the jewellery; in one case, this was estimated to have a value of around £20,000. There is a familiar ring to the story of Mrs Bianka Promfret, who had planned to leave the majority of her estate of about £60,000 to Dr Shipman, but was persuaded by her ex-husband, to change her will just two weeks before she died. When Shipman killed the unfortunate woman with a morphine injection, she had probably not told him that she had cut him out of her will.

As the Shipman case is so recent, the archival sources of the police investigation are not available, so a detailed analysis of their findings has not been possible. There had been gossip and rumour around Hyde about Dr Shipman before the case of Mrs Grundy set off the full-blown police enquiry but the familiar belief that Dr Shipman was simply 'easing the passing' of his patients held any doubts at bay. This was an explanation people wanted to believe, as they did with Dr Adams. In neither case was it true. What is much more chilling about Dr Adams is the sophisticated planning that went into his selection and grooming of his victims, inducing them to become drug addicts and testing out different drugs till he found the right combinations. Beside him, Dr Shipman looks like a naive opportunist and rather crude operator.

It is difficult to make any detailed comparison in the family backgrounds of Dr Shipman and Dr Adams. In both cases, there seems to have been some distance between father and son – a trait which is common in the lives of serial killers: Dr Shipman would not take time off to attend his father's funeral in 1985; Dr Adams had an extremely strict and religious father. Both men had dominant mothers who brought them up to believe that they were clever and superior. Both were isolated in childhood and adolescence, not being allowed to play with other children. Trauma came earlier to Dr Adams with the death of his father when he was 15, followed by his younger brother, two years later; Dr Shipman's mother died when he was 17.

When the detective in charge of the Shipman case, Detective Chief Superintendent Postles, pondered Shipman's motives, he concluded that Dr Shipman thought himself to be superior and had a desire to dominate and control. Dr Adams was brought up by his Plymouth Brethren parents to believe that he was one of God's chosen. He was also encouraged by his ambitious mother to emulate his great uncle, who had crowned a lifetime of achievement, firstly as a result of his academic performance and secondly as a missionary, by being made a Mandarin. In case after case, it was evident that Dr Adams had a desperate need to control and dominate his patients. Driven for half his life by his hugely determined mother, he had a single-minded ambition from the start of his career to achieve status and wealth.

## Comparison with Dr Michael Swango

In America, in June 2000, another doctor serial killer, Michael Swango, was convicted, sentenced for killing four patients, but thought to have killed possibly thirty-five. Like Dr Adams, he was the son of a distant and strict father and an undemonstrative mother who focussed entirely on him. Where Dr Adams' childhood was tightly disciplined by his parents' religious beliefs, Dr Swango was brought up in an institutional family atmosphere with military exercises enforced by his ex-army father.

Dr Swango became a hospital doctor with a particular predilection for 'accident and emergency'; Dr Adams served as a houseman in Bristol in charge of the A&E department. Like Dr Adams, Dr Swango was preoccupied with control and manipulation; he was narcissistic, highly self-absorbed, and with a strong sense of his own entitlement. He lacked empathy for others and, in his case, this was sometimes strongly apparent to colleagues. This same trait was seen in both Dr Shipman and Dr Adams, particularly after a patient's death in an abrupt and unfeeling manner towards relatives. Witnesses reported Dr Adams giving the deceased scant attention, signing the death certificate, then picking up some memento of the occasion on his way out with some comment to the effect that it had been promised to him or simply that he wanted it.

Dr Swango too had some bizarre habits with food, gobbling pies and cakes whole, hoarding cream cheese pastries at the hospital and storing piles of bacon sandwiches. Hannam had found Adams' surgery cupboards '…very untidy. Numerous bottles (including morphine) were either on top or lying on each other. There were several boxes and slabs of chocolate, some packets of sugar, some pieces of margarine and butter. Some of the chocolate had actually stuck to the shelves…' The hoarding of food probably developed after his mother's death; it seems unlikely that she would have permitted it in her lifetime.

It was apparent even in medical school that Dr Swango had an unusual fascination for accident and emergency situations and violent deaths; it was even noticeable that there was a sexual element. Dr Adams' fascination was with drugs and anaesthetics, death and funerals. In the case of Dr Swango, the Ohio State doctors knew that he had probably murdered patients but did not refer their suspicions to the police. After an F.B.I. investigation, a warrant was issued for Swango's arrest, but he had managed to obtain a post at a mission hospital in Zimbabwe. It was not until July 1995, when patients were dying and he was found to be injecting patients from a syringe concealed in his coat pocket and there were suspicious deaths that the police were called and discovered large amounts of dangerous drugs and hospital equipment in his home.

## The Conduct of the Prosecution's Case against Dr Adams

Substantial research has led to the conclusion that the prosecution's case was interfered with and that, at some point, the intention switched from trying to hang Dr Adams to trying to ensure that he would be found not guilty. One is led to this conclusion by three separate pieces of evidence.

First, there is the handling of the Nurses' Notes, with which the Defence punctured the Prosecution case on the second day of the trial.

Second, there was the conduct of the Prosecution, which was so flat-footed and incompetent that questions were raised in Parliament.

Third, I believe that important Tory politicians were shocked by the media interest in the case and its potential implications at a time when the Government was extremely vulnerable and that they yielded to the advice being given by influential figures, such as Lord Beaverbrook, the Canadian magnate who owned, *inter alia*, *The Daily Express*, which championed Dr Adams' cause.

## The Strange Case of the Nurses' Notes

It was normal practice for the nurses in private nursing homes to maintain patient notes. In practice, they were fairly informal documents – usually simple exercise books – in which the nurses would record changes in the patient's condition, changes in the patient's mood, doctor's visits, meals or medication taken and any other events which seemed relevant. It is important to realise that they were not intended as an 'official' medical record. Their purpose was simply to assist with the change over between different shifts of nurses, so that the incoming nurse could get quickly up to speed. There was no set practice that would specify ownership of the notes or responsibility for their destruction once the patient's treatment was over.

Geoffrey Lawrence's genius in his cross-examination of the nurses was that he managed to present these documents as accurate accounts of what actually happened, day by day, in the treatment of Mrs Morrell and as much more reliable than the nurses' memories. Thus, he was able to undermine their testimony and destroy, at an early stage of the trial, a key pillar of the Prosecution's case. He produced the documents with a dramatic flourish and apparently to the general astonishment of the court. They were accepted surprisingly quickly into evidence by the Prosecution with only the mildest of protests from Manningham-Buller that the Prosecution had not yet had time to study them.

Lawrence's account of how the documents came into his hands is not very convincing and is at odds with the accounts given both by Dr Adams and by Dr Adams' solicitors. Dr Adams had three versions of how the notes came into his possession. One was that the notes were sent on to him by Mrs Morrell's son in a parcel, which he had never opened thinking they were 'some small effects'. The other was that the notes were delivered anonymously to his door some time after Mrs Morrell's death.

It seems most unlikely that Claude Morrell would have been in a position to send Dr Adams the Nurses's Notes. Firstly, the notes were in the charge of the nurses and were not part of the patient's effects; the nurses would normally have destroyed them at the conclusion of the case and would have no reason to pass them on to the patient's relatives – in fact they deliberately would not do so in case they caused distress with graphic details of the illness. Claude Morrell would not have known of their existence, so would not have thought of asking for them. Secondly, as the interview which Hannam conducted with Claude Morrell revealed, Morrell recognised in retrospect that Dr Adams had deliberately misinformed him about the quantities of drugs he was giving Mrs Morrell. Given Dr Adams' secretive behaviour, he would not have left evidence of the actual treatment for her son to find.

The second version offered by Dr Adams was that the papers were left on his doorstep by an anonymous donor. What use the sender believed these normally no-value notebooks could be to Dr Adams is not clear. The sender's motives for delivering these ephemera and for remaining anonymous are also obscure. Remembering that there was no legal requirement to keep these informal records, Dr Adams' version of what happened next is even more bizarre; he decided not only to preserve these apparently useless documents, but also to entrust them to his secretary for filing. When later quizzed on this point by journalists, he resorted to obfuscation and referred to 'Providence'.

When quizzed by Chief Superintendent Hannam on the evening of his arrest whether he had any documents relating to Mrs Morrell's care, he did not apparently remember the Nurses's Notes, in spite of the fact that having had them returned to him was such an unusual occurrence. It was only much later, at 3 a.m. the following day, after he had been charged by Chief Superintendent Hannam and he and his solicitor, James, had returned to his surgery, that he remembered the books and they were found stuffed in the back of a filing cabinet in his surgery. In another interview, Dr Adams had yet another version, claiming that the notebooks were found in the Anderson air-raid shelter in the garden. Whatever the case, he claimed they were subsequently transferred to his defence team. (Actually, he had no defence team at that point in time.)

His solicitor told his family a somewhat different story. According to the solicitor's son, his father's version was that, when the importance of the nurses notes were recognised by the Defence team, shortly before the trial, James was dispatched to Dr Adam's surgery to search for the notes and he found them.

None of these versions fits with the evidence in the Police files. Amongst Hannam's own prepared papers, there is a list of exhibits for the Committal Hearing which he had passed over to the DPP's Office. The Nurses' Notes are clearly mentioned as one of the exhibits. Either Superintendent Hannam or Inspector Pugh had found these notes in Dr Adams' surgery on the crucial evening when they came to interview and charge Dr Adams and had taken charge of them. This is the only way they could have been passed with the other exhibits to the DPP's office. So Dr Adams' versions of events – certainly the timing and who made the discovery – were fabrications.

The interesting questions are how and why did the Notes find their way to Geoffrey Lawrence's team and why, since they could have reached the Defence team only via the DPP's office, did the Prosecution claim to have had no prior sight of the notes? If one supposes that the DPP considered the documents to be of no use to the Prosecution, then the right course of action would have been to reveal the presence of the documents to the Defence in the normal way. But surely someone would have checked the nurses' statements with the Notes? Surely then the discrepancies would have been revealed and the full significance of the documents would have been recognised? In any case, Hannam would have realised as soon as he read the notebooks. Is there another possibility that the Police procedures in obtaining the notes were in some way at fault, in which case the documents might not have been admissible in support of the Prosecution's case? Or might it have been embarrassing to admit how the documents were obtained? Alternatively, perhaps the risk to the Prosecution's case was considered serious – but not necessarily fatal – and it was decided simply to press on with the case.

Whatever the truth, some way had to be found of handing the Notes over to the Defence. The DPP's office could have simply handed them over to the Defence in the normal way of any evidence. But the Prosecution claim during the trial not to have seen the Notes proves that this option was not followed. So it appears that the DPP opted for subterfuge. Perhaps the Notes were simply passed on to Herbert James, Dr Adams' solicitor in Eastbourne – possibly via Inspector Brynley Pugh, the local officer, who was present when the Notes were discovered in the first place and who was a friend of Dr Adams. Whatever the truth, this was probably Herbert James' last contribution to the case on his client's behalf, since he never recovered from the stroke he suffered while attending the trial at the Old Bailey and died at the Esperance Hospital in Eastbourne in 1959.

But why the need for subterfuge? One possibility is that the release of the Notes was part of a deliberate intent to undermine the case for the Prosecution. Such a decision could have been made only at the highest level and might be evidence of political interference. Certainly, given the concerns about the survival of the NHS, the timing of the trial of Dr Adams could not have been worse and finding Dr Adams not guilty had a silver lining for the Government. Many doctors had suffered a substantial reduction in their incomes due to the NHS payment system and were threatening to resign; the Government took the situation so seriously that a Royal Commission on doctors' remuneration in the NHS was set up in February 1957. Were the case to have gone against Dr Adams – worse still, were he to have been hanged – there might have been mass defections of doctors from the service, triggering off a second major political crisis.

But if this were true, why didn't Reggie simply consider the implications for the Notes and abandon the case? Hannam recorded that he submitted the papers on the case to the DPP, Theobald Mathew, in December. Those papers included the Nurses' Notes as an exhibit. Those papers would have been reviewed by Melford Stevenson, Reggie's second in command. He was extremely competent. It is not likely that he would have missed the conflicts between the nurses' statements and the Notes. The crucial decision to arrest Dr Adams was perhaps taken in Reggie's office at the House of Commons on the fateful day in December, 1956, when Hannam was summoned to receive the Attorney General's instructions. Perhaps too much impetus had been built up behind the case to delay any further and Reggie agreed with the Police that the sheer weight of evidence justified the arrest and trial. Perhaps Reggie was reluctant to let go visions of himself at the Old Bailey on a high profile case. Maybe he knew of Eden's impending resignation and recognised that to delay meant either upstaging a new Prime Minister or delaying the whole process till February. Maybe he, like the Police, was convinced of Dr Adams' guilt and simply decided to let the Committal hearing determine whether or not there was a case to answer. Whatever the case, the decision was taken to proceed against Dr Adams.

At a later stage, possibly after Macmillan became Prime Minister, there was a change of direction. Macmillan might, in any event, have had his own concerns about the case since his late brother-in-law, the Duke of Devonshire, had been a patient of Dr Adams and died in his presence. By this time, it was too late to abandon the prosecution without great loss of face. The only option left was to undermine the case. At some level, it was decided to pass the

Nurses' Notes over to the Defence. It is not clear whether Reggie was complicit in this move. The Prosecution's shocked reaction in the Old Bailey when Lawrence produced the Notes convinced the Press and the Judge.

## The Prosecution's Management of the Case

After Hannam produced the report which provided the basis of the decision to accuse and arrest Dr Adams, Reggie took an unusual step on his own initiative: he released a copy to the British Medical Association. When he was challenged on this issue, he said rather huffily that he couldn't see anything wrong with letting them have a confidential copy. The politician in Reggie was clearly trying to keep the doctors' professional body 'on-side' while he moved against one of their members. Nevertheless, the lawyer in him should have recognised that this was an extraordinary breach of confidentiality. Hannam's report contained information on many cases which were not addressed in the Trial. It also gave an account of confidential interviews with witnesses, who included doctors in the Eastbourne region who had received a letter from the BMA, reminding them that they could not discuss patients of other doctors with the Police. There was also a risk that a copy of the document might have found its way to Dr Adams.

The second question concerned Reggie's handling of the case in court. There was certainly no love lost between Reggie and Lord Devlin, the judge in the case. But in his book on the trial, the latter was scathing about Reggie's performance in court. Reading Mr Justice Devlin's summing up, it comes as no surprise that the jury took only 45 minutes to acquit. Even to the layman's eye, time and again, Reggie allowed Lawrence much too much scope to tease misleading answers out of witnesses. Reggie also managed to antagonise one of his own expert witnesses, effectively undermining his testimony, which, given the way Lawrence had already destroyed the evidence provided by the nurses, put the last nail in the coffin of the Prosecution's case.

---

# Chapter Thirty-Nine

# An Independent Medical Opinion

---

## Dr Jane Mercer

In order to obtain an up-to-date medical opinion on the Morrell case, I sought the opinion of Dr Jane Mercer, Pathologist at Eastbourne District General Hospital, who also has pharmacological expertise. She had sight of the Nurses' Notebooks detailing the last few months of Mrs Morrell's life, the prescription lists and Dr Ashby's notes. It also seemed that Mrs Morrell might have been exhibiting some of the symptoms of porphyria, so she cast her experienced eye on the evidence.

## Medical Condition

Mrs Morrell was being treated for a stroke: the treatment for a stroke is good nursing care and no medication is really necessary. Some stroke patients become confused, restless and even aggressive and mild sedation would be appropriate. There may also be difficulty sleeping so that some type of sleeping tablet might be necessary. There is unlikely to be much pain.

This patient was treated with opiates – heroin, morphine and omnopon. In pain relieving doses they cause drowsiness but are not really suitable for ensuring a good night's sleep. They would reduce aggressive behaviour and excitability but it is likely that milder medication would be effective. I think, therefore, the use of opiates at all is probably unnecessary. There are no real advantages in using a combination of two or three opiates at once and, instead of using two, it would be more usual to use a larger dose of one to give the same effect. There have always been fashions in prescribing and, perhaps at that time, this was in general use. It may simply have been Dr Adams' preference. The long term use of these drugs carries a significant risk of addiction. It would have been known that they were addictive in the 1940s.

A variety of barbiturates was used and these would be a reasonable choice for insomnia, but again there are milder preparations which might be effective. Barbiturates were widely used at this time. If they were to be prescribed for the hypnotic effect, it would be usual to give them in the evening rather than during the daytime.

Prescribing opiates and barbiturates together increases the risk of toxicity from respiratory depression. They are often used in combination during anaesthesia and Dr Adams was an anaesthetist.

I note that during 1948, Dr Adams used both barbiturates and opiates. From April to December he was using more barbiturates. In 1950, he was using opiates more often but still using some barbiturates. It is therefore likely that by the time of her death Mrs Morrell had developed tolerance to both drug types.

It is quite possible that the patient developed porphyria as a result of barbiturate use. The porphyrias are a group of diseases resulting from partial defects in the activity of the enzymes regulating haem synthesis in haemoglobin formation. The enzyme defects lead to the abnormal accumulation of porphyrin. There are eight different types of porphyria and seven of these affect the skin. The severity of the disease and the age of onset depends on the type. There are different inheritance patterns for different types. They are all rare disorders. Three types include neurological effects, including 'brain storms' during which behaviour is frankly insane. Barbiturates are contra indicated in porphyria as they make the disorder worse or induce the disease in the susceptible. The skin rash is a blistering rash which heals leaving scars. The rash is a photosensitivity and occurs mainly on the face and hands. They may suffer from hypertrichosis (excess hair on the hands and face). They are said to be the origin of the were-wolf with their hairiness, fear of daylight and mad and possibly aggressive behaviour. They may have dark urine. Most types are not severe enough to produce the full were-wolf!

I suspect that if this lady did develop porphyria she may have died much earlier as a result of continued barbiturate administration, which is often rapidly fatal. The symptoms described could be attributable to other causes. Dark urine could merely be due to dehydration. Irritability and aggressive behaviour could be hangover effects after barbiturates. Both barbiturates and opiates can cause a rash and this is usually urticarial (extremely itchy with some blistering). This rash would not be photosensitive. [The curtains in her room were always drawn across to keep the room darkened.] The contra indication of barbiturates in porphyria was described in 1962 and it is likely that Dr Adams may not have known about this. Alcohol and scopolamine are also contraindicated in porphyria.

During the last few days before her death, Mrs Morrell was given very large daily doses of opiates in frequent and relatively small amounts. These were given on an 'as required' basis. This manner of treatment would only be justified for a terminally ill patient with intractable pain. There does not seem to be any evidence that she was terminally ill or in much pain. The daily doses are at a level where there is a strong possibility of killing the patient. She survived several days on high doses and this indicates that she had developed an enormous tolerance to high doses from long term use of these drugs. The degree of tolerance would not be very predictable.

In the last days before her death, Mrs Morrell was constipated. The faecal incontinence is likely to have been 'overflow incontinence' which occurs in constipation when the bowel is overfull. This is a side effect of opiate administration to which no tolerance develops. Her intake of food and fluid during this time was low and she passed urine infrequently. This suggests that she was in some danger of circulatory collapse (a risk with high dose opiates due to the lowering effect on blood pressure and made worse by a low fluid intake). When she was awake during this time, she was restless and jerky. This may in fact be due to addiction and a craving for the next dose of opiate.

## The Cause of Death

She died 'peacefully in her sleep'. This could happen as a result of an opiate overdose, a barbiturate overdose or a paraldehyde overdose. It could also be a result of a further stroke.

There is one clue here. The nurse records that her respiratory rate was 50 at 12.45 a.m. when she was asleep. This is a high respiratory rate and the rate is normally about 40 per minute. Opiates and barbiturates cause respiratory depression in overdose. A stroke leading to death is likely to cause Cheyne Stokes respiration which is slow intermittent and noisy breathing. Paraldehyde in overdose causes a rapid respiration rate. The doses given – 2cc at 7.30 p.m. and 5cc at 10.30 p.m. – make a total of 7cc. The normal dose is 4-8cc. If the third injection, shortly before death was also paraldehyde, an overdose would be likely. From the prescription information, Dr Adams obtained 4oz of paraldehyde. I take this to mean 4 fluid ounces which is 100ml or cc – enough to dispose of a horse!

The nurses notes for 8/9th October 1950 mention the '? stroke'. She was given a special capsule and a special injection and shortly afterwards became drowsy, went to sleep and then became semicomatose. When she awoke, there seems to be no mention of paralysis or slurred speech as would be the result of a stroke. The onset of drowsiness followed by sleep and then coma would fit very well with the administration of a large dose of opiate or barbiturate or both. I feel that this could have been an unsuccessful attempt on her life. Maybe he underestimated the dose which she could tolerate at this stage.

I find it suspicious that he arranged a cremation within 36 hours of death. In 1950, cremation was relatively unusual and burial would have been far more common. Was it actually Dr Adams who arranged this? [It was.] Funeral arrangements are usually made by the relatives of the deceased and the doctor is only involved in issuing the death certificate. Also it usually takes longer than 36 hours to complete funeral arrangements now (usually about a week). Perhaps it was quicker in 1950. [It was usually a week, by tradition.]

## Special Injections

The nature of these is unknown

# Chapter Forty

## The Justified Sinner

Before the 19th Century, 'Criminal law knew only two terms, the offence and the penalty'.[1] Then another element was formulated – the criminal – emerging as 'a pale phantom',[2] but becoming more solid, more real, until he becomes the principal player, requiring an explanation of his motivation and psychological impulse to commit the crime. Foucault dubs this the 'psychiatrization of the law'. We now need an explanation as to why a person commits a crime, and more so if it appears to be an unnatural crime, such as a mother murdering her child. A doctor and a patient are viewed as having a parental-child relationship and this is why it seems so unnatural to us for a doctor to murder a patient. If insanity is ruled out another explanation is required.

Detective Superintendent Hannam summed up his view of Dr Adams in his First Report:

> 'He is a suave hypocrite and one is led to borrow from Robert Louis Stevenson the appropriate title of Dr Jekyll and Mr Hyde for he is a real life embodiment of all that colloquialism implies.'

This heading is borrowed from James Hogg's book, *The Private Memoirs and Confessions of a Justified Sinner*, which is foreshadowed by Burns' poem *Holy Willie's Prayer* and was used by Robert Louis Stevenson as the basis for *Dr Jekyll and Mr Hyde*. Since the latter book, many have explained people like Dr Adams and Dr Shipman as 'a Jekyll and Hyde'. James Hogg came much closer to the answer and his book is a subtle psychological study of the possible and logical outcome of extreme Calvinism.

Calvin's theology was based on the literal interpretation of the Bible; salvation was by the grace of God alone and not by the works of man; and those who were to be saved were already pre-destined by God to be the subjects of His salvation. This is a great simplification of his doctrines, but sometimes, down the centuries, these would engender unexpected aberrations. James Hogg explains the baptism of the 'Jusified Sinner':

> 'I depended entirely on the bounty of free grace, holding all the righteousness of man

[1] Foucault, quoting Garofalo / [2] Ibid

as filthy rags, and believing in the momentous and magnificent truth that, the more heavily loaden [sic] with transgressions, the more welcome was the believer at the throne of grace... That I was now a justified person, adopted among the number of God's children – my name written in the Lamb's book of life, and that no by-past transgression, nor any future act of my own, or of other men, could be instrumental in altering the decree, "All the powers of darkness," added he, "shall never be able to pluck you again out of your Redeemer's hand."'

As there is so much emphasis on sin in his home and he is chastised so often, the 'Justified Sinner' learns early to lie because so much is forbidden to him. The 'labyrinth of deceit' leads to 'doubling': there is the outer persona and the other self deep within. Like Edmund Gosse, explaining the same phenomenon resulting from his Plymouth Brethren upbringing in his autobiographical book *Father and Son*, he actually speaks to his other self and thinks of him as a separate person. He decides upon his work of reformation:

'...to cut off the enemies of the Lord from the face of the earth; and I rejoiced in the commission, finding it more congenial to my nature to be cutting sinners off with the sword than to be haranguing them from the pulpit, striving to produce an effect which God, by his act of absolute predestination had for ever rendered impracticable... Seeing that God had from all eternity decided the fate of every individual that was to be born of woman, how vain was it in man to endeavour to save those whom their Maker had, by an unchangeable decree, doomed to destruction... How much more wise would it be, thought I, to begin and cut sinners off with the sword! For till that is effected, the saints can never inherit the earth in peace. Should I be honoured as an instrument to begin this great work of purification, I should rejoice in it!'

And as for the sins he himself would commit whilst he was effecting this work:

'..dare you say that there is not enough of merit in His great atonement to annihilate all your sins, let them be as heinous and atrocious as they may? And moreover, do you not acknowledge that God hath pre-ordained and decreed whatsoever comes to pass? Then, how is it that you should deem it in your power to eschew one action of your life, whether good or evil?... "What thine hand findeth to do, do it with all thy might, for none of us knows what a day may bring forth."'

He believed that no act of his could ever remove him from his communion with God; he could do anything with perfect safety because the elect were infallible.

There is another interesting parallel with Edmund Gosse's book. The double of the 'Justified Sinner' persuades him to kill:

'Besides, you ought to consider what great advantages would be derived to the cause of righteousness and truth were the estate and riches of that opulent house in your possession, rather than in that of such as oppose the truth and all manner of holiness.'

Edmund Gosse tells this true story about a member of the Brethren in Devon:

'Mr Dormant (a retired solicitor) was not very well off, and in the previous year he had persuaded an aged gentleman of wealth to come and board with him. When, in the course of the winter, this gentleman died, much surprise was felt at the report that he had left almost his entire fortune, which was not inconsiderable, to Mr Dormant. Much surprise – for the old gentleman had a son to whom he had always been warmly attached, who was far away, I think in South America, practising a perfectly respectable profession of which his father entirely approved… and I am very much pleased to remember that when the legacy was first spoken of, he (my Father) regretted that Mr Dormant should have allowed the old gentleman to make this will. If he knew the intention, my Father said, it would have shown a more proper sense of his responsibility if he had dissuaded the testator from so unbecoming a disposition. That was long before any legal question arose; and now Mr Dormant came into his fortune, and began to make handsome gifts to missionary societies, and to his own meeting in the town… But in process of time we heard that the son had come back from the Antipodes, and, was making investigations. Before we knew where we were, the news burst upon us, like a bomb-shell, that Mr Dormant had been arrested on criminal charges and was now in gaol in Exeter.

Sympathy was at first much extended among us to the prisoner. But it was lessened when we understood that the old gentleman had been "converted" while under Dormant's roof, and had given the fact that his son was an "unbeliever" as a reason for disinheriting him. All doubt was set aside when it was divulged, under pressure, by the nurse who attended the old gentleman, herself one of the "saints", that Dormant had traced the signature to the will by drawing the fingers of the testator over the document when he was already and finally comatose. …My Father regretted that he had not been able to persuade him to admit any error, even of judgment. But the prisoner's attitude in the dock, when the facts were proved, and not by him denied, was still more extraordinary.

He could be induced to exhibit no species of remorse, and, to the obvious anger of the judge himself, stated that he had only done his duty as a Christian, in preventing this wealth from coming into the hands of an ungodly man, who would have spent it in the service of the flesh and of the devil. Sternly reprimanded by the judge, he made the final statement that at the very moment he was conscious of his Lord's presence, in the dock at his side, whispering to him "Well done, thou good and faithful servant!" In this frame of conscience, and, with a glowing countenance, he was hurried away to penal servitude.

Yet I was never sure, and I am not sure now, that the wretched being was a hypocrite… that Dormant, …may not have sincerely believed that it was better for the money to be used in religious propaganda than in the pleasures of the world…'

Both the Justified Sinner and Mr Dormant described the inner narrative which reflected their own interpretation of the crimes they committed. The legal interpretation of their actions would have been quite different, but it is that inner story which they would have been living. There is another parallel which is even more strange. John George Haigh, the acid-bath murderer, and the son of devout Plymouth Brethren parents, talked about one of his crimes, while he was in Brixton prison:

> 'He believed in God and would not swear. He did not like to hear others swearing and when he talked of Mrs Durand-Deacon [a victim] he put his curious philosophy of life into effect. He said that he felt as if it was his mother he was killing when he shot Mrs Durand-Deacon in the back of the head, and although he was sorry, and for a moment felt some compunction, dismissed it quickly with the thought that he was very hard up and had to have money… Then he really did give the show away on what was almost a Hitlerian theory on life, for he declared "Mrs Durand-Deacon should have been kicking up the daisies long ago. She's neither of use to the country, nor to humanity." He added that he could "put her money to better advantage in the interests of humanity, such as experimental engineering". By that reason he justified the killing and was quite satisfied in his justification though he repeated to me more than once that he could not get his mother out of his mind as he fired the shot in the little room at Leopold Road, Crawley. He said he loved his mother, that she was a very good woman. He never mentioned his father.'

David Canter, the psychological profiler, suggests it is instructive to work out what happened early in life: those small incidents, those odd phrases. Dr Adams' earliest memory was that of his father chastising him for disobeying him and refusing the gift of an apple from a friend – which was equated with refusing a gift from God, and this incident may have imprinted itself on his mind indelibly. He should take even what he did not want or need. He certainly never looked a gift-horse in the mouth again, and it may explain, for instance, his extraordinary action and persistence in pursuing gifts, even at the mere mention of the possibility of one. The gifts, apart from the Rolls Royces, were not valued for their intrinsic worth – his house was full of these items, mostly unused, at the time of his death – they were more like trophies. He related the incident of the apple after the trial, fifty-five years after it happened, also mentioning that he only once again disobeyed his father, but did not say what the second incident was about. At that time he described his father as 'strict'. The only family photograph ever seen was one probably taken in 1906 with his parents and brother sitting in his father's large open Wolseley car. His description of the photograph was 'my brother William Samuel braves the storm in the front seat with father, my mother and I shelter behind.' So the grouping suggests that he preferred to be with his mother and that she protected him. He is a huddled figure in the back seat and his small brother – aged 2, sits proprietorially in the front passenger seat. Anecdotal evidence of his childhood and student years describes him as a 'loner', which would not be surprising considering his Brethren upbringing. Dr David Canter says tellingly:

'…the child brought up in an institution almost inevitably learns that he is a commodity to be dealt with… an object. But many families create an institutional mood of their own.'[3]

Dr Adams had aspired to emulate his uncle as a missionary doctor in China and satisfy his mother's dream; in the event Professor Rendle Short, 'God's Recruiting Sergeant' had directed him to Eastbourne. He arrived there, rejected, on the rebound, but he still had to fulfil that impulse for power and glory. To the end he still remembered the medical and evangelical missions, leaving them legacies.

The earliest anecdote of his Eastbourne days is that recorded by Sister Stuart-Hemsley, recalling what Miss Mackintosh, the Matron of Upperton Maternity Home had told her, and this must have been soon after he arrived as he only had a bicycle. He had thrown the bicycle on a flower-bed in front of the nursing home and damaged the flowers. Matron had said to him: 'You won't have a bike if you do that again' and he had retorted: 'If you live in this town long enough you will see me riding in my Rolls.' In later years, he said that he had wanted to follow in his Uncle John's footsteps, 'his brilliant career' and become a doctor missionary in China, but that 'like Peter, I might only "follow from afar".' By the time he was in Eastbourne, at twenty-three or twenty-four years old, he seems to have been rather arrogant, and had decided that he was going to become a rich man. And the 'Rolls' would be something better than his father's achievement of the Wolseley. It is likely that Professor Rendle Short recognised that the young John Bodkin Adams required a comfortable and fashionable life and that this is why he encouraged him to go to Eastbourne as a GP. The 'academic' career that Dr Adams said was his prospect in Bristol was probably not something that the Professor ever had in mind for him, particularly since he had not taken an honours degree.

Although the early anecdote relates his going to a maternity home, it is worth mentioning here that obstetrics was always an area of medicine which he avoided; probably he could not do so early in his career. He could not entirely do so with his 'panel' or NHS patients though. Mrs Muddell, the bank manager's wife had recalled the treatment she had received in 1925 which was so crude that it might be thought that he was committed to the literal interpretation of *Genesis* 3 verse 16 'in sorrow shalt thou bring forth children'. It was mentioned in an interview to me that the wife of another professional man had changed to another GP when she became pregnant.

From Mrs Mawhood's stories of his early years, it can be seen that Dr Adams also thought nothing of asking for money or indeed just putting goods which he wanted on to a patient's account without informing them. The earliest statement to police about his activities with the elderly rich was made around 1930 by Mr Plummer, the accountant. There are those telling remarks he made: for instance, to Mrs Galloway when she was making out the bill for millinery for the deceased Mrs Morrell, telling her to double it as 'there was plenty of money there'. A 'Robin Hood' attitude. Did he also think of the riches of old ladies like Mrs Morrell being very

[3] Canter, *Criminal Shadows*

much undeserved riches because they were inherited? That they could be put to better use? The story of Mrs Hughes and the Thurstons is instructive because it was a will he had altered without benefiting from it; but he had moved money to the 'more deserving' in his eyes. He made his money from the rich and his father had made his money from the poor. There was considerable opportunity for justification.

The most traumatic experiences of his early life were his encounters with death: that of his father – with a cerebral haemorrhage and in coma – when he was just fifteen, and that of his brother – in the Spanish 'flu epidemic – when he was nineteen. In Brethren terms, John Adams should have become the head of the household at his father's death as men took precedence over women, but evidence indicates that his mother took immediate charge by insisting that her boys signed the pledge because it represented her 'earnest desire' after their father's death. He had kept this document and still had it in 1957, despite not adhering to his promise to forswear alcohol. The doctrine of the Brethren attested that his father and his brother had become Saints in Heaven and were in a far better place than those left behind. He left no record of what had been said to him as a child about death, but Haigh did and his account is very similar to that of Edmund Gosse:

> 'He [his father] was constantly preoccupied with thoughts of the Hereafter, and often wished the Lord would take him home. It was a sin to be content with this world, and there were constant reminders of its corruptness and evil. Often I pondered my father's references to the Heavenly places, and to the "works that will destroy this body". It was inevitable that I should develop an early inhibition regarding death.'

Between those two sudden deaths in his adolescent years, John Adams was to be confronted with cadavers for dissection and dying patients in hospital. All around him: in his family, in his religion, medicine, the Ulster of his youth and the struggle for Irish independence, the First World War and the Spanish 'flu epidemic in Belfast – the common theme of all of these was death.

There is not a great distance between death and Dr Adams' primary medical interest – anaesthesia, where patients are made unconscious. He studied anaesthetics in his spare time until he obtained his Diploma in Anaesthetics in 1941. At the time of his arrest he held posts at two hospitals in Eastbourne, spending around eight hours a week anesthetising patients for operations. He was deeply interested in hypnotic drugs and what these could do to patients and others. He did not, however, use them on himself; he was never a guinea pig. The drugs gave him power over people, but it would have been of no interest to him to dominate a person who had no power, and this equated with wealth and social status. Hannam wondered why he had bothered himself sometimes with the petty details of financial control, but it was surely all part of the process of that complete domination he needed to achieve. Each of the Brethren is a 'priest'; being a doctor as well makes a combination which is verging on the godlike, with life and death, the spiritual and the physical, both in the same pair of hands.

The life of a GP is quite ideal for anyone who wishes to have a parallel secret existence to the story of the life which is open to the public gaze. The patient-doctor relationship was always secret and even the nurses were unaware of the treatment. There was the public persona: his life with his mother, his cousin and servants, religion, the YMCA, the shooting. Hannam thought that he had another secret life and that this was with the three 'mistresses'. Then he had started to probe the connection with Lieutenant-Colonel Sir Roland Gwynne, and he had been stopped in this endeavour. He had also had his investigation into drug-trafficking halted.

When John Adams came to Eastbourne, he would not have immediately fitted in with Eastbourne society; even amongst the doctors he was the only one from Ulster, the others being mainly of Scottish origin. He and his mother and cousin would have had an introduction to the Brethren in the town in the first instance, but, as far as local society was concerned, they were not part of it. Yet he, without 'connections' aimed to be the most fashionable doctor in the town, with the richest patients. How did he set about achieving this? What was the key to his success? A new, young, attractive and unmarried doctor in the town probably caused a riffle of excitement to run through the tea-rooms, but not through the most important circles. He probably quick-ly realised that his exceptional shooting skills would be useful in gaining contacts if he could acquire invitations to shoots on local estates. Eastbourne was run by a very few people and prominent among those locally was the name of Gwynne: Rupert was the M.P. in the early '20s and had large estates on the outskirts of the town. His younger brother Roland was more acces-sible, however, living at Folkington Manor and known for his lavish spending on 'entertaining'.

There is, in the police files, an anonymous memorandum, probably emanating from the *Daily Mail* reporter, Rodney Hallworth, which suggested a homosexual relationship between Adams, Gwynne and 'a police officer'. This was promptly quashed – again an instance of a pos-sible line of investigation being turned into a hunt for the disseminator of the information – and Hallworth denied being the author. There is also evidence that Adams had threatened that he would 'bring down' three other people in the town if he was convicted. One of these was Roland Gwynne and he was a frightened man when he was interviewed by Hannam. However, he was well-protected by his connections. There was talk in the tea-rooms about the 'three mis-tresses', and this explanation was 'accepted' by the police, but was probably inaccurate. Like Haigh, Dr Adams appears not to have had a very active sex life. Perhaps his passions were sub-limated into other activity: the quest for wealth, power, position in society and the shotgun and hypodermic needle. In 1935 Dr Adams broke off his engagement to Norah O'Hara, even although her parents had bought and furnished a house for them. There has been an explana-tion that Mrs Adams prevented the marriage because Norah's parents were 'in trade'. Ellen Adams came from 'trade' herself and married 'trade' and if she had the power to stop the mar-riage why would she not have done it earlier? It seems a convenient 'cover' for a situation which had somehow got out of control, and, in the end, it seems that John Adams could not go through with any marriage. His life could not encompass such a close relationship, or a sexual relationship with a woman. Apart from the possibility that he was homosexual, it would have interfered with his relationships with his female patients who preferred him to be unmarried, and his secret other self. Norah was also a dominant character like his mother, but she remained his best and most loyal friend for the rest of his life. She does not seem to have been jealous of his friendships with other women. Whatever occurred, it was probably a crucial incident in his life. Hannam reported that Miss Ella Leach had been 'similarly turned over' by Dr Adams, and that he had given her a house 'as a peace offering'. Miss Betty Cradock of 'Little Hill', East Dean, who had been left a considerable sum by her uncle, was the 'mistress' he had taken on holiday when he went with Roland Gwynne, shooting in Scotland. He was said to visit her weekly and take her flowers. Villagers of East Dean still recall that when they saw her after these visits, she was 'uplifted', and they put it down to an excess of sherry. It may have been something rather more potent. Although Hannam stated that Scotland Yard had correspondence from Cheshire Constabulary which 'confirms the general opinion in Eastbourne that Miss Cradock is the mistress of Dr Adams', there is no evidence for heterosexual activity in his life and it may be that these women acted as 'cover' for him, and that he was grateful for their friendship. Miss Cradock would, after all, have seemed to be an attractive prospect as a wife as she was both socially acceptable and wealthy.

When did the drug-trafficking start? Probably very early in Dr Adams' career in Eastbourne. It seems a very sordid matter now when drug-taking and addiction is so open and extends throughout society and trafficking is the trade of underworld gangs. From the twenties through to the early sixties, drug-taking was very different, being mainly confined to the elite. The middle classes and the 'salt of the earth' working classes imagined the elite to be as law-abiding as they themselves were. The other group of 'customers' would be the neurotic rich who did not really want to know what they were being prescribed. A source, wishing to remain anonymous, in Eastbourne said that people 'knew where to go' if they wanted controlled drugs. Dr Adams had soon put himself above and beyond the law, and in this his beliefs and upbringing stood him in good stead: he would not be judged at all because he was already a 'Saint'.

> 'When the Brethren tell us not to expect any improvement in our nature, when they assert that our fallen nature can never be sanctified, they are, unintentionally, no doubt, teaching men to acquiesce in the existence of evils which it should be their lifelong endeavour to remove.'[4]

Haigh concluded in his prize-winning school Divinity essay that

> 'We may well learn the lesson that one fall, even though it be met by perfect grace and full restoration, does not cure a natural disposition, though it may go far to correct it.' So when he left the immediate influence of his parents: 'I did not ask myself whether I was doing right or wrong. That seemed to me to be irrelevant. I merely said: "This is what I wish to do." And as the means lay within my power, that was what I decided.'

Although it is difficult to tell because the police investigation of Dr Adams' activities only covered a ten-year period and a few other odd cases, the indications are that these escalated after his mother's death in 1943. At 44 years old he was a free agent at last. A further interesting

---

[4] *History and Teaching of the Plymouth Brethren*, Canon Teulon quoted in *Trial of John George Haigh*.

parallel with Adams was another son of strict Plymouth Brethren parents – his father a preacher – but in his case he rebelled while he was still a child and rejected his parents' religion. When he was at Cambridge University he even changed his first name from that of his father, Edward, (who died when he was 11) because of his hatred of the Brethren's doctrine, to one of his own choice. This was the remarkable Aleister Crowley, who set out upon a lifetime's quest for control, domination and the antithesis of fundamentalist Christianity.

Dr Adams also embarked on his secretive quest for control and domination. There is an early story of 1927 in the police statements made by a patient who had been diagnosed by Dr Adams as needing an immediate operation for gallstones, which he arranged for her in Southfields Nursing Home in Eastbourne, to be carried out by a London surgeon. She consulted her brother, who was an army doctor, and he was shocked when he discovered that Adams had not had an X-ray done. Her brother took her to a Harley Street surgeon, Sir Gordon Taylor who said she did not have gallstones. By the early 1930s, if not earlier, it is evident that his technique of taking over the life of a rich patient and controlling their financial affairs had been developed – as in the case of Miss Henrietta Hatton. By 1935 there was the first suspicious death noted by police – that of Mrs Matilda Whitton – which they had been directed to although their investigation did not cover the years prior to 1946 – with, from Dr Adams' point of view, a most successful outcome. He was preying on those he had in his power and there are many episodes which show that he had no real empathy with his 'dear' patients. They seem to have been objects and guinea pigs to him and his behaviour when they were dead or unconscious is particularly illustrative of this aspect. The taking of their personal belongings was obviously very significant to him; he would go to considerable lengths to obtain something even if this appeared very strange to someone else present. These activities were against the backdrop of the respectable and religious young doctor with the growing and fashionable practice, who worked longer hours than any other GP in the town and never refused to come out at night for a patient.

In other words, Dr Adams was an actor: he appeared to see the world as others did, but he did not, in fact, do so. It is unlikely that he felt any remorse or guilt for any of his actions; he was able to justify them, after all. The victims he selected were rich, elderly women, in the main. Women of some position. Many thought he was in love with them, and he encouraged this with small gifts, photographs of himself, loaning them his car and chauffeur for shopping trips. He was in control of their personal and financial worlds; most of them had cut themselves off from family and friends, or they had none left, or he refused access. The ultimate control was over life and death: the fatal injection, arranging and attending the funeral and preventing other mourners from attending; being executor of the will. His control was total. Getting patients addicted to drugs was a very good method of gaining physical and psychological control over them. He was also the doctor who would make a pact with an elderly and rich patient, promising them that he would ensure that they did not suffer 'at the end', and agreeing to cut an artery to make certain that they were dead. With such a pact in place they would stay under his control whatever happened, so they would either die in their own home or in a nursing home where he was the doctor.

By 1956, he had such confidence that he took one risk too many with Mrs Bobbie Hullett: she was over thirty years younger than his usual choice of patient. She had many friends and a prominent social position. There was the £1,000 cheque. Then somehow everything was mis-timed and his partner Dr Harris became involved. He doubtless had made a pact with her so that she had the barbiturates available and he would do nothing to interfere with her 'suicide'.

Dr Adams had given Mrs Hullett a copy of the *Daily Light*, a book of morning and evening readings from the Old and New Testaments. with some readings for 'special occasions', which had been used by the Brethren from at least the beginning of the 20th Century. Each page has several eclectic texts (most including St. Paul's epistles) which have passing similarities but are out of context. She had one place marked in this book since the death of her husband and the book was by her bedside when she died; it is not known which page this was. The following page is an educated guess but it would fit in with the further information on the Hullett case prepared for trial; it comes under the heading 'Bereavement' and is one of two such pages:

'Father, I will that they also, whom thou has given me, be with me where I am.

He shall return no more to his house, neither shall his place know him any more.

Whilst we are at home in the body, we are absent from the LORD: we are willing rather to be absent from the body, and to be present with the LORD, – I am in a strait betwixt the two, having a desire to depart, and to be with Christ; which is far better. – Whether we live or die, we are the LORD'S.

Ye have in heaven a better and an enduring substance. – It doth not yet appear what we shall be: but we know that, when he shall appear, we shall be like him; for we shall see him as he is.- Now we see through a glass darkly; but then face to face. – I will behold thy face in righteousness:

I shall be satisfied, when I awake, with thy likeness.

So shall we ever be with the LORD. Wherefore comfort one another with these words.

John 17.24. Job 7.10.-2 Cor.5.6-8.-Phil.1.23.-Ro.14.8.-He.10.34.

Jno.3.2.-1 Cor.13.12.-Ps.17.15.-1 Thess.4.17,18.'

The second text is Job's comfort indeed, and, taken together, these texts would surely encourage someone inclined to suicide. Still, if she had become a Saint, it would all have been justified.

# Chapter Forty-One

## The Political Connections

The skein of political connections with Dr Adams' case stretched beyond the Gwynne family to reach several members of the Government and Mandarins of the ruling Conservative Party.

## Lord Hailsham

Rupert Gwynne had the happy foresight to appoint two powerful men – the future Lord Selbourne and Douglas Hogg, Viscount Hailsham (his wife Stella's widowed cousin) – as his daughters' guardians. Viscount Hailsham and his family lived nearby. His two sons, Quintin – who would become Lord Chancellor as his father had been before him – and Neil, were much the same age as the Gwynne girls and the cousins saw each other frequently as they grew up.

Quintin Hogg, otherwise Lord Hailsham, lived close to his cousins and Stella Ridley; his home was in the country at Carter's Corner Place – 2½ miles from Hailsham, and in Hellingly – both just a few miles from Wootton and Folkington Manors. His father had bought the house in 1917 and Quintin Hogg was brought up there from the age of ten. He saw his cousins often. In later years, he noted that he had confided in his cousin, Elizabeth David née Gwynne, when he met her in Cairo during the Second World War. (Exactly what Elizabeth David was doing, travelling about the theatre of war with apparent freedom, has never been fully explained.) His half-brother – the barrister Edward Marjoribanks, who was the biographer of Sir Edward Marshall Hall – succeeded Rupert Gwynne as Conservative M.P. for Eastbourne at the age of 24. Sadly, he committed suicide in 1932, having been jilted for a second time.

Later, Lord Hailsham was to have closer connections with the Adams case. In 1956, he was First Lord of the Admiralty and he was appointed Minister of Education in Macmillan's first Cabinet in January 1957, so he served on both cabinets which dealt with the Suez Crisis and the Adams case. He also received reports from the Attorney General, with whom he had had a long acquaintanceship, on the investigation and trial of Dr Adams. But he had a much closer connection with the case via Theobald Mathew, who was Director of Public Prosecutions throughout the Adams affair. Theobald Mathew had been one of the most celebrated Pupil Masters in the legal profession; Quintin Hogg had been his pupil after being called to the Bar in 1932, and they remained friendly down all the years. The DPP's office handled all the evidence relating to the Adams case and would have been involved in the disposal of the controversial Nurses' Notes.

# Gwilym Lloyd-George

Gwilym Lloyd-George was Home Secretary during the police investigation of Dr Adams. He too had a close connection with Eastbourne. He was born on 4 December, 1894, the younger son of David Lloyd George. When his father was Chancellor of the Exchequer, he chose Eastbourne College, a relatively new public school, for his education. Gwilym joined the school in 1910. Not a brilliant scholar, he was 'a simple, upstanding, friendly chap, with an unusually keen sense of humour',[1] and rather good at rugby, cricket and athletics. He gained a place at Jesus College, Cambridge, but the First World War intervened at the end of his first year and he joined the Royal Welsh Fusiliers. He was soon transferred to the Royal Garrison Artillery, rose to the rank of Major and was mentioned in despatches.

Gwilym never returned to Cambridge and in 1922 was elected Liberal Member of Parliament for Pembroke. He held the seat until 1950 when he suffered his first and only electoral defeat. Deserting the Liberal Party for the Conservatives, he was re-elected as Member for Newcastle (North) in 1951. By nature, he took more after his mother, Dame Margaret Lloyd George – being placid and even-tempered – than his famous father. He was much admired and liked by Members of the Commons and on two occasions he was a candidate for the post of Speaker.

Gwilym Lloyd George's first Government appointment was as Parliamentary Secretary to the Board of Trade in 1931. He then became Parliamentary Secretary to the Ministry of Food from 1939 to 1941. Churchill made him his Minister of Fuel and Power in 1942 and 'for more than three years… Lloyd-George held this exacting post and achieved results which made an outstanding contribution to the nation's war effort'.[2] In the first Conservative administration after the Second World War in 1951, he was made Minister of Food and he always liked to recall that he had been the one who had 'seen off' food rationing. Eden then appointed him Home Secretary and Minister for Welsh Affairs, appointments which he held during 1954-1957.

Gwilym Lloyd-George had obviously been very fond of his old School and he remained loyal to it for the rest of his life; he and his wife had also sent their two sons to be educated there. When Macmillan became Prime Minister in 1957 he replaced him as Home Secretary with RA Butler, elevating 'Gil' to the House of Lords as Viscount Tenby. Perhaps there was more to his removal as Home Secretary than meets the eye. As Home Secretary, he had refused to reprieve Ruth Ellis, who had killed her abusive lover. While this decision was consistent with Conservative policy at the time, by 1957, the mood of the House was changing. RA Butler, his successor, was a known for his abolitionist sympathies. During the Adams trial, Parliament

---

[1] *The Eastbournian*  /  [2] Ibid, quoting *The Times*

duly voted to abolish capital punishment, partially reserving the death penalty for special cases *e.g.* where the victim was a police officer.

# Dukes of Devonshire

Andrew Cavendish, the Eleventh Duke of Devonshire, had succeeded to the title following his father's sudden death in 1950. He had had an elder brother, William, but he was killed in action in 1944.

Eastbourne had been planned and built by the Seventh and Eight Dukes of Devonshire. The Devonshires retained considerable influence in Eastbourne through covenants, land and property ownership, and personal involvement. The Eleventh Duke continued the interest which his father and his forbears had in Eastbourne. The family residence – a Grade 1 listed building in the heart of the town called Compton Place, where the 10th Duke had died, is now leased to a Japanese-owned School of English. This was one of the measures taken by the Eleventh Duke when he was faced with death duties; his father had died four months before the deadline for avoiding death duties and he faced a bill from the Inland Revenue for £7 million. Hardwick Hall was given to the National Trust, thousands of acres of land in Dumfries-shire and Derbyshire, some Sussex property and the Mayfair house were sold. Chatsworth was saved.

The Duke had planned to be a publisher, expecting that 'Uncle Harold' (Harold Macmillan) would give him a job at Macmillan's, the family publishing firm. After Eton and Trinity College Cambridge, he had joined the Coldstream Guards, and had won the M.C. He had married the Hon. Deborah Freeman-Mitford, in 1941.

His political career started after he became the Eleventh Duke: he was Parliamentary Under-Secretary for Commonwealth Relations from 1960 to 1962, Minister of State at the Commonwealth Relations Office from 1962 to 1964 and Minister for Colonial Affairs from 1963 to 1964. In the event, 'Uncle Harold' had given him employment; he modestly described these appointments as 'gross nepotism', saying deprecatingly, 'I think we'd given him some good shooting.'

The Duke always had an affection for Eastbourne, having visited it from 1936, when his father came to stay at Compton Place; as a Government minister, he found it more convenient than Derbyshire. He and his wife honeymooned in Eastbourne in 1941 and lived there after the War for two years. He enjoyed coming for a week's holiday every year, staying at the Cavendish Hotel on the seafront: 'In the lounge there are reproductions of Sir Joshua Reynolds' portraits of the 5th Duke and Georgiana, his wife, which are so good I wonder who has the originals.' He loved to listen to the performances of the military bands at the bandstand, to take a boat trip along the Seven Sisters and to have a pub lunch. 'I also indulge in a short snobbish walk from the statue of the 7th Duke, outside my hotel, to that of the 8th, on what is known as the Western Lawns in front of the Grand Hotel.'[3]

[3] Devonshire, *Eastbourne Local Historian,* 131

In November, 1950, Andrew Cavendish's father, the Tenth Duke of Devonshire, paid his final, fateful visit to Eastbourne. Dr Adams attended him after his heart attack and was present when he died. This event connected Dr Adams with the highest offices in the land. The Attorney-General, Sir Reginald Manningham-Buller, who would prosecute Dr Adams six years later for the murder of Mrs Edith Morrell, was also a member of the Devonshire family: he was descended from the 4th Duke, through his mother, Lilah Cavendish. The husband of Lady Dorothy, the sister of the Tenth Duke, was Harold Macmillan.

# Harold Macmillan

Born on 10th February, 1894, he had an American mother, like Winston Churchill. His father was a publisher and had created a highly successful business. Macmillan was educated at Eton and Balliol College, Oxford. He married Lady Dorothy Cavendish, sister of the 10th Duke of Devonshire. He became brother-in-law by marriage to Lord Salisbury, whose wife was a cousin of Lady Dorothy. Macmillan entered Parliament in 1924. He was resident minister at Allied Forces H.Q. in the Mediterranean in 1942, when he became friendly with Eisenhower. By 1954, he was Minister of Defence in Eden's Government and was made Foreign Secretary in 1955. After nine months, Eden moved him, much against his will, to be Chancellor of the Exchequer. Lord Salisbury, who was a grandee of the Conservative Party, Lord President of the Council and a member of the cabinet, had an audience with the youthful Queen Elizabeth II in January 1957. He then interviewed each member of the Cabinet to ask: 'Well, which is it, Wab (Rab Butler) or Hawold?' [4]

Macmillan's approach to career advancement was not handicapped by such considerations as moral scruple. Having initially supported the Suez adventure, he knew when to withdraw and align himself with Eisenhower, leaving Eden and Butler to pick up the pieces. Duplicitous, cunning, and manipulative, he achieved his aim of becoming Prime Minister on 9 January and he was determined on his course: 'if we can survive until Parliament disperses over the summer, we can go on to win' (the next general election). One of his first decisions was to sack the Home Secretary, Gwilym (Gil) Lloyd-George. As is often the custom of victors in the race for the highest office in the land, he replaced him with the colleague he had just trumped, RA Butler. Lloyd-George went to the Lords as Viscount Tenby.

Though he loved his wife, Lady Dorothy, devotedly, she had been having an affair with Robert Boothby – another Conservative MP and Eton and Oxford man – since 1930. Boothby was Minister of Food for Churchill in 1939. He had married Diana Cavendish – a cousin of Lady Dorothy – in 1935 and had divorced her two years later.[5] Macmillan and Lady Dorothy had one son and two daughters by the time the affair started. A fourth child, a daughter, is generally agreed to have been Boothby's. Macmillan would never agree to a divorce; leaving aside his his love for his wife, a messy divorce would have been enough to ruin a political career in the

---

[4] Ball / [5] Diana, daughter of Richard Cavendish, brother of 9th Duke of Westminster

1950s. The marriage was one of name only and the affair continued until Lady Dorothy's death in 1966; Macmillan even remained faithful. He also agreed to give Boothby a life peerage. Their children suffered and rumours spread. Problems with alcohol dogged them all and one committed suicide after an abortion had left her sterile.

In July 1991, Woodrow Wyatt and Queen Elizabeth the Queen Mother had a discussion about it:

> 'She said, [of Boothby] "He was a lovely man. He was a bounder but not a cad. He was very amusing."
>
> She enjoyed the frank discussion about his relations with Dorothy Macmillan, Churchill and all the rest of it. I said, "The press knew all about it", and she said, "We all knew about it". I said, "But of course in those days it was different. People hadn't decided to make public all these scandals". She said, "Now they think of nothing but nastiness whether it's about the Prince of Wales or anybody else." I said, "It's because there's growing democracy and a feeling that in the old days a privileged circle only knew about these things so why shouldn't the grown-up, modern democrats know about them too."'[6][7]

Boothby was hardly good marriage material: he was a promiscuous bisexual who was addicted to gambling and who was sacked by Churchill for lying to a Parliamentary committee. He also kept company with Tom Driberg, a left-wing Labour M.P. and supporter of Stalin.

Driberg, educated at Lancing and Oxford, was the most disreputable M.P. in the House: he had a penchant for 'cottaging' and rent-boys; he was a close friend of Guy Burgess and an agent for M.I.5, the K.G.B. and Czechoslovakia. In addition, he had homosexual friends in the London underworld of gangsters, and introduced Boothby to Ronnie Kray. Lord Beaverbrook, his one-time employer, (he had been 'William Hickey' the gossip columnist) had gone to great lengths to protect him from exposure and, at one time, had ensured that there was no mention of his Bow Street conviction in any newspaper. Many other homosexuals convicted in the '50s were less fortunate. In 1956 he travelled to Moscow to see Guy Burgess and get the story about his disappearance from London with Donald McLean and in 1957 he became Chairman of the Labour Party.

Boothby became a television celebrity during the 1950s, and it was not until July 1964 that there was a front-page story in the *Daily Mirror*: 'Peer and Gangster: Yard Probe'.

Scandals seethed under the veneer of respectability. In November 1958, Ian Harvey, the under-secretary at the Foreign Office was caught in an act of sodomy in St. James' Park. His paid partner was a guardsman. Apparently, Harvey was another 'cottager' and had been for thirteen years. Macmillan was very worried; Harvey could be more or less brushed aside as the 'one bad apple' but there were other Conservative MP's at risk of exposure. Eventually it was

---

[6] Wyatt

[7] Woodrow Wyatt also relates the story, which he had from Professor J. B. Harold, that Macmillan was expelled from Eton for buggery; the alternative story is that he left due to illness. (Ball)

a heterosexual scandal – the Profumo Affair – that ruined the image the ruling elite had cultivated from the Victorian era as the guardians of the nation's morality.

Britain of the 1950s was an intensely class-conscious society. The elite and institutions were staunchly Victorian in outlook and set the rules for the rest of society. Concurrently, the period from the end of the War until around 1960 saw a great revival of British Protestantism, with Church attendances reaching record levels.

This was also the age of mass communications. Before the Coronation in 1952, few people had a television set, but many bought their first set to watch the great event. At the time of the Coronation, Sir Edmund Hillary, a mountaineer from New Zealand conquered Everest in the company of Sherpa Tensing. This period was a highpoint of patriotism and celebration. The people thanked God and wished the young Queen long life reigning over them. The radio and television coverage of the Coronation brought the British and the rest of the Commonwealth together in one long, simultaneous, global celebration. Commercial television arrived in 1955 and by 1957 there was a TV set in the majority of homes. At the same time, the readership of daily newspapers also reached a post-war high.

It was Macmillan's close relationship with media owners like Lord Beaverbrook that helped to keep the lid on potential scandals. It may have been coincidence, but when the case of Dr Adams hit the headlines in July, 1956, Percy Hoskins, the Crime Reporter of the *Daily Express* newspaper – Beaverbrook's organ of conservative and patriotic public opinion – immediately leapt to the defence of Dr Adams. The Eden government may have initially considered the whole matter was a useful diversion for the electorate from their Egyptian activities. The Attorney-General, Sir Reginald Manningham-Buller, probably took a longer-term view, foreseeing that Macmillan would soon become Prime Minister. Manningham-Buller, a career politician more than a lawyer, and a distant cousin of Lady Dorothy, had his eye on the Woolsack. The current incumbent was Lord Kilmuir, the former Sir David Maxwell-Fyfe, who had been Home Secretary before Gwilym Lloyd-George.

Macmillan thought that the British middle classes wanted 'peace', 'nest eggs' and 'white goods'[8] more than anything else, but in truth, what they actually wanted was the National Health Service. It had transformed their health, given them longer and better lives and taken away the burden of paying for medical care. It was a Labour government that had created it just after the war, but, from then on, any government failing to protect it would pay for the damage at the polls. Voting in a Conservative government did not signal any desire on the part of the electorate to dismantle the welfare state.

In 1956, the backbone of the N.H.S., the primary care service of the general practitioners, was near to breaking-point. The doctors were totally disaffected because the payment system had proved inadequate. They were all contracted individually, so they had the power to cause the collapse of the N.H.S. by simply withdrawing their services. There was a desperate concern in Government to keep the doctors 'on-side'. In November 1956, after the second invasion of Egypt, when the downfall of the Eden administration seemed a certainty, the Attorney-General

[8] Ball

took the extraordinary step of passing a copy of Hannam's confidential report on the Adams' investigation to the British Medical Association.

During the Labour administration in 1948, there had been a majority in favour of the abolition of the death penalty. This was not sustained under the succeeding Conservative government. Several hangings during the 1950s had disturbed the general public: Derek Bentley was nineteen when he was hanged, but his mental age was much lower. His younger accomplice, who had shot the policeman victim, was merely detained 'During Her Majesty's Pleasure'. Timothy Evans, another man of limited mental ability, was hanged and some time later, John Christie was convicted of killings at the same address; 10, Rillington Place. Then Ruth Ellis was hanged for shooting her abusive lover. Lord Kilmuir had refused a reprieve for Derek Bentley and Gwilym Lloyd-George had refused one to Ruth Ellis. A Bill to abolish hanging resulted in a majority of 19 in the House of Commons, but was defeated in the Lords by 143. The result was an unhappy compromise with capital punishment being retained for two classes of murder. Murder by poison was no longer a capital offence. The Act was ratified during the Trial, creating the anomaly that Dr Adams would hang if he were convicted and yet a person indicted for the same offence just three weeks later would have been given a life sentence.

## Sir Reginald Manningham-Buller

The character of Widmerpool in Anthony Powell's *A Dance to the Music of Time* is partly based on Manningham-Buller.[9] Powell admitted basing one episode on Manningham-Buller's life, in which Widmerpool causes a schoolfellow to be expelled from Eton for making improper advances to another boy.

Manningham-Buller was Attorney-General under the Eden and Macmillan administrations. He prosecuted in the case of the Portland Spy Ring and in 1961, he played a crucial role in exposing the traitor George Blake by allowing him to be interrogated by MI6 officers. 'Just make sure you bring him back alive,' …They did, after Blake had confessed.

Patrick Devlin had fun at Manningham-Buller's expense in his book, *Easing the Passing*, which is about the Adams' case. But Devlin had a considerable grudge against Manningham-Buller, who had made the career progression Devlin had aspired to and who was instrumental not only in the rejection of Devlin's report on Nyasaland but also the preparation of the rival Armitage Report. However, the politician in Reggie would always win over the lawyer. He was truly the Machiavelli of his day. That the Conservative Party remained in power, can be attributed in large part to Reggie's machinations.

Whatever his outward persona, Manningham-Buller was in fact an extremely talented political wrangler and an accomplished guardian of secrets. His patriotism was never in doubt. At the same time, he remained totally loyal to Macmillan and had his complete trust. He coveted and won the Lord Chancellorship and was satisfied with the power and sense of achievement

[9] Powell, *Journals 1990-92*

this position brought him; he was never Macmillan's rival for the Premiership. Though Lord Devlin described him rather peevishly as a 'do-badder', his judgement was generally sound. He opposed the Suez adventure and advised Eden against it. Perhaps he was instrumental in persuading Macmillan, who had initially supported it. A surprising tribute was paid to him by Tam Dalyell, a Labour MP, during a House of Commons debate concerning MI5. He described Lord Dilhorne (Reggie's title after his elevation to the House of Lords), who had helped him as a young M.P., as '…extremely kind, painstaking and nice. I think extremely well of him.'

As Foreign Secretary in the previous government, Macmillan was undoubtedly the best man to be Prime Minister in the aftermath of Suez. But the Government could have foundered on the Adams case. Given the immense media interest, soundings would also have been taken with Lord Beaverbrook. Given the connections between the Conservative Party and the unloved and unsound Lt. Col. Sir Roland Gwynne and the link – however tenuous – to Macmillan, since Dr Adams had been alone with his brother-in-law, the Duke of Devonshire, at the time of his death, the affair threatened to blow up into a long-running, media-driven, five star scandal. But perhaps the greatest concern amongst Conservative leaders was the possible impact on the NHS. The Attorney General was in contact with the BMA and was secretly updating them on the police investigation, in an effort to keep them 'on side'. Lloyd George had not been best pleased when he learned what Manningham-Buller had been up to and, on 7 January, 1957, wrote him an extremely angry letter of complaint.[10] But two days later, Harold Macmillan became Prime Minister, Lloyd George was out of office and the holder of the post of Attorney General was unchanged.

The BMA believed that, coming on top of doctors' current unhappiness with payments from the National Health Service, the prosecution of a doctor could provoke mass resignations, which would threaten a collapse in the Service. In Britain, the NHS was sacred. Any Government permitting damage to the NHS could expect serious damage at the polls.

Once it realised that, if Dr Adams were hanged, the chances of re-election were slim, the Government began to modify its approach to the whole affair. According to the evidence I have uncovered, the Attorney General embarked on a new course in prosecuting the case against Dr Adams sometime after 9 January, when Macmillan became Prime Minister, just three months prior to the trial. Macmillan was surrounded by a coterie of Conservative Party grandees; men who were not only well qualified to counsel on the Suez crisis but who were also, for different reasons, extremely well informed on the Adams affair. Given the rapid sequence of events, the decision to undermine the case against Dr Adams must have been taken during the 1956 Christmas Recess, once Eden's fate was sealed and the succession decided.

The skein of direct and indirect political connections to Dr Adams stretched from local politicians in Eastbourne, to members of Parliament, several members of Government and mandarins of the Conservative Party.

[10] See *Matters Medical*.

# The Friendship with Roland Gwynne

We can only surmise how Dr Adams first met Lt. Col. Roland Gwynne, DSO, or how the two became such firm friends. Perhaps Gwynne's wealthy neighbour, the retired steel merchant, Mawhood, who regarded the young Dr Adams as his protégé, introduced him to Gwynne. Maybe the occasion was a shoot over Mawhood's estate or Gwynne's. Dr Adams' prowess with a shotgun would certainly have drawn attention.

Perhaps it is not surprising that Gwynne, who was in constant pain from his war wound and who, perhaps unfairly, had a reputation in his family as a hypochondriac, would have engaged a newly qualified young doctor in conversation, maybe in the hope he might learn of some new treatment. The young Dr Adams would have needed little encouragement to talk to such a wealthy, well-connected individual; such social contacts would also have furnished the necessary entrée to Eastbourne society he needed, for Dr Adams was an ambitious man, who was already dreaming of his own practice. Added to which, Gwynne had good shooting on his estate, which was very convenient for Eastbourne.

But perhaps what drew Dr Adams on were not such worldly concerns. After all, he had been imbued from an early age with a profound belief in Providence. Could he have understood such a meeting as anything other than providential? He would have had little difficulty in recalling his family catechism, the stories his mother repeated to him of her uncle, the great John Bodkin, rising in favour to the top of Chinese society through the influence of the rich and powerful. Perhaps through all those years of meetings of the Plymouth Brethren, listening to his father inveighing against a sinful world, Dr Adams had developed a sense for the weakness in people. Here was a dashing, decorated, retired army officer with impeccable social credentials, political connections and all the paraphernalia of success – the estate, the big house, servants, a luxurious lifestyle and great wealth besides. Lt. Col. Gwynne embodied the success to which Dr Adams aspired. Yet, like some tragic hero in Shakespeare, Roland Gwynne also had a weakness, which would lead to his downfall. Dr Adams would soon uncover this secret and it would bind them together for fifty years.

But on first meeting, the two men had very little in common. The young Dr Adams was Irish, he was newly qualified, just arrived from Belfast via Bristol and a fledgling partner in a local medical practice. He was by no means poor according to contemporary standards, but nevertheless lived modestly in rented accommodation with his widowed mother and his cousin. When he first arrived, he even cycled to his appointments, till his partners decided that a car was a more appropriate form of transport. He was a member of Plymouth Brethren – a reactionary wing of the Protestant faith – had no influential family connections in England, could boast no military service (distinguished or otherwise) or any political affiliation, let alone influence. Gwynne was nearly seventeen years his senior. He was on the crest of a wave, financially, socially and politically. In the language of old warriors, he had had a good war. Not only had he survived the greatest conflict in human history (albeit with a leg wound which caused him to limp and would be the source of great pain in later years) but – much to the disbelief of his openly sceptical family – he had also been awarded the DSO for an act of ' – conspicuous gallantry and judgement'. His family was extremely wealthy and well-connected; his brother, Rupert, was the Member of Parliament for Eastbourne. Roland had been privately educated before attending Cambridge University and then embarking on a legal and political career. He was already a significant figure in the local Establishment which controlled Eastbourne. Perhaps what would have particularly impressed the car-mad Dr Adams was the Rolls-Royce he drove around town.

Yet there was something they did have in common – a link which Roland would certainly not have acknowledged in their early meetings. Their families both originated from Ireland. Although James Anderson Gwynne, Roland's father, and later, Roland himself, went to great lengths to lay claim to aristocratic Welsh forbears (Roland even went so far as to submit a false entry to *Burke's Peerage*) Roland Gwynne and John Bodkin Adams were of more obscure Antrim descent. Roland's grandfather, John Gwynne, and his father, James, were born in Bushmills, a small town a few miles outside Coleraine, where Dr Adams lived, went to school and now enjoys his eternal rest in the family plot.

Given the circumstances and age in which they lived, the Gwynnes' reticence and deceit about their family past is hardly surprising and would certainly not have been unusual. However, it concealed a remarkable story of initiative and enterprise. In 1846, John Gwynne, Roland's grandfather, was a 'manufacturer of edge tools, reaping hooks, axles, and all kinds of agricultural implements'.[1] John and his brother James were, however, quite remarkable entrepreneurs. 1847 was the worst year of the Great Potato Famine in Ireland and demand for agricultural tools – particularly for spades, their main product – had collapsed. James travelled to America in search of new ideas and acquired the patent rights from WD Andrews for his 'patent reaction pump', an improvement on a pump first developed in America in 1818. The Gwynnes were so successful that they were able to set up as manufacturers in London in 1851, with an investment from a merchant banker and a tea trader, a certain Mr. Twining. The endeavour was a stroke of genius. The pump had many industrial applications: 'factories, tanneries, breweries, steamers, fire engines, dry dock, distilleries, railways, mines, quarries, drainage, irrigation, water supply, etc'. Their business was given a great boost at the Great Exhibition of 1851 where a Gwynne Pump powered 'the much admired fountain at Crystal Palace' and the 'Cologne Fountain in Phalon's Bower of Perfume. Capacity of delivery 25 gallons per minute'.

[1] *Slater's Directory*, Ireland 1846

When John died four years later, his eldest son, James Anderson Gwynne, at the age of 23, took charge of the business, with his brothers Henry and John working under him. They exhibited 'the great Centrifugal [steam] pump' at the Crystal Palace Exhibition of 1862. James also diversified his business interests, to include 'Gas Blowers, sheep-shearing machines, horse clippers and electric lighting plants'. He also made considerable amounts of money from land speculation in the City of London and, from 1876 onwards, he bought significant estates near Eastbourne, which included Folkington Manor, Wootton Manor and Michelham Priory. James' expanding interests caused problems between the brothers, and his mother Agnes – who objected to his marriage to May Purvis, a Scottish Episcopalian from Edinburgh – loaned Henry and John the money to set up a works at Hammersmith in direct competition with James but concentrating solely on the pumps.

James aspired to become the archetypal English squire but the transition from the Bushmills' forge in Presbyterian Ulster was not easy. He and May raised seven children – four boys and three girls – at Folkington Manor. In spite of their wealth, theirs was not an altogether happy household; James became progressively more irascible and his bouts of anger more unpredictable. His life became a series of blunders. He first disinherited his eldest son, Reggie, when he got into debt at Oxford University, regarding him as a ne'er-do-well. Reggie went off to Canada with £50 and thrived outside his father's ambit. He joined the military and rose to the rank of General. He became well-known and highly respected in Canada, but James was never reconciled with him. Nevile, the second son, ran the family firm, but James kept him short of money and refused to modernise the works, leaving the rival firm managed by his brother John to become more successful and competitive. In August 1903, after a violent argument at Folkington, Nevile left the house and was later given notice to leave the family firm by the end of the year. James ended up having to sell his engineering business to his brother John a year later and Nevile joined his uncle in Hammersmith. The business was renamed 'Gwynnes Limited'.

Perhaps the most remarkable of the seven children was Violet, who achieved great fame as a harpsichordist, known by her married name: Violet Gordon-Woodhouse, Her niece, Katharine said:[2]

> 'She did not have to exert much charm to make me conscious of her magnetism; but I knew instinctively that she thought herself grand and different from the rest of the family, not only because she was a musical genius, but because she was a person apart, surrounded by her admirers and adorers... Aunt Violet was like a Queen, with her Lords [her husband and three other men who lived with her] and Ladies in Waiting.'

The other two sisters were totally overshadowed by Violet. There was Eva, who had engineered a marriage to an actor, Charlie Isaacson – an older man who had never intended to marry –

[2] Ayling [For the full story of Violet, see Jessica Douglas-Home's (Nevile's granddaughter) biography of her.]

'Their marriage had never been consummated and Eva did not pretend that it had been…'[3]
She succeeded in bankrupting him in her efforts to keep up with Violet. The youngest daughter
Dorothy never left home.

Rupert, the third son, turned out spectacularly well so far as James was concerned – in his
eyes he could do no wrong. He studied law and became a barrister, but even greater things were
to come. He married extremely well. His wife was the Hon. Stella Ridley, who belonged to an
aristocratic family, whose lineage went back to the Norman conquest. Stella's father was the
fifth baronet and first Viscount. He had been Home Secretary in Lord Salisbury's Conservative
government at the end of the nineteenth century. Stella had been brought up by Lord and Lady
Aberdeen in Scotland. Lord Aberdeen had been Governor General and Viceroy of Ireland and
Governor General of Canada. With such wealth and high calibre political connections, it was
not surprising that Rupert Gwynne became Member of Parliament for Eastbourne in 1910
and, later, a Junior Minister in the Conservative Government.

Roland was the whelp of this remarkable brood. He was born in 1882, when his mother was
forty-one. He was seven years younger than his sister Dorothy, his nearest sibling. By then,
May had given birth to nine children (two had died) and she moved out of the marital bedroom. James virtually ignored Roland but May doted on him. Not only did she spoil him outrageously but, in a more bizarre display of affection, she also dressed him as a girl in frocks,
bows and necklaces, his fair hair in long corkscrew ringlets, and generally treated him like a
daughter. He was taught by Dorothy's governesses at home until the age of thirteen when he
was taken out of the female attire to be tutored 'by the eccentric and unlikeable Rector of
Folkington Parish, a bachelor'.[4] Roland went up to Cambridge, where, unsurprisingly, he
seemed to have a facility for making friends with the wealthy and influential. But it appears that
not all was plain sailing in his life. Dorothy noted in her diary that he arrived home one day saying that he would never return to university; the cause of his distress was not revealed.
Nevertheless, he did go back, and, in due course, was called to the Bar. This was his first surprise for his family, who thought him quite the dunderhead. He obtained a post as a Judge's
Marshall – an official accompanying a circuit judge, dealing with secretarial and other duties –
and was 'particularly popular with the judges' elderly wives'.[5] A very good dancer, he attended
all the best balls during the London season. When he was not travelling with a judge or staying with friends, he lived at Folkington.

His niece, Katharine – just 13 years younger than Roland – described what he was like:

'…as a child I was always sorry when he arrived and glad when he left. He was not interested in children but that did not matter so much as his total lack of warmth. I could
never understand why some people said he was charming and attractive; to me he was
not even good looking. He was moderately tall and well set up, and far less dark than
Neville or Rupert; his features were regular, and he had darting, sharp, yellow brown
eyes.'

[3] Ibid / [4] Ibid / [5] Ibid

Although afterwards he developed a passionate cult for his mother, he was sometimes very rude to her in those days, and I can remember her crying on one occasion and saying that she did not think any son should speak in such a way to his mother… he was not in the least ashamed… in a way both my Grandmother and Aunt Kate [May's sister] were afraid of him. He was a bully when given the chance, and his charming manners were switched on to serve his purpose… he was not a lovable person and I did not feel there was kindness in him…

When he was in good form, he could be very amusing, but there was always a deep undercurrent of malice in his wit; he was like Kay after the Snow Queen put a splinter of ice in his heart. In his later life he became adept at getting through his victims' defences and exposing their weaknesses. He saw nearly everything through a distorting mirror, and I remember thinking that if Roland said something, you could be sure the opposite was the real if not the apparent truth. You could feel the pleasure he obtained from wounding or mortifying anyone who was not in a position to retaliate. Was he in a way hitting back because he was one of the misfits of life? Indeed, how could he be truthful when his paramount object was to conceal the truth.'[6]

If he did feel a misfit, then he had every reason to blame his family for permitting his very strange upbringing. The truth was that Roland was a homosexual.

'He was not interested in girls or women, though they were sometimes interested in him… He would start a slight flirtation… probably as a mask to hide his real inclinations, but killed it stone dead the moment he felt it was going too far for his liking.'[7]

In the early years, Roland was understandably covert about his sexuality; he obviously concealed it from his father, who would have cut him off. His sister, Dorothy, once put her foot in it: she thought that a friend of Roland's who came to stay, Bertie, was showing an interest in her and intended to propose. When confronted by her mother to state his intentions towards her, Bertie replied that it could 'never be'! Dorothy recorded in her diary on another occasion that Roland was 'like a lovesick girl' after another male friend left Folkington, so maybe the truth had slowly dawned on her that her brother was not like other men.

Roland's homosexuality was seen – by those of his family who dared acknowledge it – to be a sign of a weak character, so they had difficulty in believing that he had genuinely won the D.S.O. Perhaps they suffered from the common failing of older siblings who are jealous of the attention paid to the youngest of the family and come to despise and resent them for it in later life. Whatever the case, Roland was already thirty-two when war broke out, so he enlisted as an officer in the Sussex Yeomanry, guarding the South Coast of England. The casualty lists at the front were mounting and a woman 'friend of the family' sent him a white feather, accusing him of cowardice. His response was to volunteer for active service and in September 1916, he trans-

[6] Ibid  /  [7] Ibid

ferred to France in command of 150 soldiers to reinforce the battalion. After the Battle of the Somme, he was moved to Flanders where he won the D.S.O. in February 1917. He was twice wounded and commanded the Queen's Royal West Surrey Regiment.

He found himself able to confide his fears only to his brilliant and unconventional sister, Violet Gordon-Woodhouse, who wrote to him affectionately. He was probably already shell-shocked when:

> '…during the Third Battle of Ypres, he was wounded painfully in the knee and left out in no man's land until he could be brought in by stretcher-bearers. Among the Gwynnes, Violet and May alone understood that courage in a frightened man is greater than courage in a fearless one.'[8]

Roland was in hospital in France and England for many months and, although he recovered from the wounds, he was left with a permanent limp and a stiff knee. He returned to live at Folkington Manor, where his mother was fast deteriorating:

> 'Everyone was touched by Roland's devotion to her and his concern for her, so apparent when she entered a room leaning heavily on his arm, her steps slow and faltering, his eyes fixed anxiously on her movements.'[9]

He had written to her practically every day during the War, when he was able to; perhaps their closeness had overcome any resentment he may have felt over his upbringing. He was friendly with a woman, nearly twice his age: a rich widow, 'Lady A'[10] whom he had met when he was a Judge's Marshall. She had visited him in France when he was wounded and she exercised great influence over him:

> 'She certainly played a big part in shaping his activities and, after he returned to civilian life, she decided that he ought to have some work to do. Incredible as it seems, he actually joined my Father [Nevile] for a time as a kind of glorified salesman, and how he must have hated it. He did it quite well, however… Rumours got around that he would marry Lady A but she told her relations there was no question of it. After his mother's death, it suited Roland far better to take up the part of the devoted selfless friend, who renounced marriage with any other woman because of his great and unrequited love.'

It seems that Roland had learned by this time how to use a woman friend as 'cover' for his homosexuality and that 'Lady A.' well understood her role but members of the family and friends had simply misread the situation.

May Gwynne died in 1922. She followed James' injunction that she could inherit his money only on condition she should 'dispose of it according to his wishes'. So her will sowed further

---

[8] Douglas-Home / [9] Ayling / [10] Ibid. Her full name is not given.

conflict in the family, which, from the wording of James' will, must have been the original intention. Roland stood to be the primary beneficiary: not only did he inherit a substantial share of the estate, he was also to inherit practically everything in the event that Rupert had no sons. Rupert attempted to resolve the conflicts the will would cause, but chose a solution which was particularly to his own benefit and that of his family. He offered his brother and sisters substantial amounts of money to renounce their claims: Roland was to have Folkington for his lifetime and Dorothy the Home Farm. Dorothy had already been forced to move from the Manor to the Home Farm on her mother's death, so she demanded that repairs should be done on outhouses as part of the deal; Rupert prevaricated and they quarrelled. As a result, Rupert's deal collapsed, much to Roland's subsequent relief:[11]

> 'When he realised how near he had been to signing it all away he was both terrified and overjoyed, and told everyone that he owed it all to Dorothy… and would never be able to do enough to show her how grateful he was.'[12]

The episode seems to show Roland in a better light than Rupert.

At about this time – 1922 – the Conservative Party at Lewes were seeking a new candidate to stand for Parliament, and Nevile, who was living five miles from Lewes, heard that Roland intended to put himself forward for the nomination. Nevile was horrified:

> 'A great friend was on the Selection Committee and Nevile authorised him to tell them that, if Roland was selected, he would publicly oppose it by every means in his power. The very correct members of the Committee must have had a shock; the message was conveyed to Roland, who withdrew his name with the greatest haste.'

The inference to be drawn from this is that Nevile must have informed his friend that Roland was a practising homosexual. Rupert's reaction was more urbane than puritanical. He told his niece, Katharine Ayling and her brother John:

> "I hear Nevile was very angry at the idea of Roland trying to stand as M.P. for Lewes – a General Watson, I suppose you know him, told the Committee he couldn't be considered", he laughed. "Of course, Roland was in a state of frenzy, and couldn't withdraw quickly enough. I was rather relieved, I must say, as I should have had to write all his speeches for him."[13]

Perhaps it was the Selection Committee's rebuff that made Roland settle for local politics, where he was very successful.

When James died in 1915, Rupert inherited the estates.[14] While Reggie was perfectly aware that he had been disinherited, Nevile believed that he had been reinstated in a later will.

---

[11] Ibid / [12] Ibid / [13] Ibid / [14] This is a simplification of an extremely complicated and perverse will.

However, it was the 1903 will, in which he was not mentioned, which was proven. Even today, there are family members who are convinced that there was a later will. They suspect it was destroyed and cast Rupert and Roland as the culprits. On the other hand, James was quite capable of misleading Nevile; perhaps he had also given assurances to Stella Ridley's family that Rupert would inherit.

Rupert and Stella Gwynne had four daughters: Priscilla, Elizabeth, Diana and Felicité. Crucially, they had no sons. In the early 1920s, having no male heir, Rupert was obliged, in accordance with his father's will, to pass on Wootton Manor and all the estates to his younger brother, Roland, an irony which his younger brother must have enjoyed.

It was about this time that the well-connected, influential and now well-heeled Lt. Col. Roland Gwynne met the newly arrived Dr John Bodkin Adams. The immediate circumstances are not clear. One possibility is their common interest in shooting. The Gwynne family had large estates and Dr Adams was a truly exceptional shot. Perhaps William Mawhood, who also owned large local estates and who was a patient and, in some way, a patron of Dr Adams, introduced him to Gwynne. What is sure is that once the relationship was established, it survived for fifty years, albeit with a period of cooling between. Their relationship was extremely close: long before the police investigation into Dr Adams in 1956, they were in the habit of going on shooting holidays together in Scotland and Ireland and actually went to Scotland during the investigation. Neither of them was married but they were accompanied by a woman, Betty Cradock, who lived in East Dean, near Eastbourne. This close relationship with Roland Gwynne gave Dr Adams not only an important entrée to Eastbourne society, but also unimpeachable credentials. Much later, during the police investigation, the then (Conservative) Mayor of Eastbourne, Sir Sydney Caffyn, shocked that any suspicion should be levelled at Dr Adams, would appeal to his fellow citizens to come forward with evidence to help the enquiry. The appeal acted like a rallying call in Dr Adams' defence and brought forth a welter of support.

In the late autumn of 1924, Rupert Gwynne became seriously ill very suddenly. His kidneys failed and he died on 12th October, just after he had been re-elected as a Member of Parliament. He was aged 53. A Dr Lionel Handson certified the cause death as being disease of the mitral valve of the heart – this would have been caused by the rheumatic fever which he had suffered 32 years previously, and 'dropsy' which would have been from the same cause. Unusually, Dr Handson wrote 'No P.M.' on the certificate; it is tempting to think that, in spite of Rupert Gwynne's medical history, the doctor was uneasy about the cause of death and called the Coroner for his advice. But it is not clear why he made the note. The certificate also shows that Roland was present at his brother's death and that he registered it:

> 'Roland, who had never been close to him, was the last member of his family to see him alive. He came out to tell my father [Nevile] what had happened... he even shed tears as he described Rupert as almost dying in his arms. The moment of emotion did not last when it was disclosed that at the time of his death Rupert had been overdrawn at the bank by many thousands of pounds. The estate could well support it; but Roland,

now master, was not pleased, and I remember him making a slighting remark which shocked me.'[15]

The estates passed directly to Roland.

Stella and her daughters were allowed to remain at Wootton Manor, provided that she did not remarry. From this point on, they found Roland increasingly unpleasant and manipulative. Dorothy was moved to the Manor Farm. Roland now wanted to live his life as he wished without the constant surveillance and disapproval of his family. He transformed Folkington Manor from the austere and comfortless mansion preferred by James, to a luxurious and modernised residence.

Stella Gwynne, Rupert's widow, was somewhat eccentric, particularly in her sense of fashion; she moved, not only in political, but more and more in artistic and literary circles – she was more Bloomsbury than Virginia Woolf and the Bloomsbury set in Charleston Farmhouse, a few miles distant from Wootton Manor. She had a haughty manner, keeping people at a distance by making them feel uncomfortable. Veronica Nicholson said of the Gwynne style 'Oh, they were very "Greenery, Yallery".' A later story tells of her being ' – met off a train by a relative, far from being inconspicuous [she] stepped out of her carriage, stately and resplendent in a huge brimmed hat hung all around with little tinkling bells.'[16] Stella might have had a strong personality, but she was not a good mother.

It was Priscilla, the eldest of the four sisters, who eventually took care of the family, always making sure that they were not short of money. Three of the sisters – Priscilla, Diana and Elizabeth all married. Elizabeth became in the process, Elizabeth David, wrote books on cooking and revolutionised British cuisine. Felicité had a broken love affair early in life and never married.

Whatever Roland's treatment of his family, his public career as a local establishment figure flourished. He began by holding various offices in Sussex, including those of High Sheriff of the County for 1926-27, Chairman of the Magistrates in Eastbourne and Hailsham, a member of the County Council and Mayor of Eastbourne for two years from 1929. His portrait still hangs in the Mayor's parlour in Eastbourne Town Hall. He became well-known, however, for the parties he held at Folkington Manor: he held weekend parties all the year round and was excellent at organising them. He was particularly interested in food and had an outstanding cook. He invited the aristocracy, politicians, actors; notable guests included Lord Willingdon, Viceroy of India and his wife, and the Kiplings. Violet was not often among the guests: she felt that he was not the little brother she had once known, but a stranger. His niece, Katharine, thought him a showman, with an artificial charm, a good conversationalist but one with nothing to say. It was during this period that she came to realise that it was not women he was interested in.

Perhaps wary of the treatment meted out to his brothers, Roland had apparently bottled up a spendthrift nature until his father died in 1915. He had then spent money freely, starting with the purchase of a Rolls Royce (which he managed to crash into a tree on the estate) and he

[15] Ayling / [16] Chaney

entertained lavishly. Consequently, within a few years, he had become very short of money, and this was what induced him to accept Rupert's offer of money in return for his giving up his inheritance.

After Rupert's death, Roland continued spending money recklessly on 'entertaining' at Folkington. He was also underwriting his political career, which culminated in his becoming Mayor of Eastbourne in 1929, during the Depression. By the early 1930s, he was in debt. All this led to arguments with Stella, because he wanted her to leave Wootton so that he could let it. As his debts grew, he became increasingly unpleasant and deliberately made life as difficult as he could for her. The situation became so intolerable that, in 1933, it was a factor in her decision to remarry. Her new husband was Major John Hamilton, ADC to the Governor of Jamaica; he owned a plantation on the island. Roland got exactly what he wanted – Wootton Manor. Perhaps Stella did too – a home almost as far away from Roland Gwynne as she could get.

Some of Roland's reckless spending was flowing in the direction of his butler:

> 'The household was dominated by the sinister figure of his butler, who had a forceful personality and a cynical knowledge of human nature. He was dark and had a rather piratical look... and stories went round that no personable woman was 'safe' with him. His manner was certainly familiar, but he knew just how far it was permissible for him to go; and when it suited him he was an adept at a kind of throw-away flattery... Wilde knew his master probably better than anyone else...
>
> To a very large extent, he ran the household and his word was law. If he thought there should be a new, expensive record player or radio, Roland bought it; if he decided there should be champagne for dinner, champagne there was; and he chose and mixed the cocktails, lavishly provided for the guests by a host who did not touch alcohol himself. Relations and friends said lightly that Wilde must have some hold over Roland but in fact it was no laughing matter. Wilde knew all the details of his master's life and being the man he was... profited by his knowledge. Roland would do anything to keep his secret life intact, and so Wilde's power grew with the years.'[17]

Some time during the 1930s Wilde married and retired from service; naturally enough, he became a successful inn-keeper, but it was Roland who had provided the money for the venture. A more suitably subservient and honest butler was acquired for Folkington.

The parties went on throughout the '20s and '30s – weekends, luncheons; there was shooting and hunting on the estates. This way of life continued to some extent even during the War: he was very busy and he still entertained, though now it was to welcome Canadian army officers who were billeted in the Eastbourne area:

> 'Everyone knew that Roland had taken to drink; it had started with the Canadian officers who had almost assumed control of the house, and since then he had never looked

[17] Ayling

back. This was probably the beginning; but after the war many anxieties crowded in on him, and he turned more and more to alcohol as an anodyne.'[18]

The family had always understood that 'Lady A' intended to leave Roland a large part of her fortune, but, after years of apparently 'devoted attention' and using her as 'cover', she made the mistake, during the early years of the war, of wanting to move to the safety of Folkington Manor as her own house was in Queen Anne's Gate in Westminster. Roland was horrified at this proposal and the strictures which it would impose on his life. 'Lady A' must also have been around 80 years old at this time. Angry and offended, she spoke to Nevile and told him that Roland obviously no longer wanted her, and was 'not a gentleman'. He had certainly ended his hopes of any bequest. His niece analysed the situation:

> 'The reason why he behaved like this will always remain a mystery but there was little doubt that he was engaged in some obsessive personal affair which at the time must have meant more to him than anything else… I think that at this time… recklessness must have taken possession of Roland; there is no other explanation.'[19]

Roland's family, of course, knew very little of what went on at his parties: only a few members of the family were invited on particular occasions, and it was only the servants – such as Wilde, the butler – who were really informed about Roland's 'secret life'. One clue may lie in love letters from jockeys, which were found amongst his papers after his death.[20] Secrecy with regard to homosexual activity was absolutely essential as, even performed in private, it was a serious criminal offence, punishable with imprisonment until 1967. A man in Roland's situation was holding out an open invitation for blackmailers.

Towards the end of the Second World War, it was apparent that Roland was spending in excess of his income: taxes were high and likely to increase; he lived expensively, with a large staff and kept a considerable stable of horses; the entertaining became more extravagant. Nevile, then living in Sussex, realised that Roland was selling off land, and that in doing so he must have found a way to break James' Trust.

By 1947, Roland had squandered all his father's capital and he found it impossible to keep up his extravagant lifestyle at Folkington Manor. In 1947, when he could sell off no more land, he decided to lease Folkington Manor to a retired millionaire. He managed to get rid of the tenant he had installed at Wootton Manor and moved in there. Elizabeth David, née Gwynne, his niece, visited him several times, presumably to see Wootton rather than Uncle Roland, whom she found most objectionable.

At Wootton, he restricted the entertainment to luncheon parties. He was by now 65 years old and it is possible he had left any promiscuous lifestyle behind him. His niece and her parents, meeting him accidentally in London, were struck by the change in him: instead of his pre-

---

[18] Ibid  /  [19] Ibid

[20] A member of the family informed me that he had read and destroyed the letters.

viously pale and well-shaped face, he now appeared moon-faced with a purple complexion; they attributed this to alcohol. The news from Wootton related that:

> 'Now he mixed the drinks himself, such strong ones that people found themselves talking wildly and walking unsteadily, which was not surprising seeing that as time went on he poured anything that was to hand into his cocktail shaker – gin, brandy, vermouth, liqueurs, one was as good as another.'[21]

After one smart occasion when he had hosted a party for the cream of Sussex society, including a duchess and the Lord Lieutenant, the guests were all taken ill with symptoms of probable food poisoning. Roland telephoned Dr Adams in the early hours of the morning '…only to be told that he also was prostrate after the wonderful lunch he had enjoyed with the other guests.'[22]

Roland was devastated, and thought that there might be some conspiracy behind it all:

> '…some plot to ruin him in the eyes of the County, and were his servants in some way involved? …In the end it was traced back to a goose's egg which had been used in making the supreme ice-cream they had all so much enjoyed. Eggs were strictly rationed in those days… Roland told the story of the goose's egg in his inimitable style, and assured everyone that such a thing would never again be used in his kitchen.'

It was certainly a likely explanation and perhaps it was Dr Adams, who was qualified in Public Health, who traced the source of the food poisoning. Roland's real decline, however, certainly seems to have begun during the Committal Hearing in February 1957. He was now Lt. Col. Sir Roland Gwynne – he had been knighted in the 1957 New Year's Honours List. He had been replaced as Chairman on the bench by David Honeysett, due to his conflict of interest, since it was known that he was a close friend of Dr Adams. One evening during the committal, he dined at the White Hart Hotel in Lewes with Lord Chief Justice Goddard and Sir Hartley Shawcross Q.C., who had been Attorney-General in Attlee's post-war administration; they were both Sussex notables whom he had doubtless entertained at Folkington and Wootton. Driving home from the dinner, he had a car crash. He was apparently not drunk. In spite of all the excesses of his past life, his public image was that he was teetotal; but he did have the reputation of being a reckless driver, something he had in common with Dr Adams.

Hannam interviewed him in the nursing home while he was still recovering. The purpose was to follow up on a remark that Sir Roland was said to have made. Apparently, he had some comment to the effect that, since he had been one of Dr Adams' patients, he considered he had '– made a lucky escape'.

During the interview, he passed the remark off as a tasteless joke, indicating that Dr Adams had been his doctor for only eight years and that, during that time, he had never had a condition that required powerful drugs. But it seems that evening he had not only crashed his car;

---

[21] Ayling / [22] Dr Adams was undoubtedly his GP at the time c.1947.

he had also travelled his road to Damascus. He announced an extraordinary change of heart: he intended to break with Dr Adams entirely. Then followed a curious revelation: he had given instructions in his will that he should be buried in a lead-lined coffin. The point was not lost on Hannam; funeral directors normally used lead-lined coffins only when there was a severe risk of contamination from the body to the surrounding water table or when a corpse is transported long distances; but such a casket would also slow the process of decomposition and preserve any evidence of poisoning. It was a heavy hint that Sir Roland thought Dr Adams guilty of poisoning his patients. Perhaps he was also afraid that Dr Adams might somehow find a way of wreaking revenge at his betrayal.

All the cocks in East Sussex must have been crowing their heads off as he betrayed Dr Adams and broke his long relationship with him. The irony was that he would have been destroyed publicly if he had stood by Dr Adams and he was destroyed anyway by his betrayal. Wootton Manor itself now mirrored the emptiness of Roland's life and the fading of his glory days: visitors saw only the library, the dining-room and a bathroom. Uncared for, the gardens were overgrown; not maintained, the unused rooms succumbed to damp and mould.

If Dr Adams emerged from his ordeal somewhat sullied but unbowed, Sir Roland became a figure of tragedy. At the last party his niece attended at Wootton, an old friend confided in her:

> '…that poor Roland had no love in him and no real interest in anything but himself; was desperately unhappy, and could not bear to be alone.
>
> When there were no parties he used to walk up and down the library and the passages in his dressing-gown, weeping and wringing his hands, to the consternation of the housekeeper and butler… [who were] at their wits' end as to what to do.'[23]

He had even come to dislike his butler and cook and only his old housemaid, Ada, was congenial to him. To raise funds he had been selling off lands belonging to the estates over the years: farmland and woodland; pictures and other valuable items had gone. He would presumably have been breaking the terms of James' Trust in doing this. His niece's memoir suggests that when Roland realised that there was nothing left:

> '…he had a stroke, and for two days was at the point of death. People said that it was entirely through his clever doctor that he survived physically; and it was ironic that Roland had never cared for this man as he had for a former medical attendant, an old rogue if ever there was one.' [Dr Adams][24]

After a long illness, being no longer able to look after himself and apparently unloved by his family, he was made a ward of the Court of Protection in 1965, possibly at Priscilla's instigation; this would have prevented his controlling his own money and possessions. His last will is dated 2 February 1963 and is only two paragraphs long. He made over his entire estate to

[23] Ayling / [24] Ibid

his legal counsel, Sir Dingwall Latham Bateson; [25] the will contains a sentence which is almost a parody of his father's bequest to May:

> 'with the request (which shall not be legally binding) that he will administer my estate for the benefit of my faithful servants and friends in accordance with wishes which have long since been made known to him.'

In 1965, Sir Roland was 83 years of age and details are sketchy about what happened after his stroke: he is described in the memoir as being 'a mental wreck' and 'leaving ruin behind him' and having 'just been able to give his Solicitor Power of Attorney' before 'his collapse was complete' – Sir Dingwall Bateson administered the estate until he (Sir Dingwall) died in a shooting accident in 1968. Sir Roland was certainly taken to a nursing home in Eastbourne and he never returned to Wootton Manor: he was in both 'Edgehill' and 'The Esperance'. He apparently deteriorated rapidly into a state which required constant nursing, the cost of which 'would have been formidable' if he had returned to Wootton. He was very miserable in the first nursing home and the person who gave him devoted attention was Joe, his groom who, often with his wife, visited Roland daily:

> 'He spoke of Roland with great compassion, and then added something which we have always remembered. "The Colonel is a poor tormented soul."' [26]

During the first years of his sojourn in the nursing home, Joe was able to take him out in the car and even to visit friends or have lunch at Wootton – which does not indicate the need for round-the-clock nursing care. His memory became more cloudy, although he still recognised his niece and remembered her family. He seemed content to live in the past. It was only in the last twelve months of his life that he was more or less unconscious of his surroundings, and he died on November 15th, 1971 in his ninetieth year.

Since Sir Roland never married, Priscilla, being the eldest daughter of Rupert and Stella Gwynne, inherited the estates from him. She moved back to Wootton Manor in 1970 and her mother, Stella, returned. The now dilapidated Folkington Manor was sold to raise money for repairs to Wootton. The value of Sir Roland's estate when he died was £222,976. The will which was proved was that which named Sir Dingwall Bateson as executor. What happened to Sir Roland's estate is somewhat of a mystery. Some surviving relatives insist that he died penniless. It contains no reference to wishing to be buried in a lead lined casket. Perhaps he considered Dr Adams no longer a threat. On the other hand, the signature seems shaky and is barely legible; perhaps he was simply beyond caring.

In any event, it seems that the two men were reconciled at the end. The signature on Sir Roland's death certificate is that of Dr John Bodkin Adams. [27]

[25] Sir Dingwall, 'Dingo' to his friends, was a lawyer and past President of the Law Society
[26] Ayling / [27] Douglas-Home

Chapter Forty-Three

—◆—

# Was Dr Adams a Serial Killer?

—◆—

I imagine that Dr Camps, the Home Office pathologist at the time, must have thought so. He found grounds for concluding that 163 of the 310 deaths certified by Dr Adams between 1946 and 1956 (incidentally a death rate superior to Dr Shipman's) were suspicious. But suspicion is one thing; proof quite another. Dr Jane Mercer's view is that the evidence, certainly in the Morrell case, would be insufficient on its own to secure a conviction in court today. Nevertheless, she is convinced by the evidence that Dr Adams made at least one attempt to kill Mrs Morrell before her life was actually brought to an end.

Hannam and his team collected sufficient evidence in at least four cases to show that Dr Adams did seek the death of his patients. Of these, the Morrell case – the case that went to trial – was the weakest. Hannam did have other cases but he was harried by time pressures. All investigations were dropped following the failure of the Morrell case at the Old Bailey and the Attorney-General's decision not to proceed with the Hullett indictment; at that point, there was no likelihood that Hannam would be permitted to carry out further exhumations to search for more evidence.

The extraordinary journey made by the Nurses' Notes signals that there was a will at the highest of levels to undermine the case against Dr Adams and to find him not guilty. I believe that the rather half-hearted conduct of the case by the Attorney General and his passing of the police report to the B.M.A. reinforces this view.

## The Strongest Cases

The evidence prepared by Hannam's team provides strong reasons for suspecting that Dr Adams killed many of his patients; the best evidence they had was in the cases of:

Mrs Julia Bradnum, Miss Clara Neil-Miller, Mrs Bobbie Hullett, Mrs Morrell

In the cases of Mrs Bradnum and Miss Neil-Miller, it was clear from witness statements and (in

Miss Neil Miller's case) the autopsy, that Dr Adams' treatment led directly to the death of both patients. In both cases, he had a motive – he was a beneficiary under their wills, having previously intervened in their preparation. In both cases, he deliberately recorded a false cause of death on the death certificates. Mrs Bradnum's immediate cause of death was the injection he administered, three minutes before she died. Miss Neil Miller died of pneumonia two days after he left her lying naked in front of an open window with a freezing February wind blowing over her.

The circumstances of the deaths of Mrs Morrell and Mrs Hullett are highly suspicious and in each case Dr Adams had ample motive and opportunity, but took action by proxy. Mrs Hullett died of a drug overdose, for which Dr Adams apparently provided the means. Mrs Morrell died following an injection prepared by Dr Adams, but administered by a nurse acting under his instruction. For several months before their deaths, Dr Adams had kept both women under heavy sedation. In Mrs Hullett's case, this would have contributed greatly to her depression. In Mrs Morrell's case, sedation was not necessary, as she was not in any pain.

## Motive

The question of motive has always haunted this case. The Police actually investigated only those cases in the ten years previous to the start of their investigation where Dr Adams profited by way of a legacy from the patient's death. In the Morrell case, the police believed that Dr Adams decided to kill her before this volatile woman could change her will – which was currently in his favour – yet again. But the counter arguments (used by Dr Adams when he was arrested) are also strong. Firstly, the question of rationale: why would he decide to murder a patient who was going to die any way? Secondly, the burden of proof question: how could his treatment be proved to be murder when she was such a frail old woman with an already tenuous grip on life – after all, medicine is not a perfect science and wasn't he treating her to the best of his ability and knowledge?

The historian who strays into the realms of psychology – trying in this case, for example, to understand what might have motivated Dr Adams – is living dangerously, for that way lies a novel, not an historical account based on corroborated facts. But comparing Dr Adams with a known serial killer is a legitimate line of enquiry. Dr Shipman, for example, was not at all fictional; he was all too real and he terminated his life before his motive for killing his patients could be discovered.

In Dr Adams' case, the police concentrated on material gain but studies of other serial killers suggest that they are driven by a complex mix of physical needs, emotions and often bizarre interpretations of reality; they are seldom driven by a single motive and that motive is not necessarily money. For example, the motive of material gain was present in only a handful of Shipman's many victims. This suggests that Hannam's approach was too blinkered. Perhaps he had little room for manoeuvre: there was huge public interest in the case, Dr Adams was the known suspect, he had limited resources and he had the DPP breathing down his neck, anxious for a result.

Dr Camps, the Home Office pathologist, whose reputation has never been challenged, classified 163 of the 309 death certificates signed by Dr Adams between 1946 and 1956, as 'suspicious deaths'. This does not mean necessarily that Dr Adams murdered all 163 of these patients, but it does suggest that, had they considered a wider range of motives, the police might have been able to assemble more cases. Over the years, a number of alternatives have been suggested as motives. They fall broadly into three groups: the intentional – i.e. acts of euthanasia or murder; the unintentional: errors of diagnosis and treatment, possibly incompetence; thirdly – the patients all died simply of old age or the conditions from which they were suffering.

## Euthanasia

Euthanasia has to be considered, but, in three of the four cases identified by Hannam, the patients were not in pain; they were not suicidal and of the three, only Miss Neil-Miller was very ill. In the case of Bobbie Hullett, who was suicidal, I believe Dr Adams furnished her with the means to terminate her own life, which was still an illegal act.

It was almost certain that Dr Adams was practising euthanasia in a fifth case – that of William Mawhood. I believe the facts point to a pact between patient and practitioner – Dr Adams was induced by the lure of managing Mawhood's substantial estate to ensure that Mawhood did not suffer a painful death. This pact was scotched at the last minute by Mrs Mawhood.

## A Clinical Error

The second option is that Dr Adams simply made a mistake and lost control in each of these cases, with the result that the patients died. But there is too much in his actions which smacks of intention or premeditation.

In Bobbie Hullett's case, though she was not in actual pain, he was treating her with extremely powerful drugs and had been doing so for a number of months; he knew her state of mind and that there was a risk that she had secreted enough of her late husband's barbiturates to kill herself, if he had not actually supplied them himself. He did not inform his colleague Dr Harris of the risks to this patient and deliberately made himself absent when she was critically ill, not to attend another desperately ill patient, but to attend a YMCA meeting, which was surely a postponable engagement. He had actually checked out the dosage of the antidote for barbiturate poisoning before she took the overdose and 24 hours earlier, then, as the patient lay dying, he administered less than the amount required.

In Mrs Morrell's case, we have the evidence of Dr Mercer, who has identified a stage in his treatment which she views as a definite attempt to terminate her life. In Miss Neil-Miller's case, it is difficult to see how his treatment could have been a simple mistake of judgement. In the case of Mrs Bradnum she does not appear to have been ill at all, apart from a nervous stomach upset, yet he gave her an injection and she died within a few minutes of its administration. He even predicted to her lodgers that she would die almost immediately.

## Natural Causes

The third possibility is that these patients simply died of their illnesses, in spite of Dr Adams' best efforts to preserve their lives and make them comfortable. In the case of Miss Neil-Miller, leaving her to freeze in front of an open window at her age and in her frail state of health, seems an unlikely approach to preserving her life. In the case of Mrs Bradnum, she was in reasonably good health, she was not in pain, other than a nervous stomach and was well enough to talk to neighbours and deal with her affairs; there was no obvious purpose of the injection administered by Dr Adams other than to terminate her life and he predicted to those present that it would kill her. In the case of Mrs Morrell, it was clearly the injection delivered by the Nurse Randall – on Dr Adams' instructions – which killed Mrs Morrell. From the prescription, it is clear that he had prepared a massive injection of paraldehyde. In the case of Bobbie Hullett, the autopsy showed that she died of barbiturate poisoning.

## Incompetence

The fourth possibility is that Dr Adams was well-meaning, but old-fashioned and incompetent. But this argument does not stand up to scrutiny. Perhaps his peers did not think him the best doctor in Eastbourne, but his patient list included many elderly women and he had been treating the elderly for over thirty years; he was something of an expert in geriatrics and must have known what he was doing. He also had a diploma in anaesthetics and was a practicing anaesthetist. It seems unlikely that a doctor with such a background would make so many frequent blunders or that the propensity to make such mistakes would not have resulted in his forced retirement from hospital practice.

## Intelligence

How intelligent was Dr Adams? From the fact that he did qualify at university, we may safely conclude that he was well above average intelligence. He clearly seems to have had more savvy, for example, than Dr Shipman, who nevertheless managed to deceive everyone.

However, Professor Rendle-Short's decision that he was not missionary material suggests that he lacked the intellect of his uncle, the great Dr John Bodkin. They may have shared the same family traditions and upbringing, but his uncle had graduated with a first-class degree. Knowing that John Adams had had been ill for a year and had graduated with an ordinary degree by dint of hard work, Professor Rendle-Short invited him to Bristol to give him the chance to show what he could do. Having watched him work for less than a year, he recommended that he should pursue the post in Eastbourne. Dr Adams was clearly tenacious and hard working, but these are not the only qualities which make for a good missionary. Perhaps Dr Adams' later sybaritic life style gives a clue to what Professor Rendle-Short saw in him.

## Faith

Dr Adams was apparently so God-fearing, it seems paradoxical to suggest that he might deliberately have taken human lives. Dr Adams made frequent proclamations of his faith, which included, not only the daily prayers, but also praying for God's guidance in treating a patient. In his interviews with journalists, he reiterated his confidence in God's grace. He made constant references to the Almighty knowing what was in his heart and his innocence of evil intent. Yet according to the faith which Dr Adams practised, his salvation was assured no matter what sins he might commit, because he had been already saved. All he would have to do would be to put such wealth as he might gain to a better use in serving God. The incident in his childhood, when his father beat him for 'refusing a gift of God' also had a big impact on how he saw such opportunities.

Gosse, and Haigh, the acid bath murderer, who were also the sons of Plymouth Brethren, point to another possibility. Gosse in particular describes how, as a boy, he came to recognise the benefits, within such a closed and stifling community, of paying lip service to beliefs which he considered false – the need, as it were, to live a lie, to have a secret inner life, but to act out another. There was certainly an actor in Dr John Adams. He loved being the centre of attention, being in the public eye – everything, from his Rolls Royces, his chauffeur, his Savile Row suits, his arrogance, his turn of phrase at key moments, his explosive temperament in public meetings, his desire for influence and position... all this from a man who, from an early age, had observed his own father attracting attention with his motor cars and moving crowds of people with his sermons. Throughout his life, he put effort into maintaining a respectable appearance and the right image. Religion was his cloak of respectability; it provided perfect cover for his grooming of rich elderly widows

## Evidence of a Traumatic Childhood and Dominant Parent

His father died when he was fifteen. His brother died suddenly during the Influenza epidemic soon after John Adams went to university. From his earliest years, his mother had a huge impact on him. She it was who set him the challenge of emulating her uncle and inculcated the work ethic. She it was who forced him to sign the temperance pledge and then came with him to Eastbourne to make sure he stuck to it and made a success in Eastbourne. She would have encouraged him in the courting of the wealthy and influential, treating Eastbourne as a replacement for a province in China. She believed in the principles of hard work and thrift, but she also came from a family who owned property and would have encouraged him in the purchase of the house in Trinity Trees. When he courted Norah O'Hara, the butcher's daughter, it was reputedly his mother who had him call off the engagement because she was 'trade' and although this is unlikely to have been the reason, she undoubtedly did not want him to marry.

His life changed after 1943 when his mother died. Though the police claimed that he had three mistresses, this would have been extremely unlikely in a small community like Eastbourne. In fact, his sexuality is an area of doubt. When his mother died in 1943, he was only forty-four, not too old to get married, remembering that his father was in his forties on his wedding day. He was still close to his jilted girlfriend – they remained friends until he died. As a wealthy and successful doctor in a community short of men in the post war years, he could have had his choice and there was no shortage of wealthy widows in Eastbourne. On the other hand, he pursued a close, thirty-five-year relationship with Lt. Col. Roland Gwynne, who is known to have been an aggressive homosexual.

The image that emerges is of a lone wolf, a secretive, ambitious man, wealthy, yet never quite accepted within the upper classes whom he wooed, and despised by his peers in medicine; yet someone who worked long hours, was willing to turn out day or night for patients, and had a small number of long-term friends. He was competitive and a crack-shot, Olympic standard, but described by his fellow sportsmen as greedy – a man who would shoot the other man's birds. He had inherited his father's love of expensive motorcars, but he was an erratic driver and usually had a chauffeur.

He was self-obsessed and dishonest. A collector/thief of things, especially from his dead patients; the things had intrinsic value, he stored them and rarely used them – they were more trophies. He was insecure. He kept the things and ate too much for comfort. He stockpiled drugs and kept poor records. His files were in a perpetual mess; he kept no records, even for patients. He grew physically unattractive in his middle and later years. When his home in Trinity Trees was sold following his death, the auctioneers remarked that the house was full of valuables, but that the fabric of the house had been allowed to fall into disrepair.

The difficulties of detecting rogue doctors and then understanding their motives are legion. The odds are stacked heavily in their favour. Dr Shipman was given away only by a stupid mistake. Though he was no Einstein, Dr Adams was clearly more intelligent and sophisticated than Dr Shipman. While he did make mistakes, the environment within which he was operating was less efficient in detecting criminal activity than today and the trust in doctors was more absolute. Dr Adams had also anaesthetised suspicion through his friendships with Lt. Col. Gwynne, who served a term as mayor of Eastbourne and the Chief Constable. He was a pillar of the local community through his service to the community and through his long association with the YMCA. Like Shipman, he had several hundred N.H.S. patients who sang his praises. Even after Shipman was found guilty, there were still former patients who could not believe that their kindly doctor had committed such crimes.

Similarly, when Leslie Henson came out of the Hullett Inquest, proclaiming to everybody within earshot that the verdict was nonsense and that Dr Adams was responsible for Bobbie

Hullett's death, he was attacked by a band of elderly, umbrella wielding women, protecting their dear Doctor Adams.

## The Bobbie Hullett Case

The Police evidence in the Bobbie Hullett case was much the strongest, which raises the question why the DPP chose to pursue the case of Edith Morrell. In the Bobbie Hullett case, the Police had the forensic evidence provided by the body. The DPP could prove that Dr Adams knew that Bobbie Hullett was suicidal and that he had good reason to suspect that she had a sufficient supply of barbiturates to kill herself. They could prove that he had discussed the antidote and the dosage with an expert both a few hours before she took the overdose and on the day before she died, which proves that he expected her to make an attempt on her own life. He failed to warn his colleague, Dr Harris, of these things and was absent when Mrs Hullett went into a coma. He also admitted that he gave her insufficient of the antidote to save her life. This evidence puts the swift clearance of the £1,000 cheque and the bizarre phone call to the Coroner the day before Bobbie Hullett died in a different light.

It is also clear that Dr Adams misled the court at the Hullett Inquest on an important point. The DPP's files show clearly that Dr Adams accompanied Bobbie Hullett on her visit to Ireland. At the inquest, he claimed that he had given her medication to take with her on her trip, implying that he did not accompany her; so, according to his version, Bobbie Hullett had the opportunity to keep back a lethal dose of medication without his knowledge.

## Evidence of Drug Trafficking

There are some grounds for believing that Dr Adams was trafficking in drugs. Certainly, this was Hannam's suspicion. This might explain why he was so coy about admitting he had accompanied Bobbie Hullett to Ireland. After all, doctors do not usually accompany their patients on holiday. Witness after witness commented on the great regularity and secrecy of Dr Adams' visits to patients. He was proved to have substantial quantities dangerous drugs in his medicine cupboard and no system of accounting for them. He was frequently seen by nurses simply to produce and administer drugs from his bag, without explaining what the drugs were, where they came from or accounting for them later. In the DPP's files, there is a note that Lt. Col. Gwynne used to visit Dr Adams every morning without fail at 9 am. Yet, in his statements to Police, Lt. Col. Gwynne claimed that he had received only occasional light medication for headaches. Dr Adams was also a regular morning visitor to the home of Miss Betty Cradock, the woman who accompanied Dr Adams and Lt. Col. Gwynne on a shooting holiday to Scotland in September, 1956, during the police investigation; neighbours commented that she also looked 'uplifted' after these visits. Perhaps Lt. Col. Gwynne's visits to his surgery and Dr Adams' visits to Betty Cradock were for reasons neither patients nor Doctor could admit.

It is clear that Lt. Col. Gwynne's connection with the Dr Adams household was much closer than a simple patient/doctor relationship would suggest. When Dr Adams' former house-keeper/cook, Frances Abrams, was called to be a witness at his Lewes trial, she approached Lt. Col. Gwynne, as the chairman of the magistrates, to seek exemption. She subsequently applied to Lt. Col. Gwynne for a job and was duly hired, despite the Colonel's statement to Hannam that he had decided to have nothing further to do with Dr Adams.

Taking the many other cases into consideration, there is also ample evidence of a systematic approach to gaining control over his patients through the use of drugs – a power which was exploited to enrich himself through their wills. It is astonishing, however, that these issues were never even taken up by the GMC Ethics Committee, who must have been made fully aware of Dr Adams' unprofessional activities by Hannam's report. It is surprising that other professions – such as the Accountancy and Legal professions – whose members in Eastbourne were certainly aware of what he was doing – made no attempt to have Dr Adams struck off permanently.

## The DPP's Choice of Case to Prosecute

The choice of which case or cases to prosecute was in the hands of the DPP, who appears to have consulted Reginald Manningham-Buller and his team, but not Hannam. Hannam was frustrated at being excluded from the discussions. I surmise that he rashly made this annoyance known. The files show that, for his troubles, he received a reprimand on his conduct of the case. Ostensibly, the pretext for the reprimand was that he had leaked information about the case to journalists, which inflamed the reports in the press. While he was more expansive in his informal press briefings than would be the practice today, he was using the briefings as a rather naïve tactic to unnerve Dr Adams. It must also be recalled that Reginald Manningham-Buller leaked Hannam's Report to the BMA, which earned him a toothless reprimand from the outgoing Home Secretary.

The evidence of the tortuous path followed by Nurses' Notes and the damage they did to the prosecution case at the outset of the Trial leads directly to the conclusion that a decision was made, at the highest of levels, to lose the case. As an historian and not an investigator, I can only point to the many pressures on the government of the day – particularly the desire to win the next election and the threat to the future of the National Health Service – that might have triggered this decision. Whatever the reason, I come to the conclusion that the most powerful evidence against Dr Adams was never presented in court. The strongest evidence which might have seen him convicted, at least of manslaughter, if not murder, was contained in the Hullett case.

## The General Medical Council

The G.M.C. is the body which regulates the medical profession; it is a charity funded by doctors and therefore has a fundamental conflict of interest. It is ineffectual in policing and disciplining, having no investigative body and no means of tracking repeat complaints. It is not representative of the general public which it is supposed to protect: doctors are elected by doctors and the lay members are not elected. It also has too many roles other than the disciplinary one, including ensuring the standards of medical courses and 'good medical practice'. There is much discussion about its role and it organisational culture, particularly since the Shipman Reports have been published. Perhaps a system such as the Swedish one, where there is a government body with doctors only acting in an advisory role, would be preferable.

## Medical Training

'Doctors learn to keep other doctors' mistakes secret from almost the first day they arrive at medical school.'[1] There has been some exploration into medical training in America and the defects in the system which might lead to an attitude or perspective on death which is not that of the lay person or patient. A 1984 journal article described what occurred in a teaching hospital:

> 'Half… of the new interns interviewed in the first two months had been involved in serious patient errors, many of which caused complications or death… By the time they finish their residency, those [house officers] who perceived themselves as not having killed a patient regarded themselves as lucky…
>
> While the doctors-in-training may feel guilt and remorse over the mistakes they made, they have developed elaborate mechanisms of distancing and denial, which, while not completely successful psychologically, are artefacts of a highly insular and self-protective subculture…'[2]

A 1996 article reported a lecturer doctor's advice to his clinical medical students: 'If you communicate well and are empathetic and sympathetic you can literally get away with murder.' The students inferred that this was 'an overt reference to avoiding the personal impact of negligent practice by carefully managing interactions with patients.'[3]

## Opportunity

Dr Herbert Kinnell, a psychiatrist, in an article in the *British Medical Journal*,[4] suggests that 'arguably medicine has thrown up more serial killers than all the other professions put together'

[1] Holton, *How Doctors Have Betrayed Us All*, [*The Lancet*]

[2] Mizraki, *Managing Medical Mistakes*

[3] Annandale, *Professional Defenses*

[4] Kinnell, *Serial Homicide by Doctors: Shipman in Perspective*

and that the medical profession may 'attract some people with a pathological interest in the power of life and death'.

Dr Cameron Stark replied to this article, having, with others, carried out an analysis of serial killers in nursing: that opportunity was of paramount importance. Up to 1997 the research team identified 13 convictions of nurses for serial murder of patients. In nursing the opportunity was associated 'with the delivery of intravenous fluids, with being in a bed out of sight of a nursing station, and with evenings or nights'. It was ease of access and a low chance of observation which were important features. But the difference between doctors and nurses is that doctors are able to sign a death certificate. 'The reason for the difference in the number of reported deaths may simply relate to the doctors' greater opportunity to remain undiscovered.'[5] The true number of murders in the healthcare professions, 'the dark figure of crime', remains unknown. The only doctor in Britain who has been convicted of the serial killing of patients (other than family) is Dr Shipman.

## Autopsies and Coroners

In 1965 Professor F.E. Camps, the Home Office Pathologist, told the Cremation Society Conference that 'Homicide is not quite so infrequent as statistics may show, for it is not the undetected case which is the source of anxiety but the unsuspected case.' He quoted two examples: firstly, that during the Second World War thousands of men had been trained to kill by unarmed combat in order to silence and kill guards, so that there were a large number of people with the knowledge of how to kill but up to 1965 there had only been one murderer recorded as having used the technique. Even if there was an autopsy this was the sort of death which would be missed by a pathologist who was 'not alive to the possibility' or who had been asked to perform the autopsy because it was 'an easy case' in his spare time. Secondly, there had been shown to be a wide variation in the number of autopsies ordered per cases reported to the Coroner in different parts of the country. Doctors reporting cases to Coroners described them as 'easy' or 'natural' and Coroners would act upon this information. Deaths due to poisoning were commonly missed. Professor Camps believed that it was necessary for autopsies to be carried out by trained medico-legal pathologists, not clinical pathologists doing them as a sideline.

He also suggested the setting-up of a medico-legal service closely integrated with the Coroners' system. The standard of death certification for burial should be the same as that for cremation, because unless material was saved for possible toxicological and pathological investigation, it was unlikely that an autopsy after exhumation would yield results, as often only the skeleton remained. The medical referee, instead of being the appointed referee of the crematorium, should be an assistant Coroner and he would be responsible for referring cases to the Coroner. This would then fit in with a medico-legal autopsy service, slanted to treat cases with suspicion, and with complete facilities for toxicological and other examinations. This would

---

[5] Stark, *Opportunity may be more important than profession in serial homicide.* [bmj.com 26 January, 2001]

certainly prevent doctors having a 'cosy relationship' with a Coroner doctor – which certainly happened in the cases of Shipman and Adams. It would also close the loophole in the Coroner's Guide to Doctors of Reportable Deaths: 'A death should be referred to H.M. Coroner if the deceased was not seen by a doctor within the last 14 days prior to death'. This allowed Dr Adams to attend patients only within a very short time before death, for example in the case of the Duke of Devonshire, or, alternatively, to 'drop in' on patients who were not ill on his friendly weekly visits, and then not report these sudden deaths to the Coroner. Nearly 50 years later that loophole remains.

## Expert Medical Evidence

The trial of Dr Adams hinged, to a large extent, on the expert medical evidence. It demonstrates the difficulties involved in the use of the adversarial system in relation to this type of evidence. It proved very easy to distort the honest opinions of Doctors Douthwaite and Ashby, and made it difficult for them to make full statements of their findings and the reasons behind them. It was particularly damaging to Dr Douthwaite's reputation, and undeservedly so from the point of view of his profession. None of the three doctors were professional witnesses or even used to giving evidence in court and being cross-examined. Only Professor Camps was an expert in the medico-legal field, and unfortunately, in this trial, only had a limited role to play. There has been much recent discussion about this problem, particularly in relation to cases where parents are accused of harming or killing infants or small children, as paediatricians are reluctant to give evidence. It has been suggested that medical expert witnesses should be the subject of inquisitorial procedure – without it affecting the adversarial system of trial – and that they should be the judge's witnesses, rather than being those of the prosecution or the defence.

## The Independence of the Judiciary

The Attorney-General is a barrister member – a political appointee – of the Government who, *inter alia*, advises his government colleagues on questions of law; takes proceedings for contempt of court, e.g. against newspapers for breach of the *sub judice* rules, and seeks injunctions against bodies which have acted unlawfully. He supervises the Crown Prosecution Service, which via the Director of Public Prosecutions is answerable and accountable to Parliament through the Attorney-General. There are certain categories of prosecution, such as some offences of bribery, offences under the Official Secrets Act 1911, some offences of racial hatred, and some offences relating to prevention of terrorism and belonging to a proscribed organisation, which may only be commenced with the consent of the Attorney-General. The Attorney-General has final responsibility for the enforcing of the criminal law.

A further power of the Attorney-General – used by Sir Reginald Manningham-Buller in the case of Dr Adams – is to enter a *nolle prosequi*, the effect of which is to halt a trial on indictment. Manningham-Buller used it to halt the indictment of Dr Adams for the murder of Mrs. Hullett, but it is a discretionary power normally used on compassionate grounds where the accused has become seriously ill during the course of his trial. Lord Devlin criticised, in his book, this use of the *nolle prosequi* as an abuse of the Attorney-General's power. An alternative would have been to offer no evidence, or, of course, to proceed with the trial on the Hullett indictment. In the event, Mrs. Hullett has received no semblance of justice: the inquest verdict still stands as 'suicide' and there was no formal procedure for the medical treatment to be investigated by the G.M.C. without a complaint from a relative.

Her Majesty's Attorney-General is the chief legal adviser of the Crown in England and Wales, representing the Queen and the Government in court, and having supervisory powers over prosecutions; he is assisted by the Solicitor-General, which office is also a political appointment. The Lord Chancellor's proposals for constitutional reforms have, as one of their aims, the reinforcement of the independence of the judiciary, but do not seem to address the problems inherent in the diverse roles and allegiances of the office of Attorney-General.

## The Present Attorney-General, Lord Goldsmith

In response to my enquiries as to the position and role of a contemporary Attorney-General and the possibility for any interference in the judicial process, the Attorney-General, Lord Goldsmith, instructed a member of his staff to reply on his behalf. In view of the importance of these points it is worth quoting some parts of this letter:

'1. Originally, appearing as advocate on behalf of the Crown in cases involving serious constitutional considerations, public order or treason, was one of the primary functions of the Attorney-General. Prosecuting cases of poisoning was part of this convention, but has over the years ceased to continue. In the great majority of cases these days, of course, the Attorney-General nominates Counsel to act on his behalf in the prosecution of government cases. Prosecuting a case from start to finish would be relatively time consuming for an Attorney and generally impractical.

However, in appropriate cases (for example where the issues are of particular importance to the Government) the Attorney-General may be asked by the relevant Minister or Department to represent the government himself. The Attorney-General would in any event expect to be consulted in relation to important or difficult cases.'

Therefore, the Attorney-General does appear personally in very particular cases, but not now – as was still the case in Sir Reginald Manningham-Buller's time – as a matter of routine in cases of poisoning.

The next extract from the letter illustrates the fact that Sir Reginald Manningham-Buller was given a quite exceptional position in both the Eden and Macmillan governments:

'2. As far as I can determine, the position of Attorney-General has never officially been a Cabinet post. However, it has in the past been practice for a given Attorney-General to be appointed to the Cabinet. According to J. Edwards in his book *The Attorney-General: Politics and the Public Interest*, since 1928, it has been the practice to exclude the Attorney from the Cabinet. He concludes that:

> *On the question of the membership of the Cabinet itself, it is the outward manifestation of the Attorney-General's disassociation from the inner council of the government that assumes the greatest importance in underlining his independence in the enforcement of criminal law. By excluding the Attorney-General from actual membership of the Cabinet the tradition may well have been enhanced that the subject of criminal prosecution is outside the purview of the Cabinet's decision making functions.'*

Lord Goldsmith, the current Attorney-General:

> '...is not a member of the Cabinet but may be invited to attend Cabinet meetings or some of its committees, if legal advice is likely to be required or where his Ministerial responsibilities for policy or delivery are likely to be engaged.'

Nevertheless, the appointment of an Attorney-General is a political one: he is the chief legal adviser to the Government, but he also has public interest functions, so his role is a dual one. The statements in the letter on these matters are of considerable interest:

> 'When acting as the Government's legal adviser, the Attorney-General acts as a member of the Government and is bound by the doctrine of collective responsibility. He gives impartial legal advice. As with any other Minister of the Crown, if a point of principle were sufficiently important, he would have to consider resigning if the Government failed to heed his advice.
>
> When acting as a public officer (for example: individual criminal proceedings, contempt of court, charities) the relevant decision is for the Attorney-General to make although he is able to seek the views of ministerial colleagues. The responsibility for making decisions in public interest matters rests squarely with the Attorney-General and his decisions must not be influenced by political considerations.
>
> This matter is discussed in great detail by J. Edwards in his book [referred to above]. Having studied non-political appointments of Attorney-General in other Commonwealth countries, he argues that:

> *...no matter how entrenched constitutional safeguards may be, in the final analysis it is the strength of character, personal integrity and depth of commitment to the principles of independence and the impartial representation of the public interest, on the part of the holders of the office of Attorney-General, which is of supreme importance. Such qualities are by no*

*means associated exclusively with either the political or non-political nature of the office of Attorney-General. Instances of indefensible distortion of the Attorney-General's powers can be documented in countries which have subscribed to the non-political public servant model of Attorney-General. It is these kind of situations that induce widespread disillusionment with the ideals associated with democratic government.*

In the discharge of his functions Lord Goldsmith attaches the greatest importance to the principles of fairness, independence and accountability.'

In my view, Macmillan and Manningham-Buller adhered to no such principles in relation to the office of Attorney-General.

# The Police

The Commissioner of the Metropolitan Police is appointed by the Home Secretary. Sir John Nott-Bowyer was appointed by Sir David Maxwell-Fyfe (later Lord Kilmuir) in 1953 during Eden's administration and considered a 'safe' Conservative appointment. He was supposed to be a 'safe' professional. 'He had a good brain and all the social graces, and was an expert horseman... and a devoted bridge player... Above all, he was excessively idle.'[6] A Scotland Yard superintendent of the 1950s described him as '...a nice man when what we needed was a bit of a bastard.' As the post of Commissioner was a political appointment, the Commissioner needed all the more, to be capable of standing up for his Force. Detective Superintendent Hannam never got the backing he deserved: his investigation was hampered, curtailed and evidence he gathered withheld. He was certain, beyond any doubt, that he had discovered a serial killer and I believe that he was right.

[6] Ascoli

# APPENDICES

# Appendix I

---

# What Happened

# to the Dramatis Personae?

---

### The Judge – Patrick Devlin

Macmillan chose Devlin to conduct a Commission of Enquiry into policing in Nyasaland in 1959. According to his biographer,[1] this was a decision he came to regret. Devlin concluded that – 'Nyasaland is – no doubt temporarily – a police state where it is not safe for anyone to express approval of the policies of the Congress Party'. Further, the Devlin Report was highly critical of the Governor and of the Colonial Office.

Macmillan's response was quite unstatesmanlike He described Devlin in vitriolic terms: 'he is (a) Irish – no doubt with that Fenian blood that makes Irishmen anti-Government on principle, (b) a lapsed Roman Catholic. His brother is a Jesuit priest, (c) Hunchback, (d) bitterly disappointed at my not having made him Lord Chief Justice'. Of course, Devlin's report was wholly accurate[2] but, in order to defuse a crisis which would have caused the resignations of Lennox-Boyd, the Secretary of State for the Colonies, and the Governor of Nyasaland, the Government produced the rival Armitage Report and published it in July 1959 with the Devlin Report. As Attorney-General, Sir Reginald Manningham-Buller, played a considerable part in this manoeuvre. It was said by some commentators that Devlin was a rival of Manningham-Buller's for the job of Lord Chancellor. However, the thinking man's Press was generally on Devlin's side; Bernard Levin, the much respected journalist and commentator, wrote in *The Spectator* that – 'The Government refused to accept the Devlin Report because it told the truth…'

The General Election was held three months later and the Conservatives were returned to office. Had he written the 'right' report, Devlin would doubtless have become Lord Chief Justice. But the sting of the Devlin Report was not easily forgotten. It was a further two years before Macmillan elevated him to the House of Lords. Lord Devlin subsequently became a Lord of Appeal and was Chairman of the Press Council.

In 1983, shortly after the death of Dr Adams, he published a book – *Easing the Passing* –

---

[1] Lamb / [2] Ibid

about the famous trial over which he presided. The timing of the publication suggests that he had much of the material prepared in advance. He was quite clearly suspicious of Dr Adams but placed the blame of the failure of the trial at the door of the then Sir Reginald Manningham-Buller

Lord Devlin spent the remainder of his career writing about law and history, being particularly interested in the relation of law to morality. He died on 9th August, 1992.

### Sir Reginald Manningham-Buller, QC, M.P.

Attorney-General during the period 1954–62; he succeeded Lord Kilmuir as Lord Chancellor on 13th July, 1962 – after the 'night of the long knives', when Macmillan cleared seven sitting Ministers from his government. Reggie became 1st Viscount Dilhorne of Greens Norton, receiving his due reward for his loyalty and service from Harold Macmillan.

Selwyn Lloyd, the then Chancellor, had not thought himself a good enough lawyer to become Lord Chancellor. He commented that this was 'a judgment he was to revise when Reginald Manningham-Buller went to the Woolsack'.

But 'Reggie' was to prove his usefulness to Macmillan on future occasions. For example, he played a significant role in what came to be called 'The Profumo Affair'.

In 1962, Sir Roger Hollis, Head of MI5, British counter-intelligence, informed Macmillan that John Profumo, the Secretary of State for War in MacMillan's government had been caught in a classic 'honeytrap'. He was having an affair with a prostitute called Christine Keeler who had a connection with a KGB spy called Ivanov. A certain Dr Stephen Ward was seeking information from Christine Keeler about atomic secrets which were to be handed to West Germany by the USA. Macmillan asked Reggie, now Lord Dilhorne, the Lord Chancellor, to conduct an investigation. He was to interview 'such people as he liked "in the family", that is police, ministers, and civil servants but no one else'.[3]

Macmillan had also instructed Sir Timothy Bligh, one of his Principal Private Secretaries, to ask Sir Joseph Simpson, Commissioner of Metropolitan Police to talk to Reggie. The Director of Public Prosecutions, it had been ascertained, was now ready to proceed against Dr Ward on 4th June 1963, when Keeler returned to London. Bligh's memorandum recorded that, when the Commissioner had pointed out that 'The police could not conduct their actions on the basis of instructions from the Government', Bligh had responded that neither the Lord Chancellor nor anyone else in the Government would want to interfere with police matters.[4]

There followed a series of exchanges between the Prime Minister's Office and Sir Joseph, which were never mentioned in the Denning Report into the Profumo Affair. Lamb concludes that:

'The failure of the Government to show Denning the documents relating to Sir Joseph Simpson is sinister and confirms the author's suspicion that Macmillan was close to tampering with the course of justice by delaying Ward's arrest.'

[3] Lamb / [4] Ibid

Just as Reggie was Macmillan's foot soldier in the case against Dr Adams, so he was acting on Macmillan's behalf in relation to Dr Stephen Ward. It seems likely that, if there was tampering going on, it was Reggie who was guiding the interference, if not actually interfering himself.

John Profumo and his wife were in Venice when they received the news that Reggie was conducting an enquiry. Profumo confessed to his wife that he had lied to the House of Commons regarding his relationship with Ms Keeler and promptly returned to London. Two Cabinet meetings were held on 12th and 13th June to discuss his resignation. Reggie's report was available at the second meeting. He informed the Cabinet that the security aspect merited no further action. Harold Wilson, the leader of the Opposition, had sight of the report and was not satisfied; so Macmillan instructed Reggie to conduct a second, this time secret, enquiry.

A bizarre connection with Reggie emerged: Dr Stephen Ward was attempting to engineer secret lines of communication between the Foreign Office and Ivanov. His intermediary was Sir Godfrey Nicholson, a Member of Parliament, who was Lady Dilhorne's brother-in-law. Through Sir Godfrey, Dr Ward had already met with the Permanent Head of the Foreign Office.[5]

Reggie took the strange step of criticising the Denning Report on the Profumo Affair in a letter to Macmillan. The advice he gave also flew in the face of the irrefutable evidence that Profumo had an intimate relationship with Keeler; Reggie proffered the view that 'no sensible person' would consider that Profumo would have to resign. If the Prime Minister shared this view, then he and Reggie were in an extremely small minority in Parliament. Lord Hailsham speculated that Reggie enjoyed some strange power over Macmillan, 'Harold had done another of his somersaults under the influence of Reggie Dilhorne.'[6]

In October, 1963, Macmillan went into hospital having been diagnosed as having prostate cancer. The Prime Minister feared (incorrectly, as it turned out) that he was about to die, so a successor had to be chosen quickly. The task of assessing candidates fell to Reggie. Rab Butler described how Reggie began his informal soundings 'like a large Clumber spaniel sniffing the bottoms of the hedgerows.'[7] Whatever those soundings revealed, Reggie had determined that Lord Home (who subsequently resigned his peerage and took the name and title Sir Alex Douglas-Home) would be the next Prime Minister and that he, Reggie, would be the Kingmaker. He reported to Macmillan that ten Ministers wanted Lord Home – including Iain McLeod, the Chairman of the Conservative Party. The other three candidates – Reginald Maudling, Rab Butler and Lord Hailsham, could raise support from only nine ministers between them – four for Reginald Maudling, three for Rab Butler and only two for Lord Hailsham.

McLeod's view on these matters was, in fact, diametrically opposed to Reggie's. He believed that only two members of the Cabinet would vote for Home and, as McLeod's widow later confirmed, McLeod himself was not one of them. Later, four members of Macmillan's cabinet – Enoch Powell, Lord Butler, Lord Eccles (previously Sir David Eccles, formerly Minister for Education before the 'night of the long knives') and Lord Aldington – all told Macmillan's biographer, Alistair Horne, that Reggie 'was astray'. Nevertheless, on this occasion, Reggie prevailed. Shortly after Macmillan entered hospital, Sir Alex Douglas-Home succeeded Macmillan

[5] Ibid / [6] Hailsham / [7] Thorpe

as the leader of the Conservative Party and therefore Prime Minister. He led the party to an election defeat on 15 October, 1964 and was replaced as leader by Edward Heath, the future Prime Minister, in July 1965.

Having lost his position as Lord Chancellor, Reggie retired from full-time politics. He was made Viscount Dilhorne in the dissolution honours' list and became deputy leader of the opposition in the House of Lords. After the General Election he accepted an offer from Harold Wilson's government to become a lord of appeal in ordinary. In this role he was very successful and sat in 205 appeals until he retired at the age of 75 in 1980. He died suddenly on 7th September that same year, a month after his retirement.

His widow, Mary, died on March 25th 2004, aged ninety-three. Her obituary recorded that, during the Second World War, she trained pigeons to carry secret messages to agents.

His daughter, Eliza Manningham-Buller, is today the Director General of MI5. She was recruited into the service during the 1970s, apparently much to Reggie's distress. Nevertheless, she appears to have inherited Reggie's appetite for the role of secret mover. She was a very successful field agent and is accredited by Oleg Gordievsky, the Russian double agent, with keeping his identity secret during the Cold War.

### Detective Superintendent Hannam

He was promoted to Commander, but left the C.I.D. in 1960, becoming a security adviser – no doubt he was very disillusioned at being prevented from bringing the Adams case to a successful conclusion, having his investigations curtailed, and at the political interference in the justice system. There had also been the attempt by the Attorney-General to use him as the 'fall guy', when Hannam leaked a little information to the *Daily Mail* reporter in the interests of justice; the Attorney-General trying to cover up the fact that he had provided the whole of the police report to the Defence.

Like the meticulous detective he was, he left a clue – the one piece of evidence which was the key to the political interference in the trial – in his papers. He died just a few months before Dr Adams.

### Detective Inspector Pugh

He stayed with the C.I.D. in Eastbourne, but he developed Alzheimer's Disease and died at the age of 69 on 10th March, 1977 in a Sussex Hospital.

### Dr Arthur Douthwaite

It was said that it was due to his performance as a medical witness at the trial, that he failed to gain the Presidency of the Royal College of Physicians. Like Hannam, he had been trounced by the Attorney-General rather than Mr Lawrence – in his case by having crucial evidence withheld from him.

### Herbert Victor James, Solicitor to Dr Adams

Suffered a stroke during Dr Adams' Trial and never fully recovered. He died in the Esperance Nursing Home in 1959, having been visited regularly by his friend, former client and associate, Dr Adams.

### Geoffrey Lawrence, QC

In the year following Dr Adams' trial, he successfully defended Charles Ridge, Chief Constable of Brighton against charges – with other officers – of conspiracy to obstruct the course of justice. The allegations concerned the taking of bribes; Ridge was acquitted but two other C.I.D. officers were convicted. Lawrence was Chairman of the General Council of the Bar from 1960-62, and made an acclaimed visit to the U.S. to address the American Bar Association. He was knighted in 1963 and became a Judge. He was appointed by the government to chair the National Incomes Commission in 1962, and also chaired an independent inquiry into parliamentary remuneration which reported in 1964. In 1965 he was appointed to the High Court, although not long after he became seriously ill. He had a farm in Sussex, but his passion was for music and he was an accomplished violinist. He died on 3rd February 1967 at the age of 64.

### Sir Melford Stevenson

In the year of the Adams' trial, he was appointed judge in the Probate, Divorce, and Admiralty Division of the High Court, and knighted in the same year. But it was with his transfer to the Queen's Bench Division in 1961 that he became one of the best-known judges of the day, with his strong personality and outspokenness. The trial of the Krays brought him much notoriety, and he was frequently given difficult cases to conduct. When he retired in 1979, he made many appearances on television, which was a natural medium for him. He died on 26th December, 1987 at the age of 85.

### Detective Sergeant Hewett

Charlie Hewett – as can be seen in 'Aftermath' – remained with the C.I.D. at Scotland Yard and became a Chief Superintendent.

# The Press and the Police

## July–August 1956

Hannam was in the habit of giving informal briefings to journalists in the bar of the New Inn, just opposite Eastbourne Police Station, where he found accommodation during his lengthy investigation. He made a table of Extracts from the Daily Press – in response to criticisms about leaks to press.

| Date/Newspaper | Report and Quotes | Hannam's Comments |
| --- | --- | --- |
| 27.7 *Daily Express* | Dead widows: Police Chief speaks out. <u>Mr Walker said that murder has not been ruled out.</u> Several people had given info. about the deaths. He added, 'There is lot of talk in this town and as policemen we cannot ignore gossip. The purpose of our inquiries has been to arrive at the truth and stop these rumours. <u>Even after this case is cleared up to our satisfaction it may be that our inquiries will not necessarily cease.'</u> | If remarks underlined were in fact made by the Chief Constable what greater invitation to the Press to run sensational story could have been made. |
| 27.7 *News Chronicle* | New turn in mystery of widow's death. Three wealthy women may be exhumed. The Chief Constable said tonight that although it may be proved there was no foul play in connection with Mrs Hullett's death <u>the C.I.D. would have to continue inquiries into 'other matters'.</u> | As above |
| 27.7. *Daily Mirror* | Now deaths of four women are probed. Exhuma- | As above |

| | | |
|---|---|---|
| *27.7. Daily Mirror* (Cont.) | tions of their bodies from local cemeteries may be considered. Last night Mr Richard Walker, Chief Constable of Eastbourne, <u>disclosed that Police had taken a number of drugs and other articles from Mrs Hullett's home.</u> Mr Walker added, 'This inquiry may help to clear up rumours circulating in the town. <u>If there is a satisfactory explanation of Mrs Hullett's death it does not mean that we will not investigate the other deaths.</u>' | |
| *29.7 Empire News & Sunday Chronicle* | Wealthy widow not murdered. The Constable of Eastbourne, Mr Richard Walker revealed this to me yesterday. He said, 'I've been in conference with Dr Camps the Home Pathologist and the Eastbourne Coroner, Dr A.C. Somerville. We talked about the case in to the Press in all its aspects. Certain chemical tests have yet to be made, but as <u>I now have documentary proof that there is no question of murder</u> there is no sense of urgency.' ... 'After four days of investigation I learnt of one letter which threw an entirely different light on the whole business. There is no doubt about it they are in Mrs Hullett's handwriting all right... It has been particularly difficult for me because I know everybody in the case personally. I knew Mrs Hullett as a friend and her doctor is my doctor. The reason for the witholding of the letters may be the diffidence which some people have about revealing what they regard as their personal business. I think something I said when hard-pressed during the week may have given rise to a misundersranding. I am referring to the reported possibility of the exhumation of three other wealthy women. The exhumations were not intended and there will be no further police inquiries into these deaths.' | If true it seems almost incredible for a Chief Constable to make such disclosures. <u>All the above was apparently said 3 weeks before N.S.Y. were even consulted.</u> |
| *19.8 Sunday Dispatch* | Mystery of women's deaths – Yard called in. To make inquiries into the deaths of several wealthy women Scotland Yard's Supt. Herbert Hannam | This must have been a direct disclosure to the Press. |

| | | |
|---|---|---|
| 19.8 *Sunday Dispatch* (Cont.) | and Det. Serg. Charles Hewett will visit Eastbourne tomorrow… As a result of inquiries by the Eastbourne Police it is possible that exhumations will take place. Senior officers of Eastbourne police visited the Yard last week and talked to murder squad detectives and officials of the D. of P.P. | What could be more likely to resuscitate [speculation]. |
| 20.8 *Daily Mail* | Six women in murder riddle. Det.Supt.Herbert Hannam of Scotland Yard's murder squad has been called in by the Police at Eastbourne to start a lengthy inquiry into alleged fraud, which may develop into a murder investigation. He will interview the relatives of at least six wealthy women who have died here in the past ten years. Two women at least may be exhumed. <u>Mr Hannam is expected to interview the relatives of Mrs Edith Alice Morrell a wealthy widow who died at 82, after a stroke here in 1950. Mr Walker said tonight, 'It is true I have consulted with Mr Hannam at Scotland Yard with the result that he is expected down here very shortly.'</u> Earlier today Mr Walker spent four hours with Dr A.C. Sommerville, the East Sussex Coroner at his home at East Grinstead. | At this time I had not heard of Mrs Morrell and it did not appear in the Eastbourne Police file which had been loaned to me. |
| 20.8 *Daily Sketch* | Seaside mystery of 13 rich women. Det.Supt. Hannam of Scotland Yard's murder squad will arrive here tomorrow morning. I understand he may also investigate the deaths of at least twelve other women. Reference is made to Mr Walker's visit to East Grinstead and to Mrs Morrell about whom detailed comment is made. | |
| 20.8 *Daily Telegraph* | Yard inquiry into deaths of rich widows. Town's dossier covers ten years. – similar to above thereafter - | |
| 20.8 *Evening Standard* | Deaths of 300 women to be probed. | |
| 21.8 *The Times* | Scotland Yard to help at Eastbourne. The Chief | If true a further |

| | | |
|---|---|---|
| 21.8 *The Times* (Cont.) | Constable of Eastbourne told a Press Conference that he had called in the Yard, 'because the situation has changed during the past fortnight'. | whetting of interest and encouragement for publicity. |
| 21.8 *Daily Mail* | Yard study wills of 300 women in £1m probe. A million pounds – that is the amount involved in an investigation of alleged fraud on wealthy women which Scotland Yard men will start here tomorrow. And if a gigantic swindle is discovered an immediate murder probe will begin. | This is the day I arrived in East-bourne for the inquest but these publications preced-ed me. Press seen at E. in evening and told I had no info. to give them. |
| 22.8 All papers | Reported full details of inquest on Mrs Hullett. | |
| 22.8 *Daily Mail* | Yard probe mass poisoning. 25 deaths in the great mystery of Eastbourne. Inquiry into 400 wills. Rich women believed to be victims. Scotland Yard Murder Squad is to investigate the suspected mass poisoning of wealthy women in Eastbourne during the past 20 years. | At this time I had no conversation with the Press. |
| 22.8 *Daily Mirror* | Rich widow drama. Suicide verdict-C.I.D. to probe 12 other deaths. | |
| 22.8 *The Times* | The Coroner called Det.Supt.Hannam and said he understood that the Chief Constable of East-bourne had invoked the aid of Scotland Yard to investigate certain deaths in the neighbourhood. | |
| 22.8 *Evening Standard* | Mystery of the 300 women. Yard probing hyp-notic killer theory. Ten years of murder? Police probing the deaths of more than 300 Eastbourne women believe that a killer may have been at large in the town for 10 years. This theory has been reported to Scotland Yard and senior offi-cers have been told to investigate it. | |
| 23.8 *The Daily Herald* | 40 Yard men probe Eastbourne wills. Ten rich | |

| | |
|---|---|
| 23.8 *The Daily Herald* (Cont.) | women to be exhumed. Mrs Morrell was mentioned again in this article as also was a lady named Chessum whom we have no knowledge of to this day. |

| | |
|---|---|
| 23.8 *Daily Telegraph* | Bodies of 3 women may be exhumed. Police theory of hypnotism. Check to be made on wills. Scotland Yard officers led by Det.Supt. Herbert Hannam who are investigating the deaths of a number of women in Eastbourne and district over the past ten years will not hesitate, I understand, to apply for exhumation orders if they are considered necessary. |

| | | |
|---|---|---|
| 23.8 *Daily Express* | The truth about Eastbourne. A conference was held at Scotland Yard last night. It followed an unprecedented flood of rumours and allegations that a mass murderer was at work in Eastbourne. These reached such proportions that the Chief Constable of Eastbourne felt that an investigation by his officers would not carry sufficient weight to clear up the matter once and for all. He, therefore, asked for the help of the Yard. Allegation: – 400 wealthy widows have been murdered. Untrue. Allegation: – The murderer has been at work for 20 years. Untrue. Allegation: The sum of a million pounds is involved. Untrue. | I wrote a very brief letter to Mr Percy Hoskins the chief crime reporter of the *Daily Express* thanking him for this sensible report. |

| | |
|---|---|
| 23.8 *Daily Mail* | Yard may exhume ten women. Supt.Hannam of Scotland Yard will arrive here tomorrow with a list of ten women who may be exhumed in the Yard's most sensational murder inquiry. |

| | |
|---|---|
| 23.8 *Evening Standard* | Help the Police call by Eastbourne Mayor. Yard men tour the town. Hannam to probe 20 deaths. Det.Supt. Hannam of Scotland Yard took ten minutes to confer with local police when he arrived in Eastbourne today to probe the deaths of more than 300 women in the resort in the past |

| | | |
|---|---|---|
| *23.8 Evening Standard* (Cont.) | 10 years. Then he drove off to begin a series of interviews with Eastbourne people who may be able to help in his inquiries. | |
| *23.8 Evening Argus* | Hannam dodges the Press. Scotland Yard's Det.Supt.Hannam who is in charge of 'murder' inquiries arrived in Eastbourne today. After going to his hotel he was driven to police HQ by a roundabout route to dodge reporters waiting for him at the main entrance. He had a short conference with the Chief Constable and then went to offices which have been reserved for him by Eastbourne police to spend several hours going through reports. 'It may be days before he has anything to say to you,' said a spokesman. | At 5 p.m. this day bec. of Press overwhelming the police HQ I held a press conference. About forty were present. A shorthand note was taken and a transcript is attached. |
| *24.8 Daily Express* | Yard detective slams widow rumours. The Express rumours were dispelled at a five minute press conference by Supt.Hannam. The Supt. had nothing to say which might indicate any definite development in the inquiry. | |

No other newspaper referred on this day to my press conference but in the main continued their sensational technique. All press reports referred to herein are in my possession.

——◆——

# Dangerous Drugs Found in Dr Adams' Possession by Police

——◆——

Hannam's Second Report recorded that the two bottles of morphine concealed by Dr Adams at the time of the search of Kent Lodge on 24th November, 1956 are those in Parcel 'A'. The others were mostly in his black bag which lay unlocked on the floor of the surgery; Dr Adams, when asked 'to pick out for the Inspector all the dangerous drugs', from the brown bag which he had fetched from his car, produced one tin, which is included in this list, but, as can be seen from the brown bag list it was not all the dangerous drugs.

|  | Drug | Total Quantity D.D.A. |
|---|---|---|
| Parcel 'A' | 2 x 10cc bottles Morphine 'Hyperduric' | 5 ½ grains |

Dangerous Drug contents of Black bag, surgery and one tin from Brown Bag

| | Drug | Total Quantity D.D.A. |
|---|---|---|
| Parcel 'B' | 10cc Bottle Morphine 'Hyperduric' | 5 grains |
| | 1cc Ampoule Morphine 'Hyperduric' | ½ grain |
| | 1cc 'Tubunic' ampoule syringe Morphine | ⅙ grain |
| | ⅙th grain Morphine Sulphate tabs. | 1⅚ths grains |
| | ¼ grain Morphine Sulphate | 2¼ grains |
| | ⅓rd grain Omnopon | 5 grains |
| | ⅓rd grain Omnopon | 2⅔rds grains |
| | 1cc Ampoule | ⅓rd grain |
| | Omnopon with Scopolamine | 2 grains |
| | 1cc 'Tubunic' Ampoule Syringe Omnopon | ⅓rd grain |
| | ⅙th grain Diamorphine Hydrochloride | 2 grains |
| | ⅟₂₀th grain Cocaine Hydrochloride | ⅗ths grain |
| Parcel 'C' | 10cc Bottle Morphine 'Hyperduric' | 1 grain |

| | Drug | Total Quantity D.D.A. |
|---|---|---|
| | $\frac{1}{3}$rd grain Omnopon | 7 grains |
| | $\frac{1}{6}$th grain Diamorphine Hydrochloride | $1\frac{1}{2}$ grains |
| | $\frac{1}{50}$th grain Cocaine Hydrochloride | 223 $\frac{1}{50}$th grains |
| Parcel 'D' | 1 cc Ampoules Morphine 'Hyperduric' | 1 grain |
| | 1 cc Ampoules Omnopon | 4 grains |
| | 2 cc Ampoules Pethidine Hydrochloride | 100 mgm |
| | 25 mgm Pethidine Hydrochloride | 925 mgm |
| | 50 mgm Pethidine Hydrochloride | 400 mgm |
| | 5 mgm Physeptone | 510 mgm |
| Parcel 'E' | $\frac{1}{4}$ grain Morphine Sulphate | 3 grains |
| | $\frac{1}{6}$th grain Diamorphine Hydrochloride | $1\frac{1}{6}$ths grains |

Contents of Brown Bag

1. 1, 1cc Hyperdermic Syringe in steel container.
2. 1, cc ditto
3. 1, 2cc Hyperdermic Syringe and six needles in white container.
4. 1, white metal box containing Sphygnomanometer
5. 1, Canvas holdall containing surgical instruments.
6. 1, pair Forceps.
7. 1, pair of Surgical scissors.
8. 2, rolls of Gauze.
9. 3, rolls of Elastoplast.
10. 1, tin Elastoplast dressings.
11. 1, tin Penicillin Nonad Tulle.
12. 1, Albucid Nasal Spray.
13. 1, Tes tape in plastic container.
14. 1, Plastic container containing capsules of:
    Seconal Sodium 1½ grs. (Barbiturate), Amytal 1½ grs. (Barbiturate),
    Tuinal 1½ grs. (Barbiturate)
15. 1, Bottle containing 10 tablets of Sulpenin.
16. 1, Bottle containing 10 capsules of Carbital (Phenobarbitone Sodium)
17. 1, Bottle containing Bardase tablets. (Hyosyamine Sulphate) (Phenobarbitone)
18. Box containing 4 vials of Crystamycin
19. Box containing bottle of Albucid, eye drops.
20. 4 Vials of Penidural.
21. 1, Bottle marked Alophen containing pills. (laxative)
22. 2 tins, containing tablets marked Soneryl. (butobaritone)
23. 1, Bottle containing tablets, name J.B. Adams thereon.

24. 1, Metal tin containing finger sheaths.
25. 1, Bottle marked Numbutal containing tablets. (Pentobarbital)
26. 1, tin marked Seconal Sodium containing capsules. (Barbiturate)
27. 1, container, containing Veganin tablets.
28. 1, tin containing Amyl Nitrite sachets.
29. 10 packets marked 'Saridone' containing tablets.
30. 1, tube marked Chloromycetin Cream.
31. 1, tube marked Bornolin.
32. 1, tin marked Sedormid tablets.
33. 1, Bottle marked Nembudeine, containing tablets. (Phenobarbitone sodium + codeine.
34. 1, Green tube marked "A.H." [Alfred Hullett?]
35. 1, Vial of iodine.
36. 1, Box containing 3 ampules of Apyrogen. (sterile fluid)
37. 1, Blue box containing tablets.
38. 1, Box marked Sodium Morrhuate containing 3 ampules. [Very dangerous except to obliterate varicose veins - causes blood clots.]
39. 1, card containing seven safety pins.
40. 1, box containing 6 ampule syringes.
41. 1, Carton marked Mersalyl B.D.H. containing 2 ampules. [toxic mercury salt, formerly used as diuretic.]
42. 1, box marked Emergency Sutures, containing 8 phials.
43. 1, carton marked Omnopon Scopolamine, containing 2 ampules. [Scopolamine causes amnesia]
44. 6, Bottles containing tablets and 2 bottles containing liquid. [unmarked]
45. 1, pad of Form E.C.10.
46. 1, memo pad.
47. 2, bandages.
48. 2 pieces of rubber tubing.
49. 1, Box containing Inspection instruments.

All handed back to Hempsons, Defence solicitors on 11.2.57 by Sergeant Hewett and not used as Exhibits.

Note: 1 grain = 0.0648 grams

# Dr Ashby's Summary of Drugs used by Dr Adams

**Morphine**   Derivative of Opium / Depresses respiration / Lowers appreciation of pain / Some general depressing effect on brain / Hypnotic / Spinal cord is stimulated [Not true – See 'An Independent Medical Opinion'. Was not known in 1957.] / Normal dose, $\frac{1}{8}$th to $\frac{1}{3}$rd grain, maximum $\frac{1}{2}$ grain.
Main Points: There is only one purpose for which this drug can be given for prolonged periods, and that is severe pain due to incurable disease, which for practical purposes means inoperable cancer. The grave dangers of producing addiction prevent its prolonged use otherwise.

**Heroin**   Synthetic drug made from Morphine, action very similar / More dangerous as depresser of respiration / Much more dangerous as regards addiction / A greater stimulating effect on spinal cord. [Not true – see above Morphine] / Convulsions can be caused by over-dosage. / Dose $\frac{1}{12}$th to $\frac{1}{6}$th grain, maximum quantity in 24 hours, $\frac{1}{4}$ grain.

**Omnopon**   Prepared from Opium and contains all ingredients including 50% by weight of Morphine / In practice $\frac{1}{3}$rd grain Omnopon = $\frac{1}{4}$ grain morphine / 4 grains of Omnopon = 3 grains of Morphine / Action similar to Morphine and mainly resulting from the Morphine contents.

**Pethidine**   Synthetic substitute for Morphine / Reduced appreciation of pain with less of a depressing effect on brain as compared with Morphine / Addiction is a danger / Maximum therapeutic dose, $1\frac{1}{2}$ grains.

**Barbiturates**   Action: Depress the whole central nervous system, brain and spinal cord / Negligible effect on pain / Coma from overdose shows no stimulation effects such as spasms or convulsions / Liable to produce loss of memory, drowsiness, lassitude and depression / General mental and physical sluggishness.

**Pheno-barbitone**  Slow acting, lasting 6-8 hours / May accumulate as eliminated slowly.

**Allonal**  Barbiturate drug of addiction contains amidopyrine to help suppress pain, but this latter is dangerous as a blood poison and has been largely given up as death can result [See An Independent Medical Opinion] / Dose, 1-2 tablets as sedative or Hypnotic / 2-4 tablets as analgesic and Hypnotic.

**Veramon**  Similar to Allonal / Also contains Amidopyrine / Dose 1-2 tablets.

**Medinal**  Barbiturate / Sodium Barbitone, used mainly as an Hypnotic / Dose, 5-10 grains.

**Nembutal**  Pentobarbitone / Rapidly acting barbiturate / Dose, 1½ to 3 grains / Regarded as dangerous if used with more than very small doses of Morphia.

**Amytal**  Barbiturate / Slow acting like Phenobarbitone / Dose, as Sedative ⅓rd to ¾qtrs grain / Hypnotic 1½ to 5 grains.

**Seconal**  Quick and short acting Barbiturate / Dose, ¾qtrs to 3 grains

**Sedormid**  The proprietary name for sleeping drug which is not a barbiturate but which has a similar action to barbitone though milder / Each tablet contains 4 grains / Dose, 1 to 2 tablets.

**Thiopentone (Pentothal)**  Barbiturate given as an anaesthetic / Acts very quickly when put into a vein.

**Paraldehyde**  A relatively safe soporific used as a sedative, to induce sleep and to suppress convulsions / It may be given by mouth or intramuscular injection / The full dose by either route is 120 minims = 8cc (4 oz. = 120cc is 15 times the full dose) / Death may follow 5 times the normal dose / [See also 'An Independent Medical Opinion'].

**Methedrine**  Stimulates the brain, can counteract the depressive effect of barbiturates and other sedatives.

# Notes on Medicines

**Anethaine Ointment**   Local anaesthetic ointment.

**Benzedrine Tablets**   Given before breakfast to awaken patient.

**Dexedrine Tablets**   Similar to Benzedrine and Methedrine [Dexadrine is an amphetamine, now a controlled drug. In the past it was often used as an appetite suppressant. Benzedrine is a more potent cousin, and methedrine is also an amphetamine. All are addictive. Amphetamines work by suppressing all spontaneous behaviour, reducing socialising characteristics and causes an increase in obsessive-compulsive behaviours. Side effects can include: irritability, liver irritation/toxicity, increased heart rate, tics, Tourette's syndrome, insomnia, dry mouth, behaviour disturbances, thought disorder, and high blood pressure.]

**Nupercainal**   Ointment – local anaesthetic / Irritation or piles.

**Balmosa Liniment**   Wintergreen cream for muscular pain.

**Luminal**   Proprietary name for Phenobarbitone.

**Opium Tablets**   This could be either Oral Omnopon or Dover Tablet.

**Coramine Injection**   Nikethamide by proprietary name / Stimulant.

**Enema Saponis**   Enema of warm water and green soft soap.

**Atropine**   Given by injection / First stimulates and then depresses central nervous system / Lessens secretions of saliva, bronchial secretions / Prevents sickness. / Given with morphine to reduce bronchial secretion / Used in treatment of renal and biliary colic.

# Eastbourne Doctors

---+---

These are notes from *A Century of Eastbourne Doctors 1883-1983* in the Eastbourne Medical Society Centenary Edition of the Eastbourne Medical Gazette. When this was compiled, Dr Adams was still alive and practising.

ADAMS, John B. MB BCh BAO 1921 (Belfast) DPH MD DA. Joined the 6 College Road (Red House) practice in 1922 after hospital posts in Bristol. Became anaesthetist on the staff of the Princess Alice hospital. During the 1939-45 war helped to keep the practice going with Laurie and Gwen Snowball. Resigned from the practice in 1958. Still active in medicine and his favourite sport of clay pigeon shooting.

BARKWORTH, F. Basil S. MB BS 1945 (Guys). Worked as Medical Officer at the Mildmay Mission hospital before RAMC service, mostly in Palestine and North Africa as a graded Radiologist. On July 1st 1948 became a partner at the 6 College Road practice. Married Beryl a Guy's nurse and has three sons – one an accountant in Bristol, one teaches chemistry and John is a local osteopath. Retired 1982. Main interests are Christian witness locally through the work of the Victoria Baptist Church. President of the Medical Society 1971.

ESTCOURT, H. Geoffrey. MBE MRCS LRCP (Middlesex) MB BS FRCSE. Born 1901 he qualified in 1924 an joined the White House practice in 1926. In 1936 he was appointed to the staff of the Princess Alice hospital and developed a special interest in abdominal and thyroid surgery. During the 1939-45 war he was with a field surgical unit and took part in the landings in Sicily, Salerno, Castellamare and Anzio. President of Eastbourne Medical Society in 1947. He retired in 1966. Died 1980. His charming manner made him a popular figure.

GRAY, Norman HDD RCS (Edin.) LDS (Liverpool) Well known Dental Practitioner. Consultant Dental Surgeon to the Eastbourne hospitals 1948-60. After spending a year in the Angle School in Philadelphia, USA, he became one of the few people in this country treating cases with fixed appliances and using gold wire before the introduction of stainless steel. Was Secretary of the European Orthodontic Society and President of the British Society for the Study of Orthodontics. [Member of Plymouth Brethren and friend of Dr Adams.]

HARRIS, R. Vincent MB BS MRCS LRCP 1933 (St. Barts.) DCH MD. Was House Physician at the Royal Northern Hospital. Came to Eastbourne in 1937 and joined the Adams, Williams and Snowball practice, also worked as a Clinical Assistant at the St. John's Hospital for Diseases of the Skin, London. Joined the T.A. in 1939 and at the outbreak of war was with the local 21st BMH. Later sent to India as Specialist in Dermatology and was Adviser in Dermatology to the 14th Army. On returning to Eastbourne started the first skin clinic in 1947 at the Princess Alice Hospital. Retired from hospital work in 1975 and general practice in 1979.

MATHEW, Philip W. MRCS LRCP 1907 (Middlesex). Practised in Ceylon before joining the Rook, Wilson, Hall practice in 1923. He gave anaesthetics for the firm and was anaesthetist at Hellingly Hospital for over 20 years. Was the General Organising Secretary of the BMA 99th A.G.M. held at Eastbourne in 1931. President of the Medical Society in 1935. Secretary of the Local Medical War Committee during the 1939-45 War. Retired from NHS in 1959 and died in 1974, aged 90.

SHERA, A. Geoffrey. MA MRCS LRCP 1914 (Cambridge and UCH) MD FRCPath. Consultant Pathologist to the Eastbourne Hospitals 1919-1954. In 1915 during part of his Army Service was posted to the Military Hospital, Eastbourne. A founder member of the Association of Clinical Pathologists. Isolated Salmonella Eastbourne in 1931. Chairman Eastbourne Division BMA in 1933. President of the Medical Society 1934. Wrote many papers on intestinal spirochaetosis. Had an inventive mind – among his devices were a type of coronary artery scissors and a thermostatic bath for warming transfusion blood. He arranged the first blood transfusion in Eastbourne, giving 2 pints in 1924. Died in 1971.

SNOWBALL, Lawrence AH. MB BS MRCS LRCP 1930 (Kings) FRCSE MRCP. Great athlete and captained the hospital tennis team. Did house jobs at KCH and Hampstead. For some years he was a missionary in China. Joined the 6 College Road practice in 1935 and was appointed on the surgical staff of Princess Alice Hospital in 1937. Received a commendation for his work through the air raids, when his wife Gwen also helped out. Consultant Orthopaedic Surgeon until his retirement in 1967 when he continued as GP. Died in 1979 aged 74. Chairman of local BMA Division in 1949 and President of Sussex Branch 1950, when he was President of the Medical Society he was also an active member of the Gideons International Movement.

SOMERVILLE, Angus C. MRCS LRCP 1923 (Kings). Had a practice in East Grinstead. Assistant Coroner East Sussex, Lewes Division (which included Eastbourne) 1943-8. Coroner 1948-74. Died 1981. Shrewd and kindly, but presented a frosty, irascible exterior, all part of preserving the dignity of his office. Estimated he handled 160,000 cases. 'One can't say one has enjoyed the job, but I have found the cases interesting!' Always tried to avoid an inquest if possible for the relatives' sake – so when he broke his hip the year after retirement his former pathologists sent him a get well message with the words 'and don't worry we will put the fracture in Part II of the death certificate so it won't need an inquest'.

# Appendix VI

# Certifications of Death

# by Dr Adams

## 1946 – 1956

An asterix denotes a nursing/retirement home

| | Patient | Age | Date | Cause of Death (a) / (b) / (c) | Place of Death |
|---|---|---|---|---|---|
| 1 | Absale, Caroline Ada | 83 | 25.1.50 | Myocardial degeneration | Home |
| 2 | Adams, Annie | 75 | 19.10.49 | Myocardial failure | Home |
| 3 | Adams, Ellen (His Mother) | | 3.4.43 | | Home |
| 4 | Adams, Julia | 71 | 28.1.47 | Coronary thrombosis | S. Teresa* |
| 5 | Alexander, Cyril Wilson | 67 | 26.5.47 | Myocardial failure | Home |
| 6 | Allen, Thomas Gaskell | 87 | 22.8.55 | Syncope / Paralysis Agitens | Home |
| 7 | Anderson, John Kerr | 82 | 28.8.53 | Myocardial failure | Esperance* |
| 8 | Angell, Robert | 79 | 2.1.52 | Coronary thrombosis | Home |
| 9 | Armitage, Charlotte | 82 | 27.9.46 | Cerebral thrombosis | Olinda* |
| 10 | Armour, Margaretta Agnes | 69 | 15.2.53 | Coronary thrombosis | Home |
| 11 | Atkinson, Agnes McKinnon | 76 | 26.3.55 | Myocardial failure / Acute Nephritis | Esperance* |
| 12 | Attfield, Ellen May | 70 | 31.12.54 | Cerebral haemorrhage / Cardio vasc.deg | Olinda* |
| 13 | Avann, Florence Annie | 66 | 24.3.53 | Carcinoma of stomach / Cardio vasc deg Fractured neck of femur. | Home |
| 14 | Avann, Frank | 60 | 14.2.55 | Cerebral haemorrhage / Cardio vasc deg | Home |
| 15 | Bale, Jessie Dunbar | 78 | 16.8.48 | Cerebral thrombosis / Cardio vasc deg | Olinda* |
| 17 | Barker, William Henry | 77 | 18.11.47 | Uraemia | Home |
| 18 | Barr, Cora Evelyn | 73 | 23.3.52 | Cerebral Thrombosis / Cardio vasc deg | Olinda* |
| 19 | Barrett, Wm. James Bevins (Visitor) | 66 | 13.7.51 | Coronary Thrombosis / Carcinoma of breast | Home |
| 20 | Bates, Ethel | 69 | 24.1.51 | Myocardial failure / Cardio vasc deg | Olinda* |
| 21 | Bevan-Williams, Antonia R. | 83 | 20.1.46 | Myocardial failure / Cardio vasc deg | Olinda* |
| 22 | Bickley, Max (Visitor) | 86 | 30.7.50 | Coronary thrombosis / Pontine Haemorrhage | Berrow* |
| 23. | Billings, Edith Ann | 84 | 14.4.48 | Pernicious Anaemia / Heart block | Tredegar* |
| 24. | Blagrove, Percy Althonso Harry | 74 | 9.2.54. | Uraemia / Cardio Vasc deg | Home |
| 25. | Blanco, Angel | 57 | 22.4.47 | Cerebral thrombosis / Cardio vasc Deg | Home |
| 27. | Blanco, Esther | 54 | 27.10.46 | Uraemia / Primary carcinoma of breast | Home |
| 28. | Blundell Jane | 88 | 4.12.39 | Myocardial degeneration / Carcinoma of Sigmoid Colon | Home |

| 29. | Blunt, George | | 19.4.55 | Cerebral thrombosis | Home |
|---|---|---|---|---|---|
| 30 | Boehm, Brian Keith | 17 | 3.1.53. | Acute myocarditis | Home |
| 31 | Boles, Clara Annie | 85 | 29.12.53 | Cerebral Haemorrhage | Home |
| 32 | Bolton, Annie Dorothea Visitor | 70 | 7.11.51 | Cerebral thrombosis | Home |
| 33 | Booty, Horatio Edwin | 85 | 14.5.49 | Coronary thrombosis / Uraemia / General Arteric Sclerosis | Manor Hall* |
| 34 | Bowdler, Edith | 91 | 9.10.50 | Myocardial failure | Barton* |
| 35 | Bradnum, Julia | 84 | 27.05.52 | Cerebral haemorrhage | Home |
| 36 | Bradshaw, John | 83 | 28.9.49 | Bulbar paralysis / Cardio Vasc Deg | |
| 37 | Braidwood, Harold Lithgow | 76 | 5.7.49 | Cerebral thrombosis / Operation for acute intestinal obstruction. | Nursing Home Esperance* |
| 38 | Brierley, Constance Marion | 80 | 26.12.53 | Uraemic Coma / Chronic nephritis and pyelitis | Hotel resident |
| 39 | Bristow, Herbert George | 81 | 24.3.50 | Cerebral thrombosis / Cardio vasc deg | Manor Hall* |
| 40 | Brutton, Laura Mary | 78 | 3.12.51 | Cerebral Thrombosis / Cardio vasc deg | Esperance* |
| 41 | Bucks, Elizabeth | 92 | 3.3.47 | Cerebral thrombosis / Cardio vasc deg | Olinda* |
| 42 | Burnage, Valerie Ann | 0.6 | 3.4.46 | Acute nephritis | Home |
| 43 | Bush, Eva Margaret | 85 | 21.12.48 | Cerebral thrombosis | Barton* |
| 44 | Butler, Frederick | 76 | 23.2.47 | Myocardial failure | Home |
| 45 | Butler, Henrietta | 82 | 4.1.56 | Broncho-pneumonia | Home |
| 46 | Cannon, Clare | 84 | 14.4.48 | Uraemia / Cardio vasc deg | Home |
| 47 | Cave,Dorothy Piesse | 63 | 5.2.51 | Cerebral haemorrhage / Primary in breast | Esperance* |
| 48 | Cavendish, Edward William Duke of Devonshire | 55 | 26.11.50 | Coronary thrombosis / Cardio vasc deg | Tredegar* |
| 49 | Cavill, Florence Emily | 86 | 9.5.54 | Cerebral haemorrhage | Home |
| 50 | Cawdron, Amelia Belinda Clarke | 77 | 20.7.53 | Cerebral Haemorrhage / Asthma chronic | Home |
| 51 | Chandler, Alfred Lincoln, | 58 | 2.11.49 | Carcinoma of prostate / Cardio vasc deg | Home |
| 52 | Chasey, Ethel | 68 | 24.11.48 | Broncho pneumonia chronic bronchitis / pulmonary fibrositis / Cardio vasc deg | Esperance* |
| 53 | Chesterman, Maud Mary | 76 | 11.10.51 | Uraemia | Home |
| 54 | Chilton, Elizabeth | 64 | 6.2.51 | Pernicious anaemia / Carcinoma of rectum | Home |
| 55 | Christie, Philip Norman | 39 | 27.4.48 | Cerebral thrombosis / Renal Degeneration | Southfields* |
| 56 | Clark, Samuel Chapman | 87 | 3.6.54 | Myocardial failure / Carcinoma of ovary | Nursing Home |
| 57 | Clemence, Annie | 97 | 8.1.53 | Myocardial failure / Cirrhosis of liver / Cholaemia | Hotel resident |
| 58 | Clifford, Henry William | 86 | 11.5.53 | Myocardial failure / Cardio vasc deg | Home |
| 50 | Clogg, Gertrude Maud | 74 | 12.12.52 | Cerebral thrombosis | Home |
| 60 | Cockhead, Leslie George | 86 | 15.12.47 | Uraemia | Home |
| 61 | Cofman-Nicoresti, Joseph | 85 ' | 28.4.56 | Coronary thrombosis. | Esperance* |
| 62 | Collier, Guy | 74 | 18.4.49 | Cholaemia | Esperance* |
| 63 | Collings, Richard William | 86 | 30.4.51 | Cerebral thrombosis | Home |
| 64 | Commons, Stephen Richard | 40 | 6.1.49 | Myocardial failure / Fibrosis of lung | Hotel resident |
| 65 | Cooper, Harold St. Clare (Visitor) | 64 | 4.3.53 | Cerebral haemorrhage | Olinda* |
| 66 | Cooper, Mary Catherine (Hotel guest) | 85 | 16.4.49 | Cerebral thrombosis | Sandhurst Hotel |
| 67 | Cooper, William | 80 | 23.1.53 | Myocardial failure / Cardio vasc deg | Grassington Road* |
| 68 | Cornes, Maria Davidson (Visitor) | 75 | 14.6.44 | Occlusion of left coronary artery | Olinda* |
| 69 | Couper, Ada Lucy | 85 | 14.11.51 | Myocardial failure / Cardio vasc deg | Home |
| 70 | Couper, Edward Edmonstone | 93 | 3.11.54 | Myocardial failure / Primary carcinoma of liver. | Hotel resident |
| 71 | Cox, Frank James | 68 | 28.4.49 | Myocardial degeneration / Septic influensal septicaemia. | Hotel resident |
| 72 | Cradock, Percy Stanley | 73 | 27.9.46 | Uraemia / Cardio vasc deg | (not known) |
| 73 | Crook, Thomas William (Hotel guest) | 82 | 12.8.48 | Carcinoma of rectum | Victoria Court Hotel |
| 74 | Daniels, May | 65 | 20.3.52 | Carcinoma of lung | Home |
| 75 | Dawbarn, Emily | 87 | 20.3.46 | Gangrene of foot / Cardio vasc deg | Home |
| 76 | Dawson, Emily Ada (Hotel guest) | 78 | 24.11.55 | Uraemia    Cardio vasc deg | Grand Hotel |
| 77 | Day, Bessie Sarah | 68 | 10.3.52 | Cerebral thrombosis / Renal sclerosis | Esperance* |
| 78 | Dear, John | 82 | 16.5.53 | Uraemia | Relative's Home |

| 79 | Devis, Louise Colley | 62 | 26.8.53 | Myocardial failure / acute pyelitis | Home |
|---|---|---|---|---|---|
| 80 | Dixon, Arthur Cyril Stanley | 82 | 13.8.55 | Coronary thrombosis / Cardio vasc deg | Esperance* |
| 81 | Dodd, Edward Montague | 56 | 5.8.53 | Cerebral thrombosis / Cardio vasc deg | Olinda* |
| 82 | Downs, James Priestley | 88 | 30.5.55 | Cerebral thrombosis / Cardio vasc deg | Home |
| 83 | Downs, Jane Elizabeth I'Anson (Hotel Guest) | 71 | 26.10.49 | Carcinoma of breast / Chronic bronchitis and asthma | Victoria Court Hotel |
| 84 | Draper, William Norman | | 9.4.48 | Uraemia / Cardio vasc deg | Hotel resident |
| 85 | Eallace, Edith Mary | 78 | 30.3.50 | Myocardial failure / Carcinoma of prostate | Home |
| 86 | Eatough, Ida | 55 | 25.11.52 | Myocardial failure / Renal congestion / Cardio-vascular degeneration | Home |
| 87 | Edwards, Mary Ann | 86 | 19.2.55 | Cerebral Haemorrhage / Operation for acute intestinal obstruction | Esperance* |
| 88 | Ellison, Alice Maud | 71 | 20.2.47 | Nephritis / Cardio vasc deg | Home |
| 89 | Ellison, Clara | 75 | 29.10.50 | Myocardial failure / Cardio vasc deg | Home |
| 90 | Evans, Alfred Henry | 78 | 17.11.48 | Cerebral haemorrhage / Fibrositis of liver. | Home |
| 91 | Facer, Mary Ellen | 82 | 29.3.52 | Bulbar paralysis | Home |
| 92 | Faldo, Harry Herbert | 73 | 11.8.46 | Cerebral thrombosis / Cardio vasc deg | Home |
| 93 | Fawcett, Nancy (*otherwise* Ann Corker; Visitor) | 74 | 16.2.51 | Diabetic coma /Cardio vasc deg | Nursing Home |
| 94 | Fawcus, Gladys Constance | 62 | 2.7.49 | Carcinoma of liver / Cerebral thrombosis. | Home |
| 95 | Fielding, Frederick | 84 | 18.10.48 | Uraemia / Cardio vasc deg | Esperance* |
| 96 | Fielding, George | 89 | 18.7.49 | Cerebral thrombosis | Esperance* |
| 97 | Fletcher Susan. | 86 | 25.3.52 | Cerebral Thrombosis | Home |
| 98 | Fletcher, Edith Matilda | 53 | 27.2.48 | Malignant ovarian cyst | Esperance* |
| 99 | Foster, Dora | 65 | 13.12.50 | Uraemia and cholaemia / cerebral thrombosis. | Esperance* |
| 100 | Fowler, Albert | 74 | 20.2.47 | Cerebral haemorrhage / Cardio vasc deg | Tredegar* |
| 101 | Fox, Agnes Gertrude | 74 | 17.1.51 | Cerebral haemorrhage / Cardio vasc deg | Highland Lodge* |
| 102 | Freebody, Olive Mabel | 41 | 18.8.48 | Cerebral haemorrhage / Cardio vasc deg | Home |
| 103 | Giles, Beatrice Ethel | 72 | 31.12.50 | Uraemia / Cardio vasc deg | Manor Hall* |
| 104 | Gilford, Kathleen Vera | 64 | 19.1.49 | Cerebral thrombosis | Home |
| 105 | Gillies, Alan Merrylees | 68 | 18.11.54 | Cholaemia | Home |
| 106 | Goldsmith, Emily Ellen | 82 | 8.2.56. | Cerebral haemorrhage | Home |
| 107 | Goodrich, Mary Eliz. W. | 65 | 18.10.51 | Cerebral Thrombosis / renal degeneration | Home |
| 108 | Gore, Lilian Wilmot Reid | 84 | 31.3.49 | Myocardial failure | Home |
| 109 | Gore-Browne, Daisy Anne | 79 | 24.1.54 | Cerebral Thrombosis / Nephritis | Home |
| 110 | Goulston, John, | 77 | 5.12.50 | Uraemia / Carcinoma of Prostate | Home |
| 111 | Gover, William George | 86 | 13.10.49 | Myocardial failure / Nephritis | Home |
| 112 | Gow, Norman (Visitor) | 69 | 9.1.48 | Myocardial degeneration | Home |
| 113 | Gower, Edith Winifred | 62 | 11.10.52 | Secondary carcinoma of lung | Home |
| 114 | Greem, Annie Eliz | 90 | 27.11.52 | Cerebral Thrombosis | Home |
| 115 | Gregory, Louisa | 60 | 1.1.46 | Cerebral thrombosis / Acute nephritis | Home |
| 116 | Grinyer, Fanny Elizabeth | 81 | 25.7.49 | Cerebral haemorrhage | Home |
| 117 | Hacker, William Albert | 74 | 25.2.54 | Uraemia | Home |
| 118 | Haggar, John Robert | 81 | 9.2.53 | Cerebral thrombosis | Home |
| 119 | Haggar, Laura | 77 | 8.4.54 | Coronorary Thrombosis | Home |
| 120 | Hamblin, Rosa | 82 | 7.11.49 | Cerebral thrombosis | Home |
| 121 | Hamilton, Helen Eliza | 88 | 18.2.46 | Coronary thrombosis. | Home |
| 122 | Hansor, Fanny Edith | 73 | 17.1.46 | Myocardial failure / Senility | Home |
| 123 | Hargroves, Elizabeth Pamela | 90 | 12.11.46 | Myocardial failure / Cardio vasc deg | Home |
| 124 | Harris, Dora | 91 | 5.8.55 | Myocardial failure | Home |
| 125 | Harris, Hannah | 77 | 3.4.46 | Diabetic coma. | Home |
| 126 | Harrod, Olive Mary. | 70 | 23.3.51 | Cerebral Thrombosis | Home |
| 127 | Hawes, Rose | 88 | 16.4.50 | cerebral thrombosis | Home |
| 128 | Haynes, Sidney Harold | 66 | 20.5.51 | Myocardial failure | Home |
| 129 | Henley, Edward Cornish | 84 | 13.1.56 | Uraemia | Nursing Home |
| 130 | Henry, Sarah Florence Jane (his Cousin) | 51 | 9.6.52 | Secondary carcinoma / burns on leg | Home |
| 131 | Herbert, Irene | | 5.8.44 | (Not Signed By Dr. Adams) | Home |

| 132 | Hier-Davies, Harry | 81 | 29.6.51 | Cerebral thrombosis. | Grassington Road* |
| 133 | Highwood, Keble John | 71 | 20.7.48 | Coronary thrombosis | Nursing Home |
| 134 | Hill, Cicely Grant | 74 | 5.3.54 | Cerebral Haemorrhage | Home |
| 135 | Hill, William Henry | 54 | 13.7.51 | Carcinoma of rectum / senile arterial degeneration. | Home |
| 136 | Holland, William Heap | 78 | 22.5.52 | Cholaemia | Home |
| 137 | Hollands, Albert C. W. | 49 | 2.6.49 | Coronary thrombosis | Home |
| 138 | Holman, John | 85 | 27.1.46 | Chronic nephritis / chronic nephritis. | Home |
| 139 | Holton, Edith Daisy | 62 | 22.12.54 | Diffuse carcinomatosis | Relative's home |
| 140 | Howden, Winifred Edwards | 79 | 10.1.47 | Myocardial failure. | Home |
| 141 | Hughes, Harriett Maud | 66 | 19.11.51 | Cerebral Thrombosis | Home |
| 142 | Hullett, Alfred John | 71 | 14.3.56 | Cerebral haemorrhage /Nephritis. | Nursing Home |
| 143 | Hullett, Gertrude Joyce | 50 | 23.7.56 | Barbitone poisoning / Suicide | Home |
| 144 | Hullett, Mabel Theodora | 67 | 20.5.51 | Myocardial failure | Home |
| 145 | Hunter, Rose Ann | 74 | 21.2.46 | Carcinoma ventriculi | Home |
| 146 | Inman, Edith Maud | 67 | 22.8.55 | Anaemia and Asthenia / Nephritis | Home |
| 147 | Jackman, John Stephen | 79 | 20.2.52 | Coronary thrombosis | Nursing Home |
| 148 | Jackson, Alice Foster (Visitor) | 86 | 13.12.49 | Cerebral thrombosis | Home |
| 149 | Jackson, Mary Ellen | 83 | 13.4.55 | Cerebral thrombosis | Home |
| 150 | Jacobs, Esther | 84 | 17.2.46 | Nephritis | Tredegar* |
| 151 | James, Robert Richard | 74 | 23.3.53 | Uraemia | Esperance* |
| 152 | Jennings, Ethel Anita Dawes | 68 | 8.9.48 | Cerebral haemorrhage | Home |
| 153 | Jones, Harriett Maria | 91 | 9.3.46 | Uraemia. | Home |
| 154 | Katermark, Stanley Charles | 61 | 9.9.48 | Myocardial failure | Grassington Road* |
| 155 | Keef | | | | Home |
| 156 | Kelly, Henrietta Creery | 84 | 3.3.52 | Uraemia | Hotel resident |
| 157 | Kember, Martha | 72 | 5.2.46 | Cerebral thrombosis. | Home |
| 158 | Kilburn, Erna Carl | 82 | 19.1.52 | Carcinoma of stomach | Home |
| 159 | Kilgour, Annabella | 89 | 26.10.50 | Cerebral thrombosis | Highland* |
| 160 | King, Agnes Clara | 77 | 13.1.49 | Myocardial failure. | Hotel resident |
| 161 | King, William | 82 | 26.3.46 | Uraemia | Home |
| 162 | Kite, Margaret Wina | 75 | 10.4.52 | Uraemia | Home |
| 163 | Knight, Edith Mary | 86 | 27.10.49 | Coronary thrombosis | Home |
| 164 | Knight, Raymont | 85 | 4.5.50 | Myocardial failure | Nursing Home |
| 165 | Lawrence, Clifford Downing | 62 | 26.1.53. | Cerebral haemorrhage | Home (Visitor) |
| 166 | Lazenby, Alice | 73 | 14.5.51 | Myocardial Failure. | Esperance*, |
| 167 | Leatham, Robert E. K. | 62 | 11.5.48 | Myocardial failure / Nephritis. | Home |
| 168 | Lennard, Annie Louise | 76 | 28.4.50 | Cerebral thrombosis | Esperance* |
| 169 | Lennard, Florence Elizabeth | 75 | 17.1.55 | Coronary thrombosis | Home |
| 170 | Levey, Grace Ann | 63 | 16.2.51 | Coronary thrombosis | Home |
| 171 | Lewin, Emily Louise | 78 | 12.8.51 | Myocardial failure. | Home |
| 172 | Lindsay-Hogg, Alice Margaret Emma (Visitor) | 96 | 23.8.52 | Scirrhus carcinoma of breast / chronic nephritis | Home |
| 173 | Livesey, Thomas William | 66 | 1.8.50 | Uraemia | Home |
| 174 | Lloyd, Agnes | 63 | 23.12.47 | Aplastic pernicious anaemia | (not known) |
| 175 | Long, William | 80 | 30.9.49 | Cerebral Thrombosis / Fibrotic infiltration of lung. | Princess Alice Hospital |
| 176 | Lorden, Emma Sarah | 74 | 23.1.47 | Cerebral thrombosis / Cardio vasc deg | Home |
| 177 | Lovell, Arthur W. H. | 84 | 3.6.46 | Myocardial failure / chronic nephritis | Home |
| 178 | Luard, Constance Mary | 74 | 17.12.55 | Severe Haematemesis | Esperance* |
| 179 | Macdonald, Anne Marshall | 72 | 9.2.53 | Coronary thrombosis | Grand Hotel |
| 180 | Macdonald, Mary Ann | 96 | 28.11.52 | Cerebral Thrombosis. / chronic nephritis | Jevington Gardens* |
| 181 | MacPherson, Andrew | 81 | 22.12.49 · | Coronary thrombosis | Nursing Home |
| 182 | Maitland, Florence Annie | 81 | 29.10.50 | Cerebral haemorrhage | Home |
| 183 | Mallett, Florence Marguerite | 64 | 22.7.47 | Myocardial failure / chronic nephritis. | Home |
| 184 | Manser, Amy | 82 | 3.1.51 | Uraemia / chronic nephritis | Home |
| 185 | Manser, Robert Reuben | 81 | 20.10.50 | Cerebral thrombosis | Home |
| 186 | Marshall, Ruth Forbes Bingham | 74 | 22.10.49 | Myocardial failure / chronic nephritis. | Home |
| 187 | Martin, Gilbert Nelson | 88 | 4.8.46 | Cerebral thrombosis. | Home |

| 188 | Martindale-Vale, Laura | 81 | 19.7.51 | Cerebral Thrombosis | Home |
| 189 | Marwick, Minnie Emily | 72 | 23.10.47 | Cerebral Haemorrhage | Esperance* |
| 190 | Massey, Ellen Catherine | 91 | 19.3.51 | Cerebral Thrombosis | Esperance* |
| 191 | Mawhood, William Erskine | 89 | 8.3.49 | Carcinoma Recti | Esperance* |
| 192 | Mayhew, Annie | 88 | 23.6.52 | Coronorary Thrombosis | Southdown Hotel (Guest) |
| 193 | McKenzie, Lily Florence | 72 | 11.4.47 | Cerebral thrombosis | Esperance* |
| 194 | Meakins, Daniel Luther | 66 | 8.8.50 | Uraemia | Home |
| 195 | Mende, Sarah Ethel | 74 | 12.8.53 | Cerebral thrombosis / Chronic nephritis | Home |
| 196 | Mendoza, Charlotte Maria | 71 | 7.1.51 | Myocardial failure | Grassington Road* |
| 197 | Mesham Elizabeth | 74 | 21.8.50 | Cerebral thrombosis | Home |
| 198 | Meyer, Cerise | 70 | 28.3.51 | Cerebral Thrombosis / Cardio vasc deg | Redoubt* |
| 199 | Middleton, Robert Hugh | 70 | 22.2.53 | Myocardial failure | Home |
| 200 | Millard, Ada Selina | 78 | 10.1.48 | Myocardial failure./ Senile cardio-vascular degeneration | Home |
| 201 | Milsted, Elizabeth | 83 | 16.12.51 | Cerebral thrombosis / chronic renal degeneration | Home |
| 202 | Molyneux, Anne Cecilia | 78 | 3.3.50 | Cerebral thrombosis | Home |
| 203 | Money, Ellen Bertha Louise | 81 | 12.11.48 | Cerebral thrombosis | Home |
| 204 | Morgan-Jones, Louisa Amelia | 80 | 15.3.56 | Cerebral thrombosis. | Home |
| 205 | Morgan-Jones, Percy | 79 | 19.7.53 | Cerebral thrombosis | Home |
| 206 | Morrell, Edith Alice. | 81 | 13.11.50 | Cerebral thrombosis. | Relative's home |
| 207 | Morris, Robert | 83 | 24.12.48 | Myocardial failure | Home |
| 208 | Mortimer, Emily Louise | 75 | 24.12.46 | Cerebral thrombosis. | Home |
| 209 | Mouat, Mary Jane Matilda | 89 | 31.1.46 | Cerebral thrombosis | Home |
| 210 | Nash, Adelaide | 69 | 6.7.51 | Cerebral Haemorrhage. | Olinda* |
| 211 | Nash, Adelaide Mary | 44 | 27.2.53 | Acute and severe Malseria | Home |
| 212 | Neil-Miller, Clara | 87 | 22.2.54 | Coronorary Thrombosis | Home |
| 213 | Neil-Miller, Hilda | 86 | 15.1.53 | Cerebral Thrombosis. | Home |
| 214 | Newham, Florence Helena | 75 | 7.12.47 | Cerebral haemorrhage / Fibrous degeneration of liver | Esperance* |
| 215 | Norton, Dowding Annie A. | 79 | 9.11.52 | Toxaemia | Home |
| 216 | Nottidge, Gertrude Anne | 84 | 9.2.54 | Cerebral Thrombosis | Southdown Hotel (Guest) |
| 217 | Osborn, George William | 82 | 13.1.55 | Cerebral thrombosis | Olinda* |
| 218 | Ovens, William Digby (At club) | 93 | 29.12.48 | Uraemia | Bowling Club, Princes Park |
| 219 | Pack, Evelyn Mary | 74 | 19.11.49 | Cerebral haemorrhage | Southfields* |
| 220 | Payne, Frances Hewitt | 90 | 13.4.55 | Cerebral thrombosis | Esperance* |
| 221 | Payne, Marjorie | 63 | 17.3.49 | Cerebral thrombosis | Olinda* |
| 222 | Peach, Edmund Wilfred Ashton | 54 | 26.4.47 | Uraemia | Home |
| 223 | Pearce, George William | 82 | 10.3.56 | Cerebral thrombosis / sub acute nephritis | Olinda* |
| 224 | Pechin, Blanche (Visitor) | 81 | 6.1.55 | Diffuse carcinomatosis | Olinda* |
| 225 | Peerless, Sarah | 95 | 10.5.52 | Cerebral Thrombosis | Berrow* |
| 226 | Pidgen, Anne Allam | | 5.7.50 | Cerebral thrombosis | Esperance* |
| 227 | Popham, Henry | 95 | 27.5.47 | Uraemia / Myocardial degeneration / high blood pressure | Home |
| 228 | Pound, Percy Herbert | 80 | 11.1.51 | Cerebral thrombosis | Home |
| 229 | Powell, Lilian Eleather Jane (Visitor) | 70 | 24.4.56 | Coronary thrombosis | Esperance* |
| 230 | Prendergast, Robert John | 81 | 14.5.46 | Uraemia | Home |
| 231 | Price, Mary Jane | 91 | 18.2.50 | Uraemia | Esperance* |
| 232 | Price-Davies, Gwendoline Cholita Mary Sceynton | 78 | 15.12.48 | Cardiac failure | Burlington Hotel (resident) |
| 233 | Price-Jones, Edgar | 62 | 15.10.49 | Carcinoma of Caecum | Tredegar* |
| 234 | Prince, Mary Alice. | 74 | 7.4.51 | Cerebral Thrombosis | Home |
| 235 | Prince, Sidney Herbert | 85 | 21.12.54 | Cerebral thrombosis. | Tredegar* |
| 236 | Reader, Ada Mary | 85 | 27.4.54 | Cerebral Thrombosis | Hydro Hotel |
| 237 | Redfern, Ethel Grace | 58 | 30.11.47 | Myocardial failure | Home |
| 238 | Reeve, Ellen Laura Cleeve | 76 | 2.2.48 | Cerebral thrombosis | Home |

| 239 | Rendell, Lilian Matilda | 61 | 10.2.47 | Cerebral thrombosis / chronic interstitial nephritis | Home |
| 240 | Rennick, Alexander de Clancy | 70 | 20.8.49 | Uraemia / chronic interstitial nephritis / senility | Home |
| 241 | Richards, Eveline Louise | 76 | 26.10.49 | Cerebral thrombosis | (not known) |
| 242 | Richards, Helene Natala (Neighbour) | 66 | 6.12.51 | Cholaemia / Cardio vasc deg | Home |
| 243 | Richardson, Alice Mary | 80 | 19.2.53 | Myocardial failure / Cardio vasc deg | Esperance* |
| 244 | Ridpath, Ernest Guy | 73 | 16.8.51 | Cerebral thrombosis / Fibrosis of lungs Phthisis | Home |
| 245 | Robson, Edwin Leslie | 83 | 6.4.51 | Coronary thrombosis / Cardio vasc deg | Home |
| 246 | Rogers, Agnes Edith | 67 | 25.12.46 | Malignant ovarian cyst / Cardio vasc deg | Home |
| 247 | Roylance, Robert William | 86 | 1.3.48 | Uraemia / Cardio vasc deg | Home |
| 248 | Scott, Edith Harriette | 79 | 19.3.52 | Cerebral Thrombosis / Cardio vasc deg | Home |
| 249 | Sharp, Mary Beatrice | 78 | 16.12.50 | Coronary thrombosis | Olinda* |
| 250 | Shaw, Eleanor Grace | 79 | 31.3.50 | Cerebral thrombosis / Angina Pectoris | Cavendish Hotel (Guest) |
| 251 | Shilton, Rebecca Georgina (Visitor) | 80 | 12.7.49 | Cardiac failure / Cardio vasc deg | Home |
| 252 | Shotter, Mary | 82 | 14.4.49 | Cerebral thrombosis / chronic interstitial nephritis. | Home |
| 253 | Sidgreaves, Ethel Maud | 60 | 23.3.47 | Cerebral thrombosis / Cardio vasc deg | Home |
| 254 | Smith, Frederick Stanley | 77 | 30.11.47 | Carcinoma of lung / Toxaemia of grangrene, right foot | Berrow* |
| 255 | Smith, George Edward | 73 | 6.7.55. | Coronary thrombosis | Home |
| 256 | Smith, Jane Ann | 78 | 1.8.54 | Coronary Thrombosis | Esperance* |
| 257 | Smith, Margaret | 83 | 24.4.56 | Cerebral thrombosis / coronary thrombosis | Mansion Hotel |
| 258 | Smith, William Richard | 75 | 24.11.47 | Myocardial Failure / Cardio vasc deg | Home |
| 259 | Soden, Helen Margaret | 64 | 21.1.53 | Uraemia | Esperance* |
| 260 | South, Constance May (Hotel Resident) | 82 | 14.7.56 | Myocardial failure / carcinoma of descending colon | Chatsworth |
| 261 | Speed, Roland James Edward | 68 | 24.11.55 | Myocardial failure / Cardio vasc deg | Home |
| 262 | Stacey, Frank | 73 | 4.2.56 | Cerebral thrombosis. | Home |
| 263 | Stames, Arthur Herbert | 68 | 26.9.47 | Myocardial Haemorrhage | Esperance* |
| 264 | Stanley, Arthur | 77 | 4.11.47 | Cerebral Haemorrhage / sclerotic kidneys. | Olinda* |
| 265 | Starr, Ann | 84 | 13.3.56 | Cerebral Haemorrhage / chronic bronchitis | Home |
| 266 | Stephens, John Phillips (Visitor) | 69 | 27.10.53 | Myocardial failure / Cardio vasc deg | Home |
| 267 | Steward, Edith Emily | 87 | 16.1.49 | Myocardial failure / Cardio vasc deg | Cumberland Hotel |
| 268 | Stock, Jessie | 68 | 9.7.48 | Cerebral haemorrhage / Cardio vasc deg | Home |
| 269 | Stokes, Henry Cosby | 87 | 27.3.56 | Uraemia coma | Home |
| 270 | Strange, Frank | 74 | 23.11.48 | Cerebral thrombosis. | Home |
| 271 | Sugarman, Leah Visitor | 52 | 31.7.51 | Coronary thrombosis | Osborne Road (Relative's home) |
| 272 | Sumpster, Ernest James | 69 | 20.2.46 | Cerebral thrombosis / Cardio vasc deg | Home |
| 273 | Swift, Lionel David Piercy | 78 | 25.12.55 | Myocardial failure | Esperance* |
| 274 | Tanner, Annie | 73 | 25.7.55 | Coronary thrombosis / High blood pressure / Cardio-vascular degeneration | Home |
| 275 | Tanner, Matilda | 69 | 4.2.50 | Uraemia | Mansion Hotel |
| 276 | Tansley, John Beaumont | 91 | 27.7.55 | Cerebral haemorrhage / Cardio vasc deg | Olinda* |
| 277 | Taylor, Selina Marygetta | 72 | 2.3.49 | Cerebral haemorrhage / Fibrosis of liver | Home |
| 278 | Thacker, Ellen Annie | 82 | 15.11.49 | Cerebral thrombosis | Olinda* |
| 279 | Thomas, Edgar Burt | 84 | 21.1.54 | Cerebral thrombosis / Cardio vasc deg Renal Failure | Sandhurst Hotel (Resident) |
| 280 | Thomas, Julia Maude | 72 | 22.11.52 | Cerebral Thrombosis / Cardio vasc deg | Olinda* |
| 281 | Thompson, Arthur Robert | 65 | 24.12.49 | Pelvic sarcoma / cardio vasc renal degeneration. | Olinda* |
| 282 | Thomson, Alice Mary | 94 | 31.10.46 | Cerebral thrombosis | Esperance* |
| 283 | Tilley, Sarah Pauline | 97 | 2.12.52 | Cerebral Thrombosis / Cholaemia | Olinda* |
| 284 | Tite, Mary | 86 | 22.11.48 | Cerebral thrombosis | Olinda* |
| 285 | Tomlinson, Evelyn Hildegarde | 75 | 2.8.54 | Uraemia / chronic nephritis | Esperance* |
| 286 | Tomlinson, Walter Cyril | 77 | 26.8.54 | Coronary thrombosis | Olinda* |
| 287 | Towner, Cathreen Sarah Bond | 81 | 12.2.50 | Myocardial failure / Sprue end macrocytic anaem. | Relative's home |

| 288 | Trusler, Peter James | 0.5 | 8.6.48 | Deformity – absence of cranial vault. | Home |
| 289 | Turner, Dora Scott | 72 | 5.8.46 | Cerebral thrombosis / Cardio vasc deg | Olinda* |
| 290 | Turton, Maria Leah | 87 | 10.1.47 | Nephritis / Cardio vasc and renal degeneration | |
| | | | | Fracture of neck of femur. | Tredegar* |
| 291 | Upsdell, George Edgar Skynner | 60 | 23.8.46 | Uraemia / Cardio vasc deg | Home |
| 292 | Wager, Kate | 64 | 21.6.56 | Coronary thrombosis / carcinoma left breast. | Hydro Hotel |
| 293 | Wain, Phoebe | 68 | 13.2.51 | Cerebral thrombosis / Cardio vasc deg | Home |
| 294 | Walker, Helen | 62 | 24.8.46 | Carcinoma of uterine cervix | Nursing Home |
| 295 | Ware, Amy Constance | | | | |
| | Clavering I'Anson | 76 | 23.2.50 | Cerebral thrombosis | Sandhurst Hotel (Guest) |
| 296 | Waters, Alice Jane | 77 | 27.4.52 | Myocardial failure / Cardio vasc deg | |
| | | | | senility | Relative's home |
| 297 | Waters, William John Alfred | 73 | 19.1.51 | Myocardial failure / Myocardial infarction | |
| | | | | advanced othero sclerosis / gall stones | Home |
| 298 | Webb, Adela | 75 | 2.11.46 | Cerebral thrombosis / Cardio vasc deg | Home |
| 299 | Webb, Alexina | 80 | 21.5.49 | Carcinoma of stomach /high blood pressure | |
| | | | | renal insufficiency | Kenilworth Court Hotel (Resident) |
| 300 | Webster, Annie Eliza Mawby | 74 | 8.8.47 | Oedema of lung / carcinoma of ovary | Home |
| 301 | Wheale, Mary Elizabeth (Visitor) | 52 | 6.10.55 | Coronary thrombosis / Lower Dicker | Home |
| 302 | Whitton, Matilda | | 11.5.53 | Myocardial degeneration / rupture of a | |
| | | | | thero sclerotic blood vessel / Nephro sclerosis | (Hotel Resident) |
| 303 | Williams, Cecilia Margaret | 84 | 30.8.47 | Cerebral Haemorrhage | Nursing Home |
| 304 | Williams, Frederick | 88 | 6.1.56 | cerebral thrombosis / athero sclerosis | Beaulieu Hotel (Resident) |
| 305 | Williams, Jane | 78 | 8.11.47 | Uraemia / carcinoma of lungs | |
| | | | | carcinoma of breast. | White Hermitage Hotel |
| 306 | Williams, Kate | 78 | 1.10.48 | Cerebral thrombosis | (not known) |
| 307 | Wintle, Lily | 70 | 16.7.55 | Cerebral thrombosis / | |
| | | | | Hyperpesis & atheroma of coronary arteries | (not known) |
| 308 | Woolrych, Leslie Owen | 69 | 2.5.55 | Oedema of lung | Home |
| 309 | Yates, Ada Louisa | 86 | 23.2.49 | Cerebral thrombosis / Arterio sclerosis | Nursing Home |

# Bibliography

---

## Primary Sources

*R. v. John Bodkin Adams*, Sussex Police archive, East Sussex Record Office.

*R. v. John Bodkin Adams*, Metropolitan Police (Scotland Yard) archive, The National Archives.

*R. v. John Bodkin Adams*, Director of Public Prosecutions archive, The National Archive.

Haine's Undertakers' Archives, Eastbourne.

Local, national and international newspapers and periodicals

*A Complete Report of the Trial of Dr E.W. Pritchard*, (William Kay, Edinburgh, 1865) [reprinted from *The Scotsman*]

The Shipman Reports

Ayling, Katherine, *My Father's Family*, (Unpublished Memoirs, 1979)

Gwynne family papers


## Secondary Sources

Annandale, E., *Professional Defenses*, International Journal of Health Services 26 (1996): 751-775

Ariés, Philippe, *The Hour of Our Death*, trans. by Helen Weaver, (London, Penguin, 1987)

Arnott, Anne, *The Brethren*, (London, A.R. Mowbray, 1969)

Ascoli, David, *The Queen's Peace*, (London, Hamish Hamilton, 1979).

Ball, Simon, *The Guardsmen, Harold Macmillan, Three Friends and the World They Made*, (London, Harper Collins, 2004).

Bedford, Sybille, *The Best We Can Do*, (London, Penguin, 1961).

Boothby, Robert, *Recollections of a Rebel*, (London, Hutchinson, 1978).

Britton, Paul, *The Jigsaw Man*, (London, Corgi, 1998)

Byrne, Gerald, *John George Haigh*, (London, Headline, 1949)

Cameron, Deborah, Frazer, Elizabeth, *The Lust to Kill*, (Cambridge, Polity Press, 1987).

Camps, F.E., *The Uses and Abuses of Cremation Medical Certificates*, (Paper to The Cremation Society of Great Britain, 1957)

Camps, F.E., *What is Death?* (Paper to The Cremation Society of Great Britain, 1965)

Canter, David, *Criminal Shadows*, (London, Harper Collins, 1994)

Capper, W.M. and Johnson, D., *Arthur Rendle Short, Surgeon & Christian*, (Inter-Varsity Fellowship, London, 1954).

Capper, W.M., and Johnson, D., *The Faith of a Surgeon, Belief and experience in the life of Arthur Rendle Short*, (Exeter, Paternoster Press, 1976).

Chaney, Lisa, *Elizabeth David*, (London, Macmillan, 1998).

Cooper, Artemis, *Writing at the Kitchen Table, Elizabeth David, The Authorized Biography*, (London, Michael Joseph, 1999).

Coward, Noel, *The Noel Coward Diaries*, ed. Payn & Morley, (London, Phoenix, 1998).

Crenshaw, James L., *Ecclesiastes, A Commentary*, (Philadelphia, Westminster Press, 1987).

Devlin, Patrick, *Easing The Passing*, (London, The Bodley Head, 1985)

Devonshire, Andrew, *Accidents of Fortune*, (Norwich, Michael Russell, 2004)

Douglas-Home, Jessica, *Violet, The Live and Loves of Violet Gordon-Woodhouse*, (London, The Harvill Press, 1996)

Dunboyne, Lord (ed.), *Trial of John George Haigh*, (London, William Hodge, 1953)

Emsley, Clive, *The English Police*, (London, Longman, 2nd. Ed. 1996)

Foucault, Michel, *Essential Works of Foucault 1954-1984*, ed. J. Faubion, (London, Penguin, 2002)

Gathorne-Hardy, Jonathan, *Doctors*, (London, Weidenfeld & Nicolson, 1984).

Gatrell, V.A.C., *The Hanging Tree*, (Oxford, Oxford University Press, 1994).

Gibson, Ronald, *The Family Doctor his life and history*, (London, George Allen & Unwin, 1981).

Gilmore, Mikal, *Shot in the Heart*, (New York, Doubleday, 1994)

Gosse, Edmund, *Father and Son*, (London, Heinneman,1907)

Gribble, Leonard, *Triumphs of Scotland Yard*, (London, John Long, 1955)

Grice, Edward, *Great Cases of Sir Henry Curtis-Bennett K.C.*, (London, Hutchinson, 1937)

Hailsham, Lord, *A Sparrow's Flight, Memoirs*, (London, Collins, 1990)

Hallworth, Rodney & Williams, Mark: *Where There's a Will*, (Exeter, Capstan Press, 1983).

Hattersley, Roy, *Fifty Years On*, (London, Little, Brown & Co., 1997).

Hogg, James, *The Private Memoirs and Confessions of a Justified Sinner*, (Edinburgh, 1824)

Holton, R., *How Doctors Have Betrayed Us All*, The Independent, 14 June 1998: 1, 2

Hopkins, Harry, *The New Look, A Social History of the Forties and Fifties in Britain*, (London, Martin Secker & Warburg, 1963).

Hoskins, Percy, *Two Men Were Acquitted*, (London, Secker & Warburg,1984).

Humphrey, George, *Eastbourne at War*, (Seaford, S.B. Publications, 1998).

Kennedy, Ludovic, *Ten Rillington Place*, (London, Gollancz, 1961).

La Bern, Arthur, *Haigh, The mind of a murderer*, (London, W.H. Allen, 1973).

Lamb, Richard, *The Macmillan Years 1957-1963, The Emerging Truth*, (London, John Murray, 1995).

Lesley, Cole, *The Life of Noel Coward*, (London, Jonathan Cape, 1976).

Lewis, Peter, *The 1950s*, (London, William Heinemann, 1978).

MacCulloch, Diarmaid, *Reformation*, (London, Allen Lane, 2003).

Macmillan, Harold, *The Macmillan Diaries, The Cabinet Years, 1950-1957*, ed. Peter Catterall (London, Macmillan, 2003).

Mizrahi, T., *Managing Medical Mistakes*, Social Science and Medicine, 19 (1984): 135-146.

Neatby, William B., *A History of the Plymouth Brethren*, (Stoke-on-Trent, Tentmaker, 1901) [reprinted 2000]

O'Donnell, Michael, *One Man's Burden*, British Medical Journal, Oct. 1983.

Pugh, Peter, *Grand Hotel*, (Eastbourne, The Grand Hotel, 1987).

Rose, Clarkson, *With a Twinkle in My Eye*, (London, Museum Press, 1951)

Simpson, Keith, *Forty Years of Murder*, (London, Harrap,1978)

Stark, C., Paterson B., Henderson, T, Kidd, B., Godwin M., 'Counting the Dead', (Nursing Times, 1997 93; 46:34-47.)

Stark, C., Sloan D., 'Murder in the NHS: Audit of Critical Incidents in Patients at Risk', (British Medical Journal 1994; 308:477.)

Stock C., 'Opportunity May Be More Important than Profession', (bmj.com 26 January 2001).

Surtees, John, *Eastbourne A History*, (Chichester, Phillimore, 2002).

Surtees, John, Ed., *Eastbourne Medical Gazette Centenary Edition*, (Eastbourne Medical Society, 1983).

Surtees, John, *The Strange Case of Dr Bodkin-Adams*, (Seaford, S.B. Publications, 2000).

Thorpe, D.R., Eden: *The Life and Times of Anthony Eden*, (London, Chatto & Windus, 2003).

Thorpe, D.R., *Selwyn Lloyd*, (London, Jonathan Cape, 1989).

Walkley, Victor G., *A Church Set On a Hill*, (Eastbourne, Upperton Press,1972)

Weight, Richard, *Patriots: National Identity in Britain 1940-2000*, (London, Macmillan, 2002)

Whittle, Brian & Ritchie, Jean, *Prescription for Murder*, (London,Warner, 2000, Updated edition, 2001.)

Wu, A.W.et al., *Do House Officers Learn from Their Mistakes?*, Journal of the American Medical Association, 265 (1991):2089-2094.

Wyatt, Woodrow, *The Journals of Woodrow Wyatt*, ed. by Sarah Curtis, (London, Macmillan, 1998).

# Index

First published in Great Britain by

Elliott & Thompson Ltd
27 John Street
London  WC1N 2BX

ISBN  1 904027 19 9

First edition

Book design by Brad Thompson
Printed and bound in Great Britain by Athenaeum Press